Levels 1 & 2

BENCHMARK SERIES

Microsoft® Excel® 365

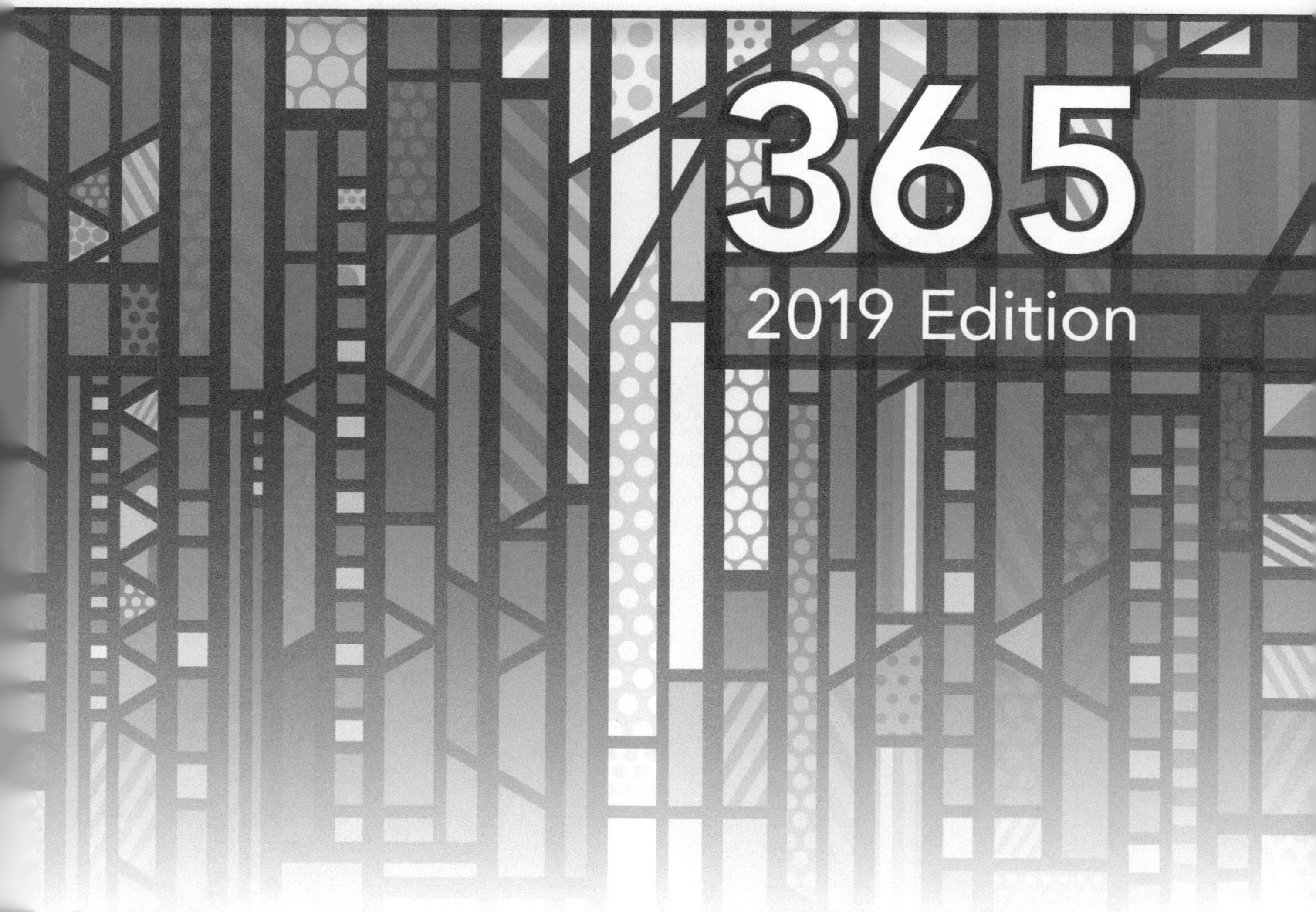

2019 Edition

[...]ta Rutkosky

Jan Davidson
Lambton College
Sarnia, Ontario

Audrey Roggenkamp
Pierce College Puyallup
Puyallup, Washington

Ian Rutkosky
Pierce College Puyallup
Puyallup, Washington

A DIVISION OF KENDALL HUNT

Minneapolis

Cover Photo Credit: © lowball-jack/GettyImages
Interior Photo Credits: Follow the Index.

ISBN 978-0-76388-722-3 (print)

7900 Xerxes Avenue S STE 310
Minneapolis, MN 55431-1118
Email: CustomerService@ParadigmEducation.com
Website: ParadigmEducation.com

Printed in the United States of America

Brief Contents

Contents

Microsoft Excel Level 2

Preface

Achieving Proficiency in Excel

The Benchmark Series, *Microsoft® Excel® 365*, 2019 Edition, is designed for students who want to learn how to use Microsoft's powerful spreadsheet program to manipulate numerical data in resolving financial and other problems requiring data management and analysis. No prior knowledge of spreadsheets is required. After successfully completing a course in Microsoft Excel using this courseware, students will be able to do the following:

- Create and edit spreadsheets and worksheets of varying complexity.
- Format cells, columns, and rows as well as entire workbooks in a uniform, attractive style.
- Analyze numerical data and project outcomes to make informed decisions.
- Plan, research, create, revise, and publish worksheets and workbooks to meet specific needs.
- Given a workplace scenario requiring a numbers-based solution, assess the information requirements and then prepare the materials that achieve the goal efficiently and effectively.

Well-designed pedagogy is important, but students learn technology skills through practice and problem solving. Technology provides opportunities for interactive learning as well as excellent ways to quickly and accurately assess student performance. To this end, this course is supported with Cirrus, Paradigm's cloud-based training and assessment learning management system. Details about Cirrus as well as its integrated student courseware and instructor resources can be found on page xii.

Proven Instructional Design

The Benchmark Series has long served as a standard of excellence in software instruction. Elements of the series function individually and collectively to create an inviting, comprehensive learning environment that leads to full proficiency in computer applications. The following visual tour highlights the structure and features that comprise the highly popular Benchmark model.

Unit Openers display the unit's four chapter titles. Each level of the course contains two units with four chapters each.

Chapter Openers Present Learning Objectives

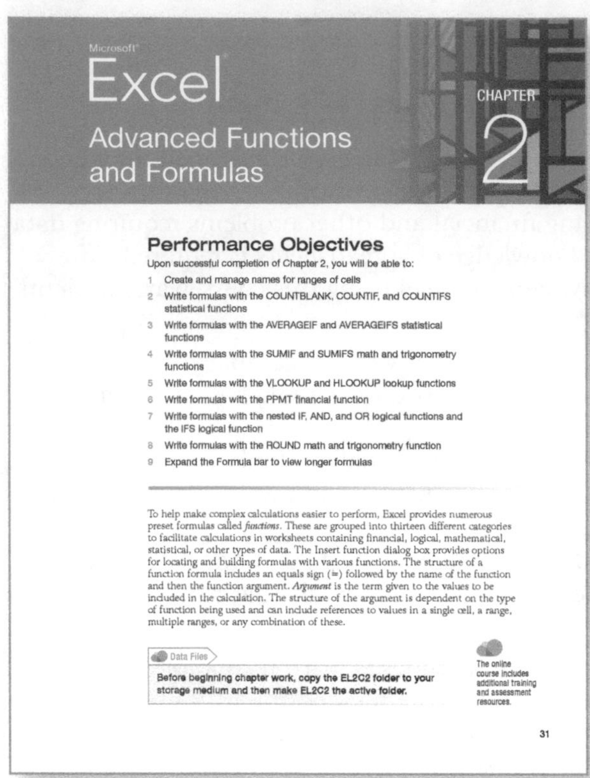

Microsoft®

Excel®

Advanced Functions and Formulas

CHAPTER 2

Performance Objectives

Upon successful completion of Chapter 2, you will be able to:

1. Create and manage names for ranges of cells
2. Write formulas with the COUNTBLANK, COUNTIF, and COUNTIFS statistical functions
3. Write formulas with the AVERAGEIF and AVERAGEIFS statistical functions
4. Write formulas with the SUMIF and SUMIFS math and trigonometry functions
5. Write formulas with the VLOOKUP and HLOOKUP lookup functions
6. Write formulas with the PPMT financial function
7. Write formulas with the nested IF, AND, and OR logical functions and the IFS logical function
8. Write formulas with the ROUND math and trigonometry function
9. Expand the Formula bar to view longer formulas

To help make complex calculations easier to perform, Excel provides numerous preset formulas called *functions*. These are grouped into thirteen different categories to facilitate calculations in worksheets containing financial, logical, mathematical, statistical, or other types of data. The Insert function dialog box provides options for locating and building formulas with various functions. The structure of a function formula includes an equals sign (=) followed by the name of the function and then the function argument. *Argument* is the term given to the values to be included in the calculation. The structure of the argument is dependent on the type of function being used and can include references to values in a single cell, a range, multiple ranges, or any combination of these.

Data Files

Before beginning chapter work, copy the EL2C2 folder to your storage medium and then make EL2C2 the active folder.

The online course includes additional training and assessment resources.

31

Chapter Openers present the performance objectives and an overview of the skills taught.

Data Files are provided for each chapter.

Activities Build Skill Mastery within Realistic Context

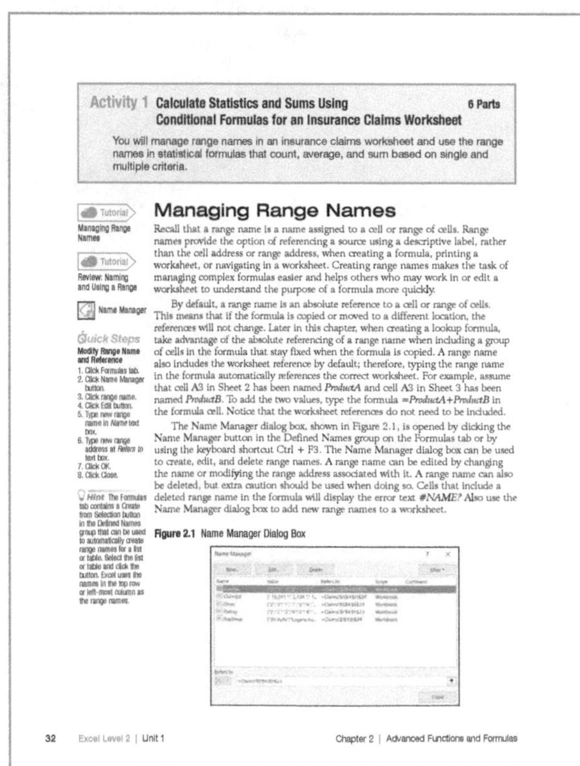

Activity 1 Calculate Statistics and Sums Using Conditional Formulas for an Insurance Claims Worksheet — **6 Parts**

You will manage range names in an insurance claims worksheet and use the range names in statistical formulas that count, average, and sum based on single and multiple criteria.

Managing Range Names

Tutorial: Managing Range Names

Tutorial: Review: Naming and Using a Range

Name Manager

Recall that a range name is a name assigned to a cell or range of cells. Range names provide the option of referencing a source using a descriptive label, rather than the cell address or range address, when creating a formula, printing a worksheet, or navigating in a worksheet. Creating range names makes the task of managing complex formulas easier and helps others who may work in or edit a worksheet to understand the purpose of a formula more quickly.

By default, a range name is an absolute reference to a cell or range of cells. This means that if the formula is copied or moved to a different location, the references will not change. Later in this chapter, when creating a lookup formula, take advantage of the absolute referencing of a range name when including a group of cells in the formula that stay fixed when the formula is copied. A range name also includes the worksheet reference by default; therefore, typing the range name in the formula automatically references the correct worksheet. For example, assume that cell A3 in Sheet 2 has been named *ProductA* and cell A3 in Sheet 3 has been named *ProductB*. To add the two values, type the formula =*ProductA*+*ProductB* in the formula cell. Notice that the worksheet references do not need to be included.

The Name Manager dialog box, shown in Figure 2.1, is opened by clicking the Name Manager button in the Defined Names group on the Formulas tab or by using the keyboard shortcut Ctrl + F3. The Name Manager dialog box can be used to create, edit, and delete range names. A range name can be edited by changing the name or modifying the range address associated with it. A range name can also be deleted, but extra caution should be used when doing so. Cells that include a deleted range name in the formula will display the error text *#NAME?* Also use the Name Manager dialog box to add new range names to a worksheet.

Quick Steps

Modify Range Name and Reference

1. Click Formulas tab.
2. Click Name Manager button.
3. Click range name.
4. Click Edit button.
5. Type new range name in *Name* text box.
6. Type new range address at *Refers to* text box.
7. Click OK.
8. Click Close.

Hint The Formulas tab contains a Create from Selection button in the Defined Names group that can be used to automatically create range names for a list or table. Select the list or table and click the button. Excel uses the names in the top row or left-most column as the range names.

Figure 2.1 Name Manager Dialog Box

32 Excel Level 2 | Unit 1 — Chapter 2 | Advanced Functions and Formulas

Multipart Activities provide a framework for instruction and practice on software features. An activity overview identifies tasks to accomplish and key features to use in completing the work.

Tutorials provide interactive, guided training and measured practice.

Quick Steps in the margins allow fast reference and review of the steps needed to accomplish tasks.

Hints offer useful tips on how to use features efficiently and effectively.

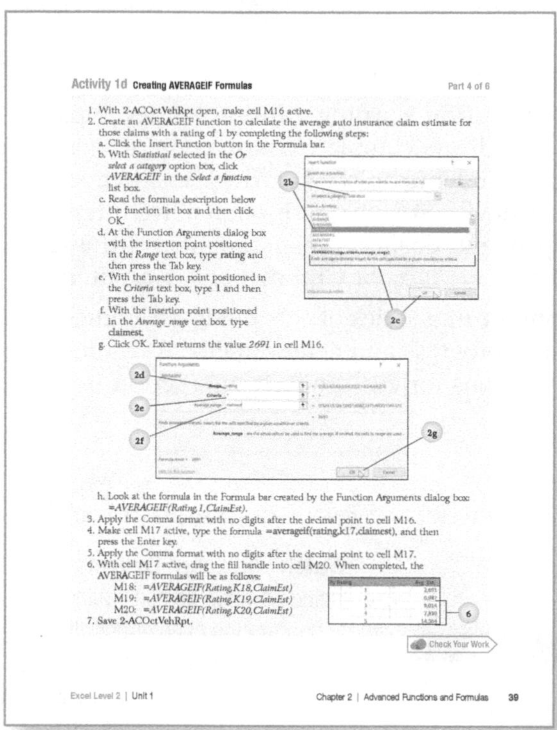

Activity 1d **Creating AVERAGEIF Formulas** Part 4 of 6

1. With 2-ACOctVehRpt open, make cell M16 active.
2. Create an AVERAGEIF function to calculate the average auto insurance claim estimate for those claims with a rating of 1 by completing the following steps:
   a. Click the Insert Function button in the Formula bar.
   b. With *Statistical* selected in the *Or select a category* option box, click *AVERAGEIF* in the *Select a function* list box.
   c. Read the formula description below the function list box and then click OK.
   d. At the Function Arguments dialog box with the insertion point positioned in the *Range* text box, type **rating** and then press the Tab key.
   e. With the insertion point positioned in the *Criteria* text box, type **1** and then press the Tab key.
   f. With the insertion point positioned in the *Average_range* text box, type **claimest**.
   g. Click OK. Excel returns the value *2691* in cell M16.
   h. Look at the formula in the Formula bar created by the Function Arguments dialog box: *=AVERAGEIF(Rating,1,ClaimEst)*.
3. Apply the Comma format with no digits after the decimal point to cell M16.
4. Make cell M17 active, type the formula **=averageif(rating,k17,claimest)**, and then press the Enter key.
5. Apply the Comma format with no digits after the decimal point to cell M17.
6. With cell M17 active, drag the fill handle into cell M20. When completed, the AVERAGEIF formulas will be as follows:
   M18: *=AVERAGEIF(Rating,K18,ClaimEst)*
   M19: *=AVERAGEIF(Rating,K19,ClaimEst)*
   M20: *=AVERAGEIF(Rating,K20,ClaimEst)*
7. Save 2-ACOctVehRpt.

Excel Level 2 | Unit 1 Chapter 2 | Advanced Functions and Formulas 39

Step-by-Step Instructions guide students to the desired outcome for each activity part. Screen captures illustrate what the screen should look like at key points.

Magenta Text identifies material to type.

Check Your Work model answer images are available in the online course, and students can use those images to confirm they have completed the activity correctly.

Between activity parts, the text presents instruction on the features and skills necessary to accomplish the next section of the activity.

Typically, a file remains open throughout all parts of the activity. Students save their work incrementally. At the end of the activity, students save, print, and then close the file.

Chapter Review Tools Reinforce Learning

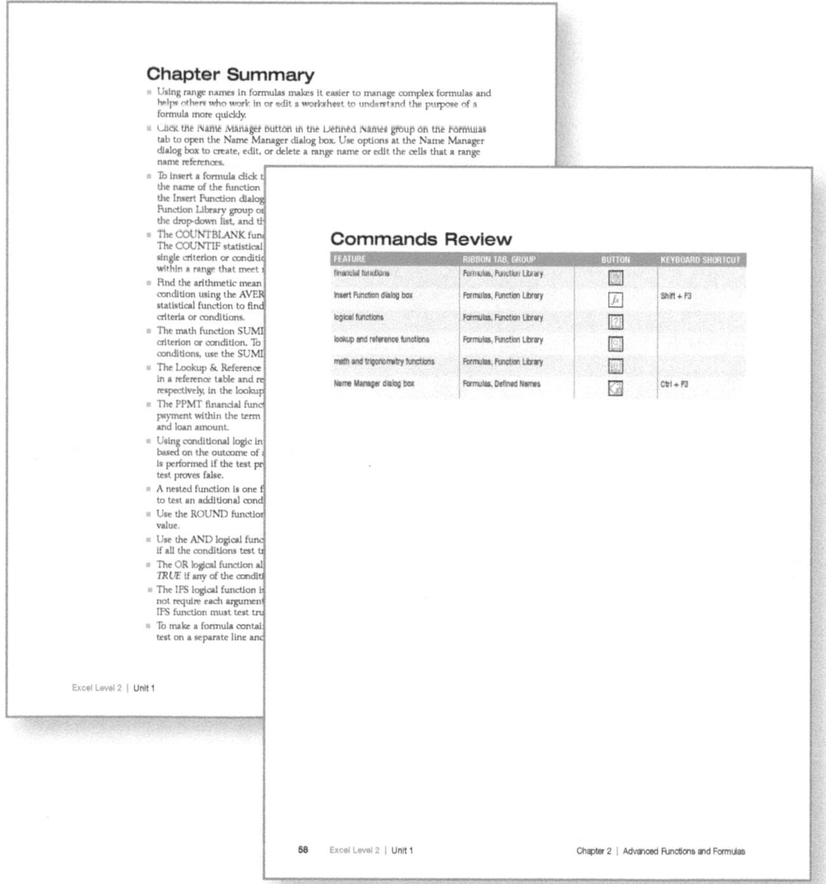

Chapter Summary

- Using range names in formulas makes it easier to manage complex formulas and helps others who work in or edit a worksheet to understand the purpose of a formula more quickly.
- Click the Name Manager button in the Defined Names group on the Formulas tab to open the Name Manager dialog box. Use options at the Name Manager dialog box to create, edit, or delete a range name or edit the cells that a range name references.
- To insert a formula click t
  the name of the function
  the Insert Function dialog
  Function Library group o
  the drop-down list, and th
- The COUNTBLANK fun
  The COUNTIF statistical
  single criterion or conditi
  within a range that meet
- Find the arithmetic mean
  condition using the AVER
  statistical function to find
  criteria or conditions.
- The math function SUMI
  criterion or condition. To
  conditions, use the SUMI
- The Lookup & Reference
  in a reference table and re
  respectively, in the lookup
- The PPMT financial func
  payment within the term
  and loan amount.
- Using conditional logic in
  based on the outcome of
  is performed if the test pr
  test proves false.
- A nested function is one f
  to test an additional cond
- Use the ROUND functior
  value.
- Use the AND logical func
  if all the conditions test t
- The OR logical function al
  TRUE if any of the conditi
- The IFS logical function i
  not require each argumen
  IFS function must test tru
- To make a formula contai
  test on a separate line and

Excel Level 2 | Unit 1

Commands Review

FEATURE	RIBBON TAB, GROUP	BUTTON	KEYBOARD SHORTCUT
financial functions	Formulas, Function Library		
Insert Function dialog box	Formulas, Function Library	*fx*	Shift + F3
logical functions	Formulas, Function Library		
lookup and reference functions	Formulas, Function Library		
math and trigonometry functions	Formulas, Function Library		
Name Manager dialog box	Formulas, Defined Names		Ctrl + F3

58 Excel Level 2 | Unit 1 Chapter 2 | Advanced Functions and Formulas

A **Chapter Summary** reviews the purpose and execution of key features.

A **Commands Review** summarizes visually the major features and alternative methods of access.

The Cirrus Solution

Elevating student success and instructor efficiency

Powered by Paradigm, Cirrus is the next-generation learning solution for developing skills in Microsoft Office. Cirrus seamlessly delivers complete course content in a cloud-based learning environment that puts students on the fast track to success. Students can access their content from any device anywhere, through a live internet connection; plus, Cirrus is platform independent, ensuring that students get the same learning experience whether they are using PCs, Macs, or Chromebook computers.

Cirrus provides Benchmark Series content in a series of scheduled assignments that report to a grade book to track student progress and achievement. Assignments are grouped in modules, providing many options for customizing instruction.

Dynamic Training

The online Benchmark Series courses include interactive resources to support learning.

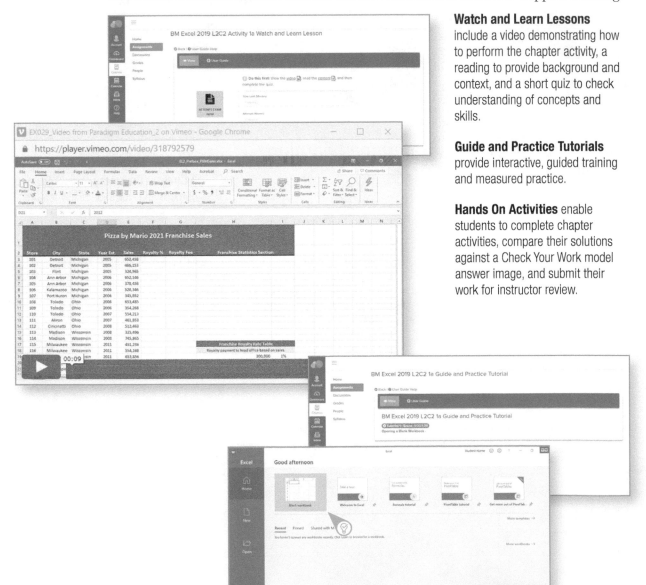

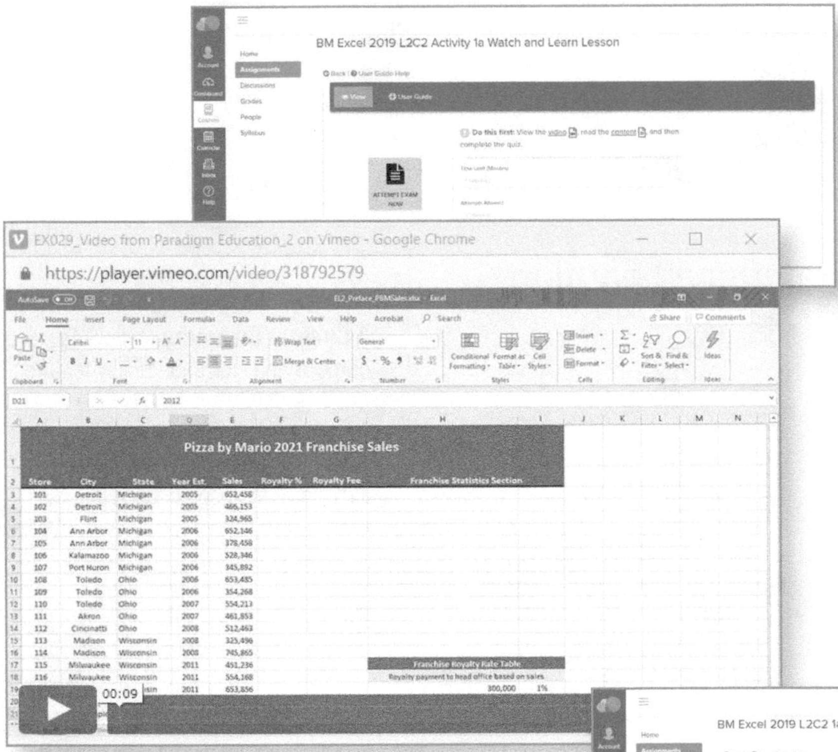

Watch and Learn Lessons include a video demonstrating how to perform the chapter activity, a reading to provide background and context, and a short quiz to check understanding of concepts and skills.

Guide and Practice Tutorials provide interactive, guided training and measured practice.

Hands On Activities enable students to complete chapter activities, compare their solutions against a Check Your Work model answer image, and submit their work for instructor review.

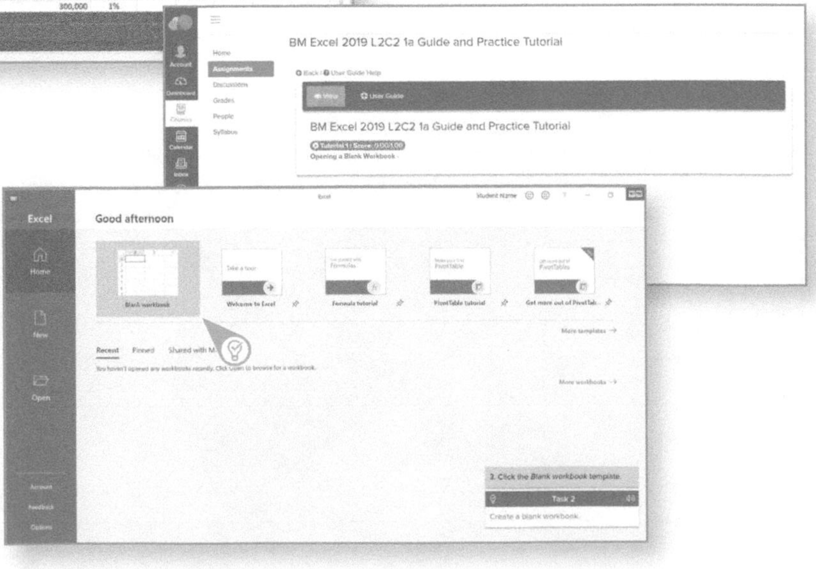

Chapter Review and Assessment

Review and assessment activities for each chapter are available for completion in Cirrus.

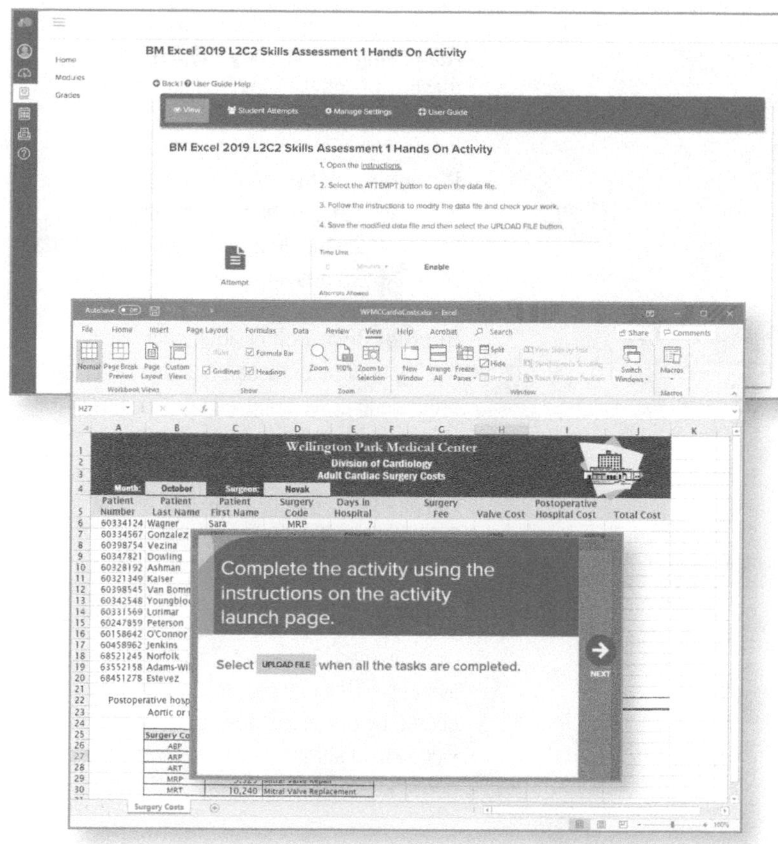

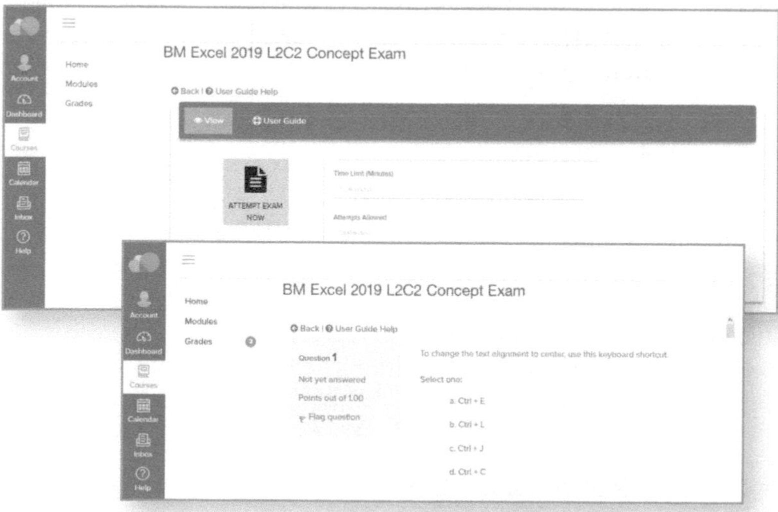

Knowledge Check completion exercises assess comprehension and recall of application features and functions as well as key terminology.

Skills Assessment Hands On Activity exercises evaluate the ability to apply chapter skills and concepts in solving realistic problems. Each is completed live in Excel and is uploaded through Cirrus for instructor evaluation.

Visual Benchmark assessments test problem-solving skills and mastery of application features.

A **Case Study** requires analyzing a workplace scenario and then planning and executing a multipart project. Students search the web and/or use the program's Help feature to locate additional information required to complete the Case Study.

Exercises and **Projects** provide opportunities to develop and demonstrate skills learned in each chapter. Each is completed live in the Office application and is automatically scored by Cirrus. Detailed feedback and how-to videos help students evaluate and improve their performance.

Skills Check Exams evaluate students' ability to complete specific tasks. Skills Check Exams are completed live in the Office application and are scored automatically. Detailed feedback and instructor-controlled how-to videos help student evaluate and improve their performance.

Multiple-choice **Concepts Exams** assess understanding of key commands and concepts presented in each chapter.

Unit Review and Assessment

Review and assessment activities for each unit of each Benchmark course are also available for completion in Cirrus.

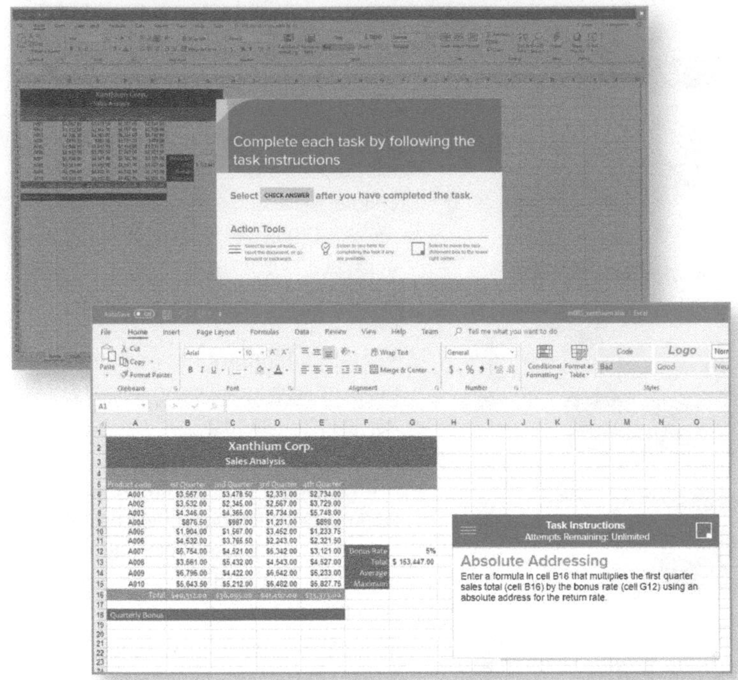

Assessing Proficiency exercises check mastery of software application functions and features.

Writing Activities challenge students to use written communication skills while demonstrating their understanding of important software features and functions.

Internet Research assignments reinforce the importance of research and information processing skills along with proficiency in the Office environment.

A **Job Study** activity at the end of Unit 2 presents a capstone assessment requiring critical thinking and problem solving.

Unit-Level Projects allow students to practice skills learned in the unit. Each is completed live in the Office application and automatically scored by Cirrus. Detailed feedback and how-to videos help students evaluate and improve their performance.

Student eBook

The Student eBook, accessed through the Cirrus online course, can be downloaded to any device (desktop, laptop, tablet, or smartphone) to make Benchmark Series content available anywhere students wish to study.

Instructor eResources

Cirrus tracks students' step-by-step interactions as they move through each activity, giving instructors visibility into their progress and missteps. With Exam Watch, instructors can observe students in a virtual, live, skills-based exam and join remotely as needed—a helpful option for struggling students who need one-to-one coaching, or for distance learners. In addition to these Cirrus-specific tools, the Instructor eResources for the Benchmark Series include the following support:

- Planning resources, such as lesson plans, teaching hints, and sample course syllabi
- Delivery resources, such as discussion questions and online images and templates
- Assessment resources, including live and annotated PDF model answers for chapter work and review and assessment activities, rubrics for evaluating student work, and chapter-based exam banks in RTF format

About the Authors

Nita Rutkosky began her career teaching business education at Pierce College in Puyallup, Washington, in 1978 and holds a master's degree in occupational education. In her years as an instructor, she taught many courses in software applications to students in postsecondary information technology certificate and degree programs. Since 1987, Nita has been a leading author of courseware for computer applications training and instruction. Her current titles include Paradigm's popular Benchmark Series, Marquee Series, and Signature Series. She is a contributor to the Cirrus online content for Office application courses and has also written textbooks for keyboarding, desktop publishing, computing in the medical office, and essential skills for digital literacy.

Jan Davidson started her teaching career in 1997 as a corporate trainer and postsecondary instructor and holds a Social Science degree, a writing certificate, and an In-Service Teacher Training certificate. Since 2001, she has been a faculty member of the School of Business and International Education at Lambton College in Sarnia, Ontario. In this role, she has developed curriculum and taught a variety of office technology, software applications, and office administration courses to domestic and international students in a variety of postsecondary programs. As a consultant and content provider for Paradigm Education Solutions since 2006, Jan has contributed to textbook and online content for various titles. She has been author and co-author of Paradigm's Benchmark Series *Microsoft® Excel®*, Level 2, and *Microsoft® Access®*, Level 2 since 2013 and has contributed to the Cirrus online courseware for the series. Jan is also co-author of *Advanced Excel® 2016.*

Audrey Roggenkamp holds a master's degree in adult education and curriculum and has been an adjunct instructor in the Business Information Technology department at Pierce College in Puyallup, Washington, since 2005. Audrey has also been a content provider for Paradigm Education Solutions since 2005. In addition to contributing to the Cirrus online content for Office application courses, Audrey co-authors Paradigm's Benchmark Series, Marquee Series, and Signature Series. Her other available titles include *Keyboarding & Applications I and II* and *Using Computers in the Medical Office: Word, PowerPoint®, and Excel®*.

Ian Rutkosky has a master's degree in business administration and has been an adjunct instructor in the Business Information Technology department at Pierce College in Puyallup, Washington, since 2010. In addition to joining the author team for the Benchmark Series and Marquee Series, he has co-authored titles on medical office computing and digital literacy and has served as a co-author and consultant for Paradigm's Cirrus training and assessment software.

Microsoft®

Office

Getting Started in Office 365

Microsoft Office is a suite of applications for personal computers and other devices. These programs, known as *software*, include Word, a word processor; Excel, a spreadsheet editor; Access, a database management system; and PowerPoint, a presentation program used to design and present slideshows. Microsoft Office 365 is a subscription service that delivers continually updated versions of those applications. Specific features and functionality of Microsoft Office vary depending on the user's account, computer setup, and other factors. The Benchmark courseware was developed using features available in Office 365. You may find that with your computer and version of Office, the appearance of the software and the steps needed to complete an activity vary slightly from what is presented in the courseware.

Identifying Computer Hardware

The Microsoft Office suite can run on several types of computer equipment, referred to as *hardware*. You will need access to a laptop or a desktop computer system that includes a PC/tower, monitor, keyboard, printer, drives, and mouse. If you are not sure what equipment you will be operating, check with your instructor. The computer system shown in Figure G.1 consists of six components. Each component is discussed separately in the material that follows.

Figure G.1 Computer System

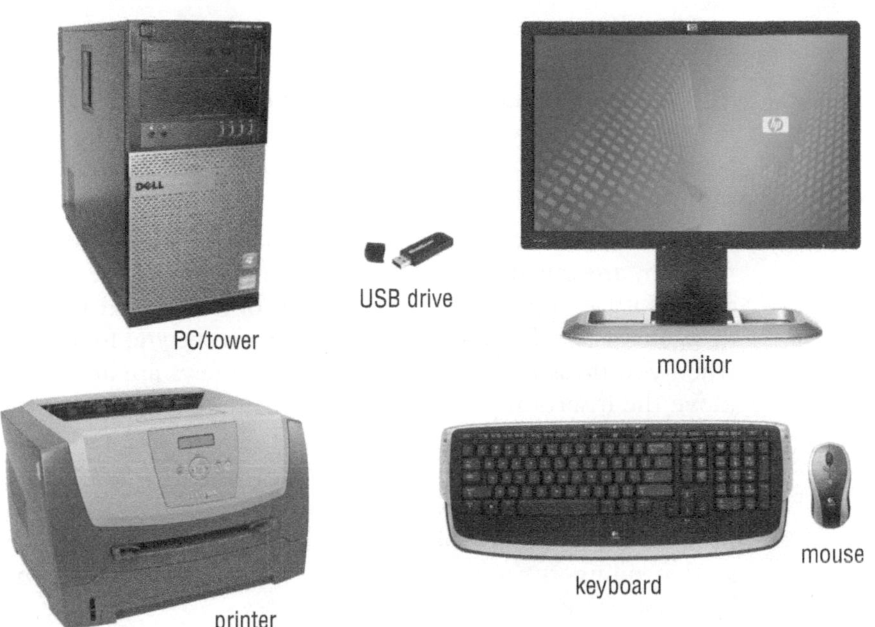

Figure G.2 System Unit Ports

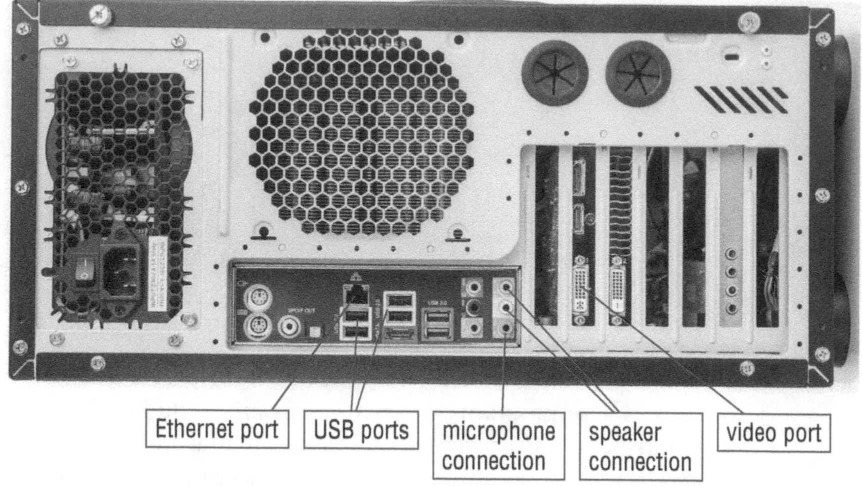

System Unit (PC/Tower)

Traditional desktop computing systems include a system unit known as the *PC (personal computer)* or *tower*. This is the brain of the computer, where all processing occurs. It contains a Central Processing Unit (CPU), hard drives, and video cards plugged into a motherboard. Input and output ports are used for attaching peripheral equipment such as a keyboard, monitor, printer, and so on, as shown in Figure G.2. When a user provides input, the PC computes it and outputs the results.

Monitor

Hint Monitor size is measured diagonally and is generally the distance from the bottom left corner to the top right corner of the monitor.

A computer monitor looks like a television screen. It displays the visual information output by the computer. Monitor size can vary, and the quality of display for monitors varies depending on the type of monitor and the level of resolution.

Keyboard

The keyboard is used to input information into the computer. The number and location of the keys on a keyboard can vary. In addition to letters, numbers, and symbols, most computer keyboards contain function keys, arrow keys, and a numeric keypad. Figure G.3 shows a typical keyboard.

The 12 keys at the top of the keyboard, labeled with the letter *F* followed by a number, are called *function keys*. Use these keys to perform functions within each of the Office applications. To the right of the regular keys is a group of special or dedicated keys. These keys are labeled with specific functions that will be performed when you press the key. Below the special keys are arrow keys. Use these keys to move the insertion point in the document screen.

Some keyboards include mode indicator lights to indicate that a particular mode, such as Caps Lock or Num Lock, has been turned on. Pressing the Caps Lock key disables the lowercase alphabet so that text is typed in all caps, while pressing the Num Lock key disables the special functions on the numeric keypad so that numbers can be typed using the keypad. When you select these modes, a light appears on the keyboard.

Figure G.3 Keyboard

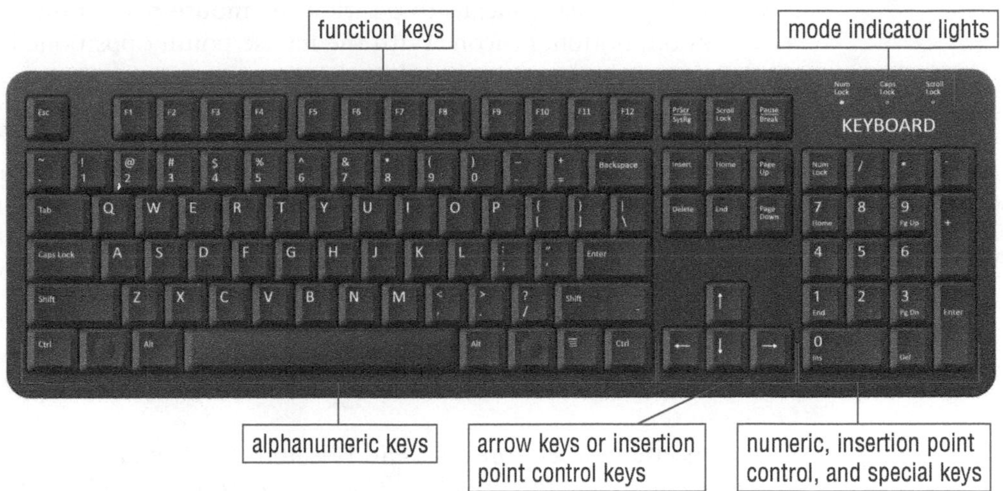

Drives and Ports

An internal hard drive is a disk drive that is located inside the PC and that stores data. External hard drives may be connected via USB ports for additional storage. Ports are the "plugs" on the PC, and are used to connect devices to the computer, such as the keyboard and mouse, the monitor, speakers, USB flash drives and so on. Most PCs will have a few USB ports, at least one display port, audio ports, and possibly an ethernet port (used to physically connect to the internet or a network).

Printer

An electronic version of a file is known as a *soft copy*. If you want to create a hard copy of a file, you need to print it. To print documents, you will need to access a printer, which will probably be either a laser printer or an ink-jet printer. A laser printer uses a laser beam combined with heat and pressure to print documents, while an ink-jet printer prints a document by spraying a fine mist of ink on the page.

Mouse

Most functions and commands in the Microsoft Office suite are designed to be performed using a mouse or a similar pointing device. A mouse is an input device that sits on a flat surface next to the computer. You can operate a mouse with your left or right hand. Moving the mouse on the flat surface causes a corresponding pointer to move on the screen, and clicking the left or right mouse buttons allows you to select various objects and commands.

Using the Mouse The applications in the Microsoft Office suite can be operated with the keyboard and a mouse. The mouse generally has two buttons on top, which you press to execute specific functions and commands. A mouse may also contain a wheel, which can be used to scroll in a window or as a third button. To use the mouse, rest it on a flat surface or a mouse pad. Put your hand over it with your palm resting on top of the mouse and your index finger resting on the left mouse button. As you move your hand, and thus the mouse, a corresponding pointer moves on the screen.

When using the mouse, you should understand four terms—*point*, *click*, *double-click*, and *drag*. To *point* means to position the mouse pointer on a desired item, such as an option, button, or icon. With the mouse pointer positioned on the item, *click* the left mouse button once to select the item. (In some cases you may *right-click*, which means to click the right mouse button, but generally, *click* refers to the left button.) To complete two steps at one time, such as choosing and then executing a function, *double-click* the left mouse button by tapping it twice in quick succession. The term *drag* means to click and hold down the left mouse button, move the mouse pointer to a specific location, and then release the button. Clicking and dragging is used, for instance, when moving a file from one location to another.

Hint Instructions in this course use the verb *click* to refer to tapping the left mouse button and the verb *press* to refer to pressing a key on the keyboard.

Using the Mouse Pointer The mouse pointer will look different depending on where you have positioned it and what function you are performing. The following are some of the ways the mouse pointer can appear when you are working in the Office suite:

- The mouse pointer appears as an I-beam (called the *I-beam pointer*) when you are inserting text in a file. The I-beam pointer can be used to move the insertion point or to select text.
- The mouse pointer appears as an arrow pointing up and to the left (called the *arrow pointer*) when it is moved to the Title bar, Quick Access Toolbar, ribbon, or an option in a dialog box, among other locations.
- The mouse pointer becomes a double-headed arrow (either pointing left and right, pointing up and down, or pointing diagonally) when you perform certain functions such as changing the size of an object.
- In certain situations, such as when you move an object or image, the mouse pointer displays with a four-headed arrow attached. The four-headed arrow means that you can move the object left, right, up, or down.
- When a request is being processed or when an application is being loaded, the mouse pointer may appear as a moving circle. The moving circle means "please wait." When the process is completed, the circle is replaced with a normal mouse pointer.
- When the mouse pointer displays as a hand with a pointing index finger, it indicates that more information is available about an item. The mouse pointer also displays as a hand with a pointing index finger when you hover over a hyperlink.

Touchpad

If you are working on a laptop computer, you may be using a touchpad instead of a mouse. A *touchpad* allows you to move the mouse pointer by moving your finger across a surface at the base of the keyboard (as shown in Figure G.4). You click and right-click by using your thumb to press the buttons located at the bottom of the touchpad. Some touchpads have special features such as scrolling or clicking something by tapping the surface of the touchpad instead of pressing a button with a thumb.

Figure G.4 Touchpad

Touchscreen

Smartphones, tablets, and touch monitors all use touchscreen technology (as shown in Figure G.5), which allows users to directly interact with the objects on the screen by touching them with fingers, thumbs, or a stylus. Multiple fingers or both thumbs can be used on most touchscreens, giving users the ability to zoom, rotate, and manipulate items on the screen. While many activities in this textbook can be completed using a device with a touchscreen, a mouse or touchpad might be required to complete a few activities.

Figure G.5 Touchscreen

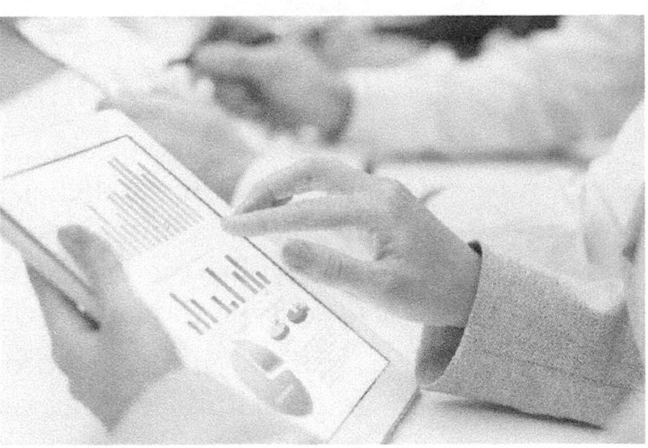

Choosing Commands

A *command* is an instruction that tells an application to complete a certain task. When an application such as Word or PowerPoint is open, the *ribbon* at the top of the window displays buttons and options for commands. To select a command with the mouse, point to it and then click the left mouse button.

Notice that the ribbon is organized into tabs, including File, Home, Insert, and so on. When the File tab is clicked, a *backstage area* opens with options such as opening or saving a file. Clicking any of the other tabs will display a variety of commands and options on the ribbon. Above the ribbon, buttons on the Quick Access Toolbar provide fast access to frequently used commands such as saving a file and undoing or redoing an action.

Using Keyboard Shortcuts and Accelerator Keys

As an alternative to using the mouse, keyboard shortcuts can be used for many commands. Shortcuts generally require two or more keys. For instance, in Word, press and hold down the Ctrl key while pressing P to display the Print backstage area, or press Ctrl + O to display the Open backstage area. A complete list of keyboard shortcuts can be found by searching the Help files in any Office application.

Office also provides shortcuts known as *accelerator keys* for every command or action on the ribbon. These accelerator keys are especially helpful for users with motor or visual disabilities or for power users who find it faster to use the keyboard than click with the mouse. To identify accelerator keys, press the Alt key on the keyboard. KeyTips display on the ribbon, as shown in Figure G.6. Press the keys indicated to execute the desired command. For example, to begin checking

Figure G.6 Word Home Tab KeyTips

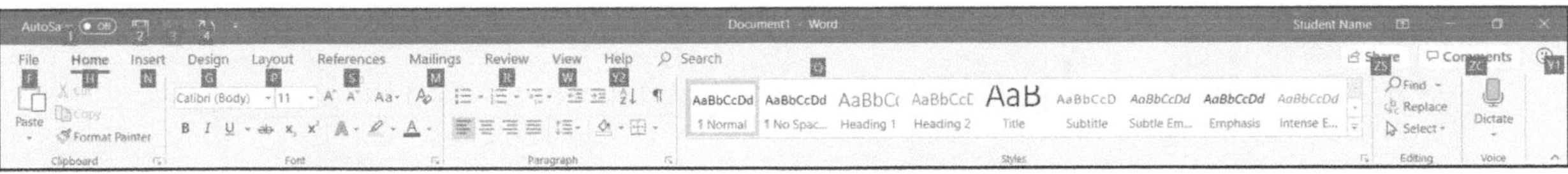

the spelling and grammar in a document, press the Alt key, press the R key on the keyboard to display the Review tab, and then press the letter C and the number 1 on the keyboard to open the Editor task pane.

Choosing Commands from a Drop-Down List

Some buttons include arrows that can be clicked to display a drop-down list of options. Point and click with the mouse to choose an option from the list. Some options in a drop-down list may have a letter that is underlined. This indicates that typing the letter will select the option. For instance, to select the option *Insert Table*, type the letter I on the keyboard.

If an option in a drop-down list is not available to be selected, it will appear gray or dimmed. If an option is preceded by a check mark, it is currently active. If it is followed by an ellipsis (…), clicking the option will open a dialog box.

Choosing Options from a Dialog Box or Task Pane

Some buttons and options open a *dialog box* or a task pane containing options for applying formatting or otherwise modifying the data in a file. For example, the Font dialog box shown in Figure G.7 contains options for modifying the font and adding effects. The dialog box contains two tabs—the Font tab and the Advanced tab. The tab that displays in the front is the active tab. Click a tab to make it active or press Ctrl + Tab on the keyboard. Alternately, press the Alt key and then type the letter that is underlined in the tab name.

Figure G.7 Word Font Dialog Box

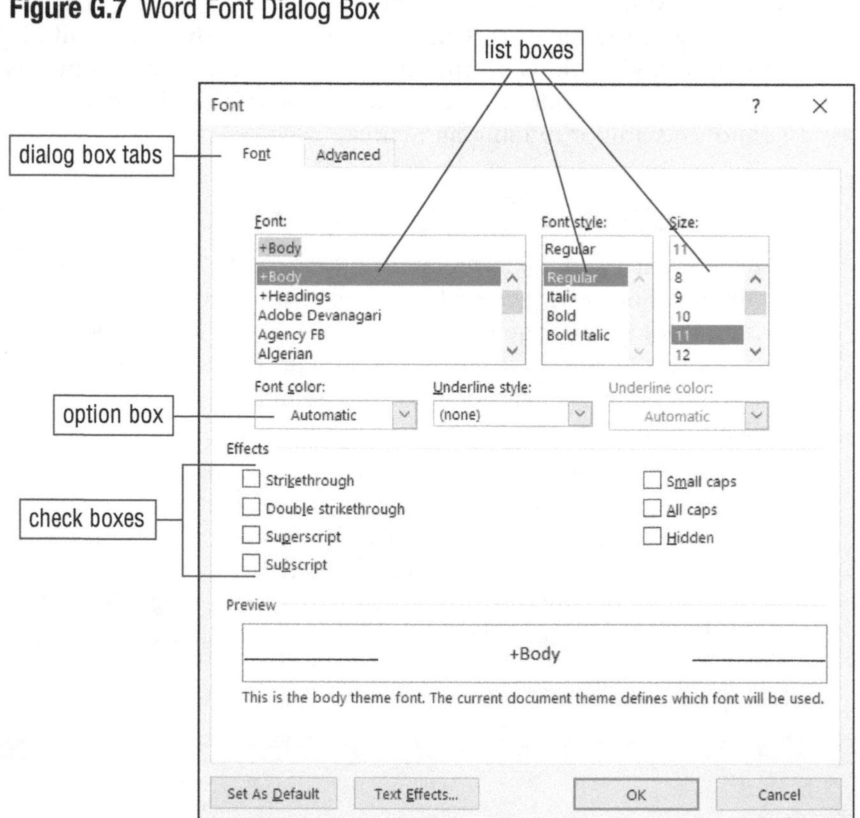

To choose an option from a dialog box using the mouse, position the arrow pointer on the option and then click the left mouse button. To move forward from option to option using the keyboard, you can press the Tab key. Press Shift + Tab to move back to a previous option. If the option displays with an underlined letter, you can choose it by pressing the Alt key and the underlined letter. When an option is selected, it is highlighted in blue or surrounded by a dotted or dashed box called a *marquee*. A dialog box contains one or more of the following elements: list boxes, option boxes, check boxes, text boxes, command buttons, radio buttons, and measurement boxes.

List Boxes and Option Boxes The fonts available in the Font dialog box, shown in Figure G.7 (on the previous page), are contained in a *list box*. Click an option in the list to select it. If the list is long, click the up or down arrows in the *scroll bar* at the right side of the box to scroll through all the options. Alternately, press the up or down arrow keys on the keyboard to move through the list, and press the Enter key when the desired option is selected.

Option boxes contain a drop-down list or gallery of options that opens when the arrow in the box is clicked. An example is the *Font color* option box in Figure G.8. To display the different color options, click the arrow at the right side of the box. If you are using the keyboard, press Alt + C.

Check Boxes Some options can be selected using a check box, such as the effect options in the dialog box in Figure G.7. If a check mark appears in the box, the option is active (turned on). If the check box does not contain a check mark, the option is inactive (turned off). Click a check box to make the option active or inactive. If you are using the keyboard, press Alt + the underlined letter of the option.

Text Boxes Some options in a dialog box require you to enter text. For example, see the Find and Replace dialog box shown in Figure G.8. In a text box, type or edit text with the keyboard, using the left and right arrow keys to move the insertion point without deleting text and use the Delete key or Backspace key to delete text.

Command Buttons The buttons at the bottom of the dialog box shown in Figure G.8 are called *command buttons*. Use a command button to execute or cancel a command. Some command buttons display with an ellipsis (...), which means another dialog box will open if you click that button. To choose a command button, click with the mouse or press the Tab key until the command button is surrounded by a marquee and then press the Enter key.

Figure G.8 Excel Find and Replace Dialog Box

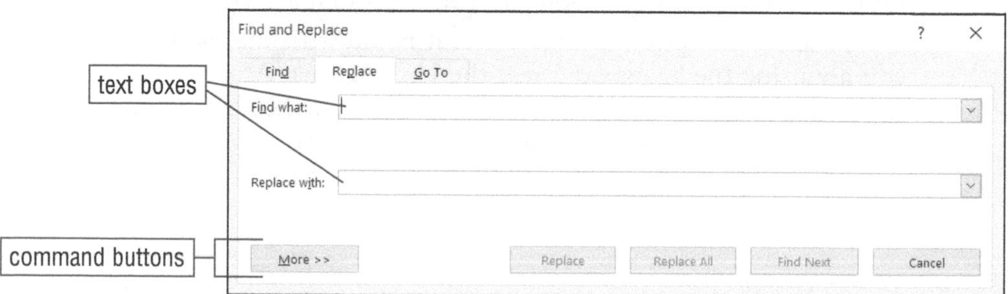

Figure G.9 Word Insert Table Dialog Box

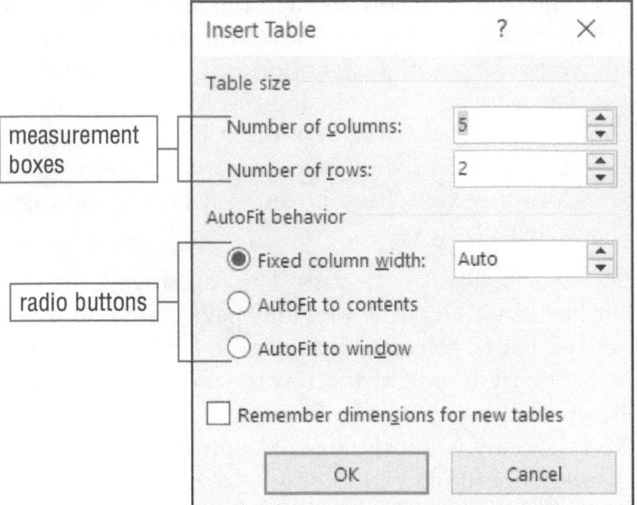

Radio Buttons The Insert Table dialog box shown in Figure G.9 contains an example of *radio buttons*. Only one radio button can be selected at any time. When the button is selected, it is filled with a dark circle. Click a button to select it, or press and hold down the Alt key, press the underlined letter of the option, and then release the Alt key.

Measurement Boxes A *measurement box* contains an amount that can be increased or decreased. An example is shown in Figure G.9. To increase or decrease the number in a measurement box, click the up or down arrow at the right side of the box. Using the keyboard, press and hold down the Alt key and then press the underlined letter for the option, press the Up Arrow key to increase the number or the Down Arrow key to decrease the number, and then release the Alt key.

Choosing Commands with Shortcut Menus

The Office applications include shortcut menus that contain commands related to different items. To display a shortcut menu, point to the item for which you want to view more options with the mouse pointer and then click the right mouse button, or press Shift + F10. The shortcut menu will appear wherever the insertion point is positioned. In some cases, the Mini toolbar will also appear with the shortcut menu. For example, if the insertion point is positioned in a paragraph of text in a Word document, clicking the right mouse button or pressing Shift + F10 will display the shortcut menu and Mini toolbar, as shown in Figure G.10.

To select an option from a shortcut menu with the mouse, click the option. If you are using the keyboard, press the Up or Down Arrow key until the option is selected and then press the Enter key. To close a shortcut menu without choosing an option, click outside the menu or press the Esc key.

Figure G.10 Shortcut Menu and Mini Toolbar

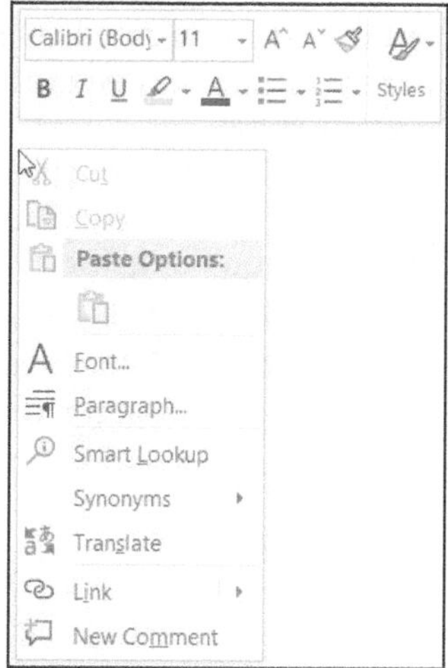

Working with Multiple Applications

As you learn the various applications in the Microsoft Office suite, you will notice many similarities between them. For example, the steps to save, close, and print are virtually the same whether you are working in Word, Excel, or PowerPoint. This consistency greatly enhances your ability to transfer knowledge learned in one application to another within the suite. Another benefit to using Microsoft Office is the ability to have more than one application open at the same time and to integrate content from one program with another. For example, you can open Word and create a document, open Excel and create a worksheet, and then copy a worksheet from the workbook into Word.

The Windows taskbar at the bottom of the screen displays buttons representing all the programs that are currently open. For example, Figure G.11 shows the taskbar with Word, Excel, Access, and PowerPoint open. To move from one program to another, click the taskbar button representing the desired application.

Maintaining Files and Folders

Windows includes a program named File Explorer that can be used to maintain files and folders. To open File Explorer, click the folder icon on the Windows taskbar. Use File Explorer to complete tasks such as copying, moving, renaming, and deleting files and folders and creating new folders. Some file management tasks can also be completed within Word, Excel, PowerPoint, or Access by clicking File and then *Open* or *Save As* and then clicking the *Browse* option to browse folders and files in a dialog box.

Directions and activities in this course assume that you are managing files and folders stored on a USB flash drive or on your computer's hard drive. If you are using your OneDrive account or another cloud-based storage service, some of the file and folder management tasks may vary.

Figure G.11 Windows Taskbar with Word, Excel, Access, and PowerPoint Open

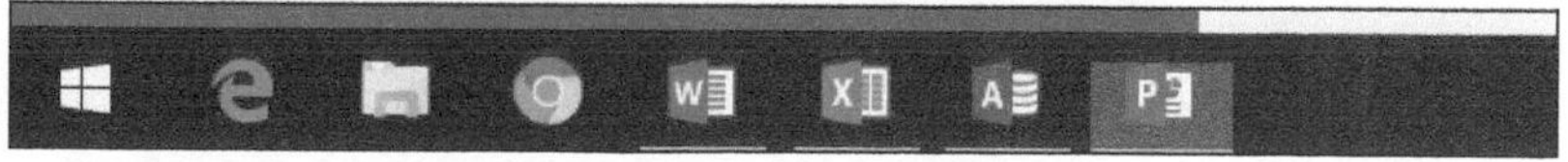

Creating and Naming a Folder

Files (such as Word documents, Excel workbooks, PowerPoint presentations, and Access databases) are easier to find again when they are grouped logically in folders. In File Explorer and in the Open or Save As dialog box, the names of files and folders are displayed in the Content pane. Each file has an icon showing what type of file it is, while folders are identified with the icon of a folder. See Figure G.12 for an example of the File Explorer window.

Create a new folder by clicking the New folder button at the top of the File Explorer window or in the dialog box. A new folder displays with the name *New folder* highlighted. Type a name for the folder to replace the highlighted text, and then press the Enter key. Folder names can include numbers, spaces, and some symbols.

Selecting and Opening Files and Folders

Select files or folders in the window to be managed. To select one file or folder, simply click on it. To select several adjacent files or folders, click the first file or folder, hold down the Shift key, and then click the last file or folder. To select files or folders that are not adjacent, click the first file or folder, hold down the Ctrl key, click any other files or folders, and then release the Ctrl key. To deselect, click anywhere in the window or dialog box.

When a file or folder is selected, the path to the folder displays in the Address bar. If the folder is located on an external storage device, the drive letter and name may display in the path. A right-pointing arrow displays to the right of each folder name in the Address bar. Click the arrow to view a list of subfolders within a folder.

Double-click a file or folder in the Content pane to open it. You can also select one or more files or folders, right-click, and then click the *Open* option in the shortcut menu.

Figure G.12 File Explorer Window

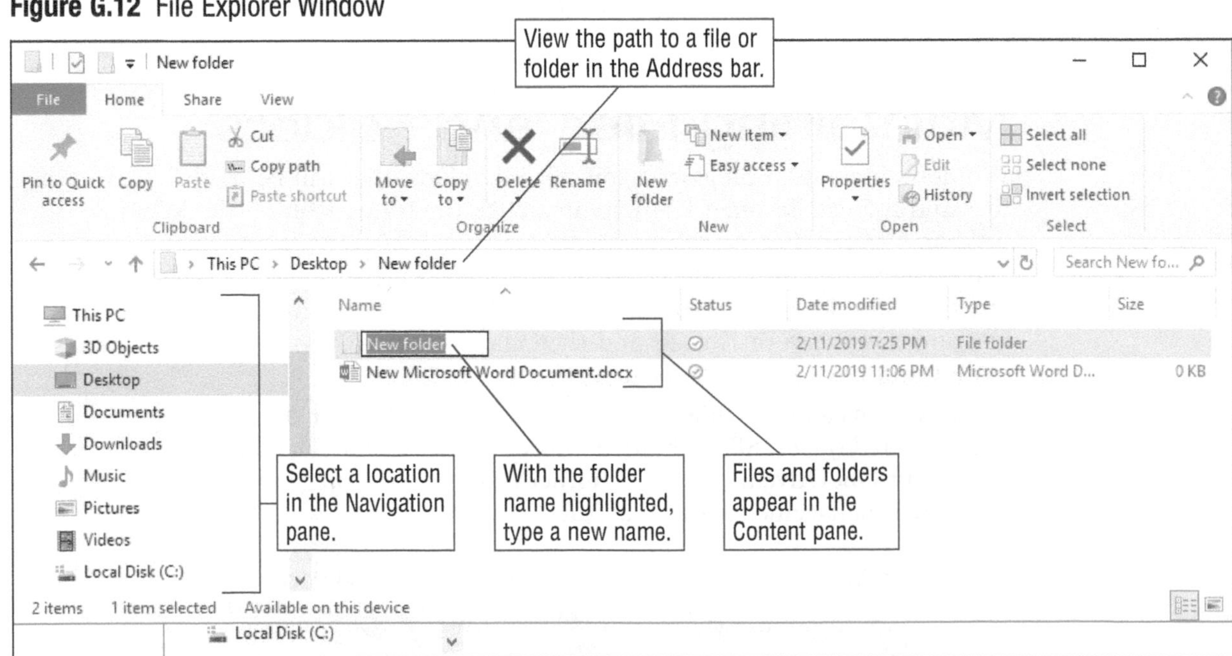

Deleting Files and Folders

Deleting files and folders is part of file maintenance. To delete a file or folder, select it and then press the Delete key. Alternatively, use the Delete button on the Home tab of the File Explorer window, or click the Organize button and then *Delete* in the dialog box. You can also right-click a file or folder and then choose the *Delete* option in the shortcut menu.

Files and folders deleted from the hard drive of the computer are automatically sent to the Recycle Bin, where they can easily be restored if necessary. If a file or folder is stored in another location, such as an external drive or online location, it may be permanently deleted. In this case, a message may appear asking for confirmation. To confirm that the file or folder should be deleted, click Yes.

To view the contents of the Recycle Bin, display the Windows desktop and then double-click the *Recycle Bin* icon. Deleted items in the Recycle Bin can be restored to their original locations, or the Recycle Bin can be emptied to free up space on the hard drive.

Moving and Copying Files and Folders

A file or folder may need to be moved or copied to another location. In File Explorer, select the file or folder and then click the Copy button at the top of the window, use the keyboard shortcut Ctrl + C, or right-click the file and select *Copy* in the shortcut menu. Navigate to the destination folder and then click the Paste button, use the keyboard shortcut Ctrl + P, or right-click and select *Paste*. If a copy is pasted to the same folder as the original, it will appear with the word *Copy* added to its name. To copy files in the Open or Save As dialog box, use the Organize button drop-down list or right-click to access the shortcut menu.

To move a file or folder, follow the same steps, but select *Cut* instead of *Copy* or press Ctrl + X instead of Ctrl + C. Files can also be dragged from one location to another. To do this, open two File Explorer windows. Click a file or folder and drag it to the other window while holding down the left mouse button.

Renaming Files and Folders

To rename a file or folder in File Explorer, click its name to highlight it and then type a new name, or right-click the file or folder and then select *Rename* at the shortcut menu. You can also select the file or folder and then click the Rename button on the Home tab of the File Explorer window or click *Rename* from the Organize button drop-down list at the Open or Save As dialog box. Type in a new name and then press the Enter key.

Viewing Files and Folders

Change how files and folders display in the Content pane in File Explorer by clicking the View tab and then clicking one of the view options in the Layout group. View files and folders as large, medium, or small icons; as tiles; in a list; or with details or information about the file or folder content. At the Open or Save As dialog box, click the Change your view button arrow and a list displays with similar options for viewing folders and files. Click to select an option in the list or click the Change your view button to see different views.

Displaying File Extensions Each file has a file extension that identifies the program and what type of file it is. Excel files have the extension *.xlsx;* Word files end with *.docx,* and so on. By default, file extensions are turned off. To view file extensions, open File Explorer, click the View tab, and then click the *File name extensions* check box to insert a check mark. Click the check box again to remove the check mark and stop viewing file extensions.

Displaying All Files The Open or Save As dialog box in an Office application may display only files specific to that application. For example, the Open or Save As dialog box in Word may only display Word documents. Viewing all files at the Open dialog box can be helpful in determining what files are available. Turn on the display of all files at the Open dialog box by clicking the file type button arrow at the right side of the *File Name* text box and then clicking *All Files* at the drop-down list.

Managing Files at the Info Backstage Area

The Info backstage area in Word, Excel, and PowerPoint provides buttons for managing files such as uploading and sharing a file, copying a path, and opening File Explorer with the current folder active. To use the buttons at the Info backstage area, open Word, Excel, or PowerPoint and then open a file. Click the File tab and then click the *Info* option. If a file is opened from the computer's hard drive or an external drive, four buttons display near the top of the Info backstage area as shown in Figure G.13.

Click the Upload button to upload the open file to a shared location such as a OneDrive account. Click the Share button and a window displays indicating that the file must be saved to OneDrive before it can be shared and provides an option that, when clicked, will save the file to OneDrive. Click the Copy Path button and a copy of the path for the current file is saved in a temporary location. This path can be pasted into another file, an email, or any other location where you want to keep track of the file's path. Click the Open file location button and File Explorer opens with the current folder active.

Figure G.13 Info Backstage Buttons

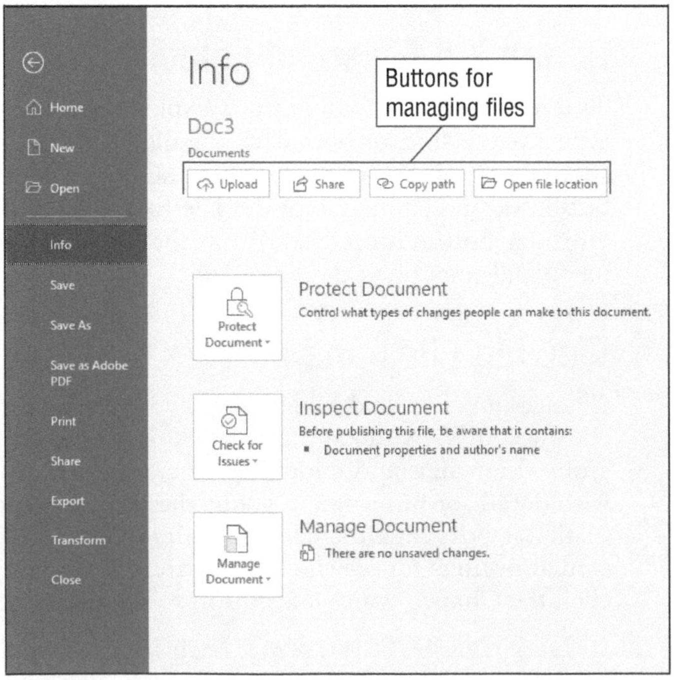

If you open Word, Excel, or PowerPoint and then open a file from OneDrive, only two buttons display—Share and Open file location. Click the Share button to display a window with options for sharing the file with others and specifying whether the file can be viewed and edited, or only viewed. Click the Open file location button to open File Explorer with the current folder active.

Customizing Settings

Before beginning computer activities in this textbook, you may need to customize your monitor's settings and change the DPI display setting. Activities in the course assume that the monitor display is set at 1920 × 1080 pixels and the DPI set at 125%. If you are unable to make changes to the monitor's resolution or the DPI settings, the activities can still be completed successfully. Some references in the text might not perfectly match what you see on your screen, so you may not be able to perform certain steps exactly as written. For example, an item in a drop-down gallery might appear in a different column or row than what is indicated in the step instructions.

Before you begin learning the applications in the Microsoft Office suite, take a moment to check the display settings on the computer you are using. Your monitor's display settings are important because the ribbon in the Microsoft Office suite adjusts to the screen resolution setting of your computer monitor. A computer monitor set at a high resolution will have the ability to show more buttons in the ribbon than will a monitor set to a low resolution. The illustrations in this textbook were created with a screen resolution display set at 1920 × 1080 pixels, as shown in Figure G.14.

Figure G.14 Word Ribbon Set at 1920 x 1080 Screen Resolution

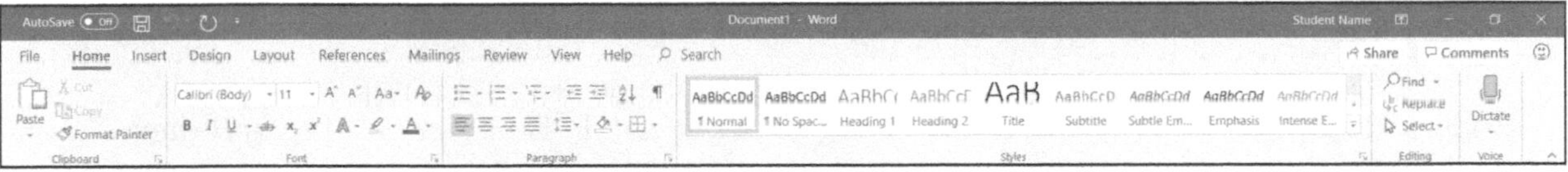

Activity 1 Adjusting Monitor Display

Note: The resolution settings may be locked on lab computers. Also, some laptop screens and small monitors may not be able to display in a 1920 × 1080 resolution or change the DPI setting.

1. At the Windows desktop, right-click in a blank area of the screen.
2. In the shortcut menu, click the *Display settings* option.

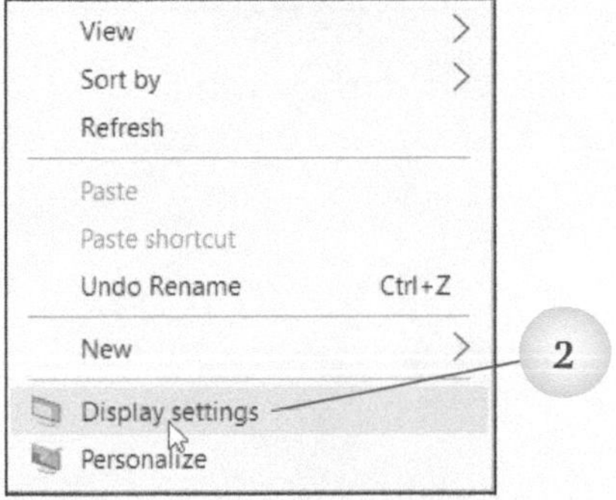

3. At the Settings window with the *Display* option selected, scroll down and look at the current setting displayed in the *Resolution* option box. If your screen is already set to 1920 × 1080, skip ahead to Step 6.

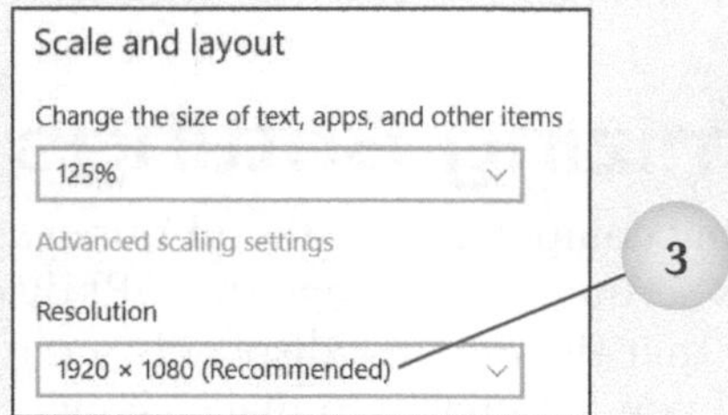

4. Click the Resolution option box and then click the *1920 × 1080* option. ***Note: Depending on the privileges you are given on a school machine, you may not be able to complete Steps 4–5. If necessary, check with your instructor for alternative instructions.***

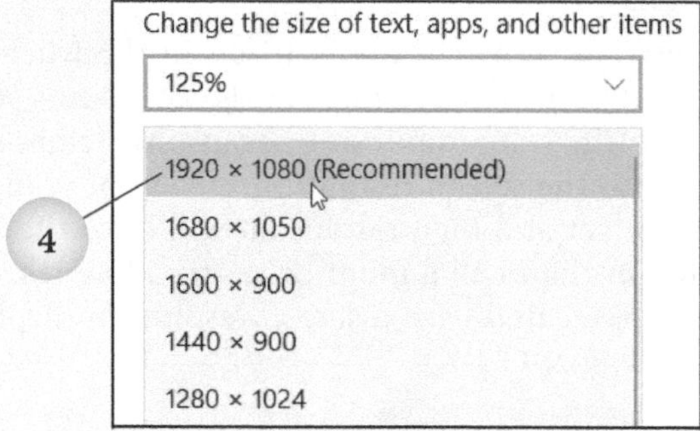

5. Click the Keep Changes button.
6. At the Settings window, take note of the current DPI percentage next to the text *Change the size of text, apps, and other items*. If the percentage is already set to 125%, skip to Step 8.
7. Click the option box below the text *Change the size of text, apps, and other items,* and then click the *125%* option in the drop-down list

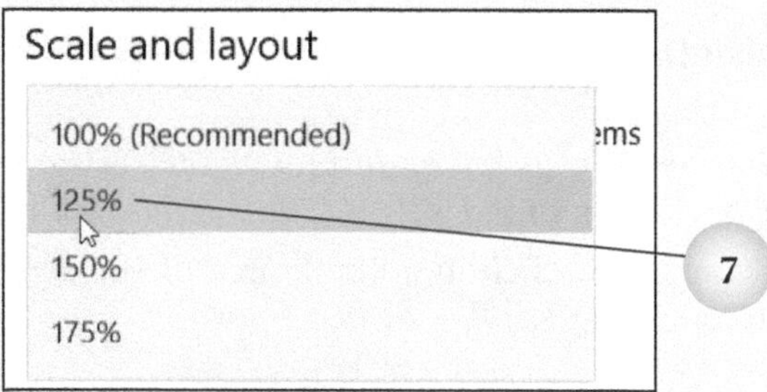

8. Click the Close button to close the Settings window.

Retrieving and Copying Data Files

While working through the activities in this course, you will often be using data files as starting points. These files are provided through your Cirrus online course, and your instructor may post them in another location such as your school's network drive. You can download all the files at once (described in the activity below), or download only the files needed for a specific chapter.

Activity 2 Downloading Files to a USB Flash Drive

Note: In this activity, you will download data files from your Cirrus online course. Make sure you have an active internet connection before starting this activity. Check with your instructor if you do not have access to your Cirrus online course.

1. Insert your USB flash drive into an available USB port.
2. Navigate to the Course Resources section of your Cirrus online course. ***Note: The steps in this activity assume you are using the Chrome browser. If you are using a different browser, the following steps may vary.***
3. Click the Student Data Files link in the Course Resources section. A zip file containing the student data files will automatically begin downloading from the Cirrus website.
4. Click the button in the lower left corner of the screen once the files have finished downloading.

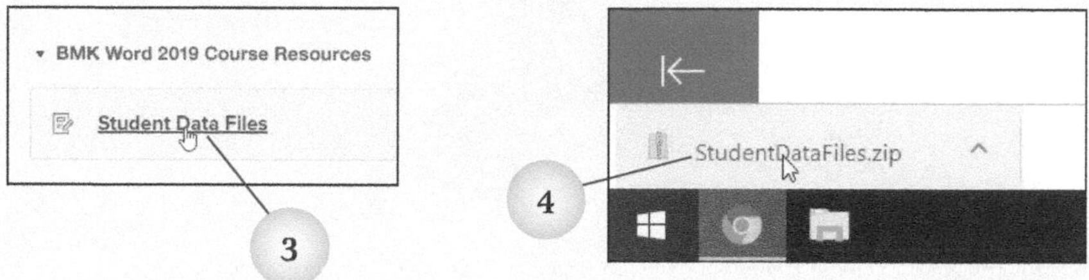

5. Right-click the *StudentDataFiles* folder in the Content pane.
6. Click the *Copy* option in the shortcut menu.
7. Click the USB flash drive that displays in the Navigation pane at the left side of the File Explorer window.
8. Click the Home tab in the File Explorer window.
9. Click the Paste button in the Clipboard group.

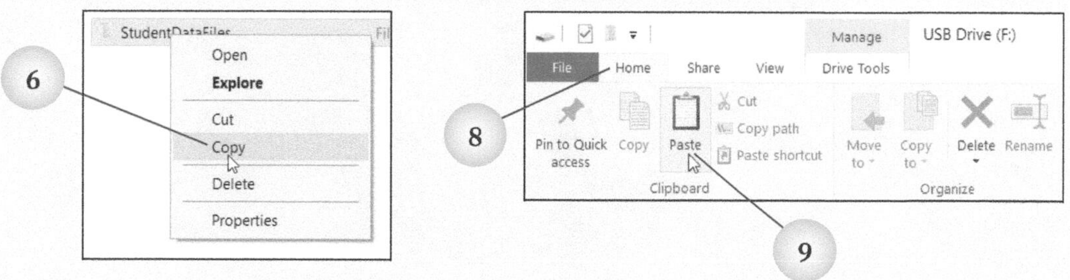

10. Close the File Explorer window by clicking the Close button in the upper right corner of the window.

Microsoft®

Excel® Level 1

Unit 1

Preparing and Formatting Worksheets

Microsoft®

Excel®

Preparing an Excel Workbook

Performance Objectives

Upon successful completion of Chapter 1, you will be able to:

1 Identify the various elements of an Excel workbook
2 Create a worksheet
3 Enter data in a worksheet
4 Save a workbook
5 Edit data in a cell
6 Print a worksheet
7 Close a workbook and close Excel
8 Use the AutoComplete, AutoCorrect, and AutoFill features
9 Open a workbook
10 Pin and unpin a workbook and folder to and from the *Recent* option list
11 Insert a formula using the AutoSum button
12 Copy a formula using the fill handle
13 Select cells and data within cells
14 Apply basic formatting to cells in a workbook
15 Use the Tell Me feature
16 Use the Help feature

Microsoft Excel is a spreadsheet program that allows users to organize, analyze, and evaluate numerical and financial data. An Excel spreadsheet can be used for such activities as creating financial statements, preparing budgets, managing inventory, and analyzing cash flow. This chapter will introduce the basics of creating a worksheet, opening workbooks, and saving workbooks. In a worksheet, learn to enter data, as well as the use of formulas to calculate sums and averages. Learn to enter data quickly and efficiently using features such as the fill handle and to apply basic formatting to data in conventional accounting style.

Before beginning the chapter work, copy the EL1C1 folder to your storage medium and then make EL1C1 the active folder.

The online course includes additional training and assessment resources.

Activity 1 Prepare a Worksheet with Employee Information **3 Parts**

You will create a worksheet containing employee information, edit the contents, and then print, save and close the workbook.

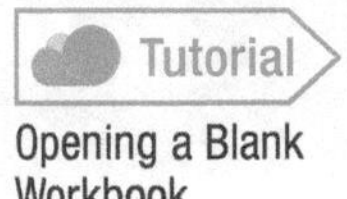

Opening a Blank Workbook

Creating a Worksheet

Open Excel by clicking the *Excel* tile at the Windows Start menu, or by following other steps as needed depending on the operating system. At the Excel opening screen, click the *Blank workbook* template. This displays a workbook with a blank worksheet, as shown in Figure 1.1. The elements of a blank Excel worksheet are described in Table 1.1.

A file created in Excel is referred to as a *workbook*. An Excel workbook consists of an individual worksheet (or *sheet*) by default but it can contain multiple worksheets, like the sheets of paper in a notebook. Notice the tab named *Sheet1*, at the bottom of the Excel window. The area containing the gridlines in the Excel window is called the *worksheet area*. Figure 1.2 identifies the elements of the worksheet area. Create a worksheet in the worksheet area that will be saved as part of a workbook. Columns in a worksheet are labeled with letters of the alphabet and rows are labeled with numbers. The intersection of a column and a row creates a box, which is referred to as a *cell*. A cell is where data and formulas are entered.

Figure 1.1 Blank Excel Worksheet

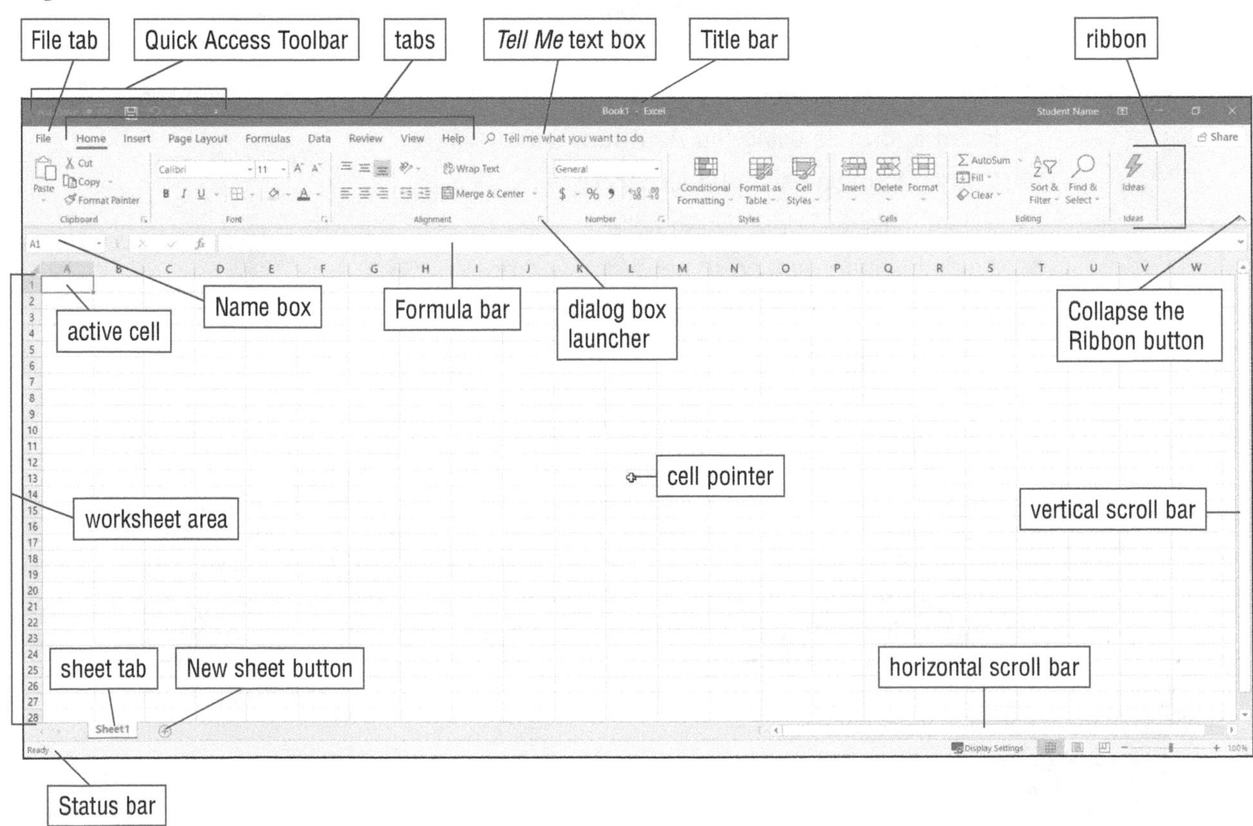

Table 1.1 Elements of an Excel Worksheet

Feature	Description
active cell	the currently selected cell, surrounded by a thick green border
cell pointer	when this icon appears, select cells by clicking or dragging the mouse
Collapse the Ribbon button	when clicked, removes the ribbon from the screen (Redisplay the ribbon by double-clicking a tab, except the File tab.)
dialog box launcher	click to open a dialog box with more options for that group
File tab	displays the backstage area that contains options for working with and managing files
Formula bar	displays the contents stored in the active cell
horizontal and vertical scroll bars	used to scroll left and right or up and down to view various parts of the worksheet
Name box	displays the active cell address or name assigned to the active cell
New sheet button	click to insert a new worksheet in the workbook
Quick Access Toolbar	contains buttons for commonly used commands that can be executed with a single mouse click
ribbon	contains the tabs with commands and buttons
sheet tab	identifies the current worksheet in the workbook
Status bar	displays the current mode, action messages, view buttons, and Zoom slider bar
tab	contains commands and buttons organized into groups
Tell Me text box	provides information and guidance on how to perform an action
Title bar	displays the workbook name followed by the application name
worksheet area	contains the cells used to create a worksheet

Figure 1.2 Elements of the Worksheet Area

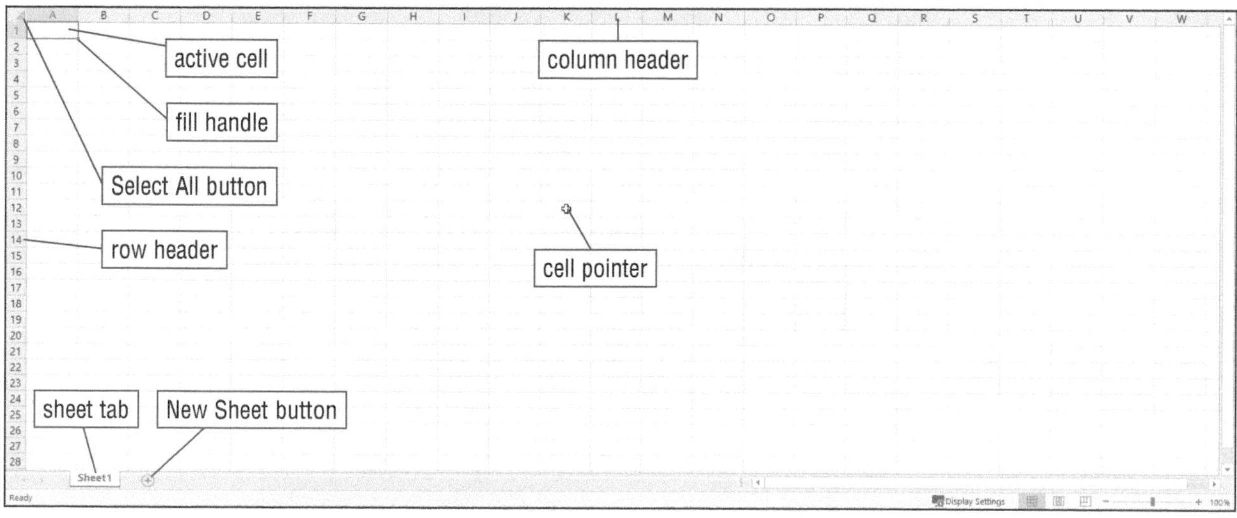

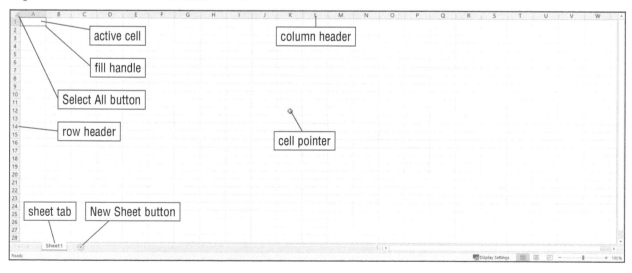

The horizontal and vertical lines that define the cells in the worksheet area are called *gridlines*. When a cell is clicked, it becomes active and a thick green border appears around it. The cell address, also called the *cell reference*, appears in the Name box. The cell reference includes the column letter and row number. For example, if the first cell of the worksheet is active, the cell reference *A1* is shown in the Name box. Any number of adjacent cells can be made active and form a range. A range is typically identified by the first cell reference and last cell reference separated by a colon. For example, the range A1:C1 contains the cells A1, B1, and C1.

Entering Data in a Worksheet

Entering Data

Navigating and Scrolling

Find & Select

Hint To make a cell active, position the cell pointer in the cell and then click the left mouse button.

Hint Ctrl + G is the keyboard shortcut to display the Go To dialog box.

Enter data such as text, a number, or a value in a cell. To enter data in a cell, make the cell active and then type the data. To make the next cell active, press the Tab key. Table 1.2 shows additional commands for making a specific cell active.

Another method for making a cell active is to use the Go To feature. To use this feature, click the Find & Select button in the Editing group on the Home tab and then click *Go To*. At the Go To dialog box, type the cell reference in the *Reference* text box and then click OK.

Before typing data into the active cell, check the Status bar. The word *Ready* should display at the left. As data is typed in a cell, the word *Ready* changes to *Enter*. Data typed in a cell is shown in the cell and in the Formula bar. If the data entered in a cell is longer than the cell can accommodate, the data overlaps the next cell to the right. (It does not become a part of the next cell—it simply overlaps it. How to change column widths to accommodate data is explained later in this chapter.)

Table 1.2 Commands for Making a Specific Cell Active

To make this cell active	Press
cell below current cell	Enter
cell above current cell	Shift + Enter
next cell	Tab
previous cell	Shift + Tab
cell at beginning of row	Home
next cell in direction of arrow	Up, Down, Left, or Right Arrow key
last cell in worksheet	Ctrl + End
first cell in worksheet	Ctrl + Home
cell in next window	Page Down
cell in previous window	Page Up
cell in window to right	Alt + Page Down
cell in window to left	Alt + Page Up

If data entered in a cell consists of text and the text does not fit in the cell, it overlaps the next cell to the right. If, however, a number is entered in a cell and the number is too long to fit in the cell, Excel changes the display of the number to number symbols *(###)*. This change is made because Excel does not want to mislead users by showing only part of a number in a cell.

Along with the keyboard, the mouse can be used to make a specific cell active. To make a specific cell active with the mouse, position the mouse pointer, which appears as a white plus symbol (✚) (called the *cell pointer*), in the cell and then click the left mouse button. The pointer appears as a white plus sign when positioned in a cell in the worksheet and as an arrow when positioned on other elements of the Excel window, such as options and buttons on tabs and scroll bars.

Scroll through a worksheet using the horizontal and/or vertical scroll bars. Scrolling shifts the display of cells in the worksheet area but does not change the active cell. Scroll through a worksheet until the desired cell is visible and then click in the cell to make it active.

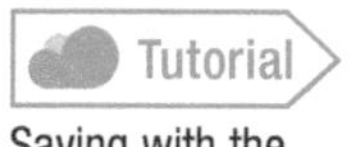

Saving with the Same Name

Saving with a New Name

Save

Quick Steps

Save Workbook
1. Click Save button on Quick Access Toolbar.
2. At Save As backstage area, click *Browse* option.
3. At Save As dialog box, navigate to folder.
4. Type workbook name.
5. Press Enter key.

Hint Ctrl + S is the keyboard shortcut to save a workbook.

Saving a Workbook

Save an Excel workbook, including all sheets within it, by clicking the Save button on the Quick Access Toolbar or by clicking the File tab and then clicking the *Save As* option at the backstage area. At the Save As backstage area, click the *Browse* option and the Save As dialog box displays. At the Save As dialog box, click the desired location in the Navigation pane, type a name for the workbook in the *File name* text box, and then press the Enter key or click the Save button. Bypass the Save As backstage area and go directly to the Save As dialog box by using the keyboard shortcut F12.

To save an Excel workbook in the EL1C1 folder, display the Save As dialog box, navigate to the correct drive in the Navigation pane, and then double-click *EL1C1* in the Content pane.

A workbook file name can contain up to 255 characters, including the drive letter and any folder names, and it can include spaces. Each file should have a distinct name. Excel will not allow two workbooks to be saved with the same file name in the same folder, even if one is in uppercase and one is lowercase. (For example, one file cannot be named *EXPENSES* and another *expenses*.) Also, some symbols cannot be used in a file name, such as the following:

forward slash (/)	question mark (?)
backslash (\)	quotation mark (")
greater-than symbol (>)	colon (:)
less-than symbol (<)	asterisk (*)
pipe symbol (|)	

If changes are made to a workbook, save the file again before closing it. It is a good practice to save periodically while working with a file to be sure no changes are lost if the application crashes or freezes or if power is interrupted.

Note: If an Excel workbook is stored in a cloud location such as Microsoft OneDrive, OneDrive for Business, or SharePoint Online, any changes to it will be saved automatically with the AutoSave feature. Multiple users can edit a file and AutoSave will save the workbook every few seconds so that changes can be seen by everyone. AutoSave can be turned on or off by clicking the toggle switch in the upper left corner of the Excel screen.

Activity 1a Creating and Saving a Workbook

Part 1 of 3

1. Open Excel by clicking the *Excel* tile at the Windows Start menu. (Depending on your operating system, the steps to open Excel may vary.)
2. At the Excel opening screen, click the *Blank workbook* template. (This opens a workbook with a blank worksheet.)
3. At the blank Excel worksheet, create the worksheet shown in Figure 1.3 by completing the following steps:
   a. Press the Enter key to make cell A2 the active cell.
   b. Type Employee in cell A2.
   c. Press the Tab key. (This makes cell B2 active.)
   d. Type Location and then press the Tab key. (This makes cell C2 active.)
   e. Type Benefits and then press the Enter key to move the insertion point to cell A3.
   f. Type Avery in cell A3.
   g. Continue typing the data shown in Figure 1.3. (For commands that make specific cells active, refer to Table 1.2.)
4. After typing the data shown in the cells in Figure 1.3, save the workbook by completing the following steps:
   a. Click the Save button on the Quick Access Toolbar.
   b. At the Save As backstage area, click the *Browse* option.
   c. At the Save As dialog box, navigate to your EL1C1 folder in the Navigation pane and then double-click the *EL1C1* folder in the Content pane.
   d. Select the text in the *File name* text box and then type 1-EmpBene.
   e. Press the Enter key or click the Save button.

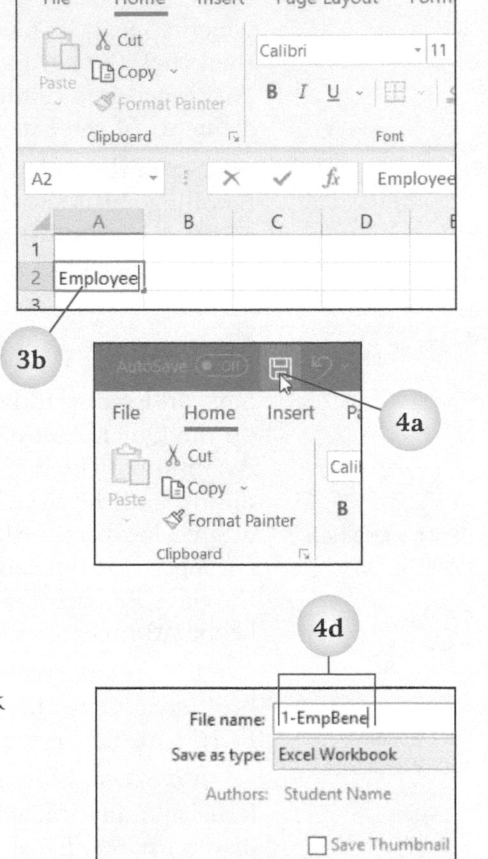

Check Your Work

Figure 1.3 Activity 1a

	A	B	C	D
1				
2	Employee	Location	Benefits	
3	Avery			
4	Connors			
5	Estrada			
6	Juergens			
7	Mikulich			
8	Talbot			
9				

Editing Data

Editing Data in a Cell

Edit data being typed in a cell by pressing the Backspace key to delete the character to the left of the insertion point or pressing the Delete key to delete the character to the right of the insertion point. To change the data in a cell, click in the cell to make it active and then type the new data. When a cell containing data is active, anything typed will take the place of the existing data.

If only a portion of the data in a cell needs to be edited, double-click in the cell. This makes the cell active, moves the insertion point inside the cell, and displays the word *Edit* at the left side of the Status bar. Move the insertion point using the arrow keys or the mouse and then make the needed corrections. Press the Home key to move the insertion point to the first character in the cell or Formula bar or press the End key to move the insertion point to the last character.

When the editing of data in a cell is complete, be sure to change out of the Edit mode. To do this, make another cell active by pressing the Enter key, the Tab key, or Shift + Tab. Two other ways to change out of the Edit mode and return to the Ready mode are to click in another cell and to click the Enter button on the Formula bar.

Cancel

Enter

If the active cell does not contain data, the Name box displays only the cell reference (by column letter and row number). As data is typed, two buttons become active on the Formula bar to the right of the Name box, as shown in Figure 1.4. Click the Cancel button to delete the current cell entry. (A cell entry can also be deleted by pressing the Delete key.) Click the Enter button when finished typing or editing the cell entry. Click the Enter button on the Formula bar and the word *Enter* (or *Edit*) at the left of the Status bar changes to *Ready*.

Figure 1.4 Buttons on the Formula Bar

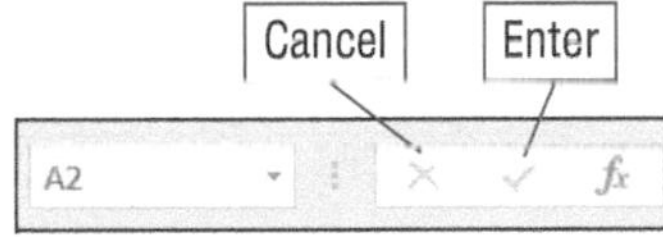

Activity 1b **Editing Data in a Cell** — Part 2 of 3

1. With **1-EmpBene** open, double-click in cell A7 (contains *Mikulich*).
2. Move the insertion point immediately left of the *k* and then type c. (This changes the spelling to *Mickulich*.)
3. Click in cell A4 (contains *Connors*), type Bryant, and then press the Tab key. (Clicking only once allows you to type over the existing data.)
4. Edit cell C2 by completing the following steps:
   a. Click the Find & Select button in the Editing group on the Home tab and then click *Go To* at the drop-down list.

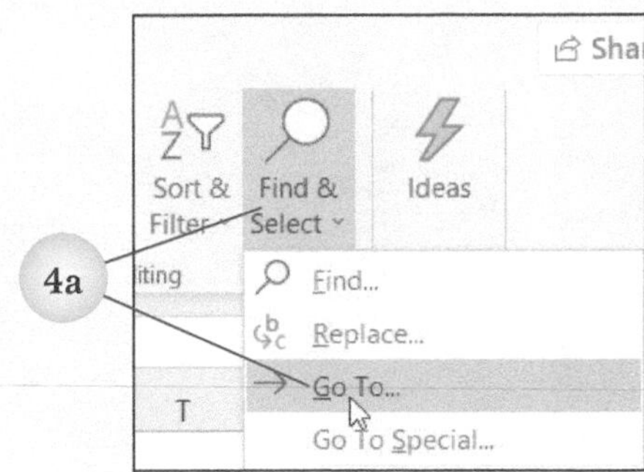

b. At the Go To dialog box, type c2 in the *Reference* text box and then click OK.
c. Type Classification (over *Benefits*).

5. Click in any other cell.
6. Click the Save button on the Quick Access Toolbar to save the workbook again.

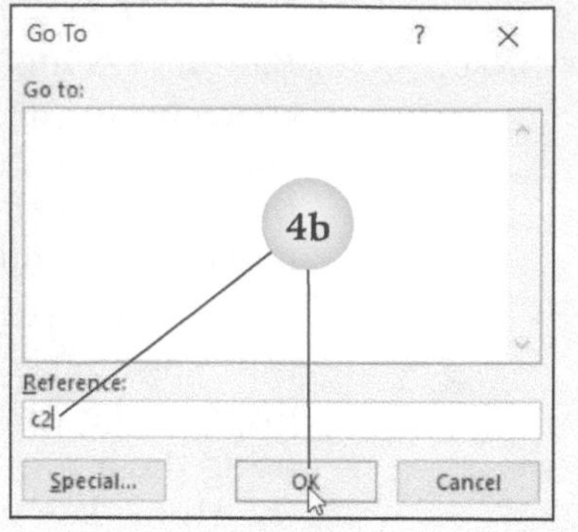

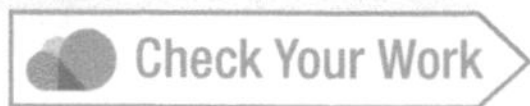

Printing a Worksheet

Hint Ctrl + P is the keyboard shortcut to display the Print backstage area.

Printing a Worksheet

With a workbook open, click the File tab and the Home backstage area displays, as shown in Figure 1.5. Use buttons and options at the backstage area to perform actions such as opening, closing, saving, and printing a workbook. Click the Back button (in the upper left corner of the backstage area) to exit the backstage area without completing an action or press the Esc key on the keyboard.

Print a worksheet from the Print backstage area, as shown in Figure 1.6. To display this backstage area, click the File tab and then click the *Print* option. The Print backstage area can also be displayed with the keyboard shortcut Ctrl + P.

Figure 1.5 Home Backstage Area

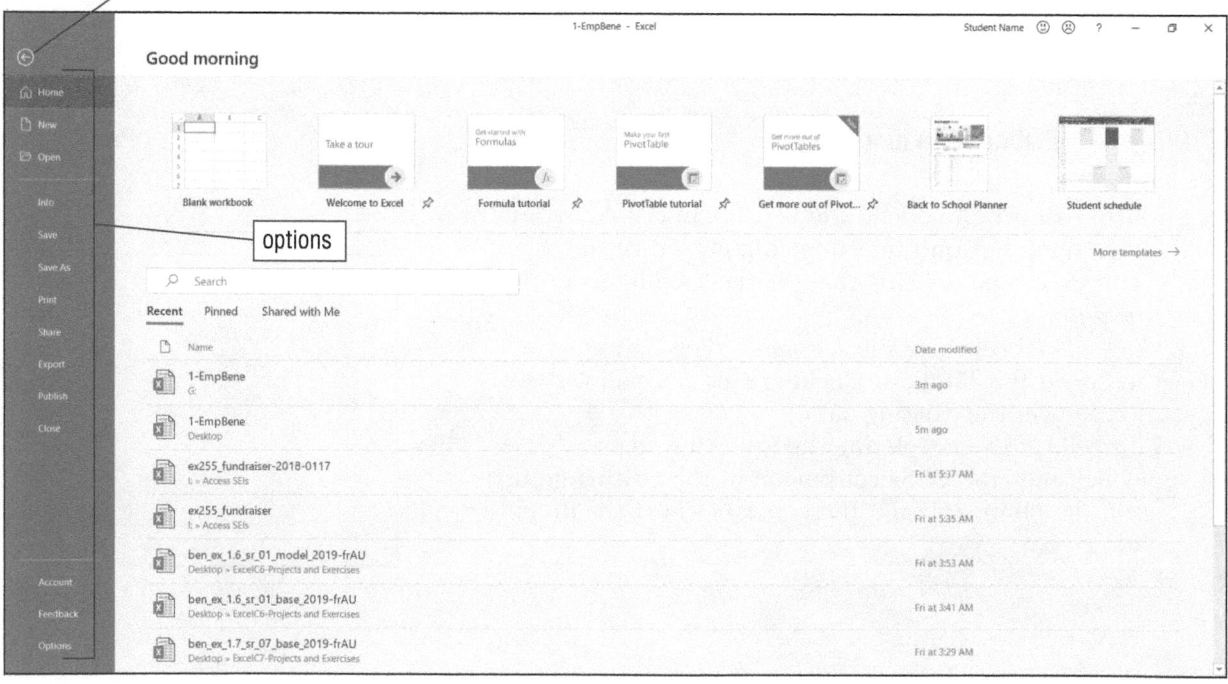

Figure 1.6 Print Backstage Area

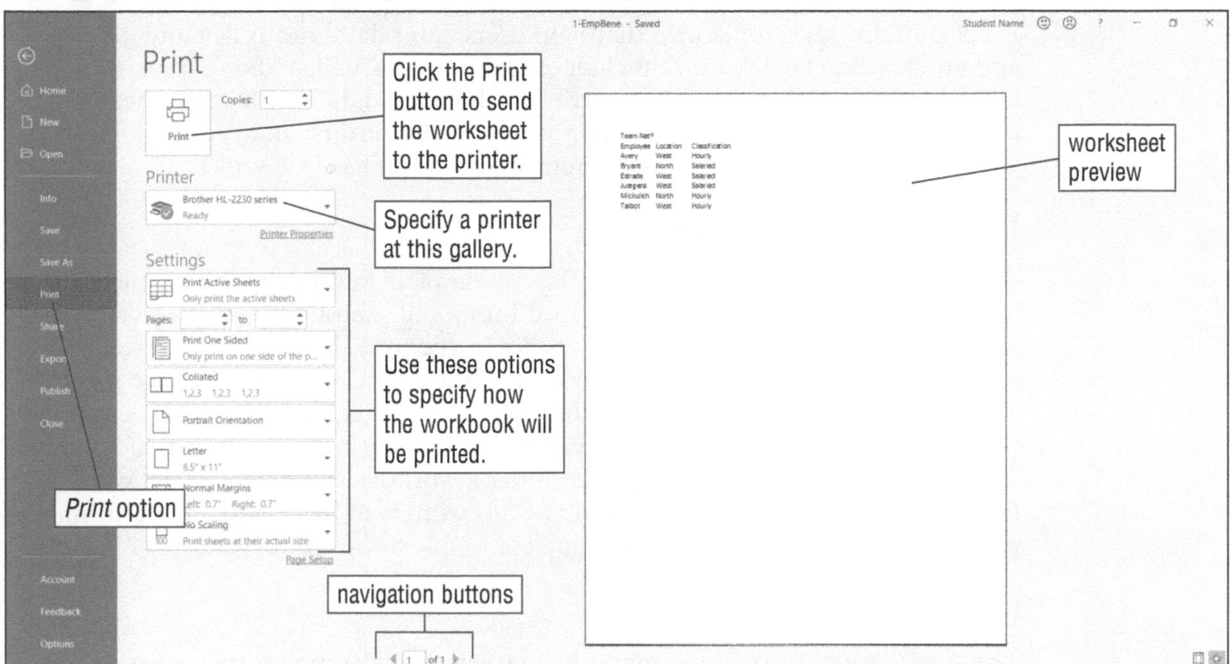

Print
Click the Print button to send the worksheet to the printer.
Printer
Specify a printer at this gallery.
Settings
Use these options to specify how the workbook will be printed.
worksheet preview
Print option
navigation buttons

Quick Steps

Print Worksheet

1. Click File tab.
2. Click *Print* option.
3. Click Print button.

Click the Print button in the Print backstage area to send the worksheet to the printer and use the *Copies* measurement box to specify the number of copies to be printed. Below the Print button are two categories: *Printer* and *Settings*. Use the gallery in the *Printer* category to specify the printer. The *Settings* category contains a number of galleries, each with options for specifying how the workbook will be printed. Use the galleries to specify whether the pages are collated when printed; what page orientation, page size, and margins the workbook should have; and whether the worksheet will be scaled to print all rows and columns of data on one page.

Another method for printing is to click the Quick Print button on the Quick Access Toolbar to send the workbook directly to the printer. To insert this button on the Quick Access Toolbar, click the arrow button at the right of the toolbar and then click *Quick Print* at the drop-down list. To remove the button, right-click it and then click *Remove from Quick Access Toolbar* at the drop-down list.

Tutorial

Closing a Workbook and Closing Excel

Closing a Workbook and Closing Excel

To close an Excel workbook without closing Excel, click the File tab and then click the *Close* option. Using the keyboard shortcut Ctrl + F4 will also close a workbook. To close Excel, click the Close button in the upper right corner of the screen. The Close button contains an *X*, and if the mouse pointer is positioned on the button, the button background changes from green to red and a ScreenTip displays with the name *Close*. Pressing the keyboard shortcut Alt + F4 will also close Excel.

Quick Steps

Close Workbook

1. Click File tab.
2. Click *Close* option.

OR

Press Ctrl + F4.

Close Excel

Click Close button.

OR

Press Alt + F4.

Close

Using Automatic Entering Features

Excel contains several features that help users enter data into cells more quickly and efficiently. These features include AutoComplete, which allows users to automatically complete multiple entries of the same data; AutoCorrect, which automatically corrects many common typographical errors; and AutoFill, which automatically inserts words, numbers, or formulas in a series.

Using AutoComplete and AutoCorrect

Using AutoComplete

The AutoComplete feature makes it easy to complete multiple entries of the same data. As the first few characters are typed into a cell, AutoComplete predicts what will be typed next based on previous entries in the worksheet, and will automatically complete the entry based on its prediction. If the AutoComplete entry is correct, accept it by pressing the Tab key or the Enter key. If it is incorrect, simply continue typing the correct data. This feature can be very useful in a worksheet that contains repetitive data entries. For example, consider a worksheet that repeats the word *Payroll*. The second and subsequent times this word is to be inserted in a cell, simply typing the letter *P* will cause AutoComplete to insert the entire word.

Using AutoCorrect

The AutoCorrect feature automatically corrects many common typing errors. To see what symbols and words are included in AutoCorrect, click the File tab and then click *Options*. At the Excel Options dialog box, click *Proofing* in the left panel and then click the AutoCorrect Options button in the right panel. This displays the AutoCorrect dialog box with the AutoCorrect tab selected, as shown in Figure 1.7, with a list box containing the replacement data.

At the AutoCorrect dialog box, type the text shown in the first column in the list box and then press the spacebar and the text in the second column is inserted in the cell. Along with symbols, the AutoCorrect dialog box contains commonly misspelled words and common typographical errors.

Figure 1.7 AutoCorrect Dialog Box with the AutoCorrect Tab Selected

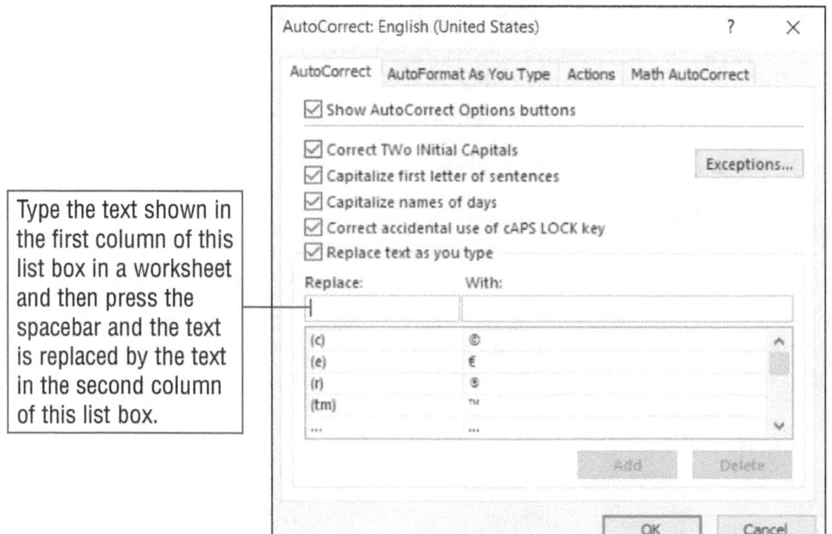

Activity 1c Inserting Data in Cells with AutoCorrect and AutoComplete

Part 3 of 3

1. With **1-EmpBene** open, make cell A1 active.
2. Type text in cell A1 as shown in Figure 1.8. Insert the ® symbol by typing (r) and then pressing the Enter key. (AutoCorrect will change (r) to ®.)
3. Type the remaining text in the cells. When you type the *W* in *West* in cell B5, the AutoComplete feature will insert *West*. Accept this by pressing the Tab key. (Pressing the Tab key accepts *West* and also makes the cell to the right active.) Use the AutoComplete feature to enter *West* in cells B6 and B8 and *North* in cell B7. Use AutoComplete to enter the second and subsequent occurrences of *Salaried* and *Hourly*.
4. Click the Save button on the Quick Access Toolbar.
5. Print **1-EmpBene** by clicking the File tab, clicking the *Print* option, and then clicking the Print button at the Print backstage area. (The gridlines will not print.)

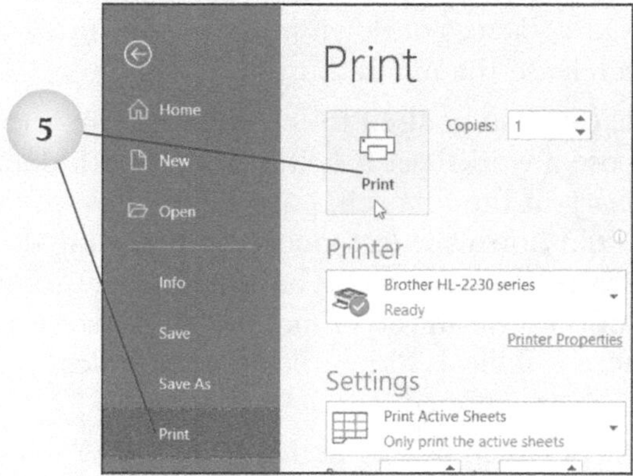

6. Close the workbook by clicking the File tab and then clicking the *Close* option at the backstage area.

Figure 1.8 Activity 1c

	A	B	C	D
1	Team Net®			
2	Employee	Location	Classification	
3	Avery	West	Hourly	
4	Bryant	North	Salaried	
5	Estrada	West	Salaried	
6	Juergens	West	Salaried	
7	Mickulich	North	Hourly	
8	Talbot	West	Hourly	
9				

Activity 2 Open and Format a Workbook and Insert Formulas **3 Parts**

You will open an existing workbook and insert formulas to find the sums and averages of numbers.

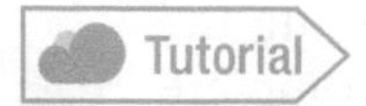

Entering Data Using the Fill Handle

Using AutoFill

When a cell is active, a thick green border surrounds it and a small green square appears in the bottom right corner. This green square is called the AutoFill *fill handle* (see Figure 1.2 on page 5). Use the fill handle to fill a range of cells with the same data or with consecutive data. For example, suppose the year 2021 is to be inserted into a row or column of cells. To do this quickly, type *2021* in the first cell, position the mouse pointer on the fill handle, click and hold down the left mouse button, drag across or down into the cells in which the year is to be inserted, and then release the mouse button.

Hint When filling cells with the fill handle, press and hold down the Ctrl key if you want to copy the same data instead of displaying the next instance in the series.

The fill handle can also be used to insert a series in a row or column of cells. For example, suppose a worksheet is being created with data for all the months in the year. Type *January* in the first cell, position the mouse pointer on the fill handle, click and hold down the left mouse button, drag down or across into 11 more cells, and then release the mouse button. Excel automatically inserts the other 11 months of the year in the proper order. When using the fill handle, the cells must be adjacent. Table 1.3 identifies the sequences inserted in cells when specific types of data are entered.

Certain sequences—such as *2, 4* and *Jan 12, Jan 13*—require that both cells be selected before using the fill handle. If only the cell containing *2* is active, the fill handle will insert *2*s in the selected cells. The list in Table 1.3 is only a sampling of what the fill handle can do. A variety of other sequences can be inserted in a worksheet using the fill handle.

Auto Fill Options

An Auto Fill Options button appears when cells are filled with data using the fill handle. Click this button and a list of options displays for filling the cells. By default, data and formatting are filled in each cell. Use the Auto Fill Options button to choose to fill only the formatting in the cells or to fill only the data without the formatting. Other fill options include choosing to copy data into the selected cells or to fill the data as a series.

Table 1.3 AutoFill Fill Handle Series

Enter this data*	And the fill handle will insert this sequence in adjacent cells*
January	February, March, April, and so on
Jan	Feb, Mar, Apr, and so on
Jan 15, Jan 16	17-Jan, 18-Jan, 19-Jan, and so on
Monday	Tuesday, Wednesday, Thursday, and so on
Product 1	Product 2, Product 3, Product 4, and so on
Qtr 1	Qtr 2, Qtr 3, Qtr 4
2, 4	6, 8, 10, and so on

* Commas represent data in separate cells.

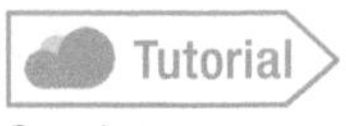

Opening a Workbook

Opening a Workbook

Open an Excel workbook at the Open dialog box. To display this dialog box, click the File tab and then click the *Open* option. This displays the Open backstage area. Other methods of displaying the Open backstage area include using the keyboard shortcut Ctrl + O and inserting an Open button on the Quick Access Toolbar. At the Open backstage area, click the *Browse* option. At the Open dialog box, navigate to the desired folder and then double-click the workbook name in the Content pane. Bypass the Open backstage area and go directly to the Open dialog box by using the keyboard shortcut Ctrl + F12.

Opening from the *Recent* Option List

Quick Steps

Open Workbook

1. Click File tab.
2. Click *Open* option.
3. Click *Browse* option.
4. Navigate to folder.
5. Double-click workbook name.

Pin Workbook to *Recent* Option List

1. Click File tab.
2. Click *Open* option.
3. Position mouse pointer over workbook name.
4. Click left-pointing push pin icon.

Unpin Workbook from *Recent* Option List

1. Click File tab.
2. Click *Open* option.
3. Position mouse pointer over workbook name.
4. Click down-pointing push pin icon.

Opening a Workbook from the *Recent* Option List

With the *Recent* option selected in the middle panel at the Open backstage area, a list displays with the most recently opened workbooks. Up to 50 workbook names appear in the list by default. Open a workbook from this list by clicking the workbook name.

Pinning and Unpinning Workbooks and Folders

If a workbook is opened on a regular basis, consider pinning it to the *Recent* option list so it can be found more easily. To pin a workbook, position the mouse pointer over the workbook name and then click the left-pointing push pin icon at the right of the workbook name. The left-pointing push pin icon changes to a down-pointing push pin icon and the pinned workbook appears in the *Pinned* category at the top of the *Recent* option list, where it can be easily found whenever the Open backstage area is displayed.

A workbook can also be pinned to the Recent list at the Excel opening screen and the Home backstage area. To unpin a workbook from the Recent or *Recent* option list, click the pin icon to change it from a down-pointing push pin icon to a left-pointing push pin icon. More than one workbook can be pinned to a list. Another method for pinning and unpinning documents is to use the shortcut menu. Right-click a workbook name and then click the option *Pin to list* or *Unpin from list*.

In addition to workbooks, folders can be pinned to a list at the Save As backstage area with the *Recent* option selected. The third panel in the Save As backstage area shows a list of the most recently opened folders and groups them into categories such as *Today*, *Yesterday*, and *Last Week*. Pin a folder or folders to the list to display them in the *Pinned* category at the top of the list.

Activity 2a Inserting Data in Cells with the Fill Handle — Part 1 of 3

1. Open **FillCells** by completing the following steps:
   a. Click the File tab and then click the *Open* option, if necessary.
   b. Click the *Browse* option.
   c. Navigate to the EL1C1 folder on your storage medium and then double-click *FillCells*.
2. Save the workbook with the name **1-FillCells** by completing the following steps:
   a. Press the F12 function key to display the Save As dialog box.
   b. Press the Home key on the keyboard to position the insertion point at the beginning of the name in the *File name* text box and then type 1-.
   c. Click the Save button.
3. Add data to cells as shown in Figure 1.9. Begin by making cell B1 active and then typing January.

4. Position the mouse pointer on the fill handle for cell B1, click and hold down the left mouse button, drag across into cell G1, and then release the mouse button.
5. Type a sequence and then use the fill handle to fill the remaining cells by completing the following steps:
   a. Make cell A2 active and then type Year 1.
   b. Make cell A3 active and then type Year 3.
   c. Select cells A2 and A3 by clicking in cell A2 and holding down the left mouse button, dragging into cell A3, and then releasing the mouse button.
   d. Drag the fill handle for cell A3 into cell A5. (This inserts *Year 5* in cell A4 and *Year 7* in cell A5.)
6. Use the fill handle to fill adjacent cells with a number but not the formatting by completing the following steps:
   a. Make cell B2 active. (This cell contains *100* with bold formatting.)
   b. Drag the fill handle for cell B2 to the right into cell E2. (This inserts *100* in cells C2, D2, and E2.)
   c. Click the Auto Fill Options button at the bottom right of the selected cells.
   d. Click the *Fill Without Formatting* option at the drop-down list.

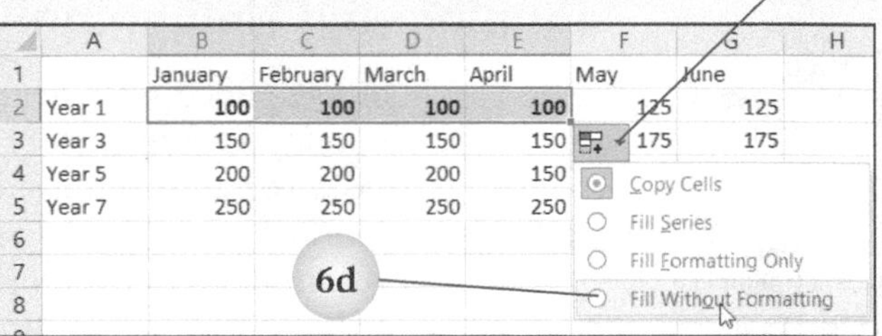

7. Use the fill handle to apply formatting only by completing the following steps:
   a. Make cell B2 active.
   b. Drag the fill handle into cell B5.
   c. Click the Auto Fill Options button and then click *Fill Formatting Only* at the drop-down list.
8. Make cell A10 active and then type Qtr 1.
9. Drag the fill handle for cell A10 into cell A13.
10. Save **1-FillCells**.

Figure 1.9 Activity 2a

	A	B	C	D	E	F	G
1		January	February	March	April	May	June
2	Year 1	**100**	100	100	100	125	125
3	Year 3	**150**	150	150	150	175	175
4	Year 5	**200**	200	200	150	150	150
5	Year 7	**250**	250	250	250	250	250
6							
7							
8							
9							
10	Qtr1	$5,500	$6,250	$7,000	$8,500	$5,500	$4,500
11	Qtr2	$6,000	$7,250	$6,500	$9,000	$4,000	$5,000
12	Qtr3	$4,500	$8,000	$6,000	$7,500	$6,000	$5,000
13	Qtr4	$6,500	$8,500	$7,000	$8,000	$5,500	$6,000

Entering Formulas

Quick Steps
Enter Formula Using AutoSum button
1. Click in cell.
2. Click AutoSum button.
3. Check range identified and make changes if necessary.
4. Press Enter key.

Formulas in Excel allow users to perform calculations on data and get a result in return. For example, the total cost of an item can be determined by inputting the individual costs of the item into a sum formula and the result will be the total of those costs. An active cell that contains a formula will display the results in the cell and the formula in the Formula bar. Formulas can be inserted using various methods, such as typing, using the mouse, and using buttons on the ribbon.

Formulas in Excel begin with an equals sign and may contain one or more of the following: mathematical operators (such as + or -), numerical values, references to a cell or range of cells, and/or a function (such as the SUM function, described below). For example, the formula *=A1+A2* can be inserted in cell A3. When values are added to cells A1 and A2, their sum will automatically appear in cell A3. Formulas can be written that add, subtract, multiply, and/or divide values. Formulas can also be written that calculate averages, percentages, minimum and maximum values, and much more.

Entering Formulas Using the AutoSum Button

Hint You can use the keyboard shortcut Alt + = to insert the SUM function in a cell.

Using the AutoSum Button to Add Numbers

Use the AutoSum button in the Editing group on the Home tab to insert a formula for calculating the sum of numbers in a range of cells. Clicking the AutoSum button will create a formula that adds numbers automatically using the SUM function. Make active the cell in which the formula will be inserted (this cell should be empty) and then click the AutoSum button. Excel looks for a range of cells containing numbers above the active cell. If no cell above contains numbers, then Excel looks to the left of the active cell. Excel suggests the range of cells to be added. If the suggested range is not correct, drag through the range of cells with the mouse and then press the Enter key. Double-click the AutoSum button to automatically insert the SUM function with the range Excel chooses.

Activity 2b Adding Values with the AutoSum Button Part 2 of 3

1. With **1-FillCells** open, make cell A6 active and then type Total.
2. Make cell B6 active and then calculate the sum of the cells by clicking the AutoSum button in the Editing group on the Home tab.
3. Excel inserts the formula *=SUM(B2:B5)* in cell B6. This is the correct range of cells, so press the Enter key.

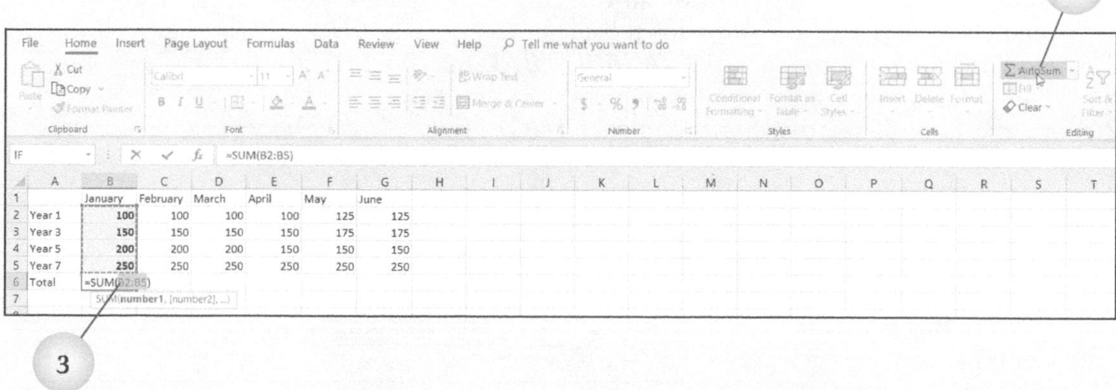

4. Make cell C6 active and then click the AutoSum button in the Editing group.

5. Excel inserts the formula *=SUM(C2:C5)* in cell C6. This is the correct range of cells, so press the Enter key.
6. Make cell D6 active.
7. Double-click the AutoSum button. This inserts the formula *=SUM(D2:D5)* in cell D6 and inserts the sums *700*.
8. Insert the sums in cells E6, F6, and G6.
9. Save **1-FillCells**.

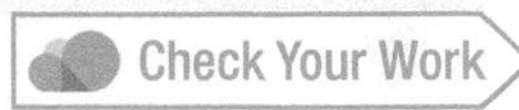

Quick Steps

Insert Average Formula Using AutoSum Button

1. Click in cell.
2. Click AutoSum button arrow.
3. Click *Average*.
4. Specify range.
5. Press Enter key.

Using the AutoSum Button to Average Numbers

A common function in a formula is the AVERAGE function. With this function, a range of cells are added together and then the total is divided by the number of cell entries. The AVERAGE function is available on the AutoSum button. Click the AutoSum button arrow and a drop-down list displays with a number of common functions.

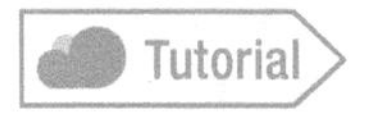

Copying Formulas

Quick Steps

Copy Formula Using Fill Handle

1. Insert formula in cell.
2. Make active cell containing formula.
3. Drag fill handle across or down to fill cells.

Using the Fill Handle to Copy a Formula

The same basic formula can be inserted in other cells in a worksheet. When copying a formula to other locations in a worksheet, use a relative cell reference. Copy a formula containing relative cell references and the cell references change. For example, insert the formula *=SUM(A2:C2)* in cell D2 and then copy it relatively to cell D3 and the formula in cell D3 displays as *=SUM(A3:C3)*. Use the fill handle to copy a formula relatively in a worksheet. To do this, position the mouse pointer on the fill handle until the mouse pointer turns into a thin black cross, click and hold down the left mouse button, drag and select the cells, and then release the mouse button.

Activity 2c Inserting the AVERAGE Function and Copying a Formula Relatively — Part 3 of 3

1. With **1-FillCells** open, make cell A14 active and then type Average.
2. Insert the average of the range B10:B13 by completing the following steps:
   a. Make cell B14 active.
   b. Click the AutoSum button arrow in the Editing group and then click *Average* at the drop-down list.
   c. Excel inserts the formula *=AVERAGE(B10:B13)* in cell B14. This is the correct range of cells, so press the Enter key.
3. Copy the formula relatively to the range C14:G14 by completing the following steps:
   a. Make cell B14 active.
   b. Position the mouse pointer on the fill handle, click and hold down the left mouse button, drag across into cell G14, and then release the mouse button.
4. Save, print, and then close **1-FillCells**.

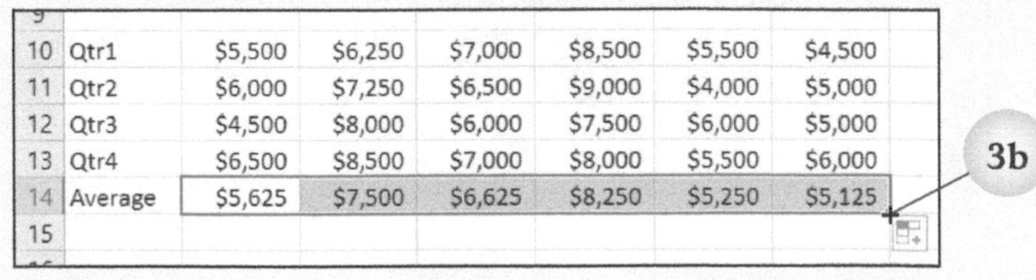

10	Qtr1	$5,500	$6,250	$7,000	$8,500	$5,500	$4,500
11	Qtr2	$6,000	$7,250	$6,500	$9,000	$4,000	$5,000
12	Qtr3	$4,500	$8,000	$6,000	$7,500	$6,000	$5,000
13	Qtr4	$6,500	$8,500	$7,000	$8,000	$5,500	$6,000
14	Average	$5,625	$7,500	$6,625	$8,250	$5,250	$5,125
15							

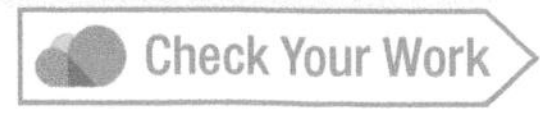

Activity 3 Format a Monthly Expenses Worksheet 2 Parts

You will open a workbook containing a monthly expenses worksheet and then change the column width, merge and center cells, and apply number formatting to numbers in cells.

Selecting Cells

Selecting Cells

Cells in a worksheet can be formatted in a variety of ways. For example, change the alignment of data in cells or rows or add character formatting. To identify the cells that are to be affected by the formatting, select the specific cells.

Selecting Cells Using the Mouse

Hint The first cell in a range has a white background and is the active cell.

Select specific cells, columns, or rows in a worksheet using the mouse. Table 1.4 displays the methods for selecting cells using the mouse.

Selected cells, except the active cell, display with a gray background (this may vary) rather than a white background. The active cell is the first cell in the selection block and displays in the normal manner (white background with black data). Selected cells remain selected until another cell is clicked with the mouse or an arrow key is pressed on the keyboard.

Selecting Cells Using the Keyboard

Keys on the keyboard can be used to select specific cells within a worksheet. Table 1.5 shows the commands for selecting specific cells. If a worksheet contains data, Ctrl + A selects all the cells containing data. If a worksheet contains groups of data separated by empty cells, Ctrl + A or Ctrl + Shift + spacebar selects a group of cells rather than all the cells.

Table 1.4 Selecting with the Mouse

To select this	Do this
column	Position the cell pointer on the column header (a letter) and then click the left mouse button.
row	Position the cell pointer on the row header (a number) and then click the left mouse button.
adjacent cells	Drag with the mouse into specific cells to select them.
nonadjacent cells	Press and hold down the Ctrl key while clicking the column header, row header, or specific cells.
all cells in worksheet	Click the Select All button. (Refer to Figure 1.2 on page 5.)

Table 1.5 Selecting Cells Using the Keyboard

To select	Press
cells in direction of arrow key	Shift + arrow key
from active cell to beginning of row	Shift + Home
from active cell to beginning of worksheet	Shift + Ctrl + Home
from active cell to last cell in worksheet containing data	Shift + Ctrl + End
entire column	Ctrl + spacebar
entire row	Shift + spacebar
cells containing data	Ctrl + A
groups of data separated by empty cells	Ctrl + Shift + spacebar

Selecting Data within Cells

Hint Select nonadjacent columns or rows by holding down the Ctrl key while selecting cells.

The selection commands presented in Table 1.4 and Table 1.5 select the entire cell. Specific characters within a cell can also be selected. To do this with the mouse, position the cell pointer in a cell and then double-click the left mouse button. Drag with the I-beam pointer through the data to be selected. Data selected within a cell appears with a gray background. To select data in a cell using the keyboard, press and hold down the Shift key and then press the arrow key that moves the insertion point in the desired direction. All the data the insertion point passes through will be selected. Press the F8 function key to turn on the Extend Selection mode, move the insertion point in the desired direction to select the data, and then press F8 to turn off the Extend Selection mode. When the Extend Selection mode is on, the words *Extend Selection* are shown at the left of the Status bar.

Applying Basic Formatting

Quick Steps

Change Column Width

Drag column boundary line.
OR
Double-click column boundary line.

Merge and Center Cells

1. Select cells.
2. Click Merge & Center button on Home tab.

Excel provides a wide range of formatting options that can be applied to cells in a worksheet. Some basic formatting options that are helpful when creating a worksheet include changing the column width, merging and centering cells, and formatting numbers.

Changing Column Width

If data in a cell overlaps into the next column, increase the width of the column to accommodate the data. To do this, position the mouse pointer on the gray boundary line between columns in the column header (Figure 1.2 on page 5 identifies the column header) until the pointer turns into a double-headed arrow pointing left and right and then drag the boundary to the new location. If the column contains data, double-click the column boundary line at the right to automatically adjust the width of the column to accommodate the longest entry.

A more precise way to change the width of a column is to display the Column Width dialog box, type in the desired width and then press the OK button. Open the Column Width dialog box by clicking the Format button in the Cells group and then click the *Column Width* option in the drop-down list. Alternatively, right-click the column header and then click *Column width* at the shortcut menu.

Merging and Centering Cells

Merge & Center

Merging and Centering Cells

In some cases, as with a title or subtitle, it may look better to merge two or more cells and then center the text within the cells instead of allowing the text to overlap into the next column. To merge cells, first check to make sure that the cells to be merged do not contain any other data. (If other cells contain data, only the data in the first cell will be placed in the newly merged cell.) Select cells to be merged and then click the Merge & Center button in the Alignment group on the Home tab.

Activity 3a Changing Column Width and Merging and Centering Cells

Part 1 of 2

1. Open **MoExps** and then save it with the name **1-MoExps**.
2. Change column widths by completing the following steps:
   a. Position the mouse pointer in the column header on the boundary line between columns A and B until the pointer turns into a double-headed arrow pointing left and right.

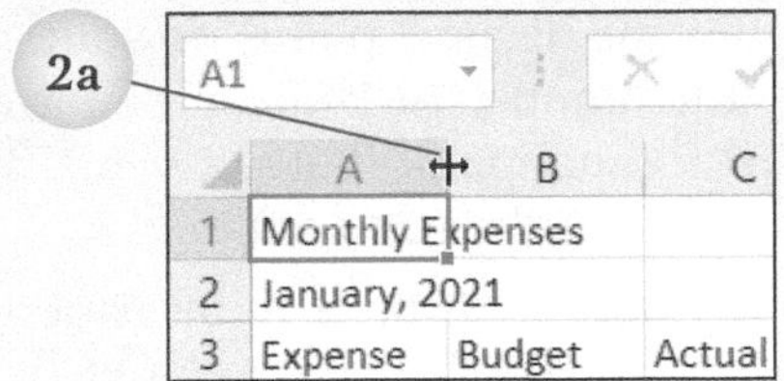

   b. Double-click the left mouse button.
   c. Position the mouse pointer in the column header on the boundary line between columns E and F and then double-click the left mouse button.
   d. Click in any cell in column F, click the Format button in the Cells group on the Home tab and then click the *Column Width* option at the drop down list.
   e. At the Column Width dialog box, type 10.25, and then click OK.
3. Merge and center cells by completing the following steps:
   a. Select the range A1:C1.
   b. Click the Merge & Center button in the Alignment group on the Home tab.

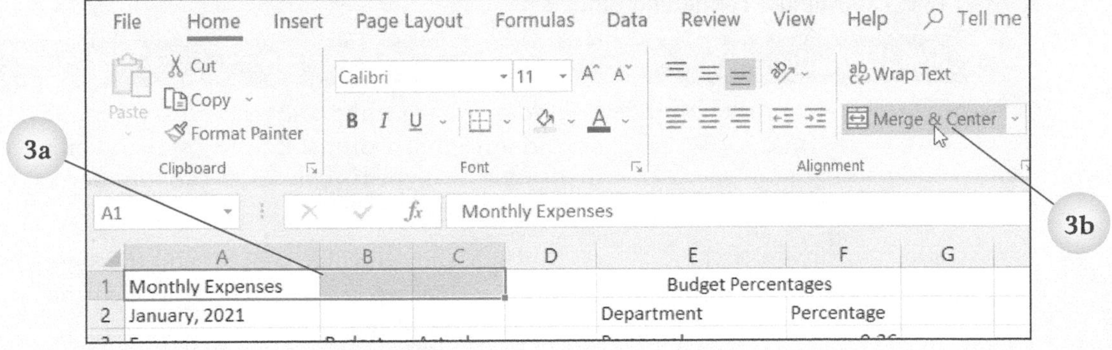

   c. Select the range A2:C2.
   d. Click the Merge & Center button.
   e. Select cells E1 and F1 and then click the Merge & Center button.
4. Save **1-MoExps**.

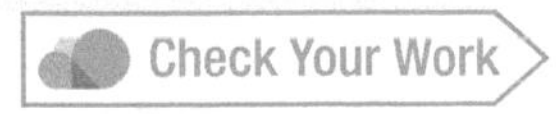

Applying Number Formatting

Formatting Numbers

Numbers in cells can be formatted to include a decimal point (45.00), comma separators (1,000,000), or symbols such as a dollar sign ($) or percentage symbol (%). As numbers are typed, Excel will recognize the formatting. For example, if *$45.50* is typed in a cell, Excel automatically applies the Currency format to the cell. If *45%* is entered in a cell, Excel automatically applies the Percentage format. Currency format, Percentage format, and other formats recognized by Excel are shown in the *Number Format* option box in the Number group on the Home tab.

Number formatting can also be applied to cells in a worksheet before or after the data is typed. To do this, select the cell or cells and then click an option in the *Number Format* option box, or click one of the buttons in the Number group on the Home tab (described in Table 1.6). For example, if the number 4500 is typed and the Accounting number formatting is applied to it, it will be formatted as $4,500.00. If the number .45 is typed and the Percentage format is applied, it will be displayed as 45%.

Use the Increase Decimal and Decrease Decimal buttons to control how many digits are displayed after the decimal point, without changing the actual value in the cell. For example, the number *1.0245* can be formatted so none or all of the digits display after the decimal point, but the value shown in the Formula bar remains the same to keep calculations accurate.

A general guideline in accounting is to insert a dollar symbol before the first amount in a column and before the total amount but not before the number amounts between them. To follow this guideline, format the first amount and total amount using the Accounting Number Format button and applying the Comma format to the number amounts between them. The Accounting number format and Comma number format are the same, except the Accounting number format includes the dollar sign. To differentiate between the two Accounting formats, steps in this textbook will use the term *Accounting format* when the Accounting Number Format button in the Number group on the Home tab is to be clicked. The term *Comma format* will be used when the Comma Style button is to be clicked.

Table 1.6 Number Formatting Buttons

Click this button		To do this
$	Accounting Number Format	Add a dollar symbol, any necessary commas, and a decimal point followed by two digits even if none are typed; right-align the number in the cell.
%	Percent Style	Multiply the cell value by 100 and display the result with a percent symbol; right-align the number in the cell.
,	Comma Style	Add any necessary commas and a decimal point followed by two digits even if none are typed; right-align the number in the cell.
←.0 .00	Increase Decimal	Increase the number of digits displayed after the decimal point in the selected cell.
.00 →.0	Decrease Decimal	Decrease the number of digits displayed after the decimal point in the selected cell.

Activity 3b Formatting Numbers

1. With **1-MoExps** open, make cell B13 active and then double-click the AutoSum button. (This inserts the total of the numbers in the range B4:B12.)
2. Make cell C13 active and then double-click the AutoSum button.
3. Apply the Accounting format to cells by completing the following steps:
   a. Select cells B4 and C4.
   b. Click the Accounting Number Format button in the Number group on the Home tab.
   c. Decrease the number of digits displayed after the decimal point to none by clicking the Decrease Decimal button in the Number group two times.

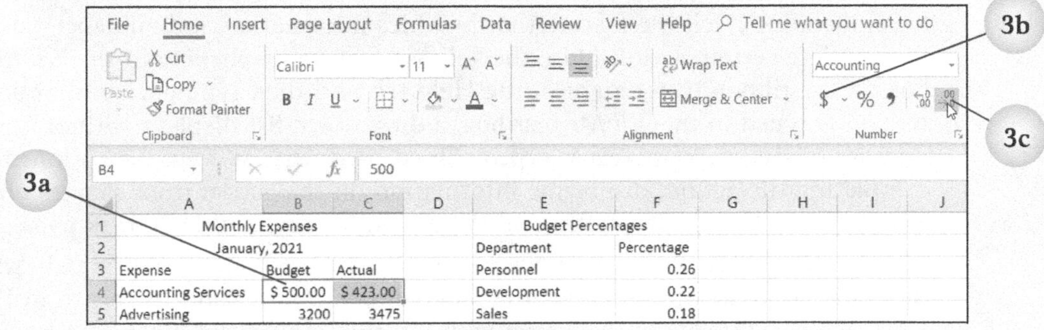

   d. Select cells B13 and C13.
   e. Click the Accounting Number Format button.
   f. Click the Decrease Decimal button two times.
4. Apply the Comma format to numbers by completing the following steps:
   a. Select the range B5:C12.
   b. Click the Comma Style button in the Number group.
   c. Click the Decrease Decimal button two times.

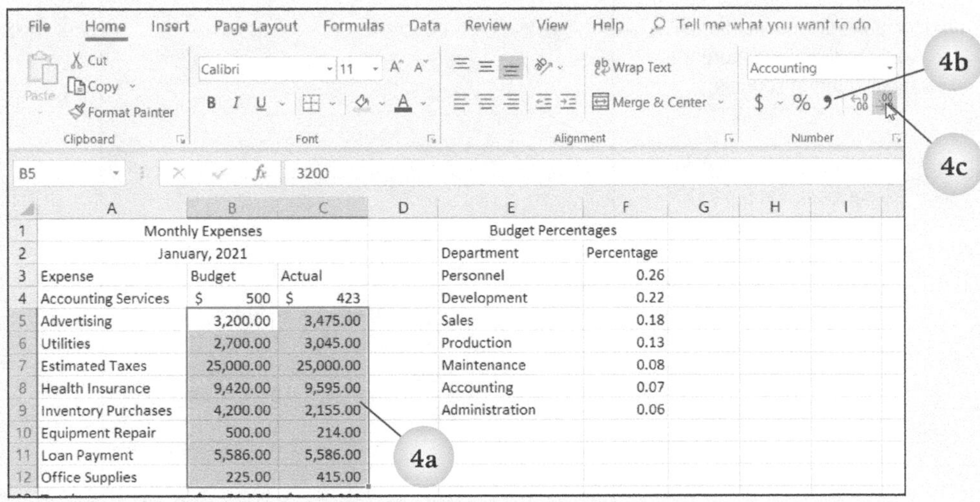

5. Apply the Percentage format to numbers by completing the following steps:
   a. Select the range F3:F9.
   b. Click the Percent Style button in the Number group on the Home tab.
6. Click in cell A1.
7. Save **1-MoExps**.

Activity 4 Use the Tell Me and Help Features **3 Parts**

You will use the Tell Me feature to learn how to change the font size of text and display the Excel Help window with information about wrapping text. You will use the Help feature to learn more about entering data in cells, changing the font color, and printing a workbook.

Using the Tell Me Feature

Quick Steps

Use Tell Me Feature

1. Click in *Tell Me* text box.
2. Type topic or feature.
3. Click option at drop-down list.

Using the Tell Me Feature

Excel includes a Tell Me feature that provides information and guidance on how to complete certain actions. Use the Tell Me feature by clicking in the *Tell Me* text box on the ribbon to the right of the Help tab and then typing a term, or action. As text is typed in the *Tell Me* text box, a drop-down list displays with options that are refined as more text is typed. The drop-down list contains options for completing the action, displaying information on the action from sources on the web, and displaying information on the action in the Excel Help task pane.

The Tell Me drop-down list also includes a Smart Lookup option. Clicking the Smart Lookup option opens the Smart Lookup task pane, as shown in Figure 1.10, at the right side of the screen with information on the typed text from a variety of internet sources. Smart Lookup can also be accessed using the Smart Lookup button on the Review tab or by selecting a cell, right-clicking in the selected cell, and then clicking the *Smart Lookup* option at the shortcut menu.

Figure 1.10 Smart Lookup Task Pane

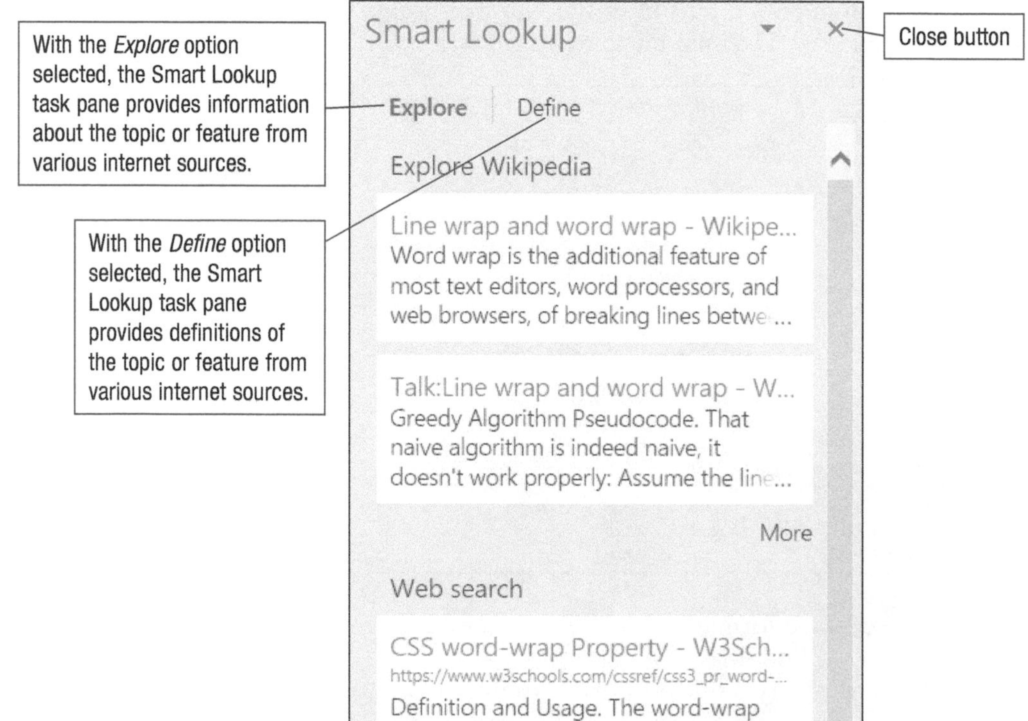

Activity 4a Using the Tell Me Feature

1. With **1-MoExps** open, select the range A1:E1.
2. Click in the *Tell Me* text box and then type font size.
3. At the drop-down list, click the *Font Size* option.
4. At the side menu, click the *14* option. (This increases the font size of the text in the range A1:E1, and the height of row 1 automatically adjusts to accommodate the larger text.)
5. Use the Tell Me feature to display the Help task pane with information on wrapping text by completing the following steps:
   a. Click in the *Tell Me* text box and then type wrap text.
   b. Position the mouse pointer over the *Get Help on "wrap text"* option and then click the *Wrap text in a cell* option at the side menu.

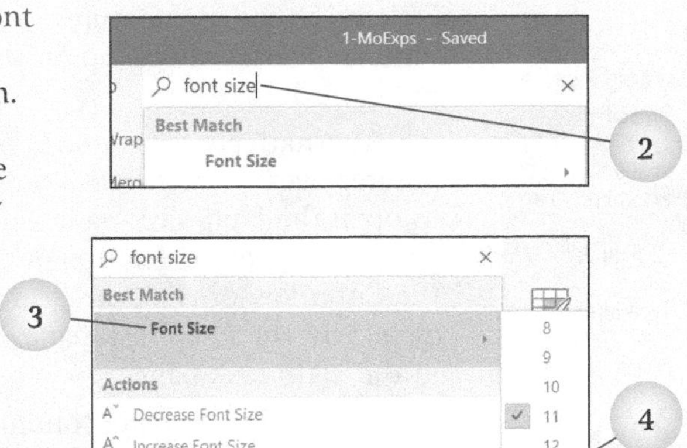

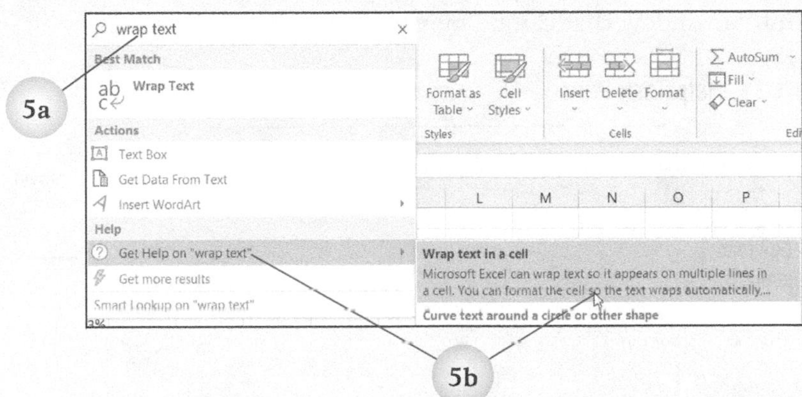

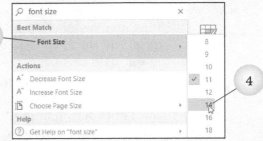

   c. At the Help task pane, read the information on wrapping text and then close the Help task pane by clicking the Close button in the upper right corner of the task pane.
6. Display information on scrolling in a workbook in the Smart Lookup task pane by completing the following steps:
   a. Click in the *Tell Me* text box and then type scrolling.
   b. Click the *Smart Lookup on "scrolling"* option. (The first time you use the Smart Lookup feature, a message may appear asking to turn on Intelligent Services. In a school setting, ask your instructor for assistance.)
   c. If two options—*Explore* and *Define*—are shown at the top of the Smart Lookup task pane, click the *Define* option. This will display a definition of the word *scrolling* in the Smart Lookup task pane.
   d. Close the Smart Lookup task pane by clicking the Close button in the upper right corner of the task pane.
7. Save, print, and then close **1-MoExps**.

Using the Help Feature

Quick Steps

Use Help Feature

1. Press F1.
2. Type term or action in search text box.
3. Press Enter key.

OR

1. Click in *Tell Me* text box.
2. Type term or action.
3. Click *Get Help on* option.

Using Help

Microsoft Excel includes a Help feature that contains information about Excel features and commands. This on-screen reference manual is similar to Windows Help and the Help features in Word, PowerPoint, and Access. Click the Help button in the Help group on the Help tab to display the Help task pane, as shown in Figure 1.11.

Alternatively, type a term or action in the *Tell Me* text box, position the mouse pointer over the *Get Help on* option, and then click an option at the side menu to open the Help task pane with the selected article displayed. In the Help task pane, type a topic, feature, or question in the search text box and then press the Enter key or click the Search help button. Articles related to the search text display in the Help task pane. Click an article and the article information displays in the Help task pane.

The Help task pane contains buttons at the top, as identified in Figure 1.11. Use the Back button to navigate to the previous page in the task pane. Click the three dots button to display more options, such as *Home*, *Office help center*, and *Contact us*. Resize or move the task pane by clicking the down arrow left of the Close button. The Help task pane can be made larger so it is easier to read the articles. The Help task pane can also be moved to the other side of the screen or made into a window that can be moved anywhere on the screen.

Figure 1.11 Help Task Pane

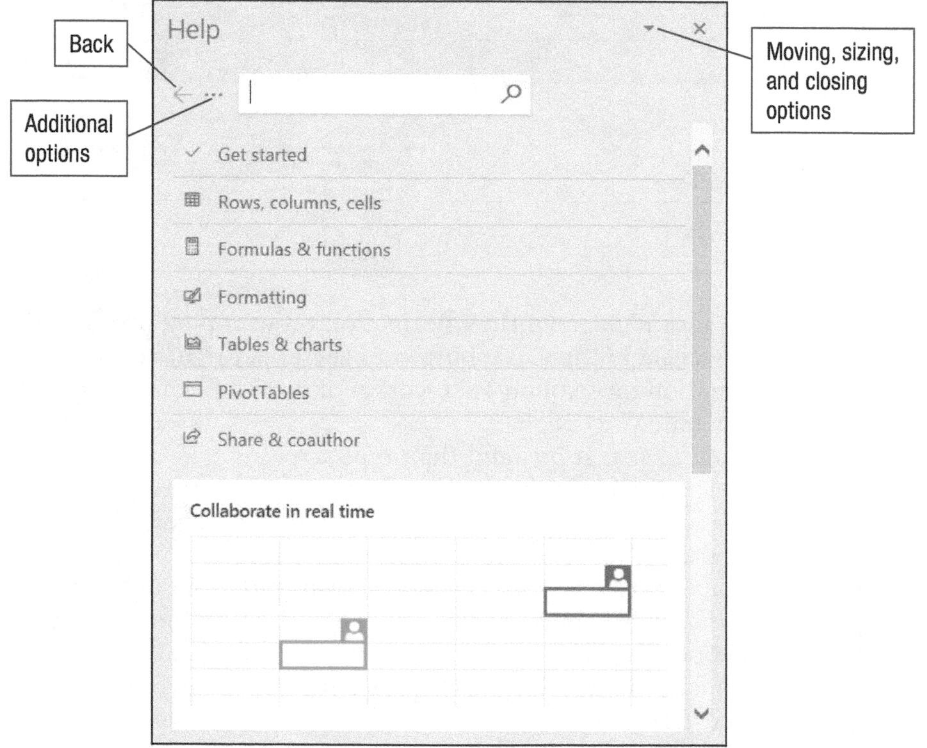

Getting Help from a ScreenTip

Hover the mouse pointer over a button and a ScreenTip displays with information about the button. Some button ScreenTips display with a Help icon and the Tell me more hyperlink. Click the Tell me more hyperlink text or press the F1 function key and the Help task pane opens with information about the button feature.

Activity 4b **Using the Help Feature** Part 2 of 3

1. At a blank screen, press Ctrl + N to display a blank workbook. (Ctrl + N is the keyboard shortcut to open a blank workbook.)
2. Click the Help tab and then click the Help button.

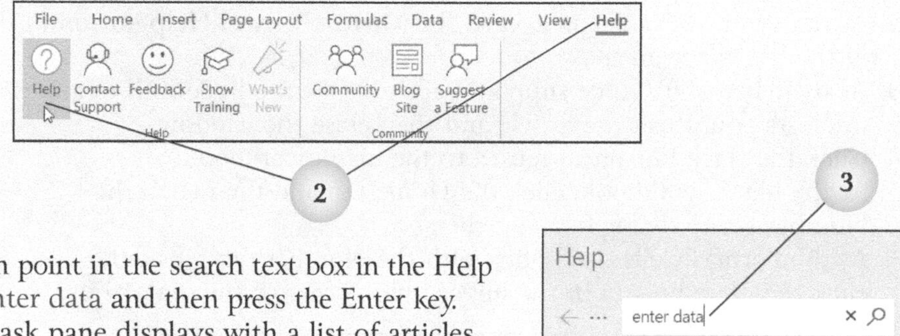

3. With the insertion point in the search text box in the Help task pane, type enter data and then press the Enter key.
4. When the Help task pane displays with a list of articles, click the article Enter data manually in worksheet cells hyperlink.
5. In the displayed article, expand some of the topics in the article and then read the information about entering data in cells.
6. Click the down arrow button in the Help task pane and then click the *Size* option at the drop-down list.

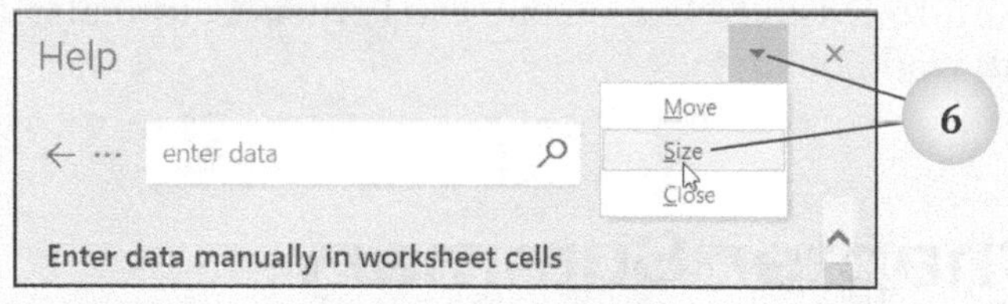

7. Resize the Help task pane to make the information in the article easier to read by moving the mouse pointer to a desired point (approximately one inch wider than it was previously) and then clicking the left mouse button.
8. Click the Back button to return to the previous page.
9. Click another article hyperlink in the Help task pane and then read in the information in the article.
10. Click the three dots button and then click the *Home* option at the drop-down list.
11. Click the Close button to close the Help task pane.
12. Click the Home tab, hover the mouse pointer over the Font Color button in the Font group until the ScreenTip displays, and then click the Tell me more hyperlink at the bottom of the ScreenTip.
13. Read the information that displays in the Help task pane, and then close the task pane.

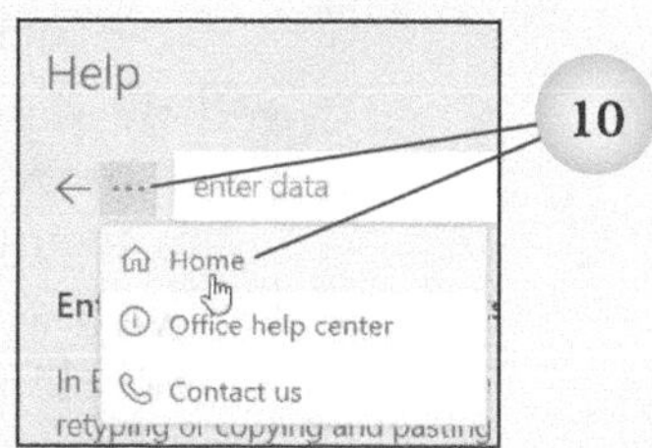

Getting Help in a Dialog Box or at the Backstage Area

Some dialog boxes and the backstage area contain a Help button, labeled with a question mark (?). Click this button and the Microsoft Office support website opens in a browser window with specific information about the dialog box or backstage area. After reading the information, close the browser window and return to Excel. If a dialog box is open in Excel, close it by clicking the Close button in the upper right corner. Exit the backstage area by clicking the Back button or pressing the Esc key.

Activity 4c **Getting Help in a Dialog Box and Backstage Area** Part 3 of 3

1. At the blank workbook, click the File tab and then click the *Print* option.
2. At the Print backstage area, click the Microsoft Excel Help button in the upper right corner of the backstage area.
3. At the Microsoft Office support website, click the hyperlink to an article on printing that interests you. Read the article and then close the window.
4. Click the Back button to return to the blank workbook.
5. At the blank workbook, click the Home tab and then click the Number group dialog box launcher.
6. At the Format Cells dialog box with the Number tab selected, click the Help button in the upper right corner of the dialog box.

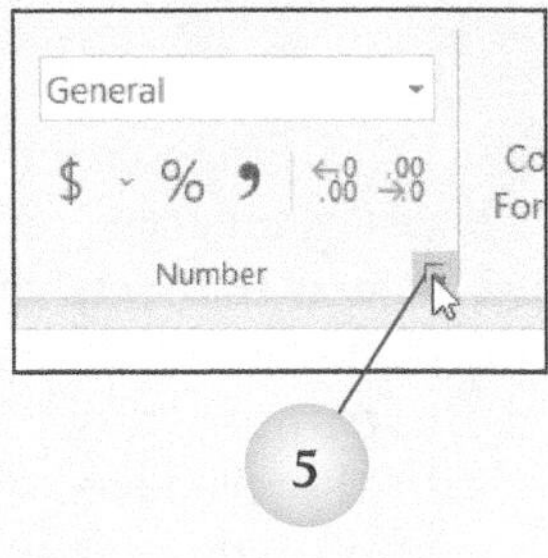

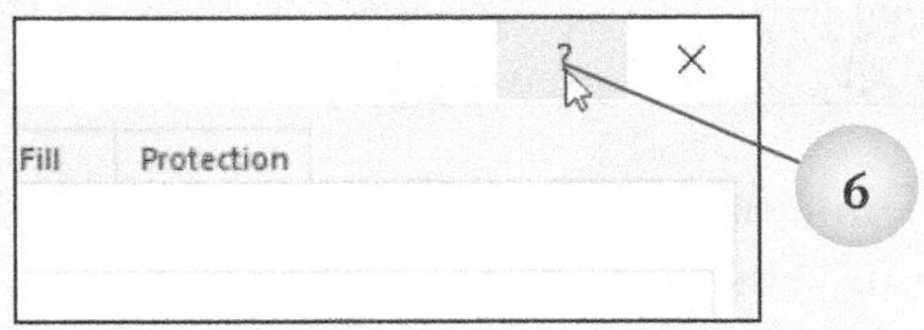

7. Read the information at the Microsoft Office support website and then close the browser window to return to Excel. In Excel, close the Format Cells dialog box.
8. Close the blank workbook.

Chapter Summary

- A file created in Excel is called a *workbook* and consists of one or more individual worksheets.
- The intersection of a column and a row in a worksheet is referred to as a *cell*. Gridlines are the horizontal and vertical lines that define cells.
- When the insertion point is positioned in a cell, the cell name (also called the *cell reference*) displays in the Name box at the left of the Formula bar. The cell name includes the column letter and row number.
- If the data entered in a cell consists of text (letters) and does not fit into the cell, it overlaps the cell to the right. If the data consists of numbers and does not fit into the cell, the numbers change to number symbols (###).
- Save a workbook by clicking the Save button on the Quick Access Toolbar or by clicking the File tab and then clicking the *Save As* option. At the Save As backstage area, click the *Browse* option. At the Save As dialog box, navigate to the desired folder, type the workbook name in the *File name* text box, and then press the Enter key.

- To replace data in a cell, click in the cell and then type the new data. To edit data within a cell, double-click in the cell and then make the necessary changes.
- Print a worksheet by clicking the File tab, clicking the *Print* option, and then clicking the Print button.
- Close a workbook by clicking the File tab and then clicking the *Close* option or by using the keyboard shortcut Ctrl + F4.
- Close Excel by clicking the Close button in the upper right corner of the screen or by using the keyboard shortcut Alt + F4.
- The AutoComplete feature automatically inserts a previous entry if the character or characters being typed in a cell match a previous entry. The AutoCorrect feature corrects many common typing errors. The AutoFill fill handle adds the same or consecutive data into a range of cells.
- Open a workbook by clicking the File tab and then clicking the *Open* option. At the Open backstage area, click the *Browse* option. At the Open dialog box, double-click the workbook name.
- Workbooks can be pinned to the *Recent* option list at the Open backstage area or the Recent list at the Home backstage area so that they can be easily accessed in the future.
- Use the AutoSum button in the Editing group on the Home tab to find the total or average of data in columns or rows.
- Use the fill handle to copy a formula in a cell to adjacent cells. The fill handle is the solid box in the bottom right of an active cell.
- Select all the cells in a column by clicking the column header. Select all the cells in a row by clicking the row header. Select all the cells in a worksheet by clicking the Select All button immediately to the left of the column headers.
- Change the column width by dragging or double-clicking the column boundary line.
- Merge and center adjacent cells by selecting them and then clicking the Merge & Center button in the Alignment group on the Home tab.
- Format numbers in cells with buttons in the Number group on the Home tab.
- The Tell Me feature provides information and guidance on how to complete certain actions. The *Tell Me* text box is located on the ribbon to the right of the Help tab.
- Use the Tell Me feature, click a hyperlink in a button ScreenTip, or press F1 to display the Help task pane. At this task pane, type a topic in the search text box and then press the Enter key.
- Some dialog boxes and the backstage area contain a Help button that, when clicked, displays the Microsoft Office support website with information specific to the dialog box or backstage area.

Commands Review

FEATURE	RIBBON TAB, GROUP/OPTION	BUTTON	KEYBOARD SHORTCUT
Accounting format	Home, Number		
AutoSum	Home, Editing		Alt + =
close Excel			Alt + F4
close workbook	File, *Close*		Ctrl + F4
Comma format	Home, Number		
decrease decimal place	Home, Number		
Go To dialog box	Home, Editing		Ctrl + G
Help task pane	Help, Help		F1
increase decimal place	Home, Number		
merge and center cells	Home, Alignment		
Open backstage area	File, *Open*		Ctrl + O
Percentage format	Home, Number		Ctrl + Shift + %
Print backstage area	File, *Print*		Ctrl + P
Save As backstage area	File, *Save As*		Ctrl + S

Microsoft®

Excel®

Inserting Formulas in a Worksheet

CHAPTER 2

Performance Objectives

Upon successful completion of Chapter 2, you will be able to:

1 Write formulas with mathematical operators
2 Type a formula in the Formula bar
3 Copy a formula
4 Determine the order of operations
5 Identify common formula and function errors
6 Use the Insert Function dialog box to insert a function in a cell
7 Write formulas with the AVERAGE, MAX, MIN, COUNT, COUNTA, NOW, and TODAY functions
8 Display formulas
9 Use absolute and mixed cell references in formulas

Excel is a powerful decision-making tool that contains data that can be manipulated in "What if?" situations. Insert a formula in a worksheet and then manipulate the data to make projections, answer specific questions, and plan for the future. For example, the owner of a company might prepare a worksheet on production costs and then determine the impact on company revenues if production is increased or decreased.

As explained in Chapter 1, formulas can be inserted into Excel worksheets to add, subtract, multiply, and/or divide values as well as calculate averages, percentages, and much more. Chapter 1 described how to use the AutoSum button to insert formulas for calculating totals and averages. In Chapter 2, you will learn to use the Formulas tab to create formulas with a variety of different functions.

Before beginning chapter work, copy the EL1C2 folder to your storage medium and then make EL1C2 the active folder.

The online course includes additional training and assessment resources.

Activity 1 Insert Formulas in a Worksheet — 4 Parts

You will open a worksheet containing data and then insert formulas to calculate differences, salaries, and percentages of budgets and equipment usage down time.

Entering Formulas Using the Keyboard

Hint After typing a formula in a cell, press the Enter key, the Tab key, or Shift + Tab.

Writing Formulas with Mathematical Operators

As explained in Chapter 1, the AutoSum button in the Editing group on the Home tab creates a formula for calculating the sum or average of values. A formula can also be written using mathematical operators. Commonly used mathematical operators and their purposes are shown in Table 2.1. When writing a formula, begin it with the equals sign (=). For example, to create a formula that divides the contents of cell B2 by the contents of cell C2 and inserts the result in cell D2, make D2 the active cell and then type *=b2/c2*. The column reference letters used in formulas can be entered as either lowercase or uppercase letters. If the column reference letters are entered in a formula in lowercase, Excel will automatically convert the column reference letters to uppercase. Formulas entered in a cell will also display in the Formula bar, where the formula can be modified.

Copying Formulas

Copying a Formula with Relative Cell References

In many worksheets, the same basic formula is used repetitively. In a situation where a formula is copied to other locations in a worksheet, use a relative cell reference. Copy a formula containing relative cell references and the cell references change. For example, if the formula *=SUM(A2:C2)* is entered in cell D2 and then copied relatively into cell D3, the formula in cell D3 appears as *=SUM(A3:C3)*. (Additional information on cell references is provided later in this chapter in the section "Using an Absolute Cell Reference in a Formula.")

 Fill

Quick Steps

Copy Formulas with Relative Cell References

1. Insert formula in cell.
2. Select cell containing formula and all cells to which formula is to be copied.
3. Click Fill button.
4. Click direction option.

To copy a formula with a relative cell reference, use the Fill button or the fill handle. (You used the fill handle to copy a formula in Chapter 1.) To use the Fill button, select the cell containing the formula and all the cells to which the formula is to be copied and then click the Fill button in the Editing group on the Home tab. At the Fill button drop-down list, click the direction. For example, click the *Down* option if the formula is being copied down the worksheet.

Table 2.1 Mathematical Operators

Operator	Purpose	Operator	Purpose
+	addition	/	division
-	subtraction	%	percentage
*	multiplication	^	exponentiation

Activity 1a Finding Differences by Inserting and Copying a Formula

Part 1 of 4

1. Open **HCReports** and then save it with the name **2-HCReports**.
2. Insert a formula by completing the following steps:
   a. Make cell D3 active.
   b. Type the formula =c3-b3.
   c. Press the Enter key.
3. Copy the formula to the range D4:D10 by completing the following steps:
   a. Select the range D3:D10.
   b. Click the Fill button in the Editing group on the Home tab and then click *Down* at the drop-down list.

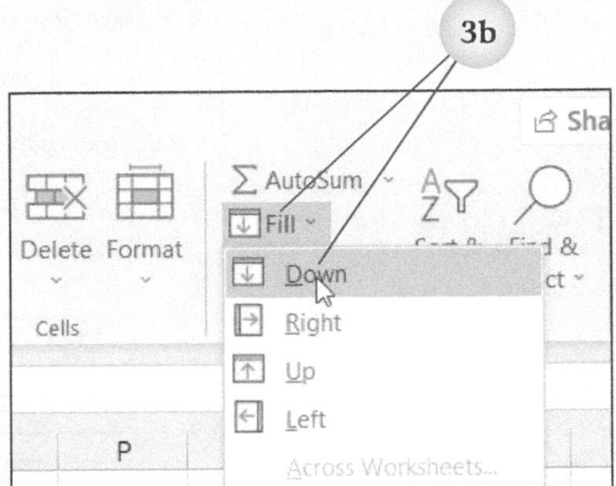

4. Save **2-HCReports**.
5. With the worksheet open, make the following changes to cell contents:
   B4: Change *48,290* to *46425*
   C6: Change *61,220* to *60000*
   B8: Change *55,309* to *57415*
   B9: Change *12,398* to *14115*
6. Make cell D3 active, apply the Accounting format by clicking the Accounting Number Format button in the Number group on the Home tab, and then click the Decrease Decimal button two times to decrease the digits displayed past the decimal point to none.
7. Save **2-HCReports**.

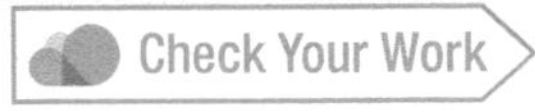

Hint Use the fill handle to copy a relative version of a formula.

As explained in Chapter 1, the fill handle can be used to copy a formula up, down, left, or right within a worksheet. To use the fill handle, insert the data in the cell (text, value, formula, etc.). With the cell active, position the mouse pointer on the fill handle until the mouse pointer turns into a thin black cross. Click and hold down the left mouse button, drag and select the cells, and then release the mouse button. When dragging a cell containing a formula, a relative version of the formula is copied to the selected cells.

Checking Cell References in a Formula

To verify if a formula is using the correct cell references, double-click in a cell containing the formula and the cells referenced in the formula display with a colored border and shading in the worksheet. This feature makes it easy to identify which cells are being referenced in a formula and is helpful when trying to identify errors that may occur in a formula.

Activity 1b Calculating Salaries by Inserting and Copying a Formula with the Fill Handle

Part 2 of 4

1. With **2-HCReports** open, insert a formula by completing the following steps:
   a. Make cell D15 active.
   b. Click in the Formula bar text box and then type =c15*b15.
   c. Click the Enter button on the Formula bar.
2. Copy the formula to the range D16:D20 by completing the following steps:
   a. Make sure cell D15 is still the active cell.
   b. Position the mouse pointer on the fill handle at the lower right corner of cell D15 until the pointer turns into a thin black cross.
   c. Click and hold down the left mouse button, drag into cell D20, and then release the mouse button.
3. Save **2-HCReports**.
4. Double-click in cell D20 to display the formula with cell references color coded to ensure the formula was copied relatively and then press the Enter key to exit the Edit mode.
5. Make the following changes to cell contents in the worksheet:
   B16: Change *20* to *28*
   C17: Change *18.75* to *19.10*
   B19: Change *15* to *24*
6. Select the range D16:D20 and then apply the Comma format by clicking the Comma Style button in the Number group on the Home tab.
7. Save **2-HCReports**.

1c 1b

PMT =c15*b15

	A	B	C	D
1	Highland Construction			
2	Customer	Actual	Planned	Difference
3	Sellar Corporation	$ 30,349	$ 34,109	$ 3,760
4	Main Street Photos	46,425	48,100	1,675
5	Sunset Automotive	34,192	32,885	(1,307)
6	Linstrom Enterprises	63,293	60,000	(3,293)
7	Morcos Media	29,400	30,500	1,100
8	Green Valley Optics	57,415	58,394	979
9	Detailed Designs	14,115	13,100	(1,015)
10	Arrowstar Company	87,534	86,905	(629)
11				
12				
13				
14	Name	Hours	Rate	Salary
15	Carolyn Bentley	35	$ 23.15	=c15*b15

	A	B	C	D
13				
14	Name	Hours	Rate	Salary
15	Carolyn Bentley	35	$ 23.15	$ 810.25
16	Lindon Cassini	20	19.00	$ 380.00
17	Michelle DeFord	40	18.75	$ 750.00
18	Javier Farias	24	16.45	$ 394.80
19	Deborah Gould	15	11.50	$ 172.50
20	William Jarman	15	11.50	$ 172.50
21				

2c

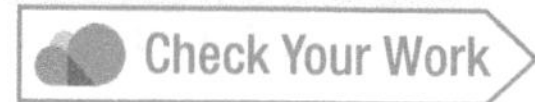

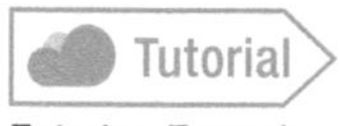

Entering Formulas Using the Mouse

Quick Steps

Write Formula by Pointing

1. Click in cell that will contain formula.
2. Type equals sign.
3. Click in cell to be referenced in formula.
4. Type mathematical operator.
5. Click in next cell reference.
6. Press Enter key.

Writing a Formula by Pointing

The formulas written in Activity 1a and Activity 1b used cell references such as *=c3-b3*. Another method for writing a formula is to "point" to the specific cells that are to be part of the formula. Creating a formula by pointing is more accurate than typing the cell reference because a mistake can be made when the cell reference is typed.

To write a formula by pointing, click in the cell that will contain the formula, type the equals sign to begin the formula, and then click in the cell to be referenced in the formula. This inserts a moving border around the cell and changes the mode from Enter to Point. (The word *Point* displays at the left side of the Status bar.) Type the mathematical operator and then click in the next cell reference. Continue in this manner until all the cell references are specified and then press the Enter key. This ends the formula and inserts the result of the calculation in the active cell. When a formula is written by pointing, the range of cells to be included in the formula can be selected.

Activity 1c Writing a Formula by Pointing That Calculates the Percentage of Actual to Budget

Part 3 of 4

1. With **2-HCReports** open, enter a formula by pointing that calculates the percentage of actual to budget by completing the following steps:
   a. Make cell D25 active.
   b. Type an equals sign (=).
   c. Click in cell B25. (This inserts a moving border around the cell and changes the mode from Enter to Point.)
   d. Type a forward slash symbol (/).
   e. Click in cell C25.
   f. Make sure the formula in D25 is *=B25/C25* and then press the Enter key.
2. Make cell D25 active, click the fill handle and hold down the left mouse button, drag into cell D31, and then release the mouse button.

	Expense	Actual	Budget	% of Budget
23				
24	Expense	Actual	Budget	% of Budget
25	Salaries	$126,000	$124,000	=B25/C25
26	Commissions	58,000	54,500	
27	Media space	8,250	10,100	
28	Travel expenses	6,350	6,000	
29	Dealer display	4,140	4,500	
30	Payroll taxes	2,430	2,200	
31	Telephone	1,450	1,500	

1a-1f

Budget	% of Budget
$124,000	102%
54,500	106%
10,100	82%
6,000	106%
4,500	92%
2,200	110%
1,500	97%

2

3. Save **2-HCReports**.

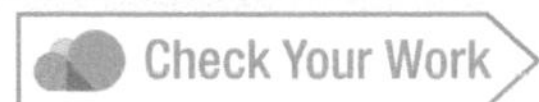

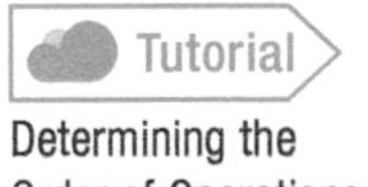

Determining the Order of Operations

Determining the Order of Operations

If a formula contains two or more operators, Excel uses the same order of operations used in algebra. From left to right in a formula, this order is negations (negative number—a number preceded by -) first, then percentages (%), then exponentiations (^), followed by multiplications (*), divisions (/), additions (+), and subtractions (-). To change the order of operations, put parentheses around the part of the formula that is to be calculated first. For example, if cells A1, B1, and C1 all contain the value 5, the result of the formula *=a1+b1*c1* will be 30 (because 5*5=25 and 5+25=30). However, if parentheses are placed around the first two cell references so the formula appears as *=(a1+b1)*c1*, the result will be 50 (because 5+5=10 and 10*5=50).

Excel requires each left parenthesis to be paired with a right parenthesis. If a formula is missing a left or right parenthesis, a message box will display explaining that an error exists in the formula and providing a possible correction, which can be accepted or declined. This feature is useful when creating a formula that contains multiple layers of parentheses (called *nested parentheses*) because it will identify any missing left or right parentheses in the formula. Parentheses can also be used in various functions to further determine the order of operations.

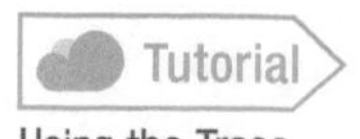

Using the Trace Error Button

Trace Error

Using the Trace Error Button

When typing or editing data in a worksheet, a button may display near the active cell. The general term for this button is a *smart tag*. The display of the smart tag button varies depending on the action performed. In Activity 1d, you will insert a formula that causes a smart tag button named the Trace Error button to appear. When the Trace Error button appears, a small dark-green triangle also appears in the upper left corner of the cell. Click the Trace Error button and a drop-down list displays with options for updating the formula to include specific cells, getting help with the error, ignoring the error, editing the error in the Formula bar, and completing an error check. In Activity 1d, two of the formulas you insert return the correct results. You will click the Trace Error button, read about what Excel perceives to be the error, and then tell Excel to ignore the error.

Identifying Common Formula Errors

Excel is a sophisticated program that requires data input and formula creation to follow strict guidelines in order to function properly. When guidelines that specify how data or formulas are entered are not followed, Excel will display one of many error codes. When an error is identified with a code, determining and then fixing the problem is easier than if no information is provided. Table 2.2 lists some common error codes.

Most errors in Excel result from the user incorrectly inputting data into a worksheet. However, most error messages will not display until the data is used in a formula or function. Common mistakes made while inputting data include placing text in a cell that requires a number, entering data in the wrong location, and entering numbers in an incorrect format. Other errors result from entering a formula or function improperly. A formula will often produce an error message if it is trying to divide a number by 0 or contains a circular reference (that is, when a formula within a cell uses the results of that formula in the same cell).

Table 2.2 Common Error Codes

Error Code	Meaning
#DIV/O	A formula is attempting to divide a number by 0.
#N/A	An argument parameter has been left out of a function.
#NAME?	A function name is not entered correctly.
#NUM!	An argument parameter does not meet a function's requirements.
#REF!	A referenced cell no longer exists within a worksheet.
#VALUE	The data entered is the wrong type (for example, text instead of numbers).

Activity 1d Writing a Formula by Pointing That Calculates the Percentage of Down Time

Part 4 of 4

1. With **2-HCReports** open, enter a formula by pointing that calculates the percentage of equipment down time by completing the following steps:
   a. Make cell B45 active.
   b. Type an equals sign followed by a left parenthesis (=().
   c. Click in cell B37. (This inserts a moving border around the cell and changes the mode from Enter to Point.)
   d. Type a minus symbol (-).
   e. Click in cell B43.
   f. Type a right parenthesis followed by a forward slash ()/).
   g. Click in cell B37.
   h. Make sure the formula in cell B45 is *=(B37-B43)/B37* and then press the Enter key.

	A	B	C	D
34				
35		EQUIPMENT USAGE REPORT		
36	Hours	January	February	March
37	Total hours available	2,300	2,430	2,530
38	Avoidable delays	19	12	16
39	Unavoidable delays	9	8	6
40	Repairs	5	7	12
41	Servicing	6	13	7
42	Unassigned	128	95	85
43	In use	2,040	2,105	2,320
44				
45	% of down time	=(B37-B43)/B37		
46	Jan - March hours			
47	April - June hours			

1a-1h

2. Make cell B45 active, click the fill handle and press and hold down the left mouse button, drag into cell G45, and then release the mouse button.
3. Enter a formula by dragging to a range of cells by completing the following steps:
   a. Click in cell B46 and then click the AutoSum button in the Editing group on the Home tab.
   b. Select the range B37:D37.
   c. Click the Enter button on the Formula bar. (This inserts *7,260* in cell B46.)

3b

	A	B	C	D	E
34					
35		EQUIPMENT USAGE REPORT			
36	Hours	January	February	March	Ap
37	Total hours available	2,300	2,430	2,530	
38	Avoidable delays	19	12	16	
39	Unavoidable delays	9	8	6	
40	Repairs	5	7	12	
41	Servicing	6	13	7	
42	Unassigned	128	95	85	
43	In use	2,040	2,105	2,320	
44					
45	% of down time	11%	13%	8%	
46	Jan - March hours	=SUM(B37:D37)			
47	April - June hours	SUM(**number1**, [number2], ...)			

4. Click in cell B47 and then complete steps similar to those in Step 3 to create a formula that totals hours available from April through June (the range E37:G37). (This inserts *7,080* in cell B47.)
5. Click in cell B46 and notice the Trace Error button. Complete the following steps to read about the error and then tell Excel to ignore it:
   a. Click the Trace Error button.
   b. At the drop-down list, click the *Help on this Error* option.
   c. Read the information in the Excel Help window and then close the window.
   d. Click the Trace Error button again and then click *Ignore Error* at the drop-down list.

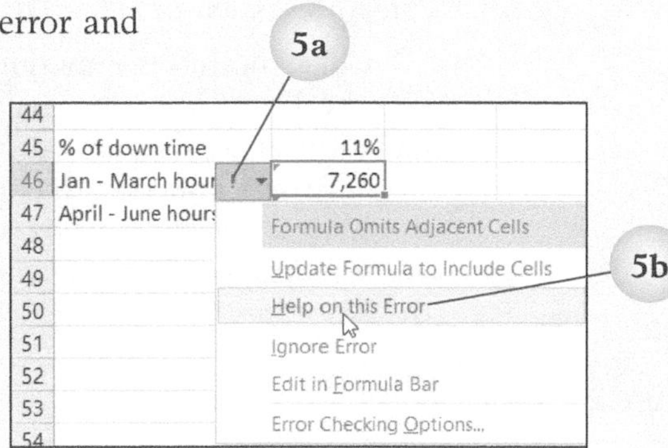

6. Remove the dark-green triangle from cell B47 by completing the following steps:
   a. Click in cell B47.
   b. Click the Trace Error button and then click *Ignore Error* at the drop-down list.
7. Save, print, and then close **2-HCReports**.

Check Your Work

Activity 2 Insert Formulas with Statistical Functions — 4 Parts

You will use the AVERAGE function to determine average test scores, use the MINIMUM and MAXIMUM functions to determine lowest and highest averages, use the COUNT function to count the number of students taking a test, and use the COUNTA function to determine the number of tests administered. You will also use date and time functions and display a formula in a cell rather than the result of a formula.

Inserting Formulas with Functions

In Activity 2b in Chapter 1, the AutoSum button was used to insert the formula *=SUM(b2:b5)* in a cell. The beginning section of the formula, *=SUM*, is called a *function*. Functions are built-in formulas. Inserting a formula takes fewer keystrokes than creating one from scratch. For example, using the *=SUM* function made it unnecessary to type a string of cell references with the plus symbol (+) between each one.

Excel provides other functions for writing formulas. A function operates on what is referred to as an *argument*. An argument may consist of a constant, a cell reference, or another function. In the formula *=SUM(b2:b5)*, the cell range *(b2:b5)* is an example of a cell reference argument. An argument may also contain a *constant*. A constant is a value entered directly into the formula. For example, in the formula *=SUM(b3:b9,100)*, the cell range *b3:b9* is a cell reference argument and *100* is a constant. In this formula, 100 is always added to the sum of the cells.

The phrase *returning the result* is used to describe when a value calculated by the formula is inserted in a cell. The term *returning* refers to the process of calculating the formula and the term *result* refers to the value inserted in the cell.

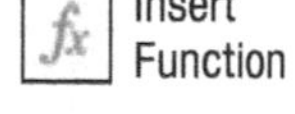

Type a function in a cell in a worksheet or use the Insert Function button on the Formula bar or the Formulas tab to write the formula. Figure 2.1 shows the Formulas tab, which provides the Insert Function button and other buttons for inserting functions in a worksheet. The Function Library group on the Formulas tab contains a number of buttons for inserting functions from a variety of categories, such as *Financial*, *Logical*, *Text*, and *Date & Time*.

Click the Insert Function button on the Formula bar or the Formulas tab and the Insert Function dialog box displays, as shown in Figure 2.2. The Insert Function dialog box can also be accessed using the keyboard shortcut Shift + F3. At the Insert Function dialog box, the most recently used functions display in the *Select a function* list box. Choose a function category by clicking the *Or select a category* option box arrow and then clicking the category at the drop-down list. Use the *Search for a function* search box to locate a specific function.

Figure 2.1 Formulas Tab

File Home Insert Page Layout Formulas Data Review View Help Tell me what you want to do

Insert Function | AutoSum | Recently Used | Financial | Logical | Text | Date & Time | Lookup & Reference | Math & Trig | More Functions — Function Library

Name Manager | Define Name | Use in Formula | Create from Selection — Defined Names

Trace Precedents | Trace Dependents | Remove Arrows | Show Formulas | Error Checking | Evaluate Formula | Watch Window — Formula Auditing

Calculation Options | Calculate Now | Calculate Sheet — Calculation

Figure 2.2 Insert Function Dialog Box

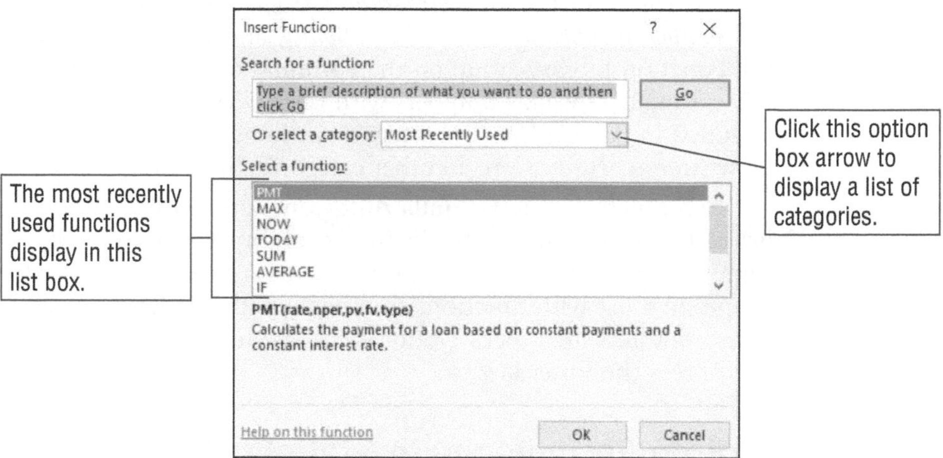

Hint You can also display the Insert Function dialog box by clicking the AutoSum button arrow and then clicking *More Functions.*

With the function category selected, choose a function in the *Select a function* list box and then click OK. This displays a Function Arguments dialog box, like the one shown in Figure 2.3. At this dialog box, enter in the *Number1* text box the range of cells to be included in the formula, any constants to be included as part of the formula, or another function.

Type a cell reference or a range of cells in an argument text box or point to a cell or select a range of cells with the mouse pointer. Pointing to cells or selecting a range of cells using the mouse pointer is the preferred method of entering data into an argument text box because there is less chance of making errors. After entering a range of cells, a constant, or another function, click OK.

More than one argument can be included in a function. If the function contains more than one argument, click in the *Number2* text box or press the Tab key to move the insertion point to the *Number2* text box and then enter the second argument. If the function dialog box covers a specific cell or cells, move the dialog box by positioning the mouse pointer on the dialog box title bar, clicking and holding down the left mouse button, dragging the dialog box to a different location, and then releasing the mouse button.

Figure 2.3 Example of a Function Arguments Dialog Box

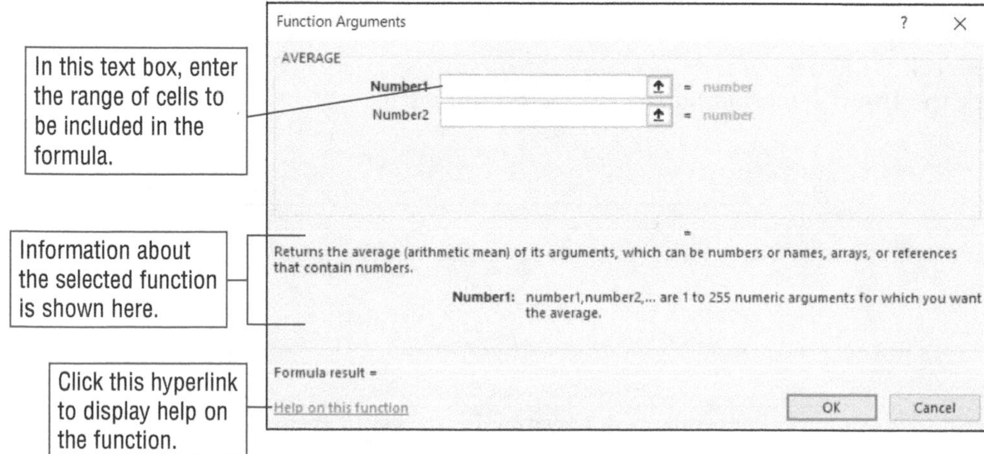

Hint Click the AutoSum button arrow on the Formulas tab and common functions display in a drop-down list.

Excel performs over 300 functions that are divided into 13 categories: *Financial*, *Date & Time*, *Math & Trig*, *Statistical*, *Lookup & Reference*, *Database*, *Text*, *Logical*, *Information*, *Engineering*, *Cube*, *Compatibility*, and *Web*. Clicking the AutoSum button in the Function Library group on the Formulas tab or the Editing group on the Home tab automatically adds numbers with the SUM function. The SUM function is included in the *Math & Trig* category. In some activities in this chapter, formulas will be written with functions in other categories, including *Statistical* and *Date & Time*.

Excel includes the Formula AutoComplete feature, which displays a drop-down list of functions. To use this feature, click in the cell or in the Formula bar text box, type the equals sign, and then type the first letter of the function. This displays a drop-down list with functions that begin with the letter. The list is further refined as more letters are typed. Double-click the function, enter the cell references, and then press the Enter key.

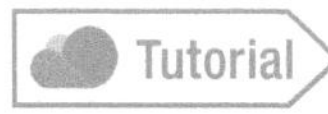

Using Statistical Functions

Writing Formulas with Statistical Functions

Write formulas with statistical functions such as AVERAGE, MAX, MIN, and COUNT. The AVERAGE function returns the average (arithmetic mean) of the arguments. The MAX function returns the largest value in a set of values and the MIN function returns the smallest value in a set of values. Use the COUNT or COUNTA functions to count the number of cells that contain numbers or letters within the specified range.

Finding Averages A common function in a formula is the AVERAGE function. With this function, the values in a range of cells are added together and then divided by the number of cells. In Activity 2a, you will use the AVERAGE function to add all the test scores for a student and then divide that number by the total number of scores. You will use the Insert Function button to simplify the creation of the formula containing an AVERAGE function.

One of the advantages to using formulas in a worksheet is that the data can be easily manipulated to answer certain questions. In Activity 2a, you will learn how retaking certain tests affects the final average score.

Activity 2a Averaging Test Scores in a Worksheet

Part 1 of 4

1. Open **DWTests** and then save it with the name **2-DWTests**.
2. Use the Insert Function button to find the average of test scores by completing the following steps:
   a. Make cell E4 active.
   b. Click the Insert Function button on the Formula bar.

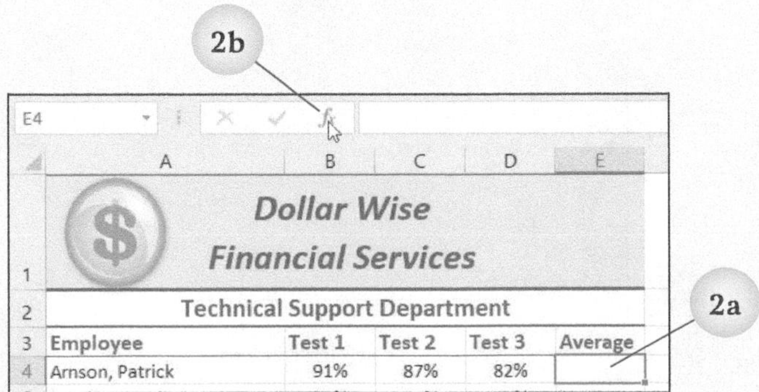

c. At the Insert Function dialog box, click the *Or select a category* option box arrow and then click *Statistical* at the drop-down list.
d. Click *AVERAGE* in the *Select a function* list box.
e. Click OK.
f. At the Function Arguments dialog box, make sure *B4:D4* displays in the *Number1* text box. (If not, type b4:d4 in the *Number1* text box.)
g. Click OK.

3. Copy the formula by completing the following steps:
   a. Make sure cell E4 is still active.
   b. Position the mouse pointer on the fill handle until the pointer turns into a thin black cross.
   c. Click and hold down the left mouse button, drag into cell E16, and then release the mouse button.
4. Save and then print **2-DWTests**.
5. After viewing the averages of test scores, you notice that a couple of students have low averages. You decide to see what happens to these average scores if students retake the tests on which they scored the lowest. You decide that a student can score a maximum of 70% on a retake of the test. Make the following changes to test scores to see how the changes affect the test averages:
   B9: Change *50* to *70*
   C9: Change *52* to *70*
   D9: Change *60* to *70*
   B10: Change *62* to *70*
   B14: Change *0* to *70*
   D14: Change *0* to *70*
   D16: Change *0* to *70*
6. Save and then print **2-DWTests**. (Compare the test averages of Teri Fisher-Edwards, Stephanie Flanery, Claude Markovits, and Douglas Pherson to see how retaking the tests affects their final test averages.)

When a function such as the AVERAGE function calculates cell entries, it ignores certain cell entries. The AVERAGE function will ignore text in cells and blank cells (not zeros). For example, in the worksheet containing test scores, a couple of cells contained *0%*. These entries were included in the averaging of the test scores. To exclude a particular test from the average, enter text in the cell such as *N/A* (for *not applicable*) or leave the cell blank.

Finding Maximum and Minimum Values The MAX function in a formula returns the maximum value in a cell range and the MIN function returns the minimum value in a cell range. For example, the MAX and MIN functions in a worksheet containing employee hours can be used to determine which employee worked the most hours and which worked the least. In a worksheet containing sales commissions, the MAX and MIN functions can be used to identify the salesperson who earned the highest commission and the one who earned the lowest.

Insert a MAX or a MIN function into a formula in the same manner as an AVERAGE function. In Activity 2b, you will use the Formula AutoComplete feature to insert the MAX function in cells to determine the highest test score average and the Insert Function button to insert the MIN function to determine the lowest test score average.

Activity 2b Finding Maximum and Minimum Values in a Worksheet

Part 2 of 4

1. With **2-DWTests** open, type the following in the specified cells:
   A19: Highest Test Average
   A20: Lowest Test Average
   A21: Average of Completed Tests
2. Insert a formula to identify the highest test score average by completing the following steps:
   a. Make cell B19 active.
   b. Type =m. (This displays the Formula AutoComplete list.)
   c. Double-click *MAX* in the Formula AutoComplete list.
   d. Type e4:e16) and then press the Enter key.

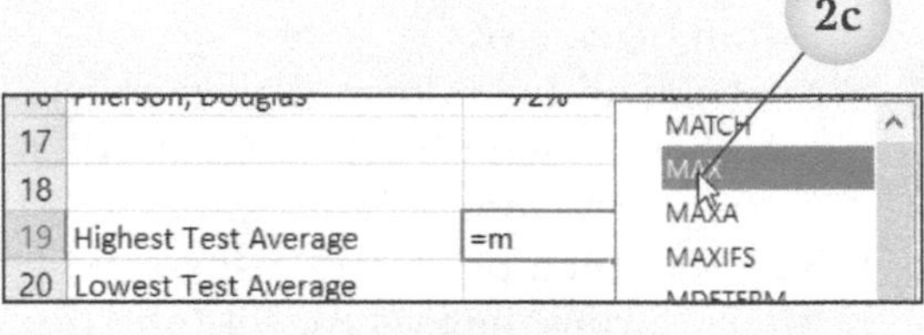

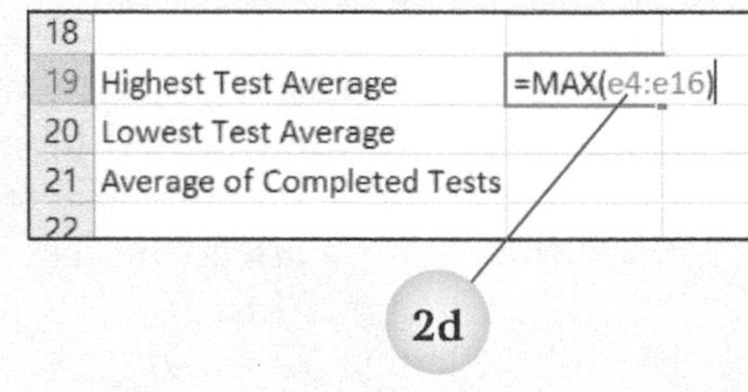

3. Insert a formula to identify the lowest test score average by completing the following steps:
   a. Make sure cell B20 is active.
   b. Click the Insert Function button on the Formula bar.
   c. At the Insert Function dialog box, make sure *Statistical* is selected in the *Or select a category* option box and then click *MIN* in the *Select a function* list box. (You will need to scroll down the list to locate *MIN*.)
   d. Click OK.
   e. At the Function Arguments dialog box, type e4:e16 in the *Number1* text box.
   f. Click OK.

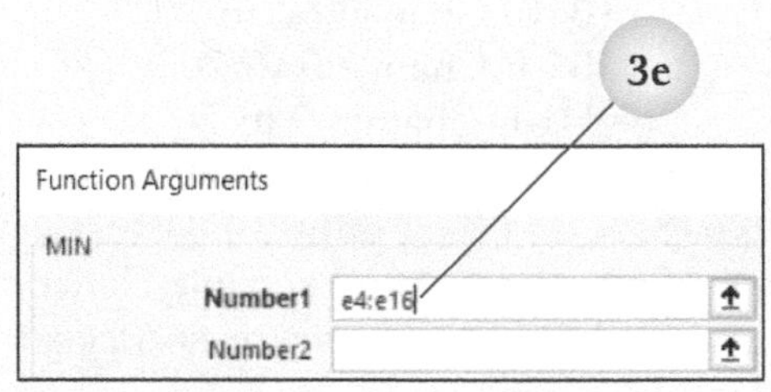

4. Insert a formula to determine the average of the completed test scores by completing the following steps:
   a. Make cell B21 active.
   b. Click the Formulas tab.
   c. Click the Insert Function button in the Function Library group.
   d. At the Insert Function dialog box, make sure *Statistical* is selected in the *Or select a category* option box and then click *AVERAGE* in the *Select a function* list box.

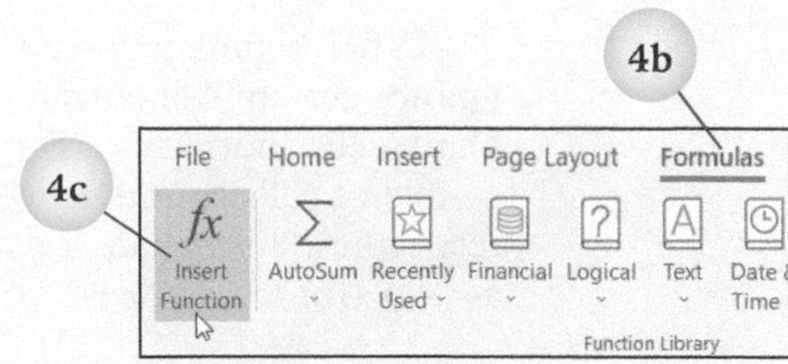

   e. Click OK.
   f. At the Function Arguments dialog box, make sure the insertion point is positioned in the *Number1* text box with existing text selected, use the mouse pointer to select the range E4:E16 in the worksheet (you may need to move the dialog box to display the cells), and then click OK.

5. Save and then print **2-DWTests**.
6. Change the *70%* values (which were previously *0%*) in cells B14, D14, and D16 to *N/A*. (This will cause the average test scores for Claude Markovits and Douglas Pherson to increase and will change the average of completed tests.)
7. Save and then print **2-DWTests**.

Counting Numbers in a Range Use the COUNT function to count the numeric values in a range and use the COUNTA function to count the cells in a range containing any characters. In Activity 2c, you will use the COUNT function to specify the number of students who have completed Test 3. In the worksheet, the cells containing the text *N/A* are not counted by the COUNT function. Additionally, you will use the COUNTA function to determine how many students should have completed Test 3 by counting the cells that contain test scores and the text N/A.

Activity 2c **Counting the Number of Students Taking Tests** Part 3 of 4

1. With **2-DWTests** open, make cell A22 active.
2. Type Test 3 Completed.
3. Make cell B22 active.
4. Insert a formula counting the number of students who have completed Test 3 by completing the following steps:
   a. With cell B22 active, click in the Formula bar text box.
   b. Type =c.
   c. At the Formula AutoComplete list, scroll down the list until *COUNT* displays and then double-click *COUNT*.
   d. Type d4:d16) and then press the Enter key.

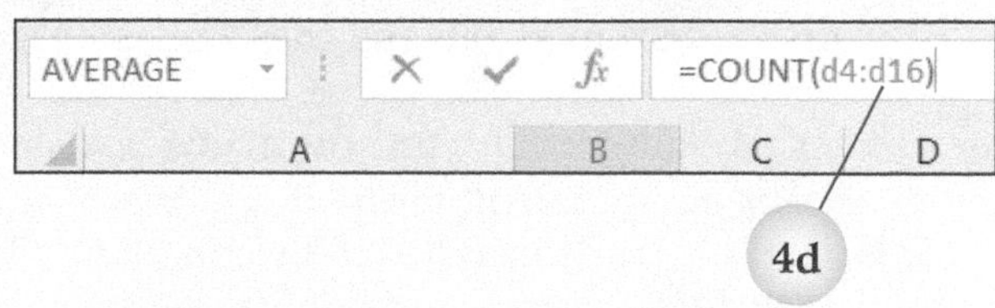

5. Count the number of students who have been given Test 3 by completing the following steps:
   a. Make cell A23 active.
   b. Type Test 3 Administered.
   c. Make cell B23 active.
   d. Click the Insert Function button on the Formula bar.
   e. At the Insert Function dialog box, make sure *Statistical* is selected in the *Or select a category* option box.
   f. Scroll down the list of functions in the *Select a function* list box until *COUNTA* is visible and then double-click *COUNTA*.
   g. At the Function Arguments dialog box, type d4:d16 in the *Value1* text box and then click OK.
6. Save and then print **2-DWTests**.

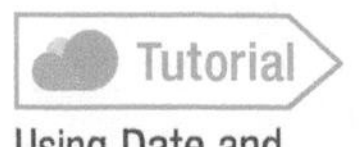

Using Date and Time Functions

Date & Time

Calculate Now

Writing Formulas with the NOW and TODAY Functions

The NOW and TODAY functions are part of the *Date & Time* category of functions. The NOW function returns the current date and time in a date-and-time format. The TODAY function returns the current date in a date format. Both the NOW and TODAY functions automatically update when a workbook is opened. To access the NOW and TODAY functions, click the Date & Time button in the Function Library group on the Formulas tab. The formulas can also be accessed at the Insert Function dialog box.

The NOW and TODAY functions can also be updated without closing and then reopening the workbook. To update a workbook that contains a NOW or TODAY function, click the Calculate Now button in the Calculation group on the Formulas tab or press the F9 function key.

Displaying Formulas

Show Formulas

Hint Press Ctrl + ` to display the formulas in a worksheet rather than the results.

Displaying Formulas

In some situations, displaying the formulas in a worksheet, rather than the results, may be useful—for example, to display formulas for auditing purposes or to check formulas for accuracy. Display all the formulas in a worksheet, rather than the results, by clicking the Formulas tab and then clicking the Show Formulas button in the Formula Auditing group. The display of formulas can also be turned on with the keyboard shortcut Ctrl + `. (This symbol is the grave accent, generally to the left of the 1 key on the keyboard.) To turn off the display of formulas, press Ctrl + ` or click the Show Formulas button on the Formulas tab.

Activity 2d Using the NOW Function and Displaying Formulas — Part 4 of 4

1. With **2-DWTests** open, make cell A26 active and then type Prepared by:.
2. Make cell A27 active and then type your first and last names.
3. Insert the current date and time by completing the following steps:
   a. Make cell A28 active.
   b. Click the Date & Time button in the Function Library group on the Formulas tab and then click *NOW* at the drop-down list.
   c. At the Function Arguments dialog box stating that the function takes no argument, click OK.
4. Update the time in cell A28 by completing the following steps:
   a. Wait for 1 minute.
   b. Click the Calculate Now button in the Calculation group on the Formulas tab.
5. Click the Show Formulas button in the Formula Auditing group to turn on the display of formulas.
6. Print the worksheet with the formulas. (The worksheet will print on two pages.)
7. Press Ctrl + ` to turn off the display of formulas.
8. Save, print, and then close **2-DWTests**.

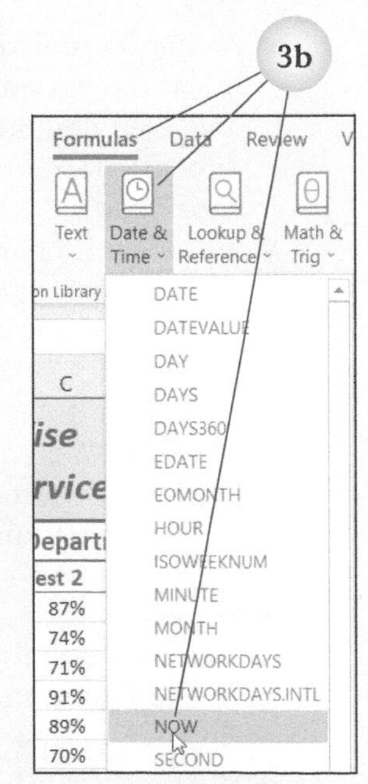

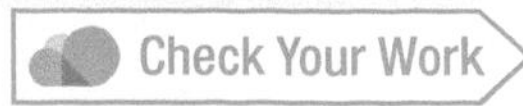

Activity 3 Insert Formulas Using Absolute and Mixed Cell References — 4 Parts

You will insert a formula containing an absolute cell reference that determines the effect on earnings with specific increases, insert a formula with multiple absolute cell references that determines the weighted average of scores, and use mixed cell references to determine simple interest.

Using Absolute and Mixed Cell References in Formulas

A reference identifies a cell or range of cells in a worksheet and can be relative, absolute, or mixed. A relative cell reference refers to a cell relative to a position in a formula. An absolute cell reference refers to a cell in a specific location. When a formula is copied, a relative cell reference adjusts whereas an absolute cell reference remains constant. A mixed cell reference does both: either the column remains absolute and the row is relative or the column is relative and the row remains absolute. Distinguish among relative, absolute, and mixed cell references using the dollar symbol ($). Type a dollar symbol before the column and/or row cell reference in a formula to specify that the column or row is an absolute cell reference.

Absolute Addressing

Using an Absolute Cell Reference in a Formula

In this chapter, you have learned to copy a relative formula. For example, if the formula *=SUM(A2:C2)* in cell D2 is copied relatively into cell D3, it changes to *=SUM(A3:C3)*. In some situations, a formula may contain an absolute cell reference, which always refers to a cell in a specific location. In Activity 3a, you will add a column for projected job earnings and then consider "What if?" situations using a formula with an absolute cell reference. To identify an absolute cell reference, insert a dollar symbol before the row and the column. For example, the absolute cell reference *C12* is typed as *c12* in a formula.

Activity 3a Inserting and Copying a Formula with an Absolute Cell Reference — Part 1 of 4

1. Open **CCReports** and then save it with the name **2-CCReports**.
2. Determine the effect of a 10% pay increase on actual job earnings by completing the following steps:
   a. Make cell C3 active, type the formula =b3*b12, and then press the Enter key.
   b. Make cell C3 active and then use the fill handle to copy the formula to the range C4:C10.
   c. Make cell C3 active, click the Accounting Number Format button on the Home tab, and then click the Decrease Decimal button two times.

A	B	C
	Cedarview	
Customer	Planned	Actual
r Corporation	$ 34,109	=b3*b12
n Street Photos	48,100	
set Automotive	32,885	
trom Enterprises	61,220	
cos Media	30,500	
en Valley Optics	58,394	
iled Designs	13,100	
wstar Company	86,905	
crease/Decrease	1.1	

2a

Cedarview	
Planned	Actual
$ 34,109	37,520
48,100	52,910
32,885	36,174
61,220	67,342
30,500	33,550
58,394	64,233
13,100	14,410
86,905	95,596

2b

3. Save and then print **2-CCReports**.
4. With the worksheet still open, determine the effect of a 10% pay decrease on actual job earnings by completing the following steps:
   a. Make cell B12 active.
   b. Type 0.9 and then press the Enter key.
5. Save and then print the **2-CCReports**.
6. Determine the effect of a 20% pay increase on actual job earnings. (To do this, type 1.2 in cell B12 and then press the Enter key.)
7. Save and then print **2-CCReports**.

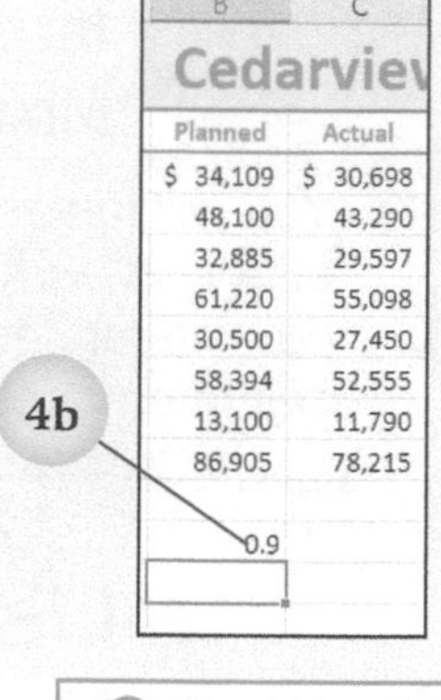

B	C
Cedarview	
Planned	Actual
$ 34,109	$ 30,698
48,100	43,290
32,885	29,597
61,220	55,098
30,500	27,450
58,394	52,555
13,100	11,790
86,905	78,215
0.9	

Check Your Work

In Activity 3a, you created a formula with one absolute cell reference. A formula can also be created with multiple absolute cell references. For example, in Activity 3b, you will create a formula that contains both relative and absolute cell references to determine the average of training scores based on specific weight percentages. In a weighted average, some scores have more value (weight) than others. For example, in Activity 3b, you will create a formula that determines the weighted average of training scores that gives more weight to the *Carpentry* percentages than the *Plumbing* or *Electrical* percentages.

Activity 3b Inserting and Copying a Formula with Multiple Absolute Cell References

Part 2 of 4

1. With **2-CCReports** open, insert the following formulas:
   a. Insert a formula in cell B23 that averages the percentages in the range B17:B22.
   b. Copy the formula in cell B23 to cells C23 and D23.
2. Insert a formula that determines the weighted average of training scores by completing the following steps:
   a. Make cell E17 active.
   b. Type the following formula:
      =b24*b17+c24*c17+d24*d17
   c. Press the Enter key.
   d. Copy the formula in cell E17 to the range E18:E22.
   e. With the range E17:E22 selected, click the Decrease Decimal button three times.
3. Save and then print **2-CCReports**.
4. With the worksheet still open, determine the effect on weighted training scores if the weighted values change by completing the following steps:
   a. Make cell B24 active, type 30, and then press the Enter key.
   b. Make cell D24 active, type 40, and then press the Enter key.
5. Save and then print **2-CCReports**.

15	Employee Training				
16	Name	Plumbing	Electrical	Carpentry	Weighted Average
17	Allesandro	76%	80%	84%	80%
18	Ellington	66%	72%	64%	67%
19	Goodman	90%	88%	94%	91%
20	Huntington	76%	82%	88%	83%
21	Kaplan-Downing	90%	84%	92%	89%
22	Larimore	58%	62%	60%	60%
23	Training Averages	76%	78%	80%	
24	Training Weights	30%	30%	40%	
25					

4a 4b

Check Your Work

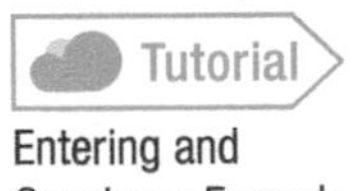

Entering and Copying a Formula with Mixed Cell References

Using a Mixed Cell Reference in a Formula

The formula you created in Step 2a in Activity 3a contained a relative cell reference (b3) and an absolute cell reference (b12). A formula can also contain a mixed cell reference. As stated earlier, in a mixed cell reference, either the column remains absolute and the row is relative or the column is relative and the row remains absolute. In Activity 3c, you will insert a number of formulas—two of which will contain mixed cell references. You will insert the formula *=e29*e$26* to calculate withholding tax and *=e29*h$36* to calculate social security tax. The dollar symbol before each row number indicates that the row is an absolute reference.

Activity 3c Determining Payroll Using Formulas with Absolute and Mixed Cell References

Part 3 of 4

1. With **2-CCReports** open, make cell E29 active and then type the following formula that calculates the gross pay, including overtime (press the Enter key after typing each formula):
   =(b29*c29+(b29*b36*d29))
2. Copy the formula in cell E29 to the range E30:E34.
3. Make cell F29 active and then type the following formula that calculates the amount of withholding tax:
   =e29*e$36
4. Copy the formula in cell F29 to the range F30:F34.
5. Make cell G29 active and then type the following formula that calculates the amount of social security tax:
   =e29*h$36
6. Copy the formula in cell G29 to the range G30:G34.
7. Make cell H29 active and then type the following formula that calculates net pay:
   =e29-(f29+g29)
8. Copy the formula in cell H29 to the range H30:H34.
9. Select the range E29:H29 and then click the Accounting Number Format button.
10. Save **2-CCReports**.

As you learned in Activity 3c, a formula can contain a mixed cell reference. In Activity 3d, you will create the formula *=$a41*b$40*. In the first cell reference in the formula, *$a41*, the column is absolute and the row is relative. In the second cell reference, *b$40*, the column is relative and the row is absolute. The formula containing the mixed cell reference allows you to fill in the column and row data using only one formula.

Identify an absolute or mixed cell reference by typing a dollar symbol before the column and/or row reference or press the F4 function key to cycle through the various cell references. For example, type *=a41* in a cell, press the F4 function key, and the cell reference changes to *=a41*. Press F4 again and the cell reference changes to *=a$41*. Press F4 a third time and the cell reference changes to *=$a41* and press F4 a fourth time and the cell reference changes back to *=a41*.

Activity 3d Determining Simple Interest Using a Formula with Mixed Cell References

Part 4 of 4

1. With **2-CCReports** open, make cell B41 the active cell and then insert a formula containing mixed cell references by completing the following steps:
   a. Type =a41 and then press the F4 function key three times. (This changes the cell reference to *$A41*.)
   b. Type *b40 and then press the F4 function key two times. (This changes the cell reference to *B$40*.)
   c. Make sure the formula displays as =*$A41*B$40* and then press the Enter key.

	A	B	C
39			SIMP
40		$ 1,000	$ 2,0
41	5%	=$A41*B$40	

1c

2. Copy the formula to the right by completing the following steps:
   a. Make cell B41 active and then use the fill handle to copy the formula to cell F41.

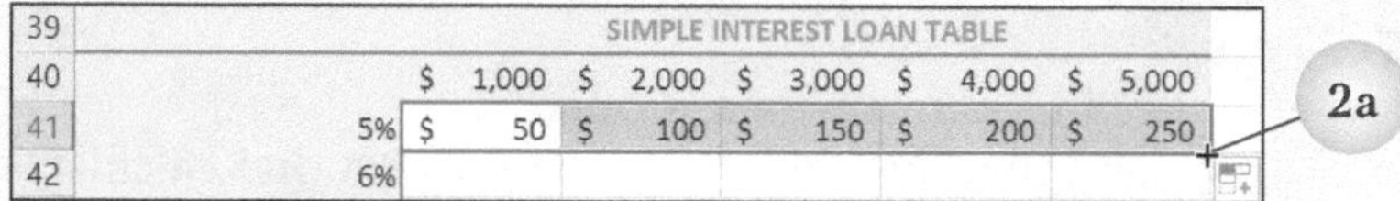

39		SIMPLE INTEREST LOAN TABLE				
40		$ 1,000	$ 2,000	$ 3,000	$ 4,000	$ 5,000
41	5%	$ 50	$ 100	$ 150	$ 200	$ 250
42	6%					

2a

   b. With the range B41:F41 selected, use the fill handle to copy the formula to cell F51.

39		SIMPLE INTEREST LOAN TABLE				
40		$ 1,000	$ 2,000	$ 3,000	$ 4,000	$ 5,000
41	5%	$ 50	$ 100	$ 150	$ 200	$ 250
42	6%	$ 60	$ 120	$ 180	$ 240	$ 300
43	7%	$ 70	$ 140	$ 210	$ 280	$ 350
44	8%	$ 80	$ 160	$ 240	$ 320	$ 400
45	9%	$ 90	$ 180	$ 270	$ 360	$ 450
46	10%	$ 100	$ 200	$ 300	$ 400	$ 500
47	11%	$ 110	$ 220	$ 330	$ 440	$ 550
48	12%	$ 120	$ 240	$ 360	$ 480	$ 600
49	13%	$ 130	$ 260	$ 390	$ 520	$ 650
50	14%	$ 140	$ 280	$ 420	$ 560	$ 700
51	15%	$ 150	$ 300	$ 450	$ 600	$ 750

2b

3. Save, print, and then close **2-CCReports**.

Chapter Summary

- Type a formula in a cell and the formula displays in the cell and in the Formula bar. If cell entries are changed, a formula automatically recalculates the values and inserts the result in the cell.
- Write a formula using commonly used operators, such as addition (+), subtraction (-), multiplication (*), division (/), percentage (%), and exponentiation (^). When writing a formula, begin with the equals sign (=).
- Copy a formula to other cells in a row or column with the Fill button in the Editing group on the Home tab or with the fill handle in the bottom right corner of the active cell.
- Double-click in a cell containing a formula and the cell references display with a colored border and cell shading.

- Another method for writing a formula is to point to specific cells that are part of the formula as the formula is being built.
- Excel uses the same order of operations as algebra and that order can be modified by adding parentheses around certain parts of a formula.
- If Excel detects an error in a formula, a Trace Error button appears and a small dark-green triangle displays in the upper left corner of the cell containing the formula.
- Excel provides different error codes for different formula errors. An error code helps identify an error in a formula by providing information on the specific issue.
- A function operates on an argument, which may consist of a cell reference, a constant, or another function. When a value calculated by a formula is inserted in a cell, this is referred to as *returning the result*.
- Excel performs over 300 functions that are divided into 13 categories.
- The AVERAGE function returns the average (arithmetic mean) of the arguments. The MAX function returns the largest value in a set of values and the MIN function returns the smallest value in a set of values. The COUNT function counts the number of cells containing numbers within the list of arguments. The COUNTA function counts the number of cells containing any data, numerical or alphabetical.
- The NOW function returns the current date and time and the TODAY function returns the current date.
- Turn on the display of formulas in a worksheet with the Show Formulas button in the Formula Auditing group on the Formulas tab or with the keyboard shortcut Ctrl + ` (grave accent).
- A reference identifies a cell or a range of cells in a worksheet and can be relative, absolute, or mixed. Identify an absolute cell reference by inserting a dollar symbol ($) before the column and row. Cycle through the various cell reference options by typing the cell reference and then pressing the F4 function key.

Commands Review

FEATURE	RIBBON TAB, GROUP	BUTTON	KEYBOARD SHORTCUT
cycle through cell references			F4
display formulas	Formulas, Formula Auditing		Ctrl + `
Insert Function dialog box	Formulas, Function Library	*fx*	Shift + F3
SUM function	Home, Editing OR Formulas, Function Library	Σ	Alt + =
update formulas	Formulas, Calculation		F9

Microsoft®

Excel®

CHAPTER 3

Formatting a Worksheet

Performance Objectives

Upon successful completion of Chapter 3, you will be able to:

1 Change column widths and row heights
2 Insert rows and columns
3 Delete cells, rows, and columns
4 Clear data in cells
5 Apply formatting to data in cells
6 Apply formatting to selected data using the Mini toolbar
7 Apply a theme and customize the theme font and colors
8 Format numbers
9 Apply formatting at the Format Cells dialog box
10 Repeat the last action
11 Automate formatting with Format Painter
12 Hide and unhide rows and columns

The appearance of a worksheet on screen and how it looks when printed is called the *format*. In Chapter 1, you learned how to apply basic formatting to cells in a worksheet. Additional types of formatting include changing column width and row height; applying character formatting such as bold, italic, and underlining; specifying number formatting; inserting and deleting rows and columns; and applying borders, shading, and patterns to cells. You can also apply formatting to a worksheet with a theme. A theme is a set of formatting choices that include colors and fonts.

Before beginning chapter work, copy the EL1C3 folder to your storage medium and then make EL1C3 the active folder.

The online course includes additional training and assessment resources.

Activity 1 Format a Product Pricing Worksheet 7 Parts

You will open a workbook containing a worksheet with product pricing data and then format it by changing column widths and row heights, inserting and deleting rows and columns, and clearing data in cells. You will also apply font and alignment formatting as well as borders and fill.

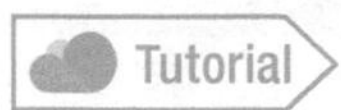

Adjusting Column Width and Row Height

Changing Column Width

The columns in a worksheet are the same width by default. In some worksheets, column widths may need to be changed to accommodate more or less data. Change column widths using the mouse on column boundary lines or at a dialog box.

Changing Column Width Using Column Boundaries

Hint To change the width of all the columns in a worksheet, click the Select All button and then drag a column boundary line to the desired position.

As explained in Chapter 1, column width can be adjusted by dragging the column boundary line or adjusted to the longest entry by double-clicking the boundary line. When the boundary line is being dragged, the column width is shown in a box above the mouse pointer. The number that is shown represents the average number of characters in the standard font that can fit in a cell.

The width of selected adjacent columns can be changed at the same time. To do this, select the columns and then drag one of the column boundary lines within the selected columns. When the boundary line is being dragged, the column width changes for all the selected columns. To select adjacent columns, position the cell pointer on the first column header to be selected (the mouse pointer turns into a black down-pointing arrow), click and hold down the left mouse button, drag the cell pointer into the last column header, and then release the mouse button.

Activity 1a Changing Column Width Using a Column Boundary Line Part 1 of 7

1. Open **CMProducts** and then save it with the name **3-CMProducts**.
2. Insert a formula in cell D2 that multiplies the price in cell B2 with the number in cell C2. Copy the formula in cell D2 to the range D3:D14.
3. Change the width of column D by completing the following steps:
   a. Position the mouse pointer on the column boundary line in the column header between columns D and E until it turns into a double-headed arrow pointing left and right.
   b. Click and hold down the left mouse button, drag the column boundary line to the right until *Width: 11.00* displays in the box, and then release the mouse button.

3b

4. Make cell D15 active and then insert the sum of the values in the range D2:D14.
5. Change the width of columns A and B by completing the following steps:
   a. Select columns A and B. To do this, position the cell pointer on the column A header, click and hold down the left mouse button, drag the cell pointer into the column B header, and then release the mouse button.
   b. Position the cell pointer on the column boundary line between columns A and B until it turns into a double-headed arrow pointing left and right.

c. Click and hold down the left mouse button, drag the column boundary line to the right until *Width: 10.43* displays in the box, and then release the mouse button.

6. Adjust the width of column C to accommodate the longest entry by double-clicking on the column boundary line between columns C and D.
7. Save **3-CMProducts**.

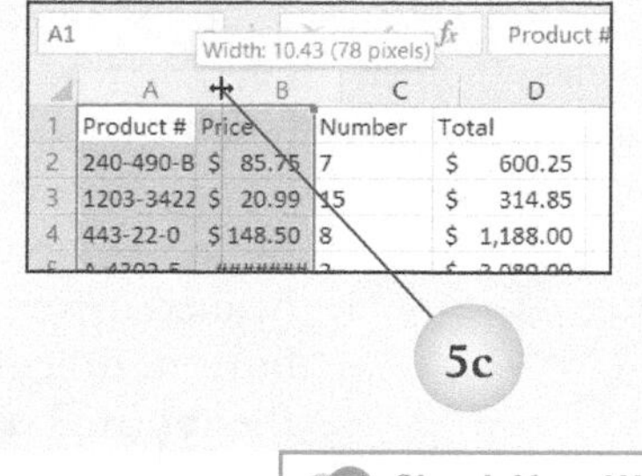

Changing Column Width at the Column Width Dialog Box

Use the *Column width* measurement box in the Column Width dialog box, shown in Figure 3.1, to specify a column width number. Increase the number to make the column wider and decrease the number to make the column narrower.

Format

Quick Steps

Change Column Width

Drag column boundary line.
OR
Double-click column boundary line.
OR
1. Click Format button.
2. Click *Column Width.*
3. Type width.
4. Click OK.

Display the Column Width dialog box by clicking the Format button in the Cells group on the Home tab and then clicking *Column Width* at the drop-down list. At the Column Width dialog box, type a measurement number (the number represents the number of characters in the standard font that can fit in the column) and then press the Enter key or click OK.

Figure 3.1 Column Width Dialog Box

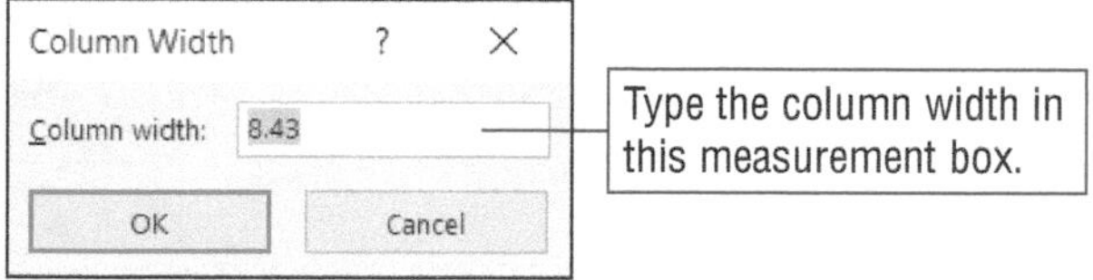

Activity 1b **Changing Column Width at the Column Width Dialog Box** Part 2 of 7

1. With **3-CMProducts** open, change the width of column A by completing the following steps:
   a. Make any cell in column A active.
   b. Click the Format button in the Cells group on the Home tab and then click *Column Width* at the drop-down list.
   c. At the Column Width dialog box, type 12.7 in the *Column width* measurement box.
   d. Click OK to close the dialog box.
2. Make any cell in column B active and then change the width of column B to 12.5 characters by completing steps similar to those in Step 1.
3. Make any cell in column C active and then change the width of column C to 8 characters by completing steps similar to those in Step 1.
4. Save **3-CMProducts**.

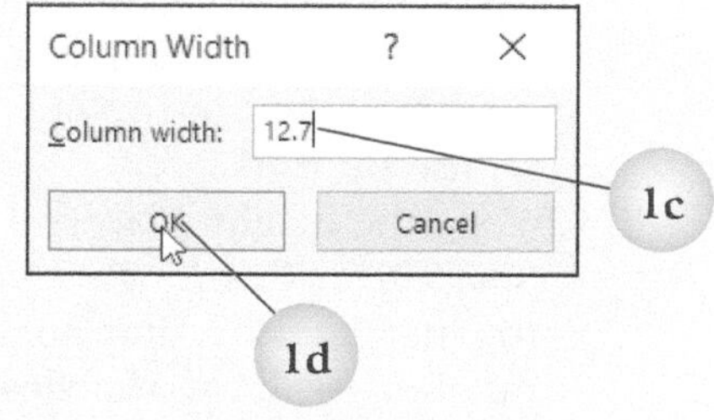

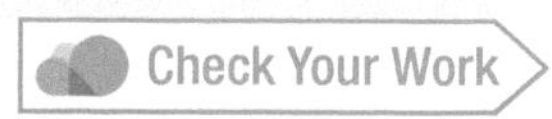

Changing Row Height

Quick Steps

Change Row Height

Drag row boundary line.
OR
1. Click Format button.
2. Click *Row Height*.
3. Type height.
4. Click OK.

Hint To change the height of all the rows in a worksheet, click the Select All button and then drag a row boundary line to the desired position.

Hint Excel measures row height in points and column width in characters.

Change row height in much the same manner as column width. Change row height using the mouse on a row boundary line or at the Row Height dialog box. Change row height using a row boundary line by positioning the cell pointer on the boundary line between rows in the row header until it turns into a double-headed arrow pointing up and down, clicking and holding down the left mouse button, dragging up or down until the row is the desired height, and then releasing the mouse button.

Change the height of adjacent rows by selecting the rows and then dragging one of the row boundary lines within the selected rows. As the boundary line is being dragged, the row height changes for all the selected rows.

As a row boundary line is being dragged, the row height displays in a box above the mouse pointer. The number that is shown represents a point measurement. Increase the point size to increase the row height; decrease the point size to decrease the row height.

Another method for changing row height is to use the *Row height* measurement box at the Row Height dialog box, shown in Figure 3.2. Display this dialog box by clicking the Format button in the Cells group on the Home tab and then clicking *Row Height* at the drop-down list.

Figure 3.2 Row Height Dialog Box

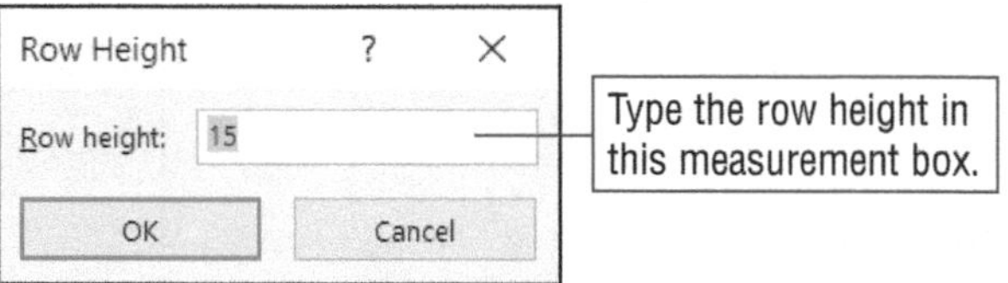

Activity 1c **Changing Row Height** Part 3 of 7

1. With **3-CMProducts** open, change the height of row 1 by completing the following steps:
   a. Position the cell pointer in the row header on the row boundary line between rows 1 and 2 until it turns into a double-headed arrow pointing up and down.
   b. Click and hold down the left mouse button, drag the row boundary line down until *Height: 19.50* displays in the box, and then release the mouse button.

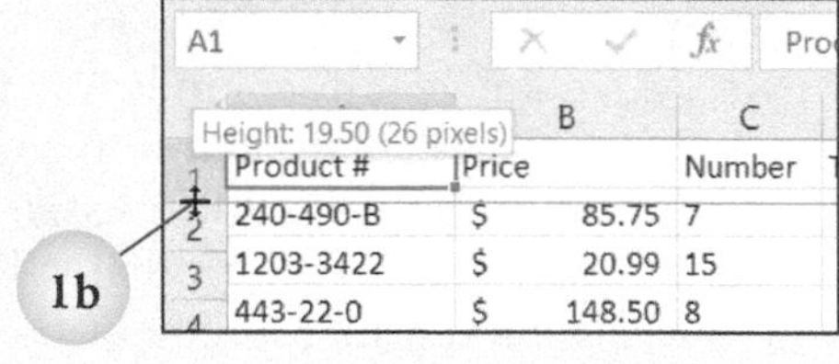

2. Change the height of rows 2 through 14 by completing the following steps:
   a. Select rows 2 through 14. To do this, position the cell pointer on the number *2* in the row header, click and hold down the left mouse button, drag the cell pointer to the number *14* in the row header, and then release the mouse button.
   b. Position the cell pointer on the row boundary line between rows 2 and 3 until it turns into a double-headed arrow pointing up and down.

c. Click and hold down the left mouse button, drag the row boundary line down until *Height: 16.50* displays in the box, and then release the mouse button.
3. Change the height of row 15 by completing the following steps:
   a. Make cell A15 active.
   b. Click the Format button in the Cells group on the Home tab and then click *Row Height* at the drop-down list.
   c. At the Row Height dialog box, type 20 in the *Row height* measurement box and then click OK.

2c

Height: 16.50 (22 pixels)

	A	B
2	240-490-B	$ 85.
3	1203-3422	$ 20.
4	443-22-0	$ 148.
5	A-4302-5	$ 1,540.
6	43-GB-39	$ 45.
7	341-453	$ 19.
8	CT-342	$ 304.
9	83-492	$ 9.
10	L-756-M	$ 95.
11	340-19	$ 15.
12	T-3491-S	$ 450.
13	900-599	$ 35.
14	43-49CE	$ 120.
15	Total	

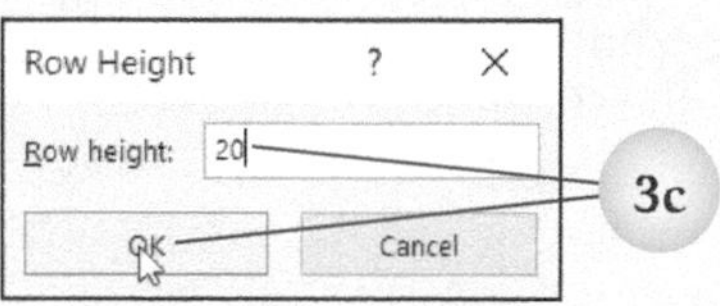

4. Save **3-CMProducts**.

Inserting Columns and Rows

Inserting and Deleting Cells, Rows, and Columns

New data may need to be included in an existing worksheet. For example, a row or several rows of new data may need to be inserted into a worksheet or data may need to be removed from a worksheet.

Inserting Rows

Hint When you insert cells, rows, or columns in a worksheet, all the references affected by the insertion automatically adjust.

A row or rows can be inserted in an existing worksheet. Insert a row with the Insert button in the Cells group on the Home tab or with options at the Insert dialog box. By default, a row is inserted above the row containing the active cell. To insert a row in a worksheet, select the row below where the row is to be inserted and then click the Insert button. To insert more than one row, select the number of rows to be inserted in the worksheet and then click the Insert button.

Insert

Quick Steps

Insert Row

Click Insert button.
OR
1. Click Insert button arrow.
2. Click *Insert Sheet Rows.*

OR
1. Click Insert button arrow.
2. Click *Insert Cells.*
3. Click *Entire row.*
4. Click OK.

Another method for inserting a row is to make a cell active in the row below where the row is to be inserted, click the Insert button arrow, and then click *Insert Sheet Rows*. A row can also be inserted by clicking the Insert button arrow and then clicking *Insert Cells*. This displays the Insert dialog box, as shown in Figure 3.3. At the Insert dialog box, click *Entire row* and then click OK. This inserts a row above the active cell.

Figure 3.3 Insert Dialog Box

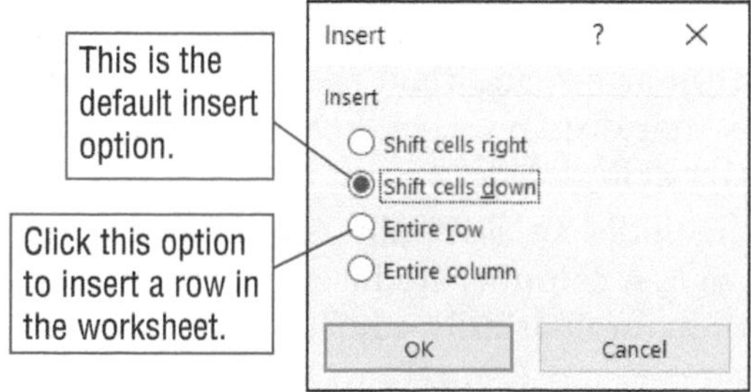

Activity 1d Inserting Rows

Part 4 of 7

1. With **3-CMProducts** open, insert two rows at the beginning of the worksheet by completing the following steps:
   a. Make cell A1 active.
   b. Click the Insert button arrow in the Cells group on the Home tab.
   c. At the drop-down list that displays, click *Insert Sheet Rows*.
   d. With cell A1 active, click the Insert button arrow and then click *Insert Sheet Rows* at the drop-down list.
2. Type the text Capstan Marine Products in cell A1.
3. Make cell A2 active and then type Purchasing Department.
4. Change the height of row 1 to 42 points.
5. Change the height of row 2 to 21 points.
6. Insert two rows by completing the following steps:
   a. Select rows 7 and 8 in the worksheet.
   b. Click the Insert button in the Cells group on the Home tab.
7. Type the following data in the specified cells. For the cells that contain money amounts, you do not need to type the dollar symbols:
   A7: 855-495
   B7: 42.75
   C7: 5
   A8: ST039
   B8: 12.99
   C8: 25
8. Make cell D6 active and then use the fill handle to copy the formula into cells D7 and D8.
9. Save **3-CMProducts**.

Inserting Columns

Quick Steps

Insert Column
Click Insert button.
OR
1. Click Insert button arrow.
2. Click *Insert Sheet Columns*.

OR
1. Click Insert button arrow.
2. Click *Insert Cells*.
3. Click *Entire column*.
4. Click OK.

Insert columns in a worksheet in much the same way as rows. Insert a column with options from the Insert button drop-down list or with options at the Insert dialog box. By default, a column is inserted immediately to the left of the column containing the active cell. To insert a column in a worksheet, make a cell active in the column immediately to the right of where the new column is to be inserted, click the Insert button arrow, and then click *Insert Sheet Columns* at the drop-down list. To insert more than one column, select the number of columns to be inserted in the worksheet, click the Insert button arrow, and then click *Insert Sheet Columns*.

Another method for inserting a column is to make a cell active in the column immediately to the right of where the new column is to be inserted, click the Insert button arrow, and then click *Insert Cells* at the drop-down list. At the Insert dialog box that displays, click *Entire column*. This inserts a column immediately left of the active cell.

Excel includes an especially helpful and time-saving feature related to inserting columns. When columns are inserted in a worksheet, all the references affected by the insertion automatically adjust.

Activity 1e Inserting Columns

Part 5 of 7

1. With **3-CMProducts** open, insert a column to the left of column A by completing the following steps:
   a. Click in any cell in column A.
   b. Click the Insert button arrow in the Cells group on the Home tab and then click *Insert Sheet Columns* at the drop-down list.
2. Type the following data in each specified cell:
   A3: Company
   A4: RD Manufacturing
   A8: Smithco, Inc.
   A11: Sunrise Corporation
   A15: Geneva Systems
3. Make cell A1 active and then adjust the width of column A to accommodate the longest entry.
4. Insert another column to the left of column B by completing the following steps:
   a. Make cell B1 active.
   b. Click the Insert button arrow and then click *Insert Cells* at the drop-down list.
   c. At the Insert dialog box, click *Entire column*.
   d. Click OK.
5. Type Date in cell B3 and then press the Enter key.
6. Save **3-CMProducts**.

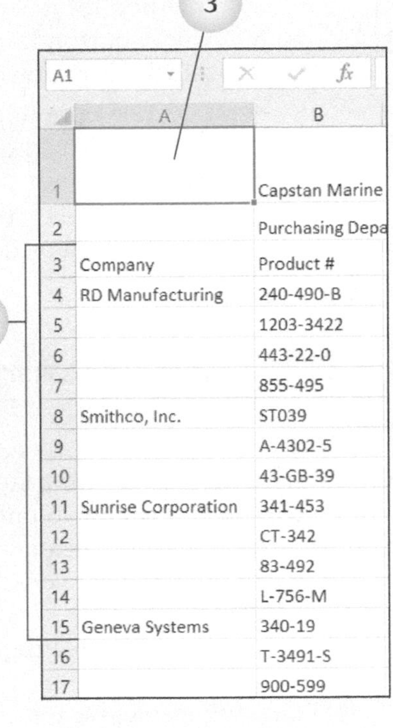

Deleting Columns and Rows

Hint Display the Delete dialog box by positioning the cell pointer in the worksheet, clicking the right mouse button, and then clicking *Delete* at the shortcut menu.

Deleting Cells, Rows, or Columns

Specific cells in a worksheet or rows or columns in a worksheet can be deleted. To delete a row, select it and then click the Delete button in the Cells group on the Home tab. To delete a column, select it and then click the Delete button. Delete a specific cell by making it active, clicking the Delete button arrow, and then clicking *Delete Cells* at the drop-down list. This displays the Delete dialog box, shown in Figure 3.4. At the Delete dialog box, specify what is to be deleted and then click OK. Delete adjacent cells by selecting them and then displaying the Delete dialog box.

Figure 3.4 Delete Dialog Box

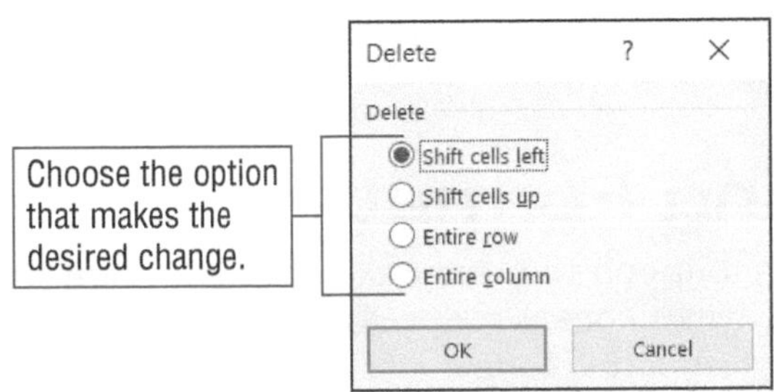

Clearing Cell Contents and Formatting

Clear

Quick Steps

Clear Data in Cells
1. Select cells.
2. Press Delete key.

OR

1. Select cells.
2. Click Clear button.
3. Click *Clear Contents*.

Clearing Data in Cells

To delete the cell contents but not the cell, make the cell active or select cells and then press the Delete key. A quick method for clearing the contents of a cell is to right-click in the cell and then click *Clear Contents* at the shortcut menu. Another method for deleting cell contents is to make the cell active or select cells, click the Clear button in the Editing group on the Home tab, and then click *Clear Contents* at the drop-down list.

Use options at the Clear button drop-down list to clear the contents of the cell or selected cells as well as the formatting and comments. Click the *Clear Formats* option to remove the formatting from the cell or selected cells but leave the data. Click the *Clear All* option to clear the contents of the cell or selected cells as well as the formatting.

Activity 1f Deleting and Clearing Rows in a Worksheet — Part 6 of 7

1. With **3-CMProducts** open, delete column B in the worksheet by completing the following steps:
   a. Click in any cell in column B.
   b. Click the Delete button arrow in the Cells group on the Home tab and then click *Delete Sheet Columns* at the drop-down list.
2. Delete row 5 by completing the following steps:
   a. Select row 5.
   b. Click the Delete button in the Cells group.
3. Clear row contents by completing the following steps:
   a. Select rows 7 and 8.
   b. Click the Clear button in the Editing group on the Home tab and then click *Clear Contents* at the drop-down list.
4. Type the following data in each specified cell:
   A7: Ray Enterprises
   B7: S894-T
   C7: 4.99
   D7: 30
   B8: B-3448
   C8: 25.50
   D8: 12
5. Make cell E6 active and then copy the formula into cells E7 and E8.
6. Save **3-CMProducts**.

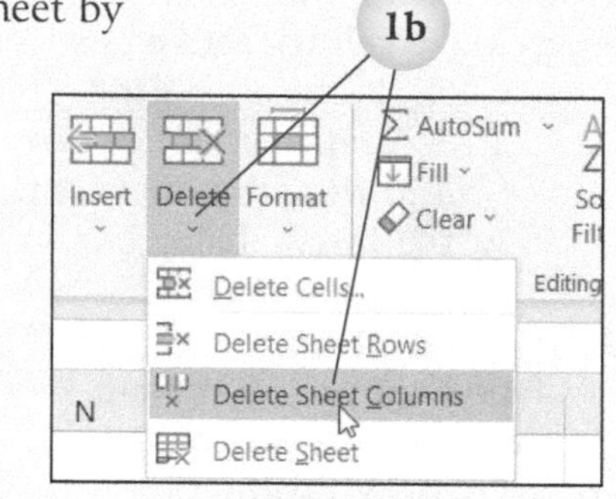

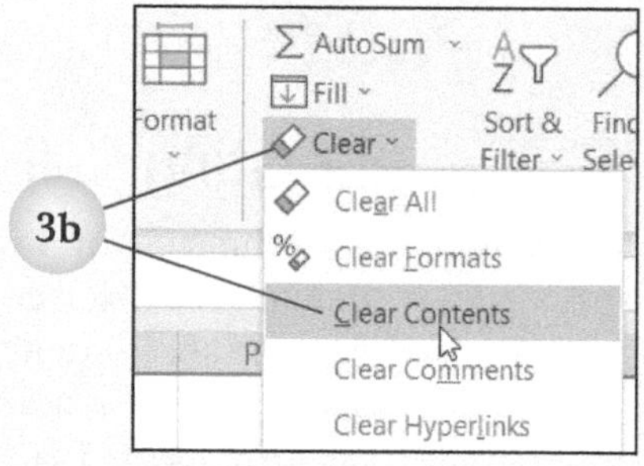

4

6		855-495	$	42.75	5	$	213.75
7	Ray Enterprises	S894-T	$	4.99	30		
8		B-3448	$	25.50	12		
9		43-GB-39	$	45.00	20	$	900.00

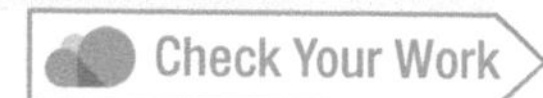

Applying Formatting

Many of the groups on the Home tab contain options for applying formatting to text in the active cell or selected cells. Use buttons and options in the Font group to apply font formatting to text and use buttons in the Alignment group to apply alignment formatting.

Figure 3.5 Font Group

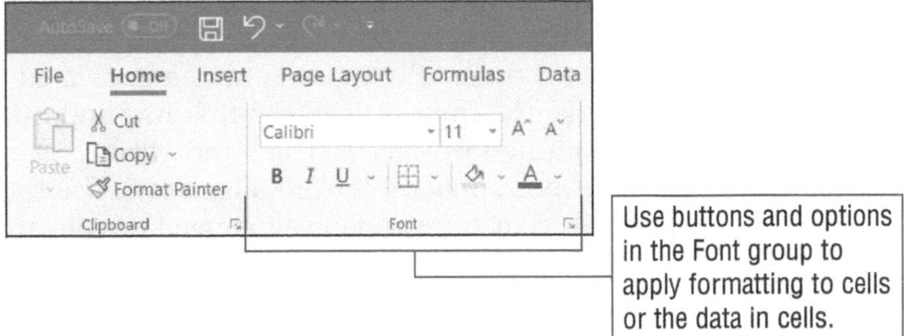

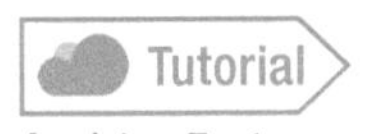

Applying Font Formatting

Applying Font Formatting

Apply a variety of formatting to cells in a worksheet with buttons and options in the Font group on the Home tab. Use buttons and options in the Font group, shown in Figure 3.5, to change the font, font size, and font color; to bold, italicize, and underline data in cells; to change the text color; and to apply a border or add fill to cells.

Bold

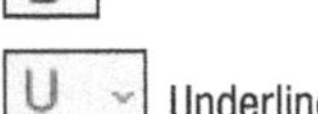
Italic

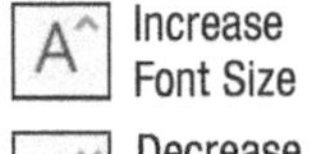
Underline

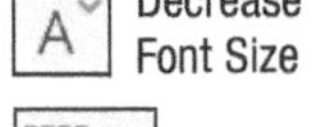
Increase Font Size

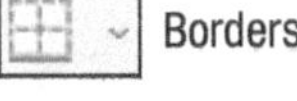
Decrease Font Size

Borders

Fill Color

Font Color

Use the *Font* option box in the Font group to change the font of the text in a cell and use the *Font Size* option box to specify the size of the text. Apply bold formatting to text in a cell with the Bold button, italic formatting with the Italic button, and underlining with the Underline button, or use the keyboard shortcuts Ctrl + B, Ctrl + I, and Ctrl + U.

Click the Increase Font Size button and the text in the active cell or selected cells increases to the next font size in the *Font Size* option box drop-down gallery. Click the Decrease Font Size button and the text in the active cell or selected cells decreases to the next point size.

Use the Borders button in the Font group to insert a border on any or all sides of the active cell or any or all sides of selected cells. The name of the button changes depending on the most recent border applied to a cell or selected cells. Use the Fill Color button to insert color in the active cell or in selected cells. Change the color of the text within a cell with the Font Color button.

Formatting with the Mini Toolbar

Double-click in a cell and then select the data within it and the Mini toolbar displays above the selected data. The Mini toolbar also displays when right-clicking in a cell. The Mini toolbar contains buttons and options for applying font formatting, such as font, font size, and font color, as well as bold and italic formatting. Click a button or option on the Mini toolbar to apply formatting to selected text.

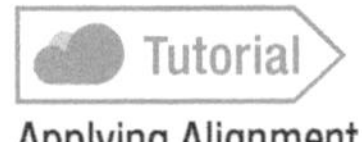

Applying Alignment Formatting

Applying Alignment Formatting

The alignment of data in cells depends on the type of data entered. Enter words or text combined with numbers in a cell and the text aligns at the left edge of the cell. Enter numbers in a cell and the numbers align at the right of the cell. Use buttons in the Alignment group to align data at the left, center, or right of the cell; align data at the top, center, or bottom of the cell; increase and/or decrease the indent of data in a cell; and change the orientation of data in a cell.

Merge & Center

As explained in Chapter 1, selected cells can be merged by clicking the Merge & Center button. If cells are merged, the merged cell can be split into the original cells by selecting the cell and then clicking the Merge & Center button. Click the

Merge & Center button arrow and a drop-down list of options displays. Click the *Merge & Center* option to merge all the selected cells and to apply center cell alignment. Click the *Merge Across* option to merge each row of selected cells. For example, if three cells and two rows are selected, clicking the *Merge Across* option will merge the three cells in the first row and merge the three cells in the second row, resulting in two cells. Click the *Merge Cells* option to merge all the selected cells but not apply center cell alignment. Use the last option, *Unmerge Cells*, to split cells that were previously merged. If cells that are selected and then merged contain data, only the data in the upper left cell remains. Data in the other merged cells is deleted.

Click the Orientation button in the Alignment group and a drop-down list displays with options for rotating data in a cell. If the data typed in a cell is longer than the cell, it overlaps the next cell to the right. To wrap the data to the next line within the cell, click the Wrap Text button in the Alignment group.

Activity 1g Applying Font and Alignment Formatting — Part 7 of 7

1. With **3-CMProducts** open, make cell B1 active and then click the Wrap Text button in the Alignment group on the Home tab. (This wraps the company name within the cell.)
2. Select the range B1:C2, click the Merge & Center button arrow in the Alignment group on the Home tab, and then click *Merge Across* at the drop-down list.
3. After looking at the merged cells, you decide to merge additional cells and horizontally and vertically center the text in the cells by completing the following steps:
   a. With the range B1:C2 selected, click the Merge & Center button arrow and then click *Unmerge Cells* at the drop-down list.
   b. Select the range A1:E2.
   c. Click the Merge & Center button arrow and then click the *Merge Across* option at the drop-down list.
   d. Click the Middle Align button in the Alignment group and then click the Center button.

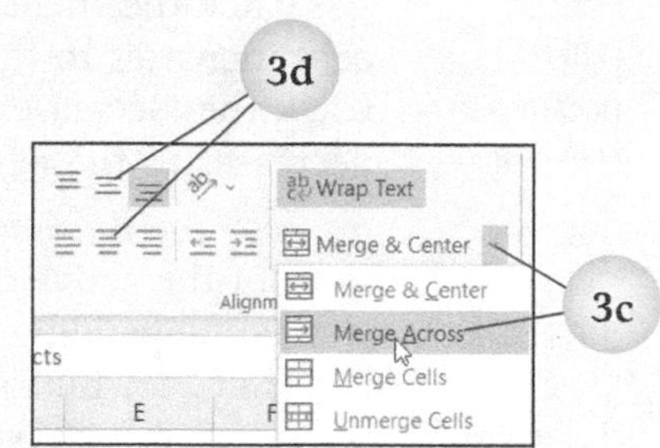

4. Rotate the text in the third row by completing the following steps:
   a. Select the range A3:E3.
   b. Click the Orientation button in the Alignment group and then click *Angle Counterclockwise* at the drop-down list.
   c. After looking at the rotated text, you decide to return the orientation to horizontal by clicking the Undo button on the Quick Access Toolbar.

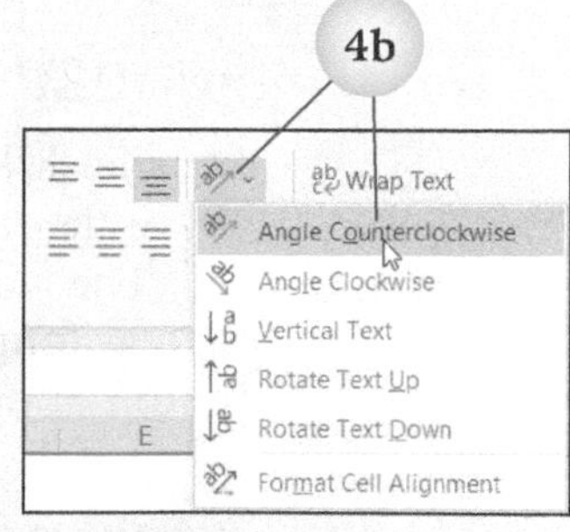

5. Change the font, font size, and font color for the text in specific cells by completing the following steps:
   a. Make cell A1 active.
   b. Click the *Font* option box arrow in the Font group, scroll down the drop-down gallery, and then click *Bookman Old Style*.
   c. Click the *Font Size* option box arrow in the Font group and then click *22* at the drop-down gallery.

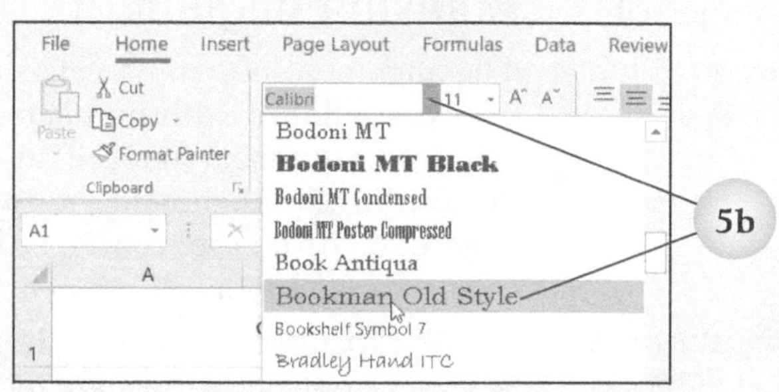

d. Click the Font Color button arrow and then click the *Dark Blue* option (ninth option in the *Standard Colors* section).

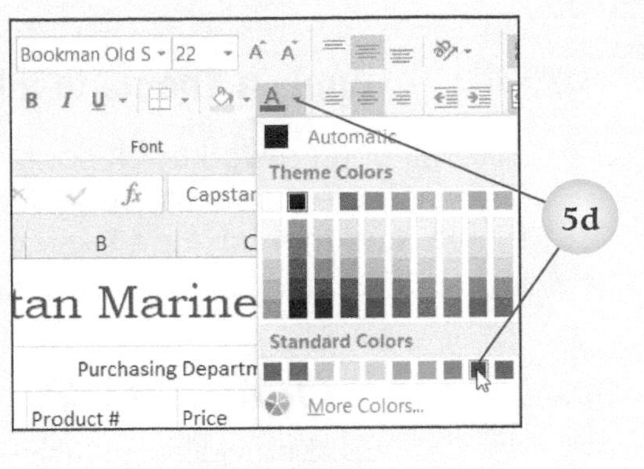

6. Make cell A2 active and then complete steps similar to those in Step 5 to change the font to Bookman Old Style, the font size to 16 points, and the font color to Dark Blue.
7. Select the range A3:E3 and then click the Center button in the Alignment group.
8. With the range A3:E3 still selected, click the Bold button in the Font group and then click the Italic button.
9. Select the range A3:E18 and then change the font to Bookman Old Style.
10. Use the Mini toolbar to apply formatting to selected data by completing the following steps:
    a. Double-click in cell A4.
    b. Select the letters *RD*. (This displays the Mini toolbar above the selected word.)
    c. Click the Increase Font Size button on the Mini toolbar.
    d. Double-click in cell A14.
    e. Select the word *Geneva* and then click the Italic button on the Mini toolbar.

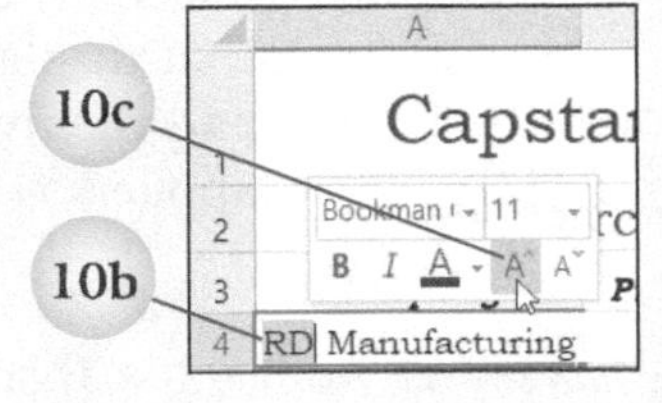

11. Adjust columns A through E to accommodate the longest entry in each column. To do this, select columns A through E and then double-click any selected column boundary line.
12. Select the range D4:D17 and then click the Center button in the Alignment group.
13. Add a double-line bottom border to cell A2 by completing the following steps:
    a. Make cell A2 active.
    b. Click the Borders button arrow in the Font group. (The name of this button varies depending on the last option selected.)
    c. Click the *Bottom Double Border* option at the drop-down list.

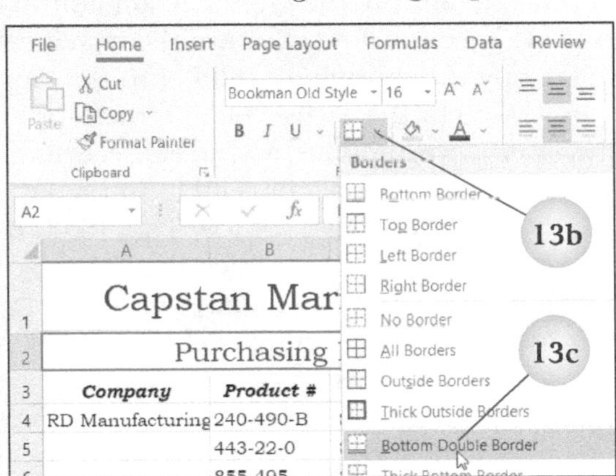

14. Add a single-line bottom border to the range A3:E3 by completing the following steps:
    a. Select the range A3:E3.
    b. Click the Borders button arrow and then click the *Bottom Border* option.
15. Apply a fill color to specific cells by completing the following steps:
    a. Select the range A1:E3.
    b. Click the Fill Color button arrow in the Font group.
    c. Click the *Blue, Accent 5, Lighter 80%* color option (ninth column, second row in the *Theme Colors* section).

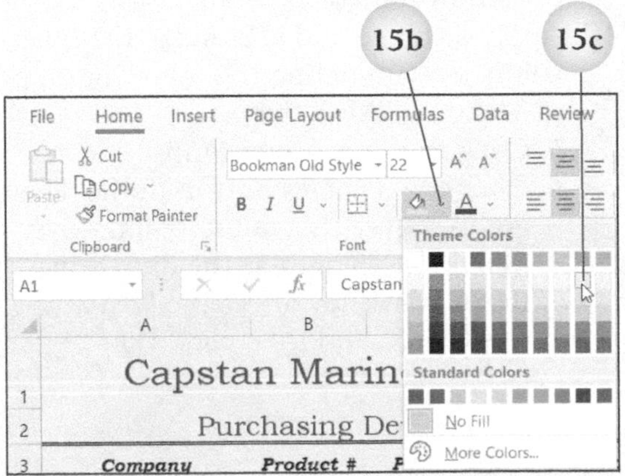

16. Select the range C5:C17 and then click the Comma Style button.
17. Select the range E5:E17 and then click the Comma Style button.
18. Save, print, and then close **3-CMProducts**.

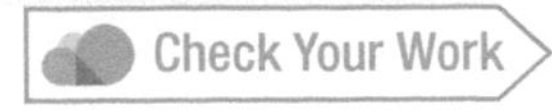

Activity 2 Apply a Theme to a Payroll Worksheet — 1 Part

You will open a workbook containing a worksheet with payroll information and then insert text in cells, apply formatting to the cells and cell contents, apply a theme, and then change the theme font and colors.

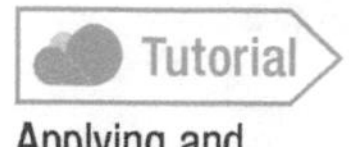

Applying and Modifying Themes

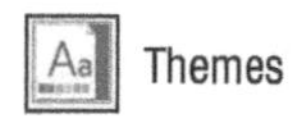

Themes

Hint Apply a theme to give your worksheet a professional look.

Applying a Theme

Excel provides a number of themes that can be used to format text and cells in a worksheet. A theme is a set of formatting choices that includes a color theme (a set of colors), a font theme (a set of heading and body text fonts), and an effects theme (a set of lines and fill effects). To apply a theme, click the Page Layout tab and then click the Themes button in the Themes group. At the drop-down gallery that displays, click the desired theme. Position the mouse pointer over a theme and the live preview feature displays the worksheet with the theme formatting applied.

Activity 2 Applying a Theme — Part 1 of 1

1. Open **SBAPayroll** and then save it with the name **3-SBAPayroll.**
2. Make cell G4 active and then insert a formula that calculates the amount of social security tax. (Multiply the gross pay amount in cell E4 with the social security rate in cell H11; you will need to use the mixed cell reference H$11 when writing the formula.)
3. Copy the formula in cell G4 to the range G5:G9.
4. Make H4 the active cell and then insert a formula that calculates the net pay (gross pay minus withholding and social security tax).
5. Copy the formula in cell H4 to the range H5:H9.
6. Increase the height of row 1 to 36.00 points.
7. Make cell A1 active, click the Middle Align button in the Alignment group, click the *Font Size* option box arrow, click *18* at the drop-down gallery, and then click the Bold button.
8. Type Stanton & Barnett Associates in cell A1.
9. Select the range A2:H3 and then click the Bold button in the Font group.
10. Apply a theme and customize the font and colors by completing the following steps:
    a. Make cell A1 active.
    b. Click the Page Layout tab.
    c. Click the Themes button in the Themes group, hover the mouse pointer over individual themes at the drop-down gallery to see how they affect the formatting of the worksheet, and then click *Wisp*.

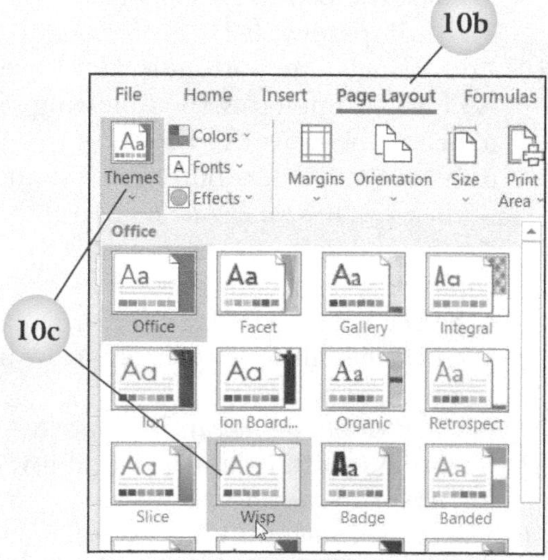

d. Click the Colors button in the Themes group and then click *Red Orange* at the drop-down gallery.

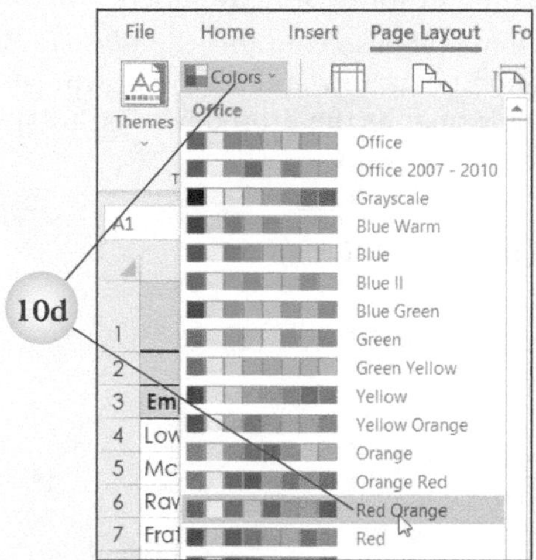

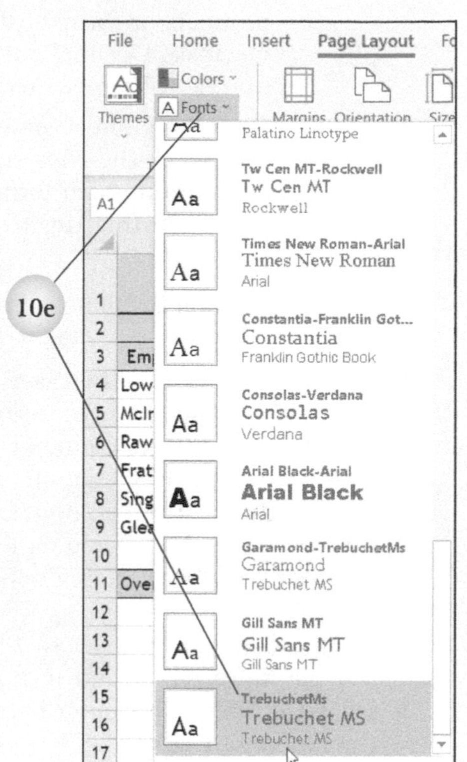

e. Click the Fonts button in the Themes group, scroll down the drop-down gallery, and then click *Trebuchet MS*.

11. Select columns A through H and adjust the width of the columns to accommodate the longest entries.
12. Save, print, and then close **3-SBAPayroll**.

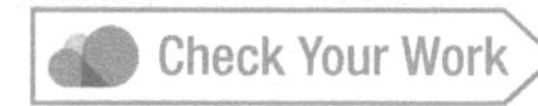

Activity 3 Format an Invoices Worksheet — 2 Parts

You will open a workbook containing an invoice worksheet and apply number formatting to the numbers in the cells.

Applying Number Formatting

Formatting Numbers

By default, the numbers in a cell align at the right and decimals and commas do not appear unless they are typed in the cell. Change the format of numbers with buttons in the Number group on the Home tab or with options at the Format Cells dialog box with the Number tab selected.

Formatting Numbers Using Number Group Buttons

The format symbols available for formatting numbers include a percent symbol (%), comma (,), and dollar symbol ($). For example, type *$45.50* in a cell and Excel automatically applies the Currency format to the number. Type *45%* in a cell and Excel automatically applies the Percentage format to the number. The Number group on the Home tab contains five buttons for formatting numbers in cells. (These buttons were explained in Chapter 1.)

Specify the formatting for numbers in cells in a worksheet before typing the numbers or format existing numbers in a worksheet. Use the Increase Decimal and Decrease Decimal buttons in the Number group on the Home tab to change the number of digits after the decimal point for existing numbers only.

The Number group on the Home tab also contains the *Number Format* option box. Click the *Number Format* option box arrow and a drop-down list displays common number formats. Click a format at the drop-down list to apply the number formatting to the cell or selected cells.

Activity 3a Formatting Numbers with Buttons in the Number Group

Part 1 of 2

1. Open **RPInvoices** and then save it with the name **3-RPInvoices**.
2. Make the following changes to column widths:
   a. Change the width of column C to 17.00 characters.
   b. Change the width of column D to 10.00 characters.
   c. Change the width of column E to 7.00 characters.
   d. Change the width of column F to 12.00 characters.
3. Select row 1 and then click the Insert button in the Cells group on the Home tab.
4. Change the height of row 1 to 42.00 points.
5. Select the range A1:F1 and then make the following changes:
   a. Click the Merge & Center button in the Alignment group on the Home tab.
   b. With cell A1 active, change the font size to 24 points and the font color to Green, Accent 6, Darker 50% (last column, sixth row in the *Theme Colors* section).
   c. Click the Fill Color button arrow in the Font group and then click *Gray, Accent 3, Lighter 60%* (seventh column, third row in the *Theme Colors* section).
   d. Click the Borders button arrow in the Font group and then click the *Top and Thick Bottom Border* option.
   e. With cell A1 active, type REAL PHOTOGRAPHY and then press the Enter key.
6. Change the height of row 2 to 24.00 points.
7. Select the range A2:F2 and then make the following changes:
   a. Click the Merge & Center button in the Alignment group.
   b. With cell A2 active, change the font size to 18 points.
   c. Click the Fill Color button in the Font group. (This will fill the cell with the gray color applied in Step 5c.)
   d. Click the Borders button arrow in the Font group and then click the *Bottom Border* option.
8. Make the following changes to row 3:
   a. Change the height of row 3 to 18.00 points.
   b. Select the range A3:F3, click the Bold button in the Font group, and then click the Center button in the Alignment group.
   c. With the cells still selected, click the Borders button.

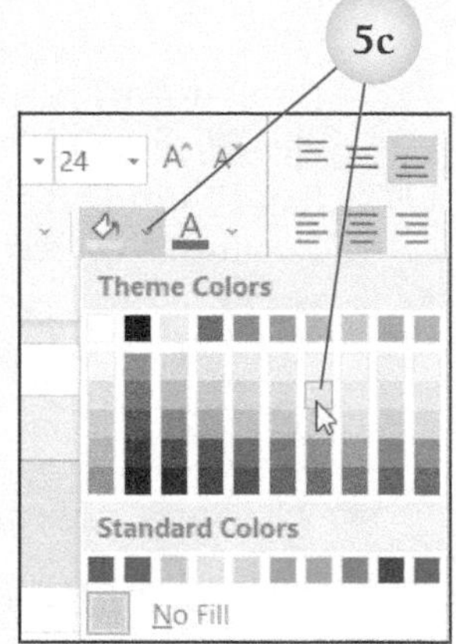

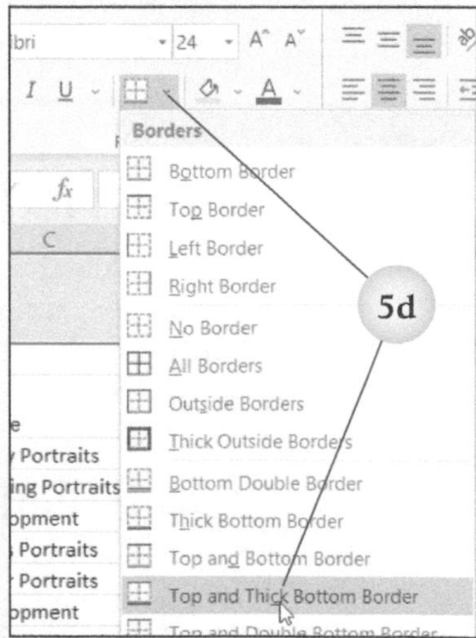

9. Make the following number formatting changes:
   a. Select the range E4:E16 and then click the Percent Style button in the Number group on the Home tab.
   b. With the cells still selected, click the Increase Decimal button in the Number group. (The percentages should include one digit after the decimal point.)

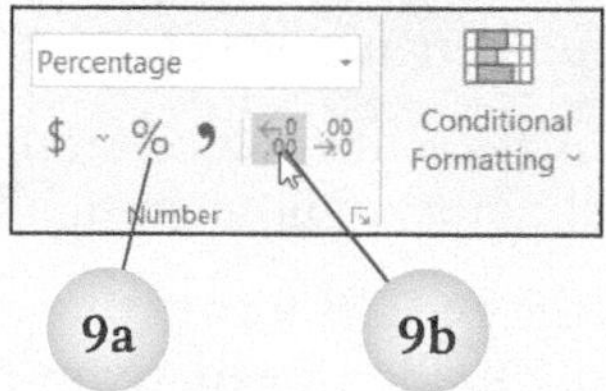

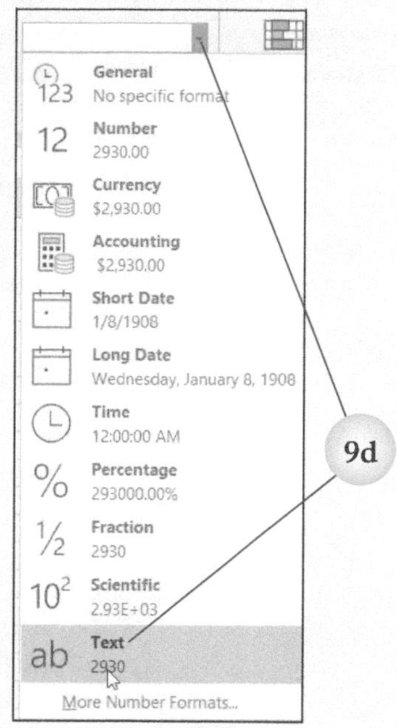

   c. Select the range A4:B16.
   d. Click the *Number Format* option box arrow, scroll down the drop-down list, and then click *Text*.
   e. With the range A4:B16 still selected, click the Center button in the Alignment group.
10. Save **3-RPInvoices**.

Applying Number Formatting at the Format Cells Dialog Box

In addition to using buttons in the Number group, numbers can be formatted with options at the Format Cells dialog box with the Number tab selected, as shown in Figure 3.6. Display this dialog box by clicking the Number group dialog box launcher or by clicking the *Number Format* option box arrow and then clicking *More Number Formats* at the drop-down list. The left side of the dialog box shows number categories; the default category is *General*. At this setting, no specific formatting is applied to numbers except right alignment in cells. The other number categories are described in Table 3.1.

Figure 3.6 Format Cells Dialog Box with the Number Tab Selected

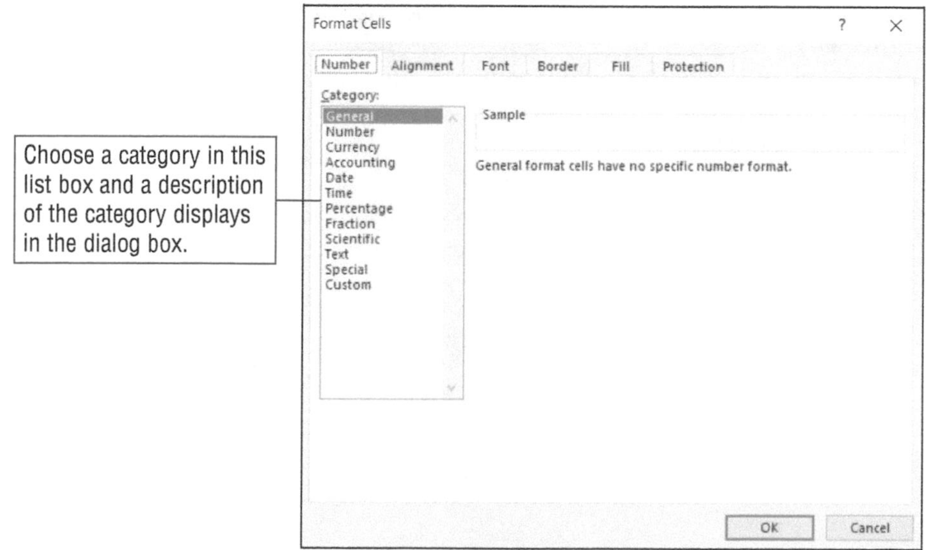

Table 3.1 Number Formatting Options at the Format Cells Dialog Box

Category	Formatting
Number	Specify the number of digits after the decimal point and whether a "thousand" separator should be used; choose the appearance of negative numbers; right-align numbers in the cell.
Currency	Apply general monetary values; add a dollar symbol as well as commas and decimal points, if needed; right-align numbers in the cell.
Accounting	Line up the currency symbols and decimal points in a column; add a dollar symbol and two digits after the decimal point; right-align numbers in the cell.
Date	Show the date as a date value; specify the type of formatting desired by clicking an option in the *Type* list box; right-align the date in the cell.
Time	Show the time as a time value; specify the type of formatting desired by clicking an option in the *Type* list box; right-align the time in the cell.
Percentage	Multiply the cell value by 100 and show the result with a percent symbol; add a decimal point followed by two digits by default; change the number of digits with the *Decimal places* option; right-align numbers in the cell.
Fraction	Specify how a fraction appears in the cell by clicking an option in the *Type* list box; right-align a fraction in the cell.
Scientific	Use for very large or very small numbers; use the letter *E* to have Excel move the decimal point a specified number of digits.
Text	Treat a number in the cell as text; the number is shown in the cell exactly as typed.
Special	Choose a number type, such as *Zip Code, Phone Number*, or *Social Security Number*, in the *Type* option list box; useful for tracking list and database values.
Custom	Specify a numbering type by choosing an option in the *Type* list box.

Activity 3b Formatting Numbers at the Format Cells Dialog Box

Part 2 of 2

1. With **3-RPInvoices** open, make cell F4 active, type the formula =(d4*e4)+d4, and then press the Enter key.
2. Make cell F4 active and then copy the formula to the range F5:F16.
3. Apply the Accounting format by completing the following steps:
   a. Select the range D4:D16.
   b. Click the Number group dialog box launcher.

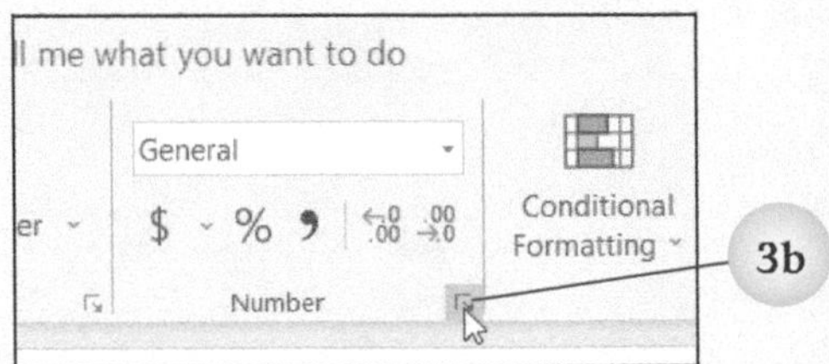

c. At the Format Cells dialog box with the Number tab selected, click *Accounting* in the *Category* list box.
d. Make sure a *2* appears in the *Decimal places* option box and a *$* (dollar symbol) appears in the *Symbol* option box.
e. Click OK.
4. Apply the Accounting format to the range F4:F16 by completing actions similar to those in Step 3.
5. Save, print, and then close **3-RPInvoices**.

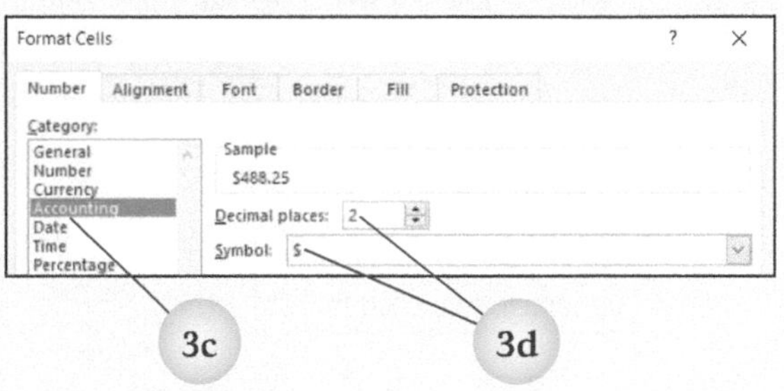

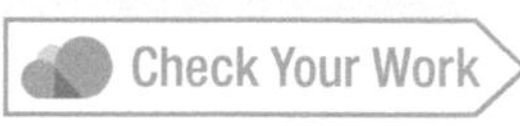

Activity 4 **Format a Company Budget Worksheet** **6 Parts**

You will open a workbook containing a company budget worksheet and then apply formatting to cells with options at the Format Cells dialog box, use Format Painter to apply formatting, and hide and unhide rows and columns.

Applying Formatting Using the Format Cells Dialog Box

Applying Formatting Using the Format Cells Dialog Box

As explained earlier in this chapter, the Format Cells dialog box with the Number tab selected provides options for formatting numbers. This dialog box also contains other tabs with options for formatting cells.

Aligning and Indenting Data

Align and indent data in cells using buttons in the Alignment group on the Home tab or using options at the Format Cells dialog box with the Alignment tab selected, as shown in Figure 3.7. Display this dialog box by clicking the Alignment group dialog box launcher.

Use options in the *Orientation* section to rotate data. A portion of the *Orientation* section shows points on an arc. Click a point on the arc to rotate the text along that point. Or type a rotation degree in the *Degrees* measurement box. Type a positive number to rotate selected text from the lower left to the upper right side of the cell. Type a negative number to rotate selected text from the upper left to the lower right side of the cell.

If the data typed in a cell is longer than the cell, it overlaps the next cell to the right. To wrap text to the next line within a cell, insert a check mark in the *Wrap text* check box in the *Text control* section of the dialog box. Insert a check mark in the *Shrink to fit* check box to reduce the size of the text font so all the data fits within the cell. Insert a check mark in the *Merge cells* check box to combine two or more selected cells into a single cell. To enter data on more than one line within a cell, enter the data on the first line and then press Alt + Enter. Pressing Alt + Enter moves the insertion point to the next line within the same cell.

Figure 3.7 Format Cells Dialog Box with the Alignment Tab Selected

Format Cells

Number | Alignment | Font | Border | Fill | Protection

Text alignment
Horizontal:
General
Indent:
0
Vertical:
Bottom
Justify distributed
Text control
Wrap text
Shrink to fit
Merge cells
Right-to-left
Text direction:
Context
Orientation
Text
Text
0 Degrees
OK
Cancel

Specify horizontal and vertical alignment with options in this section.

Use options in this section to control how text fits in a cell.

Rotate text in a cell by clicking a point on the arc or by entering a number in the *Degrees* measurement box.

Activity 4a Aligning and Rotating Data in Cells at the Format Cells Dialog Box

Part 1 of 6

1. Open **HBCJobs** and then save it with the name **3-HBCJobs**.
2. Make the following changes to the worksheet:
   a. Insert a new row at the beginning of the worksheet.
   b. Change the height of row 1 to 66.00 points.
   c. Merge and center the range A1:E1.
   d. Type Harris & Briggs in cell A1 and then press Alt + Enter. (This moves the insertion point down to the next line in the same cell.)
   e. Type Construction and then press the Enter key.
   f. With cell A2 active, type Preferred, press Alt + Enter, type Customer, and then press the Enter key.
   g. Change the width of column A to 22.00 characters.
   h. Change the width of column B to 7.00 characters.
   i. Change the widths of columns C, D, and E to 10.00 characters.
3. Make cell E3 active and then type the formula =d3-c3. Copy this formula to the range E4:E11.
4. Change the number formatting for specific cells by completing the following steps:
   a. Select the range C3:E3.
   b. Click the Number group dialog box launcher.
   c. At the Format Cells dialog box with the Number tab selected, click *Accounting* in the *Category* list box.
   d. Click the *Decimal places* measurement box down arrow until *0* displays.
   e. Make sure a *$* (dollar symbol) appears in the *Symbol* option box.
   f. Click OK.

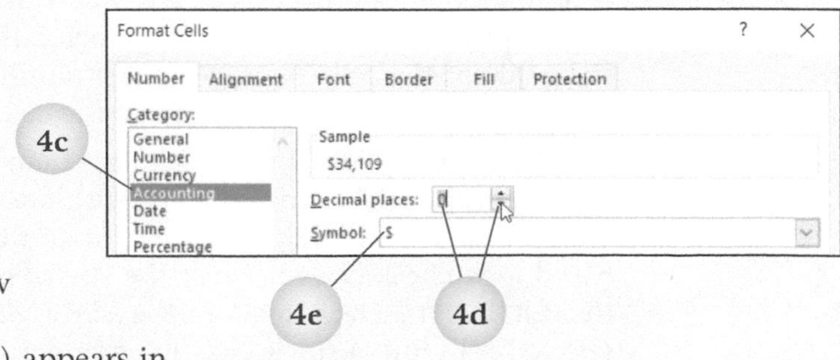

5. Select the range C4:E11, click the Comma Style button in the Number group on the Home tab, and then decrease the number of digits after the decimal point to 0.

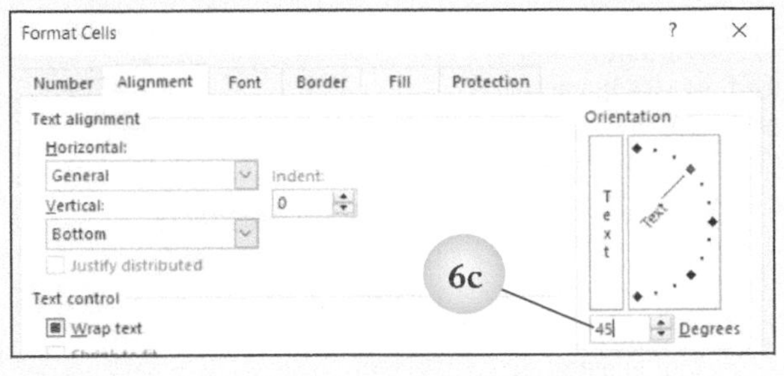

6. Change the orientation of data in cells by completing the following steps:
   a. Select the range B2:E2.
   b. Click the Alignment group dialog box launcher.
   c. At the Format Cells dialog box with the Alignment tab selected, select *0* in the *Degrees* measurement box and then type 45.
   d. Click OK.

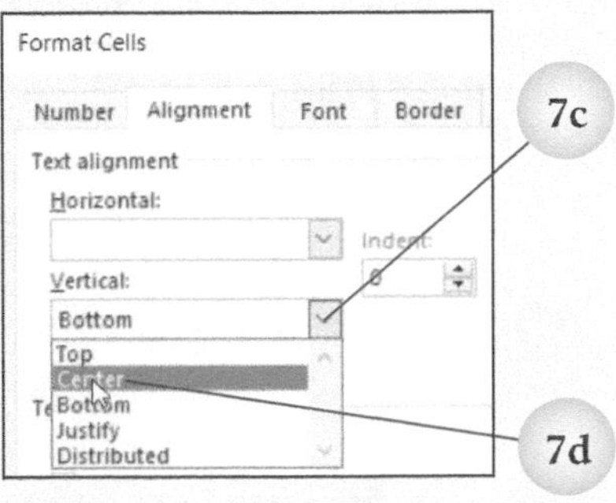

7. Change the vertical alignment of text in cells by completing the following steps:
   a. Select the range A1:E2.
   b. Click the Alignment group dialog box launcher.
   c. At the Format Cells dialog box with the Alignment tab selected, click the *Vertical* option box arrow.
   d. Click *Center* at the drop-down list.
   e. Click OK.

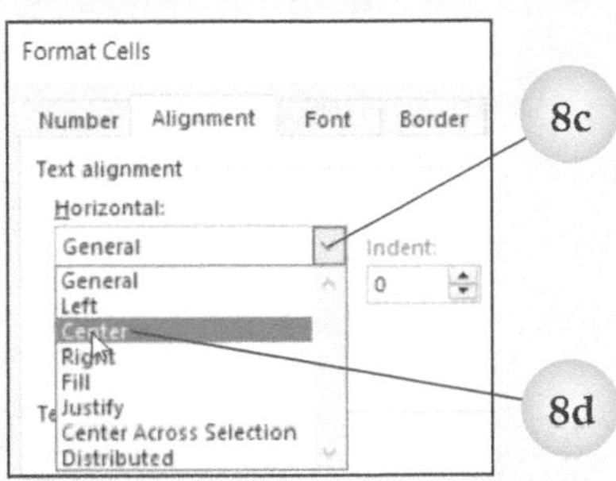

8. Change the horizontal alignment of text in cells by completing the following steps:
   a. Select the range A2:E2.
   b. Click the Alignment group dialog box launcher.
   c. At the Format Cells dialog box with the Alignment tab selected, click the *Horizontal* option box arrow.
   d. Click *Center* at the drop-down list.
   e. Click OK.

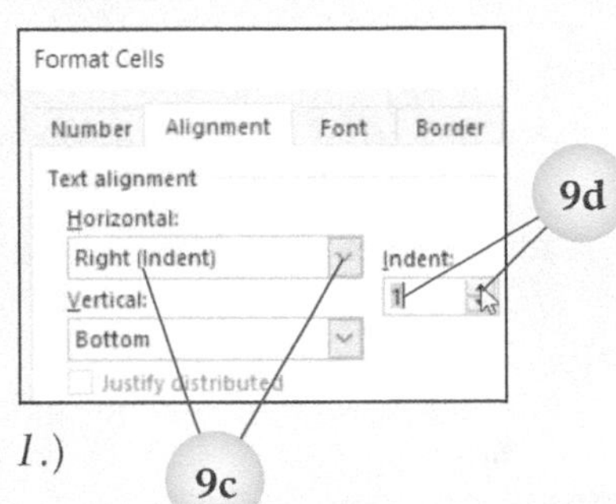

9. Change the horizontal alignment and indent of text in cells by completing the following steps:
   a. Select the range B3:B11.
   b. Click the Alignment group dialog box launcher.
   c. At the Format Cells dialog box with the Alignment tab selected, click the *Horizontal* option box arrow and then click *Right (Indent)* at the drop-down list.
   d. Click the *Indent* measurement box up arrow. (This displays *1*.)
   e. Click OK.
10. Save **3-HBCJobs**.

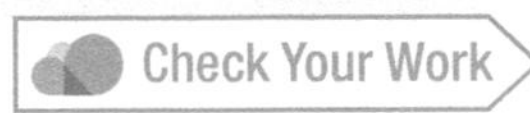

Changing the Font

As explained earlier in this chapter, the Font group on the Home tab contains buttons and options for applying font formatting to data in cells. The font for data in cells can also be changed with options at the Format Cells dialog box with the Font tab selected, as shown in Figure 3.8. Use options at the Format Cells dialog box with the Font tab selected to change the font, font style, font size, and font color; to change the underlining method; and to add effects such as superscript and subscript. Click the Font group dialog box launcher to display this dialog box.

Figure 3.8 Format Cells Dialog Box with the Font Tab Selected

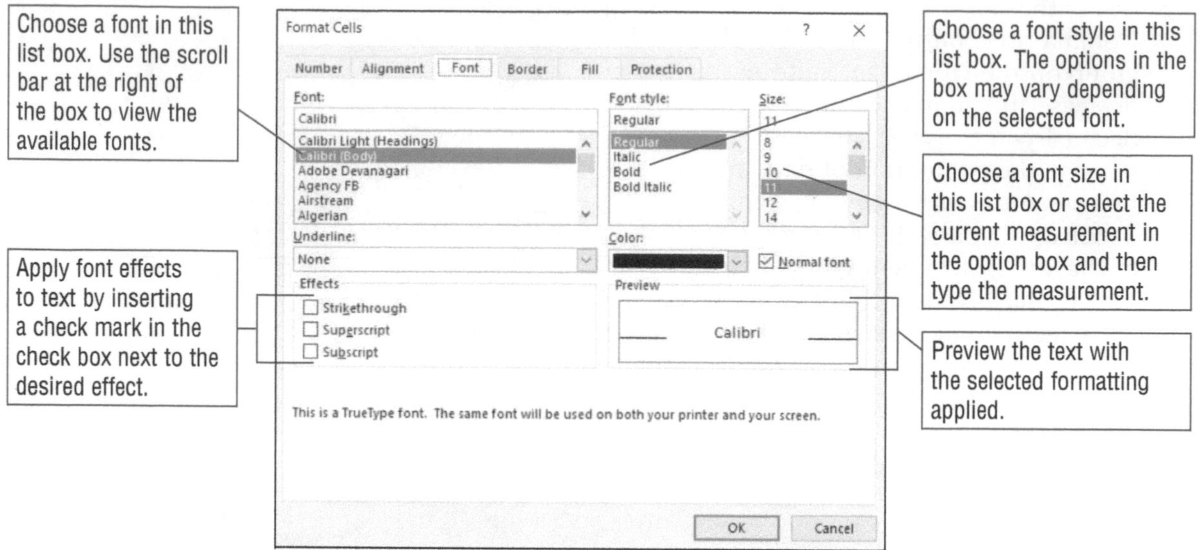

Activity 4b Applying Font Formatting at the Format Cells Dialog Box

Part 2 of 6

1. With **3-HBCJobs** open, change the font and font color by completing the following steps:
   a. Select the range A1:E11.
   b. Click the Font group dialog box launcher.
   c. At the Format Cells dialog box with the Font tab selected, scroll down the *Font* option list box and then click *Garamond*.
   d. Click *12* in the *Size* list box.
   e. Click the *Color* option box arrow.
   f. At the color palette, click the *Dark Red* color (first option in the *Standard Colors* section).
   g. Click OK to close the dialog box.
2. Make cell A1 active and then change the font size to 24 points and apply bold formatting.
3. Select the range A2:E2 and then apply bold formatting.
4. Save and then print **3-HBCJobs**.

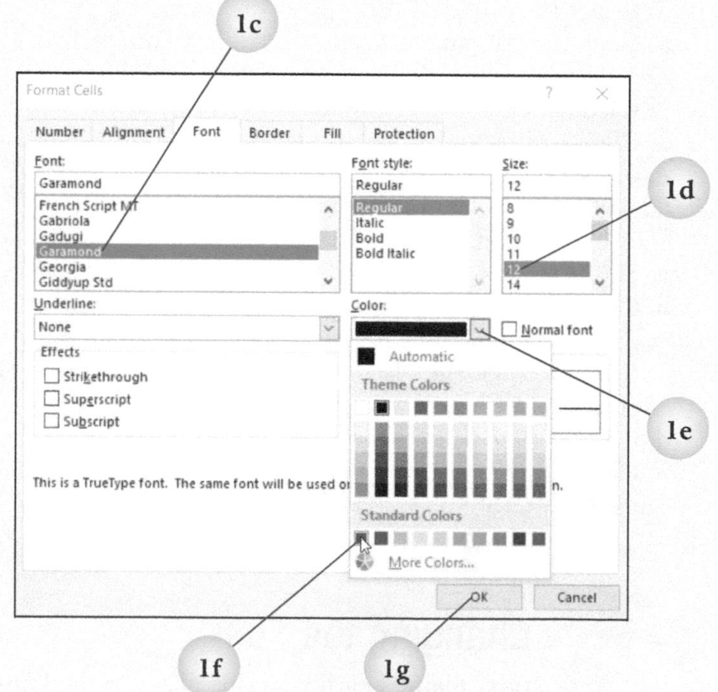

Check Your Work

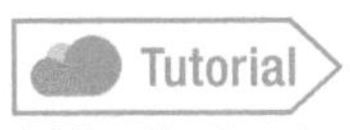

Adding Borders to Cells

Quick Steps

Add Borders to Cells

1. Select cells.
2. Click Borders button arrow.
3. Click border.

OR

1. Select cells.
2. Click Borders button arrow.
3. Click *More Borders.*
4. Use options in dialog box to apply border.
5. Click OK.

Adding Borders to Cells

The gridlines in a worksheet do not print. As explained earlier in this chapter, use the Borders button in the Font group to add borders to cells that will print. Borders can also be added to cells with options at the Format Cells dialog box with the Border tab selected, as shown in Figure 3.9. Display this dialog box by clicking the Borders button arrow in the Font group and then clicking *More Borders* at the drop-down list.

With options in the *Presets* section, remove borders with the *None* option, add only outside borders with the *Outline* option, and add borders to the insides of selected cells with the *Inside* option. In the *Border* section of the dialog box, specify the side of the cell or selected cells to which the border is to be applied. Choose the line style for the border with options in the *Style* list box. Add color to border lines by clicking the *Color* option box arrow and then clicking a color at the color palette that displays.

Figure 3.9 Format Cells Dialog Box with the Border Tab Selected

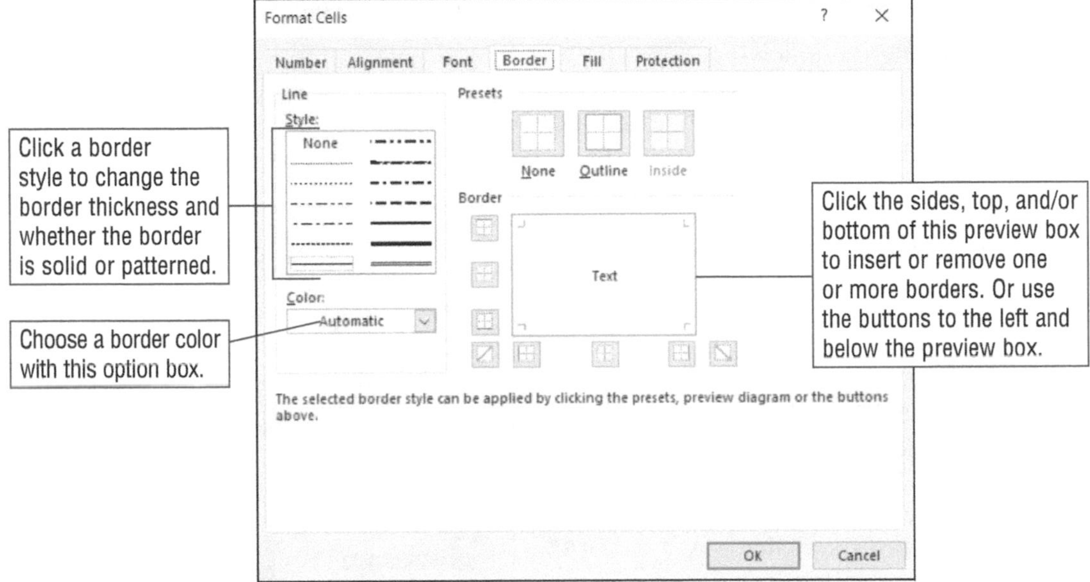

Activity 4c **Adding Borders to Cells at the Format Cells Dialog Box**

Part 3 of 6

1. With **3-HBCJobs** open, remove the 45-degree orientation you applied in Activity 4a by completing the following steps:
   a. Select the range B2:E2.
   b. Click the Alignment group dialog box launcher.
   c. At the Format Cells dialog box with the Alignment tab selected, select *45* in the *Degrees* measurement box and then type 0.
   d. Click OK.
2. Change the height of row 2 to 33.00 points.

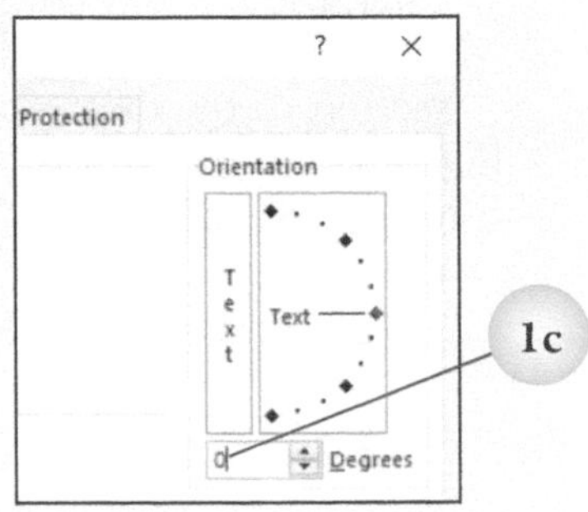

3. Add a thick, dark red border line to cells by completing the following steps:
   a. Select the range A1:E11.
   b. Click the Borders button arrow and then click the *More Borders* option at the drop-down list.
   c. At the Format Cells dialog box with the Border tab selected, click the *Color* option box arrow and then click the *Dark Red* color (first option in the *Standard Colors* section).
   d. Click the thick single-line option in the *Style* list box in the *Line* section (sixth option in the second column).
   e. Click the *Outline* option in the *Presets* section.
   f. Click OK.

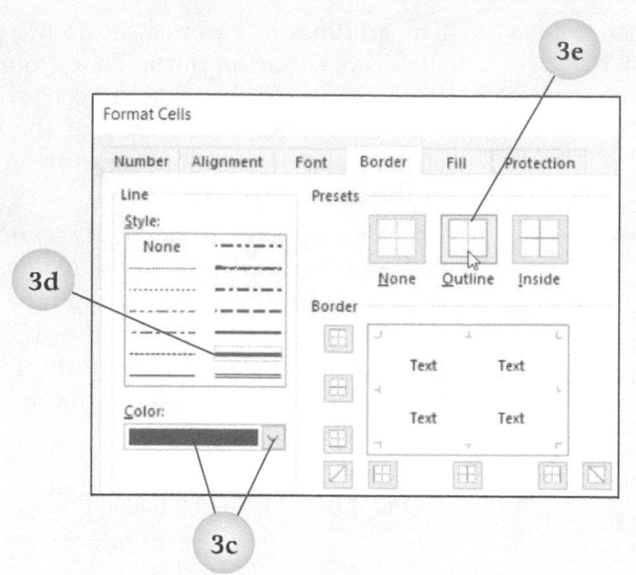

4. Add borders above and below cells by completing the following steps:
   a. Select the range A2:E2.
   b. Click the Borders button arrow and then click *More Borders* at the drop-down list.
   c. At the Format Cells dialog box with the Border tab selected, make sure the color is still Dark Red.
   d. Make sure the thick single-line option is still selected in the *Style* list box in the *Line* section.
   e. Click the top border of the sample cell in the *Border* section of the dialog box.
   f. Click the double-line option in the *Style* list box (last option in the second column).
   g. Click the bottom border of the sample cell in the *Border* section of the dialog box.
   h. Click OK.
5. Save **3-HBCJobs**.

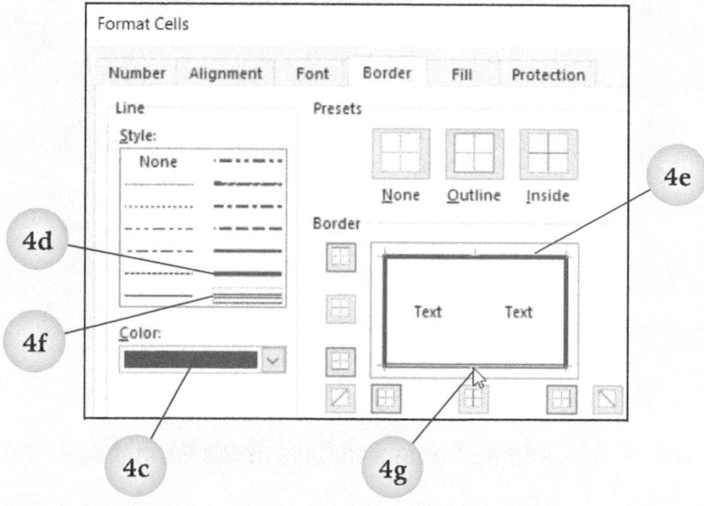

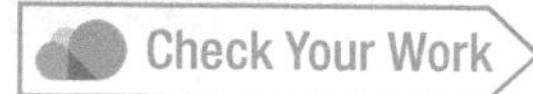

Adding Fill Color to Cells

Quick Steps

Add Fill and Shading

1. Select cells.
2. Click Fill Color button arrow.
3. Click color.

OR

1. Select cells.
2. Click Format button.
3. Click *Format Cells.*
4. Click Fill tab.
5. Use options in dialog box to apply shading.
6. Click OK.

Adding Fill and Shading to Cells

To enhance the appearance of cells and data within cells, consider adding fill color. As explained earlier in this chapter, fill color can be added to cells with the Fill Color button in the Font group. Fill color can also be added to cells in a worksheet with options at the Format Cells dialog box with the Fill tab selected, as shown in Figure 3.10. Display the Format Cells dialog box by clicking the Format button in the Cells group and then clicking *Format Cells* at the drop-down list. The dialog box can also be displayed by clicking the Font group, Alignment group, or Number group dialog box launcher. At the Format Cells dialog box, click the Fill tab or right-click in a cell and then click *Format Cells* at the shortcut menu. Choose a fill color for a cell or selected cells by clicking a color choice in the *Background Color* section. To add gradient fill to a cell or selected cells, click the Fill Effects button and then click a style at the Fill Effects dialog box.

Using Format Painter and the Repeat Command

Quick Steps

Repeat Last Action

1. Apply formatting.
2. Move to location.
3. Press F4 or Ctrl + Y.

Repeating the Last Action

To apply the same formatting to other cells in a worksheet, use the Repeat command by pressing the F4 function key or the keyboard shortcut Ctrl + Y. The Repeat command repeats the last action performed.

Figure 3.10 Format Cells Dialog Box with the Fill Tab Selected

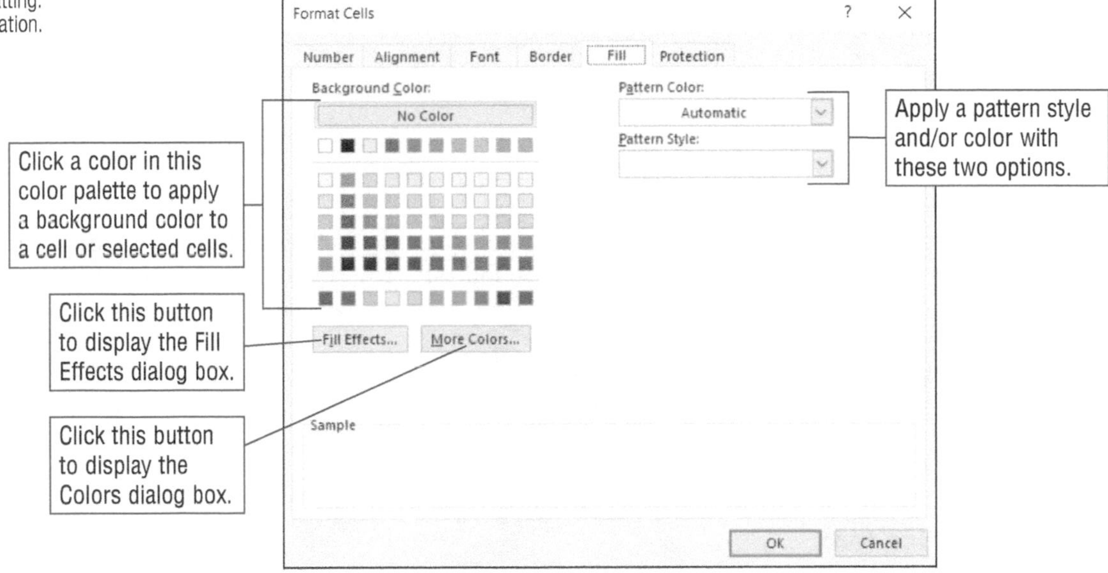

Activity 4d Adding Fill Color and Shading to Cells at the Format Cells Dialog Box

Part 4 of 6

1. With **3-HBCJobs** open, add a fill color to cell A1 and repeat the formatting by completing the following steps:
   a. Make cell A1 active.
   b. Click the Format button in the Cells group and then click *Format Cells* at the drop-down list.
   c. At the Format Cells dialog box, click the Fill tab.
   d. Click the light gold color in the *Background Color* section (eighth column, second row).

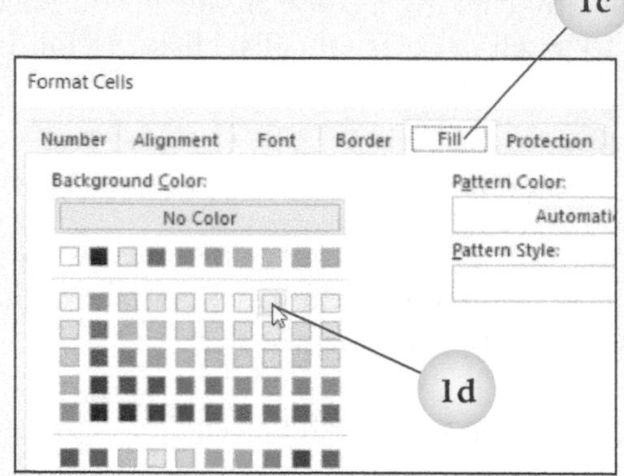

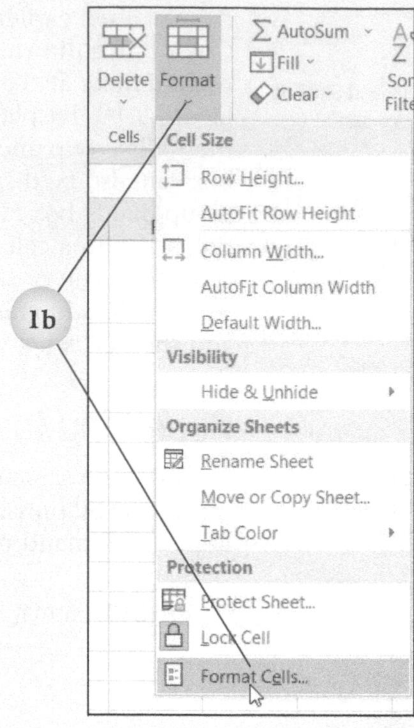

   e. Click OK.
   f. Select the range A2:E2 and then press the F4 function key. (This repeats the application of the light gold fill.)
2. Select row 2, insert a new row, and then change the height of the new row to 12.00 points.
3. Add gradient fill to cells by completing the following steps:
   a. Select the range A2:E2.
   b. Click the Format button in the Cells group and then click *Format Cells* at the drop-down list.
   c. At the Format Cells dialog box, click the Fill tab, if necessary.
   d. Click the Fill Effects button.
   e. At the Fill Effects dialog box, click the *Color 2* option box arrow and then click the *Gold, Accent 4* option (eighth column, first row in the *Theme Colors* section).
   f. Click OK to close the Fill Effects dialog box.
   g. Click OK to close the Format Cells dialog box.
4. Save **3-HBCJobs**.

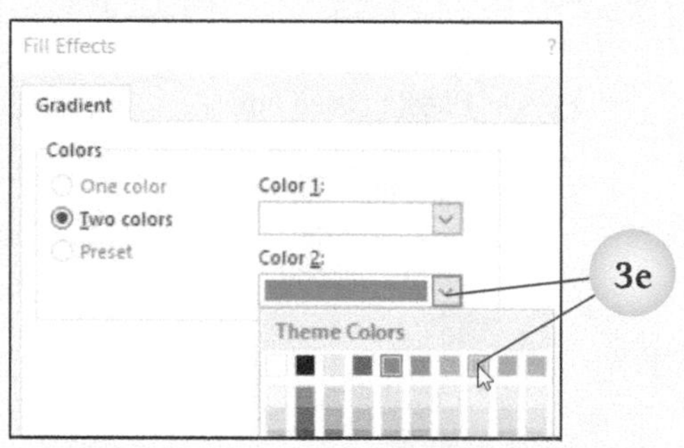

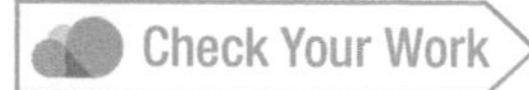

Formatting with Format Painter

Quick Steps

Format with Format Painter

1. Select cells with formatting.
2. Double-click Format Painter button.
3. Select cells.
4. Click Format Painter button.

Use the Format Painter button in the Clipboard group on the Home tab to copy formatting to different locations in the worksheet. To use the Format Painter button, make active a cell or selected cells that contain the desired formatting, click the Format Painter button, and then click in the cell or selected cells to which the formatting is to be applied.

Format Painter

Click the Format Painter button and the mouse pointer displays with a paintbrush attached. To apply formatting in a single location, click the Format Painter button. To apply formatting in more than one location, double-click the Format Painter button, select the desired cells, and then click the Format Painter button to turn off the feature.

Activity 4e Formatting with Format Painter Part 5 of 6

1. With **3-HBCJobs** open, select the range A5:E5.
2. Click the Font group dialog box launcher.
3. At the Format Cells dialog box, click the Fill tab.
4. Click the light green color in the *Background Color* section (last column, second row).
5. Click OK to close the dialog box.
6. Use Format Painter to apply the light green color to rows by completing the following steps:
   a. With the range A5:E5 selected, double-click the Format Painter button in the Clipboard group.
   b. Select the range A7:E7.
   c. Select the range A9:E9.
   d. Select the range A11:E11.
   e. Turn off Format Painter by clicking the Format Painter button.
7. Save and then print **3-HBCJobs**.

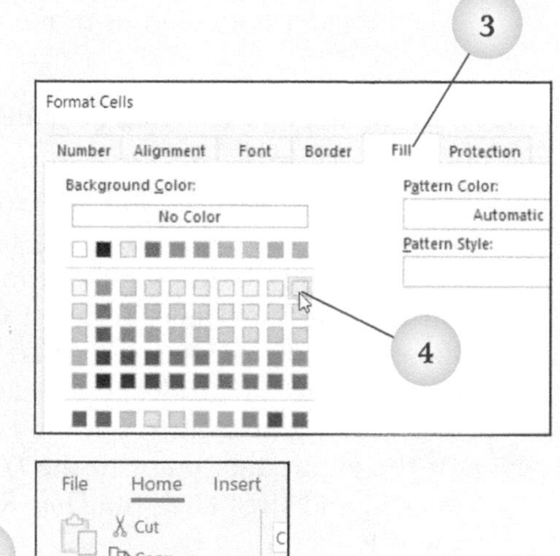

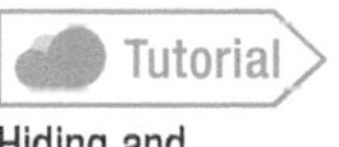

Hiding and Unhiding Columns and Rows

Quick Steps

Hide Columns
1. Select columns.
2. Click Format button.
3. Point to *Hide & Unhide*.
4. Click *Hide Columns*.

Hide Rows
1. Select rows.
2. Click Format button.
3. Point to *Hide & Unhide*.
4. Click *Hide Rows*.

Hint Set the column width to 0 and the column is hidden. Set the row height to 0 and the row is hidden.

Hiding and Unhiding Columns and Rows

If a worksheet contains columns and/or rows of data that is not being used or should not be viewed, consider hiding the columns and/or rows. To hide columns in a worksheet, select the columns, click the Format button in the Cells group on the Home tab, point to *Hide & Unhide*, and then click *Hide Columns*. To hide rows, select the rows, click the Format button in the Cells group, point to *Hide & Unhide*, and then click *Hide Rows*. To make a hidden column visible, select the columns to the left and the right of the hidden column, click the Format button in the Cells group, point to *Hide & Unhide*, and then click *Unhide Columns*. To make a hidden row visible, select the rows above and below the hidden row, click the Format button in the Cells group, point to *Hide & Unhide*, and then click *Unhide Rows*.

If the first row or column is hidden, use the Go To feature to make it visible. To do this, click the Find & Select button in the Editing group on the Home tab and then click *Go To* at the drop-down list. At the Go To dialog box, type *A1* in the *Reference* text box and then click OK. At the worksheet, click the Format button in the Cells group, point to *Hide & Unhide*, and then click *Unhide Columns* or click *Unhide Rows*.

The mouse can also be used to unhide columns or rows. If a column or row is hidden, the light-gray boundary line in the column or row header displays as a slightly thicker gray line. To unhide a column, position the mouse pointer on the slightly thicker gray line in the column header until the mouse pointer changes into a left-and-right-pointing arrow with a double line in the middle. (Make sure the mouse pointer displays with two lines between the arrows. If a single line displays, only the size of the visible column will change.) Click and hold down the left mouse button, drag to the right until the column displays at the desired width, and then release the mouse button. Unhide a row in a similar manner. Position the mouse pointer on the slightly thicker gray line in the row header until the mouse pointer changes into an up-and-down-pointing arrow with a double line in the middle. Drag down until the row is visible and then release the mouse button. If two or more adjacent columns or rows are hidden, unhide each column or row separately.

Activity 4f Hiding and Unhiding Columns and Rows

Part 6 of 6

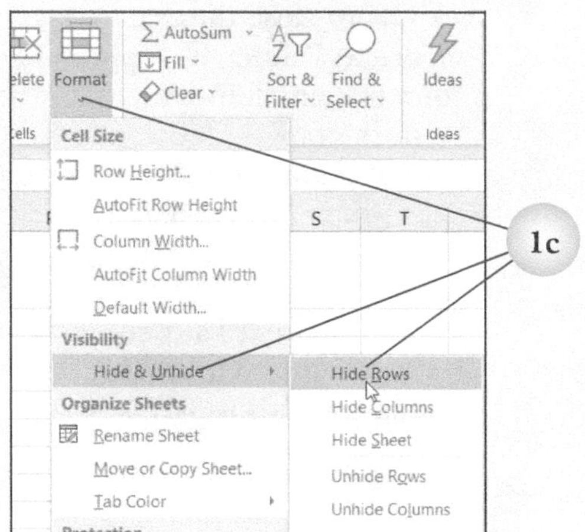

1. With **3-HBCJobs** open, hide the row for Linstrom Enterprises and the row for Summit Services by completing the following steps:
   a. Click the row 7 header to select the entire row.
   b. Press and hold down the Ctrl key and then click the row 11 header to select the entire row.
   c. Click the Format button in the Cells group on the Home tab, point to the *Hide & Unhide* option, and then click the *Hide Rows* option at the side menu.
2. Hide the column containing the dollar amounts by completing the following steps:
   a. Click in cell D3 to make it the active cell.
   b. Click the Format button in the Cells group, point to the *Hide & Unhide* option, and then click the *Hide Columns* option at the side menu.
3. Save and then print **3-HBCJobs**.
4. Unhide the rows by completing the following steps:
   a. Select rows 6 through 12.
   b. Click the Format button in the Cells group, point to *Hide & Unhide*, and then click *Unhide Rows*.
   c. Click in cell A4.
5. Unhide column D by completing the following steps:
   a. Position the mouse pointer on the thicker gray line between columns C and E in the column header until the pointer turns into a left-and-right-pointing arrow with a double line in the middle.
   b. Click and hold down the left mouse button, drag to the right until *Width: 9.29* displays in a box above the mouse pointer, and then release the mouse button.

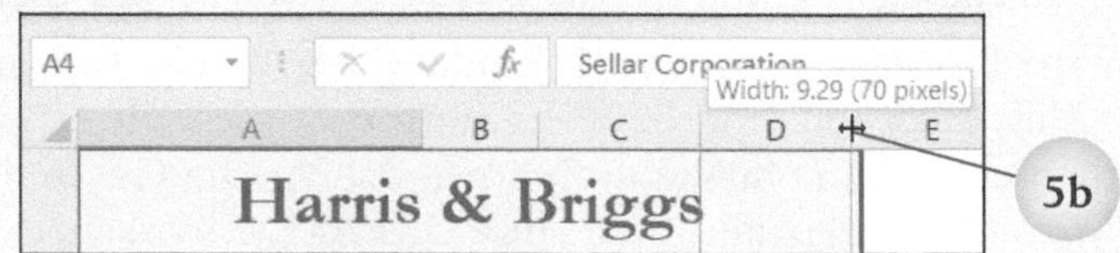

6. Save, print, and then close **3-HBCJobs**.

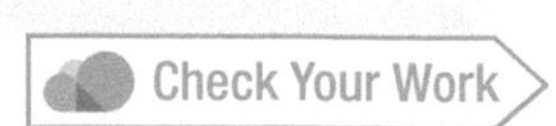

Chapter Summary

- Change column width using the mouse on column boundary lines or using options at the Column Width dialog box. Change row height using the mouse on row boundary lines or using options at the Row Height dialog box.
- Insert a row or column in a worksheet with the Insert button in the Cells group on the Home tab or with options at the Insert dialog box.
- Delete a selected row or column or multiple rows or columns by clicking the Delete button in the Cells group.
- Delete a specific cell by clicking the Delete button arrow and then clicking *Delete Cells* at the drop-down list. At the Delete dialog box, specify if only the cell should be deleted or an entire row or column.
- Delete the cell contents by pressing the Delete key or clicking the Clear button in the Editing group on the Home tab and then clicking *Clear Contents*.
- Apply font formatting with buttons and options in the Font group on the Home tab. Use the Mini toolbar to apply font formatting to selected data in a cell.
- Apply alignment formatting with buttons in the Alignment group on the Home tab.
- Use the Themes button in the Themes group on the Page Layout tab to apply a theme to cells in a worksheet, which includes formatting such as color, font, and effects. Use the other buttons in the Themes group to customize the theme.
- Format numbers in cells with buttons in the Number group on the Home tab or with options at the Format Cells dialog box with the Number tab selected.
- Apply formatting to cells in a worksheet with options at the Format Cells dialog box, which includes the Number, Alignment, Font, Border, and Fill tabs.
- Press the F4 function key or the keyboard shortcut Ctrl + Y to repeat the last action performed.
- Use the Format Painter button in the Clipboard group on the Home tab to apply formatting to several locations in a worksheet.
- Hide selected columns or rows in a worksheet by clicking the Format button in the Cells group on the Home tab, pointing to *Hide & Unhide*, and then clicking *Hide Columns* or *Hide Rows*.
- To make a hidden column visible, select the columns to the left and right, click the Format button in the Cells group, point to *Hide & Unhide*, and then click *Unhide Columns*.
- To make a hidden row visible, select the rows above and below, click the Format button in the Cells group, point to *Hide & Unhide*, and then click *Unhide Rows*.

Commands Review

FEATURE	RIBBON TAB, GROUP	BUTTON	KEYBOARD SHORTCUT
bold text	Home, Font	B	Ctrl + B
borders	Home, Font		
bottom-align (in row)	Home, Alignment		
center-align (in column)	Home, Alignment		

FEATURE	RIBBON TAB, GROUP	BUTTON	KEYBOARD SHORTCUT
clear cell or cell contents	Home, Editing		
column width	Home, Cells		
decrease font size	Home, Font		
decrease indent	Home, Alignment		
delete cells, rows, or columns	Home, Cells		
fill color	Home, Font		
font	Home, Font		
font color	Home, Font		
font size	Home, Font		
Format Painter	Home, Clipboard		
hide & unhide	Home, Cells		
increase font size	Home, Font		
increase indent	Home, Alignment		
insert cells, rows, or columns	Home, Cells		
italicize text	Home, Font		Ctrl + I
left-align (in column)	Home, Alignment		
merge and center cells	Home, Alignment		
middle-align (in row)	Home, Alignment		
number format	Home, Number		
orientation	Home, Alignment		
repeat last action			F4 or Ctrl + Y
right-align (in column)	Home, Alignment		
row height	Home, Cells		
themes	Page Layout, Themes		
top-align (in row)	Home, Alignment		
underline text	Home, Font		Ctrl + U
wrap text	Home, Alignment		

Microsoft®

Excel®

CHAPTER

4

Enhancing a Worksheet

Performance Objectives

Upon successful completion of Chapter 4, you will be able to:

1. Change the margins in a worksheet
2. Center a worksheet horizontally and vertically on the page
3. Change page orientation and paper size
4. Insert and remove page breaks in a worksheet
5. Print column and row titles on multiple pages
6. Scale data
7. Insert a background picture
8. Print gridlines and row and column headings
9. Set and clear a print area
10. Insert headers and footers
11. Customize a print job
12. Complete a spelling check
13. Use the Undo and Redo buttons
14. Find and replace data and cell formatting
15. Sort data
16. Filter data

Excel contains features you can use to enhance and control the formatting of a worksheet. In this chapter, you will learn how to change worksheet margins, orientation, size, and scale; print column and row titles; print gridlines; and center a worksheet horizontally and vertically on the page. You will also learn how to complete a spelling check on the text in a worksheet, find and replace specific data and formatting in a worksheet, and sort and filter data.

Before beginning chapter work, copy the EL1C4 folder to your storage medium and then make EL1C4 the active folder.

The online course includes additional training and assessment resources.

Activity 1 Format a Yearly Budget Worksheet 12 Parts

You will format a yearly budget worksheet by inserting formulas; changing margins, page orientation, and paper size; inserting a page break; printing column headings on multiple pages; scaling data to print on one page; inserting a background picture; inserting headers and footers; and identifying a print area and customizing a print job.

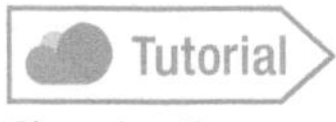

Changing Page Layout Options

Formatting a Worksheet Page

An Excel worksheet has default page formatting. For example, a worksheet has left and right margins of 0.7 inch and top and bottom margins of 0.75 inch. In addition, a worksheet prints in portrait orientation and its paper size is 8.5 inches by 11 inches. These defaults, along with additional settings, can be changed and/or controlled with options on the Page Layout tab.

Changing Margins

The Page Setup group on the Page Layout tab contains buttons for changing the margins and the page orientation and size. In addition, it contains buttons for establishing a print area, inserting a page break, applying a picture background, and printing titles.

Margins

Quick Steps

Change Worksheet Margins

1. Click Page Layout tab.
2. Click Margins button.
3. Click predesigned margin.

OR

1. Click Page Layout tab.
2. Click Margins button.
3. Click *Custom Margins* at drop-down list.
4. Change top, left, right, and/or bottom measurements.
5. Click OK.

Change the worksheet margins by clicking the Margins button in the Page Setup group on the Page Layout tab. This displays a drop-down list of predesigned margin choices. If one of the predesigned choices applies the desired margins, click that option. To customize the margins, click the *Custom Margins* option at the bottom of the Margins button drop-down list. This displays the Page Setup dialog box with the Margins tab selected, as shown in Figure 4.1.

Figure 4.1 Page Setup Dialog Box with the Margins Tab Selected

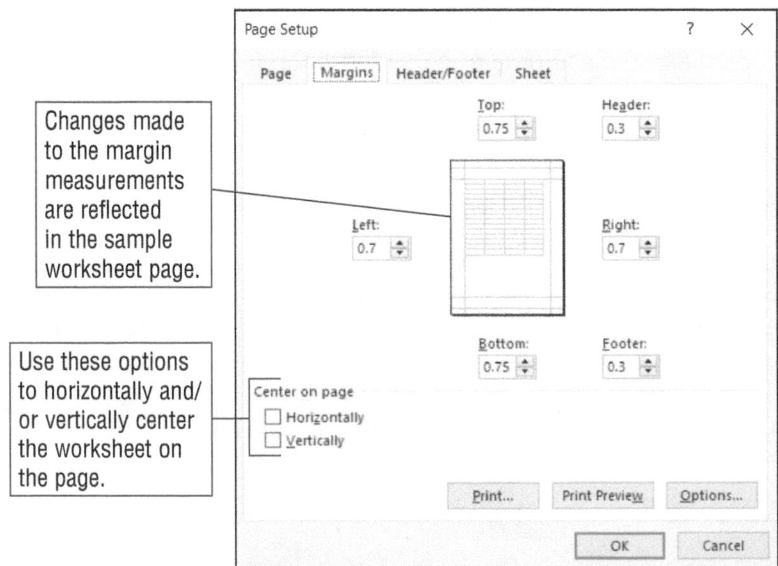

A worksheet page showing the cells and margins displays in the dialog box. As the top, bottom, left, or right margin measurements are increased or decreased, the sample worksheet page reflects the change. The measurement from the top of the page to the header can be increased or decreased with the *Header* measurement box and the measurement from the footer to the bottom of the page can be changed with the *Footer* measurement box. (Headers and footers are covered later in this chapter.)

Quick Steps

Center Worksheet Horizontally and/or Vertically

1. Click Page Layout tab.
2. Click Margins button.
3. Click *Custom Margins*.
4. Click *Horizontally* option and/or click *Vertically* check box.
5. Click OK.

Centering a Worksheet Horizontally and/or Vertically

By default, a worksheet prints in the upper left corner of the page. A worksheet can be centered on the page by changing the margins. However, an easier method for centering a worksheet is to use the *Horizontally* and/or *Vertically* check boxes that appear in the Page Setup dialog box with the Margins tab selected. Choose one or both of these check boxes and the worksheet page in the preview section displays how the worksheet will print on the page.

Activity 1a Changing Margins and Horizontally and Vertically Centering a Worksheet

Part 1 of 12

1. Open **RPBudget** and then save it with the name **4-RPBudget**.
2. Insert the following formulas in the worksheet:
   a. Insert a SUM function in cell N5 that sums the range B5:M5. Copy the formula to the range N6:N10.
   b. Insert a SUM function in cell B11 that sums the range B5:B10. Copy the formula to the range C11:N11.
   c. Insert a SUM function in cell N14 that sums the range B14:M14. Copy the formula to the range N15:N19.
   d. Insert a SUM function in cell B20 that sums the range B14:B19. Copy the formula to the range C20:N20.
   e. Insert a formula in cell B21 that subtracts the total expenses from the income. (Make cell B21 active and then type the formula =b11-b20. Copy this formula to the range C21:N21.
   f. Apply the Accounting format with no digits after the decimal point to cell N5 and cell N14.
3. Click the Page Layout tab.
4. Click the Margins button in the Page Setup group and then click *Custom Margins* at the drop-down list.

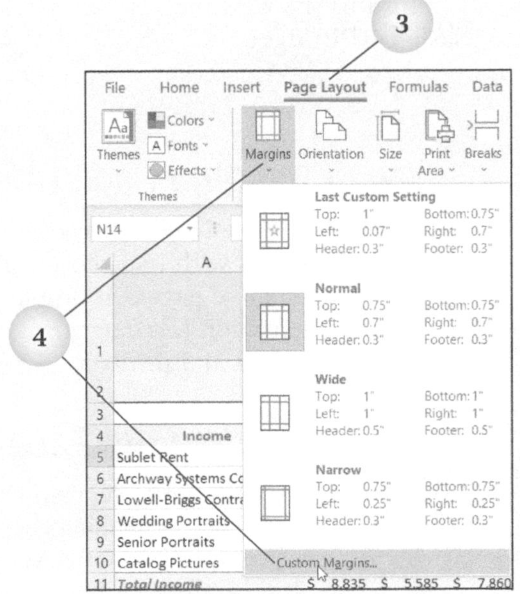

5. At the Page Setup dialog box with the Margins tab selected, click the *Top* measurement box up arrow until *3.5* displays.
6. Click the *Bottom* measurement box up arrow until *1.5* displays.
7. Preview the worksheet by clicking the Print Preview button at the bottom of the Page Setup dialog box. The worksheet appears to be a little low on the page so you decide to horizontally and vertically center it by completing the following steps:
   a. Click the Page Setup hyperlink below the galleries in the *Settings* category in the Print backstage area.
   b. Click the Margins tab at the Page Setup dialog box.
   c. In the *Top* and *Bottom* measurement boxes, change the measurements to *1*.
   d. Click the *Horizontally* check box to insert a check mark.
   e. Click the *Vertically* check box to insert a check mark.
   f. Click OK to close the dialog box.
   g. Look at the preview of the worksheet (notice the entire worksheet is not visible) and then click the Back button to return to the worksheet.
8. Save **4-RPBudget**.

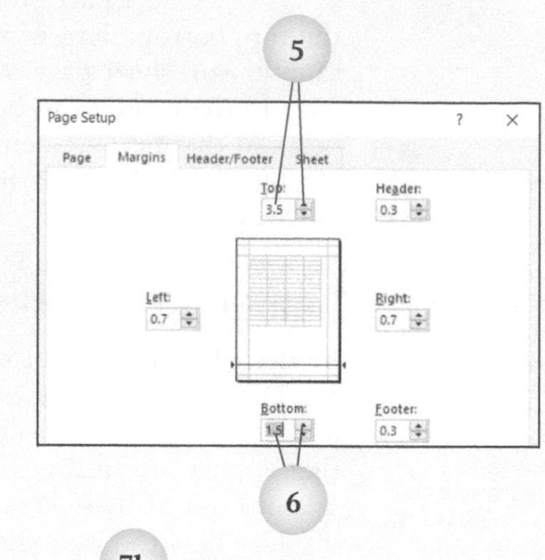

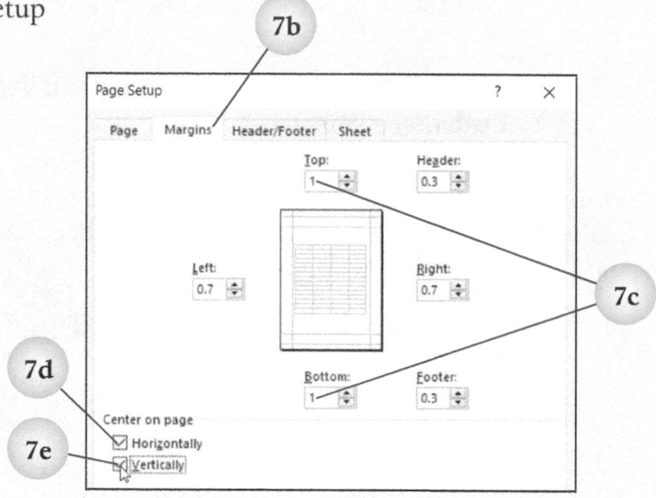

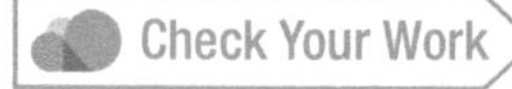

Changing Page Orientation

Click the Orientation button in the Page Setup group and a drop-down list displays with two choices: *Portrait* and *Landscape*. The two choices are represented by sample pages. A sample page that is taller than it is wide shows how the default orientation (*Portrait*) prints data on the page. The other choice, *Landscape*, rotates the data and prints it on a page that is wider than it is tall.

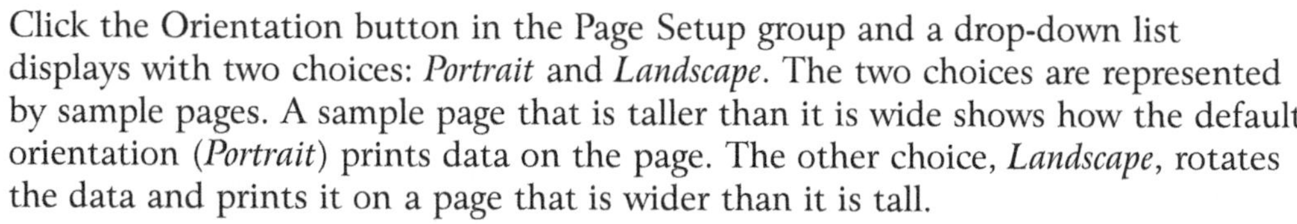

Quick Steps

Change Orientation
1. Click Page Layout tab.
2. Click Orientation button.
3. Click orientation at drop-down list.

Change Paper Size
1. Click Page Layout tab.
2. Click Size button.
3. Click size at drop-down list.

Changing the Paper Size

By default, an Excel worksheet paper size is 8.5 inches by 11 inches. Change this default size by clicking the Size button in the Page Setup group. At the drop-down list that appears, notice that the default setting is *Letter* and that the measurement *8.5"× 11"* displays below *Letter*. This drop-down list also contains a number of paper sizes, such as *Executive* and *Legal*, and a number of envelope sizes.

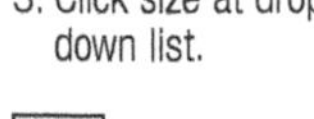

Activity 1b Changing Page Orientation and Paper Size

Part 2 of 12

1. With **4-RPBudget** open, click the Orientation button in the Page Setup group on the Page Layout tab and then click *Landscape* at the drop-down list.

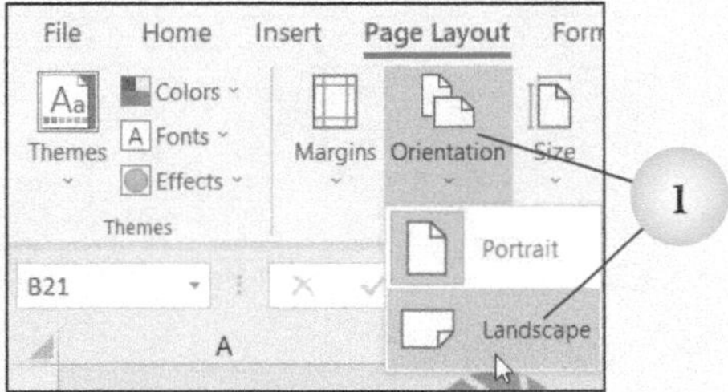

2. Click the Size button in the Page Setup group and then click *Legal* at the drop-down list.

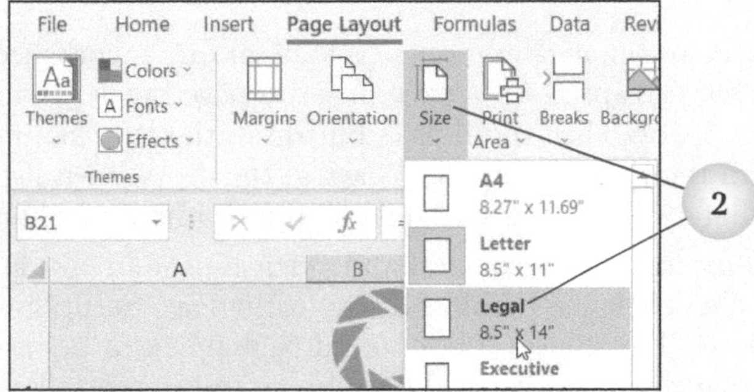

3. Preview the worksheet by clicking the File tab and then clicking the *Print* option. After viewing the worksheet in the Print backstage area, press the Esc key to return to the worksheet.
4. Save **4-RPBudget**.

Using Page Break Preview

Quick Steps

Insert Page Break
1. Select column or row.
2. Click Page Layout tab.
3. Click Breaks button.
4. Click *Insert Page Break*.

Inserting and Removing Page Breaks

The default left and right margins of 0.7 inch allow approximately 7 inches of cells across the page (8.5 inches minus 1.4 inches equals 7.1 inches). If a worksheet contains more than 7 inches of cells across the page, a vertical page break is inserted and the remaining columns are moved to the next page. A page break displays as a dashed line along cell borders. Figure 4.2 shows the page break in **4-RPBudget** when the paper size is set to *Letter*.

A page break also displays horizontally in a worksheet. By default, a worksheet can contain approximately 9.5 inches of cells down the page. This is because the paper size is set by default at 11 inches. With the default top and bottom margins of 0.75 inch, this allows 9.5 inches of cells to print vertically on one page.

Figure 4.2 Page Break

	A	B	C	D	E	F	G	H	I	J	K	L	M	N
1	Real Photography													
2	Yearly Budget													
3		*January*	*February*	*March*	*April*	*May*	*June*	*July*	*August*	*September*	*October*	*November*	*December*	*Total*
4	Income													
5	Sublet Rent	$ 1,100	$ 1,100	$ 1,100	$ 1,100	$ 1,100	$ 1,100	$ 1,100	$ 1,100	$ 1,100	$ 1,100	$ 1,100	$ 1,100	$ 13,200
6	Archway Systems Contract	235	235	235	235	235	235	235	235	235	235	235	235	2,820
7	Lowell-Briggs Contract	750	750	525	525	-	-	450	450	450	575	575	575	5,625
8	Wedding Portraits	4,500	2,000	1,500	2,800	4,000	8,250	7,500	6,850	4,500	3,500	3,500	7,000	55,900
9	Senior Portraits	2,250	1,500	4,500	5,000	3,250	1,000	300	500	650	650	400	400	20,400
10	Catalog Pictures	-	-	-	-	500	500	500	500	500	-	-	-	2,500
11	*Total Income*	$ 8,835	$ 5,585	$ 7,860	$ 9,660	$ 9,085	$ 11,085	$ 10,085	$ 9,635	$ 7,435	$ 6,060	$ 5,810	$ 9,310	$ 100,445
12														
13	Expenses													
14	Mortgage	$ 4,230	$ 4,230	$ 4,230	$ 4,230	$ 4,230	$ 4,230	$ 4,230	$ 4,230	$ 4,230	$ 4,230	$ 4,230	$ 4,230	$ 50,760
15	Utilities	625	550	600	425	400	500	650	700	700	500	550	650	6,850
16	Insurance	375	375	375	375	375	375	375	375	375	375	375	375	4,500
17	Equipment Purchases	525	1,250	950	3,500	-	-	-	-	-	-	-	-	6,225
18	Supplies	750	750	1,500	1,250	1,500	2,500	2,250	1,750	950	850	850	2,000	16,900

page break

Breaks

Excel automatically inserts page breaks in a worksheet. To have more control over what cells print on a page, insert a page break. To insert a page break, select a column or row, click the Breaks button in the Page Setup group on the Page Layout tab, and then click *Insert Page Break* at the drop-down list. A page break is inserted immediately left of the selected column or immediately above the selected row.

To insert both horizontal and vertical page breaks at the same time, make a cell active, click the Breaks button in the Page Setup group, and then click *Insert Page Break*. This causes a horizontal page break to be inserted immediately above the active cell and a vertical page break to be inserted at the left of the active cell. To remove a page break, select the column or row or make the cell active, click the Breaks button in the Page Setup group, and then click *Remove Page Break* at the drop-down list.

A page break that is automatically inserted by Excel may not be visible in a worksheet. One way to display the page break is to display the worksheet in the Print backstage area. Return to the worksheet and the page break will display in the worksheet.

Page Break Preview

Hint You can edit a worksheet in Page Break Preview.

Excel provides a page break view that displays worksheet pages and page breaks. To display this view, click the Page Break Preview button in the view area at the right side of the Status bar or click the View tab and then click the Page Break Preview button in the Workbook Views group. This causes the worksheet to display similarly to the worksheet shown in Figure 4.3. The word *Page* along with the page number appears in gray behind the cells in the worksheet. A dashed blue line indicates a page break inserted automatically by Excel and a solid blue line indicates a page break inserted manually.

Normal

Move a page break by positioning the mouse pointer on the blue line, clicking and holding down the left mouse button, dragging the line to the desired location, and then releasing the mouse button. To return to Normal view, click the Normal button in the view area on the Status bar or click the View tab and then click the Normal button in the Workbook Views group.

Figure 4.3 Worksheet in Page Break Preview

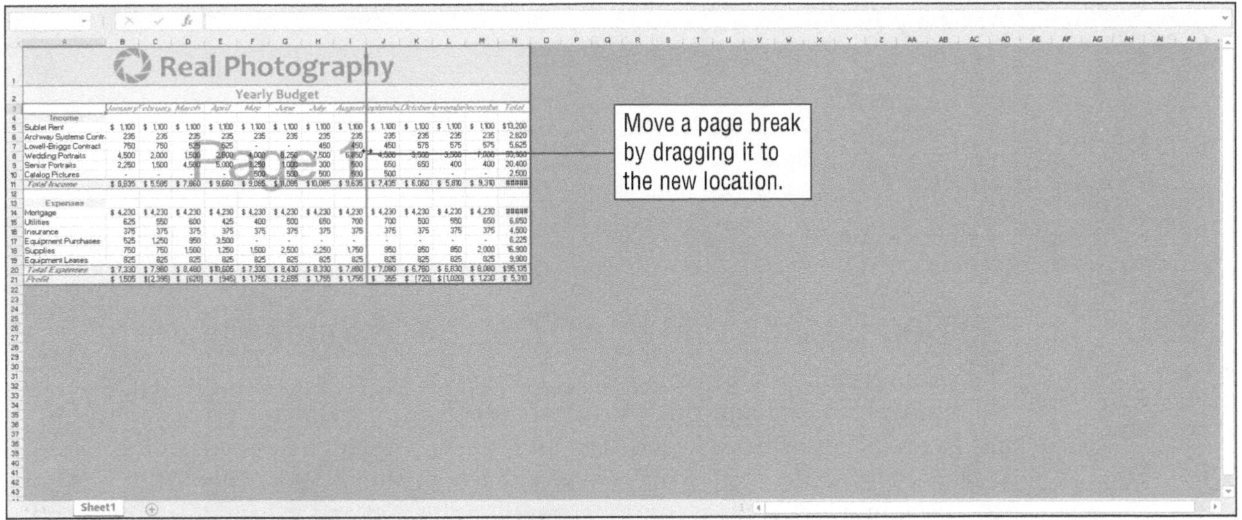

Activity 1c Inserting a Page Break in a Worksheet

Part 3 of 12

1. With **4-RPBudget** open, click the Size button in the Page Setup group on the Page Layout tab and then click *Letter* at the drop-down list.
2. Click the Margins button and then click *Custom Margins* at the drop-down list.
3. At the Page Setup dialog box with the Margins tab selected, click in the *Horizontally* check box to remove the check mark, click in the *Vertically* check box to remove the check mark, and then click OK to close the dialog box.
4. Insert a page break between columns I and J by completing the following steps:
   a. Select column J.
   b. Click the Breaks button in the Page Setup group and then click *Insert Page Break* at the drop-down list. Click in any cell in column I.

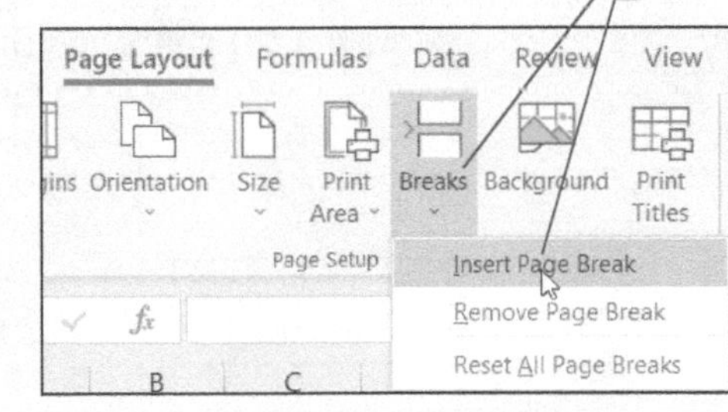

5. View the worksheet in Page Break Preview by completing the following steps:
   a. Click the Page Break Preview button in the view area at the right side of the Status bar.
   b. View the pages and page breaks in the worksheet.
   c. You decide to include the first six months of the year on one page. To do this, position the mouse pointer on the vertical blue line until the mouse pointer displays as a left-and-right-pointing arrow, click and hold down the left mouse button, drag the line left so it is between columns G and H, and then release the mouse button.

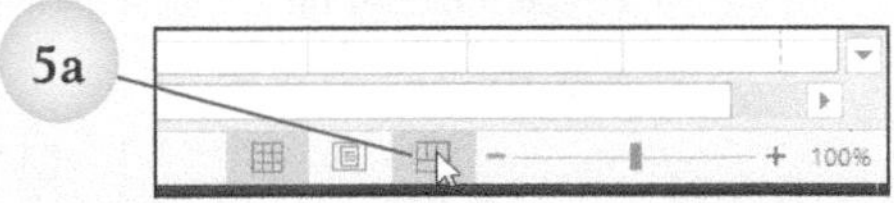

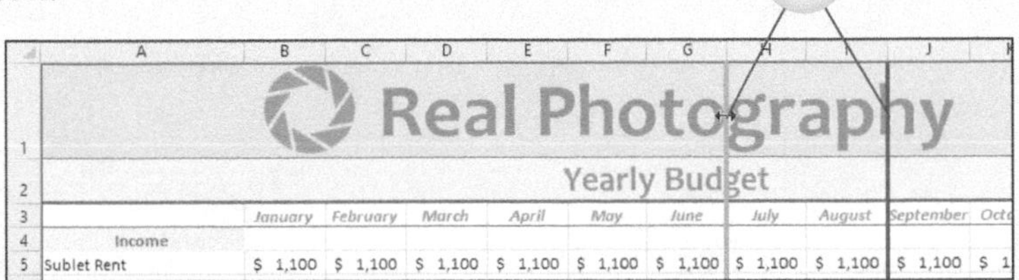

d. Click the Normal button in the view area on the Status bar.

6. Save **4-RPBudget**.

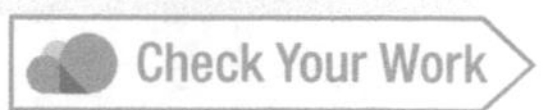

Printing Column Headers on Multiple Pages

Print Titles

Quick Steps

Print Column and Row Titles

1. Click Page Layout tab.
2. Click Print Titles button.
3. Type row range in *Rows to repeat at top* option.
4. Type column range in *Columns to repeat at left* option.
5. Click OK.

Printing Column and Row Titles on Multiple Pages

The columns and rows in a worksheet usually have titles. For example, in 4-RPBudget, the column titles include *Income*, *Expenses*, *January*, *February*, *March*, and so on. The row titles include the income and expenses categories. If a worksheet prints on more than one page, having column and/or row titles print on each page provides context for understanding the text and values in columns and rows. To do this, click the Print Titles button in the Page Setup group on the Page Layout tab. This displays the Page Setup dialog box with the Sheet tab selected, as shown in Figure 4.4.

At the Page Setup dialog box with the Sheet tab selected, specify the range of row cells to print on every page in the *Rows to repeat at top* text box. Type a cell range using a colon. For example, to print the range A1:J1 on every page, type *a1:j1* in the *Rows to repeat at top* text box. Type the range of column cells to print on every page in the *Columns to repeat at left* text box. To make rows and columns easy to identify on the printed page, specify that row and/or column headings print on each page.

Figure 4.4 Page Setup Dialog Box with the Sheet Tab Selected

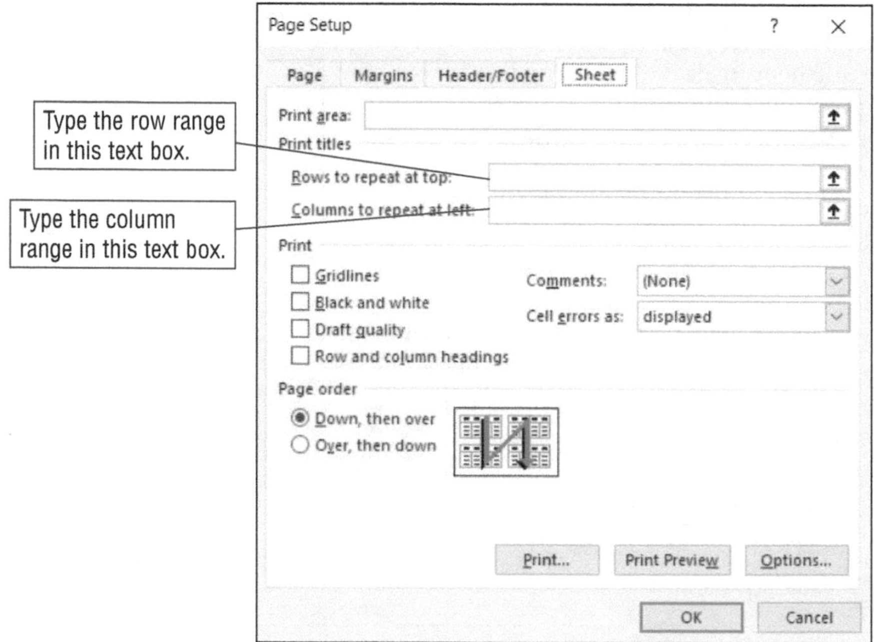

Activity 1d Printing Column Titles on Each Page of a Worksheet

Part 4 of 12

1. With **4-RPBudget** open, click the Page Layout tab and then click the Print Titles button in the Page Setup group.
2. At the Page Setup dialog box with the Sheet tab selected, click in the *Columns to repeat at left* text box.
3. Type a1:a21.
4. Click OK to close the dialog box.
5. Save and then print **4-RPBudget**.

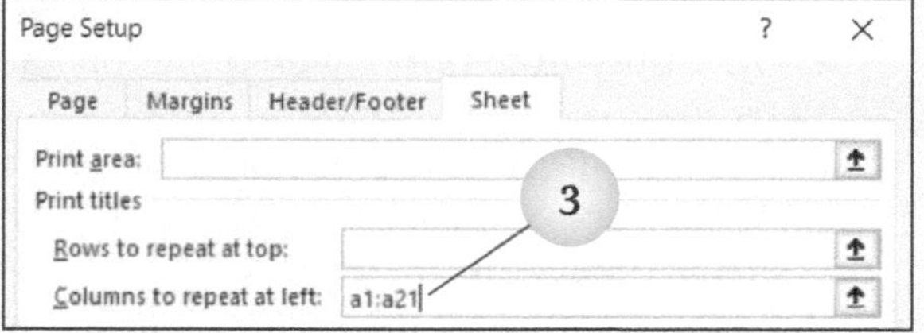

Changing Print Scaling

Width

Scaling Data

Use buttons in the Scale to Fit group on the Page Layout tab to adjust the printed output by a percentage to fit the number of pages specified. For example, if a worksheet contains too many columns to print on one page, click the *Width* option box arrow in the Scale to Fit group on the Page Layout tab and then click *1 page*. This reduces the size of the data so all the columns appear and print on one page. Manually adjust the scale of a worksheet by clicking the up or down arrows in the *Scale* measurement box or by typing a percentage in the *Scale* measurement box and then pressing the Enter key.

Activity 1e Scaling Data to Fit on One Page and Printing Row Titles on Each Page

Part 5 of 12

1. With **4-RPBudget** open, display the Page Setup dialog box with the Sheet tab selected.
2. Select and then delete the text in the *Columns to repeat at left* text box and then click the OK button.
3. Click the *Width* option box arrow in the Scale to Fit group on the Page Layout tab and then click the *1 page* option at the drop-down list.
4. Display the Print backstage area, notice that all the cells that contain data appear on one page in the worksheet, and then return to the worksheet.
5. Change the margins by completing the following steps:
   a. Click the Margins button in the Page Setup group and then click *Custom Margins* at the drop-down list.
   b. At the Page Setup dialog box with the Margins tab selected, select the current number in the *Top* measurement box and then type 3.5.
   c. Select the current number in the *Left* measurement box and then type 0.3.
   d. Select the current number in the *Right* measurement box and then type 0.3.
   e. Click OK to close the Page Setup dialog box.
6. Specify that you want row titles to print on each page by completing the following steps:
   a. Click the Print Titles button in the Page Setup group on the Page Layout tab.
   b. Click in the *Rows to repeat at top* text box and then type a3:n3.
   c. Click OK to close the dialog box.

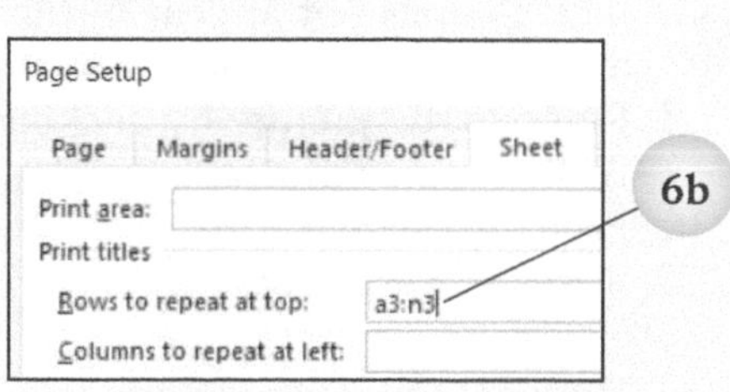

7. Save and then print **4-RPBudget**. (The worksheet prints on two pages and the row titles are repeated on the second page.)
8. At the worksheet, return to the default margins by clicking the Page Layout tab, clicking the Margins button, and then clicking the *Normal* option at the drop-down list.
9. Prevent titles from printing on the second and subsequent pages by completing the following steps:
   a. Click the Print Titles button in the Page Setup group.
   b. At the Page Setup dialog box with the Sheet tab selected, select and then delete the text in the *Rows to repeat at top* text box.
   c. Click OK to close the dialog box.
10. Change the scaling back to the default by completing the following steps:
   a. Click the *Width* option box arrow in the Scale to Fit group and then click *Automatic* at the drop-down list.
   b. Click the *Scale* measurement box up arrow until *100%* displays in the box.
11. Save **4-RPBudget**.

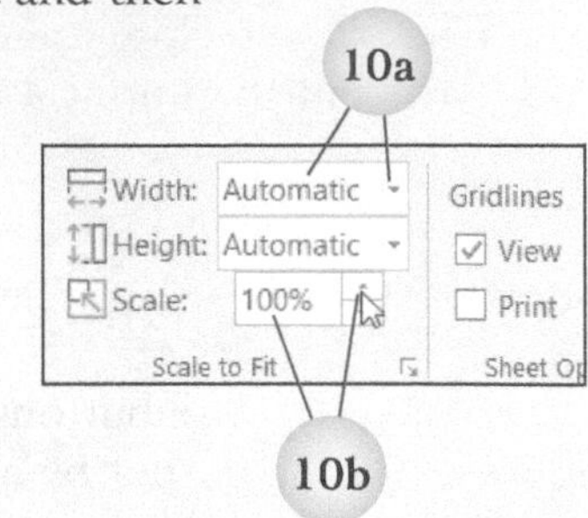

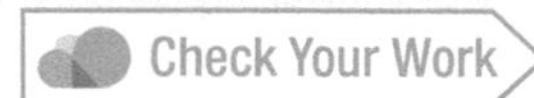

Inserting a Background Picture

Quick Steps

Insert Background Picture

1. Click Page Layout tab.
2. Click Background button.
3. Navigate to picture and double-click picture.

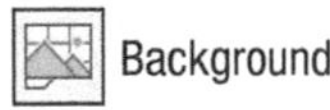

Insert a picture as a background for a worksheet with the Background button in the Page Setup group on the Page Layout tab. The picture displays only on the screen and does not print. To insert a picture, click the Background button in the Page Setup group and then click the *From a file* option at the Insert Pictures window. At the Sheet Background dialog box, navigate to the folder containing the picture and then double-click the picture. To remove the picture from the worksheet, click the Delete Background button.

Activity 1f Inserting a Background Picture

Part 6 of 12

1. With **4-RPBudget** open, insert a background picture by completing the following steps:
   a. Click the Background button in the Page Setup group on the Page Layout tab.
   b. At the Insert Pictures window, click the *From a file* option.
   c. At the Sheet Background dialog box, navigate to your EL1C4 folder and then double-click ***Ship***.
   d. Scroll down the worksheet until the ship is visible.
2. Display the Print backstage area, notice that the picture does not appear in the preview worksheet, and then return to the worksheet.
3. Remove the picture by clicking the Delete Background button in the Page Setup group on the Page Layout tab.
4. Save **4-RPBudget**.

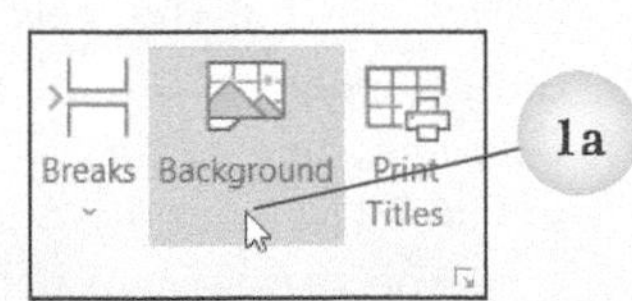

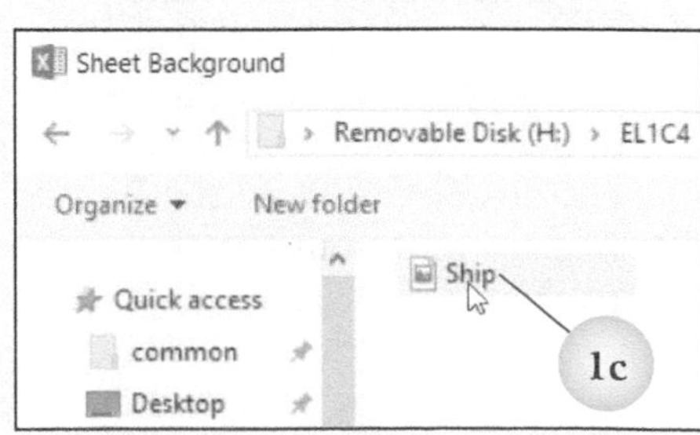

Printing Gridlines and Row and Column Headings

Quick Steps

Print Gridlines and/or Row and Column Headings

1. Click Page Layout tab.
2. Click *Print* check boxes in *Gridlines* and/or *Headings* section in Sheet Options group.

OR

1. Click Page Layout tab.
2. Click Sheet Options dialog box launcher.
3. Click *Gridlines* and/or *Row and column headings* check boxes.
4. Click OK.

Printing Gridlines and Row and Column Headings

By default, the gridlines that create the cells in a worksheet and the row numbers and column letters that label the cells do not print. The Sheet Options group on the Page Layout tab contains check boxes for gridlines and headings. The *View* check boxes for gridlines and headings contain check marks. At these settings, gridlines and row and column headings show on the screen but do not print. To print gridlines and headings, insert check marks in the *Print* check boxes. Complex worksheets may be easier to read with the gridlines printed.

The display and printing of gridlines and headings can also be controlled with options at the Page Setup dialog box with the Sheet tab selected. Display this dialog box by clicking the Sheet Options group dialog box launcher. To print gridlines and headings, insert check marks in the check boxes in the *Print* section of the dialog box. The *Print* section contains two additional options: *Black and white* and *Draft quality*. When printing with a color printer, insert a check mark in the *Black and white* check box to print the worksheet in black and white. Insert a check mark in the *Draft quality* option to print a draft of the worksheet. With this option checked, some types of formatting, such as shading and fill, do not print.

Activity 1g Printing Gridlines and Row and Column Headings — Part 7 of 12

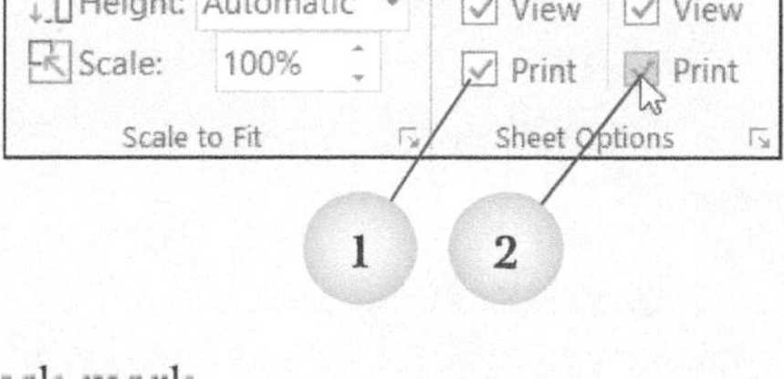

1. With **4-RPBudget** open, click in the *Print* check box below *Gridlines* in the Sheet Options group on the Page Layout tab to insert a check mark.
2. Click in the *Print* check box below *Headings* in the Sheet Options group to insert a check mark.
3. Click the Margins button in the Page Setup group and then click *Custom Margins* at the drop-down list.
4. At the Page Setup dialog box with the Margins tab selected, click in the *Horizontally* check box to insert a check mark.
5. Click in the *Vertically* check box to insert a check mark.
6. Click OK to close the dialog box.
7. Save and then print **4-RPBudget**.
8. Click in the *Print* check box below *Headings* in the Sheet Options group to remove the check mark.
9. Click in the *Print* check box below *Gridlines* in the Sheet Options group to remove the check mark.
10. Save **4-RPBudget**.

Setting a Print Area

Printing a Specific Area of a Worksheet

Use the Print Area button in the Page Setup group on the Page Layout tab to select and print specific areas of a worksheet. To do this, select the cells to print, click the Print Area button in the Page Setup group, and then click *Set Print Area* at the drop-down list. This inserts a border around the selected cells. Display the Print backstage area and click the Print button to print the cells within the border.

More than one print area can be specified in a worksheet. To do this, select the first group of cells, click the Print Area button in the Page Setup group, and then click *Set Print Area*. Select the next group of cells, click the Print Area button, and then click *Add to Print Area*. Clear a print area by clicking the Print Area button in the Page Setup group and then clicking *Clear Print Area* at the drop-down list.

Each area specified as a print area prints on a separate page. To print nonadjacent print areas on the same page, consider hiding columns and/or rows in the worksheet to bring the areas together.

Activity 1h Printing Specific Areas

Part 8 of 12

1. With **4-RPBudget** open, print the first half of the year's income and expenses by completing the following steps:
   a. Select the range A3:G21.
   b. Click the Print Area button in the Page Setup group on the Page Layout tab and then click *Set Print Area* at the drop-down list.
   c. With the border surrounding the range A3:G21, click the File tab, click the *Print* option, and then click the Print button at the Print backstage area.
   d. Clear the print area by clicking the Print Area button in the Page Setup group and then clicking *Clear Print Area* at the drop-down list.

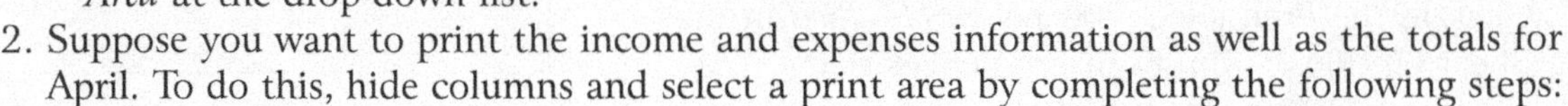

2. Suppose you want to print the income and expenses information as well as the totals for April. To do this, hide columns and select a print area by completing the following steps:
   a. Select columns B through D.
   b. Click the Home tab.
   c. Click the Format button in the Cells group, point to *Hide & Unhide*, and then click *Hide Columns*.
   d. Click the Page Layout tab.
   e. Select the range A3:E21. (Columns A and E are now adjacent.)
   f. Click the Print Area button in the Page Setup group and then click *Set Print Area* at the drop-down list.
3. Click the File tab, click the *Print* option, and then click the Print button.
4. Clear the print area by ensuring that the range A3:E21 is selected, clicking the Print Area button in the Page Setup group, and then clicking *Clear Print Area* at the drop-down list.
5. Unhide the columns by completing the following steps:
   a. Click the Home tab.
   b. Select columns A and E. (These columns are adjacent.)
   c. Click the Format button in the Cells group, point to *Hide & Unhide*, and then click *Unhide Columns*.
   d. Deselect the text by clicking in any cell containing data in the worksheet.
6. Save **4-RPBudget**.

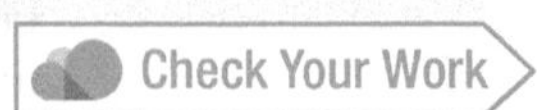

Inserting Headers and Footers

Inserting Headers and Footers

Text that prints at the top of each worksheet page is called a *header* and text that prints at the bottom of each worksheet page is called a *footer*. Create a header and/or footer with the Header & Footer button in the Text group on the Insert tab in Page Layout view or with options at the Page Setup dialog box with the Header/Footer tab selected.

Header & Footer

To create a header with the Header & Footer button, click the Insert tab, click the Text button and then click the Header & Footer button. This displays the worksheet in Page Layout view and displays the Header & Footer Tools Design tab. Use buttons on this tab, shown in Figure 4.5, to insert predesigned headers and/or footers or to insert header and footer elements such as page numbers, date, time, path name, and file name. A different header or footer can be created on the first page of the worksheet or one header or footer can be created for even pages and another for odd pages.

Quick Steps

Insert Header or Footer

1. Click Insert tab.
2. Click the Text button.
3. Click Header & Footer button.
4. Click Header button and then click predesigned header or click Footer button and then click predesigned footer.

OR

1. Click Insert tab.
2. Click the Text button.
3. Click Header & Footer button.
4. Click header or footer elements.

At the Print backstage area, preview headers and footers before printing. Click the File tab and then click the *Print* option to display the Print backstage area. A preview of the worksheet is shown at the right side of the backstage area. If the worksheet will print on more than one page, view the different pages by clicking the Next Page button or the Previous Page button. These buttons are below and to the left of the preview worksheet at the Print backstage area. Two buttons display in the bottom right corner of the Print backstage area. Click the Zoom to Page button to zoom in or out of the preview of the worksheet. Click the Show Margins button to display margin guidelines and handles on the preview page. The handles, which appear as black squares, can be used to increase or decrease the page margins and column widths. To do this, position the mouse pointer on the desired handle, click and hold down the left mouse button, drag to the new position, and then release the mouse button.

Figure 4.5 Header & Footer Tools Design Tab

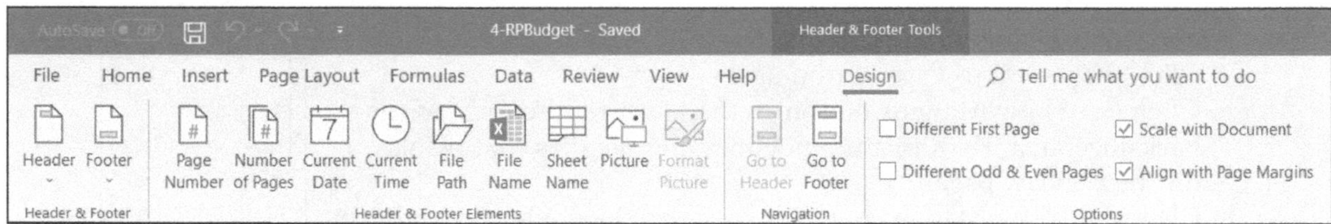

Activity 1i **Inserting a Header in a Worksheet** — Part 9 of 12

1. With **4-RPBudget** open, create a header by completing the following steps:
   a. Click the Insert tab.
   b. Click the Text button and then click the Header & Footer button.

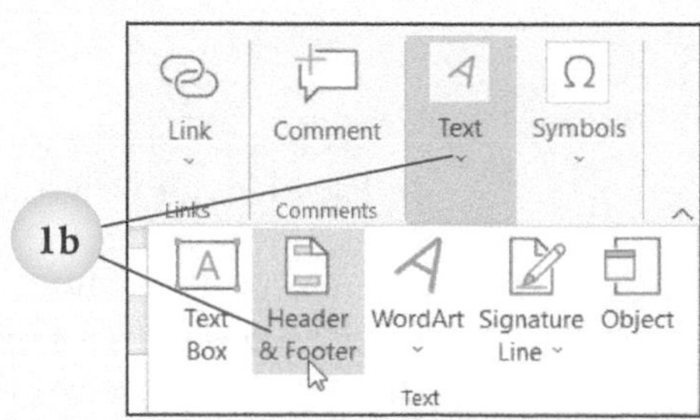

c. Click the Header button at the left side of the Header & Footer Tools Design tab and then click *Page 1, 4-RPBudget* at the drop-down list. (This inserts the page number in the middle header box and the workbook name in the right header box.)

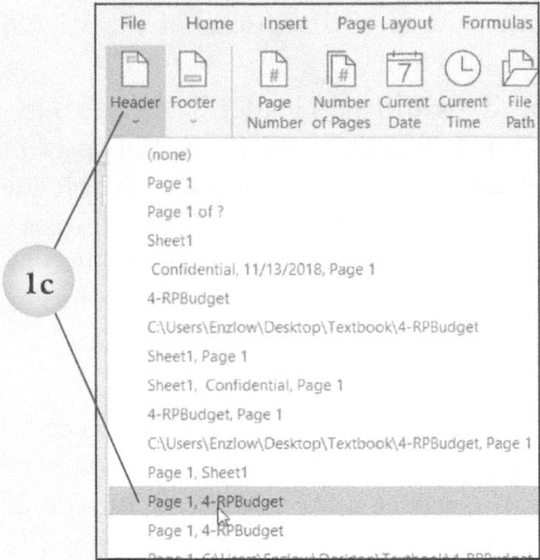

2. Preview the worksheet by completing the following steps:
   a. Click the File tab and then click the *Print* option.
   b. At the Print backstage area, look at the preview worksheet at the right side of the backstage area.
   c. View the next page of the worksheet by clicking the Next Page button below and to the left of the preview worksheet.
   d. View the first page by clicking the Previous Page button left of the Next Page button.
   e. Click the Zoom to Page button in the lower right corner of the backstage area. (Notice that the preview page has zoomed in on the worksheet.)
   f. Click the Zoom to Page button again.
   g. Click the Show Margins button in the lower right corner of the backstage area. (Notice the guidelines and handles that display on the preview page.)
   h. Click the Show Margins button to remove the guidelines and handles.
   i. Click the Back button to return to the worksheet.
3. Save **4-RPBudget**.

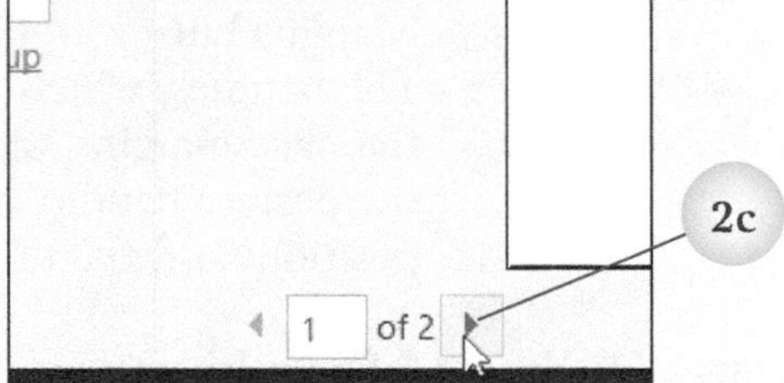

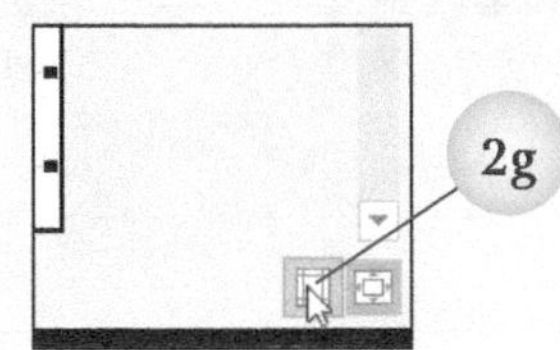

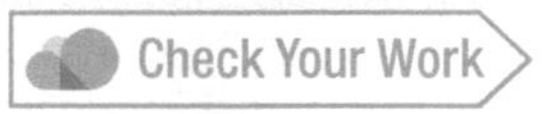

A header and/or footer can also be inserted by working in Page Layout view. In Page Layout view, the text *Add header* appears at the top of the worksheet page. Click this text and the insertion point is positioned in the middle header box. Type the header in this box or click in the left box or right box and then type the header. Create a footer in a similar manner. Scroll down the worksheet until the bottom of the page is visible and then click the text *Add footer*. Type the footer in the center footer box or click the left box or right box and then type the footer.

Activity 1j Inserting a Footer and Modifying a Header in a Worksheet
Part 10 of 12

1. With **4-RPBudget** open, make sure the workbook displays in Page Layout view.
2. Scroll down the worksheet until the text *Add footer* is visible and then click the text.

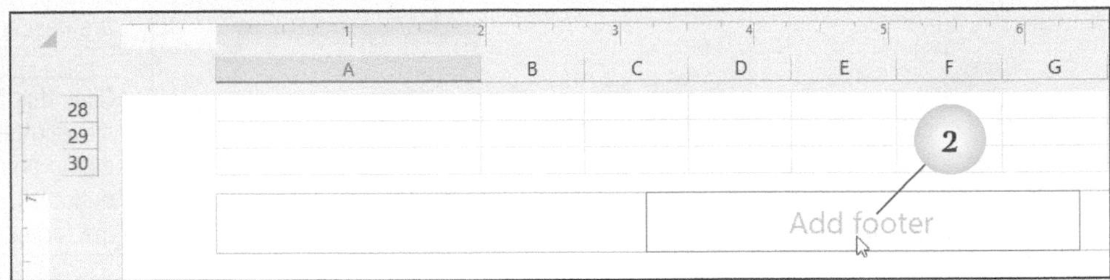

3. Type your first and last names.
4. Click in the left footer box, click the Header & Footer Tools Design tab, and then click the Current Date button in the Header & Footer Elements group. (This inserts a date code. The date will display when you click outside the footer box.)
5. Click in the right footer box and then click the Current Time button in the Header & Footer Elements group. (This inserts the time as a code. The time will display when you click outside the footer box.)
6. View the header and footer at the Print backstage area and then return to the worksheet.
7. Modify the header by completing the following steps:
   a. Scroll to the beginning of the worksheet and display the header text.
   b. Click the page number in the middle header box. (This displays the Header & Footer Tools Design tab, changes the header to a field, and selects the field.)
   c. Press the Delete key to delete the header.
   d. Click the header text in the right header box and then press the Delete key.
   e. With the insertion point positioned in the right header box, insert the page number by clicking the Header & Footer Tools Design tab and then clicking the Page Number button in the Header & Footer Elements group.
   f. Click in the left header box and then click the File Name button in the Header & Footer Elements group.
8. Click in any cell in the worksheet that contains data.
9. View the header and footer at the Print backstage area and then return to the worksheet.
10. Save **4-RPBudget**.

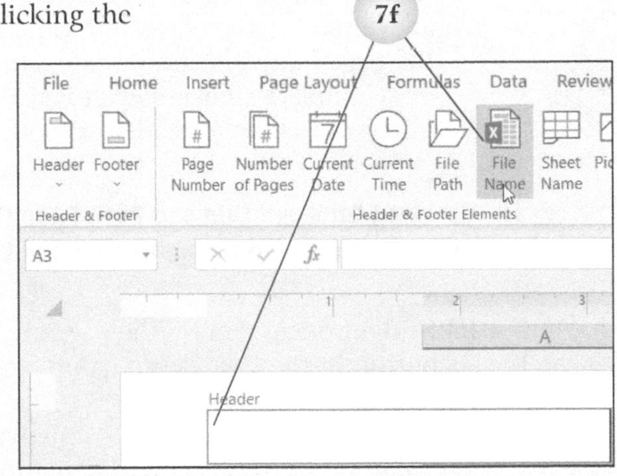

Headers and footers can also be inserted and customized using options at the Page Setup dialog box with the Header/Footer tab selected, as shown in Figure 4.6. Display this dialog box by clicking the Page Layout tab and then clicking the Page Setup group dialog box launcher. At the Page Setup dialog box, click the Header/Footer tab. If a worksheet contains headers or footers, they will appear in the dialog box. Use the check box options in the lower left corner of the dialog box to insert different odd and even page headers and/or footers or to insert a different

Figure 4.6 Page Setup Dialog Box with the Header/Footer Tab Selected

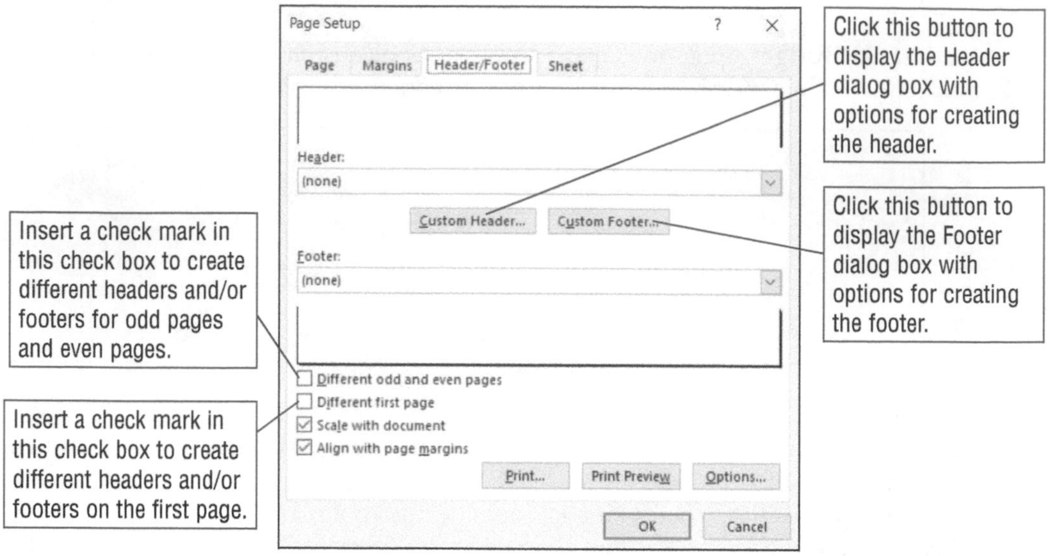

Click this button to display the Header dialog box with options for creating the header.

Click this button to display the Footer dialog box with options for creating the footer.

Insert a check mark in this check box to create different headers and/or footers for odd pages and even pages.

Insert a check mark in this check box to create different headers and/or footers on the first page.

first page header and/or footer. The bottom two check box options are active by default. These defaults scale the header and footer text with the worksheet text and align the header and footer with the page margins.

To create different odd and even page headers, click the *Different odd and even pages* check box to insert a check mark and then click the Custom Header button. This displays the Header dialog box with the Odd Page Header tab selected. Type or insert the odd page header data in the *Left section*, *Center section*, or *Right section* text box and then click the Even Page Header tab. Type or insert the even page header data in the desired section text box and then click OK. Use the buttons above the section boxes to format the header text and insert information such as the page number, current date, current time, file name, worksheet name, and so on. Complete similar steps to create different odd and even page footers and a different first page header or footer.

Activity 1k Creating Different Odd and Even Page Headers and Footers and a Different First Page Header and Footer

Part 11 of 12

1. With **4-RPBudget** open, remove the page break by clicking the Page Layout tab, clicking the Breaks button in the Page Setup group, and then clicking *Reset All Page Breaks* at the drop-down list.
2. Change the margins by completing the following steps:
   a. Click the Margins button in the Page Setup group on the Page Layout tab and then click *Custom Margins* at the drop-down list.
   b. At the Page Setup dialog box with the Margins tab selected, select the current number in the *Left* measurement box and then type 3.
   c. Select the current number in the *Right* measurement box and then type 3.
   d. Click OK to close the dialog box.

3. Click the Page Setup group dialog box launcher on the Page Layout tab.
4. At the Page Setup dialog box, click the Header/Footer tab.
5. At the Page Setup dialog box with the Header/Footer tab selected, click the *Different odd and even pages* check box to insert a check mark and then click the Custom Header button.
6. At the Header dialog box with the Odd Page Header tab selected, click the Format Text button (above the *Left section* text box).
7. At the Font dialog box, click *12* in the *Size* list box and then click OK.
8. At the Header dialog box with the file name code (&[File]) highlighted in the *Left section* text box, type Yearly Budget.

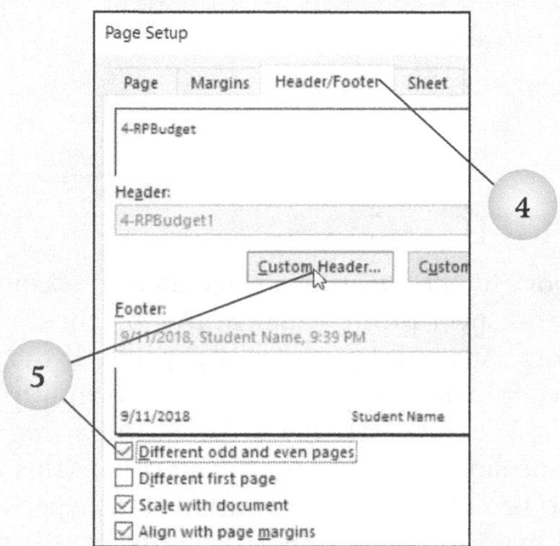

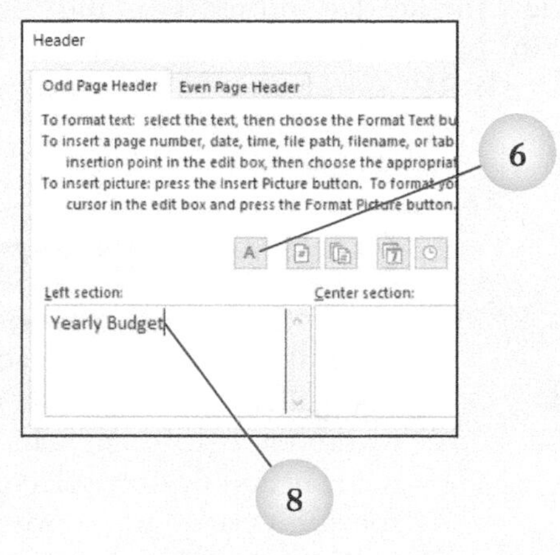

9. Click the Even Page Header tab, click in the *Left section* text box, and then click the Insert Page Number button.
10. Click in the *Right section* text box and then type Yearly Budget.
11. Select the text *Yearly Budget*, click the Format Text button, click *12* in the *Size* list box, and then click OK.
12. Click OK to close the Header dialog box.
13. Click the Custom Footer button. At the Footer dialog box with the Odd Page Footer tab selected, delete the data in the *Left section* text box and then select and delete the data in the *Right section* text box. (The footer should contain only your name.)
14. Select your name, click the Format Text button, click *12* in the *Size* list box, and then click OK.
15. Click the Even Page Footer tab, type your name in the *Center section* text box, select your name, and then change the font size to 12 points.
16. Click OK to close the Footer dialog box and then click OK to close the Page Setup dialog box. (View the header and footer in the Print backstage area and then return to the worksheet.)
17. Click the Page Setup group dialog box launcher on the Page Layout tab.
18. At the Page Setup dialog box, click the Header/Footer tab.
19. Click the *Different odd and even pages* check box to remove the check mark.
20. Click the *Different first page* check box to insert a check mark and then click the Custom Header button.

21. At the Header dialog box with the Header tab selected, click the First Page Header tab.
22. Click in the *Right section* text box and then click the Insert Page Number button.
23. Click OK to close the Header dialog box and then click OK to close the Page Setup dialog box.
24. View the header and footer in the Print backstage area and then return to the worksheet.
25. Save **4-RPBudget**.

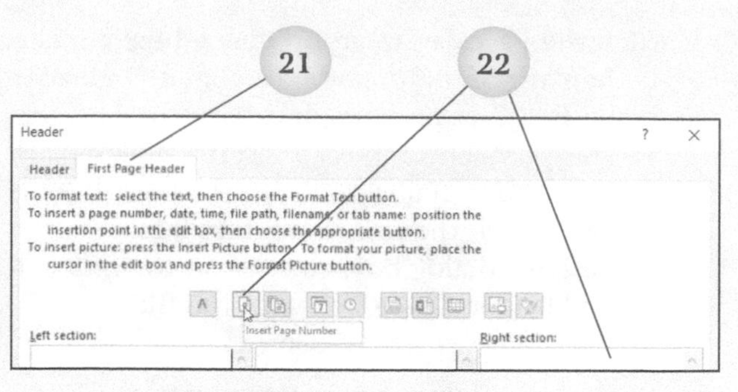

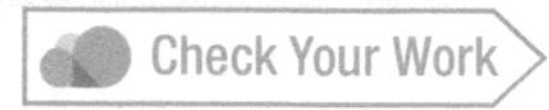

Customizing Print Jobs

Use options in the *Settings* category at the Print backstage area to specify what to print. By default, the active worksheet prints. Change this by clicking the first gallery in the *Settings* category. At the drop-down list, specify if the entire workbook is to print (which is useful when a workbook contains multiple worksheets) or only selected cells. With the other galleries in the *Settings* category, specify if pages are to print on one side or both sides of the paper (this depends on the printer) and if they are to be collated. With other options, specify the worksheet orientation, size, and margins and whether the worksheet is to be scaled to fit all the columns or rows on one page.

With the *Pages* text boxes in the *Settings* category, specify the pages of the worksheet to be printed. For example, to print pages 2 and 3 of the active worksheet, type *2* in the *Pages* measurement box in the *Settings* category and then type *3* in the *to* measurement box. Or click the up- and down-pointing arrows to select page numbers.

Activity 1l Printing Specific Pages of a Worksheet — Part 12 of 12

1. With **4-RPBudget** open, print the first two pages of the worksheet by completing the following steps:
   a. Click the File tab and then click the *Print* option.
   b. At the Print backstage area, click in the *Pages* measurement box below the first gallery in the *Settings* category and then type 1.
   c. Click in the *to* measurement box in the *Settings* category and then type 2.
   d. Click the Print button.

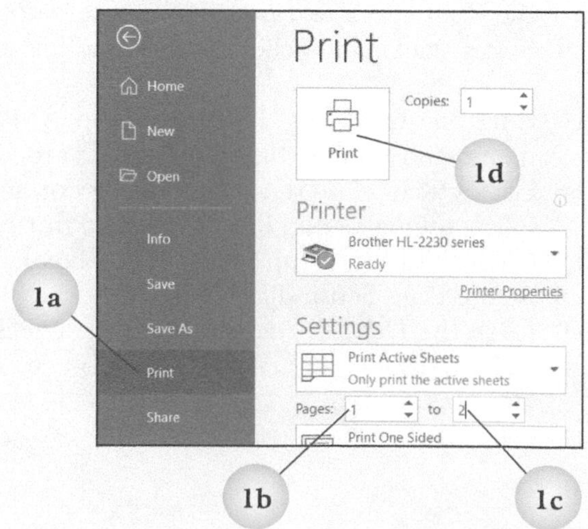

2. Print selected cells by completing the following steps:
   a. Display the worksheet in Normal view.
   b. Select the range A3:D11.
   c. Click the File tab and then click the *Print* option.
   d. At the Print backstage area, select and then delete the number in the *Pages* measurement box and the number in the *to* measurement box. (These are the numbers you inserted in Steps 1b and 1c.)
   e. Click the first gallery in the *Settings* category (displays with *Print Active Sheets*) and then click *Print Selection* at the drop-down list.
   f. Click the Print button.
3. Save and then close **4-RPBudget**.

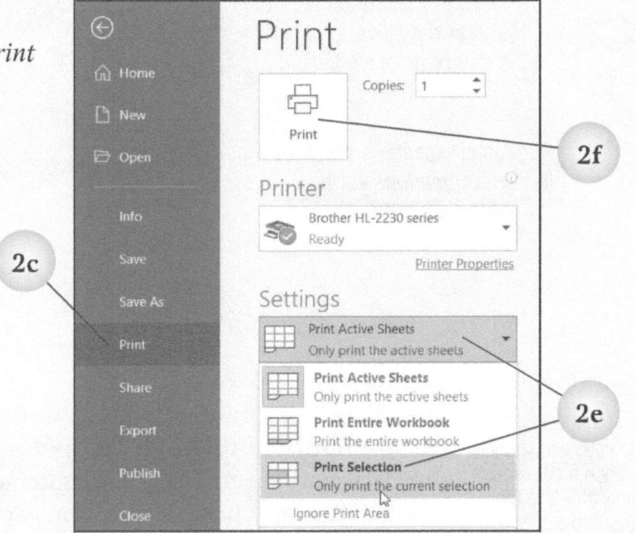

Activity 2 Format a Sales and Commissions Worksheet **3 Parts**

You will format a sales commission worksheet by inserting a formula, completing a spelling check, and finding and replacing data and cell formatting.

Checking Spelling

Spelling

Checking Spelling
1. Click Review tab.
2. Click Spelling button.
3. Replace or ignore selected words.

Checking Spelling

Excel provides a spelling check feature that verifies the spelling of text in a worksheet. The spelling check uses an electronic dictionary to identify misspelled words and suggest alternatives. Before checking the spelling in a worksheet, make the first cell active. The spelling check reviews the worksheet from the active cell to the last cell in the worksheet that contains data.

To use the spelling check, click the Review tab and then click the Spelling button in the Proofing group. Figure 4.7 shows the Spelling dialog box. At this dialog box, tell Excel to ignore a word or to replace a misspelled word with a word from the *Suggestions* list box using one of the available buttons.

Using Undo and Redo

Undo

Redo

Using Undo and Redo

Excel includes an Undo button on the Quick Access Toolbar that reverses certain commands or deletes the last data typed in a cell. For example, apply formatting to cells in a worksheet and then click the Undo button on the Quick Access Toolbar and the formatting is removed. To reapply the formatting, click the Redo button on the Quick Access Toolbar.

Figure 4.7 Spelling Dialog Box

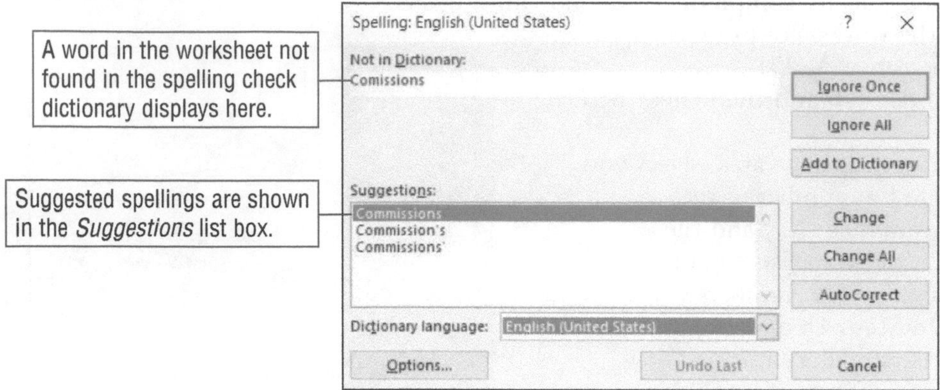

Hint Ctrl + Z is the keyboard shortcut to undo a command and Ctrl + Y is the keyboard shortcut to redo a command.

Excel maintains actions in temporary memory. To undo an action, click the Undo button arrow and a drop-down list displays containing the actions performed on the worksheet. Click a specific action at the drop-down list and that action along with any preceding actions are undone. Click the Redo button and click a specific action at the drop-down list and that action along with any preceding actions are redone. Multiple actions must be undone or redone in sequence.

Activity 2a Spell Checking and Formatting a Worksheet

Part 1 of 3

1. Open **MRSales** and then save it with the name **4-MRSales**.
2. Complete a spelling check on the worksheet by completing the following steps:
   a. If necessary, make cell A1 active.
   b. Click the Review tab.
   c. Click the Spelling button in the Proofing group.
   d. Click the Change button as needed to correct misspelled words in the worksheet. (When the spelling check stops at the proper names *Pirozzi* and *Yonemoto*, click the Ignore All button.)
   e. At the message stating the spelling check is complete, click OK.

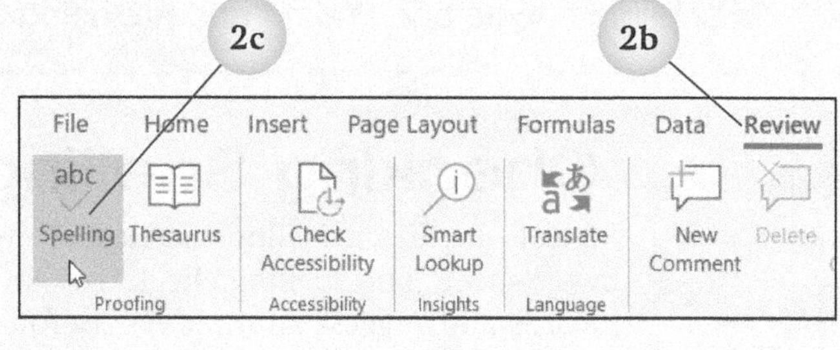

3. Insert a formula and then copy the formula without the formatting by completing the following steps:
   a. Make cell G4 active and then insert a formula that multiplies the sale price by the commission percentage.
   b. Copy the formula to the range G5:G26.
   c. Some of the cells contain shading that you do not want removed, so click the Auto Fill Options button at the bottom right of the selected cells and then click the *Fill Without Formatting* option at the drop-down list.

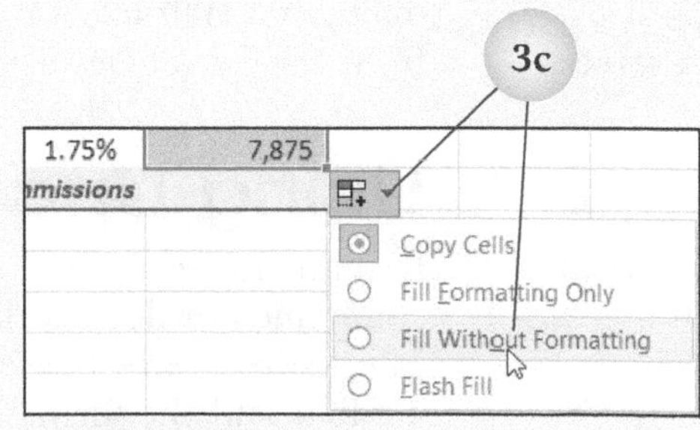

4. Make cell G27 active and then insert the sum of the range G4:G26.
5. Apply the Accounting format with no digits after the decimal point to cell G4 and cell G27.

6. Apply a theme by clicking the Page Layout tab, clicking the Themes button, and then clicking *Ion* at the drop-down gallery.
7. After looking at the worksheet with the Ion theme applied, you decide that you want to return to the original formatting. To do this, click the Undo button on the Quick Access Toolbar.

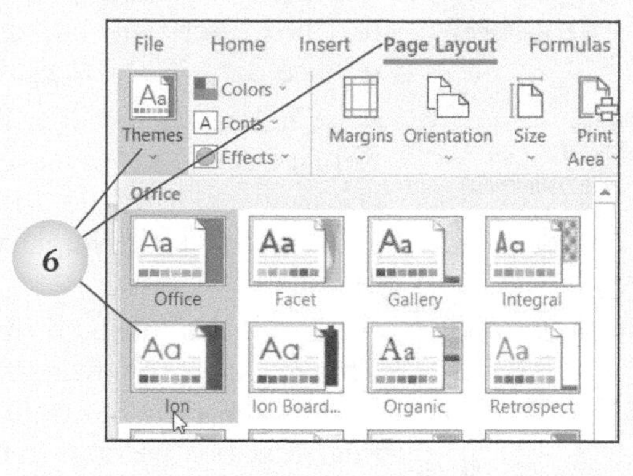

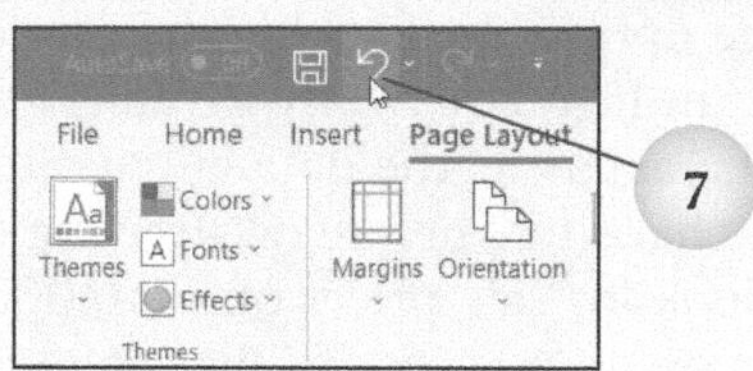

8. Save **4-MRSales**.

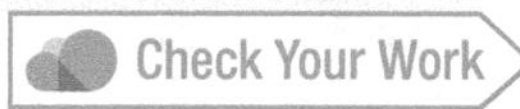

Finding Data

Replacing Data

Replacing Formatting

Quick Steps

Find Data

1. Click Find & Select button.
2. Click *Find.*
3. Type data in *Find what* text box.
4. Click Find Next button.

Find & Select

Finding and Replacing Data and Cell Formatting

Use Excel's find feature to look for specific data and either replace it with nothing or replace it with other data. This feature is particularly helpful for finding data quickly in a large worksheet. Excel also includes a find and replace feature. Use this feature to look for specific data in a worksheet and replace it with other data.

To find specific data in a worksheet, click the Find & Select button in the Editing group on the Home tab and then click *Find* at the drop-down list. This displays the Find and Replace dialog box with the Find tab selected, as shown in Figure 4.8. Type the find data in the *Find what* text box and then click the Find Next button. Continue clicking the Find Next button to move to the next occurrence of the data. If the Find and Replace dialog box blocks the view of the worksheet, use the mouse pointer on the title bar to drag the dialog box to a different location.

To find specific data in a worksheet and replace it with other data, click the Find & Select button in the Editing group on the Home tab and then click *Replace* at the drop-down list. This displays the Find and Replace dialog box with the

Figure 4.8 Find and Replace Dialog Box with the Find Tab Selected

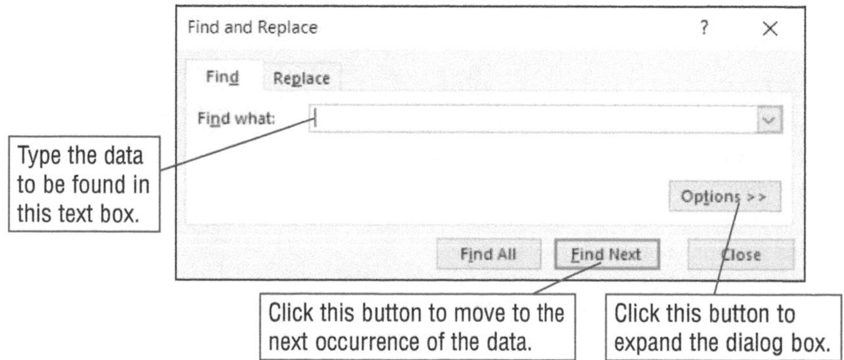

Quick Steps
Find and Replace Data
1. Click Find & Select button.
2. Click *Replace*.
3. Type data in *Find what* text box.
4. Type data in *Replace with* text box.
5. Click Replace button or Replace All button.

Hint Ctrl + F is the keyboard shortcut to display the Find and Replace dialog box with the Find tab selected.

Hint Ctrl + H is the keyboard shortcut to display the Find and Replace dialog box with the Replace tab selected.

Replace tab selected, as shown in Figure 4.9. Enter the find data in the *Find what* text box. Press the Tab key or click in the *Replace with* text box and then enter the replace data in the *Replace with* text box.

Click the Find Next button to find the next occurrence of the data. Click the Replace button to replace the data and find the next occurrence. To replace all the occurrences of the data in the *Find what* text box with the data in the *Replace with* text box, click the Replace All button. Click the Close button to close the Replace dialog box.

Display additional find and replace options by clicking the Options button. This expands the dialog box, as shown in Figure 4.10. By default, Excel will look for any data that contains the same characters as the data entered in the *Find what* text box without concern for the characters before or after the entered data. For example, in Activity 2b, you will look for sale prices of $450,000 and replace them with sale prices of $475,000. If you do not specify that you want to find only cells that contain *450000,* Excel will stop at any cell containing *450000.* For example, Excel will stop at a cell containing *$1,450,000* and a cell containing *$2,450,000.* To specify that the only data to be contained in the cell is what is entered in the *Find what* text box, click the Options button to expand the dialog box and then insert a check mark in the *Match entire cell contents* check box.

If the *Match case* option is active (contains a check mark), Excel will look for only that data that matches the case of the data entered in the *Find what* text box. Remove the check mark from this check box and Excel will find the data entered in the *Find what* text box in any case. By default, Excel will search in the current worksheet. If the workbook contains more than one worksheet, change the *Within* option to *Workbook*. By default, Excel searches by rows in a worksheet. This can be changed to by columns with the *Search* option.

Figure 4.9 Find and Replace Dialog Box with the Replace Tab Selected

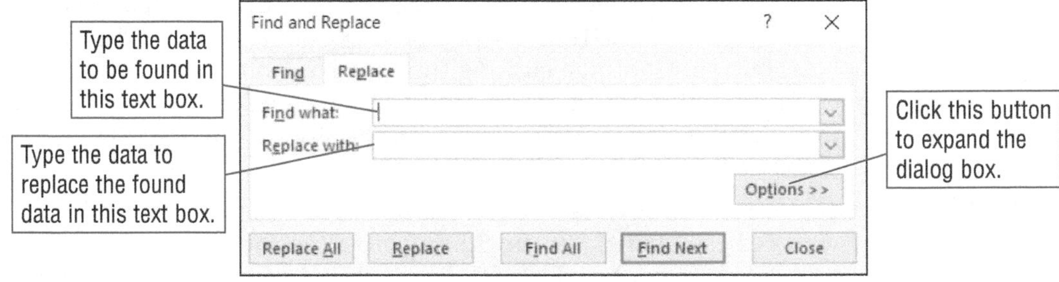

Figure 4.10 Expanded Find and Replace Dialog Box

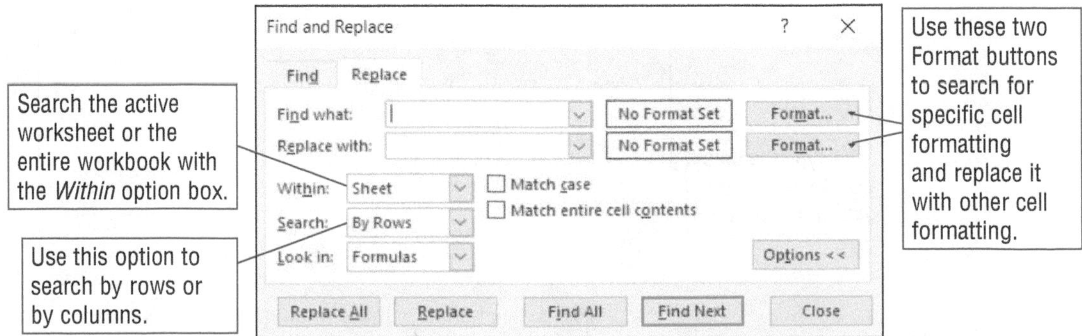

Activity 2b Finding and Replacing Data

Part 2 of 3

1. With **4-MRSales** open, find all occurrences of *Land* in the worksheet and replace them with *Acreage* by completing the following steps:
   a. Click the Find & Select button in the Editing group on the Home tab and then click *Replace* at the drop-down list.
   b. At the Find and Replace dialog box with the Replace tab selected, type Land in the *Find what* text box.
   c. Press the Tab key. (This moves the insertion point to the *Replace with* text box.)
   d. Type Acreage.
   e. Click the Replace All button.
   f. At the message stating that four replacements were made, click OK.
   g. Click the Close button to close the Find and Replace dialog box.

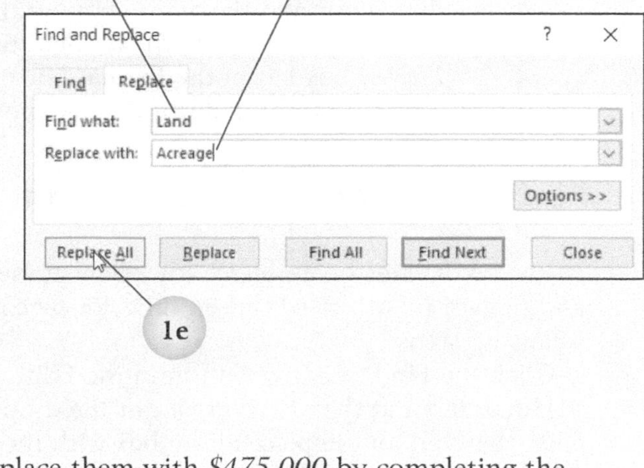

2. Find all occurrences of *$450,000* and replace them with *$475,000* by completing the following steps:
   a. Click the Find & Select button in the Editing group and then click *Replace* at the drop-down list.
   b. At the Find and Replace dialog box with the Replace tab selected, select any text in the *Find what* text box and then type 450000.
   c. Press the Tab key.
   d. Type 475000.
   e. Click the Options button to display additional options. (If additional options are already visible, skip this step.)
   f. Click the *Match entire cell contents* check box to insert a check mark.
   g. Click the Replace All button.
   h. At the message stating that two replacements were made, click OK.
   i. At the Find and Replace dialog box, click the *Match entire cell contents* check box to remove the check mark.
   j. Click the Close button to close the Find and Replace dialog box.
3. Save **4-MRSales**.

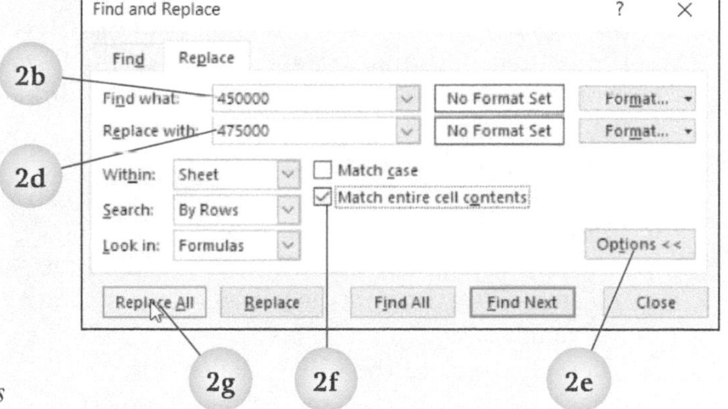

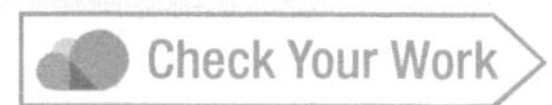

Use the Format buttons at the expanded Find and Replace dialog box (see Figure 4.10 (on page 100)) to search for specific cell formatting and replace it with other formatting. Click the Format button arrow and a drop-down list displays. Click the *Format* option and the Find Format dialog box displays with the Number, Alignment, Font, Border, Fill, and Protection tabs. Specify formatting at this dialog box. Click the *Choose Format From Cell* option from the Format button drop-down list or click the Choose Format From Cell button in the Find Format dialog box and the mouse pointer displays with a pointer tool attached. Click in the cell containing the desired formatting and the formatting displays in the *Preview* box left of the Format button. Click the *Clear Find Format* option at the Find button drop-down list and any formatting in the *Preview* box is removed.

Activity 2c Finding and Replacing Cell Formatting

Part 3 of 3

1. With **4-MRSales** open, search for a light-turquoise fill color and replace it with a light-green fill color by completing the following steps:
   a. Click the Find & Select button in the Editing group on the Home tab and then click *Replace* at the drop-down list.
   b. At the Find and Replace dialog box with the Replace tab selected, make sure the dialog box is expanded. (If not, click the Options button.)
   c. Select and then delete any text in the *Find what* text box.
   d. Select and then delete any text in the *Replace with* text box.
   e. Make sure the boxes immediately before the two Format buttons display with the text *No Format Set*. (If not, click the Format button arrow and then click the *Clear Find Format* or *Clear Replace Format* option at the drop-down list. Do this for each Format button.)
   f. Click the top Format button.
   g. At the Find Format dialog box, click the Fill tab.
   h. Click the More Colors button.
   i. At the Colors dialog box with the Standard tab selected, click the light-turquoise color, as shown at the right.
   j. Click OK to close the Colors dialog box.
   k. Click OK to close the Find Format dialog box.
   l. Click the bottom Format button.
   m. At the Replace Format dialog box with the Fill tab selected, click the light-green color (last column, second row), as shown at the right.
   n. Click OK to close the dialog box.
   o. At the Find and Replace dialog box, click the Replace All button.
   p. At the message stating that 10 replacements were made, click OK.

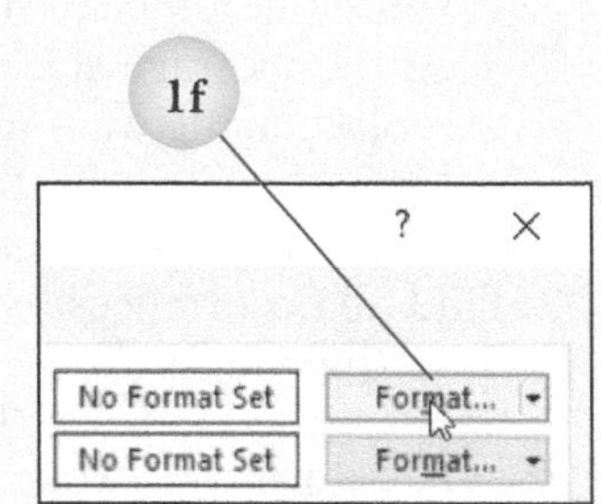

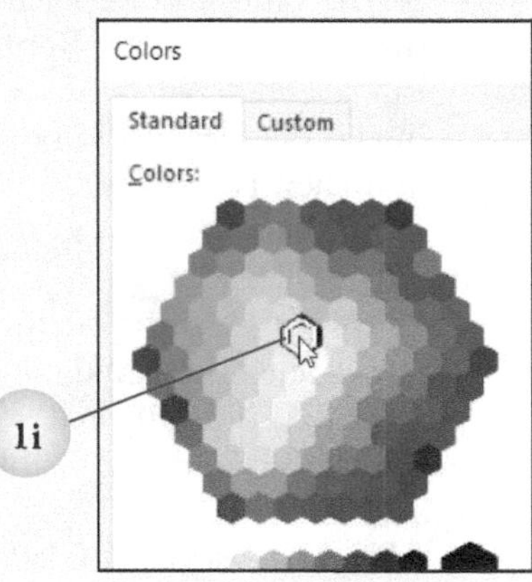

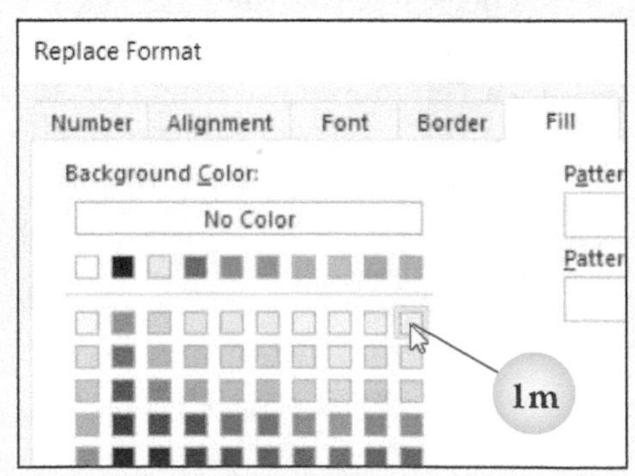

2. Search for a light-gray fill color and replace it with a light-yellow fill color by completing the following steps:
   a. At the Find and Replace dialog box, click the top Format button.
   b. At the Find Format dialog box with the Fill tab selected, click the light-gray color (fourth column, second row), as shown at the right.
   c. Click OK to close the Find Format dialog box.
   d. Click the bottom Format button.
   e. At the Replace Format dialog box with the Fill tab selected, click the yellow color (eighth column, second row), as shown below and to the right.
   f. Click OK to close the dialog box.
   g. At the Find and Replace dialog box, click the Replace All button.
   h. At the message stating that 78 replacements were made, click OK.

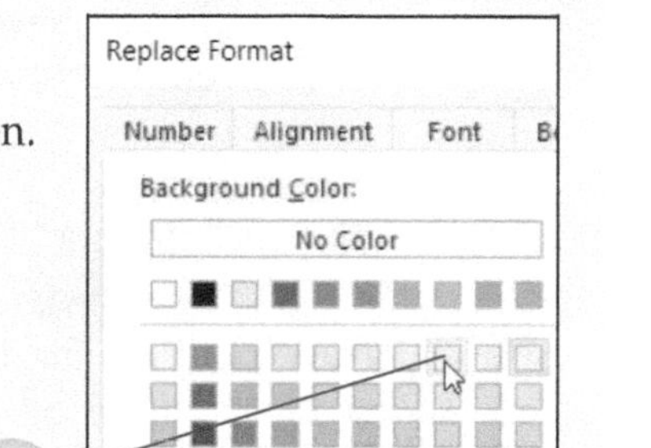

3. Search for 11-point Calibri formatting and replace it with 10-point Arial formatting by completing the following steps:
   a. With the Find and Replace dialog box open, clear formatting from the top Format button by clicking the top Format button arrow and then clicking the *Clear Find Format* option at the drop-down list.
   b. Clear formatting from the bottom Format button by clicking the bottom Format button arrow and then clicking *Clear Replace Format.*
   c. Click the top Format button.
   d. At the Find Format dialog box, click the Font tab.
   c. Scroll down the *Font* list box and then click *Calibri.*
   f. Click *11* in the *Size* list box.
   g. Click OK to close the dialog box.
   h. Click the bottom Format button.
   i. At the Replace Format dialog box with the Font tab selected, scroll down the *Font* list box and then click *Arial.*
   j. Click *10* in the *Size* list box.
   k. Click OK to close the dialog box.
   l. At the Find and Replace dialog box, click the Replace All button.
   m. At the message stating that 174 replacements were made, click OK.
   n. At the Find and Replace dialog box, clear formatting from both Format buttons.
   o. Click the Close button to close the Find and Replace dialog box.

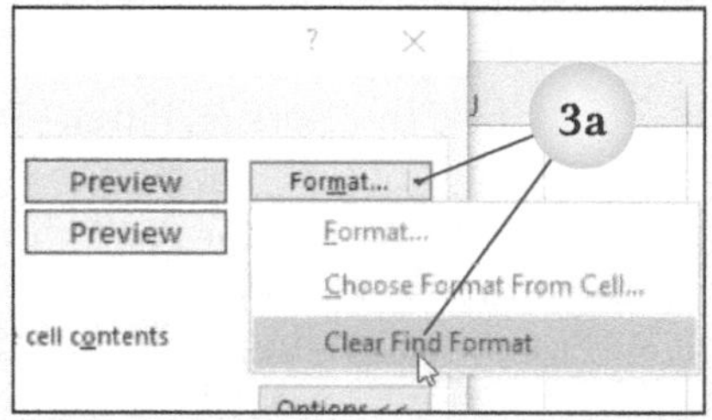

4. Save, print, and then close **4-MRSales**.

Activity 3 Insert a Formula and Sort and Filter Data in a Billing Worksheet — 4 Parts

You will insert a formula in a weekly billing worksheet and then sort and filter specific data in the worksheet.

Sorting Data

Sorting Data

Excel is primarily a spreadsheet program but it also includes some basic database functions, such as sorting data in alphabetic or numeric order. To sort data in a worksheet, use the Sort & Filter button in the Editing group on the Home tab.

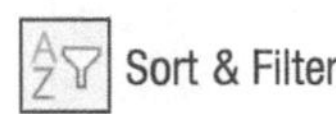

To sort data in a worksheet, select the cells containing the data to be sorted, click the Sort & Filter button in the Editing group and then click the option representing the desired sort. The sort option names vary depending on the data in selected cells. For example, if the first column of selected cells contains text, the sort options at the drop-down list are *Sort A to Z* and *Sort Z to A*. If the selected cells contain dates, the sort options at the drop-down list are *Sort Oldest to Newest* and *Sort Newest to Oldest*. If the cells contain numbers or values, the sort options are *Sort Smallest to Largest* and *Sort Largest to Smallest*. If more than one column is selected in a worksheet, Excel sorts the data in the first selected column.

Quick Steps

Sort Data

1. Select cells.
2. Click Sort & Filter button.
3. Click sort option at drop-down list.

Activity 3a **Sorting Data** Part 1 of 4

1. Open **APTBilling** and then save it with the name **4-APTBilling**.
2. Insert a formula in cell F4 that multiplies the rate by the hours. Copy the formula to the range F5:F29.
3. Sort the data in the first column in descending order by completing the following steps:
   a. Make cell A4 active.
   b. Click the Sort & Filter button in the Editing group on the Home tab.
   c. Click the *Sort Largest to Smallest* option at the drop-down list.
4. Sort in ascending order by clicking the Sort & Filter button and then clicking *Sort Smallest to Largest* at the drop-down list.
5. Save **4-APTBilling**.

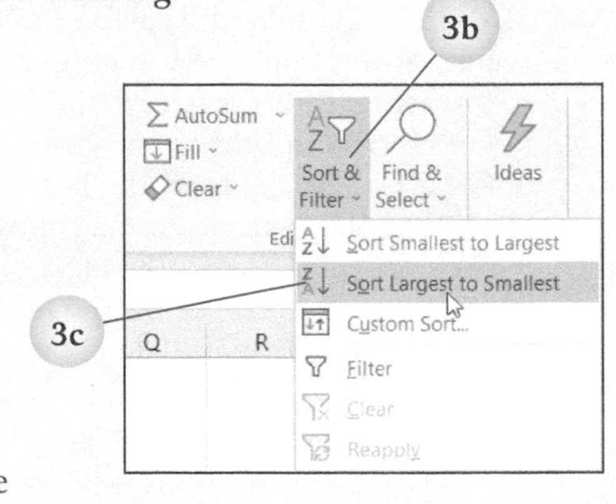

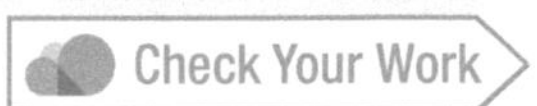

Completing a Custom Sort

To sort data in a column other than the first column, use options at the Sort dialog box. Select one column in a worksheet, click the Sort & Filter button, and then click the desired sort option; only the data in that column is sorted. If this data is related to data to the left or right that relationship is broken. For example, after sorting the range C4:C29 in 4-APTBilling, the client number, treatment, hours, and total no longer match the date.

Use options at the Sort dialog box to sort data and maintain the relationship among all the cells. To sort using the Sort dialog box, select the cells to be sorted, click the Sort & Filter button, and then click *Custom Sort*. This displays the Sort dialog box, shown in Figure 4.11.

Quick Steps

Complete Custom Sort

1. Select cells.
2. Click Sort & Filter button.
3. Click *Custom Sort* at drop-down list.
4. Specify options at Sort dialog box.
5. Click OK.

Figure 4.11 Sort Dialog Box

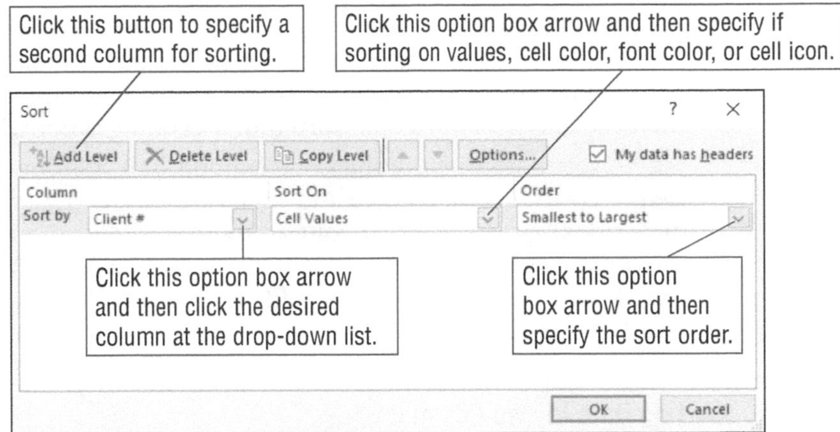

The data that displays in the *Sort by* option box will vary depending on what is selected. Generally, the data that displays is the title of the first column of selected cells. If the selected cells do not have a title, the data may display as *Column A*. Use this option to specify what column is to be sorted. Using the Sort dialog box to sort data in a column maintains the relationship among the data.

Activity 3b **Sorting Data Using the Sort Dialog Box** Part 2 of 4

1. With **4-APTBilling** open, sort the rates in the range E4:E29 in descending order and maintain the relationship to the other data by completing the following steps:
   a. Select the range A3:F29.
   b. Click the Sort & Filter button and then click *Custom Sort*.
   c. At the Sort dialog box, click the *Sort by* option box arrow and then click *Rate* at the drop-down list.
   d. Click the *Order* option box arrow and then click *Largest to Smallest* at the drop-down list.

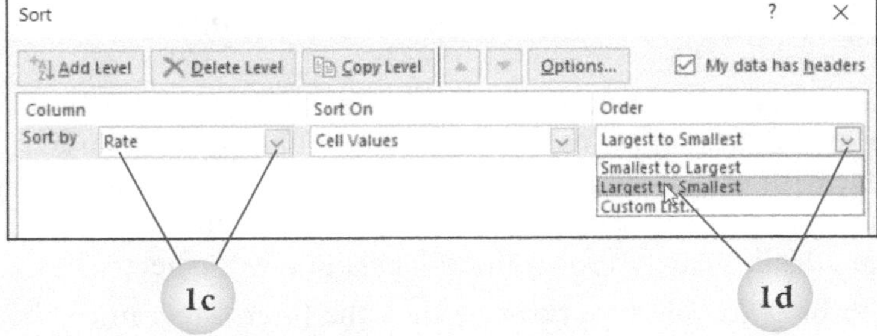

   e. Click OK to close the Sort dialog box.
   f. Deselect the cells.
2. Sort the dates in ascending order (oldest to newest) by completing steps similar to those in Step 1.
3. Save and then print **4-APTBilling**.

Sorting More Than One Column

When sorting data in cells, data in more than one column can be sorted. For example, in Activity 3c, you will sort the dates from oldest to newest and the client numbers from lowest to highest. In this sort, the dates are sorted first and then the client numbers are sorted in ascending order within the same date.

To sort data in more than one column, select all the columns in the worksheet that need to remain relative and then display the Sort dialog box. At the Sort dialog box, specify the first column to be sorted in the *Sort by* option box, click the *Add Level* button, and then specify the second column in the first *Then by* option box. To sort multiple columns, add additional *Then by* option boxes by clicking the *Add Level* button.

Activity 3c **Sorting Data in Two Columns** Part 3 of 4

1. With **4-APTBilling** open, select the range A3:F29.
2. Click the Sort & Filter button and then click *Custom Sort*.
3. At the Sort dialog box, click the *Sort by* option box arrow and then click *Date* at the drop-down list. (Skip this step if *Date* already displays in the *Sort by* option box.)
4. Make sure *Oldest to Newest* displays in the *Order* option box.
5. Click the Add Level button.
6. Click the *Then by* option box arrow and then click *Client #* at the drop-down list.
7. Click OK to close the dialog box.
8. Deselect the cells.
9. Save and then print **4-APTBilling**.

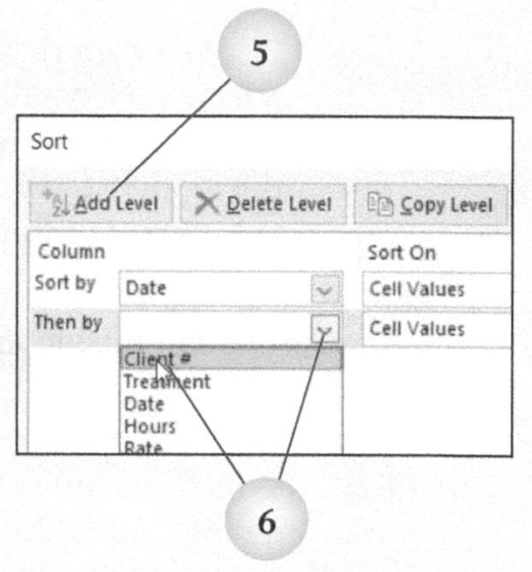

Filtering Data

Quick Steps

Filter List
1. Select cells.
2. Click Sort & Filter button.
3. Click *Filter* at drop-down list.
4. Click filter arrow in heading to filter.
5. Click option at drop-down list.

Filtering Data

A restriction called a *filter* can be placed temporarily on data in a worksheet to isolate specific data. To turn on filtering, make a cell containing data active, click the Sort & Filter button in the Editing group on the Home tab, and then click *Filter* at the drop-down list. This turns on filtering and causes a filter arrow to appear with each column label in the worksheet, as shown in Figure 4.12. Data does not need to be selected before turning on filtering because Excel automatically searches for column labels in a worksheet.

To filter data in a worksheet, click the filter arrow in the heading to be filtered. This causes a drop-down list to display with options to filter all the records, create a custom filter, or select an entry that appears in one or more of the cells in the column. When data is filtered, the filter arrow changes to a funnel icon. The funnel icon indicates that rows in the worksheet have been filtered. To turn off filtering, click the Sort & Filter button and then click *Filter*.

If a column contains numbers, click the filter arrow and point to *Number Filters* and a side menu displays with options for filtering numbers. For example, numbers can be filtered that are equal to, greater than, or less than a specified number; the top 10 numbers can be filtered; and numbers can be filtered that are above or below a specified number.

Figure 4.12 Filtering Data

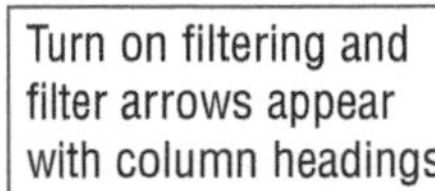

Turn on filtering and filter arrows appear with column headings.

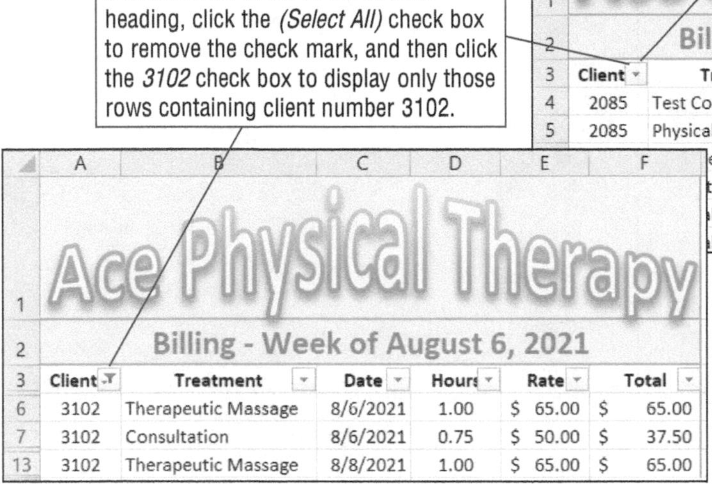

Activity 3d **Filtering Data**

Part 4 of 4

1. With **4-APTBilling** open, click in cell A4.
2. Turn on filtering by clicking the Sort & Filter button in the Editing group on the Home tab and then clicking *Filter* at the drop-down list.
3. Filter rows for client number 3102 by completing the following steps:
   a. Click the filter arrow in the *Client #* heading.
   b. Click the *(Select All)* check box to remove the check mark. (This also removes the check marks for all the items in the list.)
   c. Scroll down the list box and then click *3102* to insert a check mark in the check box.
   d. Click OK.
4. Redisplay all the rows containing data by completing the following steps:
   a. Click the funnel icon in the *Client #* heading.
   b. Click the *(Select All)* check box to insert a check mark. (This also inserts check marks for all the items in the list.)
   c. Click OK.

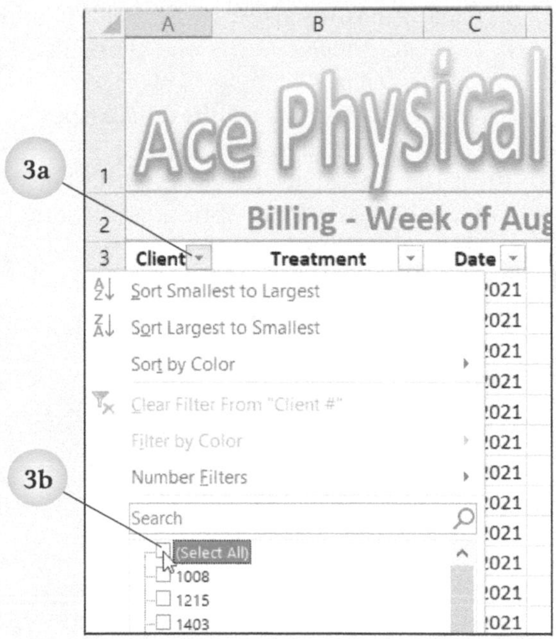

5. Filter a list of clients who receive physical therapy by completing the following steps:
   a. Click the filter arrow in the *Treatment* heading.
   b. Click the *(Select All)* check box to remove the check mark.
   c. Click the *Physical Therapy* check box to insert a check mark.
   d. Click OK.
6. Redisplay all the rows containing data by completing the following steps:
   a. Click the funnel icon in the *Treatment* heading.
   b. Click the *Clear Filter From "Treatment"* option.
7. Display the two highest rates by completing the following steps:
   a. Click the filter arrow in the *Rate* heading.
   b. Point to *Number Filters* and then click *Top 10* at the side menu.
   c. At the Top 10 AutoFilter dialog box, select the *10* in the middle measurement box and then type 2.
   d. Click OK to close the dialog box.

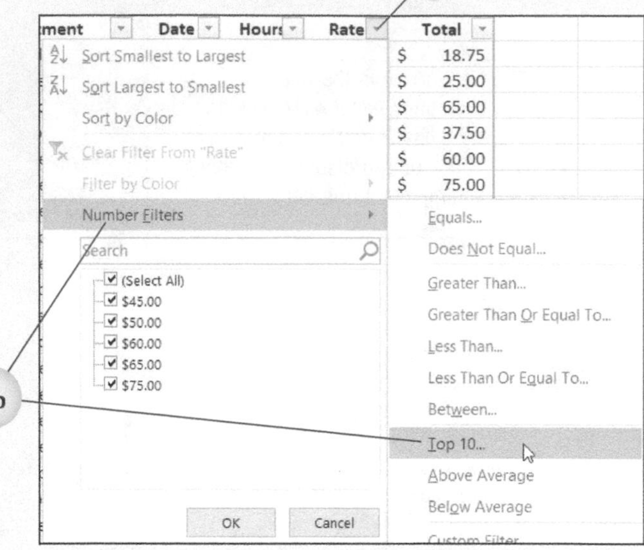

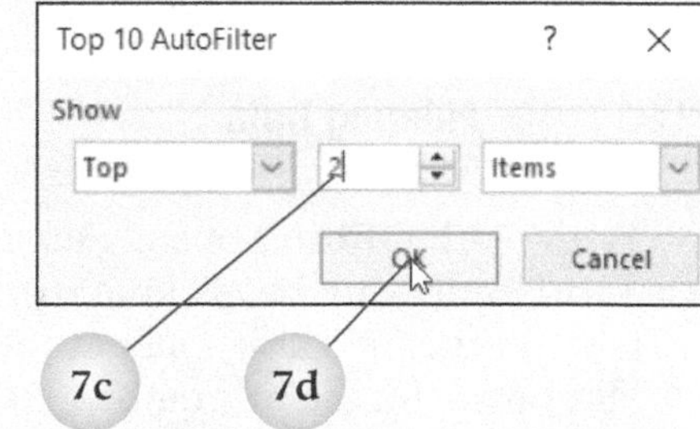

8. Redisplay all the rows that contain data by completing the following steps:
   a. Click the funnel icon in the *Rate* heading.
   b. Click the *Clear Filter From "Rate"* option.
9. Display totals greater than $60 by completing the following steps:
   a. Click the filter arrow in the *Total* heading.
   b. Point to *Number Filters* and then click *Greater Than*.
   c. At the Custom AutoFilter dialog box, type 60 and then click OK.

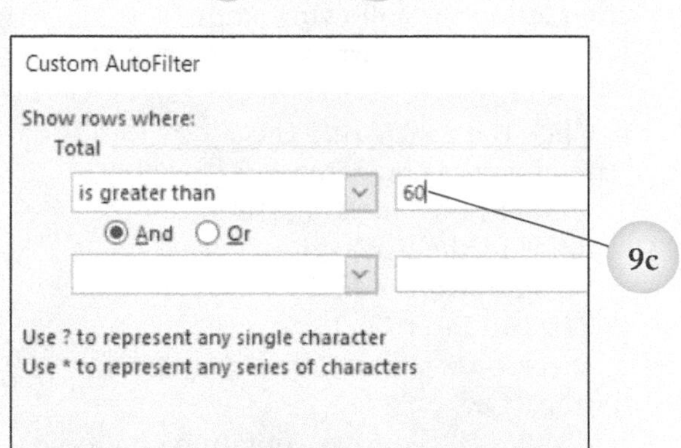

10. Print the worksheet by clicking the File tab, clicking the *Print* option, and then clicking the Print button.
11. Turn off the filtering feature by clicking the Sort & Filter button and then clicking *Filter* at the drop-down list.
12. Save and then close **4-APTBilling**.

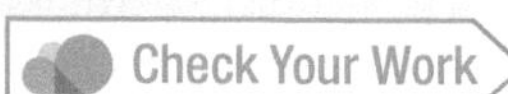

Chapter Summary

- The Page Setup group on the Page Layout tab contains buttons for changing the margins and page orientation and size, as well as buttons for establishing the print area, inserting a page break, applying a picture background, and printing titles.
- The default left and right margins are 0.7 inch and the default top and bottom margins are 0.75 inch. Change these default margins with the Margins button in the Page Setup group on the Page Layout tab.
- Display the Page Setup dialog box with the Margins tab selected by clicking the Margins button in the Page Setup group on the Page Layout tab and then clicking *Custom Margins* at the drop-down list.
- Center a worksheet on the page with the *Horizontally* and *Vertically* check boxes at the Page Setup dialog box with the Margins tab selected.
- Click the Orientation button in the Page Setup group on the Page Layout tab to display the two orientation choices: *Portrait* and *Landscape*.
- Insert a page break by selecting the column or row, clicking the Breaks button in the Page Setup group on the Page Layout tab, and then clicking *Insert Page Break* at the drop-down list.
- To insert both horizontal and vertical page breaks at the same time, make a cell active, click the Breaks button, and then click *Insert Page Break* at the drop-down list.
- Preview the page breaks in a worksheet by clicking the Page Break Preview button in the view area on the Status bar or clicking the View tab and then clicking the Page Break Preview button in the Workbook Views group.
- Use options at the Page Setup dialog box with the Sheet tab selected to specify printing column and/or row titles on each page. Display this dialog box by clicking the Print Titles button in the Page Setup group on the Page Layout tab.
- Use buttons in the Scale to Fit group on the Page Layout tab to scale data to fit on a specific number of pages.
- Use the Background button in the Page Setup group on the Page Layout tab to insert a worksheet background picture. A background picture displays on the screen but does not print.
- Use options in the Sheet Options group on the Page Layout tab to specify whether to view and/or print gridlines and headings.
- Specify the print area by selecting cells, clicking the Print Area button in the Page Setup group on the Page Layout tab, and then clicking *Set Print Area* at the drop-down list. Add another print area by selecting the cells, clicking the Print Area button, and then clicking *Add to Print Area* at the drop-down list.
- Create a header and/or footer with the Header & Footer button in the Text group on the Insert tab, in Page Layout view, or with options at the Page Setup dialog box with the Header/Footer tab selected.
- Customize odd and even page headers and footers at the Page Setup dialog box with the Header/Footer tab selected.
- Customize a print job with options at the Print backstage area.
- To check spelling in a worksheet, click the Review tab and then click the Spelling button.

- Click the Undo button on the Quick Access Toolbar to reverse the most recent action and click the Redo button to redo a previously reversed action.
- Use options at the Find and Replace dialog box with the Find tab selected to find specific data and/or formatting in a worksheet.
- Use options at the Find and Replace dialog box with the Replace tab selected to find specific data and/or formatting and replace it with other data and/or formatting.
- Sort data in a worksheet with options at the Sort & Filter button in the Editing group on the Home tab.
- Create a custom sort with options at the Sort dialog box. Display this dialog box by clicking the Sort & Filter button and then clicking *Custom Sort* at the drop-down list.
- Temporarily isolate data by filtering it. Turn on the filter feature by clicking the Sort & Filter button in the Editing group on the Home tab and then clicking *Filter* at the drop-down list. This inserts a filter arrow with each column label. Click a filter arrow and then use options at the drop-down list to specify the filter data.

Commands Review

FEATURE	RIBBON TAB, GROUP	BUTTON, OPTION	KEYBOARD SHORTCUT
background picture	Page Layout, Page Setup		
filter data	Home, Editing		
Find and Replace dialog box with Find tab selected	Home, Editing	, *Find*	Ctrl + F
Find and Replace dialog box with Replace tab selected	Home, Editing	, *Replace*	Ctrl + H
header and footer	Insert, Text		
insert page break	Page Layout, Page Setup	, *Insert Page Break*	
margins	Page Layout, Page Setup		
orientation	Page Layout, Page Setup		
Page Layout view	View, Workbook Views		
Page Setup dialog box with Margins tab selected	Page Layout, Page Setup	, *Custom Margins*	
Page Setup dialog box with Sheet tab selected	Page Layout, Page Setup		
preview page break	View, Workbook Views		
print area	Page Layout, Page Setup		
redo an action			Ctrl + Y
remove page break	Page Layout, Page Setup	, *Remove Page Break*	

FEATURE	RIBBON TAB, GROUP	BUTTON, OPTION	KEYBOARD SHORTCUT
scale height	Page Layout, Scale to Fit		
scale to fit	Page Layout, Scale to Fit		
scale width	Page Layout, Scale to Fit		
size	Page Layout, Page Setup		
sort data	Home, Editing		
spelling check	Review, Proofing		F7
undo an action			Ctrl + Z

Microsoft®

Excel® Level 1

Unit 2

Enhancing the Display of Workbooks

Microsoft®

Excel®

CHAPTER

5

Moving Data within and between Workbooks

Performance Objectives

Upon successful completion of Chapter 5, you will be able to:

1 Insert and delete worksheets
2 Move, copy, and paste cells within and between worksheets
3 Move, rename, and format sheet tabs
4 Hide and unhide worksheets
5 Print a workbook containing multiple worksheets
6 Change the zoom
7 Split a worksheet into windows and freeze/unfreeze panes
8 Name a range of cells and use a range in a formula
9 Open multiple workbooks
10 Arrange, size, hide/unhide, and move workbooks
11 Move, copy, and paste data between workbooks
12 Link data between worksheets
13 Copy and paste data between programs

Up to this point, the workbooks you have worked in have consisted of single worksheets. In this chapter, you will learn to create a workbook with several worksheets and complete tasks such as copying and pasting data within and between worksheets. Moving and pasting or copying and pasting selected cells within and between worksheets is useful for rearranging data and saving time. You will also work with multiple workbooks and complete tasks such as arranging, sizing, and moving workbooks and opening and closing multiple workbooks.

The online course includes additional training and assessment resources.

Before beginning chapter work, copy the EL1C5 folder to your storage medium and then make EL1C5 the active folder.

Activity 1 Manage Data in a Multiple-Worksheet Account Workbook **7 Parts**

You will open an account workbook containing multiple worksheets and then insert and delete worksheets and move, copy, and paste data between worksheets. You will rename and apply color to sheet tabs, hide and unhide a worksheet, and format and print multiple worksheets in the workbook.

Creating a Workbook with Multiple Worksheets

Hint Creating multiple worksheets within a workbook is helpful for saving related data.

An Excel workbook contains one worksheet by default, but additional worksheets can be added. Add additional worksheets to a workbook to store related data, such as a worksheet for expenses for individual salespeople in the company and another worksheet for the monthly payroll for all the departments within the company. Another example is to record sales statistics for each quarter in individual worksheets within a workbook.

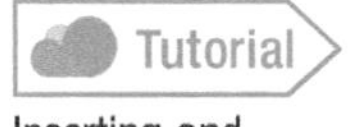

Inserting and Renaming Worksheets

Quick Steps

Insert Worksheet
Click New sheet button.
OR
Press Shift + F11.

Delete Worksheet
1. Click sheet tab.
2. Click Delete button arrow.
3. Click *Delete Sheet*.
4. Click Delete button.

Inserting a New Worksheet

Insert a new worksheet in a workbook by clicking the New sheet button to the right of the Sheet1 tab at the bottom of the worksheet area. A new worksheet can also be inserted in a workbook with the keyboard shortcut Shift + F11. A new sheet tab is inserted to the right of the active tab. To move between worksheets, click the desired tab. The active sheet tab displays with a white background and the worksheet name displays in green. Any inactive tabs display with a light-gray background and gray text.

Deleting a Worksheet

If a worksheet is no longer needed in a workbook, delete it by clicking the sheet tab, clicking the Delete button arrow in the Cells group on the Home tab, and then clicking *Delete Sheet* at the drop-down list. Another method for deleting a worksheet is to right-click the sheet tab and then click *Delete* at the shortcut menu. When deleting a worksheet, Excel displays a deletion confirmation message. At this message, click the Delete button.

Selecting Multiple Worksheets

To work with more than one worksheet at a time, select the worksheets. With multiple worksheets selected, the same formatting can be applied to cells or the selected worksheets can be deleted. To select adjacent sheet tabs, click the first tab, press and hold down the Shift key, click the last tab, and then release the Shift key. To select nonadjacent sheet tabs, click the first tab, press and hold down the Ctrl key, click any other tabs to be selected, and then release the Ctrl key.

Copying and Pasting Cells between Worksheets

Copy

Cut

Paste

Copy and Paste Cells
1. Select cells.
2. Click Copy button.
3. Click cell.
4. Click Paste button.

Hint Ctrl + C is the keyboard shortcut to copy selected data.

Copying, Cutting, and Pasting Cells

Cells in a workbook may need to be copied or moved to different locations within a worksheet or to another worksheet in the workbook. Move or copy cells in a worksheet or between worksheets or workbooks by selecting the cells and then using the Cut, Copy, and/or Paste buttons in the Clipboard group on the Home tab.

Copying and Pasting Selected Cells

Copying selected cells can be useful in worksheets that contain repetitive data. To copy cells, select the cells and then click the Copy button in the Clipboard group on the Home tab. This causes a moving dashed line border (called a *marquee*) to appear around the selected cells. To copy cells to another worksheet, click the sheet tab, click in the cell where the first selected cell is to be pasted, and then click the Paste button in the Clipboard group. Remove the moving marquee from selected cells by pressing the Esc key or double-clicking in any cell.

Selected cells in the same worksheet can be copied using the mouse and the Ctrl key. To do this, select the cells to be copied and then position the mouse pointer on any border around the selected cells until the pointer appears with a four-headed arrow attached. Press and hold down the Ctrl key, click and hold down the left mouse button, drag the outline of the selected cells to the new location, release the left mouse button, and then release the Ctrl key.

Activity 1a Inserting, Deleting, Selecting, Copying, Pasting, and Formatting Worksheets

Part 1 of 7

1. Open **RPFacAccts** and then save it with the name **5-RPFacAccts**.
2. Insert a new worksheet in the workbook by completing the following steps:
   a. Click the 2ndHalfSales sheet tab to make it active.
   b. Click the New sheet button to the right of the 2ndHalfSales sheet tab. (This inserts a new worksheet to the right of the 2ndHalfSales worksheet with the name Sheet4.)

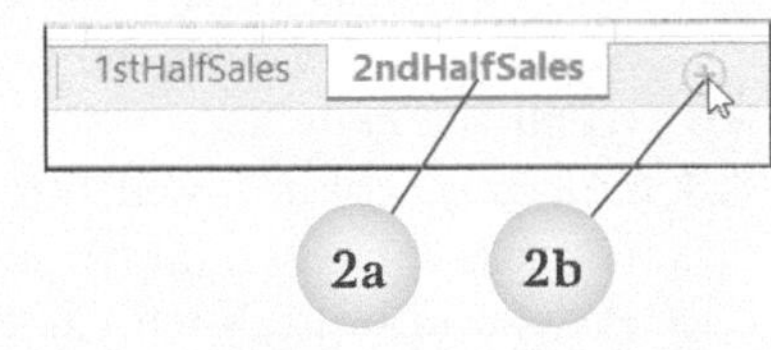

3. Delete two sheet tabs by completing the following steps:
   a. Click the 1stHalfSales sheet tab.
   b. Press and hold down the Shift key, click the 2ndHalfSales sheet tab, and then release the Shift key. (These tabs must be adjacent. If they are not, press and hold down the Ctrl key when clicking the 2ndHalfSales sheet tab.)
   c. With the two sheet tabs selected, click the Delete button arrow in the Cells group on the Home tab and then click *Delete Sheet* at the drop-down list.
   d. At the message stating that Microsoft will permanently delete the sheets, click the Delete button.

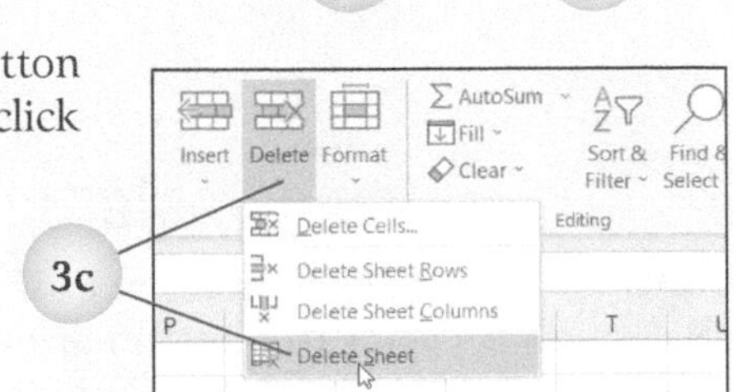

4. Copy cells from Sheet1 to Sheet4 by completing the following steps:
   a. Click the Sheet1 tab to make it the active worksheet.
   b. Select the range A1:A3 (the first three rows of data).
   c. Click the Copy button.
   d. Click the Sheet4 tab to make it the active tab.
   e. With A1 the active cell, click the Paste button.
5. Make the following changes to the new worksheet:
   a. Click in cell A3 and then type First Quarter Summary 2021.
   b. Change the width of column A to 20.00 characters.
   c. Change the width of columns B, C, and D to 12.00 characters.
   d. Type the following text in the specified cells:
      B4 January
      C4 February
      D4 March
      A5 Checks amount
      A6 Deposit amount
      A7 End-of-month balance
   e. Select the range B4:D4, click the Bold button and then click the Center button.
   f. Select the range B5:D7 and then apply the Comma format (using the Comma Style button in the Number group on the Home tab) with two digits after the decimal point.
6. Apply formatting to the cells in all four worksheets by completing the following steps:
   a. Click the Sheet1 tab to make it active and then click in cell A1 to make it the active cell.
   b. Press and hold down the Shift key, click the Sheet4 tab, and then release the Shift key. (This selects all four worksheets.)
   c. With cell A1 active, change the row height to 51.00 points.
   d. Click in cell A3.
   e. Change the font size to 14 points.
   f. Click each remaining sheet tab (Sheet2, Sheet3, and Sheet4) and notice the formatting changes applied to all the cells.
7. Change the column width for the three worksheets by completing the following steps:
   a. Click the Sheet1 tab to make it active.
   b. Press and hold down the Shift key, click the Sheet3 tab, and then release the Shift key.
   c. Select columns E, F, and G and then change the column width to 10.00 characters.
   d. Click the Sheet2 tab and then click the Sheet3 tab. Notice that the width of columns E, F, and G has changed to 10.00 characters. Click the Sheet4 tab and notice that the column width did not change.
8. Save **5-RPFacAccts**.

Using Paste Options

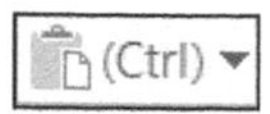

Paste Options

Using Paste Options

When pasting cells in a worksheet, specify how the cells are pasted by clicking the Paste button arrow and then clicking a paste option button at the drop-down list. Click the Paste button (not the button arrow) and a Paste Options button displays in the lower right corner of the pasted cell(s). Display a list of paste options by clicking the button or pressing the Ctrl key. This causes a drop-down list to display, as shown in Figure 5.1. The same option buttons display when the

Figure 5.1 Paste Options Buttons

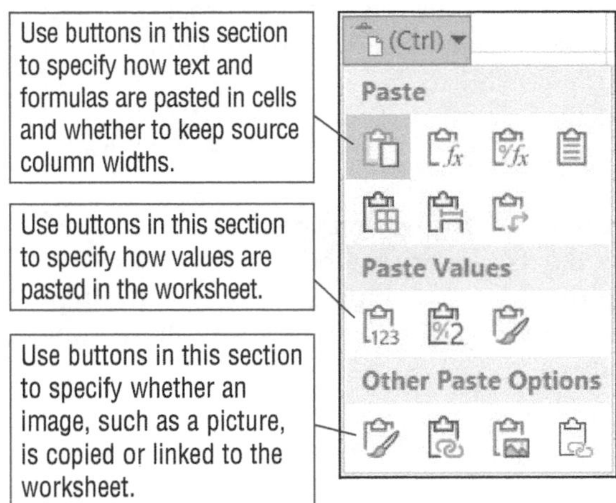
Use buttons in this section to specify how text and formulas are pasted in cells and whether to keep source column widths.
Use buttons in this section to specify how values are pasted in the worksheet.
Use buttons in this section to specify whether an image, such as a picture, is copied or linked to the worksheet.
(Ctrl)
Paste
Paste Values
Other Paste Options

Paste button arrow is clicked. Hover the mouse pointer over a button in the drop-down list and the descriptive name of the button displays along with the keyboard shortcut. Use buttons in this drop-down list to specify what is pasted.

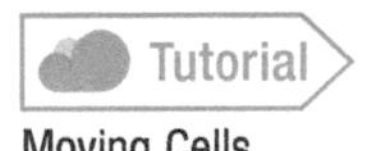
Tutorial

Moving Cells

Quick Steps

Move and Paste Cells

1. Select cells.
2. Click Cut button.
3. Click cell.
4. Click Paste button.

Hint Ctrl + X is the keyboard shortcut to cut selected data. Ctrl + V is the keyboard shortcut to paste data.

Moving Selected Cells

Selected cells and cell contents can be moved within and between worksheets. Move selected cells using the Cut and Paste buttons in the Clipboard group on the Home tab or by dragging with the mouse.

To move selected cells with buttons on the Home tab, select the cells and then click the Cut button in the Clipboard group. Click in the cell where the first selected cell is to be inserted and then click the Paste button in the Clipboard group.

To move selected cells with the mouse, select the cells and then position the mouse pointer on any border of the selected cells until the pointer appears with a four-headed arrow attached. Click and hold down the left mouse button, drag the outline of the selected cells to the new location, and then release the mouse button.

Activity 1b **Copying and Moving Cells and Pasting Cells Using Paste Options** Part 2 of 7

1. With **5-RPFacAccts** open, copy cells from Sheet2 to Sheet3 using the Paste Options button by completing the following steps:
   a. Click the Sheet2 tab to make it active.
   b. Select the range C7:E9.
   c. Click the Copy button.
   d. Click the Sheet3 tab.
   e. Click in cell C7.
   f. Click the Paste button.

g. Click the Paste Options button in the lower right corner of the pasted cells and then click the Keep Source Column Widths button at the drop-down list.
h. Make Sheet2 active and then press the Esc key to remove the moving marquee.

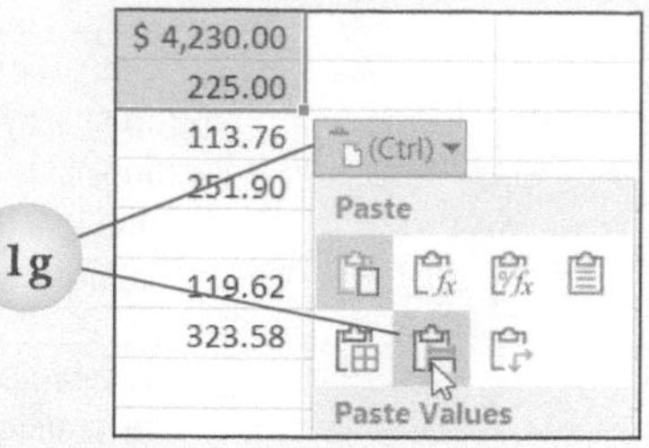

2. Click the Sheet1 tab.
3. You realize that the sublet rent deposit was recorded on the wrong day. The correct day is January 9. To move the cells containing information on the deposit, complete the following steps:
   a. Click in cell A13 and then insert a row. (The new row should appear above the row containing *Rainier Suppliers*.)
   b. Select the range A7:F7.
   c. Click the Cut button.
   d. Click in cell A13.
   e. Click the Paste button.
   f. Change the date of the deposit from January 1 to January 9.
   g. Select row 7 and then delete it.
4. Move cells using the mouse by completing the following steps: 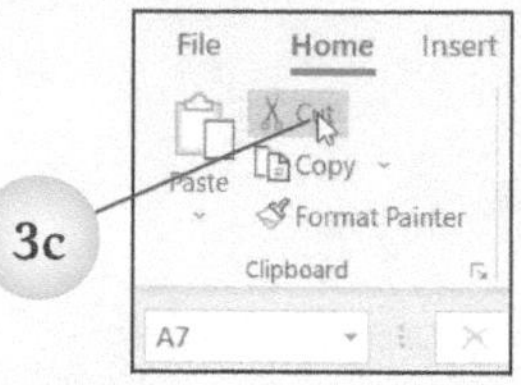
   a. Click the Sheet2 tab.
   b. Click in cell A13 and then insert a new row.
   c. Using the mouse, select the range A7:F7.
   d. Position the mouse pointer on any boundary of the selected cells until it apppears with a four-headed arrow attached. Click and hold down the left mouse button, drag the outline of the selected cells to row 13, and then release the mouse button.
   e. Change the date of the deposit to February 13. 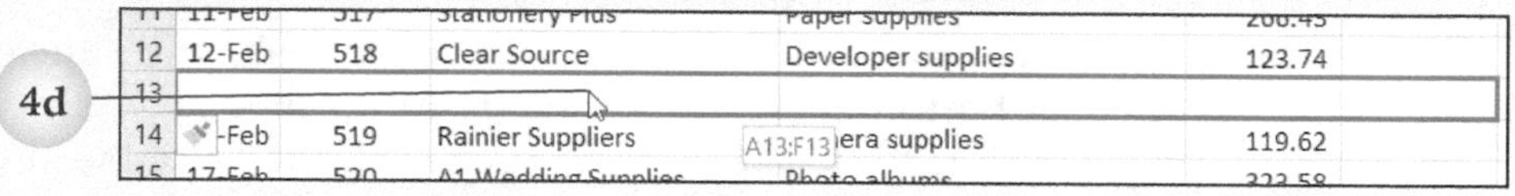
   f. Delete row 7.
5. Save **5-RPFacAccts**.

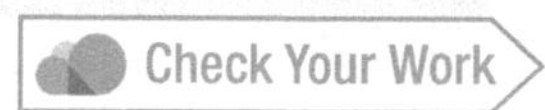

Copying and Pasting Using the Clipboard Task Pane

Quick Steps

Copy and Paste Multiple Items
1. Click Clipboard group task pane launcher.
2. Select cells.
3. Click Copy button.
4. Repeat Steps 2 and 3 as desired.
5. Make cell active.
6. Click item in Clipboard task pane to be inserted in worksheet.
7. Repeat Step 6 as desired.

Use the Clipboard task pane to copy and paste multiple items. To use the task pane, click the Clipboard group task pane launcher in the lower right corner of the Clipboard group on the Home tab. The Clipboard task pane displays at the left side of the screen similarly to what is shown in Figure 5.2.

Select data or an object to be copied and then click the Copy button in the Clipboard group. Continue selecting cells, text, or other items and clicking the Copy button. To paste an item into a worksheet, make the desired cell active and then click the item in the Clipboard task pane. If the copied item is text, the first 50 characters appear in the task pane. To paste all the selected items into a single location, make the desired cell active and then click the Paste All button in the task pane. When all the items have been pasted into the worksheet, click the Clear All button to remove any remaining items from the task pane.

Figure 5.2 Clipboard Task Pane

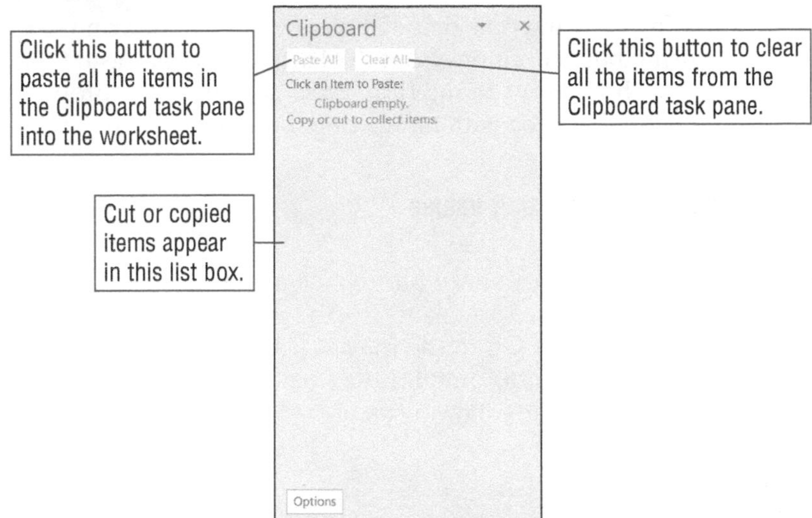

Activity 1c Copying and Pasting Cells Using the Clipboard Task Pane

Part 3 of 7

1. With **5-RPFacAccts** open, select cells for copying by completing the following steps:
   a. Display the Clipboard task pane by clicking the Clipboard group task pane launcher. (If the Clipboard task pane contains any copied data, click the Clear All button.)
   b. Click the Sheet1 tab.
   c. Select the range C15:E16.
   d. Click the Copy button.
   e. Select the range C19:E19.
   f. Click the Copy button.

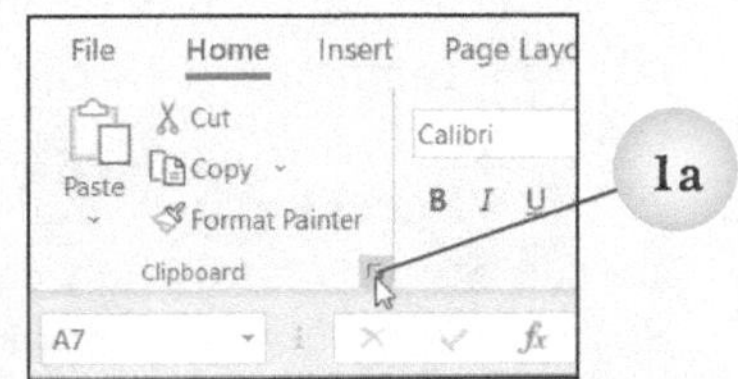

2. Paste the copied cells by completing the following steps:
   a. Click the Sheet2 tab.
   b. Click in cell C15.
   c. Click the item in the Clipboard task pane representing *General Systems Developer*.
   d. Click the Sheet3 tab.
   e. Click in cell C15.
   f. Click the item in the Clipboard task pane representing *General Systems Developer*.
   g. Click in cell C19.
   h. Click the item in the Clipboard task pane representing *Parkland City Services*.

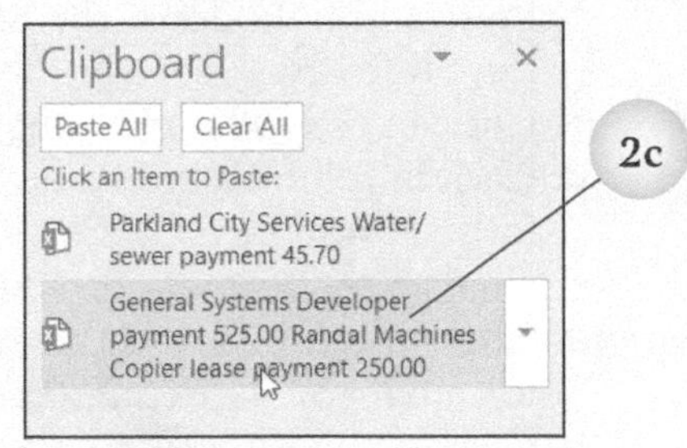

3. Click the Clear All button at the top of the Clipboard task pane.
4. Close the Clipboard task pane by clicking the Close button (contains an *X*) in the upper right corner of the task pane.
5. Save **5-RPFacAccts**.

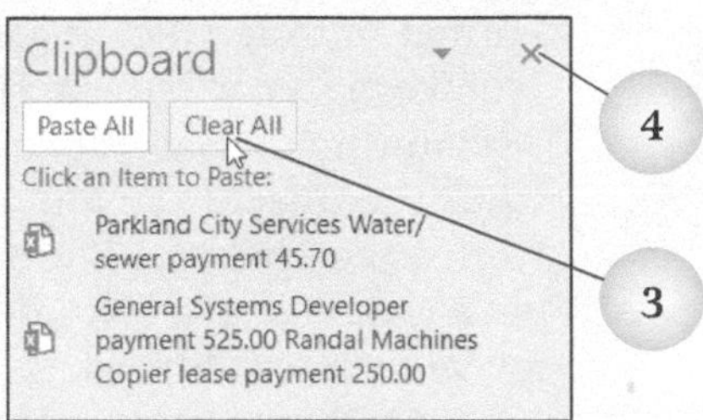

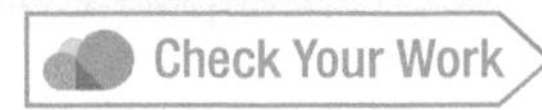

Pasting Values Only

When pasting cells that contain a value and a formula, specify what is to be pasted using button options from the Paste button or Paste Options button drop-down list. Use the buttons in the *Paste Values* section of the drop-down list to insert only the value, the value with numbering formatting, or the value with source formatting.

Activity 1d **Copying and Pasting Values** — Part 4 of 7

1. With **5-RPFacAccts** open, make Sheet1 the active tab.
2. Click in cell G6, type the formula =(f6-e6)+g5, and then press the Enter key.
3. Copy the formula in cell G6 to the range G7:G20.
4. Copy as a value (and not a formula) the final balance from Sheet1 to Sheet2 by completing the following steps:
   a. Click in cell G20.
   b. Click the Copy button.
   c. Click the Sheet2 tab.
   d. Click in cell G5 and then click the Paste button arrow.
   e. At the drop-down list, click the Values button in the *Paste Values* section of the drop-down list. (This inserts the value and not the formula.)

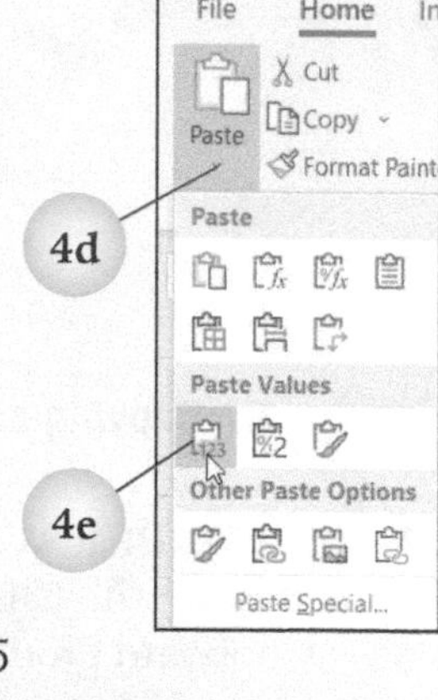

5. Click in cell G6, insert a formula that determines the balance (see Step 2), and then copy the formula to the range G7:G20.
6. Copy the amount in cell G20 and then paste the value only in cell G5 in Sheet3.
7. With Sheet3 active, make cell G6 active, insert a formula that determines the balance (see Step 2), and then copy the formula to the range G7:G20.
8. Insert formulas and apply formatting to cells in the three worksheets by completing the following steps:
   a. Click the Sheet1 tab.
   b. Press and hold down the Shift key, click the Sheet3 tab, and then release the Shift key.
   c. Click in cell D21, click the Bold button and then type Total.
   d. Click in cell E21 and then click the AutoSum button. (This inserts the formula =*SUM(E13:E20)*.)
   e. Change the formula to =*SUM(E7:E20)* and then press the Enter key.
   f. Click in cell F21 and then click the AutoSum button. (This inserts the formula =*SUM(F12:F20)*.)
   g. Change the formula to =*SUM(F6:F20)* and then press the Enter key.
   h. Select cells E21 and F21 and then click the Accounting Number Format button. Click in cell G5 and then click the Accounting Number Format button. (Cell G5 in Sheet1 already contains the Accounting format but cells G5 in Sheet2 and Sheet3 do not.)
   i. Click the Sheet2 tab and notice the text and formulas inserted in the worksheet, click the Sheet3 tab and notice the text and formulas, and then click the Sheet4 tab (to deselect the tabs).
9. Copy values from Sheet1 to Sheet4 by completing the following steps:
   a. Click the Sheet1 tab.
   b. Click in cell E21 and then click the Copy button.
   c. Click the Sheet4 tab.

d. Click in cell B5 and then click the Paste button.
e. Click the Paste Options button and then click the Values button in the *Paste Values* section of the drop-down list.
f. Click the Sheet1 tab.
g. Click in cell F21 and then click the Copy button.
h. Click the Sheet4 tab.
i. Click in cell B6, click the Paste button arrow, and then click the Values button at the drop-down list.
j. Click the Sheet1 tab.
k. Click in cell G20 and then click the Copy button.
l. Click the Sheet4 tab.
m. Click in cell B7, click the Paste button arrow, and then click the Values button at the drop-down list.

10. Complete steps similar to those in Step 9 to insert amounts and balances for February (from Sheet2) and March (from Sheet3).
11. Select the range B5:D5 and then click the Accounting Number Format button.
12. Save **5-RPFacAccts**.

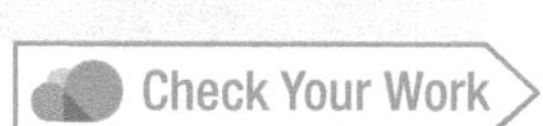

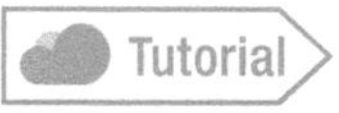

Moving, Copying, and Deleting a Worksheet

Quick Steps

Move or Copy Worksheet

1. Right-click sheet tab.
2. Click *Move or Copy*.
3. At Move or Copy dialog box, click worksheet name in *Before sheet* list box.
4. Click OK.

OR

Drag sheet tab to new position. (To copy, press and hold down Ctrl key while dragging.)

Managing Worksheets

Right-click a sheet tab and a shortcut menu displays with options for managing worksheets, as shown in Figure 5.3. For example, remove a worksheet by clicking the *Delete* option. Move or copy a worksheet by clicking the *Move or Copy* option. Clicking this option causes a Move or Copy dialog box to display with options for specifying where to move or copy the selected sheet. By default, Excel names worksheets in a workbook *Sheet1, Sheet2, Sheet3,* and so on. To rename a worksheet, click the *Rename* option (which selects the default sheet name) and then type the new name.

In addition to the shortcut menu options, the mouse can be used to move or copy worksheets. To move a worksheet, position the mouse pointer on the sheet tab, click and hold down the left mouse button (a page icon displays next to the mouse pointer), drag the page icon to the new position, and then release the mouse button. For example, to move the Sheet2 tab after the Sheet3 tab, position the mouse pointer on the Sheet2 tab, click and hold down the left mouse button, drag the page icon after the Sheet3 tab, and then release the mouse button. To copy a worksheet, press and hold down the Ctrl key and then drag the sheet tab.

Figure 5.3 Sheet Tab Shortcut Menu

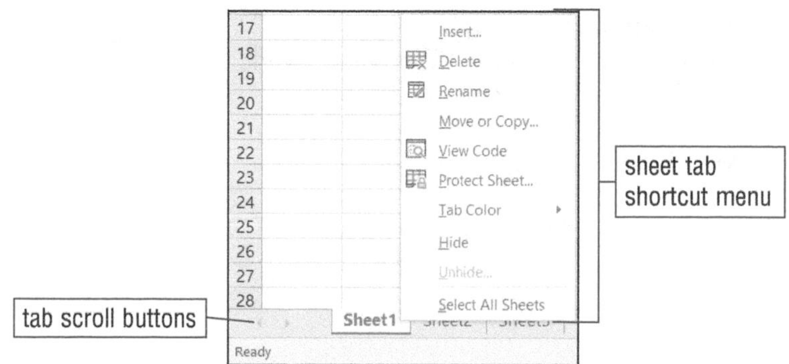

Quick Steps

Apply Color to Sheet Tab

1. Right-click sheet tab.
2. Point to *Tab Color*.
3. Click color at color palette.

Use the *Tab Color* option at the shortcut menu to apply a color to a sheet tab. Right-click a sheet tab, point to *Tab Color* at the shortcut menu, and then click a color at the color palette.

Activity 1e Selecting, Moving, Renaming, and Changing the Color of Sheet Tabs

Part 5 of 7

1. With **5-RPFacAccts** open, move Sheet4 by completing the following steps:
   a. Right-click the Sheet4 tab and then click *Move or Copy* at the shortcut menu.
   b. At the Move or Copy dialog box, make sure *Sheet1* is selected in the *Before sheet* list box and then click OK.

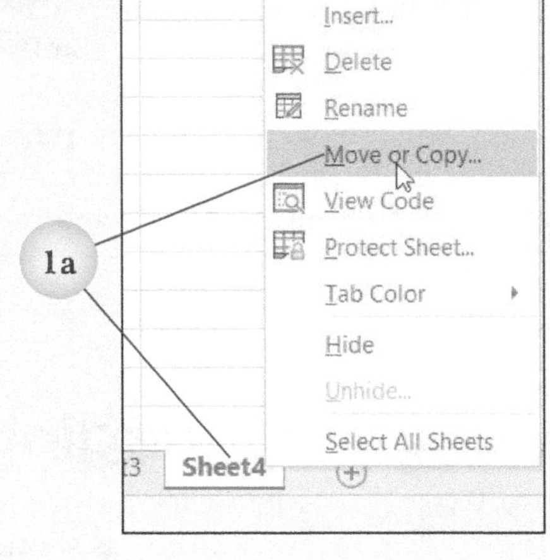

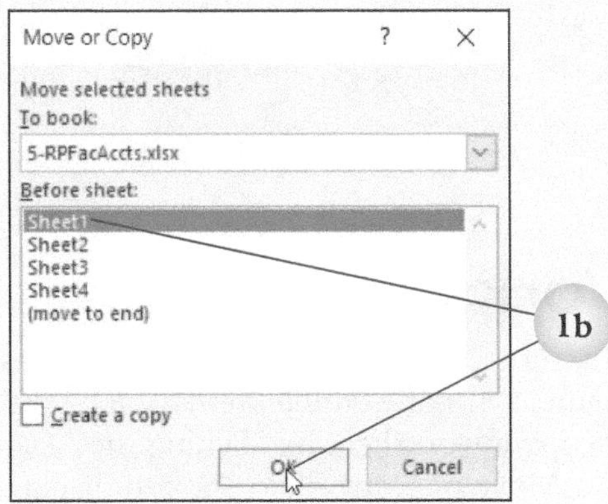

2. Rename Sheet4 by completing the following steps:
   a. Right-click the Sheet4 tab and then click *Rename*.
   b. Type Summary and then press the Enter key.
3. Complete steps similar to those in Step 2 to rename Sheet1 to *January*, Sheet2 to *February*, and Sheet3 to *March*.

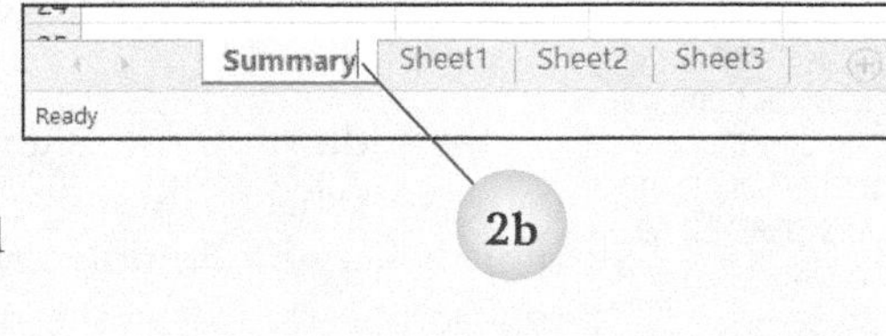

4. Change the color of the Summary sheet tab by completing the following steps:
   a. Right-click the Summary sheet tab.
   b. Point to *Tab Color* at the shortcut menu.
   c. Click the *Red* color option (second option in the *Standard Colors* section).
5. Follow steps similar to those in Step 4 to change the January sheet tab to Blue (eighth option in the *Standard Colors* section), the February sheet tab to Purple (last option in the *Standard Colors* section), and the March sheet tab to Green (sixth option in the *Standard Colors* section).
6. Save **5-RPFacAccts**.

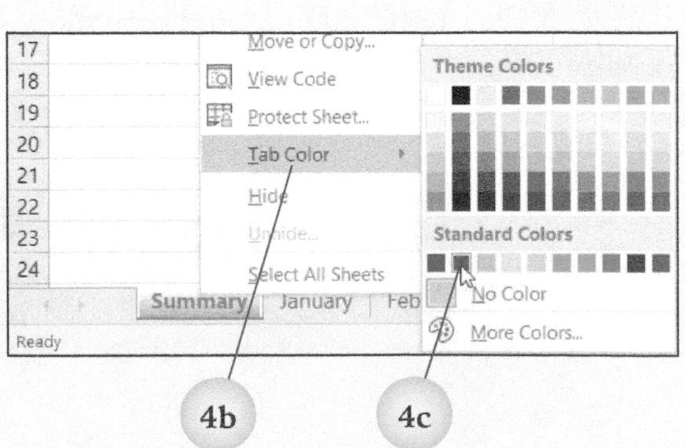

Hiding and Unhiding a Worksheet

Format

Quick Steps

Hide Worksheet

1. Click Format button.
2. Point to *Hide & Unhide*.
3. Click *Hide Sheet*.

OR

1. Right-click sheet tab.
2. Click *Hide* at shortcut menu.

Unhide Worksheet

1. Click Format button.
2. Point to *Hide & Unhide*.
3. Click *Unhide Sheet*.
4. Double-click hidden worksheet in Unhide dialog box.

OR

1. Right-click sheet tab.
2. Click *Unhide* at shortcut menu.
3. Double-click hidden worksheet in Unhide dialog box.

Hiding and Unhiding a Worksheet in a Workbook

In a workbook with multiple worksheets, a worksheet can be hidden that contains data that should not appear or print with the workbook. To hide a worksheet in a workbook, click the Format button in the Cells group on the Home tab, point to *Hide & Unhide*, and then click *Hide Sheet*. A worksheet can also be hidden by right-clicking a sheet tab and then clicking the *Hide* option at the shortcut menu.

To make a hidden worksheet visible, click the Format button in the Cells group, point to *Hide & Unhide* and then click *Unhide Sheet*, or right-click a sheet tab and then click *Unhide* at the shortcut menu. At the Unhide dialog box, shown in Figure 5.4, double-click the name of the worksheet to be unhidden.

Figure 5.4 Unhide Dialog Box

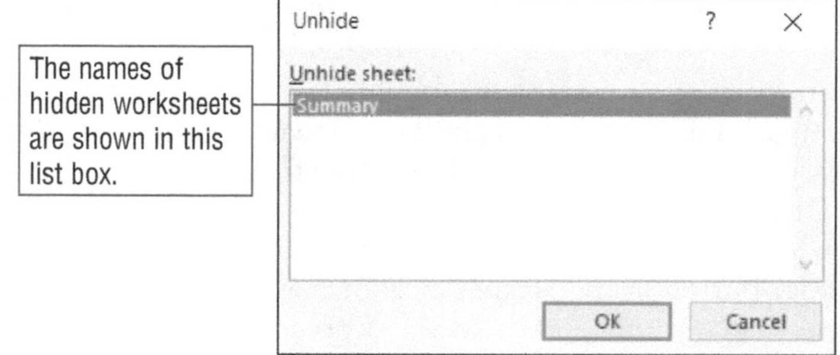

Activity 1f Hiding and Unhiding a Worksheet and Formatting Multiple Worksheets

Part 6 of 7

1. With **5-RPFacAccts** open, hide the Summary worksheet by completing the following steps:
   a. Click the Summary tab.
   b. Click the Format button in the Cells group on the Home tab, point to *Hide & Unhide*, and then click *Hide Sheet*.

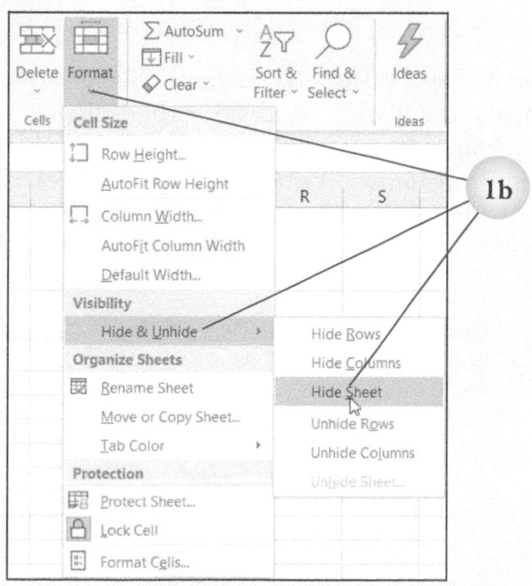

2. Unhide the worksheet by completing the following steps:
   a. Click the Format button, point to *Hide & Unhide*, and then click *Unhide Sheet*.
   b. At the Unhide dialog box, make sure *Summary* is selected in the *Unhide sheet* list box and then click OK.

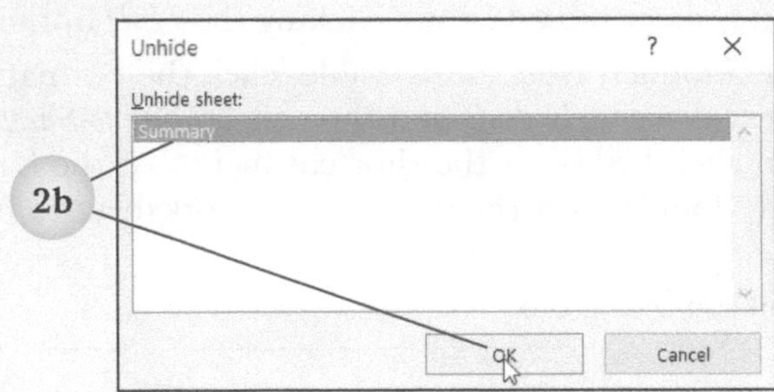

3. Insert a header for each worksheet by completing the following steps:
   a. With the Summary tab active, press and hold down the Shift key, click the March tab, and then release the Shift key. (This selects all four tabs.)
   b. Click the Insert tab.
   c. Click the Header & Footer button in the Text group.
   d. Click the Header button in the Header & Footer group on the Header & Footer Tools Design tab and then click the option at the drop-down list that prints your name at the left side of the page (if a name other than your own appears at the left side of the page, select the name and then type your first and last names), the page number in the middle, and the date at the right.
4. With all the sheet tabs selected, center each worksheet horizontally and vertically on the page. ***Hint: Do this at the Page Setup dialog box with the Margins tab selected.***
5. With all the sheet tabs still selected, change to landscape orientation. ***Hint: Do this with the Orientation button on the Page Layout tab.***
6. Save **5-RPFacAccts**.

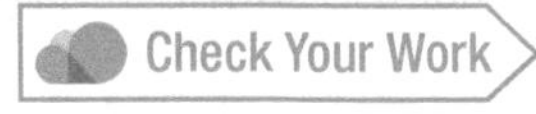

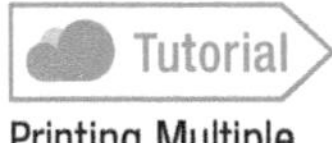

Printing Multiple Worksheets

Quick Steps

Print All Worksheets in Workbook

1. Click File tab.
2. Click *Print* option.
3. Click first gallery in *Settings* category.
4. Click *Print Entire Workbook*.
5. Click Print button.

Printing a Workbook Containing Multiple Worksheets

By default, Excel prints the currently displayed worksheet. To print all the worksheets in a workbook, display the Print backstage area, click the first gallery in the *Settings* category, click *Print Entire Workbook* at the drop-down list, and then click the Print button. Print specific worksheets in a workbook by selecting the tabs of the worksheets to be printed. With the sheet tabs selected, display the Print backstage area and then click the Print button.

Activity 1g Printing All Worksheets in a Workbook

Part 7 of 7

1. With **5-RPFacAccts** open, click the File tab and then click the *Print* option.
2. At the Print backstage area, click the first gallery in the *Settings* category and then click *Print Entire Workbook* at the drop-down list.
3. Click the Print button.
4. Save and then close **5-RPFacAccts**.

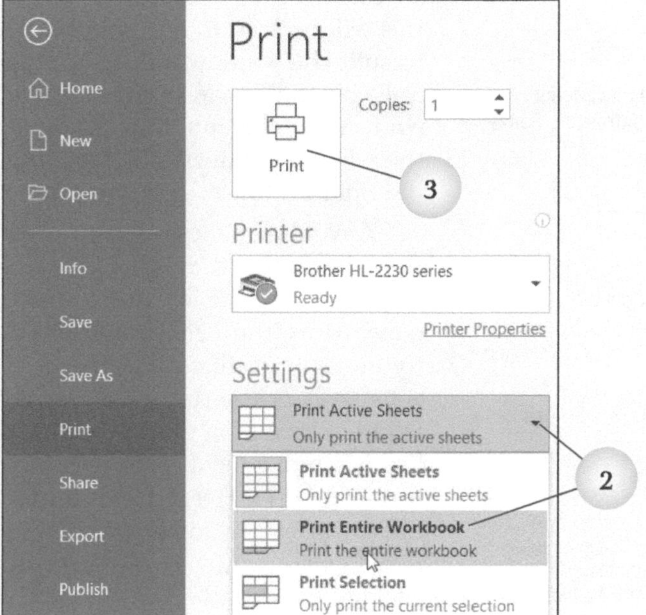

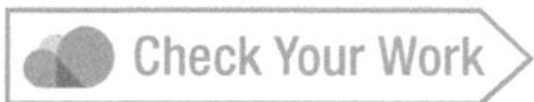

Activity 2 Write Formulas Using Ranges in an Equipment Usage Workbook

2 Parts

You will open an equipment usage workbook, view the document at different zoom percentages, and then split the window, freeze panes and edit cells. You will also name ranges and then use the range names to write formulas in the workbook.

Changing the Zoom

Changing the Zoom

The View tab contains a Zoom group with three buttons for changing zoom settings. Click the Zoom button in the Zoom group to open the Zoom dialog box, which contains options for changing the zoom percentage. Click the 100% button in the Zoom group to return the view to 100%, which is the default. Select a range of cells and then click the Zoom to Selection button to scale the zoom setting so the selected range fills the worksheet area.

Use the zoom slider bar at the right side of the Status bar to change the zoom percentage. Click the Zoom Out button (displays with a minus symbol [–]) to decrease the zoom percentage or click the Zoom In button (displays with a plus symbol [+]) to increase the zoom percentage. Another method for increasing or decreasing zoom percentage is to click and drag the zoom slider bar button on the slider bar.

Splitting a Worksheet

Freezing and Unfreezing Panes

Split

Quick Steps

Split Worksheet

1. Click View tab.
2. Click Split button.

Freeze Panes

Hint Remove a split line by double-clicking anywhere on the split line that divides the panes.

Splitting a Worksheet and Freezing and Unfreezing Panes

Depending on the size of a worksheet and the screen display settings, all cells in a worksheet may not be visible in the worksheet area at one time. (An example of this will be seen in Activity 2a.) To more easily view all the data, it can be helpful to split the window into panes. Split a worksheet window into panes with the Split button in the Window group on the View tab. Click the Split button and the worksheet splits into four panes, as shown in Figure 5.5. The panes are separated by thick light-gray lines called *split lines*. To remove split lines from a worksheet, click the Split button to deactivate it.

A window pane will display the active cell. As the insertion point is moved through the pane, another active cell may display. This additional active cell displays when the insertion point passes over one of the split lines that creates the pane. Move through a worksheet and both active cells may display. Make a change to one active cell and the change is made in the other as well. To display only one active cell, freeze the window panes by clicking the Freeze Panes button in the Window group on the View tab and then clicking *Freeze Panes* at the drop-down list. Maintain the display of column headings while editing or typing text in cells by clicking the Freeze Panes button and then clicking *Freeze Top Row*. Maintain the display of row headings by clicking the Freeze Panes button and then clicking *Freeze First Column*. Unfreeze window panes by clicking the Freeze Panes button and then clicking *Unfreeze Panes* at the drop-down list.

The split lines that divide the window can be adjusted using the mouse. To do this, position the mouse pointer on a split line until the pointer turns into a left-and-right-pointing arrow with a double line in the middle. Click and hold down the left mouse button, drag the outline of the split line to the desired location, and then release the mouse button. To move both the horizontal and vertical split lines at the same time, position the mouse pointer on the intersection of the split lines until the pointer turns into a four-headed arrow. Click and hold down the left mouse button, drag the split lines to the desired location, and then release the mouse button.

Figure 5.5 Split Window

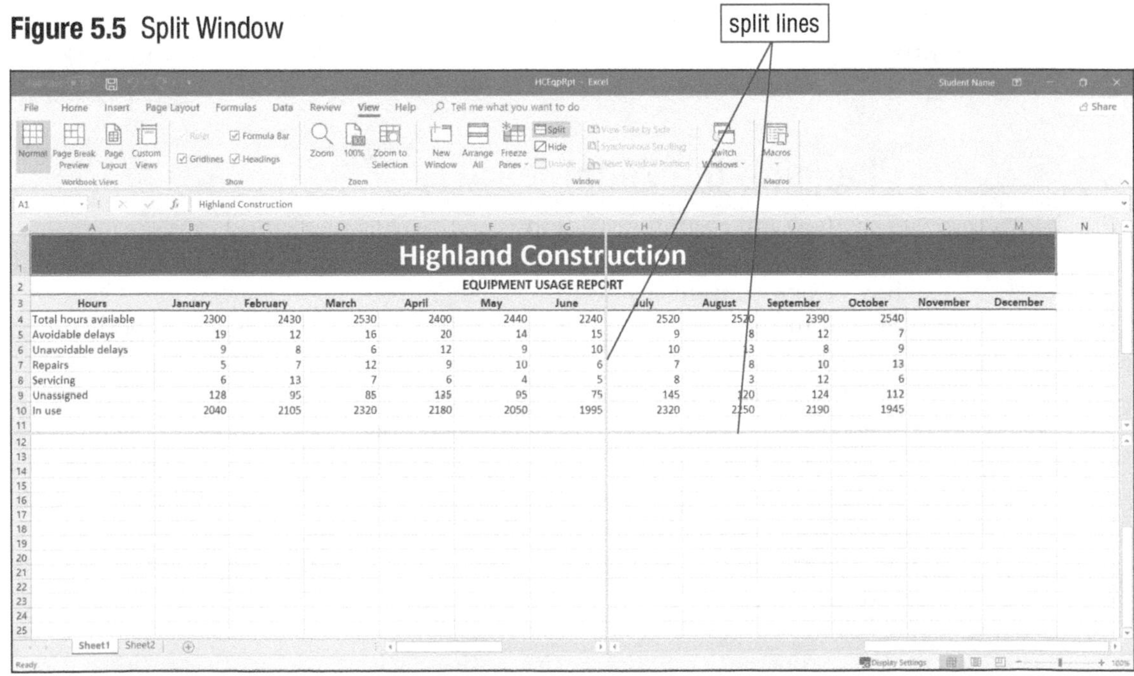

Activity 2a Using Zoom, Splitting Windows, Freezing Panes, and Editing Cells

Part 1 of 2

1. Open **HCEqpRpt** and then save it with the name **5-HCEqpRpt**.
2. Increase the Zoom percentage by clicking the Zoom In button at the right of the zoom slider bar two times.
3. Select the range G3:I10, click the View tab, and then click the Zoom to Selection button in the Zoom group.
4. Click the Zoom button in the Zoom group, click the *75%* option at the Zoom dialog box, and then click OK.

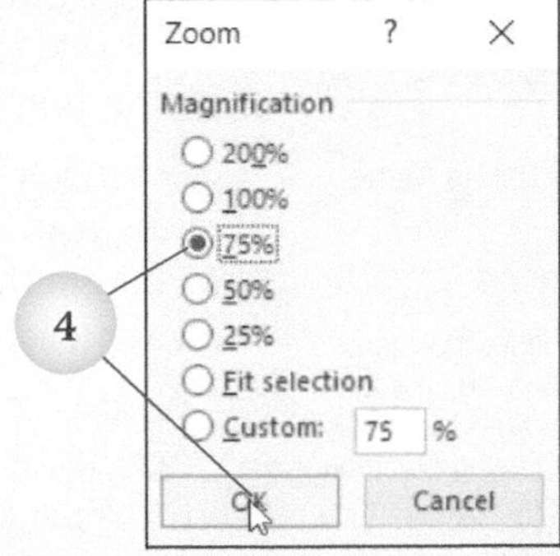

5. Click the 100% button in the Zoom group.
6. Make cell A1 active and then split the window by clicking the Split button in the Window group on the View tab. (This splits the window into four panes.)
7. Drag the vertical split line by completing the following steps:
   a. Position the mouse pointer on the vertical split line until the pointer turns into a left-and-right-pointing arrow with a double line in the middle.
   b. Click and hold down the left mouse button, drag to the left until the vertical split line is immediately to the right of the first column, and then release the mouse button.

	A	B	C	D	E	F
1					Highland C	
2						EQUIPMENT U
3	Hours	January	February	March	April	May
4	Total hours available	2300	2430	2530	2400	2440
5	Avoidable delays	19	12	16	20	14
6	Unavoidable delays	9	8	6	12	9
7	Repairs	5	7	12	9	10

7b

8. Freeze the window panes by clicking the Freeze Panes button in the Window group on the View tab and then clicking *Freeze Panes* at the drop-down list.

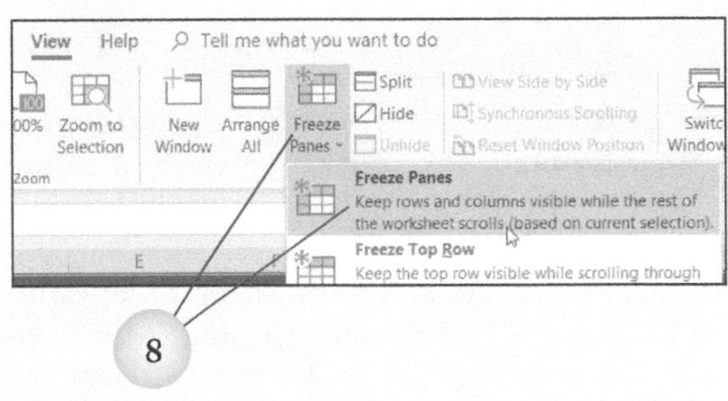

9. Make cell L4 active and then type the following data in the specified cells:

L4	2310	M4	2210
L5	12	M5	5
L6	5	M6	7
L7	9	M7	8
L8	11	M8	12
L9	95	M9	120
L10	2005	M10	1830

10. Unfreeze the window panes by clicking the Freeze Panes button and then clicking *Unfreeze Panes* at the drop-down list.
11. Remove the panes by clicking the Split button in the Window group to deactivate it.
12. Save **5-HCEqpRpt**.

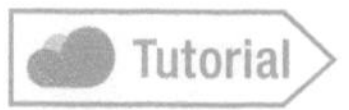

Naming and Using a Range

Naming and Using a Range

A group of adjacent cells is referred to as a *range*. A range of cells can be formatted, moved, copied, or deleted. A range can also be named and then the insertion point can be moved to the range or the named range can be used as part of a formula.

Quick Steps

Name Range

1. Select cells.
2. Click in Name box.
3. Type range name.
4. Press Enter key.

Define Name

Hint Another method for moving to a range is to click the Find & Select button in the Editing group on the Home tab and then click *Go To*. At the Go To dialog box, double-click the range name.

To name a range, select the cells and then click in the Name box to the left of the Formula bar. Type a name for the range (do not use spaces) and then press the Enter key. To move the insertion point to a specific range and select the range, click the Name box arrow and then click the range name at the drop-down list.

A range can also be named using the Define Name button in the Defined Names group on the Formulas tab. Clicking the Define Name button displays the New Name dialog box. At the New Name dialog box, type a name for the range and then click OK.

A range name can be used in a formula. For example, to insert in a cell the average of all the cells in a range named *Profit*, make the cell active and then type the formula =*AVERAGE(Profit)*. Use a named range in the current worksheet or in another worksheet within the workbook.

Activity 2b Naming a Range and Using a Range in a Formula

Part 2 of 2

1. With **5-HCEqpRpt** open, click the Sheet2 tab and then type the following text in the specified cells:

   A1 EQUIPMENT USAGE REPORT
   A2 Yearly hours
   A3 Avoidable delays
   A4 Unavoidable delays
   A5 Total delay hours
   A6 (leave blank)
   A7 Repairs
   A8 Servicing
   A9 Total repair/servicing hours

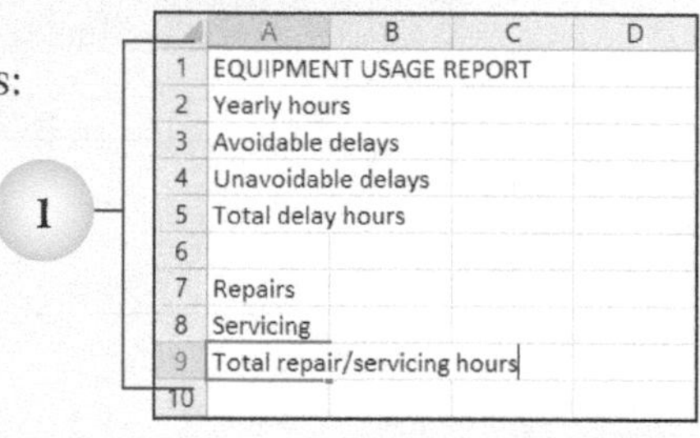

2. Make the following formatting changes to the worksheet:
   a. Automatically adjust the width of column A.
   b. Center and apply bold formatting to the text in cells A1 and A2.
3. Select a range of cells in Sheet1, name the range, and then use it in a formula in Sheet2 by completing the following steps:
   a. Click the Sheet1 tab.
   b. Select the range B5:M5.
   c. Click in the Name box to the left of the Formula bar.
   d. Type adhours (for Avoidable Delays Hours) and then press the Enter key.
   e. Click the Sheet2 tab.
   f. Click in cell B3.
   g. Type the equation =sum(adhours) and then press the Enter key.

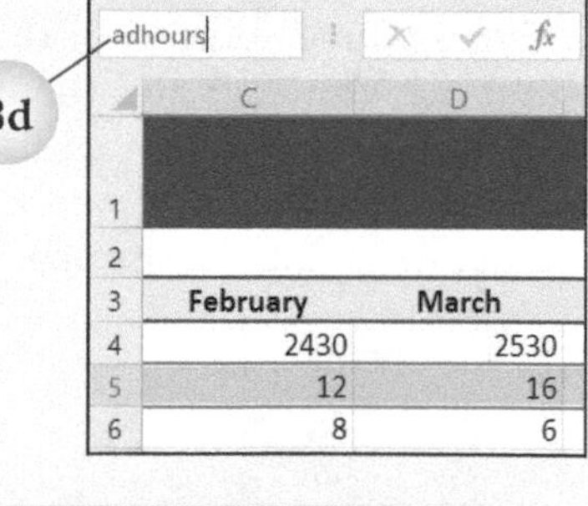

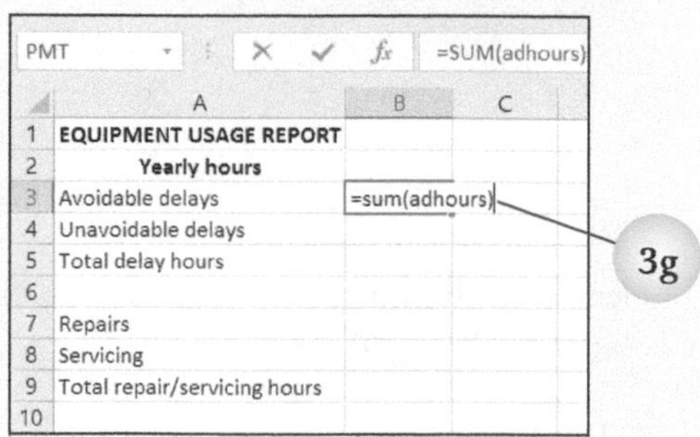

4. Click the Sheet1 tab and then complete the following steps:
   a. Select the range B6:M6.
   b. Click the Formulas tab.
   c. Click the Define Name button in the Defined Names group.
   d. At the New Name dialog box, type udhours and then click OK.
   e. Click the Sheet2 tab, make sure cell B4 is active, type the equation =sum(udhours), and then press the Enter key.
5. Click the Sheet1 tab and then complete the following steps:
   a. Select the range B7:M7 and then name the range *rhours*.
   b. Click the Sheet2 tab, make cell B7 active, type the equation =sum(rhours), and then press the Enter key.
   c. Click the Sheet1 tab.
   d. Select the range B8:M8 and then name the range *shours*.
   e. Click the Sheet2 tab, make sure cell B8 is active, type the equation =sum(shours), and then press the Enter key.
6. With Sheet2 still active, make the following changes:
   a. Make cell B5 active.
   b. Double-click the AutoSum button.
   c. Make cell B9 active.
   d. Double-click the AutoSum button.
7. Click the Sheet1 tab and then move to the adhours range by clicking the Name box arrow and then clicking *adhours* at the drop-down list.

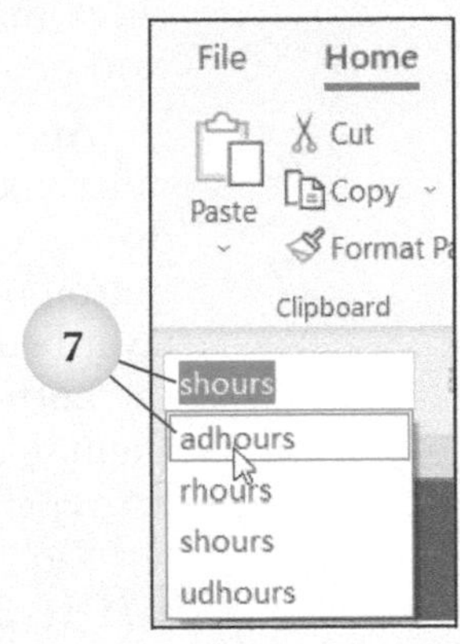

8. Select both sheet tabs, change to landscape orientation, scale the contents to fit on one page (by changing the width to *1 page* on the Page Layout tab), and then insert a custom footer with your name, the page number, and the date.
9. With both sheet tabs selected, print both worksheets in the workbook.
10. Save and then close **5-HCEqpRpt**.

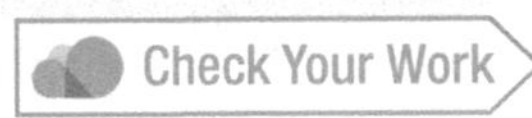

Activity 3 Arrange, Size, and Copy Data between Workbooks — 3 Parts

You will open, arrange, hide, unhide, size, and move multiple workbooks. You will also copy cells from one workbook and paste the contents in another workbook.

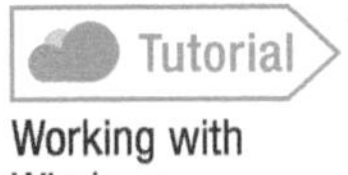

Working with Windows and Hiding and Unhiding Workbooks

Working with Windows

In Excel, multiple workbooks can be opened, a new window with the current workbook can be opened, and the open workbooks can be arranged in the Excel window. With multiple workbooks open, cell entries can be cut and pasted or copied and pasted from one workbook to another using the techniques discussed earlier in this chapter. The exception is that the destination workbook must be active before using the Paste command.

Opening Multiple Workbooks

With multiple workbooks or more than one version of the current workbook open, data can be moved or copied between workbooks and the contents of several workbooks can be compared. When a new workbook or a new window of the current workbook is opened, it is placed on top of the original workbook.

Open a new window of the current workbook by clicking the View tab and then clicking the New Window button in the Window group. Excel adds a colon followed by the number *2* to the end of the workbook title and adds a colon followed by the number *1* to the end of the originating workbook name.

Open multiple workbooks at one time at the Open dialog box. Select adjacent workbooks by clicking the name of the first workbook to be opened, pressing and holding down the Shift key, clicking the name of the last workbook to be opened, releasing the Shift key, and then clicking the Open button. If the workbooks are nonadjacent, click the name of the first workbook to be opened, press and hold down the Ctrl key, and then click the names of any other workbooks to be opened.

To see what workbooks are currently open, click the View tab and then click the Switch Windows button in the Window group. The names of the open workbooks display in a drop-down list and the workbook name preceded by a check mark is the active workbook. To make another workbook active, click the workbook name at the drop-down list.

Another method for determining which workbooks are open is to hover the mouse pointer over the Excel button on the taskbar. This causes a thumbnail to display of each open workbook. If more than one workbook is open, the Excel button on the taskbar displays additional layers in a cascaded manner. The layer behind the Excel button displays only a portion of the edge at the right of the button. Hovering the mouse over the Excel button on the taskbar displays thumbnails of all the workbooks above the button. To make another workbook active, click the thumbnail that represents the workbook.

Arranging Workbooks

If more than one workbook is open, arrange the workbooks at the Arrange Windows dialog box, shown in Figure 5.6. To display this dialog box, click the Arrange All button in the Window group on the View tab. At the Arrange Windows dialog box, click *Tiled* to display a portion of each open workbook. Figure 5.7 displays four tiled workbooks.

Quick Steps

Arrange Workbooks

1. Click View tab.
2. Click Arrange All button.
3. At Arrange Windows dialog box, click arrangement.
4. Click OK.

Figure 5.6 Arrange Windows Dialog Box

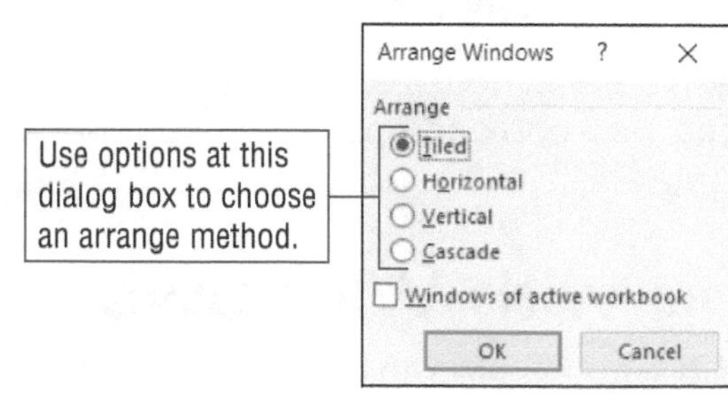

Choose the *Horizontal* option at the Arrange Windows dialog box to display the open workbooks across the screen. Choose the *Vertical* option to display the open workbooks up and down the screen. Choose the last option, *Cascade*, to display the Title bar of each open workbook. Figure 5.8 shows four cascaded workbooks.

Select the arrange option for displaying multiple workbooks based on which parts of the workbooks are most important to view simultaneously. For example, the tiled workbooks in Figure 5.7 display the company names of the workbooks.

Figure 5.7 Tiled Workbooks

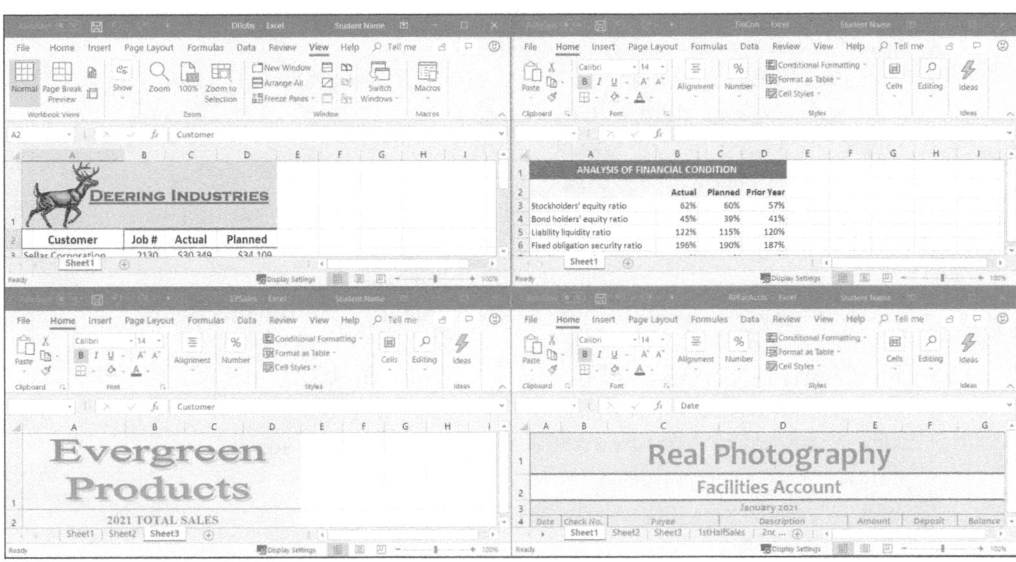

Figure 5.8 Cascaded Workbooks

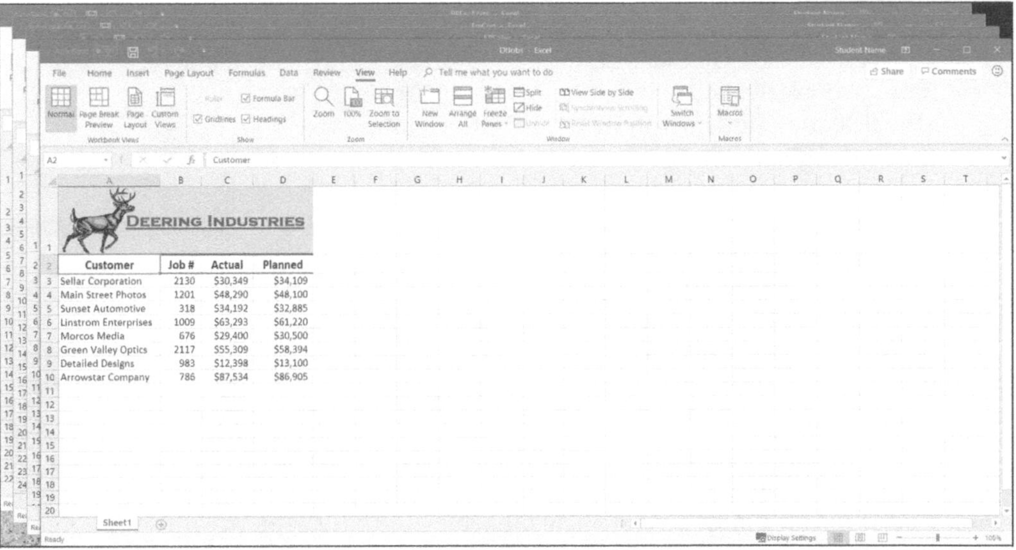

Hiding and Unhiding Workbooks

Hide

Unhide

Use the Hide button in the Window group on the View tab to hide the active workbook. If a workbook has been hidden, redisplay it by clicking the Unhide button in the Window group. At the Unhide dialog box, make sure the specific workbook is selected in the list box and then click OK.

Activity 3a Opening, Arranging, Hiding and Unhiding Workbooks — Part 1 of 3

1. Open several workbooks at the same time by completing the following steps:
   a. Display the Open dialog box with EL1C5 the active folder.
   b. Click the workbook ***DIJobs***.
   c. Press and hold down the Ctrl key, click ***EPSales***, click ***FinCon***, click ***RPFacAccts***, and then release the Ctrl key.
   d. Click the Open button in the dialog box.
2. Make **DIJobs** the active workbook by clicking the View tab, clicking the Switch Windows button, and then clicking ***DIJobs*** at the drop-down list.

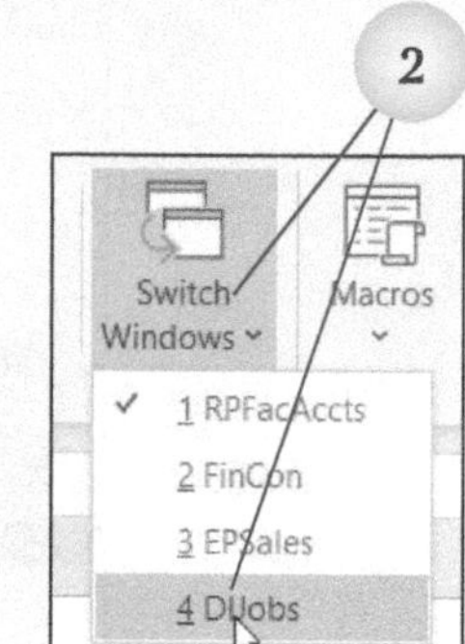

3. Tile the workbooks by completing the following steps:
   a. Click the View tab and then click the Arrange All button in the Window group.
   b. At the Arrange Windows dialog box, make sure *Tiled* is selected and then click OK.
4. Cascade the workbooks by completing the following steps:
   a. Click the Arrange All button in the **DIJobs** workbook.
   b. At the Arrange Windows dialog box, click *Cascade* and then click OK.
5. Hide and unhide workbooks by completing the following steps:
   a. Make sure **DIJobs** is the active workbook. (The file name displays on top of each workbook file.)
   b. Click the Hide button in the Window group on the View tab.
   c. Make sure **RPFacAccts** is the active workbook. (The file name displays at the top of each workbook file.)
   d. Click the Hide button in the Window group on the View tab.
   e. At the active workbook, click the View tab and then click the Unhide button.
   f. At the Unhide dialog box, click *RPFacAccts* in the list box and then click OK.
   g. Click the Unhide button.
   h. At the Unhide dialog box, make sure **DIJobs** is selected in the list box and then click OK.
6. Close all the open workbooks (without saving changes) except **DIJobs**.
7. Open a new window with the current workbook by clicking the New Window button in the Window group on the View tab. (Notice that the new window contains the workbook name followed by a hyphen and the number *2*.)
8. Switch back and forth between the two versions of the workbook.
9. Make **DIJobs-2** the active window and then close the workbook.

Sizing and Moving Workbooks

Maximize

Minimize

Close

Restore Down

Change the size of the window using the Maximize and Minimize buttons in the upper right corner of the active workbook. The Maximize button is in the upper right corner of the active workbook immediately to the left of the Close button. (The Close button is the button containing the *X*.) The Minimize button is immediately to the left of the Maximize button.

If all the open workbooks are arranged, clicking the Maximize button causes the active workbook to expand to fill the screen. In addition, the Maximize button changes to the Restore Down button. To return the active workbook back to its original size, click the Restore Down button.

Click the Minimize button in the active workbook and the workbook is reduced and displays as a layer behind the Excel button on the taskbar. To maximize a workbook that has been minimized, click the Excel button on the taskbar and then click the thumbnail representing the workbook.

Activity 3b Minimizing, Maximizing, and Restoring Workbooks — Part 2 of 3

1. Make sure **DIJobs** is open.
2. Maximize **DIJobs** by clicking the Maximize button in the upper right corner of the screen immediately to the left of the Close button.

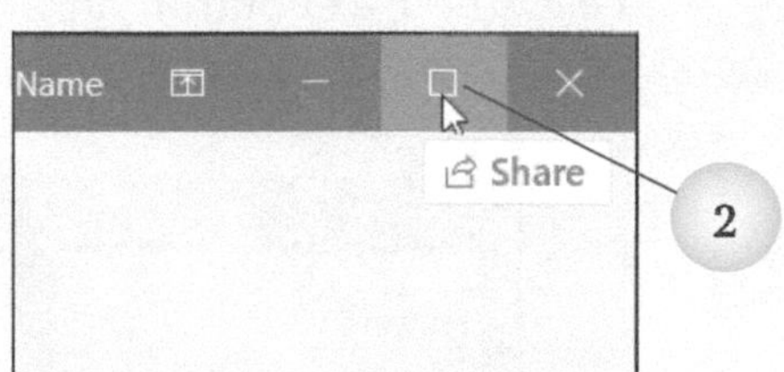

3. Open **EPSales** and **FinCon**.
4. Make the following changes to the open workbooks:
   a. Tile the workbooks.
   b. Click the **DIJobs** Title bar to make it the active workbook.
   c. Minimize **DIJobs** by clicking the Minimize button at the right side of the Title bar.

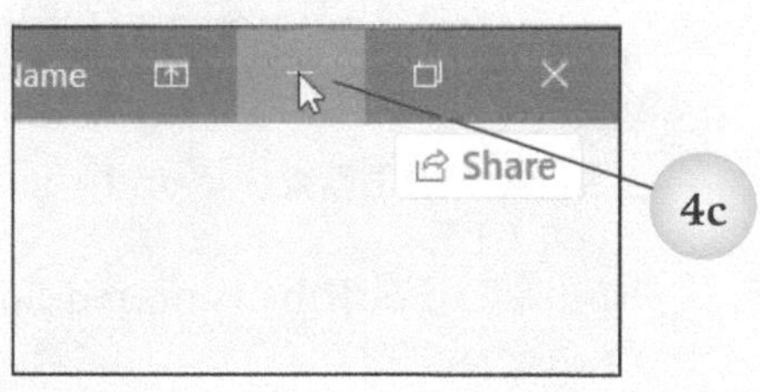

   d. Make **EPSales** the active workbook and then minimize it.
   e. Minimize **FinCon**.
5. Click the Excel button on the taskbar, click the **DIJobs** thumbnail, and then close the workbook without saving changes.
6. Complete steps similar to Step 5 to close the other two workbooks.

Moving, Linking, Copying, and Pasting Data between Workbooks

With more than one workbook open, data can be moved, linked, copied, and/or pasted from one workbook to another. To move, link, copy, and/or paste data between workbooks, use the cutting and pasting options discussed earlier in this chapter together with the information about windows.

Moving and Copying Data

Data can be moved or copied within a worksheet, between worksheets, and between workbooks and documents created in other programs, such as Word, PowerPoint, and Access. The Paste Options button provides a variety of options for pasting data in a worksheet, another workbook, or a document created in another program. In addition to being pasted, data can be linked and data can be pasted as an object or a picture object.

Activity 3c Copying Selected Cells from One Open Worksheet to Another — Part 3 of 3

1. Open **DIFebJobs**.
2. If you just completed Activity 3b, click the Maximize button so the worksheet fills the entire worksheet window.
3. Save the workbook and name it **5-DIFebJobs**.
4. With **5-DIFebJobs** open, open **DIJobs**.
5. Select and then copy text from **DIJobs** to **5-DIFebJobs** by completing the following steps:
   a. With **DIJobs** the active workbook, select the range A3:D10.
   b. Click the Copy button.
   c. Click the Excel button on the taskbar and then click the **5-DIFebJobs** thumbnail.
   d. Make cell A8 active and then click the Paste button.

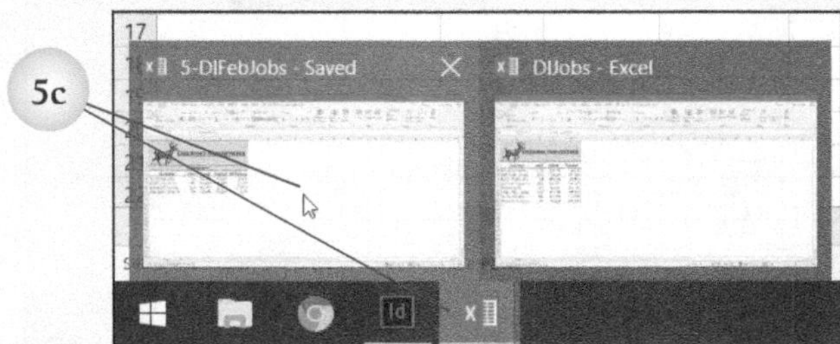

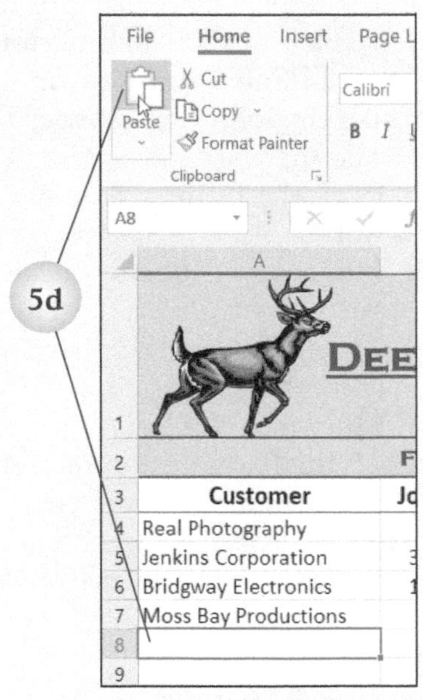

   e. Make cell E7 active and then drag the fill handle to cell E15.
6. Print **5-DIFebJobs** centered horizontally and vertically on the page.
7. Save and then close **5-DIFebJobs**.
8. Close **DIJobs**.

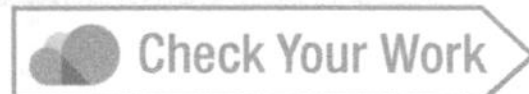

Activity 4 Linking and Copying Data within and between Worksheets and Word — 2 Parts

You will open a workbook containing four worksheets with quarterly expenses data, copy and link cells between the worksheets, and then copy and paste the worksheets into Word as picture objects.

Linking Data

Quick Steps

Link Data between Worksheets

1. Select cells.
2. Click Copy button.
3. Click sheet tab.
4. Click in cell.
5. Click Paste button arrow.
6. Click Paste Link button.

Linking Data

In addition to being copied and pasted, data can be copied and then linked within or between worksheets or workbooks. Linking data is useful for maintaining consistency and control over critical data in worksheets or workbooks. When data is linked, a change made in a linked cell is automatically made to the other cells in the link. Links can be made with individual cells or with a range of cells. When linking data, the worksheet that contains the original data is called the *source worksheet* and the worksheet that relies on the source worksheet for the data in the link is called the *dependent worksheet.*

To create a link, make active the cell containing the data to be linked (or select the cells) and then click the Copy button in the Clipboard group on the Home tab. Make active the worksheet where the cells are to be linked, click the Paste button arrow, and then click the Paste Link button in the *Other Paste Options* section in the drop-down list. Another method for creating a link is to click the Paste button, click the Paste Options button, and then click the Paste Link button in the *Other Paste Options* section in the drop-down list.

Activity 4a **Linking Cells between Worksheets** Part 1 of 2

1. Open **DWQtrlyExp** and then save it with the name **5-DWQtrlyExp**.
2. Link cells in the first-quarter worksheet to the other three worksheets by completing the following steps:
   a. With the 1st Qtr tab active, select the range C4:C10.
   b. Click the Copy button.
   c. Click the 2nd Qtr tab.
   d. Make cell C4 active.
   e. Click the Paste button arrow and then click the Paste Link button in the *Other Paste Options* section in the drop-down list.
   f. Click the 3rd Qtr tab and then make cell C4 active.
   g. Click the Paste button arrow and then click the Paste Link button.
   h. Click the 4th Qtr tab and then make cell C4 active.
   i. Click the Paste button.
   j. Click the Paste Options button and then click the Paste Link button in the *Other Paste Options* section in the drop-down list.

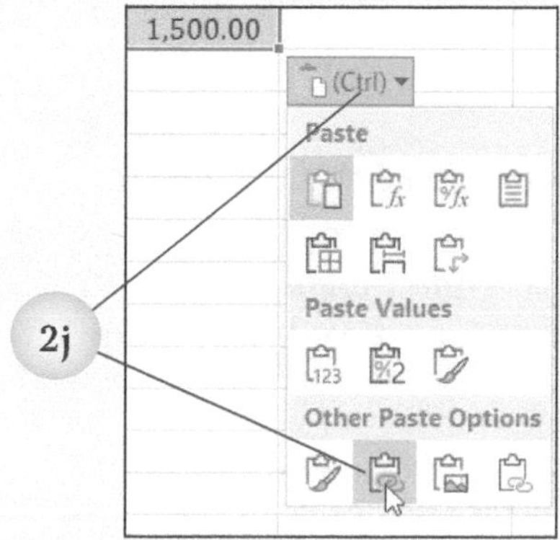

3. Click the 1st Qtr tab and then press the Esc key to remove the moving marquee.

4. Insert a formula in each worksheet that subtracts the budget amount from the variance amount by completing the following steps:
   a. Make sure the first-quarter worksheet is visible.
   b. Press and hold down the Shift key and then click the 4th Qtr tab. (This selects all four tabs.)
   c. Make cell D4 active, type the formula =c4-b4, and then press the Enter key.
   d. Copy the formula in cell D4 to the range D5:D10.
   e. Make cell D4 active and then apply the Accounting format with two digits after the decimal point and a dollar symbol.
   f. Click the 2nd Qtr tab and notice that the formula was inserted and copied in this worksheet.
   g. Click the other sheet tabs and notice the amounts in column D.
   h. Click the 1st Qtr tab.

uarter	
Budget	*Variance*
$ 126,000.00	4,000.00
54,500.00	(3,500.00)
10,100.00	1,850.00
6,000.00	(350.00)
4,500.00	360.00
2,200.00	(230.00)
1,500.00	50.00

4d

5. With the first-quarter worksheet active, make the following changes to the specified linked cells:

   C4: Change *$126,000* to *$128,000*

   C5: Change *54,500* to *56,000*

   C9: Change *2,200* to *2,400*

6. Click the 2nd Qtr tab and notice that the values in cells C4, C5, and C9 automatically changed (because they were linked to the first-quarter worksheet).
7. Click the other tabs and notice that the values changed.
8. Save **5-DWQtrlyExp** and then print all four worksheets in the workbook.

Copying and Pasting Data between Programs

Copying and Pasting Data between Programs

Microsoft Office is a suite that allows *integration*, which is the combining of data from files created by two or more programs into one file. Integration can occur by copying and pasting data between files created in different programs. For example, a worksheet can be created in Excel and specific data can be selected in the worksheet and then copied to a Word document. When pasting Excel data in a Word document, choose from among these formatting options: keep the source formatting, use destination styles, link the data, insert the data as a picture, or keep only the text.

Activity 4b **Copying and Pasting Excel Data into a Word Document** Part 2 of 2

1. With **5-DWQtrlyExp** open, open the Word program.
2. In Word, open the document **DWQtrlyRpt** in your EL1C5 folder.
3. Save the Word document with the name **5-DWQtrlyRpt**.
4. Click the Excel button on the taskbar.
5. Copy the first-quarter data into the Word document by completing the following steps:
   a. Click the 1st Qtr tab.
   b. Select the range A2:D10.
   c. Click the Copy button.
   d. Click the Word button on the taskbar.

e. In the **5-DWQtrlyRpt** document, press Ctrl + End to move the insertion point below the heading.
f. Click the Paste button arrow. (This displays a drop-down list of paste option buttons.)
g. Move the mouse over the various buttons in the drop-down list to see how each option inserts the data in the document.
h. Click the Picture button. (This inserts the data as a picture object.)
i. Press Ctrl + End and then press the Enter key two times. (This moves the insertion point below the data.)
j. Click the Excel button on the taskbar.

6. Click the 2nd Qtr tab and then complete steps similar to those in Step 5 to copy and paste the second-quarter data into the Word document. Press Ctrl + End and then press the Enter key two times.
7. Click the 3rd Qtr tab and then complete steps similar to those in Step 5 to copy and paste the third-quarter data to the Word document. Press Ctrl + End and then press the Enter key two times.
8. Click the 4th Qtr tab and then complete steps similar to those in Step 5 to copy and paste the fourth-quarter data to the Word document. (The data will display on two pages.)
9. Print the document by clicking the File tab, clicking the *Print* option, and then clicking the Print button at the Print backstage area.
10. Save and close **5-DWQtrlyRpt** and then close Word.
11. In Excel, press the Esc key to remove the moving marquee and then make cell A1 active.
12. Save and then close **5-DWQtrlyExp**.

Chapter Summary

- By default, an Excel workbook contains one worksheet. Add a new worksheet to a workbook by clicking the New sheet button or using the keyboard shortcut Shift + F11.
- Delete a worksheet with the Delete button in the Cells group on the Home tab or by right-clicking a sheet tab and then clicking *Delete* at the shortcut menu.
- To manage more than one worksheet at a time, first select the worksheets. Use the mouse together with the Shift key to select adjacent sheet tabs and use the mouse together with the Ctrl key to select nonadjacent sheet tabs.
- Copy or move selected cells and cell contents in and between worksheets using the Cut, Copy, and/or Paste buttons in the Clipboard group on the Home tab or by dragging with the mouse.
- Move selected cells with the mouse by dragging the outline of the selected cells to the new position.
- Copy selected cells with the mouse by pressing and holding down the Ctrl key while dragging the cells to the new position.
- When pasting data, specify how cells are to be pasted by clicking the Paste button arrow or pasting the cells and then clicking the Paste Options button. Clicking either button displays a drop-down list of paste option buttons. Click a button at the drop-down list.
- Use the Clipboard task pane to copy and paste data within and between worksheets and workbooks. Display the Clipboard task pane by clicking the Clipboard group task pane launcher.

- Manage worksheets by right-clicking a sheet tab and then clicking an option at the shortcut menu. Options include removing and renaming a worksheet.
- The mouse can be used to move or copy worksheets. To move a worksheet, drag the sheet tab with the mouse. To copy a worksheet, press and hold down the Ctrl key and then drag the sheet tab with the mouse.
- Use the *Tab Color* option at the sheet tab shortcut menu to apply a color to a sheet tab.
- Hide and unhide a worksheet by clicking the Format button in the Cells group on the Home tab and then clicking the desired option at the drop-down list or by right-clicking the sheet tab and then clicking the option at the shortcut menu.
- To print all the worksheets in a workbook, display the Print backstage area, click the first gallery in the *Settings* category, and then click *Print Entire Workbook* at the drop-down list. Print specific worksheets by selecting their tabs.
- Use buttons in the Zoom group on the View tab or the zoom slider bar at the right side of the Status bar to change the zoom percentage.
- Split the worksheet window into panes with the Split button in the Window group on the View tab. To remove a split from a worksheet, click the Split button to deactivate it.
- Freeze window panes by clicking the Freeze Panes button in the Window group on the View tab and then clicking *Freeze Panes* at the drop-down list. Unfreeze window panes by clicking the Freeze Panes button and then clicking *Unfreeze Panes* at the drop-down list.
- A selected group of cells is referred to as a *range*. A range can be named and used in a formula. Name a range by typing the name in the Name box to the left of the Formula bar or at the New Name dialog box.
- To open multiple workbooks that are adjacent, display the Open dialog box, click the name of the first workbook, press and hold down the Shift key, click the name of the last workbook, release the Shift key, and then click the Open button. To open workbooks that are nonadjacent, click the name of the first workbook, press and hold down the Ctrl key, click the names of the desired workbooks, release the Ctrl key, and then click the Open button.
- To see a list of open workbooks, click the View tab and then click the Switch Windows button in the Window group.
- Arrange multiple workbooks in a window with options at the Arrange Windows dialog box.
- Hide the active workbook by clicking the Hide button in the Window group on the View tab and unhide a workbook by clicking the Unhide button.
- Click the Maximize button in the upper right corner of the active workbook to make the workbook fill the entire window area. Click the Minimize button to reduce the workbook and display it as a layer behind the Excel button on the taskbar. Click the Restore Down button to return the workbook to its previous size.
- Data can be moved, copied, linked, and/or pasted between workbooks using options at the Paste Options button. Also, a workbook can be pasted as a link in a different Microsoft Office program, such a Word or PowerPoint. Changing the data in one program will change linked data that exists in a different program.

Commands Review

FEATURE	RIBBON TAB, GROUP	BUTTON, OPTION	KEYBOARD SHORTCUT
100% view	View, Zoom		
Arrange Windows dialog box	View, Window		
Clipboard task pane	Home, Clipboard		
copy selected cells	Home, Clipboard		Ctrl + C
cut selected cells	Home, Clipboard		Ctrl + X
freeze window panes	View, Window	, *Freeze Panes*	
hide workbook	View, Window		
hide worksheet	Home, Cells	, *Hide & Unhide, Hide Sheet*	
insert new worksheet			Shift + F11
maximize window			
minimize window			
New Name dialog box	Formulas, Defined Names		
new window	View, Window		
paste selected cells	Home, Clipboard		Ctrl + V
restore down			
split window into panes	View, Window		
switch windows	View, Window		
unfreeze window panes	View, Window	, *Unfreeze Panes*	
unhide workbook	View, Window		
unhide worksheet	Home, Cells	, *Hide & Unhide, Unhide Sheet*	
Zoom dialog box	View, Zoom		

Microsoft®

Excel®

CHAPTER

6

Maintaining Workbooks

Performance Objectives

Upon successful completion of Chapter 6, you will be able to:

1 Pin and unpin workbooks at the *Recent* option list
2 Copy and move worksheets between workbooks
3 Apply and modify a cell style
4 Modify, remove, and delete a cell style
5 Insert and use hyperlinks
6 Modify, edit, and remove hyperlinks
7 Create financial forms using templates
8 Insert, edit, delete, and show comments
9 Insert formulas using financial functions

After you have worked with Excel for a period of time, you will have accumulated several workbook files. Frequently used workbooks can be pinned at the Open and Home backstage areas so you can access them without needing to browse for them. In this chapter, you will also learn more methods for creating and maintaining workbooks, such as copying or moving worksheets from one workbook to another, applying cell styles and globally changing the style, inserting hyperlinks in a workbook, and using an Excel template to create a workbook. Inserting, posting, editing, and deleting comments will also be covered.

Before beginning chapter work, copy the EL1C6 folder to your storage medium and then make EL1C6 the active folder.

The online course includes additional training and assessment resources.

Activity 1 Copy and Move Worksheets into an Equipment Rental Workbook — 3 Parts

You will manage workbooks at the Open backstage area and then open multiple workbooks and copy and move worksheets between the workbooks.

Managing the *Recent* Option List

Managing the *Recent* Option List

As workbooks are opened and closed, Excel keeps a list of the most recently opened workbooks. To view this list, click the File tab and then click the *Open* option. This displays the Open backstage area, similar to what is shown in Figure 6.1. (The workbook names you see may vary from those in the figure.) Generally, the names of the 50 most recently opened workbooks are shown in the *Recent* option list and are organized in categories such as *Today*, *Yesterday*, and *Last Week*. To open a workbook, scroll down the list and then click the workbook name. The Excel opening screen and Home backstage area also display a list of the most recently opened workbooks.

Figure 6.1 Open Backstage Area

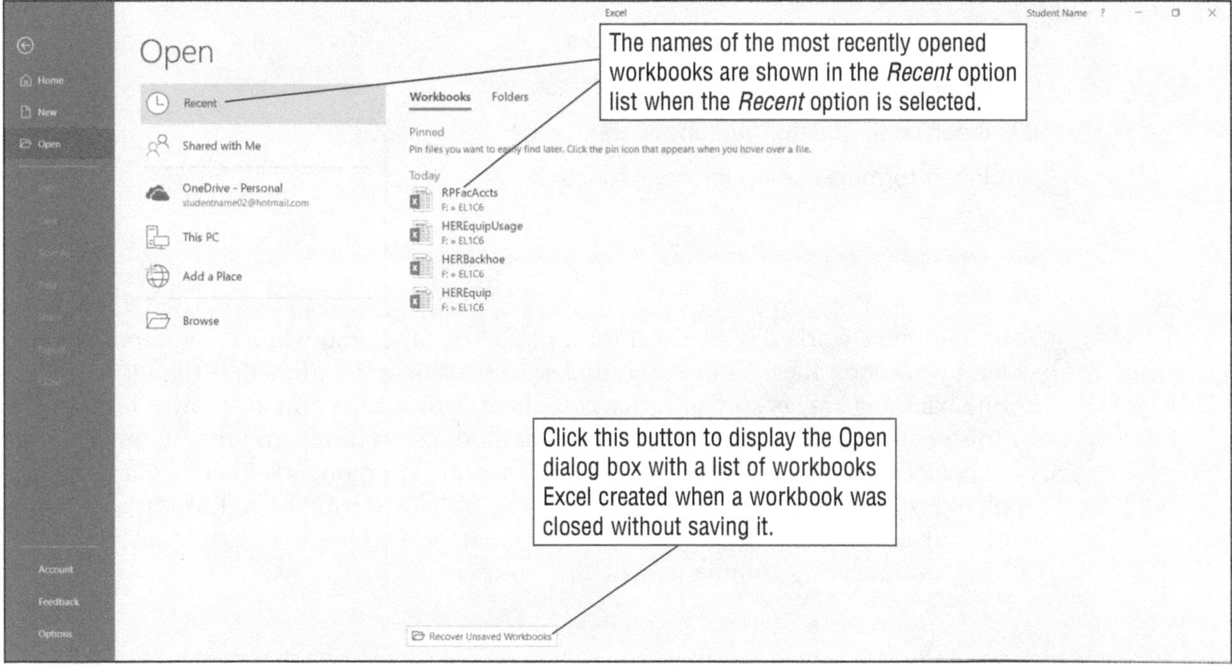

Pinning and Unpinning a Workbook

Quick Steps
Pinning/Unpinning Document
1. Click File tab.
2. Click push pin icon at right of workbook name.

OR

1. Click File tab.
2. Click *Open* option.
3. Click push pin icon at right of workbook name.

A workbook that is opened on a regular basis can be pinned to the *Recent* option list so that it can be found more easily. To pin a workbook to the *Recent* option list at the Open backstage area, hover the mouse pointer over the workbook name and then click the small left-pointing push pin icon to the right of the workbook name. The left-pointing push pin changes to a down-pointing push pin and the pinned workbook appears at the top of the list in the *Pinned* category. A workbook can also be pinned at the Home backstage area. Click the push pin icon next to a workbook name and then workbook will display in the *Pinned* tab.

To "unpin" a workbook from the *Recent* option list at the Open backstage area or the *Pinned* tab at the Home backstage area, click the push pin icon to change it from a down-pointing pin to a left-pointing pin. More than one workbook can be pinned to a list. Another method for pinning and unpinning a workbook is to use the shortcut menu. Right-click a workbook name and then click the *Pin to list* or *Unpin from list* option.

In addition to workbooks, folders can be pinned for easier access. To pin a frequently-used folder, display the Open backstage area and then click the *Folders* option. Recently opened folders are listed and grouped into categories such as *Today*, *Yesterday*, and *Last Week* to reflect the time they were last accessed. Click the push pin icon to the right of a folder and it will be pinned to the top of the list.

Recovering an Unsaved Workbook

If a workbook is closed without having been saved, it can be recovered with the Recover Unsaved Workbooks button below the *Recent* option list. Click this button and the Open dialog box displays with the names of the workbooks that Excel has saved automatically. At this dialog box, double-click the workbook name to open it.

Clearing the *Recent* Option List and the Recent List

Clear the contents (except pinned workbooks) of the *Recent* option list by right-clicking a workbook name in the list and then clicking *Clear unpinned Workbooks* at the shortcut menu. At the message asking to confirm removal of the items, click Yes. To clear a folder from the Open backstage area, right-click a folder in the list and then click *Remove from list* at the shortcut menu.

Activity 1a **Managing Workbooks at the Open Backstage Area** Part 1 of 3

1. Open Excel.
2. Click the File tab and then click the *Open* option.
3. Make sure the *Recent* option below the heading *Open* is selected. Notice the workbook names that display in the *Recent* option list.
4. Navigate to your EL1C6 folder, open **HEREquip**, and then save it with the name **6-HEREquip**.
5. Close **6-HEREquip**.
6. Open **HEREquipUsage** and then close it.

7. Open **HERBackhoe** and then close it.
8. Pin the three workbooks to the *Recent* option list (you will use them in Activity 1b) by completing the following steps:
   a. Click the File tab and then click the *Open* option. (This displays the Open backstage area with the *Recent* option selected.)
   b. Click the left-pointing push pin icon at the right of **6-HEREquip**. (This changes the pin from left pointing to down pointing and moves the workbook to the top of the list in the *Pinned* category.)

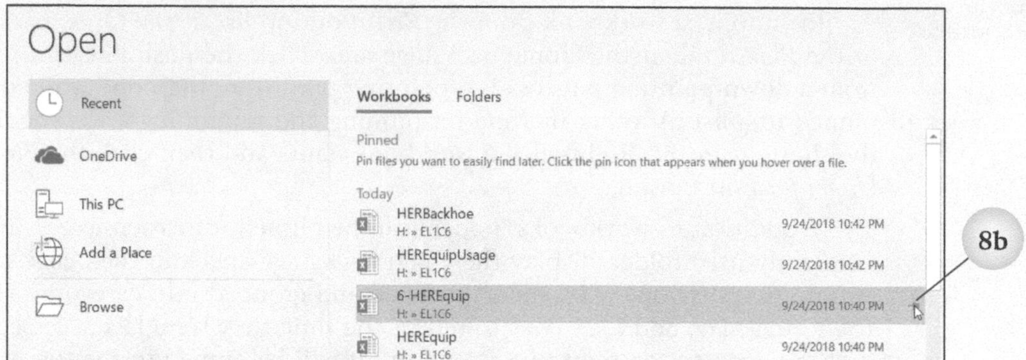

   c. Click the left-pointing push pin icon at the right of **HEREquipUsage**.
   d. Right-click ***HERBackhoe*** and then click *Pin to list* at the shortcut menu.
   e. Click the Back button to exit the Open backstage area.
9. Open **6-HEREquip** by clicking the File tab, clicking the *Open* option, and then clicking ***6-HEREquip*** in the *Recent* option list.

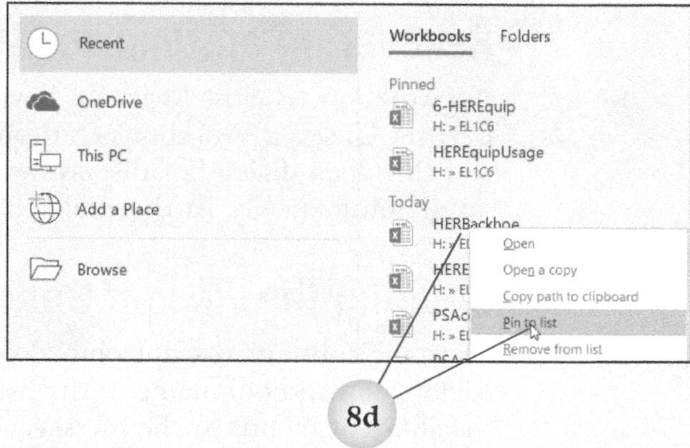

Managing Worksheets

Individual worksheets can be moved or copied within the same workbook or to another existing workbook. Exercise caution when moving sheets, since any calculations and charts based on the data in a worksheet might become inaccurate if a worksheet is moved. To duplicate a sheet in the same workbook, press and hold down the Ctrl key, click the sheet tab and hold down the left mouse button, drag to the new location, and then release the mouse button and the Ctrl key.

Copying a Worksheet to Another Workbook

Copying a Worksheet to Another Workbook

To copy a worksheet to another workbook, open both the source and the destination workbooks. Right-click the sheet tab and then click *Move or Copy* at the shortcut menu. At the Move or Copy dialog box, shown in Figure 6.2, select the name of the destination workbook in the *To book* option drop-down list, select the name of the worksheet the copied worksheet will be placed before in the *Before sheet* list box, click the *Create a copy* check box, and then click OK.

Quick Steps

Copy Worksheet to Another Workbook

1. Right-click sheet tab.
2. Click *Move or Copy.*
3. Select destination workbook.
4. Select worksheet location.
5. Click *Create a copy* check box.
6. Click OK.

Figure 6.2 Move or Copy Dialog Box

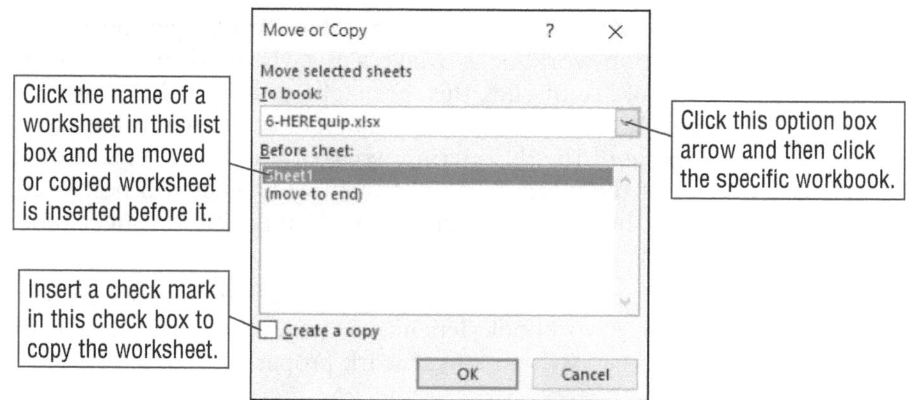

Activity 1b Copying Worksheets to Another Workbook

Part 2 of 3

1. With **6-HEREquip** open, open **HEREquipUsage**.
2. Copy the Front Loader worksheet by completing the following steps:
   a. With **HEREquipUsage** the active workbook, right-click the Front Loader tab and then click *Move or Copy* at the shortcut menu.
   b. Click the *To book* option box arrow and then click ***6-HEREquip.xlsx*** at the drop-down list.
   c. Click *(move to end)* in the *Before sheet* list box.
   d. Click the *Create a copy* check box to insert a check mark.
   e. Click OK. (Excel switches to the **6-HEREquip** workbook and inserts the copied Front Loader worksheet after Sheet1.)

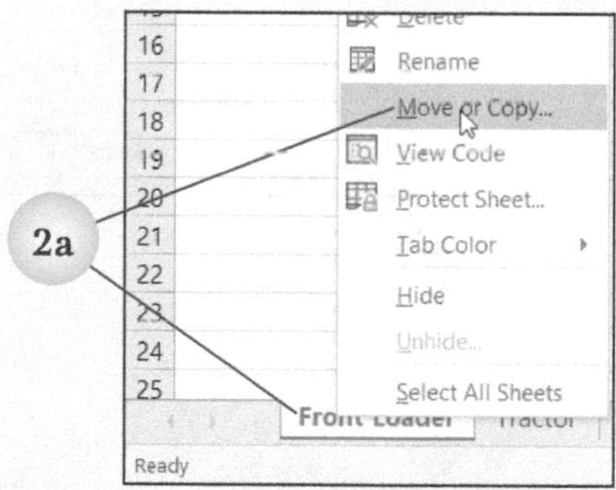

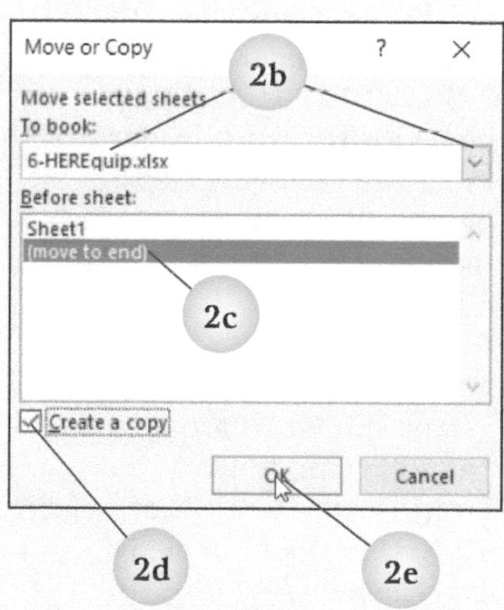

3. Complete steps similar to those in Step 2 to copy the Tractor worksheet to the **6-HEREquip** workbook.
4. Complete steps similar to those in Step 2 to copy the Forklift worksheet to the **6-HEREquip** workbook and insert the Forklift worksheet before the Tractor worksheet.
5. Save **6-HEREquip**.
6. Make **HEREquipUsage** the active workbook and then close it.

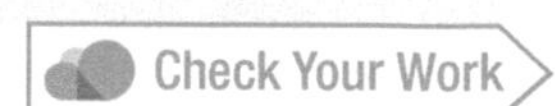

Moving a Worksheet to Another Workbook

Quick Steps

Move Worksheet to Another Workbook

1. Right-click sheet tab.
2. Click *Move or Copy*.
3. Select destination workbook.
4. Select worksheet location.
5. Click OK.

To move a worksheet to another workbook, open both the source and the destination workbooks. Make active the worksheet to be moved in the source workbook, right-click the sheet tab, and then click *Move or Copy* at the shortcut menu. At the Move or Copy dialog box, shown in Figure 6.2 (on page 147), select the name of the destination workbook in the *To book* drop-down list, select the name of the worksheet the moved worksheet will be placed before in the *Before sheet* list box, and then click OK. To reposition a sheet tab, drag the tab to the new position.

Be careful when moving a worksheet to another workbook file. If formulas in the source workbook depend on the contents of the cells in the worksheet that is moved, they will no longer work properly.

Activity 1c Moving a Worksheet to Another Workbook — Part 3 of 3

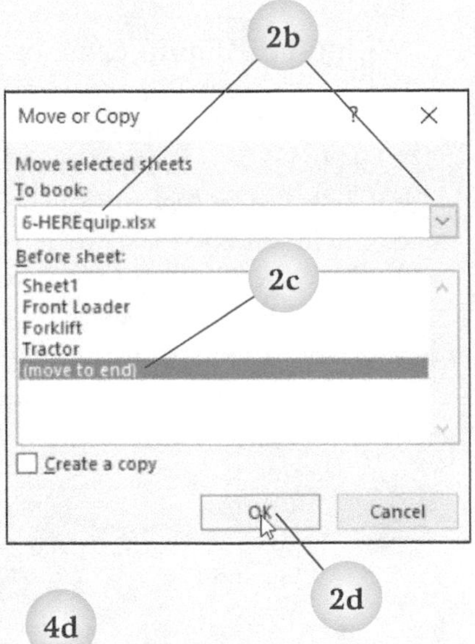

1. With **6-HEREquip** open, open **HERBackhoe**.
2. Move Sheet1 from **HERBackhoe** to **6-HEREquip** by completing the following steps:
   a. With **HERBackhoe** the active workbook, right-click the Sheet1 tab and then click *Move or Copy* at the shortcut menu.
   b. Click the *To book* option box arrow and then click ***6-HEREquip.xlsx*** at the drop-down list.
   c. Click *(move to end)* in the *Before sheet* list box.
   d. Click OK.
3. With **6-HEREquip** open, make the following changes:
   a. Rename Sheet1 as *Equipment Hours*.
   b. Rename Sheet1 (2) as *Backhoe*.
4. Create a range for the front loader total hours available by completing the following steps:
   a. Click the Front Loader tab.
   b. Select the range B4:E4.
   c. Click in the Name box.
   d. Type FrontLoaderHours.
   e. Press the Enter key.
5. Complete steps similar to those in Step 4 to create the following ranges: 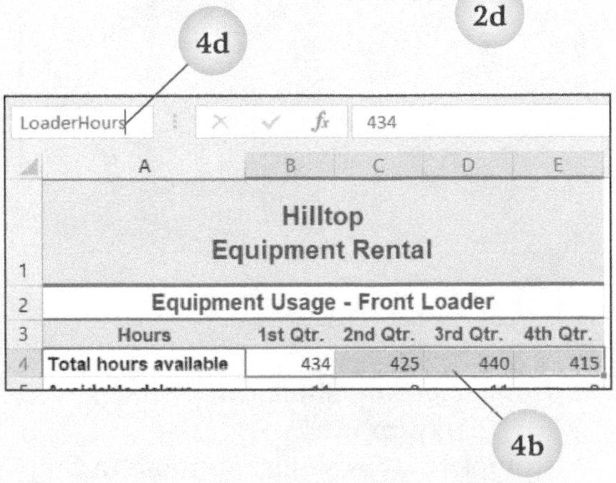
   a. In the Front Loader worksheet, select the range B10:E10 and name it *FrontLoaderHoursInUse*.
   b. Click the Forklift tab and then select the range B4:E4 and name it *ForkliftHours*. Also select the range B10:E10 and name it *ForkliftHoursInUse*.
   c. Click the Tractor tab and then select the range B4:E4 and name it *TractorHours*. Also select the range B10:E10 and name it *TractorHoursInUse*.
   d. Click the Backhoe tab and then select the range B4:E4 and name it *BackhoeHours*. Also select the range B10:E10 and name it *BackhoeHoursInUse*.

6. Click the Equipment Hours tab to make it the active worksheet and then insert a formula that calculates the total hours for the front loader by completing the following steps:
   a. Make cell C4 active.
   b. Type =sum(Fr.
   c. When you type *Fr*, a drop-down list displays with the front loader ranges. Double-click *FrontLoaderHours*.
   d. Type) (the closing parenthesis).

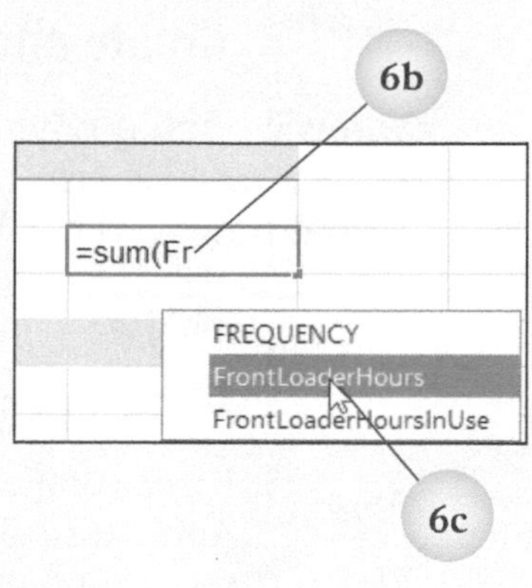

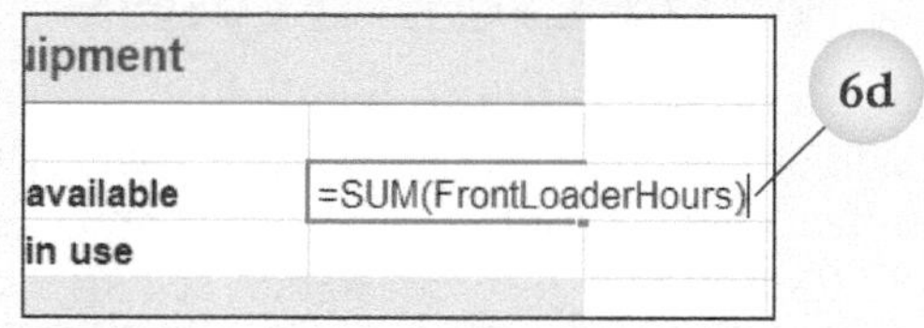

   e. Press the Enter key.
7. Complete steps similar to those in Step 6 to insert ranges in the following cells:
   a. Make cell C5 active and then insert a formula that calculates the total in-use hours for the front loader.
   b. Make cell C8 active and then insert a formula that calculates the total hours available for the forklift.
   c. Make cell C9 active and then insert a formula that calculates the total in-use hours for the forklift.
   d. Make cell C12 active and then insert a formula that calculates the total hours available for the tractor.
   e. Make cell C13 active and then insert a formula that calculates the total in-use hours for the tractor.
   f. Make cell C16 active and then insert a formula that calculates the total hours available for the backhoe.
   g. Make cell C17 active and then insert a formula that calculates the total in-use hours for the backhoe.
8. Make the following changes to specific worksheets:
   a. Click the Front Loader tab and then change the number in cell E4 from *415* to *426* and the number in cell C6 from *6* to *14*.
   b. Click the Forklift tab and then change the number in cell E4 from *415* to *426* and the number in cell D8 from *4* to *12*.
9. Select all the sheet tabs and then create a header that prints your name at the left of each worksheet, the page number in the middle, and the current date at the right.
10. Save and then print all the worksheets in **6-HEREquip**.
11. Close the workbook. (Make sure all the workbooks are closed.)
12. Make the following changes to the Open backstage area:
    a. Click the File tab and then click the *Open* option.
    b. Make sure the *Recent* option is selected.
    c. Unpin **6-HEREquip** from the *Recent* option list by clicking the down-pointing push pin icon at the right of **6-HEREquip**. (This changes the down-pointing push pin to a left-pointing push pin and moves the workbook down the list.)
    d. Unpin **HERBackhoe** and **HEREquipUsage**.
13. Click the Back button to exit the Open backstage area.

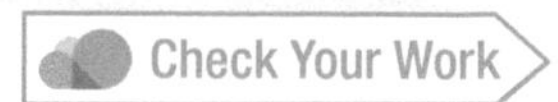

Activity 2 Create and Apply Styles to a Payroll Workbook **5 Parts**

You will open a payroll workbook, define and apply styles, and then modify the styles. You will also copy the styles to another workbook and then apply the styles in that new workbook.

Formatting with Cell Styles

Hint Cell styles are based on the workbook theme.

Formatting can be applied in a worksheet to highlight or accentuate certain cells. Apply formatting to a cell or selected cells with a cell style, which is a predefined set of formatting attributes, such as font, font size, alignment, borders, shading, and so forth. Excel provides a gallery of predesigned cell styles in the Styles group on the Home tab. Click the Cell Styles button to open the gallery. (On a wide-screen monitor, the gallery may already be open and some of the styles will be displayed. Click the More Styles arrow button at the right of the gallery to see all the available styles.)

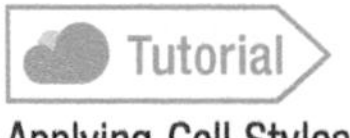

Applying Cell Styles

Quick Steps

Apply Cell Style
1. Select cell(s).
2. Click Cell Styles button.
3. Click style.

Cell Styles

Applying a Cell Style

To apply a style, select the cell(s), click the Cell Styles button in the Styles group on the Home tab, and then click the style at the drop-down gallery, shown in Figure 6.3. Hover the mouse pointer over a style in the drop-down gallery and the cell or selected cells display with the formatting applied.

Figure 6.3 Cell Styles Button Drop-Down Gallery

Activity 2a Formatting with Cell Styles

Part 1 of 5

1. Open **OEPayroll** and then save it with the name **6-OEPayroll**.
2. With Sheet1 the active worksheet, insert the necessary formulas to calculate gross pay, withholding tax amount, social security tax amount, and net pay. ***Hint: Refer to Activity 3c in Chapter 2 for assistance.*** Select the range D4:G4 and then click the Accounting Number Format button to insert dollar symbols.
3. Make Sheet2 active and then insert a formula that calculates the amount due. ***Hint: The formula in cell F4 will be =D4*(1+E4).*** Make cell F4 active and then click the Accounting Number Format button to insert a dollar symbol.
4. Make Sheet3 active and then insert a formula in the *Due Date* column that calculates the purchase date plus the number of days in the *Terms* column. ***Hint: The formula in cell F4 will be =D4+E4.***
5. Apply cell styles to cells by completing the following steps:
   a. Make Sheet1 active and then select cells A11 and A12.
   b. Click the Cell Styles button in the Styles gallery in the Styles group on the Home tab.
   c. At the drop-down gallery, hover the mouse pointer over different styles to see how the formatting affects the selected cells.
   d. Click the *Check Cell* option (second column, first row in the *Data and Model* section).
6. Select cells B11 and B12, click the Cell Styles button, and then click the *Output* option (first column, second row in the *Data and Model* section).

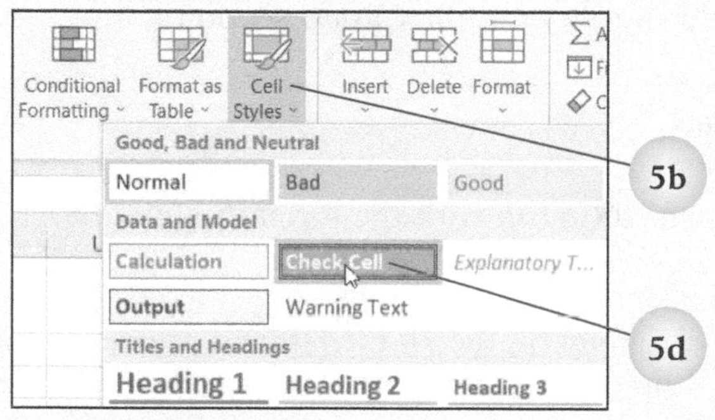

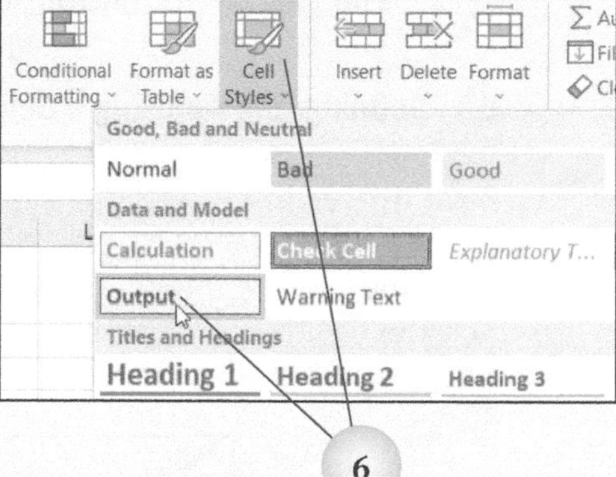

7. Save **6-OEPayroll**.

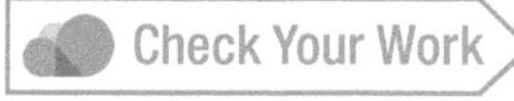

Defining a Cell Style

Quick Steps

Define Cell Style with Existing Formatting

1. Select cell containing formatting.
2. Click Cell Styles button.
3. Click *New Cell Style*.
4. Type name for new style.
5. Click OK.

Defining a Cell Style

Apply a style from the Cell Styles button drop-down gallery or create a new style. Using a style to apply formatting has several advantages. One key advantage is that it helps to ensure consistent formatting from one worksheet to another. To change the formatting, change the style and all the cells formatted with that style automatically reflect the change.

Two basic methods are available for defining a cell style. Define a style with formats already applied to a cell or display the Style dialog box, click the Format button, and then choose formatting options at the Format Cells dialog box. New styles are available only in the workbook in which they are created.

Figure 6.4 Style Dialog Box

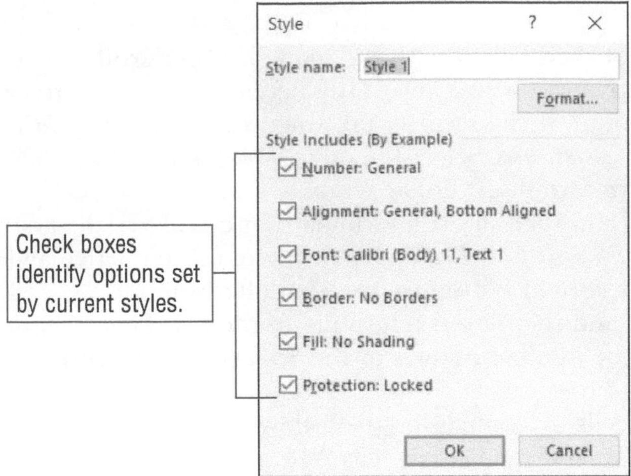

To define a style with existing formatting, select the cell or cells containing the formatting, click the Cell Styles button on the Home tab, and then click the *New Cell Style* option at the bottom of the drop-down gallery. At the Style dialog box, shown in Figure 6.4, type a name for the new style in the *Style name* text box and then click OK to close the dialog box. Custom styles are shown at the top of the Cell Styles button drop-down gallery in the *Custom* section.

Activity 2b Defining and Applying a Cell Style

Part 2 of 5

1. With **6-OEPayroll** open, define a style named *C6Title* with the formatting in cell A1 by completing the following steps:
   a. Make sure Sheet1 is active and then make cell A1 active.
   b. Click the Cell Styles button in the Styles group on the Home tab and then click the *New Cell Style* option at the bottom of the drop-down gallery.

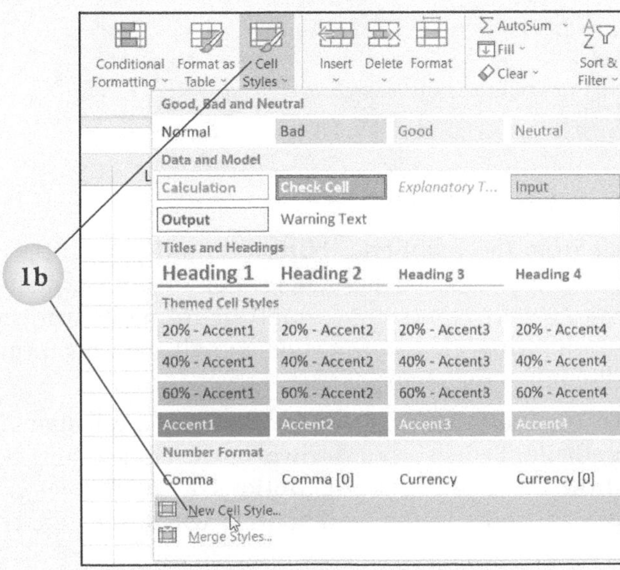

c. At the Style dialog box, type C6Title in the *Style name* text box.
d. Click OK.

2. Even though cell A1 is already formatted, the style has not been applied to it. (Later, you will modify the style and the style must be applied to the cell for the change to affect it.) Apply the C6Title style to cell A1 by completing the following steps:
   a. With cell A1 active, click the Cell Styles button.
   b. Click the *C6Title* style in the *Styles* gallery.

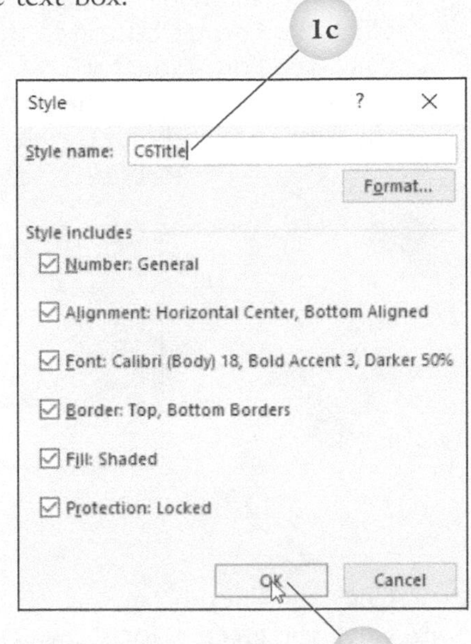

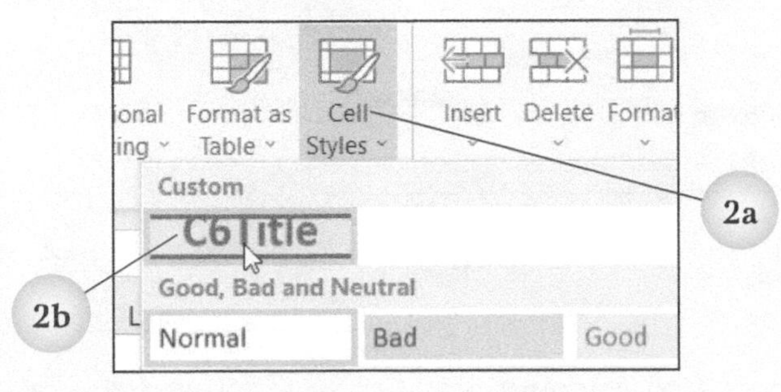

3. Apply the C6Title style to other cells by completing the following steps:
   a. Click the Sheet2 tab.
   b. Make cell A1 active.
   c. Click the *C6Title* style at the Styles gallery. (Notice that the style does not apply row height formatting. The style applies only cell formatting.)
   d. Click the Sheet3 tab.
   e. Make cell A1 active.
   f. Click the *C6Title* style at the Styles gallery.
   g. Click the Sheet1 tab.
4. Save **6-OEPayroll**.

Quick Steps
Define Cell Style
1. Click in blank cell.
2. Click Cell Styles button.
3. Click *New Cell Style*.
4. Type style name.
5. Click Format button.
6. Choose formatting options.
7. Click OK.
8. Click OK.

In addition to defining a style based on cell formatting, a custom style can be defined without first applying the formatting. To do this, display the Style dialog box, type a name for the custom style, and then click the Format button. At the Format Cells dialog box, apply the formatting and then click OK to close the dialog box. At the Style dialog box, remove the check mark from any formatting that should not be included in the style and then click OK to close the Style dialog box.

Activity 2c Defining a Cell Style without First Applying Formatting — Part 3 of 5

1. With **6-OEPayroll** open, define a custom style named *C6Subtitle* without first applying the formatting by completing the following steps:
   a. With Sheet1 active, click in any empty cell.
   b. Click the Cell Styles button and then click *New Cell Style* at the drop-down gallery.

c. At the Style dialog box, type C6Subtitle in the *Style name* text box.
d. Click the Format button in the Style dialog box.
e. Click the Font tab.
f. At the Format Cells dialog box with the Font tab selected, change the font to Candara, the font style to bold, the size to 12 points, and the color to White, Background 1.

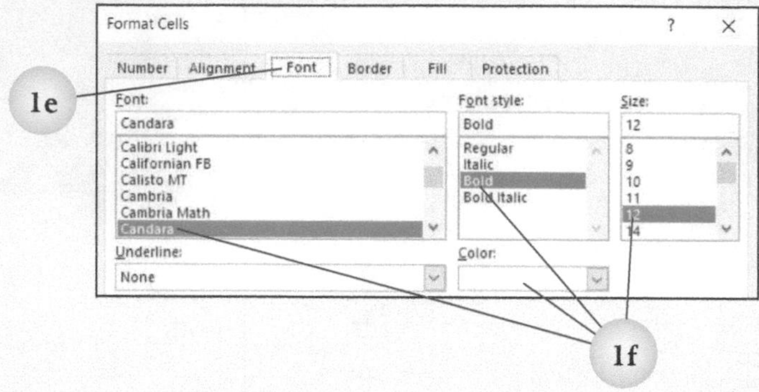

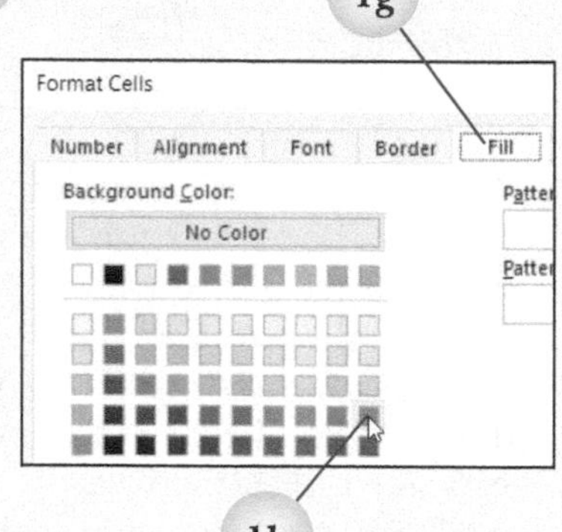

g. Click the Fill tab.
h. Click the green color shown at the right (last column, fifth row).
i. Click the Alignment tab.
j. Change the horizontal alignment to center alignment.
k. Click OK to close the Format Cells dialog box.
l. Click OK to close the Style dialog box.

2. Apply the C6Subtitle custom style by completing the following steps:
   a. Make cell A2 active.
   b. Click the Cell Styles button and then click the *C6Subtitle* style.
   c. Click the Sheet2 tab.
   d. Make cell A2 active.
   e. Click the Cell Styles button and then click the *C6Subtitle* style.
   f. Click the Sheet3 tab.
   g. Make cell A2 active.
   h. Click the Cell Styles button and then click the *C6Subtitle* style.
   i. Click the Sheet1 tab.
3. Apply the following predesigned cell styles:
   a. With Sheet1 the active tab, select the range A3:G3.
   b. Click the Cell Styles button and then click the *Heading 3* style in the *Titles and Headings* section at the drop-down gallery.
   c. Select the range A5:G5.
   d. Click the Cell Styles button and then click the *20% - Accent3* style.
   e. Apply the 20% - Accent3 style to the range A7:G7 and the range A9:G9.
   f. Click the Sheet2 tab.
   g. Select the range A3:F3 and then apply the Heading 3 style.
   h. Select the range A5:F5 and then apply the 20% - Accent3 style.
   i. Apply the 20% - Accent3 style to every other row of cells (the range A7:F7, A9:F9, and so on, finishing with the range A17:F17).
   j. Click the Sheet3 tab.
   k. Select the range A3:F3 and then apply the Heading 3 style.
   l. Apply the 20% - Accent3 style to the ranges A5:F5, A7:F7, and A9:F9.
4. With Sheet3 active, change the height of row 1 to 36.00 points.

5. Make Sheet2 active and then change the height of row 1 to 36.00 points.
6. Make Sheet1 active.
7. Save **6-OEPayroll** and then print only the first worksheet.

Modifying a Cell Style

Quick Steps

Modify Cell Style

1. Click Cell Styles button.
2. Right-click style.
3. Click *Modify*.
4. Click Format button.
5. Make formatting changes.
6. Click OK.
7. Click OK.

Modifying a Cell Style

One of the advantages to formatting cells with a style is that when the formatting is modified, all the cells formatted with that style update automatically. Modify a predesigned style and only the style in the current workbook is affected. Open a blank workbook and the cell styles available are the default styles.

To modify a style, click the Cell Styles button in the Styles group on the Home tab and then right-click the style at the drop-down gallery. At the shortcut menu, click *Modify*. At the Style dialog box, click the Format button. Make the formatting changes at the Format Cells dialog box and then click OK. Click OK to close the Style dialog box and any cells formatted with the style automatically update.

Activity 2d **Modifying Cell Styles** — Part 4 of 5

1. With **6-OEPayroll** open, modify the C6Title custom style by completing the following steps:
   a. Click in any empty cell.
   b. Click the Cell Styles button.
   c. At the drop-down gallery, right-click the *C6Title* style in the *Custom* section and then click *Modify* at the drop-down gallery.
   d. At the Style dialog box, click the Format button.
   e. At the Format Cells dialog box, click the Font tab and then change the font to Candara.
   f. Click the Alignment tab.
   g. Click the *Vertical* option box arrow and then click *Center* at the drop-down list.
   h. Click the Fill tab.
   i. Click the light blue fill color (fifth column, third row), as shown at the right.

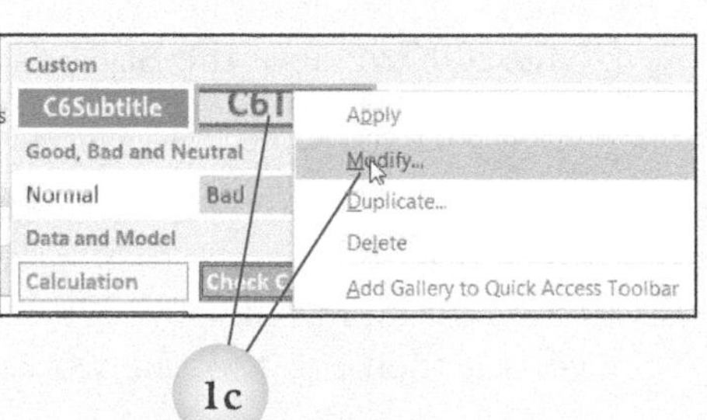

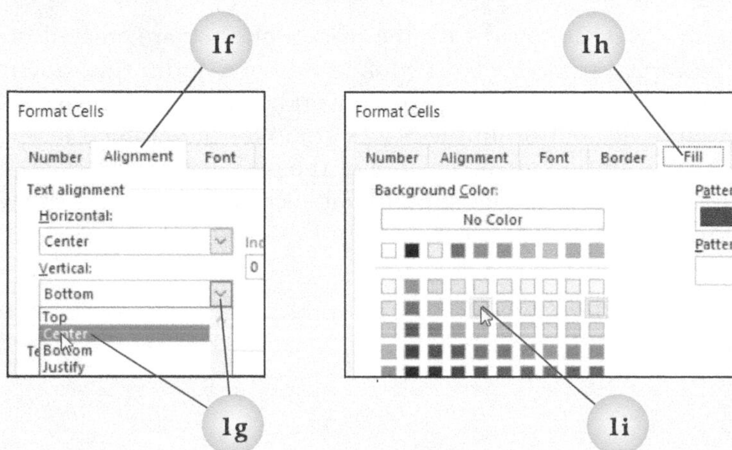

j. Click OK to close the Format Cells dialog box.
k. Click OK to close the Style dialog box.

2. Modify the C6Subtitle style by completing the following steps:
   a. Click in any empty cell.
   b. Click the Cell Styles button.
   c. At the drop-down gallery, right-click the *C6Subtitle* style in the *Custom* section and then click *Modify*.
   d. At the Style dialog box, click the Format button.
   e. At the Format Cells dialog box, click the Font tab and then change the font to Calibri.
   f. Click the Fill tab.
   g. Click the dark blue fill color, as shown at the right (fifth column, sixth row).
   h. Click OK to close the Format Cells dialog box.
   i. Click OK to close the Style dialog box.
3. Modify the predefined 20% - Accent3 style by completing the following steps:
   a. Click the Cell Styles button.
   b. At the drop-down gallery, right-click the *20% - Accent3* style and then click *Modify*.
   c. At the Style dialog box, click the Format button.
   d. At the Format Cells dialog box, click the Fill tab.
   e. Click the light blue fill color, as shown at the right (fifth column, second row).
   f. Click OK to close the Format Cells dialog box.
   g. Click OK to close the Style dialog box.
4. Click each sheet tab and notice the formatting changes made by the modified styles.
5. Change the name of Sheet1 to *Weekly Payroll*, the name of Sheet2 to *Invoices*, and the name of Sheet3 to *Overdue Accounts*.
6. Apply a different color to each of the three sheet tabs.
7. Save and then print all the worksheets in **6-OEPayroll**.

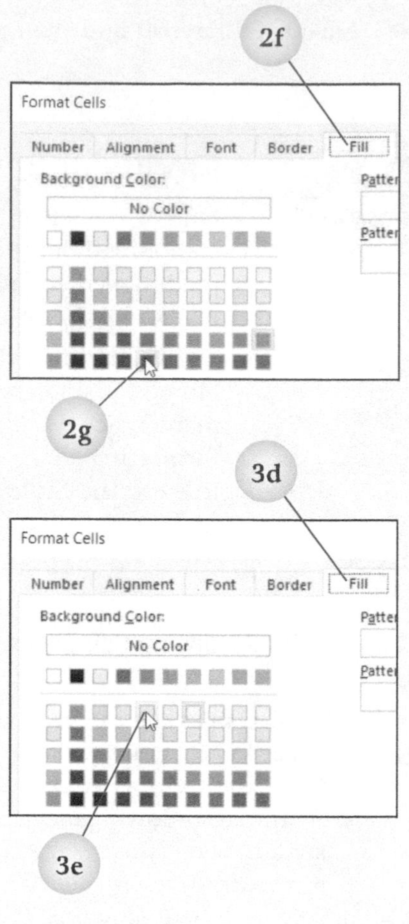

Copying Cell Styles to Another Workbook

Quick Steps

Copy Cell Styles to Another Workbook

1. Open workbook containing styles.
2. Open workbook to be modified.
3. Click Cell Styles button.
4. Click *Merge Styles* option.
5. Double-click name of workbook that contains styles.

Copying Cell Styles to Another Workbook

Custom styles are saved with the workbook they are created in. However, styles can be copied from one workbook to another. To do this, open the workbook containing the styles and open the workbook the styles will be copied into. Click the Cell Styles button in the Styles group on the Home tab and then click the *Merge Styles* option at the bottom of the drop-down gallery. At the Merge Styles dialog box, shown in Figure 6.5, double-click the name of the workbook that contains the styles to be copied.

Hint The Undo command will not reverse the merging of styles at the Merge Styles dialog box.

Figure 6.5 Merge Styles Dialog Box

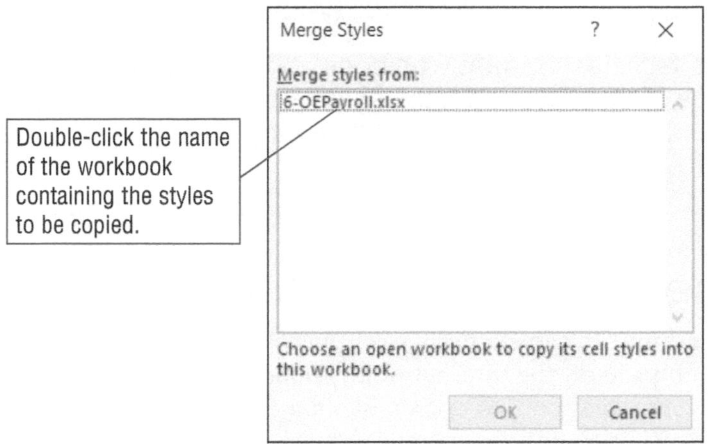

Removing a Cell Style

Quick Steps

Remove Cell Style
1. Select cells formatted with style to be removed.
2. Click Cell Styles button.
3. Click *Normal* style.

Delete Cell Style
1. Click Cell Styles button.
2. Right-click style.
3. Click *Delete*.

Remove formatting applied by a style by applying the Normal style, which is the default. To do this, select the cells, click the Cell Styles button, and then click the *Normal* style at the drop-down gallery.

Deleting a Cell Style

To delete a style, click the Cell Styles button in the Styles group on the Home tab. At the drop-down gallery, right-click the style to be deleted and then click *Delete* at the shortcut menu. Formatting applied by the deleted style is removed from cells in the workbook. The Normal cell style cannot be deleted.

Activity 2e Copying Cell Styles to Another Workbook

Part 5 of 5

1. With **6-OEPayroll** open, open **OEPlans**.
2. Save the workbook and name it **6-OEPlans**.
3. Copy the styles in **6-OEPayroll** into **6-OEPlans** by completing the following steps:
   a. With **6-OEPlans** as the active workbook, click the Cell Styles button in the Styles group on the Home tab.
   b. Click the *Merge Styles* option at the bottom of the drop-down gallery.
   c. At the Merge Styles dialog box, double-click ***6-OEPayroll.xlsx*** in the *Merge styles from* list box.
   d. At the message asking if you want to merge styles that have the same names, click Yes.
4. Apply the C6Title custom style to cell A1 and the C6Subtitle custom style to cell A2.
5. Increase the height of row 1 to 36.00 points.
6. Save, print, and then close **6-OEPlans**.
7. Close **6-OEPayroll**.

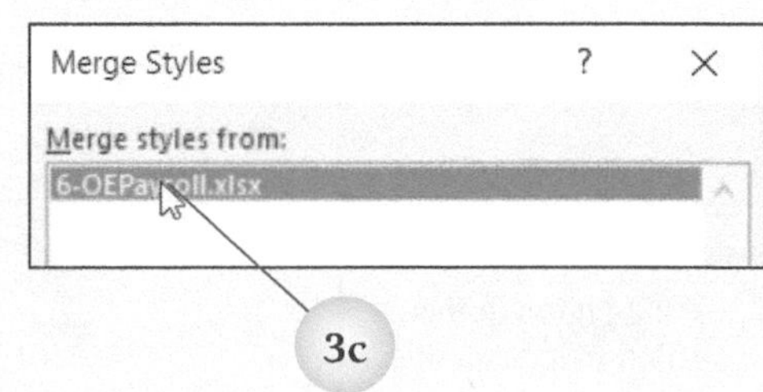

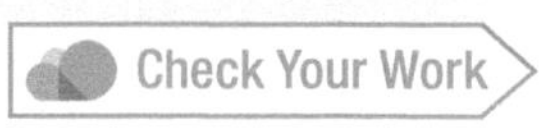

Activity 3 Insert, Modify, and Remove Hyperlinks — 3 Parts

You will open a facilities account workbook and then insert hyperlinks to a website, to cells in other worksheets in the workbook, and to another workbook. You will modify and edit hyperlinks and then remove a hyperlink from the workbook.

Inserting Hyperlinks

Quick Steps

Insert Hyperlink

1. Click Insert tab.
2. Click Link button.
3. Make changes at Insert Hyperlink dialog box.
4. Click OK.

Inserting Hyperlinks

A hyperlink can serve a number of purposes in a workbook: Click it to navigate to a web page on the internet or a specific location in the workbook, to display a different workbook, to open a file in a different program, to create a new document, or to link to an email address. Create a customized hyperlink by clicking in a cell in a workbook, clicking the Insert tab, and then clicking the Link button in the Links group. This displays the Insert Hyperlink dialog box, shown in Figure 6.6. At this dialog box, identify what is to be linked and the location of the link. Click the ScreenTip button to customize the hyperlink ScreenTip.

Linking to an Existing Web Page or File

At the Insert Hyperlink dialog box, link to a web page on the internet by typing a web address or by using the Existing File or Web Page button in the *Link to* section. To link to an existing web page, type the address of the web page, such as *www.paradigmeducation.com*.

By default, the automatic formatting of hyperlinks is turned on and the web address is formatted as a hyperlink. (The text is underlined and the color changes to blue.) Turn off the automatic formatting of hyperlinks at the AutoCorrect dialog box. Display this dialog box by clicking the File tab, clicking *Options*, and then clicking *Proofing* in the left panel of the Excel Options dialog box. Click the AutoCorrect Options button to display the AutoCorrect dialog box. At this dialog

Figure 6.6 Insert Hyperlink Dialog Box

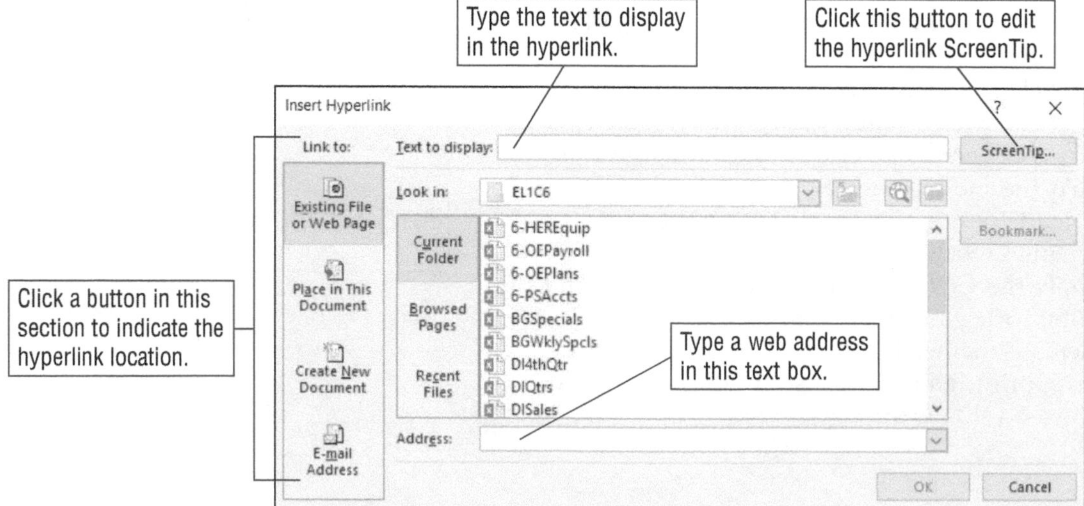

box, click the AutoFormat As You Type tab and then remove the check mark from the *Internet and network paths with hyperlinks* check box.

A hyperlink can be inserted that links to any of several sources, such as another Excel workbook, a Word document, or a PowerPoint presentation. To link an Excel workbook to a workbook or file in another application, display the Insert Hyperlink dialog box and then click the Existing File or Web Page button in the *Link to* section. Use buttons in the *Look in* section to navigate to the folder containing the file and then click the file name. Make other changes in the Insert Hyperlink dialog box as needed and then click OK.

Navigating Using Hyperlinks

Navigate to a hyperlinked location by clicking the hyperlink in the worksheet. Hover the mouse pointer over the hyperlink and a ScreenTip displays with the address of the hyperlinked location. To display specific information in the ScreenTip, click the ScreenTip button at the Insert Hyperlink dialog box, type the text in the Set Hyperlink ScreenTip dialog box, and then click OK.

Activity 3a **Linking to a Website and Another Workbook** Part 1 of 3

1. Open **PSAccts** and then save it with the name **6-PSAccts.**
2. Insert a hyperlink to information about Pyramid Sales, a fictitious company (the hyperlink will connect to the publishing company website), by completing the following steps:
   a. Make cell A13 active in the Summary sheet.
   b. Click the Insert tab and then click the Link button in the Links group.
   c. At the Insert Hyperlink dialog box, if necessary, click the Existing File or Web Page button in the *Link to* section.
   d. Type www.paradigmeducation.com in the *Address* text box. (*http://* will automatically be added to the address)
   e. Select the text in the *Text to display* text box and then type Company information.
   f. Click the ScreenTip button in the upper right corner of the dialog box.

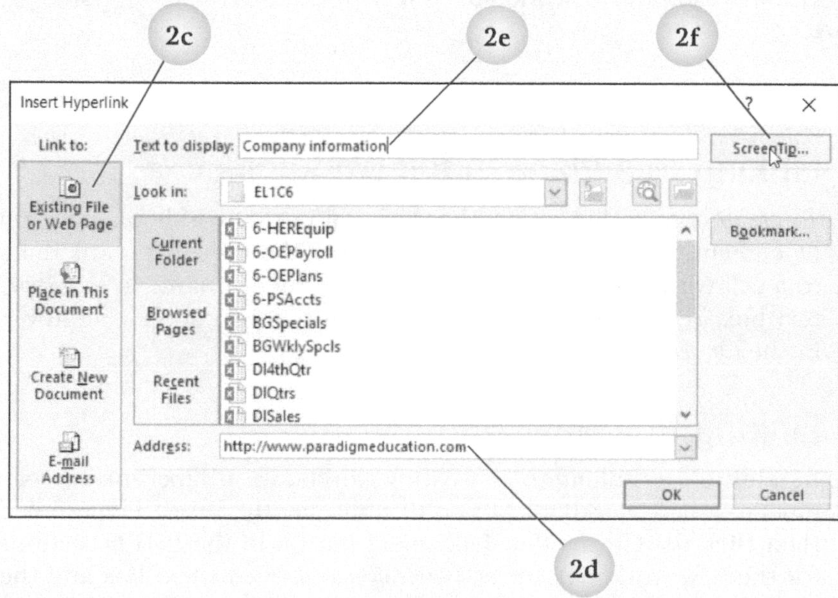

g. At the Set Hyperlink ScreenTip dialog box, type View the company website. and then click OK.
h. Click OK to close the Insert Hyperlink dialog box.

3. Navigate to the company website (in this case, the publishing company website) by clicking the Company information hyperlink in cell A13.
4. Close the web browser.
5. Create a link to another workbook by completing the following steps:
   a. Make cell A11 active, type Semiannual sales, and then press the Enter key.
   b. Make cell A11 active and then click the Link button.
   c. At the Insert Hyperlink dialog box, make sure the Existing File or Web Page button is selected.
   d. If necessary, click your *Look in* option box arrow and then navigate to your EL1C6 folder.
   e. Double-click ***PSSalesAnalysis***.

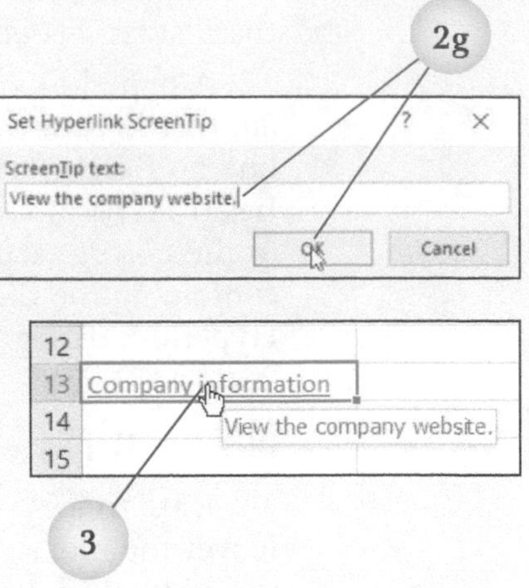

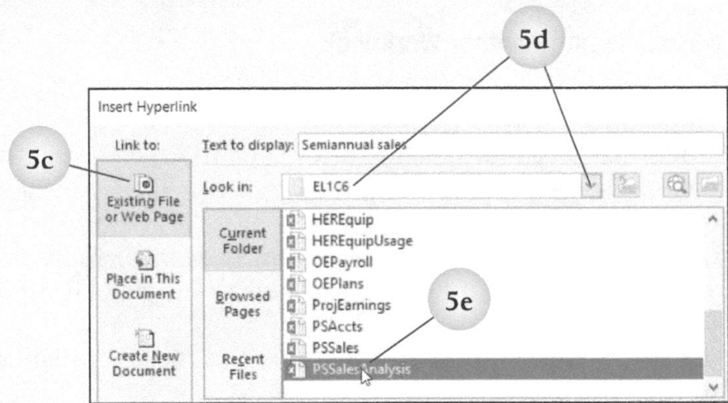

6. Click the Semiannual sales hyperlink to open **PSSalesAnalysis**.
7. Look at the information in the workbook and then close it.
8. Save **6-PSAccts**.

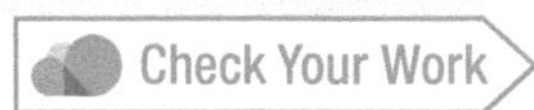

Linking to a Place in the Workbook

To create a hyperlink to another location in the workbook, click the Place in This Document button in the *Link to* section in the Edit Hyperlink dialog box. To link to a cell within the same worksheet, type the cell name in the *Type the cell reference* text box. To link to another worksheet in the workbook, click the worksheet name in the *Or select a place in this document* list box.

Linking to a New Workbook

In addition to linking to an existing workbook, a hyperlink can be inserted that links to a new workbook. To do this, display the Insert Hyperlink dialog box and then click the Create New Document button in the *Link to* section. Type a name for the new workbook in the *Name of new document* text box and then specify if the workbook will be edited now or later.

Linking Using a Graphic

A graphic—such as an image, picture, or text box—can be used to create a hyperlink to a file or website. To create a hyperlink with a graphic, select the graphic, click the Insert tab, and then click the Link button. Or right-click the graphic and then click *Link* at the shortcut menu. At the Insert Hyperlink dialog box, specify the location to be linked to and the text to display in the hyperlink.

Linking to an Email Address

At the Insert Hyperlink dialog box, a hyperlink can be inserted that links to an email address. To do this, click the E-mail Address button in the *Link to* section, type the address in the *E-mail address* text box, and then type a subject for the email in the *Subject* text box. Click in the *Text to display* text box and then type the text to display in the worksheet.

Activity 3b **Linking to a Place in a Workbook, Linking to Another Workbook, and Linking from a Graphic**

Part 2 of 3

1. With **6-PSAccts** open, create a link from the balance in cell B8 to the balance in cell G20 in the January worksheet by completing the following steps:
   a. Make cell B8 active.
   b. Click the Link button.
   c. At the Insert Hyperlink dialog box, click the Place in This Document button in the *Link to* section.
   d. Select the text in the *Type the cell reference* text box and then type g20.
   e. Click *January* in the *Or select a place in this document* list box.
   f. Click OK to close the Insert Hyperlink dialog box.

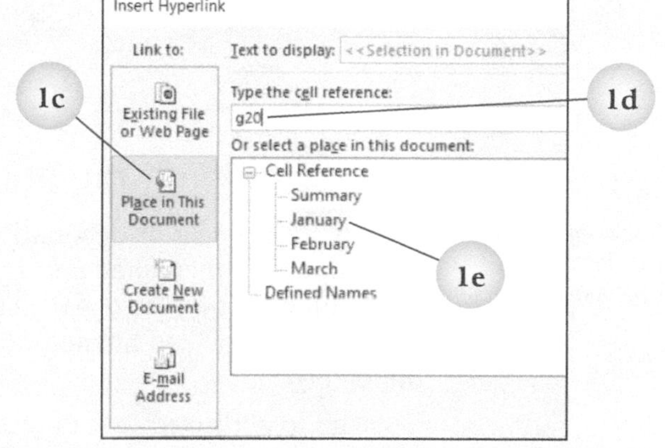

2. Make cell C8 active and then complete steps similar to those in Steps 1b through 1f except click *February* in the *Or select a place in this document* list box.
3. Make cell D8 active and then complete steps similar to those in Steps 1b through 1f except click *March* in the *Or select a place in this document* list box.
4. Click the hyperlinked amount in cell B8. (This makes cell G20 active in the January worksheet.)
5. Click the Summary sheet tab.
6. Click the hyperlinked amount in cell C8. (This makes cell G20 active in the February worksheet.)
7. Click the Summary sheet tab.
8. Click the hyperlinked amount in cell D8. (This makes cell G20 active in the March worksheet.)
9. Click the Summary sheet tab.

10. Use the first pyramid graphic image in cell A1 to create a link to the company web page by completing the following steps:
   a. Right-click the first pyramid graphic image in cell A1 and then click *Link* at the shortcut menu.
   b. At the Insert Hyperlink dialog box, if necessary, click the Existing File or Web Page button in the *Link to* section.
   c. Type www.paradigmeducation.com in the *Address* text box.
   d. Click the ScreenTip button in the upper right corner of the dialog box.
   e. At the Set Hyperlink ScreenTip dialog box, type View the company website. and then click OK.
   f. Click OK to close the Insert Hyperlink dialog box.
11. Make cell A5 active.
12. Navigate to the company website (the publishing company website) by clicking the first pyramid graphic image.
13. Close the web browser.
14. Save **6-PSAccts**.

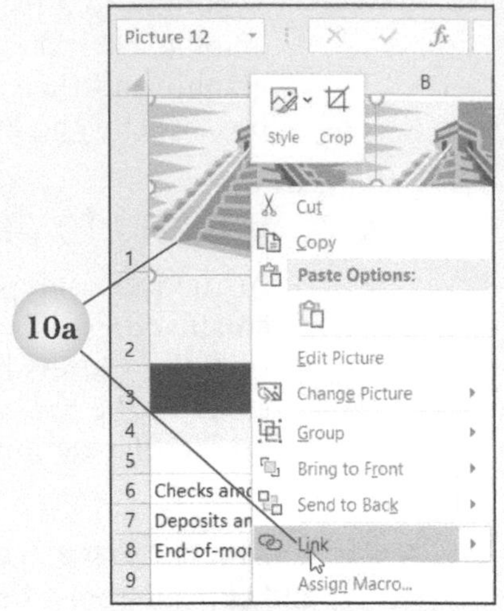

Modifying, Editing, and Removing a Hyperlink

Modifying, Editing, and Removing a Hyperlink

The hyperlink text or destination can be modified. To do this, right-click the hyperlink and then click *Edit Hyperlink* at the shortcut menu. At the Edit Hyperlink dialog box, make changes and then close the dialog box. The same options are provided at the Edit Hyperlink dialog box as the Insert Hyperlink dialog box.

The hyperlinked text in a cell can also be modified. To do this, make the cell active and then make the changes, such as applying a different font or font size, changing the text color, and adding a text effect. Remove a hyperlink from a workbook by right-clicking the cell containing the hyperlink and then clicking *Remove Hyperlink* at the shortcut menu.

Activity 3c **Modifying, Editing, and Removing a Hyperlink** Part 3 of 3

1. With **6-PSAccts** open, modify the Semiannual sales hyperlink by completing the following steps:
   a. Position the mouse pointer on the Semiannual sales hyperlink in cell A11, click the right mouse button, and then click *Edit Hyperlink* at the shortcut menu.
   b. At the Edit Hyperlink dialog box, select the text *Semiannual sales* in the *Text to display* text box and then type Customer sales analysis.

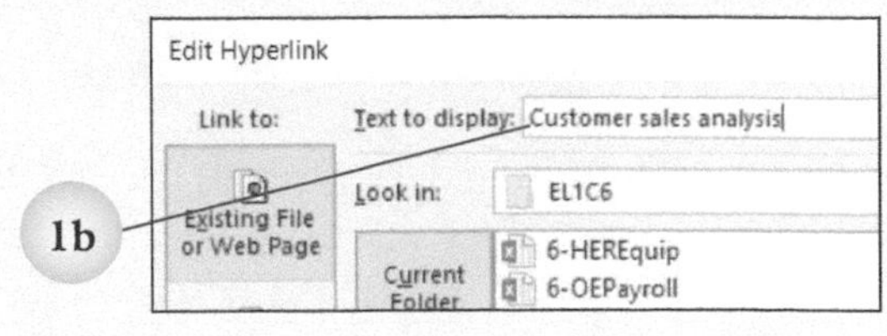

c. Click the ScreenTip button in the upper right corner of the dialog box.
d. At the Set Hyperlink ScreenTip dialog box, type Click this hyperlink to display the workbook containing customer sales analysis.
e. Click OK to close the Set Hyperlink ScreenTip dialog box.
f. Click OK to close the Edit Hyperlink dialog box.
2. Click the Customer sales analysis hyperlink.
3. After looking at the **PSSalesAnalysis** workbook, close it.
4. With cell A11 active, edit the Customer sales analysis hyperlink text by completing the following steps:
a. Click the Home tab.
b. Click the Font Color button arrow and then click the *Dark Red* color option (first option in the *Standard Colors* section).
c. Click the Bold button.
d. Click the Underline button. (This removes underlining from the text.)
5. Remove the Company information hyperlink by right-clicking in cell A13 and then clicking *Remove Hyperlink* at the shortcut menu.
6. Press the Delete key to remove the contents of cell A13.
7. Save, print only the first worksheet (the Summary worksheet), and then close **6-PSAccts**.

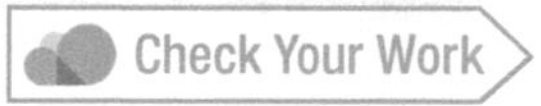

Activity 4 Create a Billing Statement Using a Template; Posting, Editing and Deleting Comments — 3 Parts

You will open a billing statement template provided by Excel, add data, and then save the template as an Excel workbook. You will also post, edit, and delete comments in the billing statement workbook.

Using Templates

Using Excel Templates

Excel provides a number of template worksheet forms for specific uses. Use Excel templates to create a variety of worksheets with specialized formatting, such as balance sheets, billing statements, loan amortizations, sales invoices, and time cards. Display installed templates by clicking the File tab and then clicking the *New* option. This displays the New backstage area, as shown in Figure 6.7.

Quick Steps

Use Excel Template
1. Click File tab.
2. Click *New* option.
3. Double-click template.

Click a template in the New backstage area and a preview of the template displays in a window. Click the Create button in the template window and a workbook based on the template opens and displays on the screen.

Locations for personalized text are shown in placeholders in the worksheet. To enter information in the worksheet, position the mouse pointer (white plus symbol [+]) in the location the data is to be typed and then click the left mouse button. After typing the data, click the next location. The insertion point can also be moved to another cell using the commands learned in Chapter 1. For example, press the Tab key to make the next cell active or press Shift + Tab to make the previous cell active. If the computer is connected to the internet, a number of templates offered by Microsoft can be downloaded.

Figure 6.7 New Backstage Area

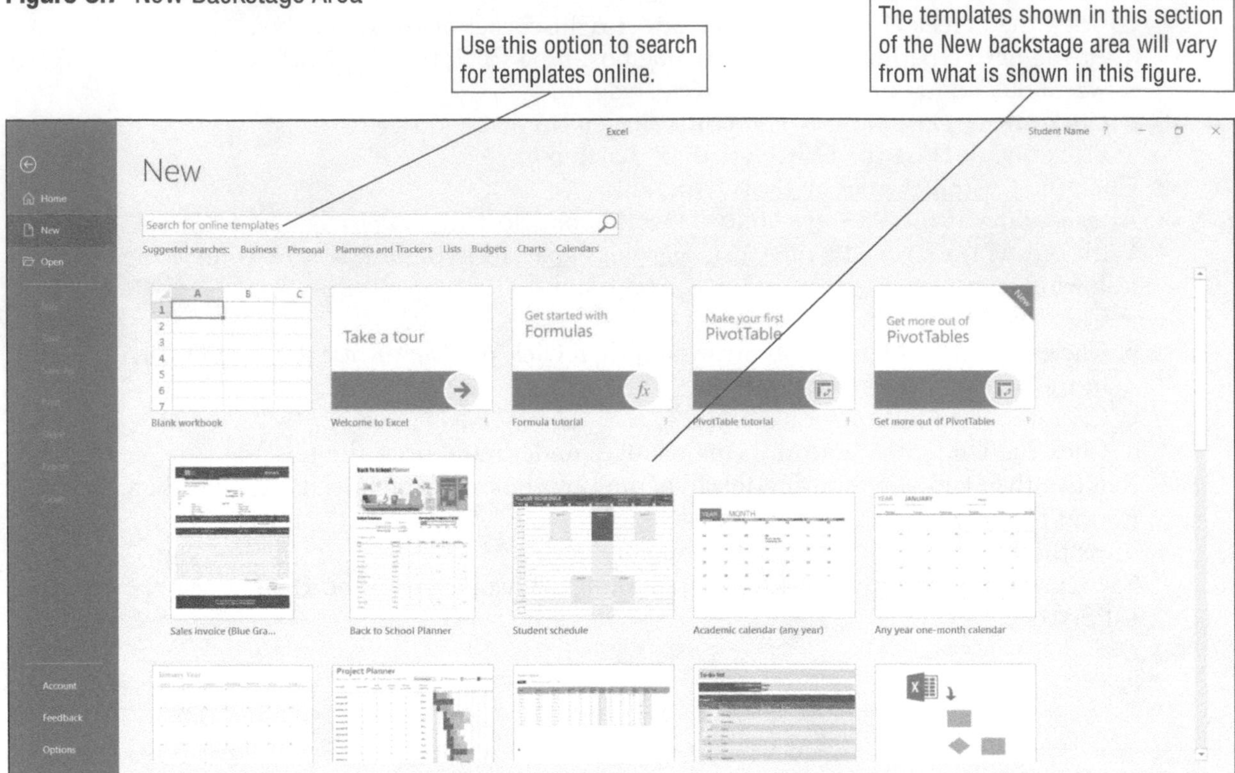

Activity 4a Preparing a Billing Statement Using a Template

Part 1 of 3

1. Click the File tab and then click the *New* option.
2. At the New backstage area, click in the search text box, type billing statement, and then press the Enter key.
3. Double-click the *Billing statement* template (see image below). If you are unable to access online templates, open the **BillingStatement** file in your EL1C6 folder.

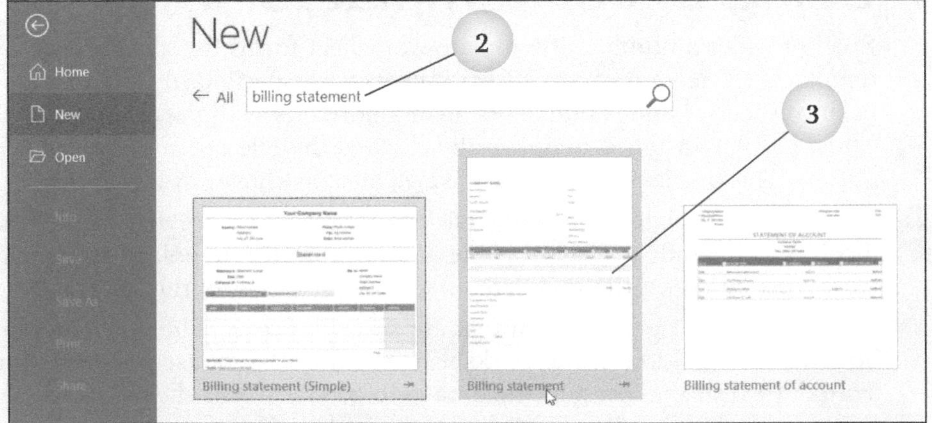

4. Make cell B1 active and then type IN-FLOW SYSTEMS.
5. Click in the cell to the right of *Street Address* (cell C2) and then type 320 Milander Way.

6. Click in each of the cells for the labels specified below and then type the text indicated:

Address 2 (cell C3): P.O. Box 2300
City, ST ZIP Code (cell C4): Boston, MA 02188
Phone (cell G2): (617) 555-3900
Fax (cell G3): (617) 555-3945
E-mail (cell G4): inflow@ppi-edu.net
Statement # (cell C6): 5432
Date (cell C7): =TODAY()
Customer ID (cell C8): 25-345
Name (cell G6): Aidan Mackenzie
Company Name (cell G7): Stanfield Enterprises
Street Address (cell G8): 9921 South 42nd Avenue
Address 2 (cell G9): P.O. Box 5540
City, ST ZIP Code (cell G10): Boston, MA 02193
Type (cell C13): System Unit
Invoice # (cell D13): 7452
Description (cell E13): Calibration Unit
Amount (cell F13): 950
Payment (cell G13): 200
Customer Name (cell C22): Stanfield Enterprises
Amount Enclosed (cell C27): 750

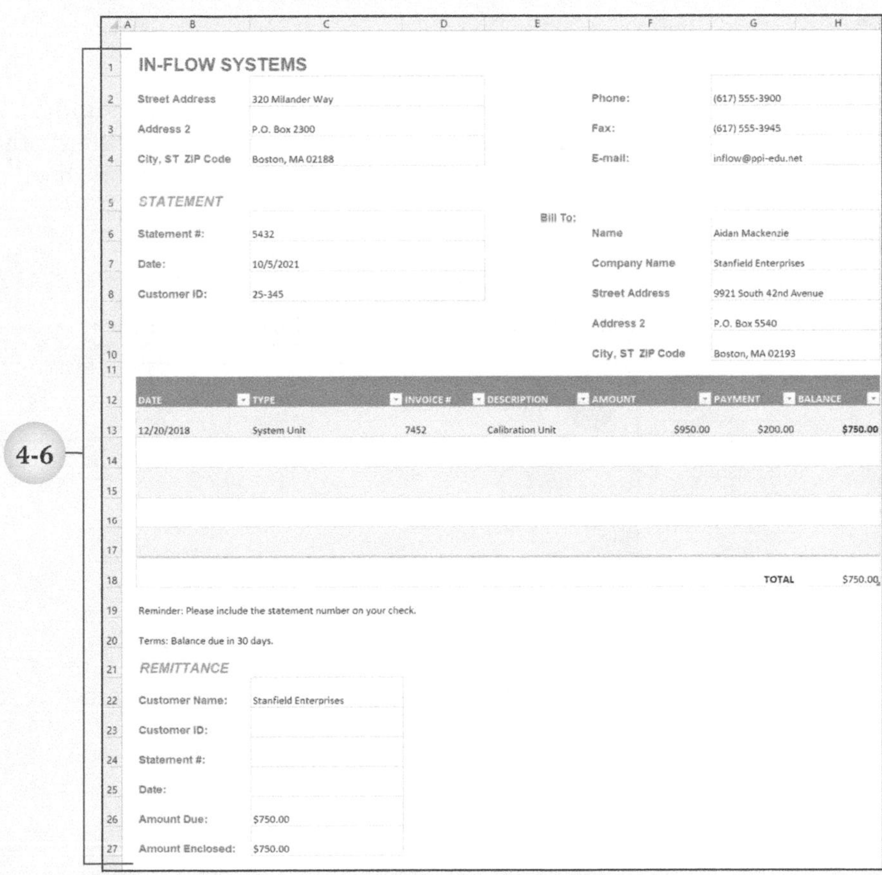

7. Save the completed invoice and name it **6-Billing**.

Inserting, Editing, and Printing Comments

Inserting and Managing Comments

Excel includes a comment feature that allows users to post, edit, reply, and delete comments. A comment is a pop-up box that is attached to a cell and contains text pertaining to the contents of the cell, as shown in Figure 6.8. Other users can post replies to a comment, starting a dialog between users to assist in reviewing a workbook. A cell that contains a comment will show a colored comment icon in the upper right corner of a cell, alerting the reader that a comment exists. Display a comment by hovering the mouse over the cell that contains a comment. Insert and manage comments with buttons in the Comments group on the Review tab, as shown in Figure 6.9.

Inserting a New Comment

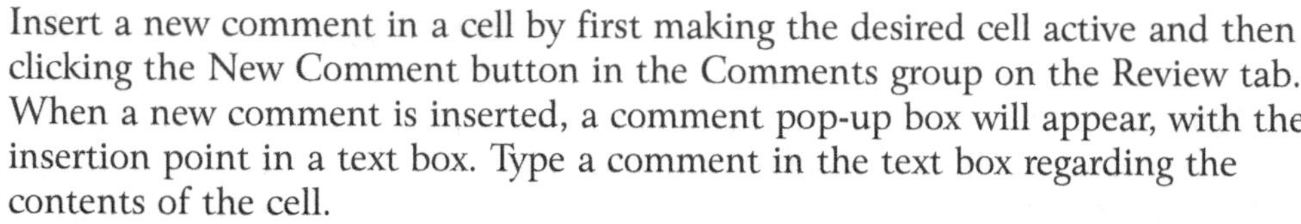

New Comment

Quick Steps

Insert New Comment

1. Click in cell.
2. Click Review tab.
3. Click New Comment button.
4. Type comment.

OR

1. Right-click cell.
2. Click *New Comment* option.
3. Type comment.

Insert a new comment in a cell by first making the desired cell active and then clicking the New Comment button in the Comments group on the Review tab. When a new comment is inserted, a comment pop-up box will appear, with the insertion point in a text box. Type a comment in the text box regarding the contents of the cell.

A new comment can also be inserted using the shortcut menu. Insert a new comment using the shortcut menu by right-clicking a cell and then clicking the *New Comment* option on the shortcut menu.

Posting a Comment

Once a comment is typed into the text box of the comment pop-up box, click the Post button to post the comment. Once a comment has been posted, other users can reply to it and additional comments can be added to the worksheet.

Figure 6.8 Comment Box

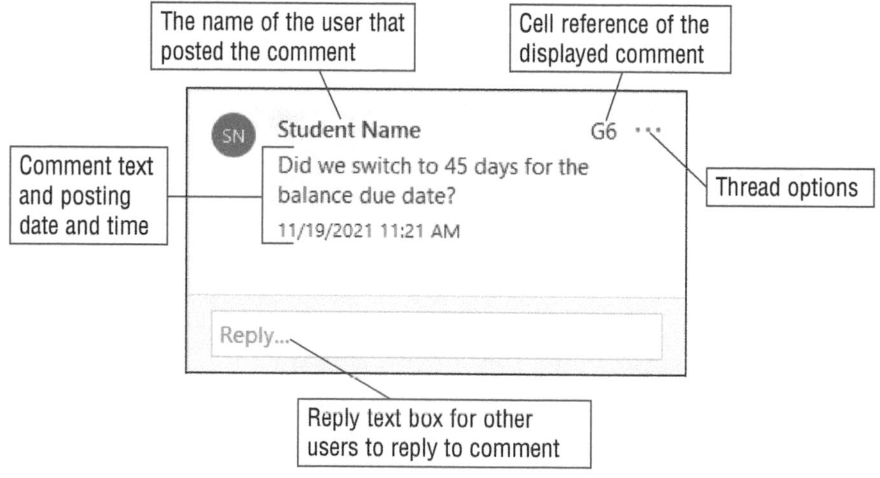

Figure 6.9 Review Tab

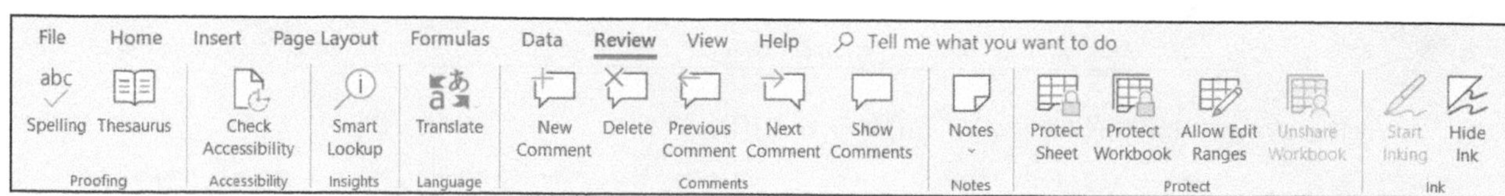

Activity 4b Inserting and Posting Comments

1. With 6-Billing open, insert a new comment by completing the following steps:
   a. Make cell C3 active.
   b. Click the Review tab.
   c. Click the New Comment button in the Comments group.

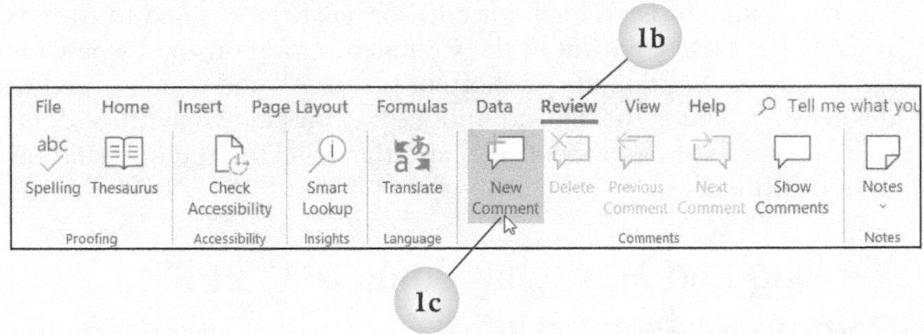

   d. Type Please enter the new P.O. Box for the Billing department here.
   e. Click the Post button.

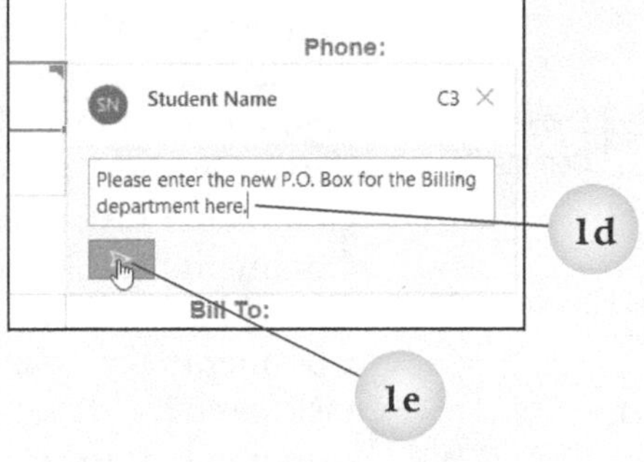

2. Insert a new comment indicating that the contact person for Stanfield Enterprises has changed by completing the following steps:
   a. Right-click cell G6.
   b. Click the *New Comment* option at the shortcut menu.
   c. Type Check with Stanfield Enterprises to learn the name of their new contact person.
   d. Click the Post button.

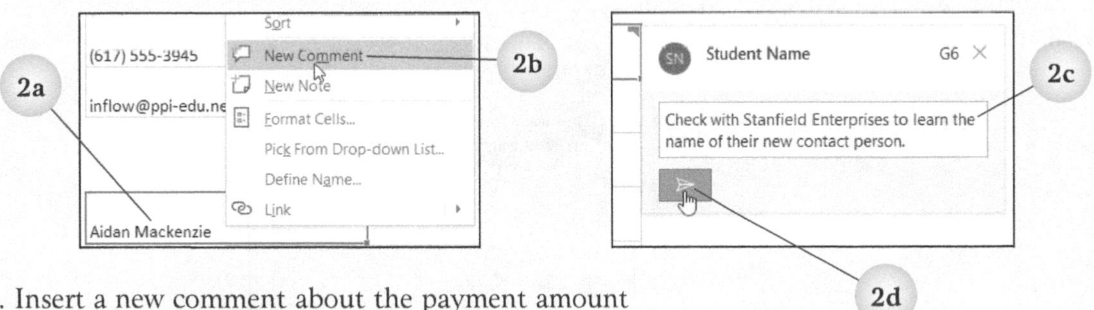

3. Insert a new comment about the payment amount by completing the following steps:
   a. Click in cell G13.
   b. Click the New Comment button.
   c. Type Ask Roger if this is the correct payment previously sent by Stanfield Enterprises.
   d. Click the Post button.
4. Insert a new comment about the balance due by completing the following steps:
   a. Click in cell B20.
   b. Click the New Comment button.
   c. Type Did we switch to 45 days for the balance due date?
   d. Click the Post button.
5. Save **6-Billing**.

Editing and Deleting a Comment

After a comment has been posted, it can be edited by using the Edit button in the comment box. Click in a cell that contains a posted comment and then position the mouse pointer anywhere inside the comment box and an Edit button appears in the lower right corner of the comment box. Click the Edit button and then use the mouse and keyboard to make edits to the comment text.

 Delete

If a comment is no longer needed or has been entered in the wrong cell, delete it using the Delete button in the Comment group on the Review tab or using the *Delete Comment* option at the shortcut menu. All comments in a thread can be deleted by clicking the Thread options button (shown as three dots in the upper right corner of the comment box) and then clicking the *Delete thread* option at the drop-down list.

Viewing and Managing Comments at the Comments Task Pane

 Show Comments

Quick Steps

Open Comments Task Pane

1. Click Review tab.
2. Click Show Comments button.

In a large worksheet, locating every cell that contains a comment may be difficult. To view all comments at a glance, open the Comments task pane, as shown in Figure 6.10. Open the Comments task pane by clicking the Show Comments button in the Comments group on the Review tab. Comments will appear in the Comments task pane in order first by row number and then by column letter. Comments can be edited, deleted, and replied to in the Comments task pane. If a worksheet contains more comments than can be shown at one time in the Comments task pane, a scroll bar is added to the task pane. Close the Comments task pane by clicking the Close button in the task pane or by clicking the Show Comments button.

Figure 6.10 Comments task pane

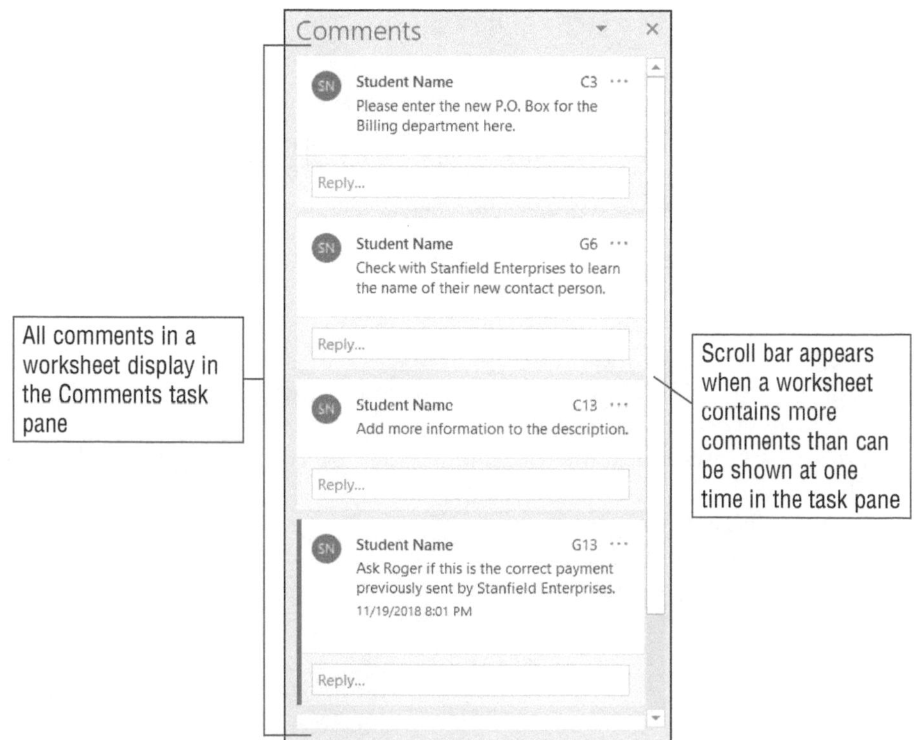

Activity 4c Editing, Deleting, and Showing Comments

Part 3 of 3

1. With 6-Billing open, edit the comment in cell G6 by completing the following steps:
   a. Click in cell G6.
   b. Position the mouse pointer anywhere in the Comment box.
   c. Click the Edit button.
   d. Move the insertion point to just before the period, press the spacebar, and then type in the Accounts department.
   e. Click the Save button.

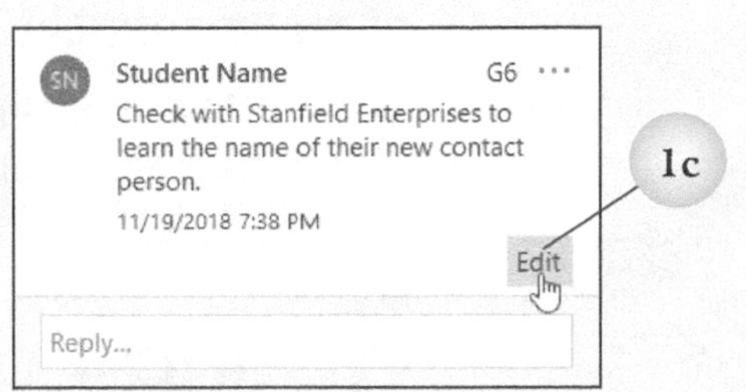

2. Click the Show Comments button in the Comments group.
3. With the Comments task pane displayed, edit the comment in cell G13 by completing the following steps:
   a. Click the comment box with the cell reference G13 in the upper right corner.
   b. Click the Edit button.
   c. Change the text *Roger* to *Richard*.
   d. Click the Save button.

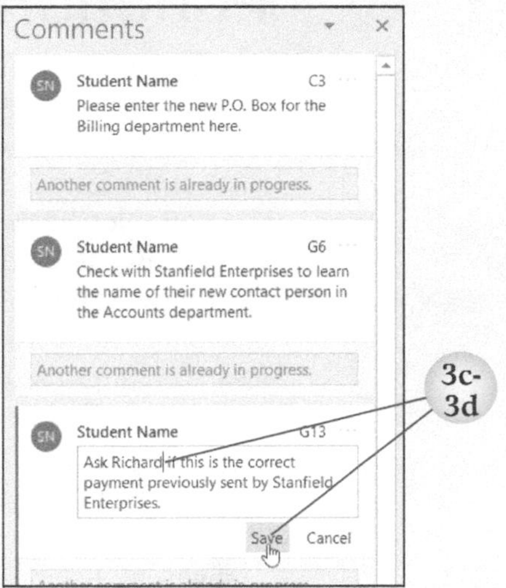

4. Click the first comment box in the Comments task pane and then click the Delete button in the Comments group.
5. Change the settings in the Page Setup dialog box in order to print the comments by completing the following steps:
   a. Click the Page Layout tab.
   b. Click the Page Setup group dialog box launcher.
   c. At the Page Setup dialog box, click the Sheet tab.
   d. Click the Comments option box arrow and then click *At end of sheet* at the drop-down list.

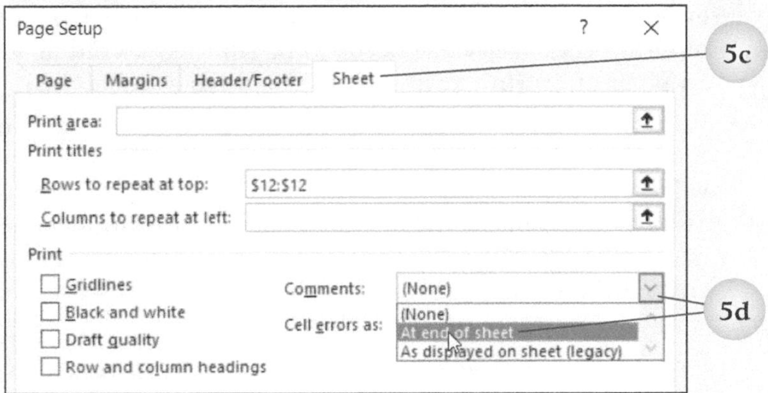

   e. Click OK.
6. Click the Close button in the Comments task pane.
7. Save, print, and then close **6-Billing**.

Activity 5 Calculate Payments and the Future Value of an Investment **2 Parts**

You will use the PMT financial function to calculate payments and the FV financial function to find the future value of an investment.

Using Financial Functions

Writing Formulas with Financial Functions

Excel provides a number of financial functions that can be used in formulas. Use financial functions to determine different aspects of a financial loan or investment, such as the payment amount, present value, future value, interest rate, and number of payment periods. Each financial function requires some of the variables listed below to return a result. Two such financial functions are the PMT function and FV function. The PMT function calculates the payment for a loan based on constant payments and a constant interest rate. The FV function calculates the future value of an investment. Financial functions use some of the following arguments:

- **Rate:** The rate is the interest rate for a payment period. The rate may need to be modified for the function to produce the desired results. For example, most rate values are given as an APR (annual percentage rate), which is the percentage rate for one year, not a payment period. So a percentage rate may be given as 12% APR but if the payment period is a month, then the percentage rate for the function is 1%, not 12%. If a worksheet contains the annual percentage rate, enter the cell reference in the function argument and specify that it should be divided by 12 months. For example, if cell B6 contains the annual interest rate, enter *b6/12* as the Rate argument.
- **Nper:** The Nper is the number of payment periods in an investment. The Nper may also need to be modified depending on what information is provided. For example, if a loan duration is expressed in years but the payments are made monthly, the Nper value needs to be adjusted accordingly. A five-year loan has an Nper of 60 (five years times 12 months in each year).
- **Pmt:** The Pmt is the payment amount for each period. This argument describes the payment amount for a period and is commonly expressed as a negative value because it is an outflow of cash. However, the Pmt value can be entered as a positive value if the present value (Pv) or future value (Fv) is entered as a negative value. Whether the Pmt value is positive or negative depends on who created the workbook. For example, a home owner lists the variable as outflow, while the lending institution lists it as inflow.
- **Pv:** The Pv is the present value of an investment, expressed in a lump sum. The Pv argument is generally the initial loan amount. For example, if a person is purchasing a new home, the Pv is the amount of money he or she borrowed to buy the home. Pv can be expressed as a negative value, which denotes it as an investment instead of a loan. For example, if a bank issues a loan to a home buyer, it enters the Pv value as negative because it is an outflow of cash.

- **Fv:** The Fv is the future value of an investment, expressed in a lump sum amount. The Fv argument is generally the loan amount plus the amount of interest paid during the loan. In the example of a home buyer, the Fv is the sum of payments, which includes both the principle and interest paid on the loan. In the example of a bank, the Fv is the total amount received after a loan has been paid off. Fv can also be expressed as either a positive or negative value, depending on which side of the transaction is being reviewed.

Finding the Periodic Payments for a Loan

The PMT function finds the payment for a loan based on constant payments and a constant interest rate. In Activity 5a, the PMT function will be used to determine monthly payments for equipment and a used van as well as monthly income from selling equipment. The formulas created with the PMT function will include Rate, Nper, and Pv arguments. The Nper argument is the number of payments that will be made on the loan or investment, Pv is the current value of amounts to be received or paid in the future, and Fv is the value of the loan or investment at the end of all periods.

To write the PMT function, click the Formulas tab, click the Financial button in the Function Library group, and then click the PMT function at the drop-down list. This displays the Function Arguments dialog box with options for inserting cell designations for Rate, Nper, and Pv. (These are the arguments displayed in bold formatting in the Function Arguments dialog box. The dialog box also contains the Fv and Type functions, which are dimmed.)

Activity 5a Calculating Payments — Part 1 of 2

1. Open **RPReports** and then save it with the name **6-RPReports**.
2. The owner of Real Photography is interested in purchasing a new developer and needs to determine monthly payments on three different models. Insert a formula that calculates monthly payments and then copy that formula by completing the following steps:
   a. Make cell E5 active.
   b. Click the Formulas tab.
   c. Click the Financial button in the Function Library group, scroll down the drop-down list, and then click *PMT*.

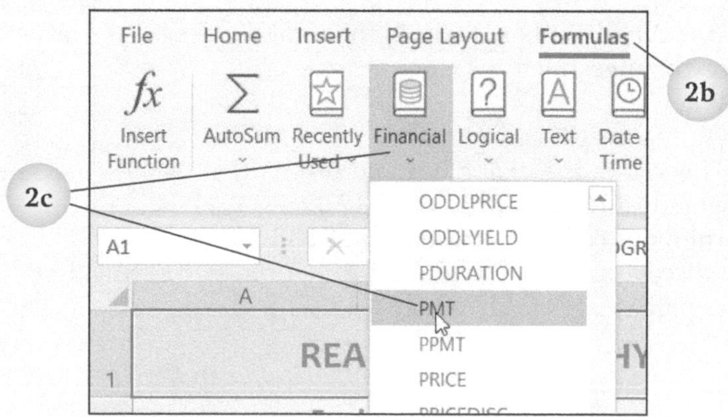

d. At the Function Arguments dialog box, type c5/12 in the *Rate* text box. (This tells Excel to divide the interest rate by 12 months.)
e. Press the Tab key. (This moves the insertion point to the *Nper* text box.)
f. Type d5. (This is the total number of months for the investment.)
g. Press the Tab key. (This moves the insertion point to the *Pv* text box.)
h. Type b5. (This is the purchase price of the developer.)
i. Click OK. (This closes the dialog box and inserts the monthly payment of *($316.98)* in cell E5. Excel shows the result of the PMT function as a negative number since the loan represents money going out of the company—a negative cash flow.)

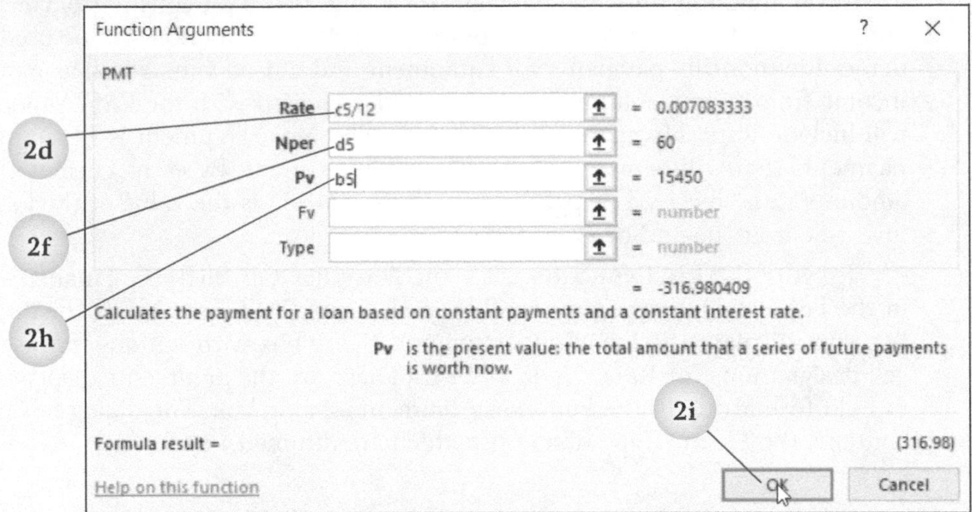

j. Copy the formula in cell E5 into cells E6 and E7.

3. The owner is interested in purchasing a used van for the company and wants an idea of what monthly payments would be at various terms and rates. Insert a formula that calculates monthly payments for a three-year loan at 5% interest by completing the following steps:
a. Make cell E12 active.
b. Make sure the Formulas tab is active.
c. Click the Financial button, scroll down the drop-down list, and then click *PMT*.
d. At the Function Arguments dialog box, type c12/12 in the *Rate* text box. (This tells Excel to divide the interest rate by 12 months.)
e. Press the Tab key.
f. Type d12 in the *Nper* text box. (This is the total number of months for the investment.)
g. Press the Tab key.
h. Type b12 in the *Pv* text box.
i. Click OK. (This closes the dialog box and inserts the monthly payment of *($299.71)* in cell E12.)
j. Copy the formula in cell E12 to the range E13:E15.

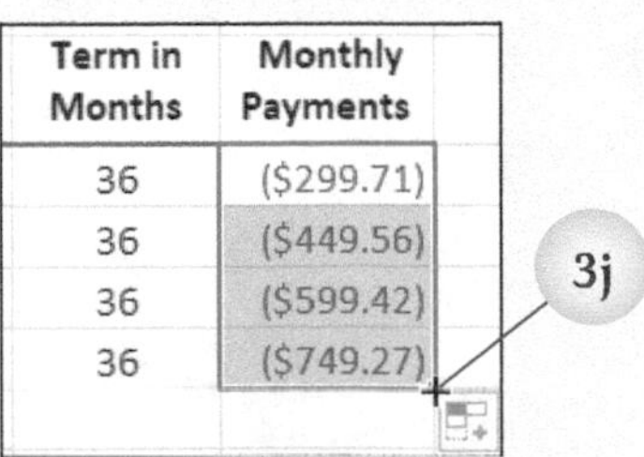

Term in Months	Monthly Payments
36	($299.71)
36	($449.56)
36	($599.42)
36	($749.27)

4. The owner has discovered that the interest rate for a used van will be 6.25% instead of 5%. Change the percentages in the range C12:C15 to 6.25%.

5. The owner is selling a camera and wants to determine the monthly payments for a two-year loan at 4.5% interest. Determine monthly payments on the camera (income to Real Photography) by completing the following steps:
   a. Make cell E20 active.
   b. Make sure the Formulas tab is active.
   c. Click the Financial button, scroll down the drop-down list, and then click *PMT*.
   d. At the Function Arguments dialog box, type c20/12 in the *Rate* text box.
   e. Press the Tab key.
   f. Type d20 in the *Nper* text box.
   g. Press the Tab key.
   h. Type -b20 in the *Pv* text box. (Enter the *Pv* cell reference preceded by a hyphen because the sale of the camera represents an outflow of an asset. Excel displays the result of the PMT function as a positive number since the camera payments represent a positive cash inflow.)
   i. Click OK. (This closes the dialog box and inserts the monthly income of *$185.92* in cell E20.)
6. Save, print, and then close **6-RPReports**.

Using the FV Function to Find the Future Value of an Investment

Finding the Future Value of a Series of Payments

The FV function calculates the future value of a series of equal payments or an annuity. Use this function to determine information such as how much money can be earned in an investment account with a specific interest rate and over a specific period of time.

Activity 5b Finding the Future Value of an Investment

Part 2 of 2

1. Open **RPInvest** and then save it with the name **6-RPInvest**.
2. The owner of Real Photography has decided to save the money needed to purchase a new developer and wants to compute how much money can be earned by investing in an investment account that returns 7.5% annual interest. The owner determines that $1,200 per month can be invested in the account for three years. Complete the following steps to determine the future value of the investment account:
   a. Make cell B6 active.
   b. Click the Formulas tab.
   c. Click the Financial button in the Function Library group.
   d. At the drop-down list, scroll down the list and then click *FV*.
   e. At the Function Arguments dialog box, type b3/12 in the *Rate* text box.
   f. Press the Tab key.
   g. Type b4 in the *Nper* text box.
   h. Press the Tab key.
   i. Type b5 in the *Pmt* text box.
   j. Click OK. (This closes the dialog box and also inserts the future value of *$48,277.66* in cell B6.)
3. Save and then print **6-RPInvest**.
4. The owner decides to determine the future return after two years. To do this, change the amount in cell B4 from *36* to *24* and then press the Enter key. (This recalculates the future investment amount in cell B6.)
5. Save, print, and then close **6-RPInvest**.

Chapter Summary

- Pin a frequently used workbook at the *Recent* options list at the Open backstage area or at the Home backstage area.
- Pinned workbooks will remain at the Open backstage area in the *Recent* options list or at the Home backstage area until unpinned.
- To move or copy a worksheet to another existing workbook, open both the source workbook and the destination workbook and then open the Move or Copy dialog box.
- Use options from the Cell Styles button drop-down gallery to apply predesigned styles to a cell or selected cells.
- Automate the formatting of cells in a workbook by defining and then applying cell styles. A style is a predefined set of formatting attributes.
- Define a cell style with formats already applied to a cell or display the Style dialog box, click the Format button, and then choose formatting options at the Format Cells dialog box.
- To apply a style, select the desired cell or cells, click the Cell Styles button in the Styles group on the Home tab, and then click the style at the drop-down gallery.
- Modify a style and all the cells to which it is applied update automatically. To modify a style, click the Cell Styles button in the Styles group on the Home tab, right-click the style, and then click *Modify* at the shortcut menu.
- Custom styles are saved in the workbook they are created in but can be copied to another workbook. Do this with options at the Merge Styles dialog box.
- Remove any new style formatting in a cell by applying the Normal style to the cell.
- Delete cell styles at the Cell Styles drop-down gallery by right-clicking a style and then clicking *Delete*.
- With options at the Insert Hyperlink dialog box, create a hyperlink to a web page, another workbook, a location within a workbook, a new workbook, or an email address. Or create a hyperlink using a graphic.
- Hyperlinks can be modified, edited, and removed.
- Excel provides templates for creating forms. Search for and download templates at the New backstage area.
- Templates contain unique areas called placeholders where information is entered at the keyboard. These areas vary depending on the template.
- Comments are a feature that allows users to provide commentary on a specific cell.
- A comment must be posted before another comment is created or before another user replies to the comment.
- Display all of the comments in a worksheet by opening the Comments task pane.
- Financial functions are available in Excel that calculate an aspect of a financial loan or investment.
- Financial functions generally use Nper, FV, PV, and Pmt as function arguments.
- Use the PMT function to determine the payments on a loan or investment.
- Use the FV function to determine the future value on a loan or investment.

Commands Review

FEATURE	RIBBON TAB, GROUP/OPTION	BUTTON, OPTION	KEYBOARD SHORTCUT
cell styles	Home, Styles		
delete comment	Review, *Comments*		
financial functions	Financial, Function Library		
Insert Hyperlink dialog box	Insert, Links		Ctrl + K
Merge Styles dialog box	Home, Styles	, *Merge Styles*	
New backstage area	File, *New*		
new comment	Review, *Comments*		
Open backstage area	File, *Open*		Ctrl + O
show comments	Review, *Comments*		
Style dialog box	Home, Styles	, *New Cell Style*	

Microsoft®

Excel®

CHAPTER

7

Creating Charts and Inserting Formulas

Performance Objectives

Upon successful completion of Chapter 7, you will be able to:

1. Create a chart with data in an Excel worksheet
2. Size, move, edit, format, and delete charts
3. Print a selected chart and print a worksheet containing a chart
4. Change a chart design
5. Change a chart location
6. Insert, move, size, and delete chart elements and shapes
7. Use the Quick Analysis feature
8. Format a chart at a task pane
9. Write formulas with the IF logical function

In previous chapters, you learned how to create and format worksheets in Excel to display and organize data. While a worksheet does an adequate job of representing data, some data are better represented visually with a chart. A chart, which is sometimes referred to as a *graph*, is a picture of numeric data. In this chapter, you will learn to create and customize charts in Excel. You will also learn how to write formulas using logical functions.

Before beginning chapter work, copy the EL1C7 folder to your storage medium and then make EL1C7 the active folder.

The online course includes additional training and assessment resources.

Activity 1 Create a Quarterly Sales Column Chart — 3 Parts

You will open a workbook containing quarterly sales data and then use the data to create a column chart. You will decrease the size of the chart, move it to a different location in the worksheet, and then make changes to sales numbers. You will also use buttons to customize and filter chart elements and styles.

Creating Charts

Creating a Chart

To provide a visual representation of data, consider inserting data in a chart. Use buttons in the Charts group on the Insert tab to create a variety of charts, such as a column chart, line chart, pie chart, and much more. Excel provides 17 basic chart types, as described in Table 7.1.

Table 7.1 Types of Charts

Chart	Description
Column	Displays values in vertical bars; useful for comparing items or showing how values vary over time.
Line	Shows trends and overall change across time at even intervals. Emphasizes the rate of change across time rather than the magnitude of change.
Pie	Shows proportions and the relationship of the parts to the whole.
Bar	Shows individual figures at a specific time or shows variations between components but not in relationship to the whole.
Area	Similar to a line chart, but with the area below the line filled in. Emphasizes the magnitude of change over time.
X Y (Scatter)	Shows the relationships among numeric values in several data series or plots the interception points between *x* and *y* values. Shows uneven intervals of data and is commonly used for scientific data.
Map	Compares values and shows categories across geographical regions.
Stock	Shows four values for a stock: open, high, low, and close.
Surface	Shows trends in values across two dimensions in a continuous curve.
Radar	Emphasizes differences and amounts of change over time as well as variations and trends. Each category has a value axis radiating from the center point. Lines connect all values in the same series.
Treemap	Provides a hierarchical view of data and compares proportions within the hierarchy.
Sunburst	Displays hierarchical data. Each level is represented by one ring; the innermost ring is the top of the hierarchy.
Histogram	Condenses a data series into a visual representation by grouping data points into logical ranges called *bins*.

continues

Table 7.1 Types of Charts—*continued*

Chart	Description
Box & Whisker	Displays medians, quartiles, and extremes of a data set on a number line to show the distribution of data. Lines extending vertically are called *whiskers* and indicate variability outside the upper and lower quartiles.
Waterfall	Illustrates how an initial value is affected by a series of positive and negative values.
Funnel	Shows values over multiple stages in a process; typically, the values decrease, making the shape of the chart resemble a funnel.
Combo	Combines two or more chart types to make data easy to understand.

Quick Steps

Create Chart
1. Select cells.
2. Click Insert tab.
3. Click chart button.
4. Click chart style.

Recommended Charts

To create a chart, select the cells in the worksheet to be charted, click the Insert tab, and then click a specific chart button in the Charts group. At the drop-down gallery, click a specific chart style. Excel will make a recommendation on the type of chart that will best illustrate the data. To let Excel recommend a chart, select the data, click the Insert tab, and then click the Recommended Charts button. This displays the data in a chart in the Insert Chart dialog box. Customize the recommended chart with options in the left panel of the dialog box. Click the OK button to insert the recommended chart in the worksheet. Another method for inserting a recommended chart is to use the keyboard shortcut Alt + F1.

Resizing, Positioning, and Moving Charts

Sizing and Moving a Chart

By default, a chart is inserted in the same worksheet as the selected cells. Figure 7.1 shows the worksheet and chart that will be created in Activity 1a. The chart is inserted in a box, which can be sized or moved within the worksheet.

Figure 7.1 Activity 1a Chart

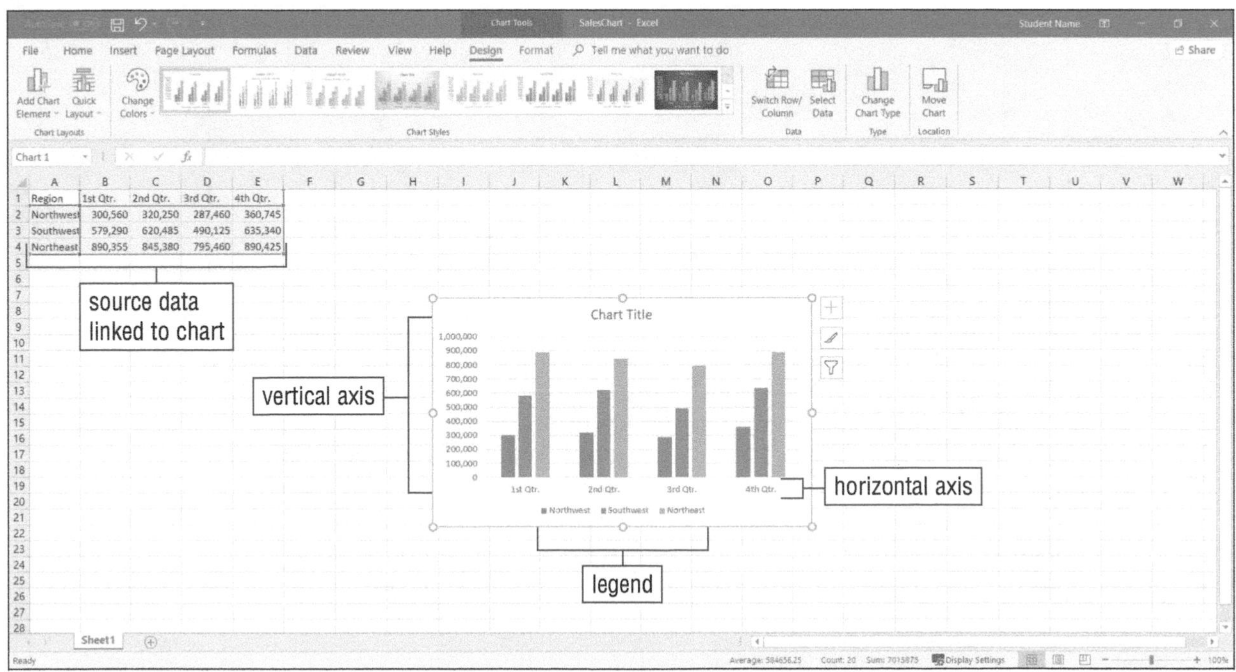

Change the size of the chart using the sizing handles (white circles) on the chart borders. Drag the top-middle and bottom-middle sizing handles to increase or decrease the height of the chart; use the left-middle and right-middle sizing handles to increase or decrease the width; and use the corner sizing handles to increase or decrease the height and width at the same time. To increase or decrease the size of the chart but maintain its proportions, press and hold down the Shift key while dragging one of the chart's corner borders.

To move the chart, make sure it is selected (a border with sizing handles appears around the chart), position the mouse pointer on a border until the pointer displays with a four-headed arrow attached, click and hold down the left mouse button, drag to the new position, and then release the mouse button.

Editing Chart Data

Editing Data and Adding a Data Series

The cells selected to create a chart are linked to it. To change the data for a chart, edit the data in the specific cells and the corresponding sections of the chart update automatically. If data is added to cells within the range of cells used for the chart, called the *source data*, the new data will be included in the chart. If a data series is added in cells next to or below the source data, click in the chart to display the source data with sizing handles and then drag with a sizing handle to include the new data.

Activity 1a **Creating a Chart** Part 1 of 3

1. Open **SalesChart** and then save it with the name **7-SalesChart.**
2. Select the range A1:E4.
3. Let Excel recommend a chart type by completing the following steps:
   a. Click the Insert tab.
   b. Click the Recommended Charts button in the Charts group.

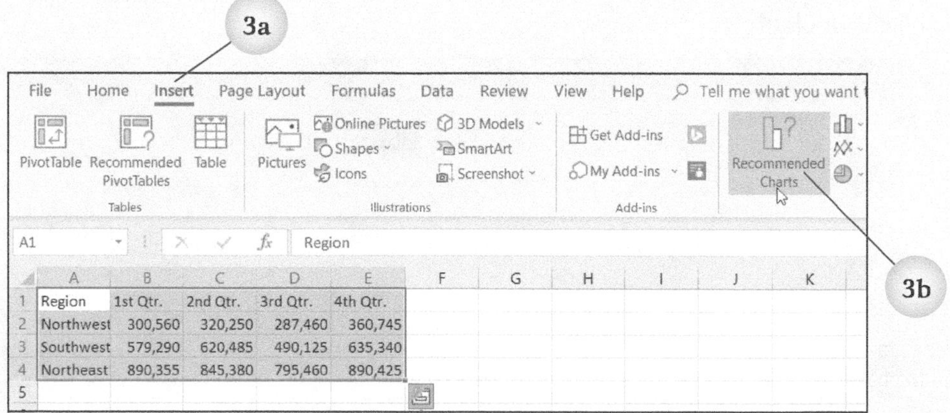

   c. At the Insert Chart dialog box, look at the options in the left panel and then click OK.
4. Slightly increase the size of the chart and maintain its proportions by completing the following steps:
   a. Position the mouse pointer on the sizing handle in the lower right corner of the chart border until the pointer turns into a two-headed arrow pointing diagonally.
   b. Press and hold down the Shift key and then click and hold down the left mouse button.

c. Drag out approximately 0.5 inch. Release the mouse button and then release the Shift key.

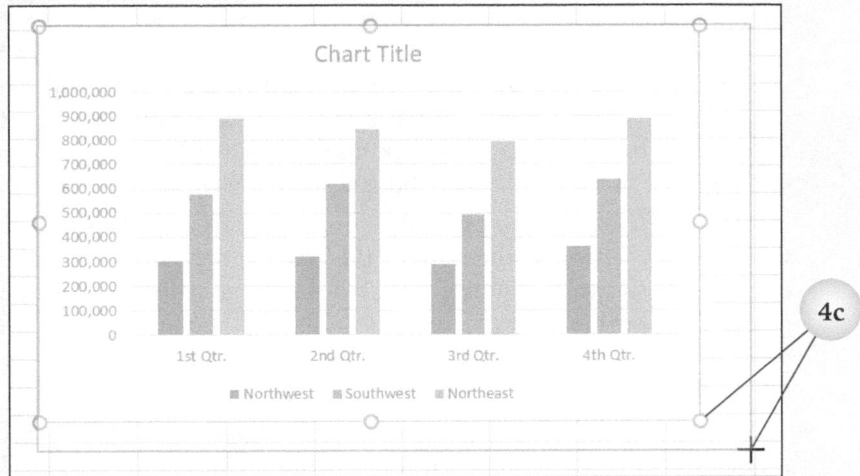

5. Move the chart below the cells containing data by completing the following steps:
   a. Make sure the chart is selected. (When the chart is selected, the border surrounding it displays with sizing handles.)
   b. Position the mouse pointer on the chart border until the pointer displays with a four-headed arrow attached.
   c. Click and hold down the left mouse button, drag the chart to row 6 below the cells containing data, and then release the mouse button.

	A	B	C	D	E
1	Region	1st Qtr.	2nd Qtr.	3rd Qtr.	4th Qtr.
2	Northwest	300,560	320,250	287,460	360,745
3	Southwest	579,290	620,485	490,125	635,340
4	Northeast	890,355	845,380	795,460	890,425
5					
6					
7			Chart Title		
8	1,000,000				

5c

6. Make the following changes to the specified cells:
   a. Make cell B2 active and then change *300,560* to *421,720*.
   b. Make cell D2 active and then change *287,460* to *397,460*.
7. Add a new data series by typing data in the following cells:
   A5 Southeast
   B5 290,450
   C5 320,765
   D5 270,450
   E5 300,455
8. Add the new data series to the chart by completing the following steps:
   a. Click in a blank area of the chart. (This selects the data source, which is the range A1:E4.)
   b. Position the mouse pointer on the sizing handle in the lower right corner of cell E4 until the pointer displays as a two-headed diagonally pointing arrow.
   c. Click and hold down the left mouse button, drag down into cell E5, and then release the mouse button. (This incorporates data row 5 in the chart.)
9. Save **7-SalesChart**.

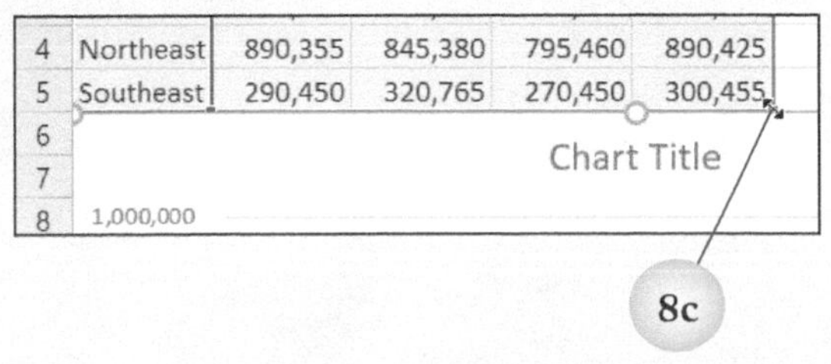

Check Your Work

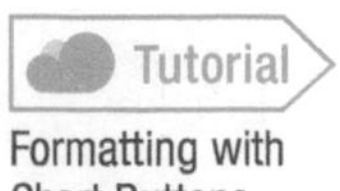
Tutorial

Formatting with Chart Buttons

Formatting with Chart Buttons

Chart Elements

When a chart is inserted in a worksheet, three buttons appear at the right of the chart border. Click the top button, Chart Elements, and a side menu displays chart elements, as shown in Figure 7.2. The check boxes containing check marks indicate the elements that are currently part of the chart. Add a new element to the chart by inserting a check mark in the check box for that element and remove an element by removing the check mark. Remove the Chart Elements side menu by clicking one of the other chart buttons or by clicking the Chart Elements button.

Chart Styles

Excel offers a variety of chart styles that can be applied to a chart. Click the Chart Styles button at the right of the chart and a side menu gallery of styles displays, as shown in Figure 7.3. Scroll down the gallery, hover the mouse pointer over a style option, and the style formatting is applied to the chart. Click the chart style that applies the desired formatting. Remove the Chart Styles side menu gallery by clicking one of the other chart buttons or by clicking the Chart Styles button.

In addition to offering a variety of chart styles, the Chart Styles button side menu gallery offers a variety of chart colors. Click the Chart Styles button and then click the Color tab to the right of the Style tab. Click a color option at the color palette. Hover the mouse pointer over a color option to view how the color change affects the elements in the chart.

Chart Filters

Use the bottom button, Chart Filters, to isolate specific data in the chart. Click the button and a side menu displays, as shown in Figure 7.4. Specify the series or categories to display in the chart. To do this, remove the check marks from those elements that should not appear in the chart. After removing the specific check marks, click the Apply button at the bottom of the side menu. Click the Names tab at the Chart Filters button side menu and options display for turning on/off the display of column and row names.

Figure 7.2 Chart Elements Button Side Menu

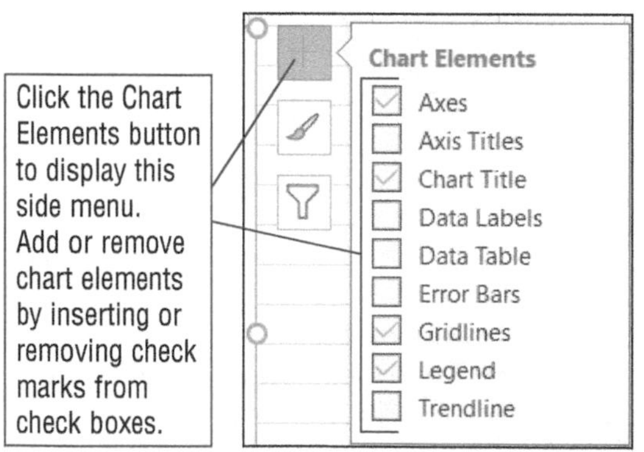
Click the Chart Elements button to display this side menu. Add or remove chart elements by inserting or removing check marks from check boxes.
Chart Elements
Axes
Axis Titles
Chart Title
Data Labels
Data Table
Error Bars
Gridlines
Legend
Trendline

Figure 7.3 Chart Styles Button Side Menu Gallery

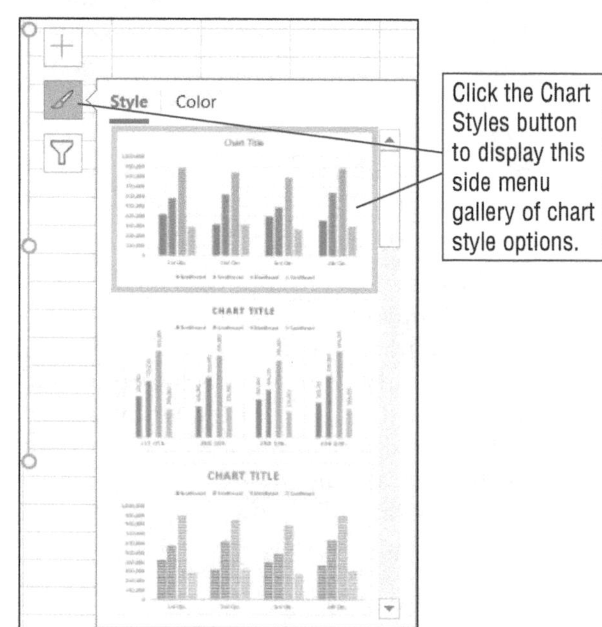
Style
Color
CHART TITLE
CHART TITLE
Click the Chart Styles button to display this side menu gallery of chart style options.

Figure 7.4 Chart Filters Button Side Menu

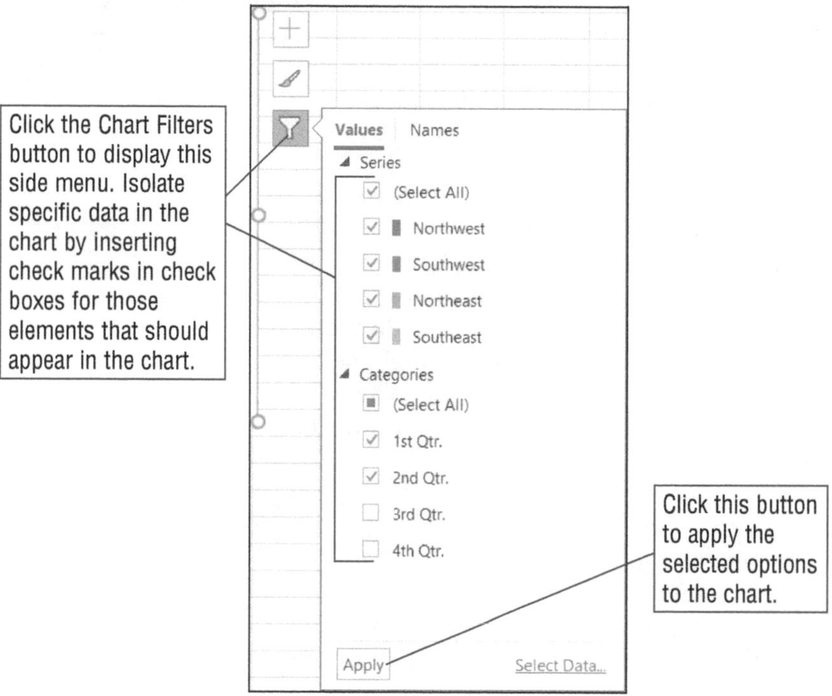

Activity 1b Formatting with Chart Buttons

Part 2 of 3

1. With **7-SalesChart** open, make the chart active by clicking inside it but outside any elements.
2. Insert and remove chart elements by completing the following steps:
   a. Click the Chart Elements button outside the upper right corner of the chart.
   b. At the side menu, click the *Chart Title* check box to remove the check mark.
   c. Click the *Data Table* check box to insert a check mark.
   d. Hover the mouse pointer over *Gridlines* in the Chart Elements button side menu and then click the right-pointing triangle.
   e. At the side menu, click the *Primary Major Vertical* check box to insert a check mark.

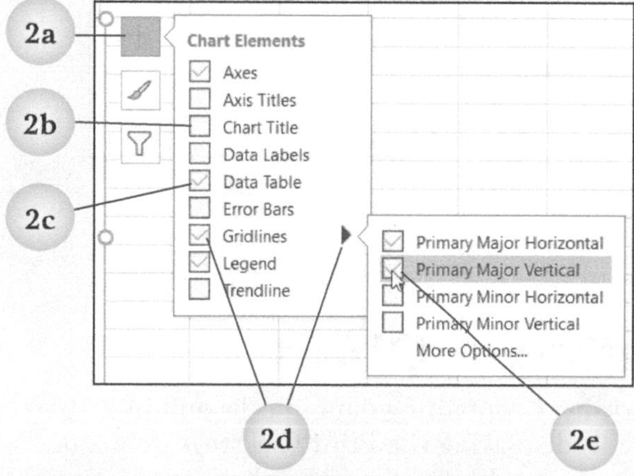

   f. Click the *Legend* check box to remove the check mark.

3. Apply a different chart style by completing the following steps:
   a. Click the Chart Styles button outside the upper right corner of the chart (immediately below the Chart Elements button). (Clicking the Chart Styles button removes the Chart Elements button side menu.)
   b. At the side menu gallery, click the *Style 3* option (third option in the gallery).
4. Display only the first-quarter and second-quarter sales by completing the following steps:
   a. Click the Chart Filters button outside the upper right corner of the chart (immediately below the Chart Styles button). (Clicking the Chart Filters button removes the Chart Styles button side menu gallery.)
   b. Click the *3rd Qtr.* check box in the *Categories* section to remove the check mark.
   c. Click the *4th Qtr.* check box in the *Categories* section to remove the check mark.
   d. Click the Apply button at the bottom of the side menu.
   e. Click the Chart Filters button to remove the side menu.

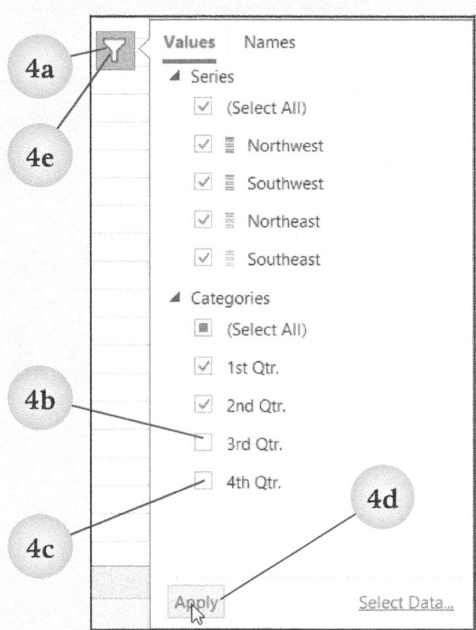

5. Save **7-SalesChart**.

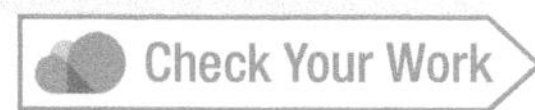

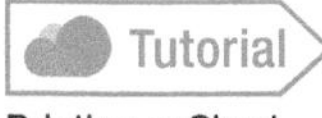

Printing a Chart

Printing a Chart

In a worksheet containing data in cells and in a chart, print only the chart by selecting it, displaying the Print backstage area, and then clicking the Print button. With the chart selected, the first gallery in the *Settings* category automatically changes to *Print Selected Chart*. A preview of the chart is shown at the right side of the Print backstage area.

Activity 1c Printing a Chart

Part 3 of 3

1. With **7-SalesChart** open, make sure the chart is selected.
2. Click the File tab and then click the *Print* option.
3. At the Print backstage area, look at the preview of the chart in the preview area and notice that the first gallery in the *Settings* category is set to *Print Selected Chart.*
4. Click the Print button.
5. Save and then close **7-SalesChart**.

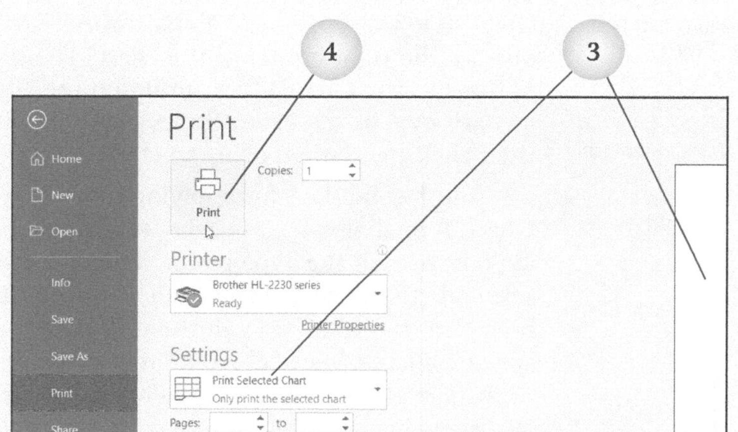

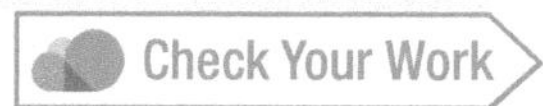

Activity 2 Create a Department Expenditures Bar Chart and Column Chart

2 Parts

You will open a workbook containing expenditure data by department and then create a bar chart with the data. You will then change the chart type, layout, and style; add chart elements; and move the chart to a new worksheet.

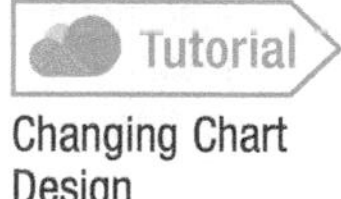

Changing Chart Design

Changing the Chart Design

Along with the buttons at the upper right corner of the chart, buttons and options on the Chart Tools Design tab can be used to apply formatting to change the chart design. This tab, shown in Figure 7.5, appears when a chart is inserted in a worksheet or a chart is selected. Use buttons and options on the tab to add chart elements, change the chart type, specify a different layout or style for the chart, and change the location of the chart so it appears in a separate worksheet.

Figure 7.5 Chart Tools Design Tab

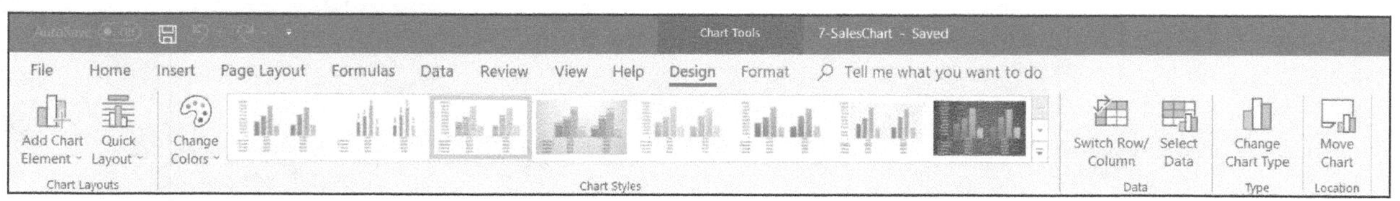

Changing the Chart Style

Quick Steps
Change Chart Type and Style
1. Make chart active.
2. Click Chart Tools Design tab.
3. Click Change Chart Type button.
4. Click chart type.
5. Click chart style.
6. Click OK.

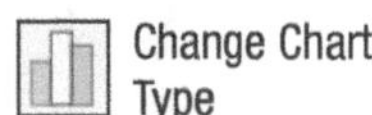
Change Chart Type

Excel offers a variety of custom charts and varying styles for each chart type. A chart style was applied to a chart in Activity 1b using the Chart Styles button outside the right border of the chart. The style of a chart can also be changed with options in the Chart Styles group on the Chart Tools Design tab. To do this, click a chart style in the Chart Styles group or click the More Chart Styles button and then click the desired chart style.

Another method for applying a chart style is to use options at the Change Chart Type dialog box. Display this dialog box by clicking the Change Chart Type button in the Type group. The dialog box displays with the All Charts tab selected, as shown in Figure 7.6. Click a chart type in the left panel of the dialog box, click the chart style in the row of options at the top right, and then click a specific chart layout below the row of styles. Click the Recommended Charts tab to display chart styles recommended for the data by Excel.

Switching Rows and Columns

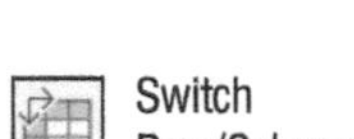
Switch Row/Column

Quick Steps
Switch Rows and Columns
1. Make chart active.
2. Click Chart Tools Design tab.
3. Click Switch Row/Column button.

When creating a chart, Excel uses row headings for grouping data along the bottom of the chart (the horizontal axis) and column headings for the legend (the area of a chart that identifies the data in the chart). Change this order by clicking the Switch Row/Column button in the Data group on the Chart Tools Design tab. Click this button and Excel uses the column headings to group data along the horizontal axis and the row headings for the legend.

Figure 7.6 Change Chart Type Dialog Box

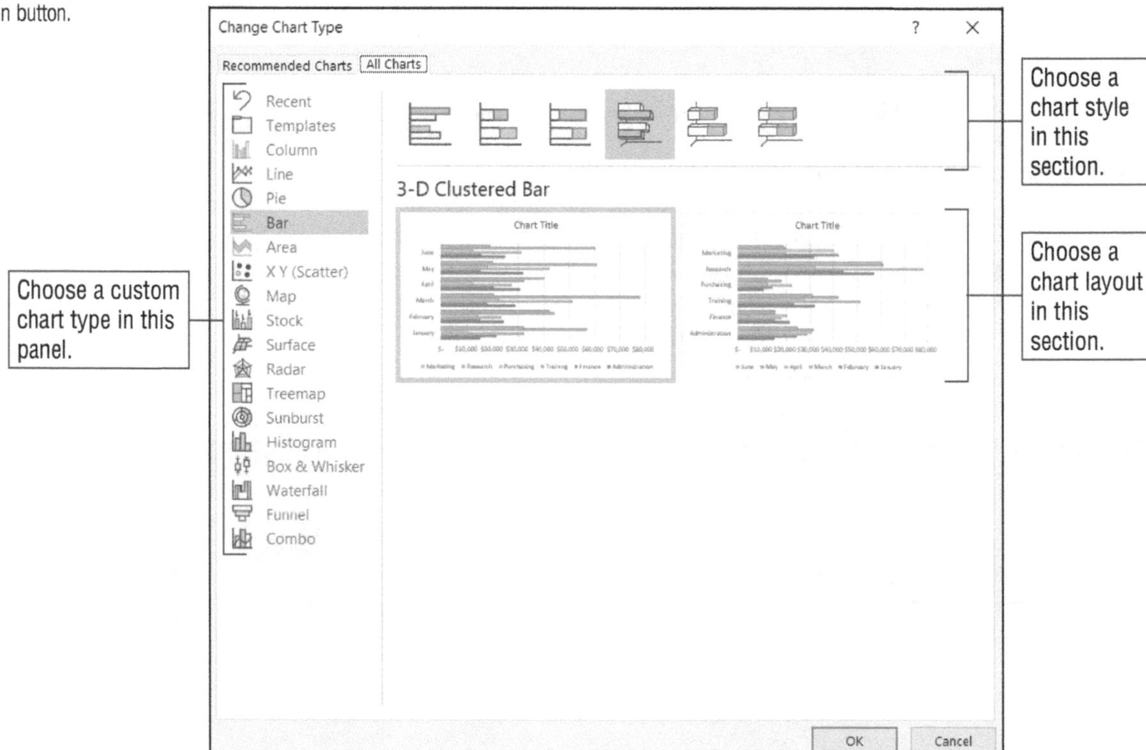

Activity 2a Creating a Chart and Changing the Design

Part 1 of 2

1. Open **DIDeptExp** and then save it with the name **7-DIDeptExp**.
2. Create a bar chart by completing the following steps:
   a. Select the range A3:G9.
   b. Click the Insert tab.
   c. Click the Insert Column or Bar Chart button in the Charts group.
   d. Click the *3-D Clustered Bar* option (first option in the *3-D Bar* section).
3. With the Chart Tools Design tab active, change the chart type by completing the following steps:
   a. Click the Change Chart Type button in the Type group.
   b. At the Change Chart Type dialog box, click the *Column* option in the left panel.
   c. Click the *3-D Clustered Column* option in the top row (fourth option from left).
   d. Click OK to close the Change Chart Type dialog box.
4. With the chart selected and the Chart Tools Design tab active, click the Switch Row/Column button in the Data group.

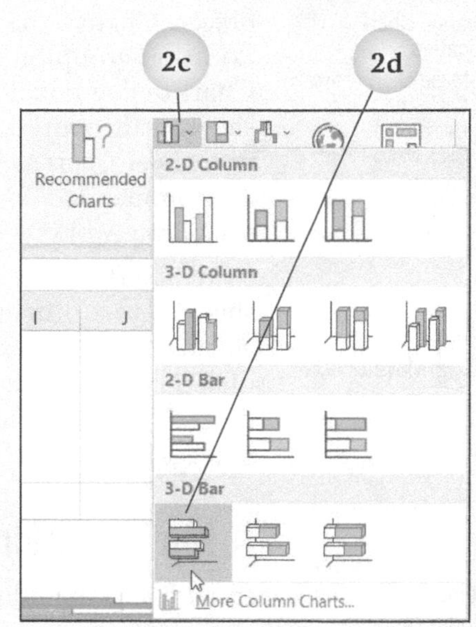

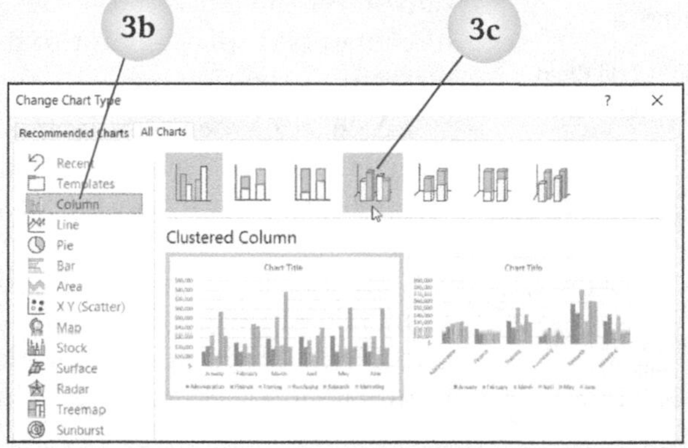

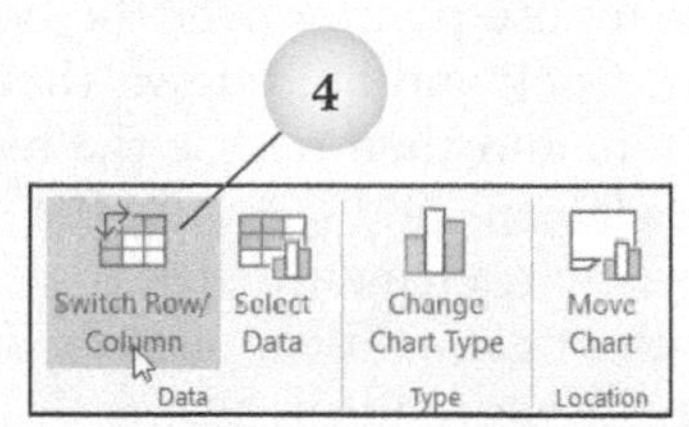

5. Save **7-DIDeptExp**.

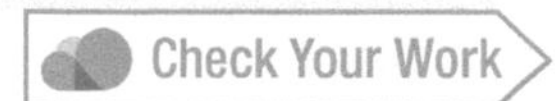

Changing Chart Layout and Colors

Quick Layout

Change Colors

The Chart Tools Design tab contains options for changing the chart layout and chart colors. Click the Quick Layout button in the Chart Layouts group and a drop-down gallery of layout options displays. Hover the mouse pointer over a layout option and the chart reflects the layout. Change the colors used in the chart by clicking the Change Colors button in the Chart Styles group and then clicking a color option at the drop-down gallery.

Changing the Chart Location

Change Chart Location

1. Make chart active.
2. Click Chart Tools Design tab.
3. Click Move Chart button.
4. Click *New sheet* option.
5. Click OK.

Move Chart

Create a chart and it is inserted in the currently open worksheet as an embedded object. Change the location of a chart with the Move Chart button in the Location group on the Chart Tools Design tab. Click this button and the Move Chart dialog box displays, as shown in Figure 7.7. To move the chart to a new sheet in the workbook, click the *New sheet* option; Excel automatically names the new sheet *Chart1*. As explained earlier in the chapter, pressing Alt + F1 will insert a recommended chart in the active worksheet. To insert a recommended chart into a separate worksheet, press the F11 function key.

A chart that is moved to a separate sheet can be moved back to the original sheet or to a different sheet within the workbook. To move a chart to a different sheet, click the Move Chart button in the Location group. At the Move Chart dialog box, click the *Object in* option box arrow and then click the sheet at the drop-down list. Click OK and the chart is inserted in the specified sheet as an object that can be moved, sized, and formatted.

Adding, Moving, and Deleting Chart Elements

Removing, Modifying, and Adding Chart Elements

Add Chart Element

Quick Steps

Delete Chart Element

1. Click chart element.
2. Press Delete key.

OR

1. Right-click chart element.
2. Click *Delete.*

In addition to adding chart elements with the Chart Elements button at the right of a selected chart, chart elements can be added with the Add Chart Element button on the Chart Tools Design tab. Click this button and a drop-down list of elements displays. Point to a category of elements and then click the desired element at the side menu.

A chart element can be moved and/or sized. To move a chart element, click the element to select it and then move the mouse pointer over the border until the pointer turns into a four-headed arrow. Click and hold down the left mouse button, drag the element to the new location, and then release the mouse button. To size a chart element, click to select the element and then use the sizing handles to increase or decrease the size. To delete a chart element, click the element to select it and then press the Delete key. A chart element can also be deleted by right-clicking it and then clicking *Delete* at the shortcut menu.

Figure 7.7 Move Chart Dialog Box

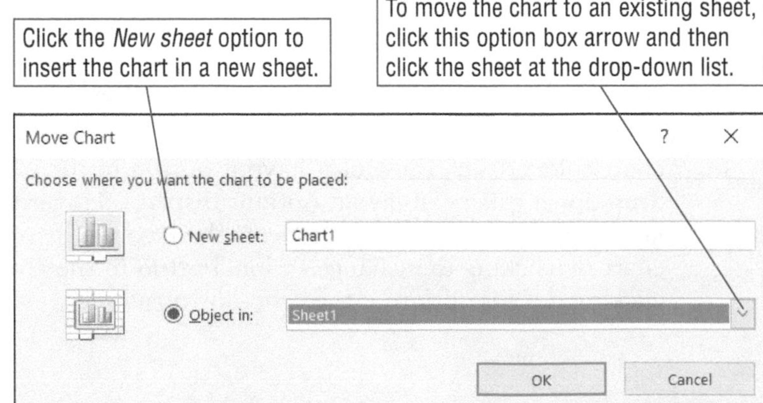

Activity 2b **Changing Chart Layout and Location and Adding Chart Elements** Part 2 of 2

1. With **7-DIDeptExp** open, make sure the Chart Tools Design tab is active. (If it is not, make sure the chart is selected and then click the Chart Tools Design tab.)
2. Change the chart style by clicking the *Style 5* option in the Chart Styles group (fifth option from the left).

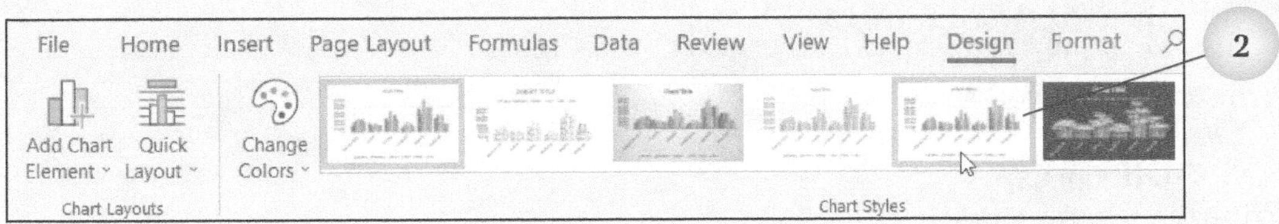

3. Change the chart colors by clicking the Change Colors button in the Chart Styles group and then clicking the *Colorful Palette 3* option (third option in the *Colorful* group).
4. Change the chart layout by clicking the Quick Layout button in the Chart Layouts group and then clicking the *Layout 1* option (first option in the drop-down gallery).

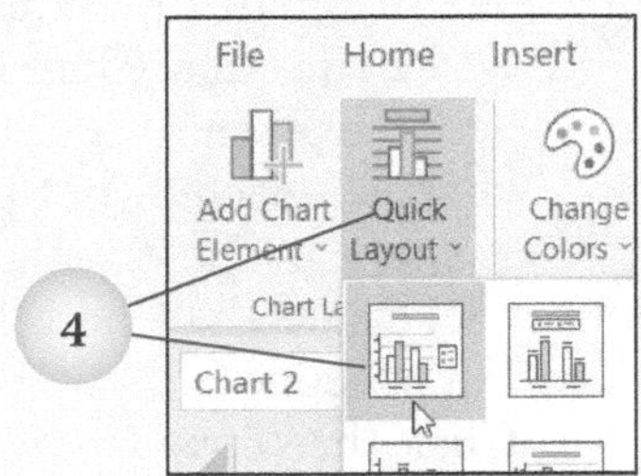

5. Add axis titles by completing the following steps:
   a. Click the Add Chart Element button in the Chart Layouts group on the Chart Tools Design tab.
   b. Point to *Axis Titles* and then click *Primary Horizontal* at the side menu.
   c. Type Department and then press the Enter key. (The word *Department* will appear in the Formula bar.)
   d. Click the Add Chart Element button, point to *Axis Titles*, and then click *Primary Vertical* at the side menu.
   e. Type Expenditure Amounts and then press the Enter key.

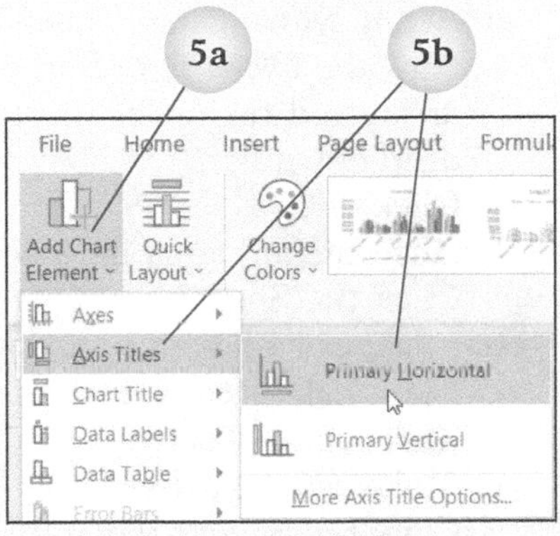

6. Click in the *Chart Title* placeholder text at the top of the chart, type Half-Yearly Expenditures, and then press the Enter key.
7. Delete the *Expenditure Amounts* axis title by clicking anywhere in it and then pressing the Delete key.
8. Move the legend by completing the following steps:
   a. Click in the legend to select it.
   b. Move the mouse pointer over the legend border until the pointer turns into a four-headed arrow.
   c. Click and hold down the left mouse button, drag up until the top border of the legend aligns with the top gridline in the chart, and then release the mouse button.

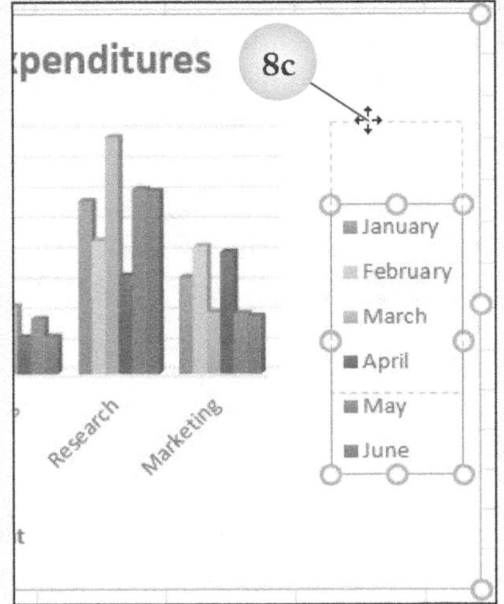

9. Move the chart to a new location by completing the following steps:
   a. Click the Move Chart button in the Location group.
   b. At the Move Chart dialog box, click the *New sheet* option and then click OK. (The chart is inserted in a worksheet named *Chart1*.)

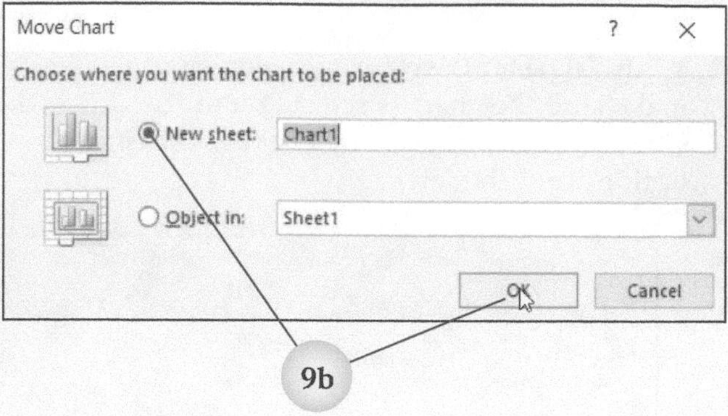

10. Save **7-DIDeptExp**.
11. Print the Chart1 worksheet.
12. Move the chart from Chart1 to Sheet2 by completing the following steps:
   a. Make sure that Chart1 is the active worksheet and that the chart is selected (not just an element in the chart).
   b. Make sure the Chart Tools Design tab is active.
   c. Click the Move Chart button in the Location group.
   d. At the Move Chart dialog box, click the *Object in* option box arrow and then click *Sheet2* at the drop-down list.
   e. Click OK.

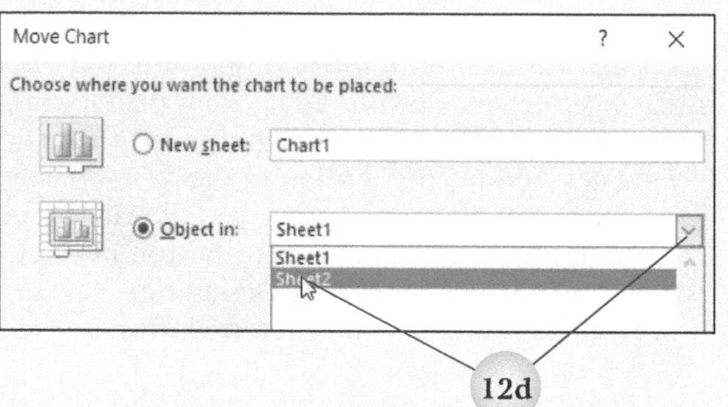

13. Change the amounts in Sheet1 by completing the following steps:
   a. Click the Sheet1 tab.
   b. Make cell B7 active and then change the amount from *10,540* to *19,750*.
   c. Make cell D8 active and then change the amount from *78,320* to *63,320*.
   d. Make cell G8 active and then change the amount from *60,570* to *75,570*.
   e. Make cell A2 active.
   f. Click the Sheet2 tab and notice that the chart displays the updated amounts.
14. Click outside the chart to deselect it.
15. Insert a header in the Sheet2 worksheet that prints your name at the left, the current date in the middle, and the workbook file name at the right.
16. Display the worksheet at the Print backstage area and make sure it will print on one page. If the chart does not fit on the page, return to the worksheet and then move and/or decrease the size of the chart until it fits on one page.
17. Print the active worksheet (Sheet2).
18. Save and then close **7-DIDeptExp**.

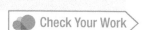

Activity 3 Create a Population Comparison Line Chart — 2 Parts

You will open a workbook containing population comparison data for Seattle and Portland and then create a line chart with the data. You will move the chart to a new worksheet, format the chart elements, and insert a shape in the chart.

Changing Chart Formatting

Changing Chart Formatting

Customize the formatting of a chart and its elements with options on the Chart Tools Format tab, as shown in Figure 7.8. Use buttons in the Current Selection group to identify specific elements in the chart and then apply formatting. Insert a shape in a chart with options in the Insert Shapes group and format shapes with options in the Shape Styles group. Apply WordArt formatting to data in a chart with options in the WordArt Styles group. Arrange, align, and size a chart with options in the Arrange and Size groups.

Formatting a Selection

Identify a specific element in a chart for formatting by clicking the *Chart Elements* option box arrow in the Current Selection group on the Chart Tools Format tab and then clicking the element at the drop-down list. This selects the specific element in the chart. Click the Reset to Match Style button to return the formatting of the element back to the original style. Use buttons in the Shape Styles group to apply formatting to a selected object and use buttons in the WordArt Styles group to apply formatting to selected data.

Figure 7.8 Chart Tools Format Tab

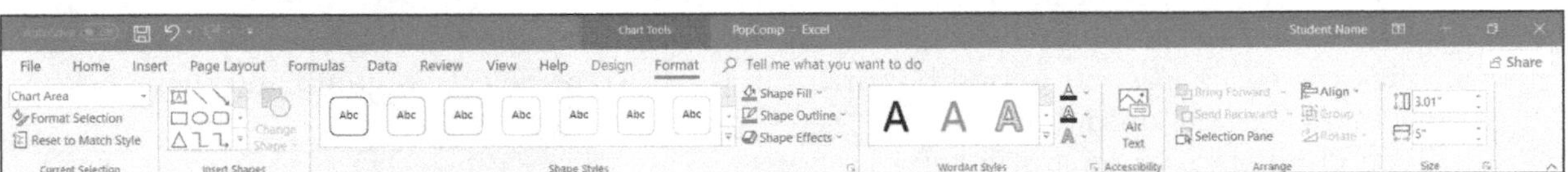

Activity 3a **Creating and Formatting a Line Chart** Part 1 of 2

1. Open **PopComp** and then save it with the name **7-PopComp**.
2. Create a line chart and add a chart element by completing the following steps:
   a. Select the range A2:I4.
   b. Click the Insert tab.
   c. Click the Insert Line or Area Chart button in the Charts group.
   d. Click the *Line with Markers* option at the drop-down list (fourth column, first row in the *2-D Line* section).
   e. Click the Chart Elements button at the upper right corner of the chart.
   f. Hover the mouse pointer over the *Data Table* option at the side menu, click the right-pointing triangle, and then click *No Legend Keys* at the side menu.
   g. Click the Chart Elements button to remove the side menu.

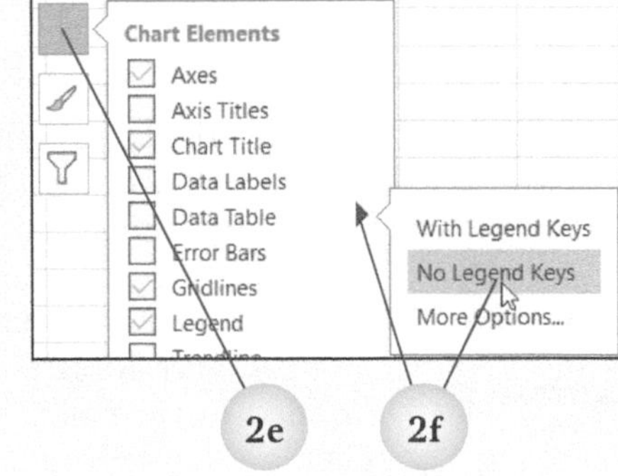

3. Move the chart to a new sheet by completing the following steps:
   a. Click the Move Chart button in the Location group on the Chart Tools Design tab.
   b. At the Move Chart dialog box, click the *New sheet* option.
   c. Click OK.

4. Format the *Portland* line by completing the following steps:
   a. Click the Chart Tools Format tab.
   b. Click the *Chart Elements* option box arrow in the Current Selection group and then click *Series "Portland"* at the drop-down list.
   c. Click the Shape Fill button arrow in the Shape Styles group and then click the *Green* color (sixth color in the *Standard Colors* section).

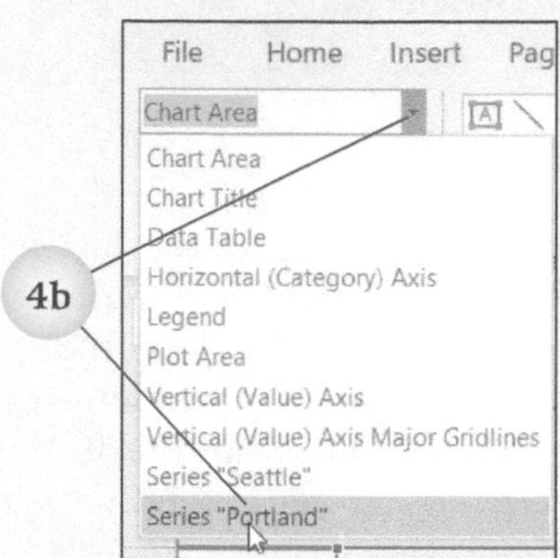

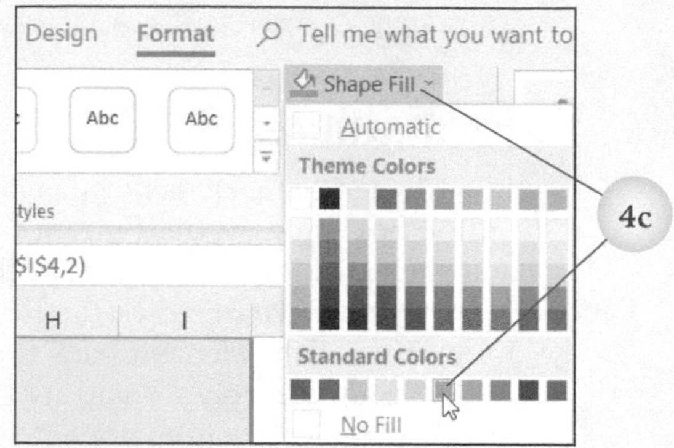

   d. Click the Shape Outline button arrow in the Shape Styles group and then click the *Green* color (sixth color in the *Standard Colors* section).
5. Type a title for the chart and format the title by completing the following steps:
   a. Click the *Chart Elements* option box arrow in the Current Selection group and then click *Chart Title* at the drop-down list.
   b. Type Population Comparison between Seattle and Portland and then press the Enter key.
   c. Click the *Fill: Black, Text color 1; Shadow* WordArt style in the WordArt Styles group (first style in the WordArt Styles gallery).

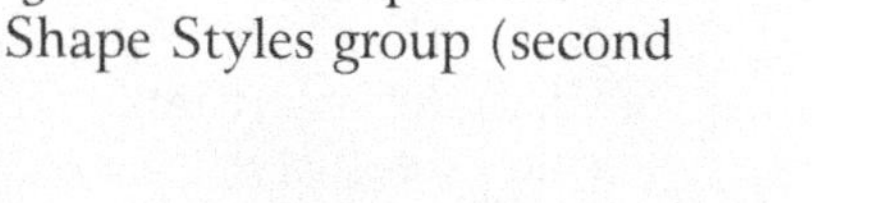

6. Format the legend by completing the following steps:
   a. Click the *Chart Elements* option box arrow and then click *Legend* at the drop-down list.
   b. Click the *Colored Outline - Blue, Accent 1* shape style in the Shape Styles group (second shape style).
7. Save **7-PopComp**.

Check Your Work

Inserting a Shape

Quick Steps

Insert Shape
1. Make chart active.
2. Click Chart Tools Format tab.
3. Click More Shapes button.
4. Click shape at drop-down list.
5. Click or drag to create shape.

The Insert Shapes group on the Chart Tools Format tab contains options for inserting shapes in a chart. Click a shape option and the mouse pointer turns into crosshairs (thin black plus symbol [+]). Click in the chart or drag with the mouse to create the shape in the chart. The shape is inserted in the chart and the Drawing Tools Format tab is active. This tab contains many of the same options as the Chart Tools Format tab. For example, a shape style or WordArt style can be applied to the shape and the shape can be arranged and sized. Size a shape by clicking the up and down arrows at the right sides of the *Shape Height* and *Shape Width* measurement boxes in the Size group on the Drawing Tools Format tab. Or select the current measurement in the *Shape Height* or *Shape Width* measurement box and then type a specific measurement.

Creating Alternative Text for an Image

Alternative text, also known as alt text, is a brief description of an object, such as a chart, that can be read by a screen reader to help a person with a visual impairment understand what objects are included in a worksheet. Create alternative text at the Alt Text task pane. Display this task pane by clicking the Alt Text button in the Accessibility group on the Chart Tools Format tab. Or, right-click a chart and then click *Edit Alt Text* at the shortcut menu. At the Alt Text task pane, type a description of the chart. If the chart is only decorative and not important for understanding the content of the worksheet, insert a check mark in the *Mark as decorative* check box. A chart marked as decorative will not include any description for screen readers.

Activity 3b **Inserting and Customizing a Shape and Adding Alt Text to a Chart** Part 2 of 2

1. With **7-PopComp** open, create a shape similar to the one shown in Figure 7.9 by completing the following steps:
   a. Click the More Shapes button in the Insert Shapes group on the Chart Tools Format tab.
   b. Click the *Callout: Up Arrow* shape (last column, second row in the *Block Arrows* section).
   c. Click in the chart to insert the shape.
   d. Click in the *Shape Height* measurement box in the Size group on the Drawing Tools Format tab, type 1.5, and then press the Enter key.
   e. Click in the *Shape Width* measurement box, type 1.5, and then press the Enter key.
   f. Apply a shape style by clicking the More Shape Styles button in the Shape Styles group and then clicking the *Subtle Effect - Blue, Accent 1* option (second column, fourth row in the *Theme Styles* section).
   g. Type Largest disparity in the shape, press the Enter key, and then type (184,411).
   h. Select the text you just typed.
   i. Click the Home tab.
   j. Click the Bold button in the Font group.
   k. Click the *Font Size* option box arrow and then click *14*.
   l. Click the Center button in the Alignment group.
2. With the shape selected, drag the shape so it is positioned as shown in Figure 7.9.
3. Select the entire chart and then create alternative text for the chart by completing the following steps:
   a. Click the Drawing Tools Format tab.
   b. Click the Alt Text button in the Accessibility group.

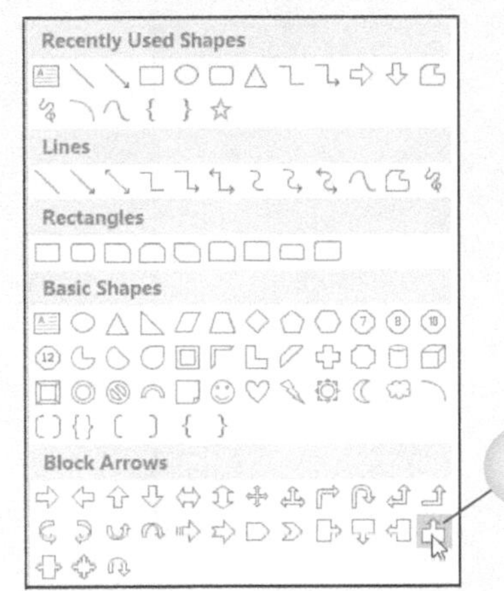

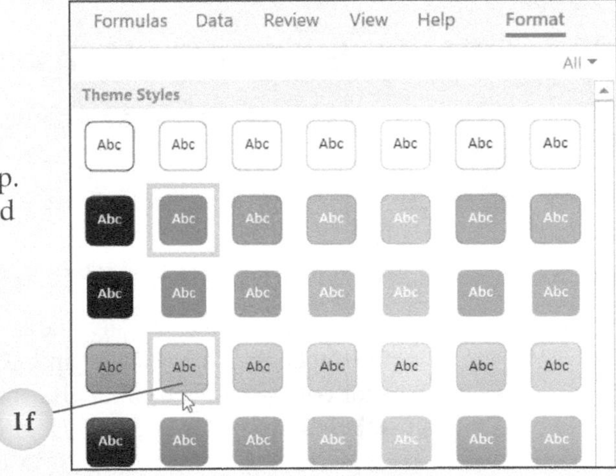

c. At the Alt Text task pane, click in the description text box and then type Chart showing a comparison between the population of Seattle and Portland.
d. Close the Alt Text task pane.
4. Save **7-PopComp**, print the Chart1 worksheet, and then close the workbook.

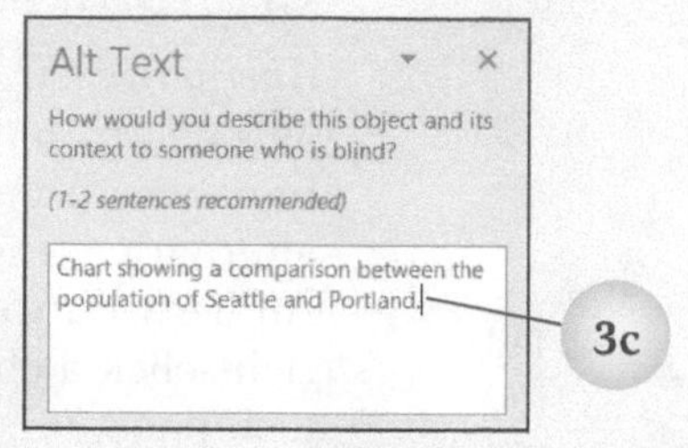

Figure 7.9 Activity 3 Chart

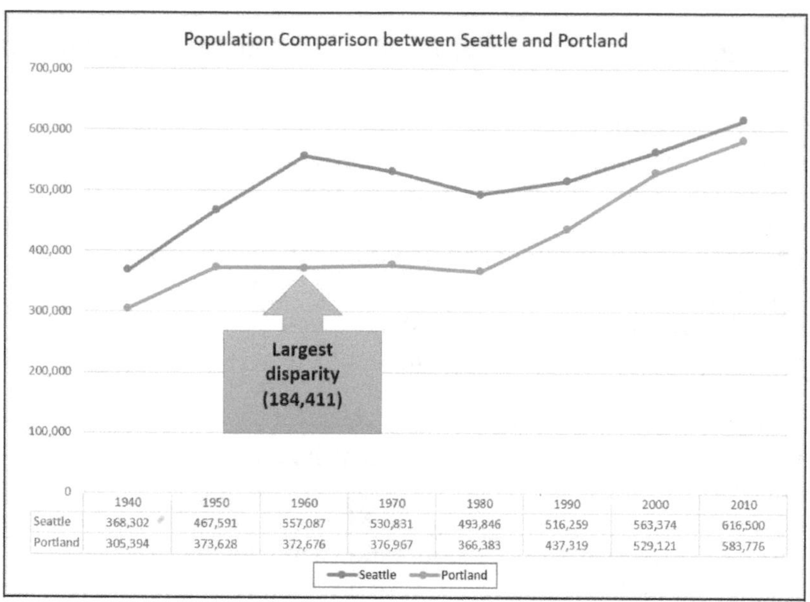

	1940	1950	1960	1970	1980	1990	2000	2010
Seattle	368,302	467,591	557,087	530,831	493,846	516,259	563,374	616,500
Portland	305,394	373,628	372,676	376,967	366,383	437,319	529,121	583,776

Activity 4 Create a Costs Pie Chart and Treemap Chart — 2 Parts

You will create a pie chart and a treemap chart, add data labels, apply a style, format chart elements, and then size and move the treemap chart.

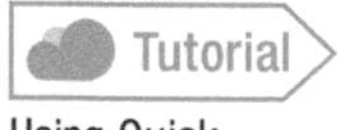

Using Quick Analysis to Create a Chart

Using the Quick Analysis Feature

A variety of methods are available for adding visual elements to a worksheet, including charts, sparklines, and conditional formatting. The Quick Analysis feature consists of a toolbar that has buttons and options for inserting all of these visual elements plus common formulas in one location. When a range is selected, Excel determines how the data in the range can be analyzed and then provides buttons and options for inserting relevant visual elements or formulas. When a range of data that is used to create a pie chart is selected, the Quick Analysis Toolbar provides buttons and options for inserting many different visual elements or formulas but also specifically including a pie chart.

Hint Ctrl + Q is the keyboard shortcut to display the Quick Analysis Toolbar for selected cells.

A Quick Analysis button appears at the bottom right corner of the selected range and when clicked, displays the Quick Analysis Toolbar, as shown in Figure 7.10. The Quick Analysis Toolbar includes the *Formatting*, *Charts*, *Totals*, *Tables*, and *Sparklines* options. Each option provides buttons that relate to how the data can be analyzed. Click a button to insert an element or formula into the worksheet.

Figure 7.10 Quick Analysis Toolbar

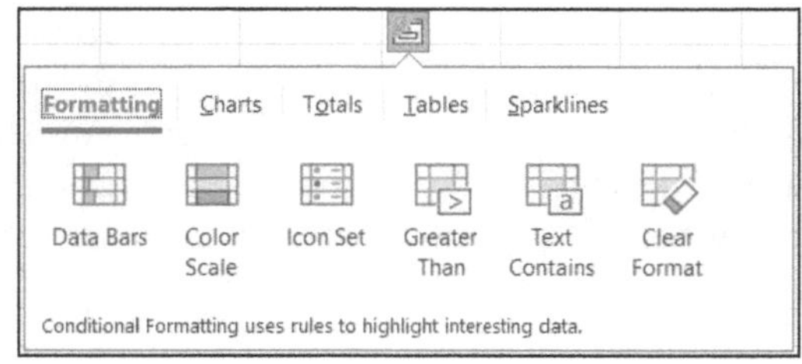

Applying Formatting at a Task Pane

Quick Steps

Display Task Pane

1. Select chart or specific element.
2. Click Chart Tools Format tab.
3. Click Format Selection button.

Format Selection

To view and apply more formatting options for charts, display the formatting task pane by clicking the Format Selection button in the Current Selection group on the Chart Tools Format tab. The task pane displays at the right side of the screen and the name of and contents in the task pane vary depending on what is selected. If the entire chart is selected, the Format Chart Area task pane displays, as shown in Figure 7.11. Format the chart by clicking formatting options in the task pane. Display additional formatting options by clicking the icons at the top of the task pane. For example, click the Effects icon in the Format Chart Area task pane and options display for applying shadow, glow, soft edges, and three-dimensional formatting.

Click a chart element and then click the Format Selection button and the task pane name and options change. Another method for displaying the task pane is to right-click a chart or chart element and then click the format option at the shortcut menu. The name of the format option varies depending on the selected element.

Figure 7.11 Format Chart Area Task Pane

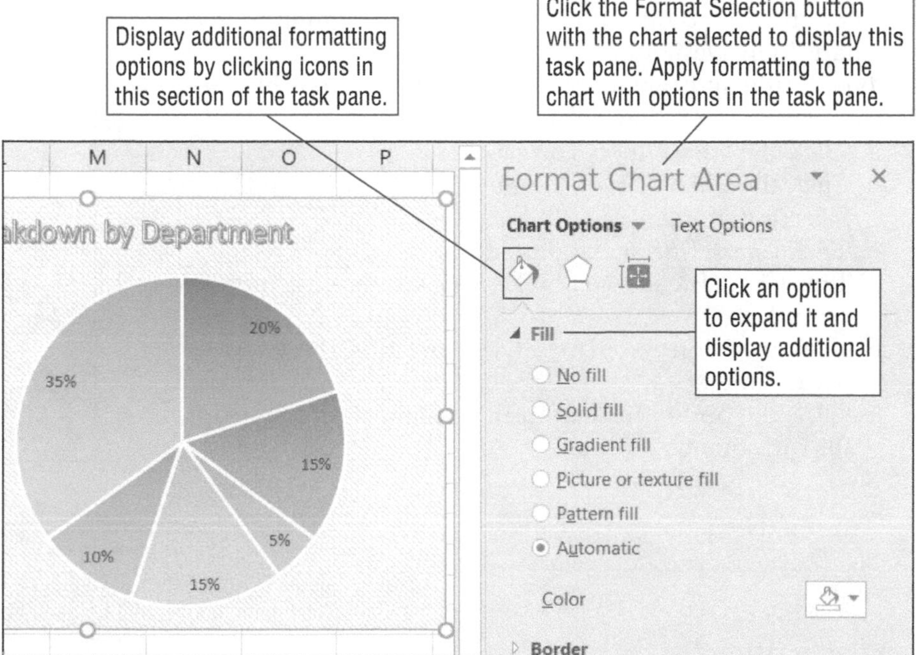

Changing Chart Height and Width Measurements

Quick Steps

Change Chart Height and/or Width

1. Make chart active.
2. Click Chart Tools Format tab.
3. Insert height and/or width with *Shape Height* and/or *Shape Width* measurement boxes.

A chart that is inserted into the current worksheet (not a separate new worksheet) can be sized by selecting it and dragging a sizing handle. A chart can also be sized with the *Shape Height* and *Shape Width* measurement boxes in the Size group on the Chart Tools Format tab. Click the up or down arrow at the right side of the measurement box to increase or decrease the size or click in the measurement box and then type a specific measurement. Another method for changing a chart size is to use options at the Format Chart Area task pane. Display this task pane by clicking the Size group task pane launcher on the Chart Tools Format tab.

Activity 4a Deleting a Chart and Creating and Formatting a Pie Chart — Part 1 of 2

1. Open **DIDeptCosts** and then save it with the name **7-DIDeptCosts**.
2. Create the pie chart shown in Figure 7.11 by completing the following steps:
   a. Select the range A3:B9.
   b. Click the Quick Analysis button at the bottom right corner of the selected range.
   c. Click the *Charts* option.
   d. Click the Pie button.

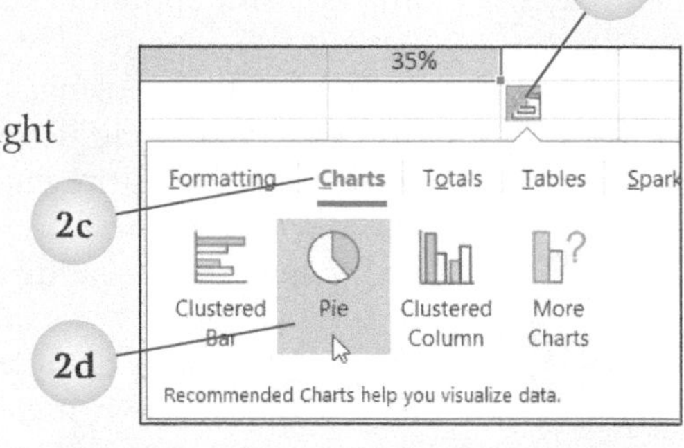

3. Insert data labels in the chart by completing the following steps:
   a. Click the Chart Elements button outside the upper right border of the chart.
   b. Hover the mouse pointer over the *Data Labels* option and then click the right-pointing triangle.
   c. Click *Inside End* at the side menu.
   d. Click the Chart Elements button to hide the side menu.
4. Click the *Style 6* option in the Chart Styles group on the Chart Tools Design tab.
5. Type a title and then apply a WordArt style to it by completing the following steps:
   a. Click the Chart Tools Format tab.
   b. Click the *Chart Elements* option box arrow in the Current Selection group.
   c. Click *Chart Title* at the drop-down list.
   d. Type Costs Breakdown by Department and then press the Enter key.
   e. Click the More WordArt Styles button in the WordArt Styles group.
   f. Click the option in the fourth column, third row (white fill with orange outline).

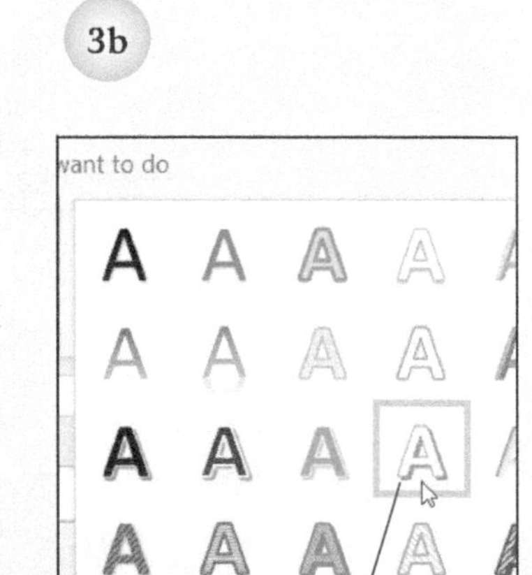

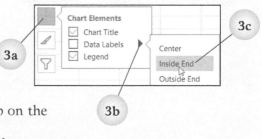

6. Use the Format Legend task pane to apply formatting to the legend by completing the following steps:
   a. Click the *Chart Elements* option box arrow and then click *Legend* at the drop-down list.
   b. Click the Format Selection button in the Current Selection group.
   c. At the Format Legend task pane, click the *Left* option in the *Legend Options* section to select it.

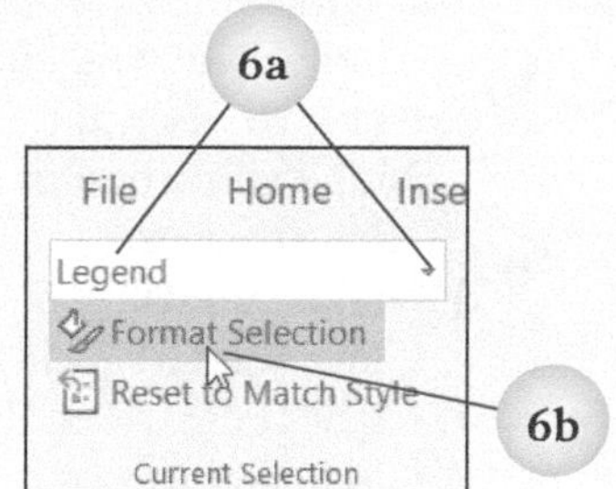

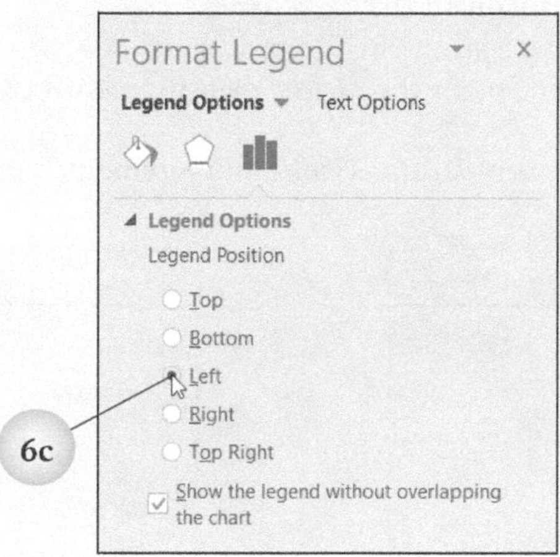

   d. Click the Effects icon in the task pane. (This changes the options in the task pane.)
   e. Click *Shadow* to expand the shadow options in the task pane.
   f. Click the Shadow button to the right of *Presets* and then click the *Offset: Bottom Right* option (first option in the *Outer* section).

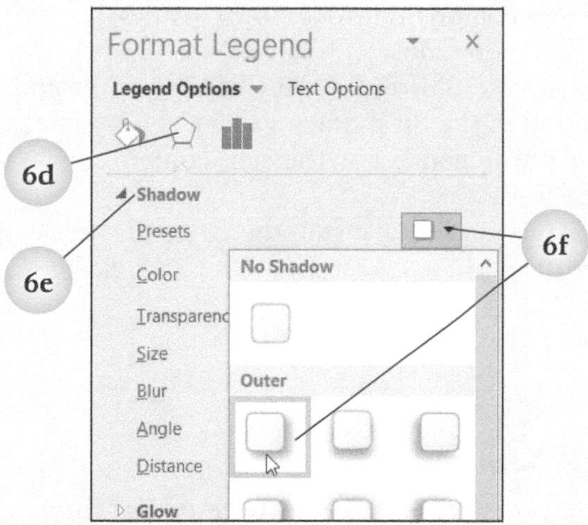

   g. Click the Fill & Line icon in the task pane.
   h. Click *Fill* to expand the fill options in the task pane.
   i. Click the *Gradient fill* option.
   j. Close the task pane by clicking the Close button in the upper right corner of the task pane.

7. Use the Format Chart Area task pane to apply formatting to the chart by completing the following steps:
   a. Click inside the chart but outside any chart elements.
   b. Click the Format Selection button in the Current Selection group.
   c. Make sure the Fill & Line icon in the Format Chart Area task pane is selected. (If not, click the icon.)
   d. Make sure the *Fill* option is expanded. (If not, click *Fill*.)
   e. Click the *Gradient fill* option.
   f. Click the Size & Properties icon in the task pane.
   g. Click *Size* to expand the size options in the task pane.
   h. Select the current measurement in the *Height* measurement box, type 3.5, and then press the Enter key.
   i. Select the current measurement in the *Width* measurement box, type 5.5, and then press the Enter key.
   j. Close the task pane.

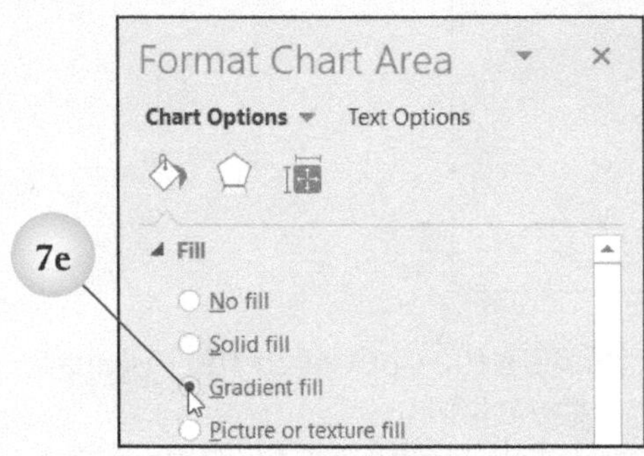

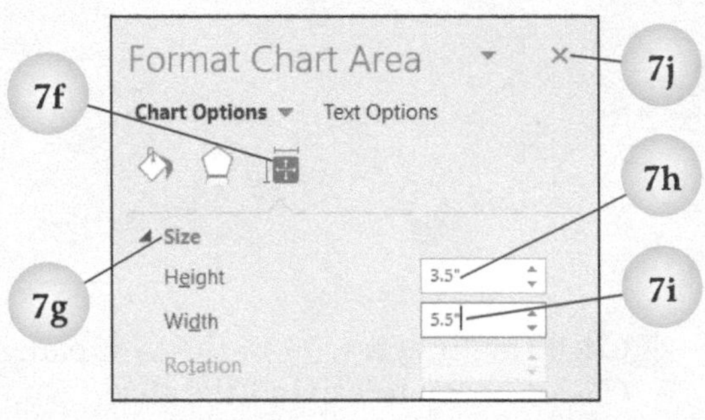

8. Save **7-DIDeptCosts** and then print only the chart.
9. Change the chart style by completing the following steps:
   a. Click the Chart Tools Design tab.
   b. Click the More Chart Styles button in the Chart Styles group.
   c. Click the *Style 9* option at the drop-down gallery.
10. Move the chart so it is positioned below the cells containing data.
11. Click outside the chart to deselect it.
12. Display the Print backstage area, make sure the chart fits on one page with the data, and then click the Print button.
13. Save **7-DIDeptCosts**.

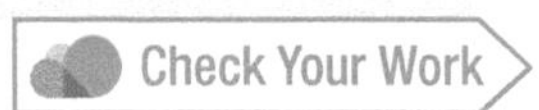

Deleting a Chart

Quick Steps

Delete Chart

1. Click chart.
2. Press Delete key.

OR

1. Right-click chart tab.
2. Click *Delete*.

Delete a chart created in Excel by clicking the chart to select it and then pressing the Delete key. If a chart has been moved to a different worksheet in the workbook, deleting the chart will delete the chart but not the worksheet. To delete the worksheet and the chart, position the mouse pointer on the sheet tab, click the right mouse button, and then click *Delete* at the shortcut menu. At the message box indicating that the selected sheet will be permanently deleted, click the Delete button.

Activity 4b Deleting a Chart and Creating and Formatting a Treemap Chart

Part 2 of 2

1. With **7-DIDeptCosts** open, click the Sheet2 tab.
2. Delete the column chart by completing the following steps:
   a. Click the column chart to select it. (Make sure the chart is selected, not a specific element in the chart.)
   b. Press the Delete key.
3. Create a treemap chart by completing the following steps:
   a. Select the range A2:C8.
   b. Click the Insert tab.
   c. Click the Insert Hierarchy Chart button in the Charts group.
   d. Click the *Treemap* option (first option).
4. Click the *Style 4* option in the Chart Styles group on the Chart Tools Design tab (fourth option from the left).
5. Click the Change Colors button in the Chart Styles group and then click the *Colorful Palette 3* option in the *Colorful* section of the drop-down gallery.
6. Click the Add Chart Element button, position the mouse pointer over the *Legend* option, click the right-pointing triangle, and then click the *None* option.
7. Click in the *Chart Title* placeholder text and then type Proportionate Departmental Expenses.
8. Change the chart height and width by completing the following steps:
   a. Make the entire chart active and then click the Chart Tools Format tab.
   b. Click in the *Shape Height* measurement box, type 5, and then press the Enter key.
   c. Click in the *Shape Width* measurement box, type 4, and then press the Enter key.
9. Move the chart so it is positioned below the cells containing data.
10. Click outside the chart to deselect it.
11. Center the worksheet horizontally and vertically.
12. Save, print, and then close **7-DIDeptCosts**.

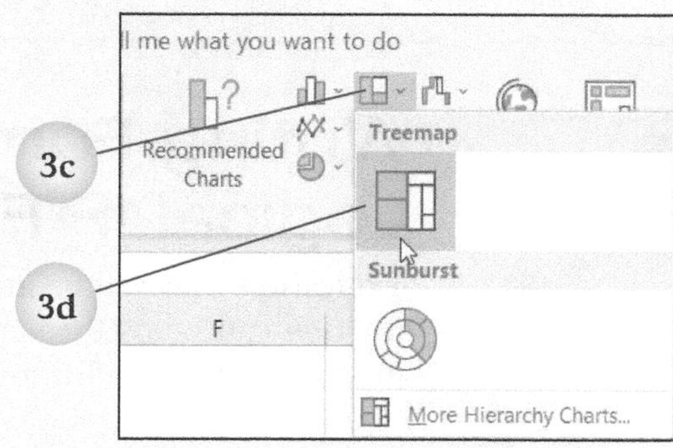

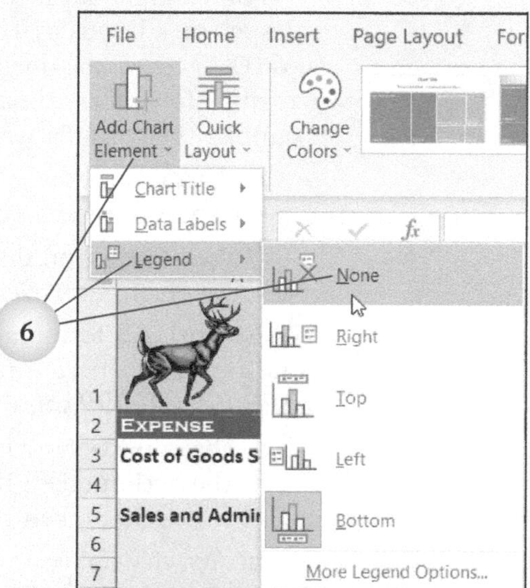

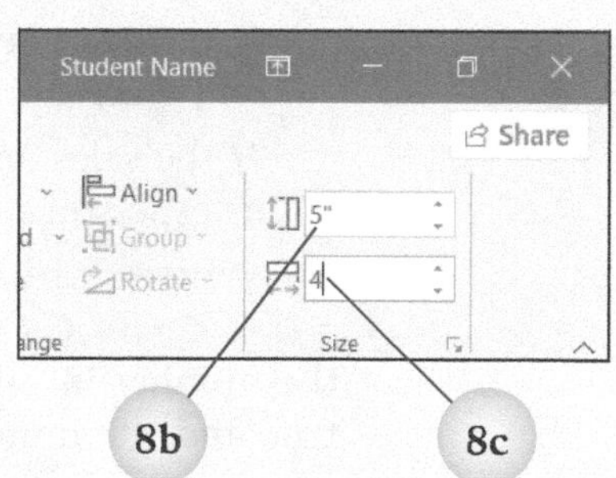

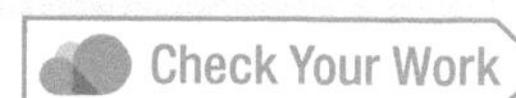

Activity 5 Insert Formulas with the IF Logical Function **3 Parts**

You will write formulas using the IF logical function to calculate sales bonuses, determine pass/fail grades based on averages, and identify discounts and discount amounts.

Using Logical IF Functions

Writing Formulas with the Logical IF Function

A question that can be answered true or false is considered a *logical test*. The ***IF function*** can be used to create a logical test that performs a particular action if the answer is true (condition met) and another action if the answer is false (condition not met).

For example, an IF function can be used to write a formula that calculates a salesperson's bonus as 10% if he or she sells more than $99,999 worth of product and 0% if he or she does not sell more than $99,999 worth of product. When writing a formula with an IF function, think about the words *if* and *then*. For example, the formula written out for the bonus example would look like this:

If the salesperson sells more than $99,999 of product, ***then*** the salesperson receives a bonus of 10%.

If the salesperson does not sell more than $99,999 of product, ***then*** the salesperson receives a bonus of 0%.

When writing a formula with an IF function, use a comma to separate the condition and the action. The formula for the bonus example would look like this: ***=IF(sales>99999,sales*0.1,0)***. The formula contains three parts:

- the condition or logical test: ***IF(sales>99999***
- the action taken if the condition or logical test is true: ***sales*0.1***
- the action taken if the condition or logical test is false: ***0***

In Activity 5a, you will write a formula with cell references rather than cell data. You will write a formula with an IF function that determines the following:

If the sales amount is greater than the quota amount, ***then*** the salesperson will receive a 15% bonus.

If the sales amount is not greater than the quota amount, ***then*** the salesperson will not receive a bonus.

Written with cell references in the activity, the formula looks like this: ***=IF(C4>B4,C4*0.15,0)***. In this formula, the condition, or logical test, is whether the number in cell C4 is greater than the number in cell B4. If the condition is true and the number is greater, then the number in cell C4 is multiplied by 0.15 (providing a 15% bonus). If the condition is false and the number in cell C4 is less than the number in cell B4, then nothing happens (no bonus). Notice how commas are used to separate the logical test from the action.

Activity 5a Writing a Formula with an IF Function

Part 1 of 3

1. Open **CMPReports** and then save it with the name **7-CMPReports**.
2. Write a formula with the IF function that determines if a sales quota has been met and if it has, inserts the bonus of 15% of actual sales. (If the quota has not been met, the formula will insert a 0.) Write the formula by completing the following steps:
   a. Make cell D4 active.
   b. Type =if(c4>b4,c4*0.15,0) and then press the Enter key.

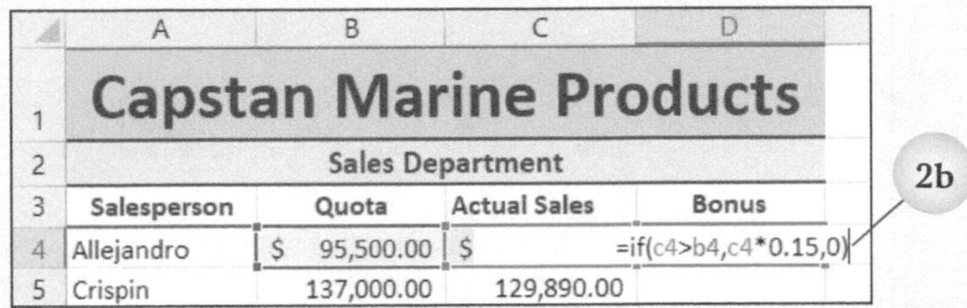

   c. Make cell D4 active and then use the fill handle to copy the formula to the range D5:D9.
3. Print the worksheet.
4. Revise the formula so it inserts a 20% bonus if the quota has been met by completing the following steps:
   a. Make cell D4 active.
   b. Click in the Formula bar, edit the formula so it displays as *=IF(C4>B4,C4*0.2,0)*, and then click the Enter button on the Formula bar.
   c. Copy the formula in cell D4 to the range D5:D9.
   d. Make cell D4 active and then apply the Accounting format with a dollar symbol ($) and two digits after the decimal point.
5. Save **7-CMPReports**.

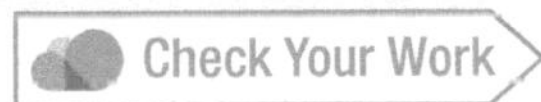

Writing Formulas with an IF Function Using the Function Arguments Dialog Box

A formula containing an IF function can be typed directly into a cell or the Function Arguments dialog box can be used to help write the formula. To use the Function Arguments dialog box to write a formula with the IF function, click the Formulas tab, click the Logical button in the Function Library group, and then click *IF* at the drop-down list. This displays the Function Arguments dialog box, shown in Figure 7.12. The Function Arguments dialog box displays the information you will type in the three argument text boxes for Activity 5b.

At the Function Arguments dialog box, click in the *Logical_test* text box and information about the *Logical_test* argument displays in the dialog box. In this text box, type the cell designation followed by what is evaluated. In the figure, the *Logical_test* text box contains *b14>599*, indicating that what is being evaluated is whether the amount in cell B14 is greater than $599. The *Value_if_true* text box contains *b14*0.95*, indicating that if the logical test is true, then the amount in cell B14 is multiplied by 0.95. (The discount for any product price greater than $599 is 5%, and multiplying the product price by 0.95 determines the price after the 5% discount is applied.) The *Value_if_false* text box contains *b14*, indicating that if the logical test is false (the product price is not greater than $599), then the amount from cell B14 is simply inserted.

Figure 7.12 Function Arguments Dialog Box

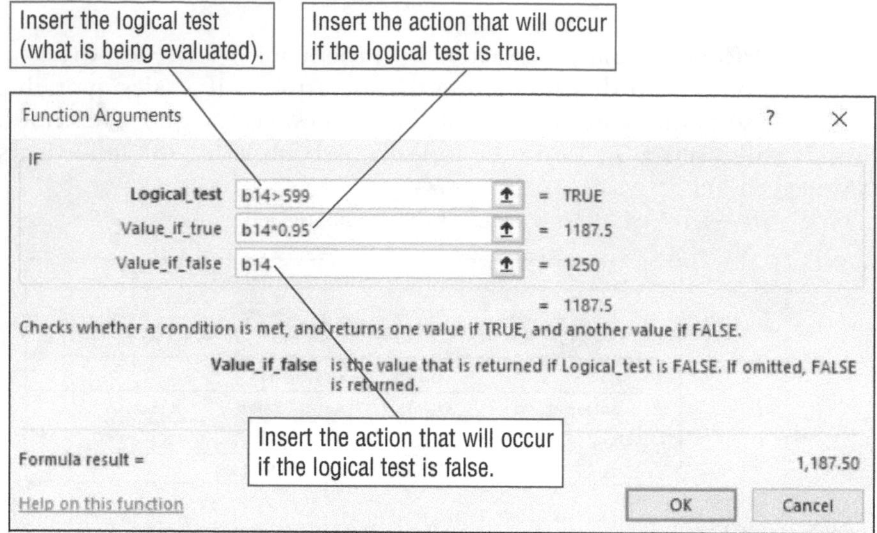

Activity 5b Writing a Formula with an IF Function Using the Function Arguments Dialog Box

Part 2 of 3

1. With **7-CMPReports** open, insert a formula with an IF function using the Function Arguments dialog box by completing the following steps:
   a. Make cell C14 active.
   b. Click the Formulas tab.
   c. Click the Logical button in the Function Library group.
   d. Click *IF* at the drop-down list.
   e. At the Function Arguments dialog box, type b14>599 in the *Logical_test* text box and then press the Tab key.
   f. Type b14*0.95 in the *Value_if_true* text box and then press the Tab key.
   g. Type b14 in the *Value_if_false* text box.

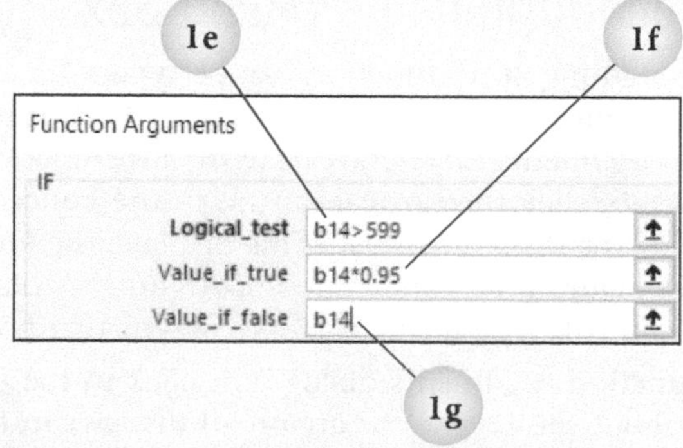

   h. Click OK to close the Function Arguments dialog box.
2. Copy the formula in cell C14 to the range C15:C26.
3. Apply the Accounting format with a dollar symbol and two digits after the decimal point to cell C14.
4. Save **7-CMPReports**.

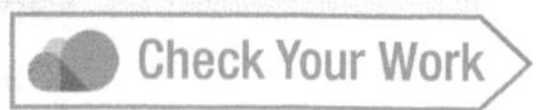

Writing IF Statements Containing Text

When writing a formula with an IF statement, if text is to be inserted in a cell rather than a value, put quotation marks around the text. For example, in Step 2 of Activity 5c, you will write a formula with an IF function that looks like this when written out:

If the new employee averages more than 79 on the quizzes, ***then*** he or she passes.

If the new employee does not average more than 79 on the quizzes, ***then*** he or she fails.

In Activity 5c, you will write the formula so the word *PASS* is inserted in a cell if the average of the new employee quizzes is greater than 79 and the word *FAIL* is inserted if the condition is not met. The formula would be ***=IF(E31>79, "PASS", "FAIL")***. The quotation marks before and after *PASS* and *FAIL* identify the data as text rather than values.

The Function Arguments dialog box can be used to write a formula with an IF function that contains text. For example, in Step 3 of Activity 5c, you will write a formula with an IF function using the Function Arguments dialog box that looks like this when written out:

If the product price is greater than $599, ***then*** insert *YES*.

If the product price is not greater than $599, ***then*** insert *NO*.

To create the formula in Step 3 using the Function Arguments dialog box, display the dialog box and then type *b14>599* in the *Logical_test* text box, *YES* in the *Value_if_true* text box and *NO* in the *Value_if_false* text box. When you press the Enter key after typing *YES* in the *Value_if_true* text box, Excel automatically inserts quotation marks around the text. Excel will do the same thing for *NO* in the *Value_if_false* text box.

Activity 5c **Writing IF Statements Containing Text** Part 3 of 3

1. With **7-CMPReports** open, insert quiz averages by completing the following steps:
   a. Make cell E31 active and then insert a formula that calculates the average of the test scores in the range B31:D31.
   b. Copy the formula in cell E31 to the range E32:E35.
2. Write a formula with an IF function that inserts the word *PASS* if the new employee quiz average is greater than 79 and inserts the word *FAIL* if the quiz average is not greater than 79. Write the formula by completing the following steps:
   a. Make cell F31 active.
   b. Type =if(e31>79,"PASS","FAIL") and then press the Enter key.

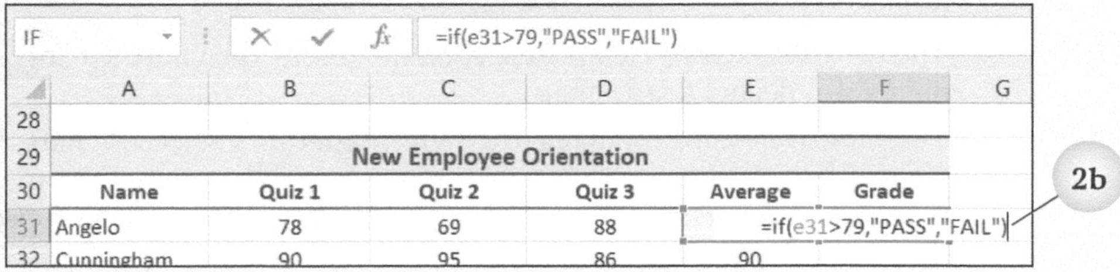

   c. Copy the formula in cell F31 to the range F32:F35.

3. Write a formula with an IF function using the Function Arguments dialog box that inserts the word *YES* in the cell if the product price is greater than $599 and inserts the word *NO* if the price is not greater than $599. Write the formula by completing the following steps:
   a. Make cell D14 active.
   b. Click the Formulas tab.
   c. Click the Logical button in the Function Library group.
   d. Click *IF* at the drop-down list.
   e. Type b14>599 in the *Logical_test* text box and then press the Tab key.
   f. Type YES in the *Value_if_true* text box and then press the Tab key.
   g. Type NO in the *Value_if_false* text box.
   h. Click OK to close the Function Arguments dialog box.
   i. Copy the formula in cell D14 to the range D15:D26.

3e
3f
Function Arguments
IF
Logical_test b14>599 = TRUE
Value_if_true "YES" = "YES"
Value_if_false NO =
3g

4. Save and then print **7-CMPReports**.
5. Press Ctrl + ` to turn on the display of formulas.
6. Print the worksheet again. (The worksheet will print on two pages.)
7. Press Ctrl + ` to turn off the display of formulas.
8. Save and then close **7-CMPReports**.

Chapter Summary

- A chart is a visual presentation of data. Excel provides 17 basic chart types: Column, Line, Pie, Bar, Area, X Y (Scatter), Map, Stock, Surface, Radar, Treemap, Sunburst, Histogram, Box & Whisker, Waterfall, Funnel, and Combo.
- To create a chart, select the cells, click the Insert tab, and then click a specific chart button in the Charts group. Click the Recommended Charts button in the Charts group and Excel will recommend a type of chart for the data.
- A chart is inserted in the same worksheet as the selected cells by default.
- Change the size of a chart using the mouse by dragging one of the sizing handles that display around the border of the chart. When changing the chart size, maintain the proportions of the chart by pressing and holding down the Shift key while dragging a sizing handle.
- Move a chart by positioning the mouse pointer on the chart border until the pointer displays with a four-headed arrow attached and then dragging with the mouse.
- The cells selected to create a chart are linked to the chart. Changes made to the data are reflected in the chart.
- Three buttons appear outside the right border of a selected chart. Use the Chart Elements button to insert or remove chart elements, use the Chart Styles button to apply chart styles, and use the Chart Filters button to isolate specific data in the chart.
- Print a chart by selecting it, displaying the Print backstage area, and then clicking the Print button.

- When a chart is inserted in a worksheet, the Chart Tools Design tab is active. Use buttons and options on this tab to add chart elements, change the chart type, specify a different layout or style for the chart, and change the location of the chart.
- Choose a chart style with options in the Chart Styles group on the Chart Tools Design tab or at the Change Chart Type dialog box.
- Click the Switch Row/Column button in the Data group on the Chart Tools Design tab to change what Excel uses to determine the grouping of data along the horizontal axis and legend.
- Use the Quick Layout button in the Chart Layouts group on the Chart Tools Design tab to change the chart layout.
- Use the Change Colors button in the Chart Styles group on the Chart Tools Design tab to apply different colors to a chart.
- Create a chart and it is inserted in the currently open worksheet. The chart can be moved to a new worksheet in the workbook with the *New sheet* option at the Move Chart dialog box.
- Add chart elements with the Add Chart Element button in the Chart Layouts group on the Chart Tools Design tab.
- Move a chart element by selecting it and then dragging it with the mouse. Use the sizing handles around a chart element to change its size. Delete a chart element by selecting it and then pressing the Delete key or by right-clicking the element and then clicking *Delete* at the shortcut menu.
- Customize the formatting of a chart and chart elements with options on the Chart Tools Format tab. Use these options to identify specific elements in the chart for formatting, insert a shape, apply formatting to a shape, apply WordArt formatting to data in a chart, insert alt text, and arrange, align, and size a chart.
- Insert a shape by clicking it in the Insert Shapes group on the Chart Tools Format tab and then clicking or dragging in the chart.
- Create alternate text for an object such as a chart and the text is read by a screen reader, helping people with a visual impairment understand what objects are included in the worksheet.
- Excel provides additional formatting options at a formatting task pane. A formatting task pane displays at the right side of the screen; the name and the contents in the task pane vary depending on whether the entire chart or an element in the chart is selected. Display a task pane by clicking the chart or element in the chart and then clicking the Format Selection button in the Current Selection group on the Chart Tools Format tab.
- Change the size of a chart with the *Shape Height* and *Shape Width* measurement boxes on the Chart Tools Format tab or at the Format Chart Area task pane.
- To delete a chart in a worksheet, click the chart to select it and then press the Delete key. To delete a chart created in a separate sheet, position the mouse pointer on the chart sheet tab, click the right mouse button, and then click *Delete*.
- A logical test is a question that can be answered with true or false. Use the IF function to create a logical test that performs one action if the answer is true (condition met) or another action if the answer is false (condition not met).

Commands Review

FEATURE	RIBBON TAB, GROUP	BUTTON	KEYBOARD SHORTCUT
add chart element	Chart Tools Design, Chart Layouts		
Change Chart Type dialog box	Chart Tools Design, Type		
change colors	Chart Tools Design, Chart Styles		
chart or chart element task pane	Chart Tools Format, Current Selection		
logical functions	Formulas, Function Library		
Move Chart dialog box	Chart Tools Design, Location		
quick layout	Chart Tools Design, Chart Layouts		
recommended chart	Insert, Charts		Alt + F1
recommended chart in separate sheet			F11
switch row/column	Chart Tools Design, Data		

Microsoft®

Excel®

CHAPTER 8

Adding Visual Interest to Workbooks

Performance Objectives

Upon successful completion of Chapter 8, you will be able to:

1 Insert symbols and special characters
2 Insert, size, move, and format images
3 Create and insert screenshots
4 Draw, format, and copy shapes
5 Insert, format, and type text in text boxes
6 Insert, format, and modify icons and 3D models
7 Insert, format, size, move, and delete SmartArt graphics
8 Insert, format, size, and move WordArt

Microsoft Excel includes a variety of features that you can use to enhance the appearance of a workbook. Some of the methods for adding visual appeal that you will learn in this chapter include inserting and modifying images, screenshots, shapes, text boxes, icons, 3D models, SmartArt, and WordArt.

Before beginning the chapter work, copy the EL1C8 folder to your storage medium and then make EL1C8 the active folder.

The online course includes additional training and assessment resources.

Activity 1 Insert Symbols, Images, and Shapes in a Financial Analysis Workbook **5 Parts**

You will open a financial analysis workbook and then insert symbols and move, size, and format an image in the workbook. You will also insert an arrow shape, type and format text in the shape, and then copy the shape.

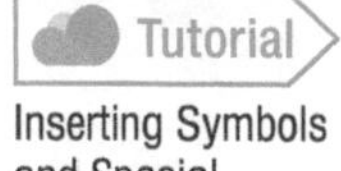

Inserting Symbols and Special Characters

Symbol

Quick Steps

Insert Symbol

1. Click in cell.
2. Click Insert tab.
3. Click Symbol button.
4. Double-click symbol.
5. Click Close.

Insert Special Character

1. Click in cell.
2. Click Insert tab.
3. Click Symbol button.
4. Click Special Characters tab.
5. Double-click special character.
6. Click Close.

Hint Increase or decrease the size of the Symbol dialog box by positioning the mouse pointer on the lower right corner until the pointer displays as a two-headed arrow and then dragging with the mouse.

Inserting Symbols and Special Characters

Use the Symbol button on the Insert tab to insert symbols in a worksheet. Click the button and the Symbol dialog box displays, as shown in Figure 8.1. At the dialog box, double-click a symbol to insert it, click the symbol and then click the Insert button, or type the code in the *Character code* text box. Click the Close button to exit the dialog box.

At the Symbol dialog box with the Symbols tab selected, additional symbols are available with different fonts. Change the font by clicking the *Font* option box arrow and then clicking a font at the drop-down list. Click the Special Characters tab at the Symbol dialog box and a list of special characters displays. Insert a special character by double-clicking a character and then clicking the Close button or by clicking the character, clicking the Insert button, and then clicking the Close button.

Figure 8.1 Symbol Dialog Box with the Symbols Tab Selected

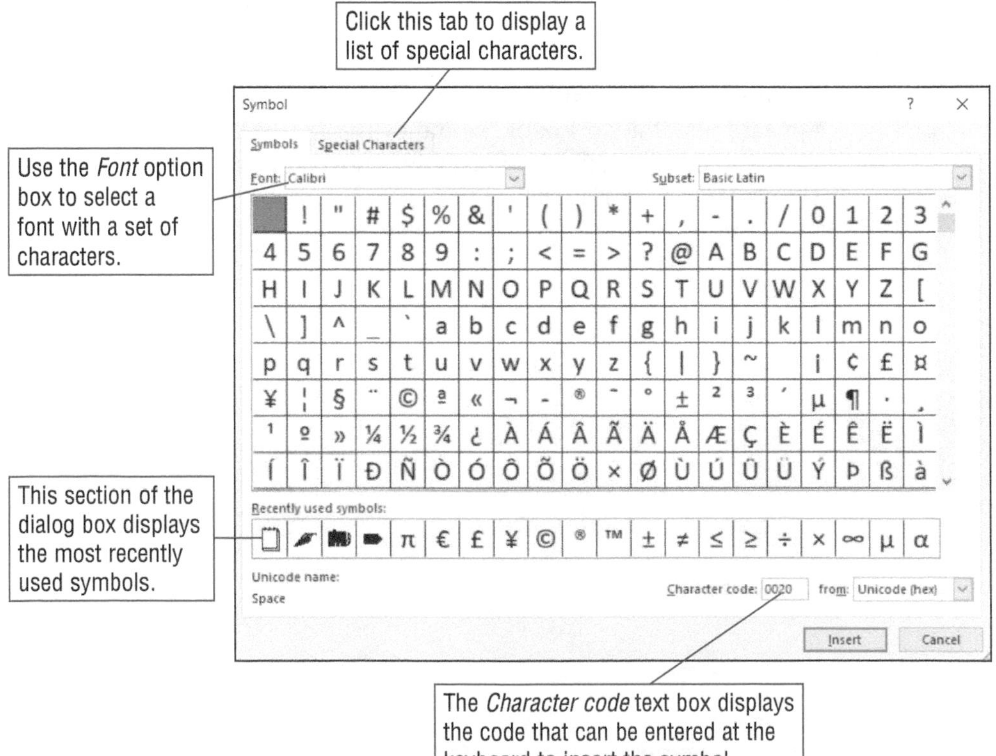

Click this tab to display a list of special characters.
Use the *Font* option box to select a font with a set of characters.
This section of the dialog box displays the most recently used symbols.
The *Character code* text box displays the code that can be entered at the keyboard to insert the symbol.
Symbol
Symbols
Special Characters
Font: Calibri
Subset: Basic Latin
Recently used symbols:
Unicode name:
Space
Character code: 0020
from: Unicode (hex)
Insert
Cancel

Activity 1a Inserting Symbols and Special Characters

Part 1 of 5

1. Open **SMFFinCon** and then save it with the name **8-SMFFinCon**.
2. Insert a symbol by completing the following steps:
   a. Double-click in cell A2.
   b. Delete the *e* at the end of *Qualite*.
   c. With the insertion point positioned immediately right of the *t* in *Qualit*, click the Insert tab.
   d. Click the Symbol button in the Symbols group.
   e. At the Symbol dialog box, scroll down the list box and then click the *é* symbol (located in approximately the ninth through eleventh rows). (You can also type *00E9* in the *Character code* text box to select the symbol.)
   f. Click the Insert button and then click the Close button.

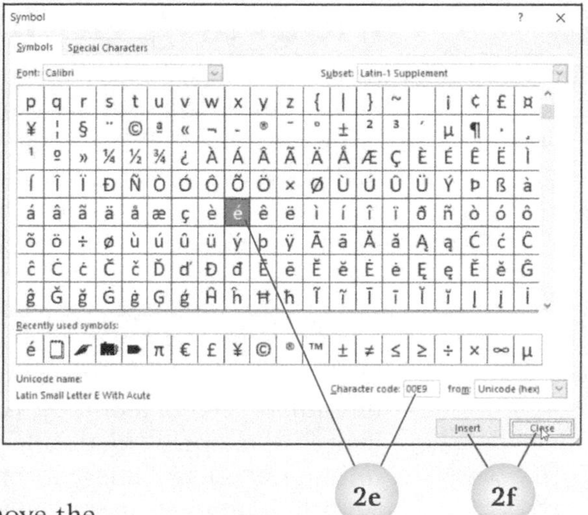

3. Insert a special character by completing the following steps:
   a. With cell A2 selected and in Edit mode, move the insertion point so it is positioned immediately right of *Group*.
   b. Click the Symbol button in the Symbols group.
   c. At the Symbol dialog box, click the Special Characters tab.
   d. Double-click the ® *Registered* symbol (tenth option from the top).
   e. Click the Close button.

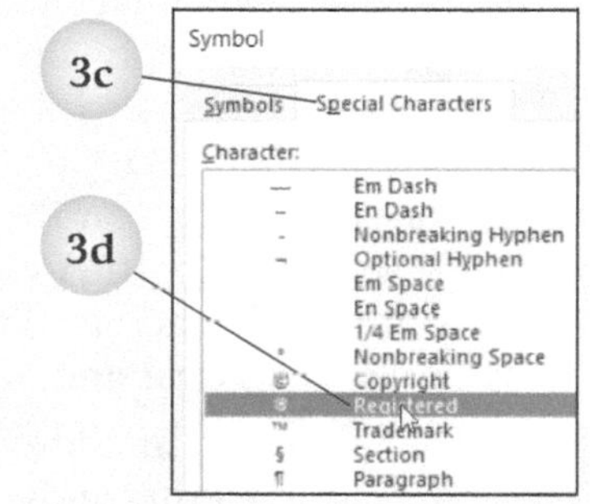

4. Insert a symbol by completing the following steps:
   a. With cell A2 selected and in Edit mode, move the insertion point so it is positioned immediately left of the *Q* in *Qualité*.
   b. Click the Symbol button in the Symbols group.
   c. At the Symbol dialog box, click the *Font* option box arrow and then click *Wingdings* at the drop-down list. (You will need to scroll down the list to see this option.)
   d. Click the ❖ symbol (located in approximately the fifth or sixth row). (You can also type *118* in the *Character code* text box to select the symbol.)
   e. Click the Insert button and then click the Close button.
5. Click in cell A3.
6. Save **8-SMFFinCon**.

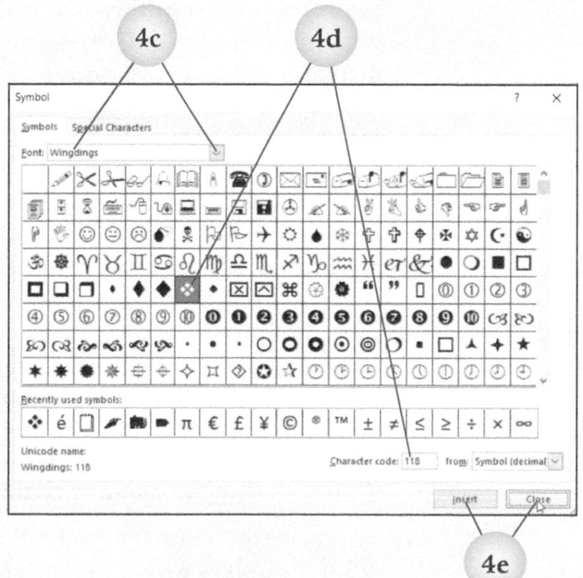

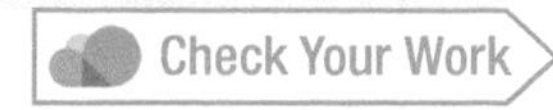

Figure 8.2 Picture Tools Format Tab

Inserting an Image

Inserting an Image

Insert an image, such as a picture or clip art image, in an Excel workbook with buttons in the Illustrations group on the Insert tab. Click the Pictures button to display the Insert Picture dialog box with options for inserting an image from a folder on the computer or a removable drive. Or click the Online Pictures button and search for images online. When an image is inserted in a worksheet, the Picture Tools Format tab appears, as shown in Figure 8.2.

Modifying Images

Quick Steps

Insert Image

1. Click Insert tab.
2. Click Pictures button.
3. Navigate to folder.
4. Double-click image.

Customizing and Formatting an Image

Use buttons in the Adjust group on the Picture Tools Format tab to remove unwanted parts of an image, correct the image brightness and contrast, change the image color, apply artistic effects to the image, change to a different image, and restore the original image formatting. Use the Compress Pictures button in the Adjust group to compress the size of an image file and reduce the amount of space the image requires on the storage medium. Use buttons in the Picture Styles group to apply a predesigned style to the image, change the image border, or apply other effects to the image. Use the Alt Text button in the Accessibility group to add alternate text for the image. With options in the Arrange group, position the image on the page, specify how text will wrap around the image, align the image with other elements in the worksheet, and rotate the image. Use the Crop button in the Size group to remove any unwanted parts of the image and use the *Shape Height* and *Shape Width* measurement boxes to specify the image size.

In addition to options at the Picture Tools Format tab, options at the shortcut menu can be used to format an image. Display this menu by right-clicking the image. Use options at the shortcut menu to change the image, choose text wrapping around the image, insert alt text, size and position the image, and display the Format Picture task pane.

Sizing and Moving an Image

Change the size of an image with the *Shape Height* and *Shape Width* measurement boxes in the Size group on the Picture Tools Format tab or with the sizing handles around the selected image. To change size with a sizing handle, position the mouse pointer on a sizing handle until the pointer turns into a double-headed arrow and then drag in or out to decrease or increase the size of the image. Use the middle sizing handles at the left and right sides of the image to make the image wider or thinner. Use the middle sizing handles at the top and bottom of the image to make the image taller or shorter. Use the sizing handles at the corners of the image to change both the width and height at the same time. Press and hold down the Shift key while dragging a sizing handle to maintain the proportions of the image.

Move an image by positioning the mouse pointer on the image border until the pointer displays with a four-headed arrow attached and then dragging the image to the new location. Rotate the image by positioning the mouse pointer on the white round rotation handle until the pointer displays as a circular arrow. Click and hold down the left mouse button, drag in the desired direction, and then release the mouse button.

Activity 1b Inserting and Formatting and Moving an Image

Part 2 of 5

1. With **8-SMFFinCon** open, insert an image by completing the following steps:
   a. Click the Insert tab and then click the Pictures button in the Illustrations group.
   b. At the Insert Picture dialog box, navigate to your EL1C8 folder and then double-click ***WallStreet***.
2. Change the size of the image by clicking in the *Shape Height* measurement box in the Size group on the Picture Tools Format tab, typing 1.8, and then pressing the Enter key.
3. Remove the yellow background from the image by completing the following steps:
   a. Click the Remove Background button in the Adjust group.
   b. Click the Keep Changes button in the Close group on the Background Removal tab.
4. Change the color by clicking the Color button in the Adjust group and then clicking the *Blue, Accent color 1 Light* option (second column, third row in the *Recolor* section).
5. Apply a correction by clicking the Corrections button in the Adjust group and then clicking the *Brightness: +20% Contrast: +20%* option (fourth column, fourth row in the *Brightness/Contrast* section).
6. Apply an artistic effect by clicking the Artistic Effects button in the Adjust group and then clicking the *Glow Edges* option (last option in the drop-down gallery).

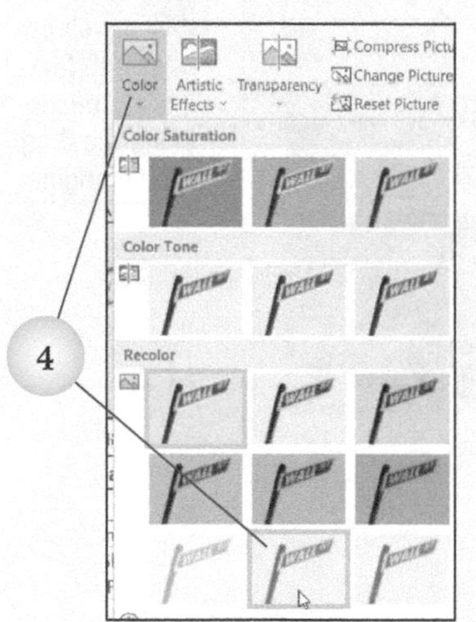

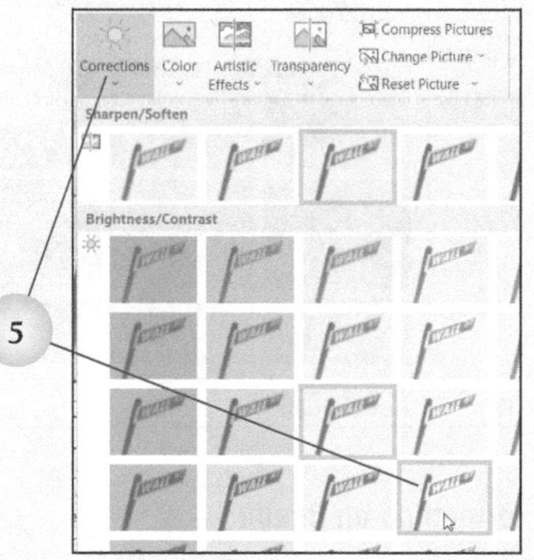

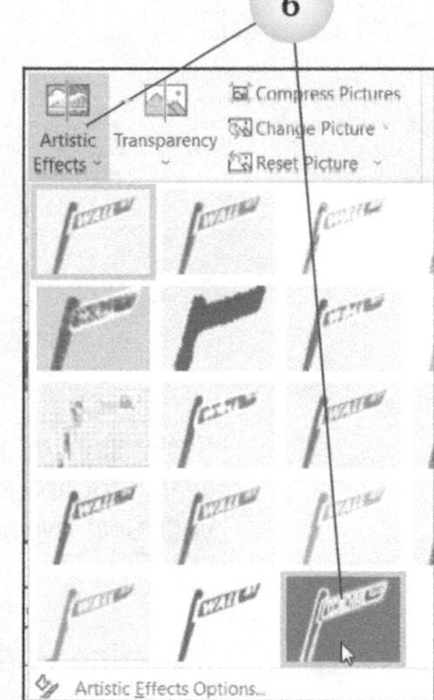

7. Move the image by completing the following steps:
   a. Position the mouse pointer on the image (displays with a four-headed arrow attached).
   b. Click and hold down the left mouse button, drag the image to the upper left corner of the worksheet, and then release the mouse button.
8. Save and then print **8-SMFFinCon**.

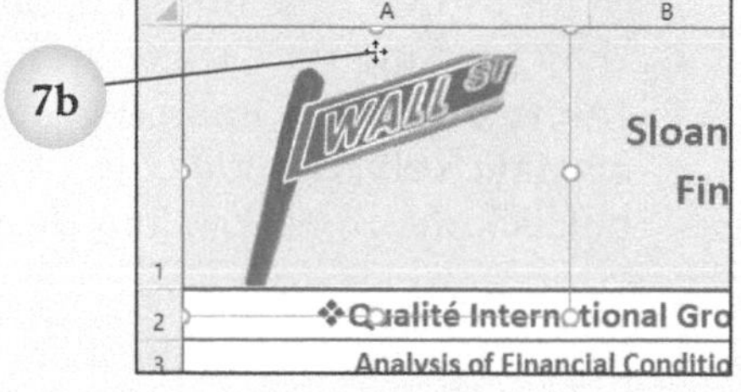

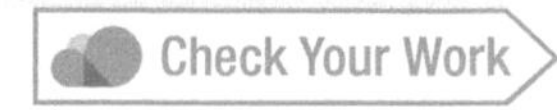

Formatting an Image at the Format Picture Task Pane

In addition to the Picture Tools Format tab, the Format Picture task pane provides options for formatting an image. Click the Picture Styles group task pane launcher or the Size group task pane launcher and the Format Picture task pane displays at the right side of the screen. Click the Picture Styles group task pane launcher and the task pane displays with the Effects icon selected; click the Size group task pane launcher and the Size & Properties icon is selected. Two other icons are also available in this task pane: the Fill & Line icon and the Picture icon. The formatting options may need to be expanded. For example, click *Size* with the Size & Properties icon selected and options for changing the size of the image display. Close the task pane by clicking the Close button in the upper right corner.

Tutorial

Inserting an Online Image

Online Pictures

Quick Steps

Insert Online Image

1. Click Insert tab.
2. Click Online Pictures button.
3. Type search word or topic.
4. Press Enter key.
5. Double-click image.

Inserting an Online Image

Use the Bing Image Search feature to search for images online. To use this feature, click the Insert tab and then click the Online Pictures button in the Illustrations group. This displays the Online Pictures window, shown in Figure 8.3. Click in the search text box, type the search term or topic, and then press the Enter key. Images that match the search term or topic display in the window. To insert an image, click the image and then click the Insert button or double-click the image. This downloads the image to the document. Customize the image with options and buttons on the Picture Tools Format tab.

Figure 8.3 Online Pictures Window

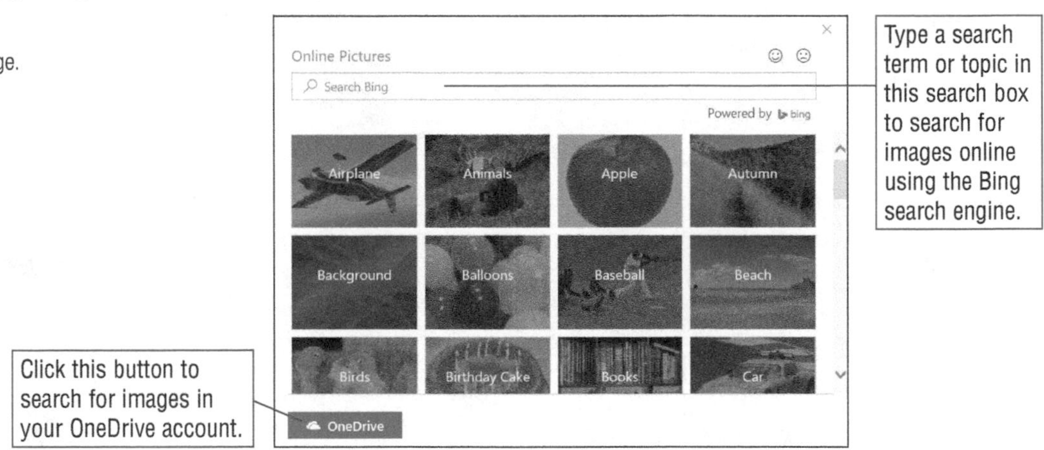
Online Pictures
Search Bing
Powered by bing
Airplane
Animals
Apple
Autumn
Background
Balloons
Baseball
Beach
Birds
Birthday Cake
Books
Car
OneDrive
Type a search term or topic in this search box to search for images online using the Bing search engine.
Click this button to search for images in your OneDrive account.

Activity 1c **Inserting and Formatting an Image** Part 3 of 5

1. With **8-SMFFinCon** open, delete the Wall Street sign image by clicking the image and then pressing the Delete key.
2. Insert a different image by completing the following steps:
   a. Make cell A1 active.
   b. Click the Insert tab and then click the Online Pictures button in the Illustrations group.

c. At the Online Pictures window, type stock market clip art in the search box and then press the Enter key.

d. Double-click the graph image shown below and to the right. (If this image is not available online, click the Pictures button on the Insert tab. At the Insert Picture dialog box, navigate to your EL1C8 folder and then double-click ***StockMarket***.)

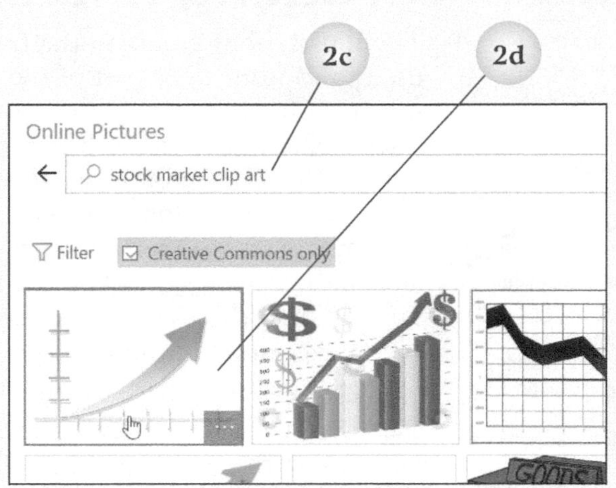

3. Display the Format Picture task pane with the Size & Properties icon selected by clicking the Size group task pane launcher on the Picture Tools Format tab.
4. If necessary, click *Size* in the task pane to display the sizing options.
5. Change the height of the image by selecting the current measurement in the *Height* measurement box, typing 1.65, and then pressing the Enter key. (The width automatically changes to maintain the proportions of the image.)

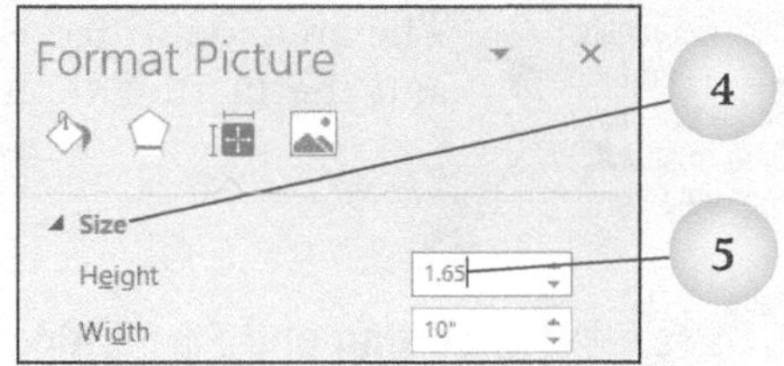

6. Change the properties of the image by clicking *Properties* in the Format Picture task pane to expand the options and then clicking the *Move and size with cells* option. (With this option selected, changing the size of the row also changes the size of the image.)
7. Make a correction to the image by completing the following steps:
   a. Click the Picture icon at the top of the task pane.
   b. Click *Picture Corrections* to expand the options.
   c. Select the current percentage in the *Brightness* text box and then type -25.
   d. Select the current percentage in the *Contrast* text box, type 40, and then press the Enter key.
8. Close the Format Picture task pane by clicking the Close button in the upper right corner.

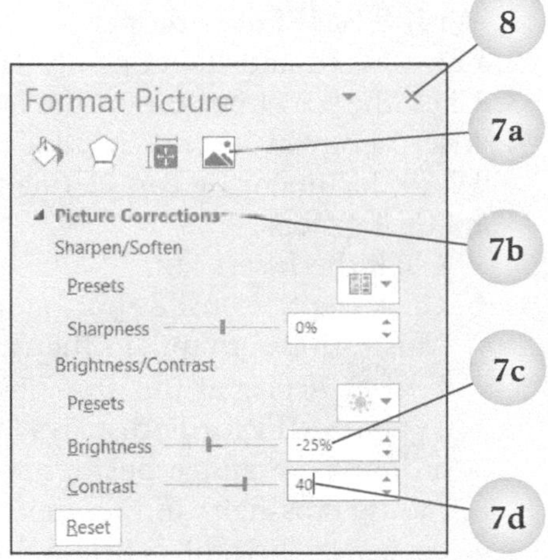

9. Create alternative text for the image by completing the following steps:
   a. Click the Alt Text button in the Accessibility group on the Picture Tools Format tab.
   b. At the Alt Text task pane, click in the description text box and then type Chart containing an up-pointing arrow.
   c. Close the Alt Text task pane.
10. Click outside the image to deselect it.
11. Increase the height of row 1 to 126.00 points and notice that the image size increases with the row height.
12. Save **8-SMFFinCon**.

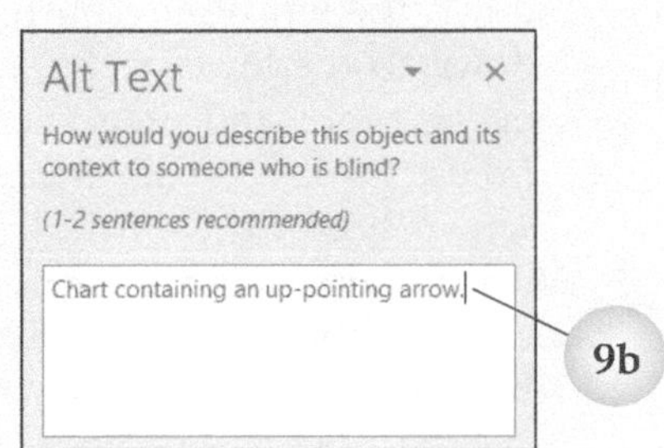

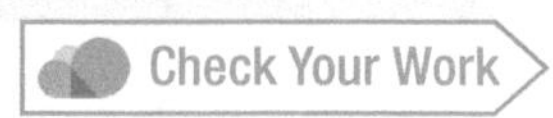

Creating and Inserting a Screenshot

Screenshot

Quick Steps

Insert Screenshot

1. Open window to be captured.
2. Make Excel active.
3. Open workbook.
4. Click Insert tab.
5. Click Screenshot button.
6. Click window at drop-down list.

OR

1. Click Screenshot button and then *Screen Clipping*.
2. Drag to specify capture area.

Creating and Inserting a Screenshot

The Illustrations group on the Insert tab contains a Screenshot button that can be used to capture all or part of the contents of a screen as an image. This is useful for capturing information from a web page or a file in another program. To create a screenshot, open the web page or file to be captured so that it is visible on the screen. Next, make Excel active and open a workbook. Click the Insert tab, click the Screenshot button, and then look in the drop-down list to see thumbnails of windows open in other programs. Click the thumbnail of the screen to be captured and the screenshot is inserted as an image in the open workbook, the image is selected, and the Picture Tools Format tab is active. Use buttons on this tab to customize the screenshot image.

A screenshot can also be made of a specific portion of the screen by clicking the *Screen Clipping* option at the Screenshot button drop-down list. Click this option and the open web page, file, or Windows desktop displays in a dimmed manner and the mouse pointer displays as crosshairs (a plus symbol [+]). Using the mouse, draw a border around the specific area of the screen to be captured. The area identified is inserted in the workbook as an image, the image is selected, and the Picture Tools Format tab is active.

Activity 1d **Inserting and Formatting a Screenshot** Part 4 of 5

1. With **8-SMFFinCon** open, make sure that no other programs are open.
2. Open Word and then open **SMFProfile** from your EL1C8 folder.
3. Click the Excel button on the taskbar.
4. Insert a screenshot of the table in the Word document by completing the following steps:
   a. Click the Insert tab.
   b. Click the Screenshot button in the Illustrations group and then click *Screen Clipping* at the drop-down list.
   c. When **SMFProfile** displays in a dimmed manner, position the mouse crosshairs in the upper left corner of the table, click and hold down the left mouse button, drag down to the lower right corner of the table, and then release the mouse button. (This creates a screenshot of the entire table.)

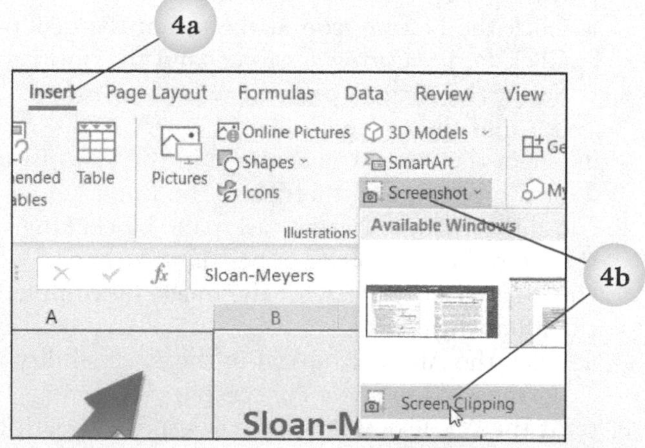

5. With the screenshot image inserted in **8-SMFFinCon**, make the following changes:
   a. Click in the *Shape Width* measurement box in the Size group on the Picture Tools Format tab, type 3.7, and then press the Enter key.

b. Click the Corrections button and then click the *Sharpen: 25%* option (fourth option in the *Sharpen/Soften* section).
c. Click the Corrections button and then click the *Brightness: 0% (Normal) Contrast: -40%* (third column, first row in the *Brightness/Contrast* section).
d. Using the mouse, drag the screenshot image one row below the data in row 10.

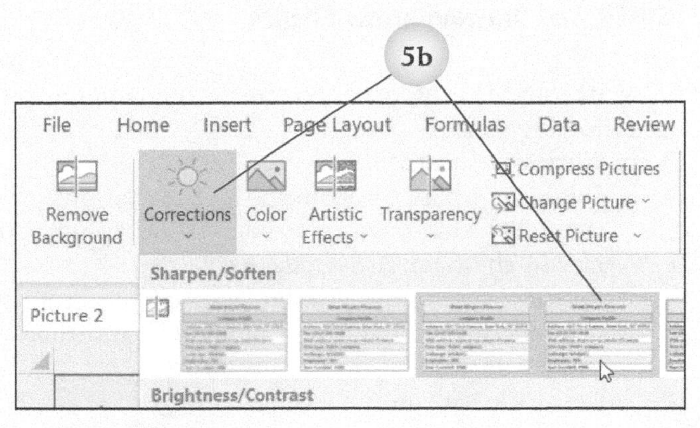

6. Make cell A4 active.
7. Save **8-SMFFinCon**.
8. Click the Word button on the taskbar, close **SMFProfile**, and then close Word.

Inserting a Shape

Formatting a Shape

Shapes

Quick Steps

Insert Shape
1. Click Insert tab.
2. Click Shapes button.
3. Click shape option at drop-down list.
4. Click or drag in worksheet.

Copy Shape
1. Select shape.
2. Click Copy button.
3. Position insertion point in new location.
4. Click Paste button.

OR
1. Select shape.
2. Press and hold down Ctrl key.
3. Drag shape to new location.

Inserting and Formatting a Shape

Chapter 7 covered how to insert shapes in a chart with options on the Chart Tools Format tab. Shapes can also be inserted in a worksheet with the Shapes button in the Illustrations group on the Insert tab. Use the Shapes button to draw shapes in a worksheet, including lines, basic shapes, block arrows, flow chart symbols, callouts, stars, and banners. Click a shape and the mouse pointer displays as crosshairs. Click in the worksheet or position the crosshairs where the shape is to begin, click and hold down the left mouse button, drag to create the shape, and then release the mouse button. Click or drag in the worksheet and the shape is inserted and the Drawing Tools Format tab, shown in Figure 8.4, becomes active. Use options and buttons on this tab to choose a shape, apply a style to a shape, arrange a shape, and change the size of a shape.

Choose a shape in the *Lines* section of the Shapes button drop-down list and the shape that is drawn is considered a line drawing. Choose an option in another section of the drop-down list and the shape drawn is considered an enclosed object. When drawing an enclosed object, maintain the proportions of the shape by pressing and holding down the Shift key while dragging with the mouse. Text can be typed in an enclosed object and then formatted using buttons in the WordArt Styles group (or options on the Home tab).

Copy a shape in a worksheet by selecting the shape and then clicking the Copy button in the Clipboard group on the Home tab. Make active the cell where the shape is to be copied and then click the Paste button. A shape can also be copied by pressing and holding down the Ctrl key while dragging the shape to the new location.

Figure 8.4 Drawing Tools Format Tab

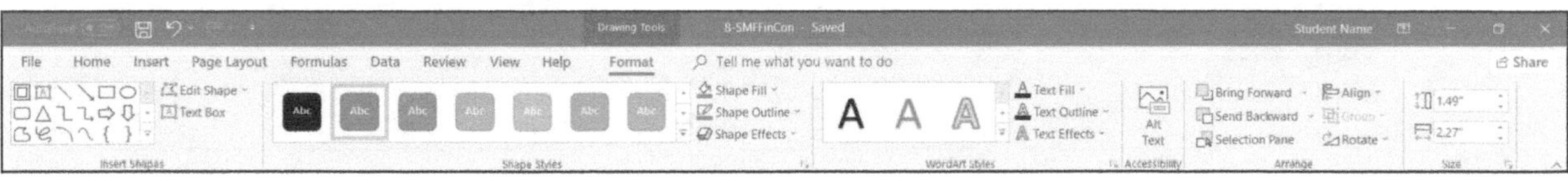

Activity 1e Drawing Arrow Shapes

1. With **8-SMFFinCon** open, create the larger arrow shown in Figure 8.5 by completing the following steps:
   a. Click the Insert tab.
   b. Click the Shapes button in the Illustrations group and then click the *Arrow: Up* shape (third column, first row in the *Block Arrows* section).
   c. Position the mouse pointer (appears as crosshairs) near the upper left corner of cell D1 and then click the left mouse button. (This inserts the arrow in the worksheet.)

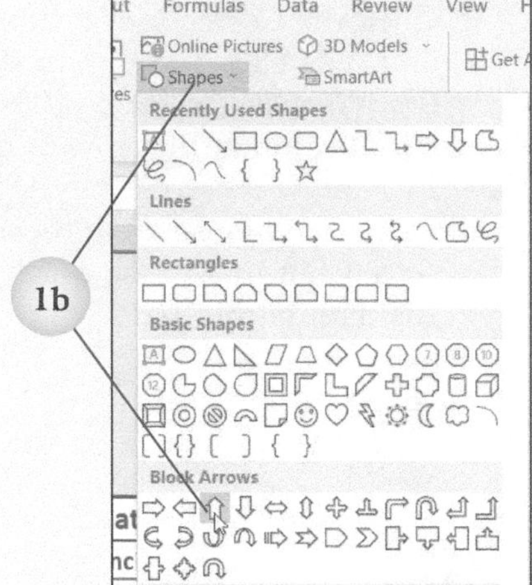

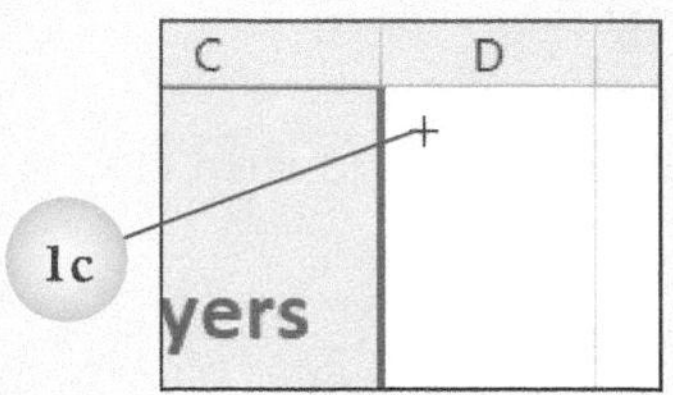

   d. Click in the *Shape Height* measurement box and then type 3.7.
   e. Click in the *Shape Width* measurement box, type 2.1, and then press the Enter key.
   f. If necessary, drag the arrow so it is positioned as shown in Figure 8.5. (To drag the arrow, position the mouse pointer on the border of the selected arrow until the pointer displays with a four-headed arrow attached, click and hold down the left mouse button, drag the arrow to the new position, and then release the mouse button.)
   g. Click the More Shape Styles button in the Shape Styles group on the Drawing Tools Format tab and then click the *Intense Effect - Blue, Accent 1* option (second column, last row in the *Theme Styles* section).
   h. Click the Shape Effects button in the Shape Styles group, point to *Glow*, and then click the *Glow: 11 point; Orange, Accent color 2* option (second column, third row in the *Glow Variations* section).

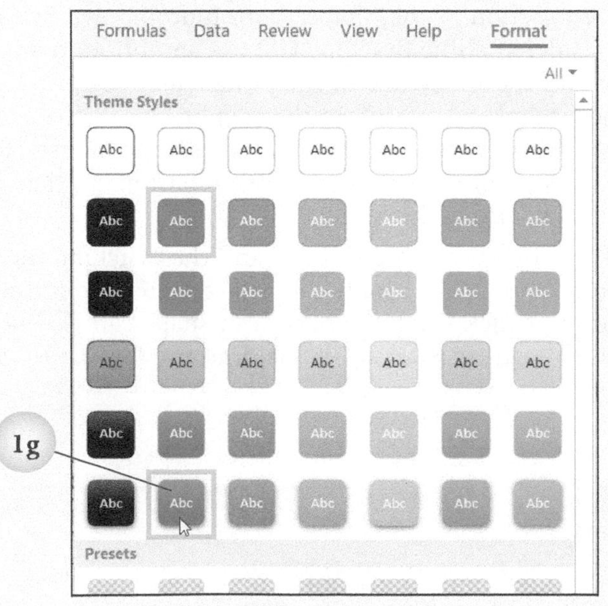

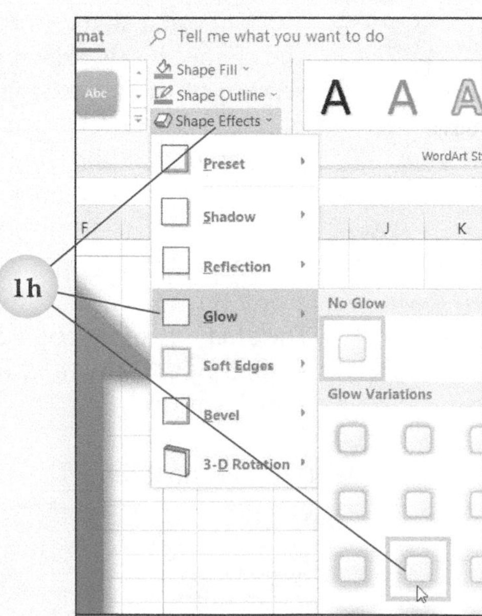

2. Insert text in the arrow by completing the following steps:
   a. With the arrow selected, type McGuire Mutual Shares 5.33%.
   b. Select the text you just typed (*McGuire Mutual Shares 5.33%*).
   c. Click the More WordArt Styles button in the WordArt Styles group and then click the option in the fourth column, third row (orange outline with white fill).
   d. Press Ctrl + E to center the text.
3. With the arrow selected, copy it by completing the following steps:
   a. Press and hold down the Ctrl key.
   b. Position the mouse pointer on the arrow border until the pointer displays with a square box and plus symbol attached.
   c. Click and hold down the left mouse button and drag to the right so the outline of the arrow is positioned at the right of the existing arrow.
   d. Release the mouse button and then release the Ctrl key.
4. Format the second arrow by completing the following steps:
   a. With the second arrow selected, click in the *Shape Height* measurement box on the Drawing Tools Format tab and then type 2.
   b. Click in the *Shape Width* measurement box, type 1.6, and then press the Enter key.
   c. Select the text *McGuire Mutual Shares 5.33%* and then type SR Linus Fund 0.22%.
   d. Drag the arrow so it is positioned as shown in Figure 8.5.
5. Change to landscape orientation. (Make sure the cells containing the data, screenshot image, and arrows will print on the same page.)
6. Save, print, and then close **8-SMFFinCon**.

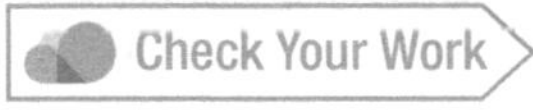

Figure 8.5 Activity 1e

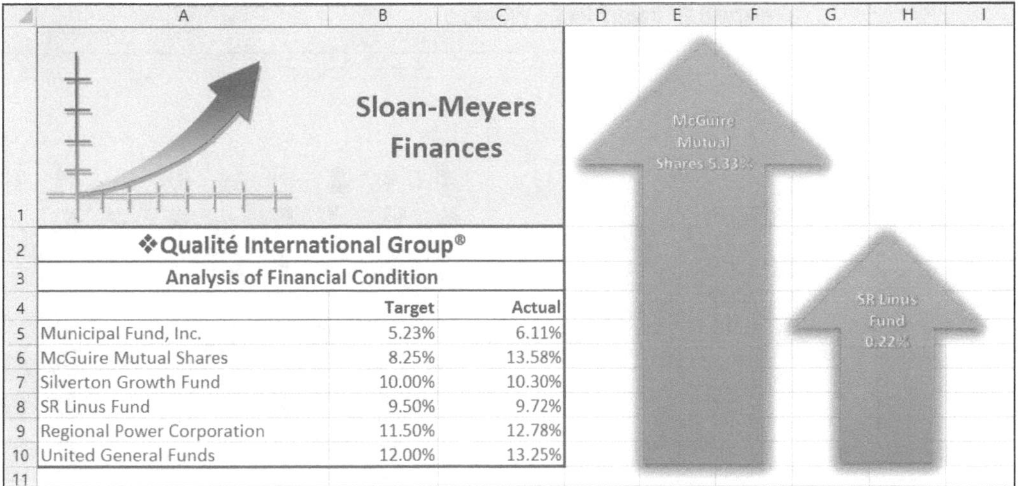

❖Qualité International Group®		
Analysis of Financial Condition		
	Target	Actual
Municipal Fund, Inc.	5.23%	6.11%
McGuire Mutual Shares	8.25%	13.58%
Silverton Growth Fund	10.00%	10.30%
SR Linus Fund	9.50%	9.72%
Regional Power Corporation	11.50%	12.78%
United General Funds	12.00%	13.25%

Activity 2 Insert an Icon, 3D Model, and Text Box in a Division Sales Workbook — 2 Parts

You will open a division sales workbook and then insert, move, and size an image, an icon, and a 3D model. You will also insert a text box and then format the text.

Inserting and Modifying Text Boxes

Text Box

Inserting and Modifying Text Boxes

To draw a text box in a worksheet, click the Insert tab and then click the Text Box button in the Text group. This causes the mouse pointer to display as a long, thin, upside-down cross (↓). Position the pointer in the worksheet and then drag to create the text box. When a text box is selected, the Drawing Tools Format tab displays with options for customizing it.

Click a text box to select it and a dashed border and sizing handles display around it. To delete the text box, click the border again to change the dashed lines to solid lines and then press the Delete key.

Tutorial

Inserting and Modifying an Icon

Quick Steps

Draw Text Box

1. Click Insert tab.
2. Click Text Box button.
3. Click or drag in worksheet to create text box.

Insert Icons

1. Click Insert tab.
2. Click Icons button.
3. Click icon.
4. Click Insert button.

Icons

Inserting and Customizing Icons

Use the Icons button in the Illustrations group on the Insert tab to insert an icon in a Word document. An icon is a simple graphic used to represent a concept or idea, such as emotions, weather, nature, the arts, and so on. Icons can be used to highlight or label data in a worksheet. These simple graphics draw the eye to important information and can be understood at a glance. Click the Icons button on the Insert tab and the Insert Icons window opens, as shown in Figure 8.6. At this window, scroll down the list box to view the various icons or click a category in the left panel to display a specific category of icons. To insert an icon in a document, double-click the icon in the list box or click the icon and then click the Insert button.

Figure 8.6 Insert Icons Window

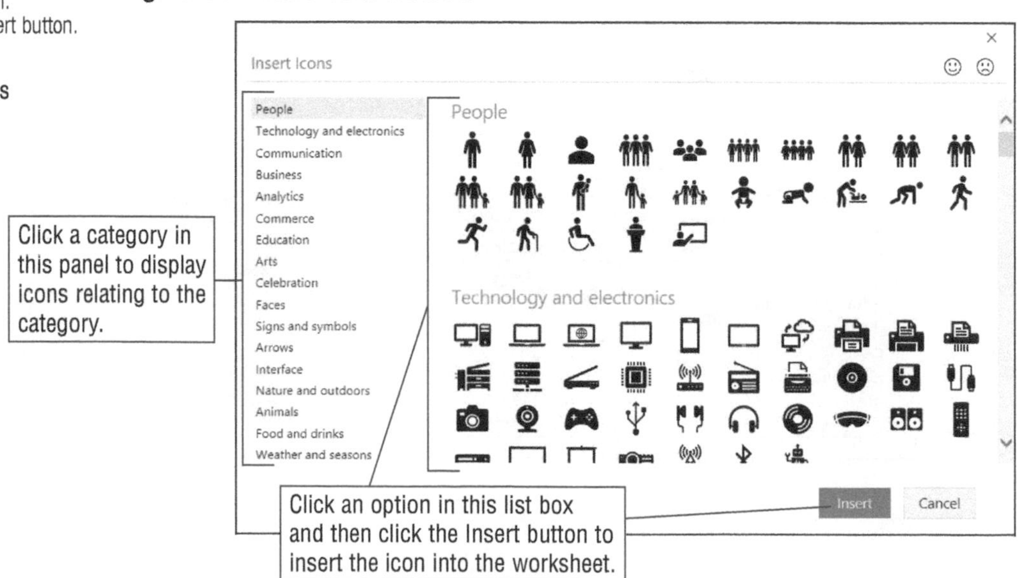

When an icon is inserted and selected in a worksheet, the Graphics Tools Format tab is active, as shown in Figure 8.7. Use options on this tab to apply a graphic style, fill, outline, and effect; type alternate text for the icon; position, align, group, rotate, and size the icon; and apply text wrapping.

Icons, like other images, can be formatted with options at the Format Graphic task pane. Display this task pane by clicking the Graphics Styles group or Size group task pane launcher. The task pane contains four icons: Fill & Line, Effects, Size & Properties, and Picture. Use options at the Format Graphic task pane to format an icon in a manner similar to formatting an image, shape, and text box.

Figure 8.7 Graphics Tools Format Tab

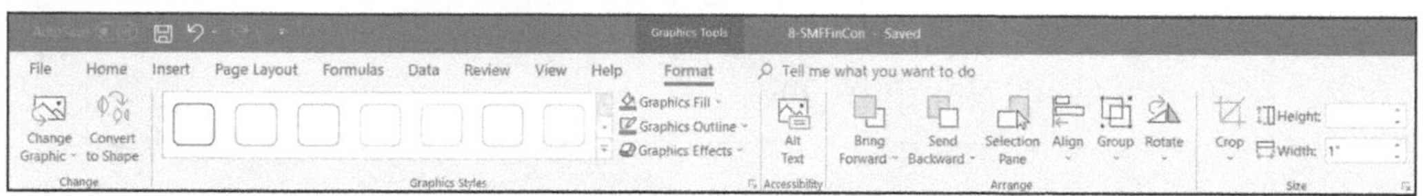

Activity 2a Inserting and Customizing an Icon and a Text Box

Part 1 of 2

1. Open **HPDivSales** and then save it with the name **8-HPDivSales**.
2. Insert and format an icon by completing the following steps:
   a. Click in cell A2.
   b. Click the Insert tab.
   c. Click the Icons button in the Illustrations group.

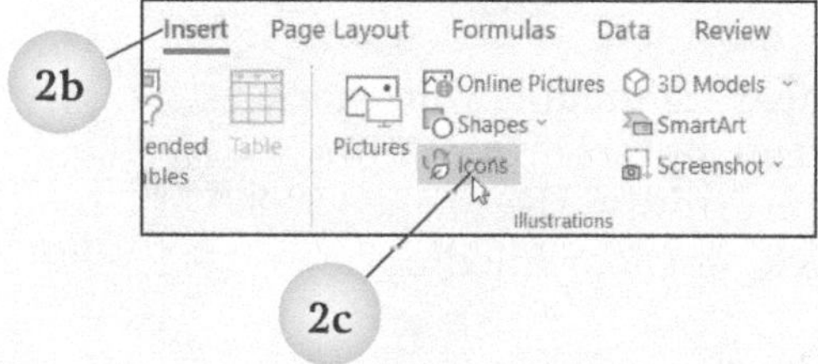

   d. At the Insert Icons window, click *Arts* at the left side of the window.
   e. Click the video camera icon shown below and then click the Insert button.

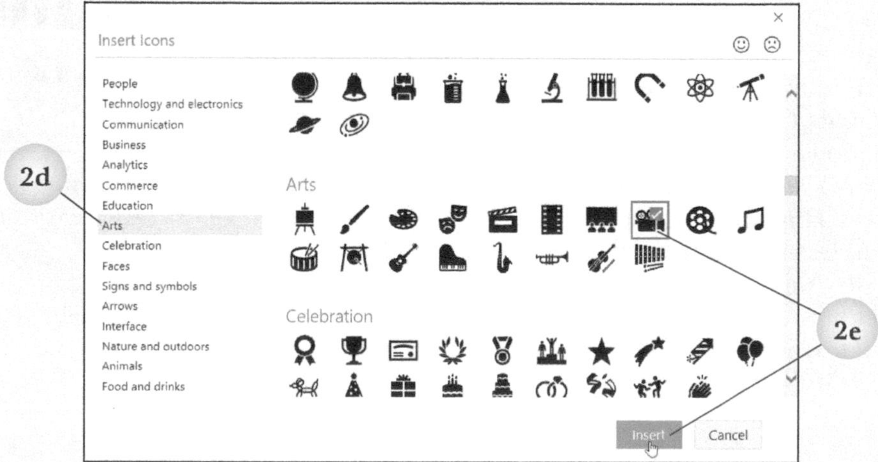

f. With the Icon selected, click the Rotate button in the Arrange group and then click the *Flip Horizontal* option at the drop-down list.
g. Click the More Graphic Styles button in the Graphics Styles group and then click the *Transparent, Colored Outline - Dark 1* option at the drop-down gallery (first column, last row).
h. Move the icon it so it is positioned as shown in Figure 8.8.

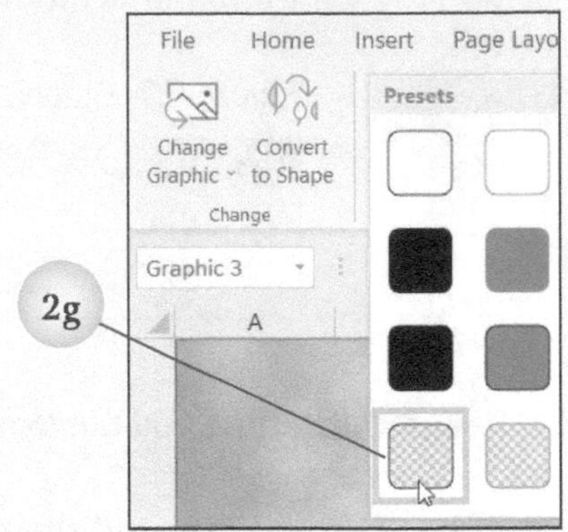

3. Draw a text box by completing the following steps:
   a. Click the Insert tab.
   b. Click the Text Box button in the Text group.
   c. Drag to cell A1 to draw a text box the approximate size and shape shown below.

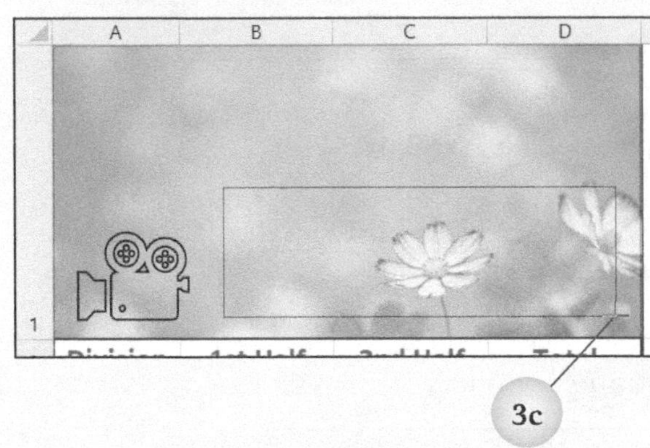

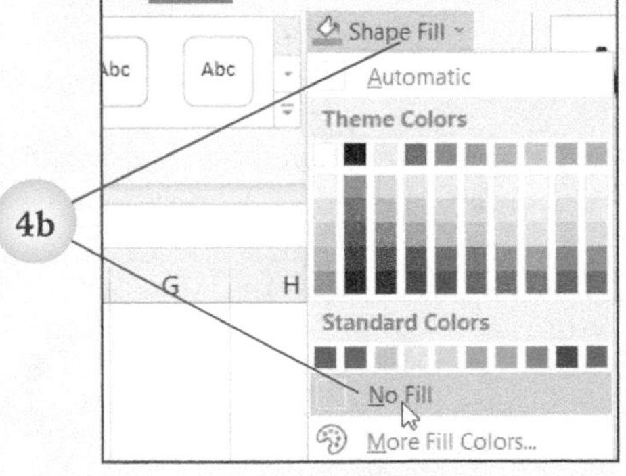

4. Format the text box by completing the following steps:
   a. Click the Drawing Tools Format tab.
   b. Click the Shape Fill button arrow in the Shape Styles group and then click *No Fill* at the drop-down gallery.
   c. Click the Shape Outline button arrow in the Shape Styles group and then click *No Outline* at the drop-down gallery.
5. Insert text in the text box by completing the following steps:
   a. With the text box selected, click the Home tab.
   b. Click the *Font* option box arrow and then click *Lucida Calligraphy* at the drop-down gallery. (Scroll down the gallery to display this font.)
   c. Click the *Font Size* option box arrow and then click *24* at the drop-down gallery.
   d. Click the Font Color button arrow and then click *Blue, Accent 1, Darker 50%* (fifth column, last row in the *Theme Colors* section).
   e. Click the Align Right button in the Alignment group.
   f. Type Hummingbird Productions.
6. Move the text box so the text is positioned in cell A1, as shown in Figure 8.8.
7. Save **8-SPDivSales**.

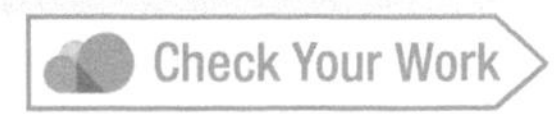

Figure 8.8 Activity 2a

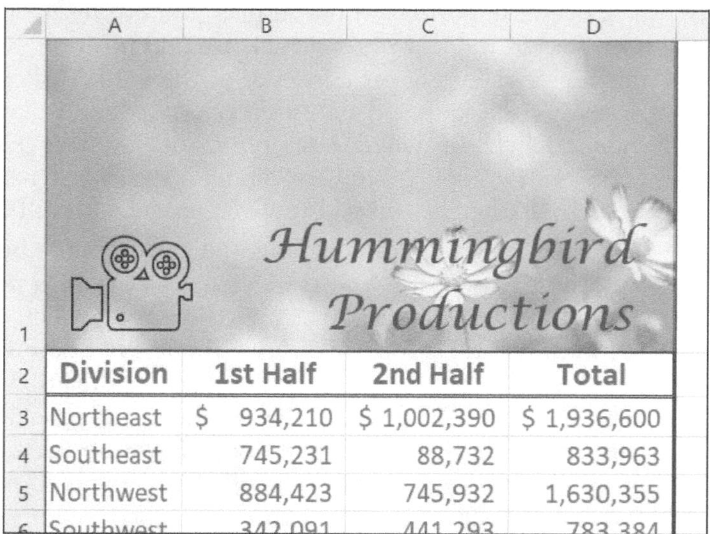

	A	B	C	D
1	Hummingbird Productions			
2	Division	1st Half	2nd Half	Total
3	Northeast	$ 934,210	$ 1,002,390	$ 1,936,600
4	Southeast	745,231	88,732	833,963
5	Northwest	884,423	745,932	1,630,355
6	Southwest	342,091	441,293	783,384

Inserting and Modifying 3D Models

Insert 3D Model

1. Click Insert tab.
2. Click 3D Models button.
3. Click category.
4. Click model.
5. Click Insert button.

3D Model

Inserting and Customizing 3D Models

A 3D model is a graphic file of an image shown in three dimensions. The model can be rotated or tilted to allow viewing from various angles or to display a specific portion or feature. Microsoft's Remix 3D library includes a collection of free 3D models that can be inserted into a Word document, PowerPoint presentation, or Excel worksheet. Access these images by clicking the 3D Models button in the Illustrations group on the Insert tab. At the Online 3D Models window, shown in Figure 8.9, click a category to view all 3D models within the category or type a keyword(s) in the search text box and then press the Enter key. Insert a 3D model in a worksheet by double-clicking the model or clicking the model and then clicking the Insert button.

Figure 8.9 Online 3D Models Window

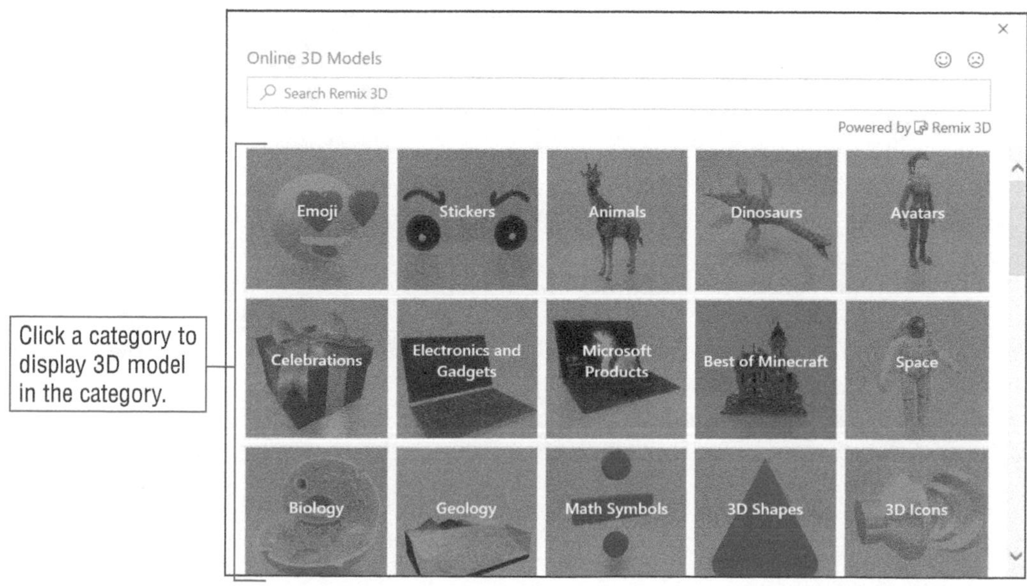

When a 3D model is inserted in a document, the 3D Model Tools Format tab is active. Use buttons in the Adjust group to insert a different 3D model or reset the selected model to its original size and position. The 3D Model Views group includes a gallery of preset views for the model. Click the Alt Text button in the Accessibility group and the Alt Text task pane displays, where a description of the model can be added. Use options in the Arrange group to position the model, apply text wrapping, send the model forward or backward, and align the model. Change the height and width of the model with options in the Size group.

The Size group also contains the Pan & Zoom button. Click this button to lock the position of the 3D model and a button (a magnifying glass with a plus symbol inside) will display at the right of the selected model. Position the mouse pointer on this button, hold down the left mouse button, and then drag up to increase the size of the model (zoom in) or drag down to decrease the size (zoom out). Use the 3D control in the middle of the model to freely rotate the model. Pan the model by clicking and dragging within the frame to change the model's position within the frame. Turn off the pan and zoom feature by clicking the Pan & Zoom button to deactivate it.

Use the 3D control that displays in the middle of a selected 3D model to rotate or tilt the model. To use the 3D control, position the mouse pointer on the control, click and hold down the left mouse button, and then drag with the mouse to rotate or tilt the model.

Options for formatting and customizing a 3D model are available at the Format 3D Model task pane. Display the task pane by clicking the 3D Model Views group or Size group task pane launcher. The task pane displays with four icons: Fill & Line, Effects, Size & Properties, and 3D Model.

Click the Fill & Line icon to display options for formatting the border line and fill of the 3D model. Use options at the task pane with the Effects icon selected to apply formatting effects, such as shadow, reflection, glow, and soft edges, and to format and rotate the model. Click the Size & Properties icon to display options for adjusting the size of the 3D model, or click the 3D Model icon to specify the rotation and camera view.

Activity 2b Inserting and Customizing a 3D Model — Part 2 of 2

1. With **8-HPDivSales** open, click in cell E1.
2. Insert a 3D model from the Remix 3D library by completing the following steps:
   a. Click the Insert tab.
   b. Click the 3D Models button in the Illustrations group.
   c. At the Online 3D Models window, click the *Animals* category.
   d. Scroll down and click the hummingbird model.
   e. Click the Insert button.
   ***Note: If you do not have access to the Online 3D Models window, open* Bird3D *from your EL1C8 folder. This workbook contains the 3D hummingbird model. Copy the model and then paste it into* 8-DivSales.**

3. Change the size of the model at the Format 3D Model task pane by completing the following steps:
   a. Click the Size group task pane launcher.
   b. Select the value in the *Width* measurement box.
   c. Type 3 and then press the Enter key.
4. Change the view of the model by clicking the *Right* view (fifth option) in the 3D Model Views gallery.

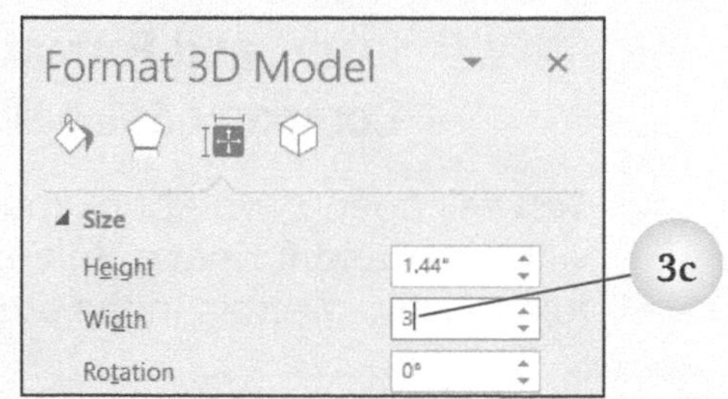

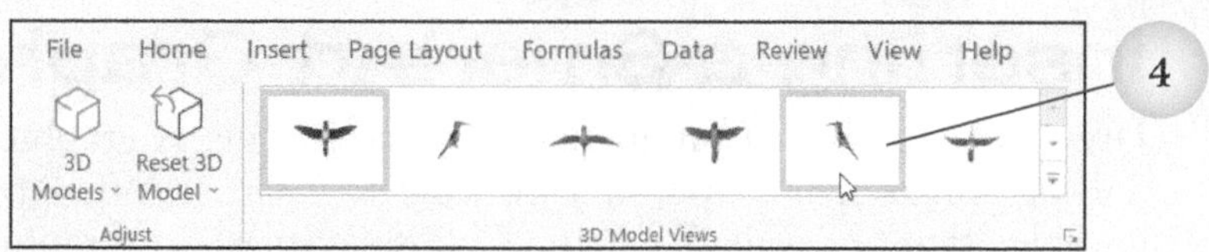

5. Reset the bird model by clicking the Reset 3D Model button in the Adjust group.

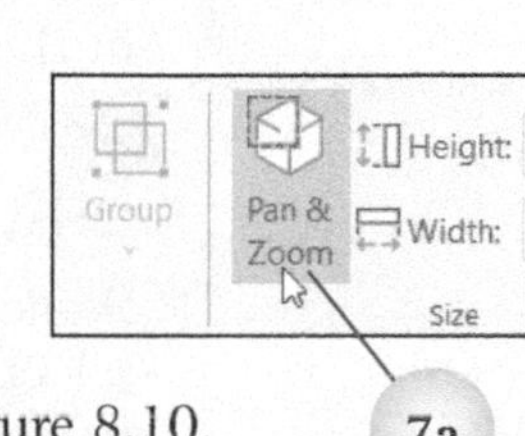

6. Use the 3D control that displays in the middle of the bird model by positioning the mouse pointer on the 3D control, pressing and holding down the left mouse button, and then dragging with the mouse to rotate the model. Rotate the model so it displays as shown in Figure 8.10.
7. Zoom in and pan the model by completing the following steps:
   a. Click the Pan & Zoom button in the Size group on the 3D Model Tools Format tab.
   b. Position the mouse pointer on the button that displays as a magnifying glass with a plus symbol inside (at the right of the model), press and hold down the left mouse button, and then drag down to decrease the size of the model so it displays as shown in Figure 8.10.
   c. Position the mouse inside the model and then pan the hummingbird within the frame by click-dragging it to the position as shown in Figure 8.10.
   d. Click the Pan & Zoom button to deactivate it.
   e. Move the model to the upper left corner of cell A1.

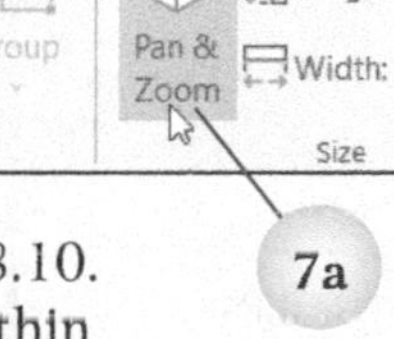

8. Close the Format 3D Model task pane.
9. Save, print, and then close **8-HPDivSales**.

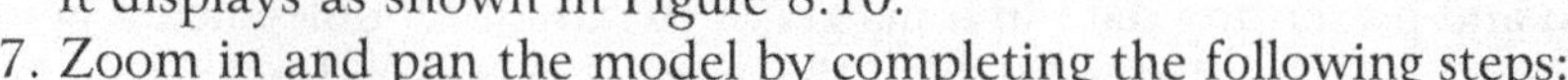

Figure 8.10 Activity 2b

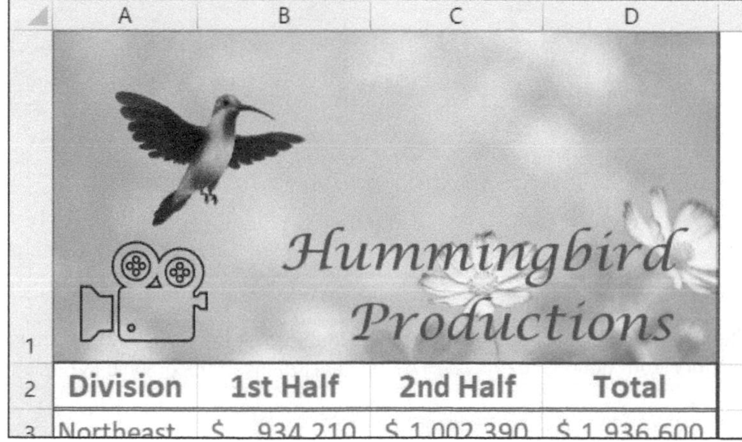

Activity 3 Insert and Format SmartArt Graphics in a Company Sales Workbook — 4 Parts

You will open a workbook that contains two company sales worksheets. You will insert and format a SmartArt cycle graphic in one worksheet and a SmartArt relationship graphic in the other. You will also create and format WordArt text.

Tutorial

Inserting a SmartArt Graphic

SmartArt

Quick Steps

Insert SmartArt Graphic

1. Click Insert tab.
2. Click SmartArt button.
3. Double-click graphic.

Inserting a SmartArt Graphic

Use the SmartArt feature included in Excel to insert graphics, such as diagrams and organizational charts, in a worksheet. SmartArt offers a variety of predesigned graphics that are available at the Choose a SmartArt Graphic dialog box, shown in Figure 8.11. Display this dialog box by clicking the Insert tab and then clicking the SmartArt button in the Illustrations group. At the dialog box, *All* is selected in the left panel and all the predesigned graphics are available in the middle panel. Use the scroll bar at the right side of the middle panel to scroll down the list of graphic choices. Click a graphic in the middle panel and the name of the graphic displays in the right panel along with a description of the graphic type. SmartArt includes graphics for presenting lists of data; showing data processes, cycles, and relationships; and presenting data in a matrix or pyramid. Double-click a graphic in the middle panel of the dialog box and the graphic is inserted in the worksheet.

Text Pane

Hint Generally, you would use a SmartArt graphic to represent text and a chart to represent numbers.

Entering Data in a SmartArt Graphic

Some SmartArt graphics are designed to include text. Type text in a graphic by selecting a shape in the graphic and then typing text in the shape, or display a text pane and then type text in the pane. Display the text pane by clicking the Text Pane button in the Create Graphic group on the SmartArt Tools Design tab. Turn off the display of the pane by clicking the Text Pane button or clicking the Close button in the upper right corner of the pane.

Figure 8.11 Choose a SmartArt Graphic Dialog Box

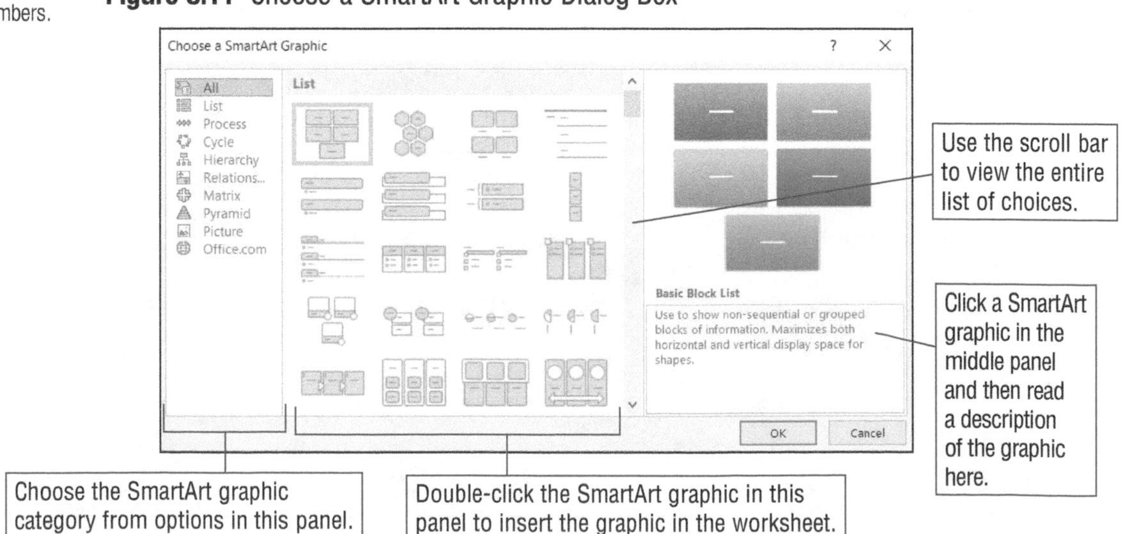
Choose a SmartArt Graphic
All
List
Process
Cycle
Hierarchy
Relations...
Matrix
Pyramid
Picture
Office.com
List
Basic Block List
Use to show non-sequential or grouped blocks of information. Maximizes both horizontal and vertical display space for shapes.
OK
Cancel
Use the scroll bar to view the entire list of choices.
Click a SmartArt graphic in the middle panel and then read a description of the graphic here.
Choose the SmartArt graphic category from options in this panel.
Double-click the SmartArt graphic in this panel to insert the graphic in the worksheet.

Modifying a SmartArt Graphic

Sizing, Moving, and Deleting a SmartArt Graphic

Increase or decrease the size of a SmartArt graphic by dragging one of the sizing handles that display around the selected graphic. Use the corner sizing handles to increase or decrease the height and width at the same time. Use the middle sizing handles to increase or decrease the height or width of the SmartArt graphic.

To move a SmartArt graphic, select it and then position the mouse pointer on the graphic border until the pointer displays with a four-headed arrow attached. Click and hold down the left mouse button, drag the graphic to the new position, and then release the mouse button. Delete a graphic by selecting it and then pressing the Delete key.

Activity 3a **Inserting, Moving, and Sizing a SmartArt Graphic in a Worksheet** Part 1 of 4

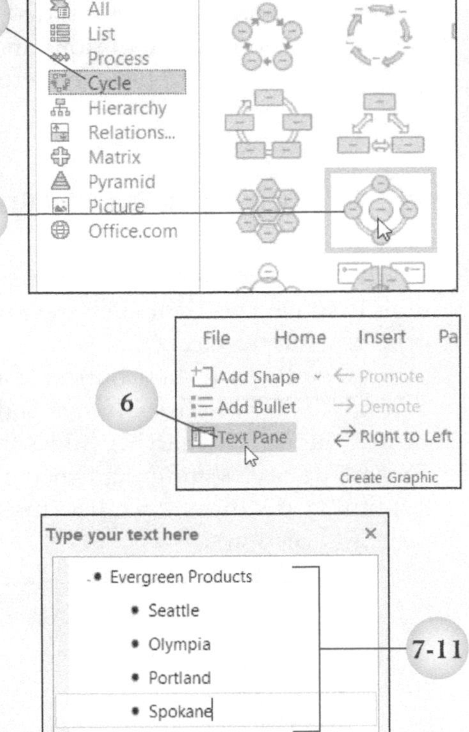

1. Open **EPCoSales** and then save it with the name **8-EPCoSales**.
2. Create the SmartArt graphic shown in Figure 8.12. To begin, click the Insert tab.
3. Click the SmartArt button in the Illustrations group.
4. At the Choose a SmartArt Graphic dialog box, click *Cycle* in the left panel.
5. Double-click *Radial Cycle* in the middle panel (as shown in the image at the right).
6. If the text pane is not open, click the Text Pane button in the Create Graphic group. (The text pane will display at the left of the SmartArt graphic.)
7. With the insertion point positioned after the top bullet in the text pane, type Evergreen Products.
8. Click in the *[Text]* placeholder below *Evergreen Products* and then type Seattle.
9. Click in the next *[Text]* placeholder and then type Olympia.
10. Click in the next *[Text]* placeholder and then type Portland.
11. Click in the next *[Text]* placeholder and then type Spokane.
12. Click the Text Pane button to close the text pane.
13. Drag the SmartArt graphic so it is positioned as shown in Figure 8.12. To drag the graphic, position the mouse pointer on the graphic border until the pointer displays with a four-headed arrow attached. Click and hold down the left mouse button, drag the graphic to the new position, and then release the mouse button.
14. Use the sizing handles around the SmartArt graphic to increase or decrease the size so it displays as shown in Figure 8.12.
15. Save **8-EPCoSales**.

Figure 8.12 Activity 3a

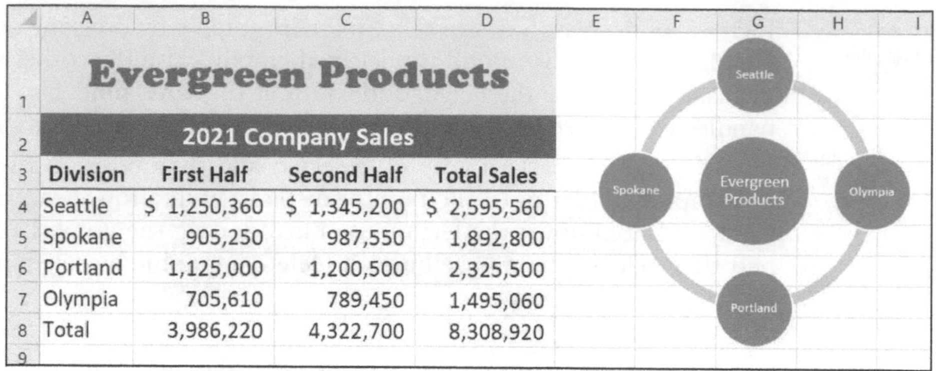

	A	B	C	D
1	Evergreen Products			
2	2021 Company Sales			
3	Division	First Half	Second Half	Total Sales
4	Seattle	$ 1,250,360	$ 1,345,200	$ 2,595,560
5	Spokane	905,250	987,550	1,892,800
6	Portland	1,125,000	1,200,500	2,325,500
7	Olympia	705,610	789,450	1,495,060
8	Total	3,986,220	4,322,700	8,308,920

Changing the SmartArt Graphic Design

Hint To restore the SmartArt default layout and color, click the Reset Graphic button in the Reset group on the SmartArt Tools Design tab.

Double-click a SmartArt graphic at the Choose a SmartArt Graphic dialog box and the graphic is inserted in the worksheet and the SmartArt Tools Design tab is active. Use options and buttons on this tab to add objects, change the graphic layout, apply a style to the graphic, and reset the original formatting of the graphic.

Activity 3b Changing the SmartArt Graphic Design — Part 2 of 4

1. With **8-EPCoSales** open, make sure the SmartArt Tools Design tab is active and then click the *Spokane* circle shape in the graphic to select it.
2. Click the Right to Left button in the Create Graphic group. (This switches *Olympia* and *Spokane*.)
3. Click the More SmartArt Styles button in the SmartArt Styles group and then click the *Polished* option at the drop-down list (first column, first row in the *3-D* section).

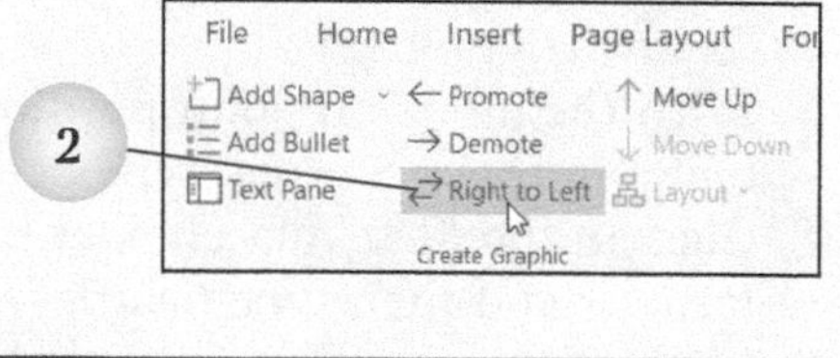

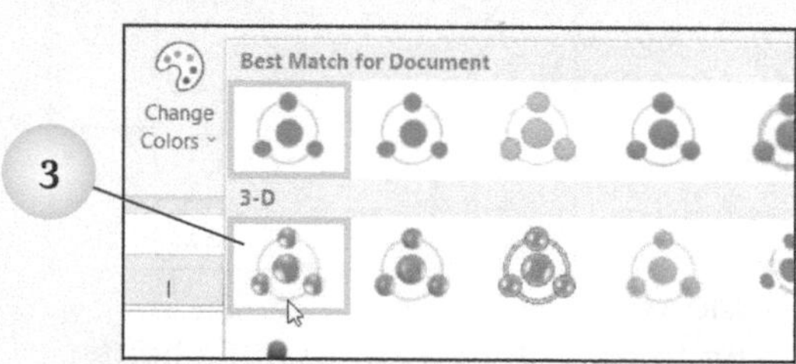

4. Click the Change Colors button in the SmartArt Styles group, scroll down the drop-down gallery, and then click the *Gradient Range - Accent 6* option (third option in the *Accent 6* section).
5. Click outside the SmartArt graphic to deselect it.
6. Change to landscape orientation. (Make sure the graphic fits on the first page.)
7. Save **8-EPCoSales** and then print the Total Sales worksheet.

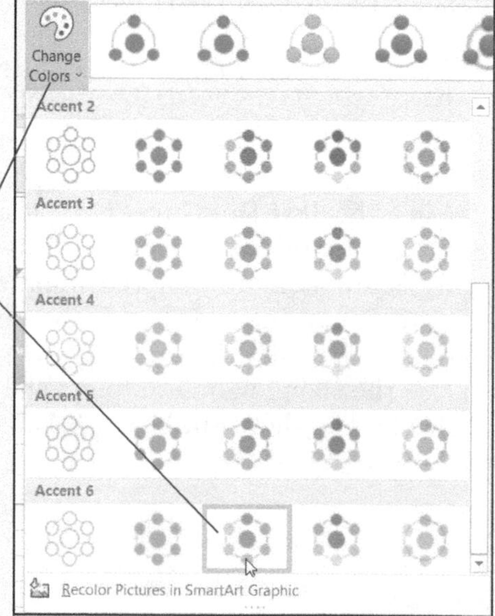

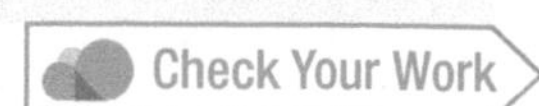

Changing the SmartArt Graphic Formatting

Click the SmartArt Tools Format tab and options display for formatting a SmartArt graphic. Use buttons on this tab to insert and customize shapes; apply a shape style; apply WordArt styles; and specify the position, alignment, rotation, wrapping style, height, and width of a graphic.

Activity 3c **Changing the SmartArt Graphic Formatting** Part 3 of 4

1. With **8-EPCoSales** open, click the Seattle Sales sheet tab.
2. Create the SmartArt graphic shown in Figure 8.13. To begin, click the Insert tab and then click the SmartArt button in the Illustrations group.
3. At the Choose a SmartArt Graphic dialog box, click *Relationship* in the left panel and then double-click *Gear* in the middle panel.

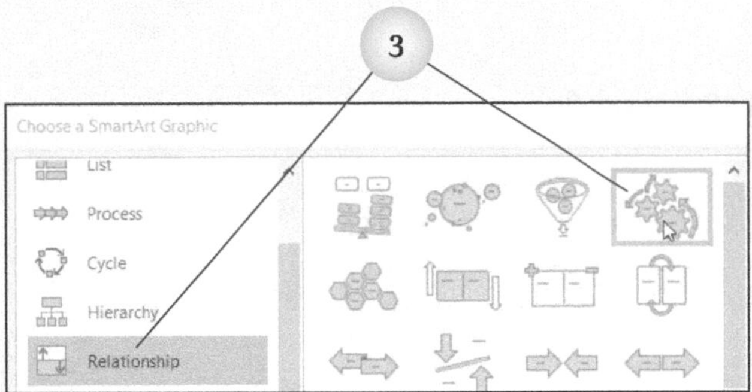

4. Click in the *[Text]* placeholder in the bottom gear and then type Quality Products.
5. Click in the *[Text]* placeholder in the left gear and then type Customized Plans.
6. Click in the *[Text]* placeholder in the top gear and then type Exemplary Service.
7. Click inside the SmartArt graphic border but outside any specific shape.
8. Click the More SmartArt Styles button in the SmartArt Styles group and then click the *Inset* option (second column, first row in the *3-D* section).
9. Click the Change Colors button and then click the *Gradient Loop - Accent 6* option (fourth option in the *Accent 6* section).
10. Click the SmartArt Tools Format tab.
11. Click in the *Height* measurement box in the Size group and then type 4.
12. Click in the *Width* measurement box, type 4.5, and then press the Enter key.

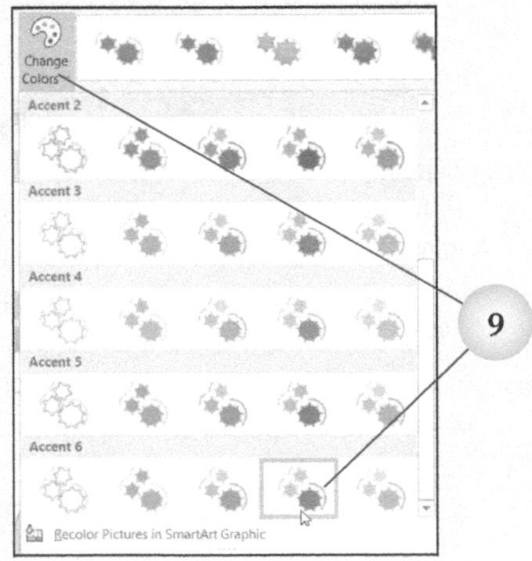

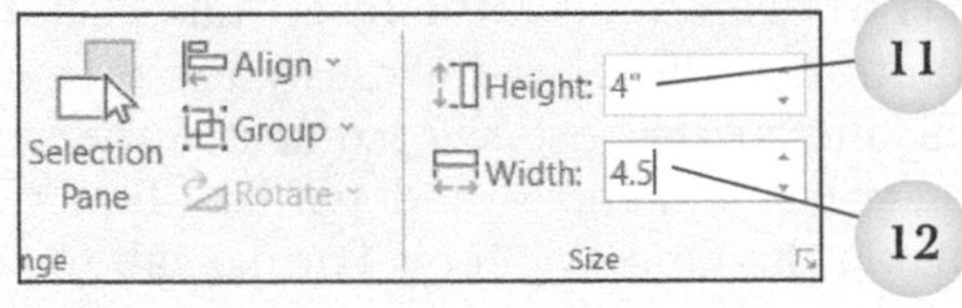

13. Click the bottom gear to select it.

14. Click the Shape Fill button arrow in the Shape Styles group and then click the *Green, Accent 6, Darker 50%* option (last column, last row in the *Theme Colors* section).
15. Click the top gear to select it.
16. Click the Shape Fill button arrow and then click the *Green, Accent 6, Darker 25%* option (last column, fifth row in the *Theme Colors* section).
17. Change to landscape orientation.
18. Move the SmartArt graphic so it fits on the first page and displays as shown in Figure 8.13.
19. Click outside the SmartArt graphic to deselect it.
20. Save **8-EPCoSales** and then print the Seattle Sales worksheet.

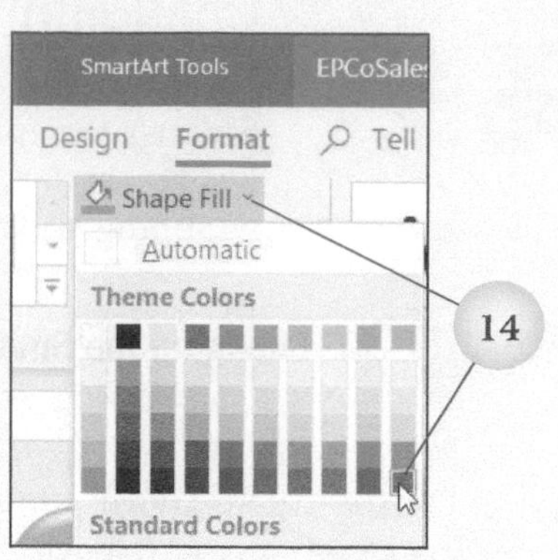

Figure 8.13 Activity 3c

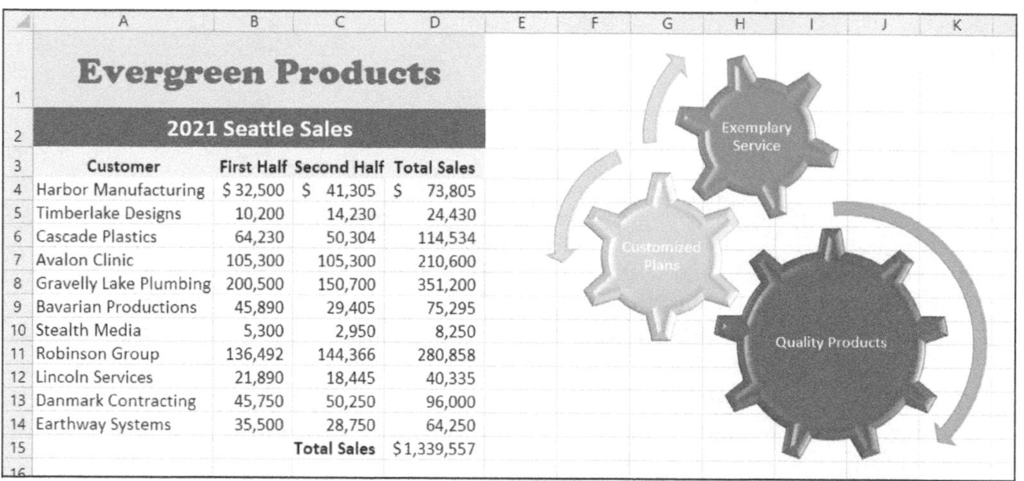

	A	B	C	D
1	**Evergreen Products**			
2	**2021 Seattle Sales**			
3	**Customer**	**First Half**	**Second Half**	**Total Sales**
4	Harbor Manufacturing	$ 32,500	$ 41,305	$ 73,805
5	Timberlake Designs	10,200	14,230	24,430
6	Cascade Plastics	64,230	50,304	114,534
7	Avalon Clinic	105,300	105,300	210,600
8	Gravelly Lake Plumbing	200,500	150,700	351,200
9	Bavarian Productions	45,890	29,405	75,295
10	Stealth Media	5,300	2,950	8,250
11	Robinson Group	136,492	144,366	280,858
12	Lincoln Services	21,890	18,445	40,335
13	Danmark Contracting	45,750	50,250	96,000
14	Earthway Systems	35,500	28,750	64,250
15			**Total Sales**	$1,339,557

Creating WordArt

WordArt

Create WordArt

1. Click Insert tab.
2. Click Text button.
3. Click WordArt button.
4. Click WordArt style at drop-down list.
5. Type text.

Creating, Sizing, and Moving WordArt

Use the WordArt feature to distort or modify text so it conforms to a variety of shapes. This is useful for creating company logos and headings. Change the font, style, and alignment of text with WordArt and use fill patterns and colors, customize border lines, and add shadow and three-dimensional effects.

To insert WordArt in an Excel worksheet, click the Insert tab, click the Text button, click the WordArt button at the drop-down list, and then click an option at the drop-down list. This inserts the text *Your text here* in the worksheet, formatted in the WordArt option selected at the drop-down list. Type text and then use the options and buttons on the Drawing Tools Format tab to format the WordArt.

Hint To remove a WordArt style from text and retain the text, click the More WordArt Styles button in the WordArt Styles group on the Drawing Tools Format tab and then click *Clear WordArt.*

WordArt text inserted in a worksheet is surrounded by white sizing handles. Use these sizing handles to change the height and width of the WordArt text. To move WordArt text, position the mouse pointer on the border of the WordArt text box until the pointer displays with a four-headed arrow attached and then drag the outline of the text box to the new location.

Make WordArt text conform to a variety of shapes using the *Transform* option from the Text Effects button drop-down list. Apply a transform shape and a small yellow circle displays below the WordArt text. Use this circle to change the slant of the WordArt text.

Activity 3d Inserting and Formatting WordArt

Part 4 of 4

1. With **8-EPCoSales** open, click the Total Sales sheet tab.
2. Make cell A1 active and then press the Delete key. (This removes the text from the cell.)
3. Increase the height of row 1 to 138 points.
4. Click the Insert tab.
5. Click the Text button, click the WordArt button, and then click the option in the first column, third row (black fill with white outline).
6. Type Evergreen, press the Enter key, and then type Products.
7. Click the WordArt border to change it to a solid line (not a dashed line).
8. Click the Text Fill button arrow in the WordArt Styles group and then click the *Green, Accent 6, Darker 50%* option (last column, last row in the Theme Colors section).
9. Click the Text Effects button in the WordArt Styles group, point to *Transform*, and then click the *Warp Up* option (third column, fourth row in the *Warp* section).
10. Position the mouse pointer (turns into a white arrow) on the small yellow circle immediately below the *d* in *Products*, click and hold down the left mouse button, drag up approximately 0.25 inch, and then release the mouse button. (This changes the slant of the text.)
11. Drag the WordArt text so it is positioned in cell A1.
12. If necessary, size the SmartArt graphic and position it so it prints on one page with the data.
13. Click the Seattle Sales sheet tab and then complete steps similar to those in Steps 2 through 11 to insert *Evergreen Products* as WordArt in cell A1.
14. Make sure the SmartArt graphic fits on one page with the data. If necessary, decrease the size of the graphic.
15. Save **8-EPCoSales** and then print both worksheets.
16. Close **8-EPCoSales**.

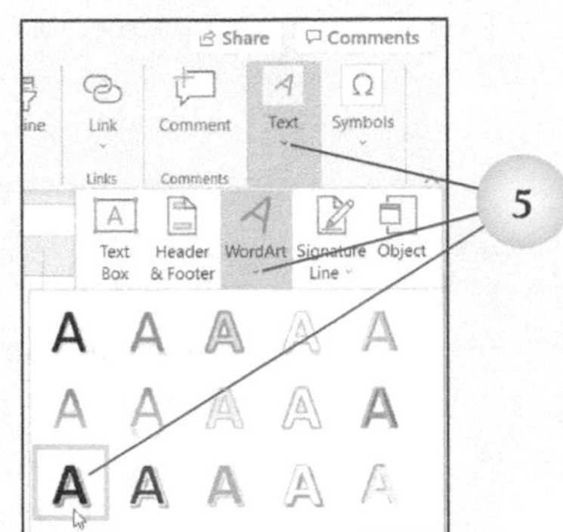

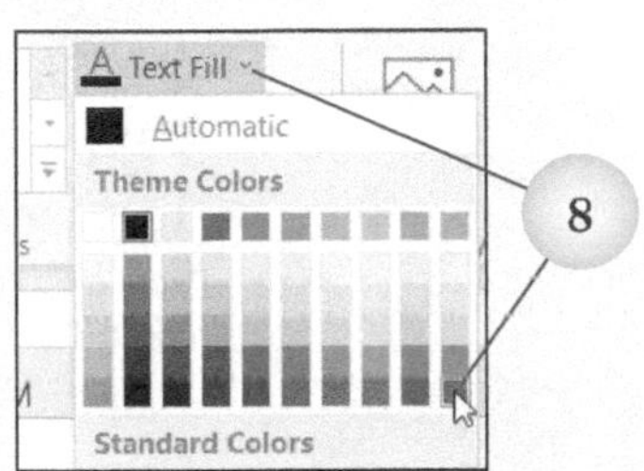

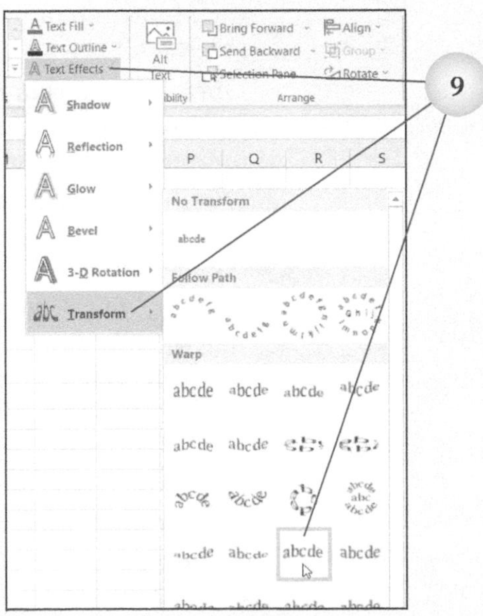

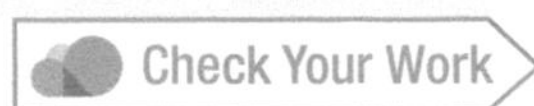

Chapter Summary

- Insert symbols with options at the Symbol dialog box with the Symbols tab or Special Characters tab selected.
- Use buttons in the Illustrations group on the Insert tab to insert an image such as a picture, clip art image, screenshot, shape, or SmartArt graphic.
- Insert an image by clicking the Insert tab, clicking the Pictures button in the Illustrations group, and then double-clicking an image at the Insert Picture dialog box.
- Insert an image in a worksheet and the Picture Tools Format tab is active. It provides options for adjusting the image, applying preformatted styles to the image, and arranging and sizing the image.
- Change the size of an image with the *Shape Height* and *Shape Width* measurement boxes in the Size group on the Picture Tools Format tab or with the sizing handles that display around a selected image.
- Move an image by positioning the mouse pointer on the image border until the pointer displays with a four-headed arrow attached and then dragging the image to the new location.
- Format and modify an image by displaying the Format Picture task pane and using the options and buttons to alter the image.
- Insert an online image with options at the Online Pictures window. Display this window by clicking the Insert tab and then clicking the Online Pictures button in the Illustrations group.
- Use the Screenshot button in the Illustrations group on the Insert tab to capture all or part of the contents of a screen as an image.
- To draw a shape in a workbook, click the Insert tab, click the Shapes button in the Illustrations group, and then click a shape at the drop-down list. Click or drag in the worksheet to insert the shape. To maintain the proportions of the shape, press and hold down the Shift key while dragging in the worksheet.
- Copy a shape by using the Copy and Paste buttons in the Clipboard group on the Home tab or by pressing and holding down the Ctrl key while dragging the shape.
- Draw a text box in a worksheet by clicking the Insert tab, clicking the Text Box button in the Text group, and then clicking or dragging in the worksheet. Use options on the Drawing Tools Format tab to format and customize the text box.
- Use the Icons button to insert simple images into a worksheet. Customize the appearance of an icon using buttons and options on the Graphics Tools Format tab and at the Format Graphic task pane.
- Insert a 3D model into a worksheet by clicking the 3D Model button in the Illustrations group on the Insert tab. Customize the appearance of a 3D model using the object control inside the model and also by using buttons and options on the 3D Models Tool Format tab and at the Format 3D Model task pane.
- Insert a SmartArt graphic in a worksheet by clicking the Insert tab, clicking the SmartArt button in the Illustrations group, and then double-clicking a graphic at the Choose a SmartArt Graphic dialog box. Customize a SmartArt graphic with options on the SmartArt Tools Design tab and SmartArt Tools Format tab.
- Use WordArt to create, distort, and modify text and to make it conform to a variety of shapes. Insert WordArt in a worksheet with the WordArt button in the Text button drop-down list on the Insert tab. Customize WordArt text with options on the Drawing Tools Format tab.

Commands Review

FEATURE	RIBBON TAB, GROUP	BUTTON
alternative text	Picture Tools Format, Accessibility	
Choose a SmartArt Graphic dialog box	Insert, Illustrations	
Insert Icons window	Insert, Illustrations	
Insert Picture dialog box	Insert, Illustrations	
Insert WordArt button drop-down list	Insert, Text	
Online 3D Models window	Insert, Illustrations	
Online Pictures window	Insert, Illustrations	
screenshot	Insert, Illustrations	
Shapes button drop-down list	Insert, Illustrations	
Symbol dialog box	Insert, Symbols	
text box	Insert, Text	

Index

D

G

H

I

Q

R

S

Interior Photo Credits

Page GS-1, © lowball-jack/GettyImages, Courtesy of Paradigm Education Solutions; *page GS-2*, © irbis picture/Shutterstock.com; page *GS-3*, © th3fisa/Shutterstock.com; page *GS-4*, © goldyg/Shutterstock.com; page *GS-5*, © Pressmaster/Shutterstock.com.

Microsoft®

Excel® Level 2

Unit 1

Advanced Formatting, Formulas, and Data Management

Microsoft®

Excel®

CHAPTER

1

Advanced Formatting Techniques

Performance Objectives

Upon successful completion of Chapter 1, you will be able to:

1 Apply conditional formatting by entering parameters for a rule
2 Create and apply new rules for conditional formatting
3 Edit and delete conditional formatting rules
4 Apply conditional formatting using icon sets, data bars, and color scales
5 Apply conditional formatting using a formula
6 Apply conditional formatting using Quick Analysis
7 Apply fraction and scientific formatting
8 Apply special number formatting
9 Create custom number formats
10 Filter a worksheet using a custom AutoFilter
11 Filter and sort data using conditional formatting or cell attributes
12 Remove a filter from a worksheet
13 Apply an advanced filter

Excel provides many options for formatting worksheets. Buttons are available in the Font, Alignment, and Number groups on the Home tab, as well as on the Mini toolbar. Excel also offers advanced formatting techniques to help users explore and analyze data. One of the most useful is *conditional formatting*. Conditional formatting allows important information to be highlighted using a different format such as a background color or font style. This formatting can help users quickly identify trends and spot critical issues that need to be investigated or monitored.

Before beginning chapter work, copy the EL2C1 folder to your storage medium and then make EL2C1 the active folder.

The online course includes additional training and assessment resources.

Activity 1 **Format Cells Based on Values in a Payroll Worksheet** **2 Parts**

Working with a payroll worksheet, you will change the appearance of cells based on criteria related to pay rate and gross pay.

Applying Conditional Formatting Using Top/Bottom Rules

Applying Conditional Formatting

Conditional formatting makes it easier to spot important information in a worksheet and analyze the data for patterns and trends. Cells within a specified range that meet a specific condition can be highlighted using a different format such as a background color or font style. For instance, values that are high or low can be formatted in red font or with a yellow background to make them stand out.

Formatting can be applied based on a specific value or a value that falls within a range or it can be applied by using a comparison operator, such as equal to (=), greater than (>), or less than (<). Conditional formats can also be based on dates, text entries, or duplicated values. Consider using conditional formatting to analyze a question, such as *Which store locations earned sales above their targets?* Using a different color to identify those stores that exceeded their target sales makes it easy to quickly identify the top performers.

Conditional Formatting

Quick Steps

Apply Conditional Formatting Using Predefined Rule

1. Select range.
2. Click Conditional Formatting button.
3. Point to rule category.
4. Click rule.
5. If necessary, enter parameter value.
6. If necessary, change format options.
7. Click OK.

Excel provides predefined conditional formatting rules that can be accessed from the Conditional Formatting button drop-down list, as shown in Figure 1.1. Unique conditional formatting rules can also be created. Using options in the *Top/Bottom Rules* drop-down list, cells can be highlighted based on a top 10 or bottom 10 value or percent or by above average or below average values.

Figure 1.1 Conditional Formatting Button Drop-Down List

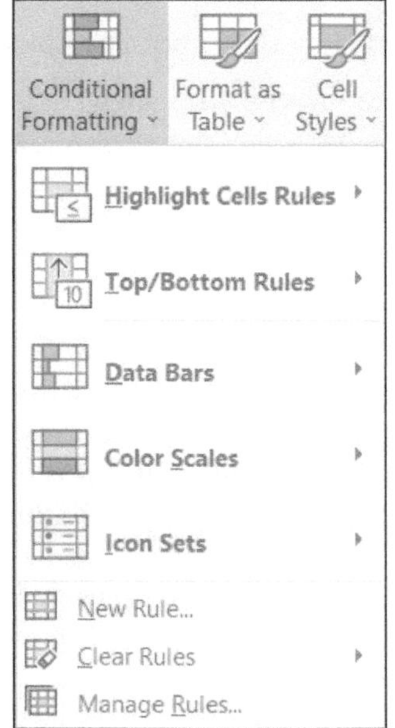

Activity 1a **Formatting Cells Using the *Highlight Cells Rules* Option** Part 1 of 2

1. Open **VRPay-Oct23**.
2. Save the workbook with the name **1-VRPay-Oct23**.
3. Using conditional formatting, apply green fill with dark green text formatting to the pay rate values to identify employees whose pay rate is less than $11.50 by completing the following steps:
   a. Select the range L6:L23.
   b. Click the Conditional Formatting button in the Styles group on the Home tab.
   c. Point to *Highlight Cells Rules* and then click *Less Than* at the drop-down list.

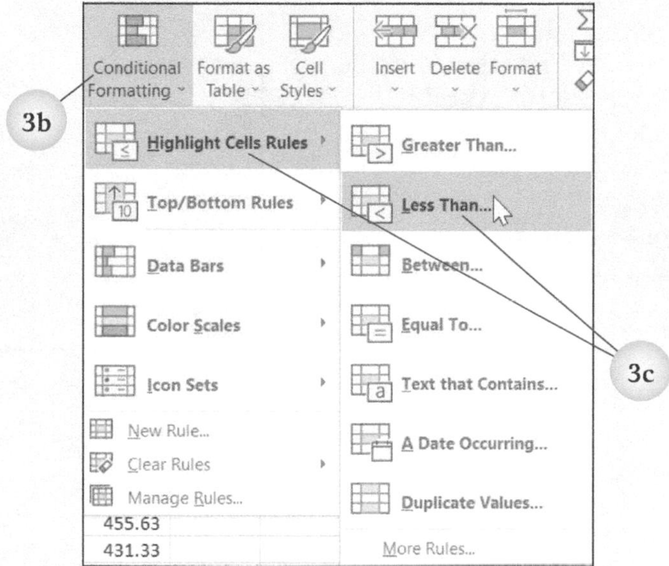

   d. At the Less Than dialog box with the text automatically selected in the *Format cells that are LESS THAN* text box, type 11.50.
   e. Click the *with* option box arrow and then click *Green Fill with Dark Green Text*.

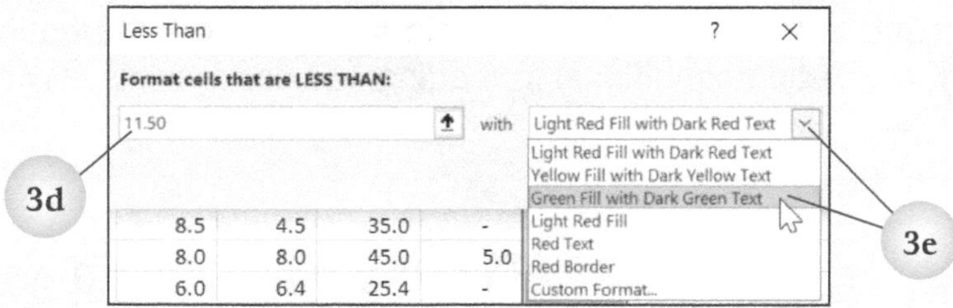

   f. Click OK.
   g. Click in any cell to deselect the range.
   h. Review the cells that have been conditionally formatted.
4. Save **1-VRPay-Oct23**.

Activity 1b Formatting Cells Based on the *Top/Bottom Rules* Option

Part 2 of 2

1. With **1-VRPay-Oct23** open, apply light red fill with dark red text conditional formatting to the gross pay values to identify employees who earned above average wages for the week by completing the following steps:
   a. Select the range M6:M23.
   b. Click the Conditional Formatting button in the Styles group on the Home tab.
   c. Point to *Top/Bottom Rules* and then click *Above Average* at the drop-down list.
   d. At the Above Average dialog box with *Light Red Fill with Dark Red Text* selected in the *Format cells that are ABOVE AVERAGE* option box, click OK.

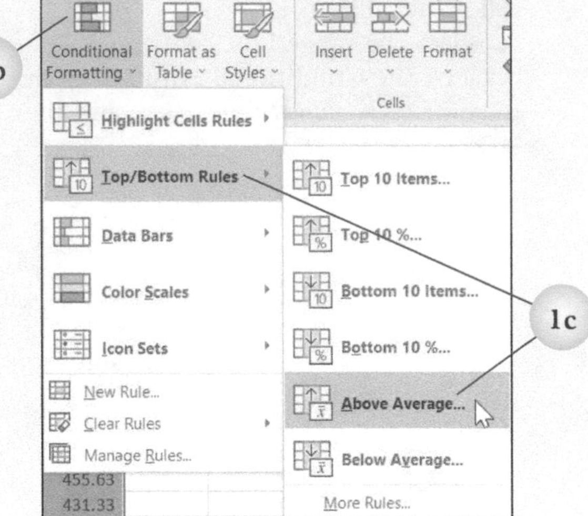

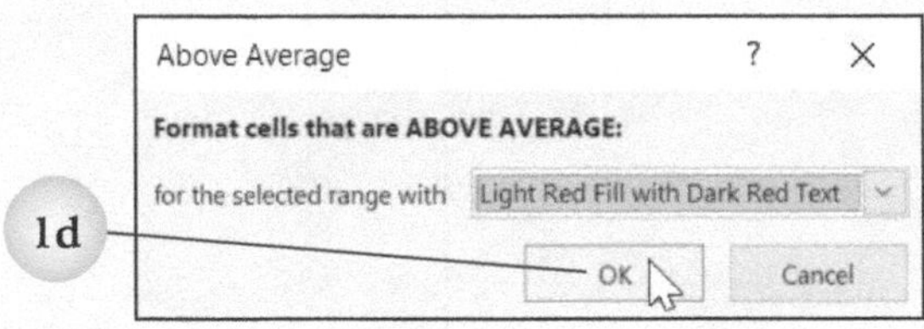

   e. Click in any cell to deselect the range.
   f. Review the cells that have been conditionally formatted.
2. Print the worksheet.
3. Save and then close **1-VRPay-Oct23**.

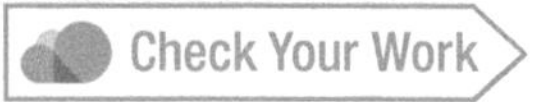

Activity 2 Apply Conditional Formatting to Insurance Policy Data

6 Parts

You will format cells in an insurance claims worksheet by creating, editing, clearing, and deleting conditional formatting rules and by visually identifying trends within the data.

Applying Conditional Formatting Using a New Rule

Hint Create a rule to format cells based on cell values, specific text, dates, blanks, or error values.

Applying Conditional Formatting Using a New Rule

Cells are conditionally formatted based on rules. A rule defines the criterion by which cells are selected for formatting and includes the formatting attributes that are applied to cells that meet the criterion. The rules that were applied in Activity 1a and Activity 1b applied conditional formatting using predefined options. At the New Formatting Rule dialog box, shown in Figure 1.2, a custom conditional formatting rule can be created that defines all the parts of the criterion and the formatting. The *Edit the Rule Description* section of the dialog box varies depending on the active option in the *Select a Rule Type* list box.

Quick Steps

Create and Apply New Formatting Rule

1. Select range.
2. Click Conditional Formatting button.
3. Click *New Rule*.
4. Click rule type.
5. Add criteria as required.
6. Click Format button.
7. Select formatting attributes.
8. Click OK to close Format Cells dialog box.
9. Click OK to close New Formatting Rule dialog box.

Figure 1.2 New Formatting Rule Dialog Box

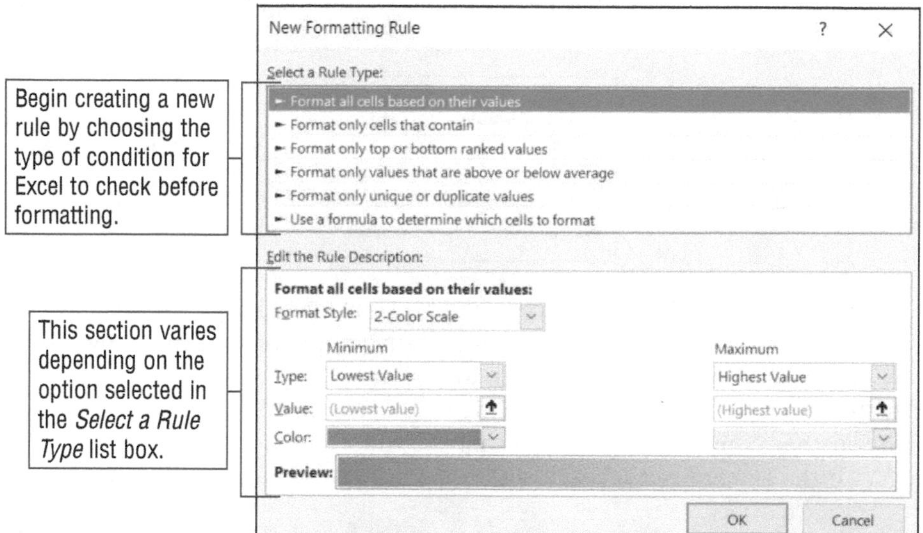

Activity 2a Applying Conditional Formatting Using a New Rule

Part 1 of 6

1. Open **ACInsce.**
2. Save the workbook with the name **1-ACInsce.**
3. The owner of AllClaims Insurance Brokers is considering changing the discount plan for customers with no claims or with only one claim. The owner would like to see the names of customers who meet either of the two claim criteria formatted in color to provide a reference for how many customers this discount would affect. Create the first formatting rule, which changes the appearance of cells in the *Claims* column that contain *0* by completing the following steps:
   a. Select the range H4:H20.
   b. Click the Conditional Formatting button in the Styles group on the Home tab.
   c. Click *New Rule* at the drop-down list.
   d. At the New Formatting Rule dialog box, click *Format only cells that contain* in the *Select a Rule Type* list box.
   e. Click the second option box arrow (which displays *between*) in the *Format only cells with* section and then click *equal to* at the drop-down list.

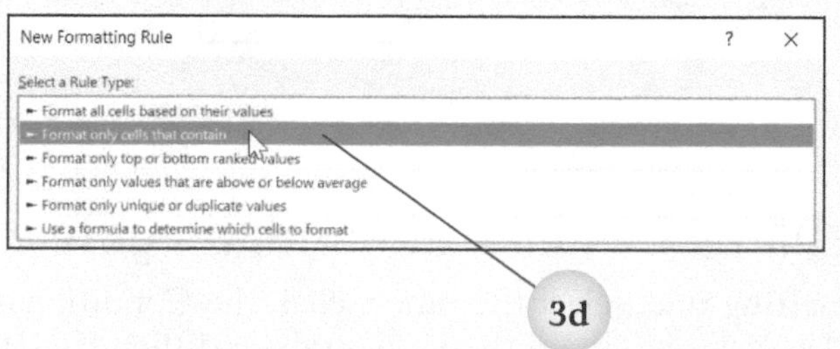

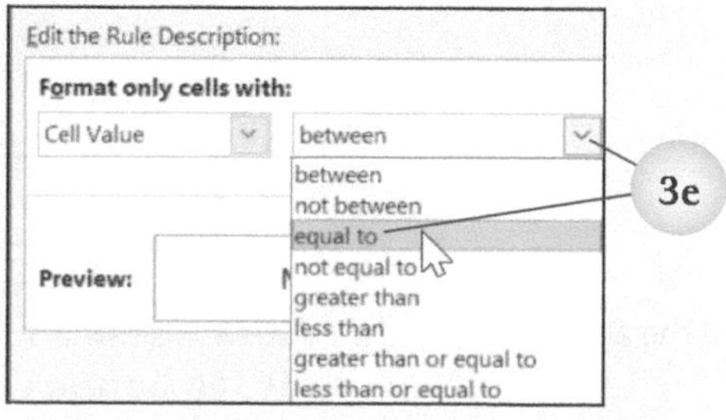

f. Click in the blank text box next to *equal to* and then type 0.
g. Click the Format button.

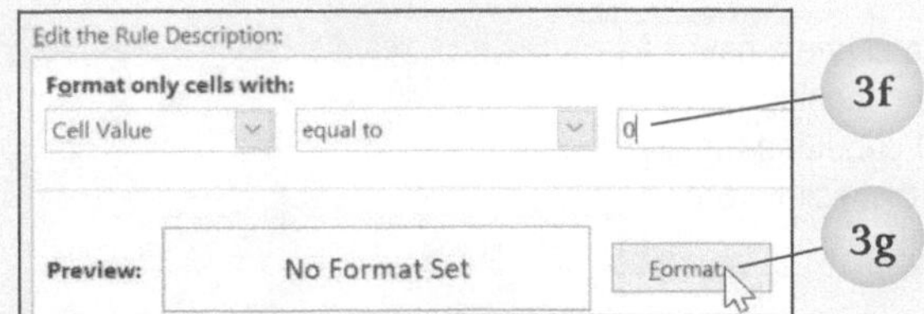

h. At the Format Cells dialog box with the Font tab selected, apply the Dark Red color (first option in the *Standard Colors* section), apply bold formatting, and then click OK.
i. Click OK at the New Formatting Rule dialog box.

4. Create a second formatting rule, which changes the appearance of cells in the *Claims* column that contain *1*, by completing the following steps:
   a. With the range H4:H20 still selected, click the Conditional Formatting button and then click *New Rule*.
   b. At the New Formatting Rule dialog box, click *Format only cells that contain* in the *Select a Rule Type* list box.
   c. Click the second option box arrow in the *Format only cells with* section (which displays *between*) and then click *equal to* at the drop-down list.
   d. Click in the blank text box next to *equal to* and then type 1.
   e. Click the Format button.
   f. At the Format Cells dialog box with the Font tab selected, apply the Blue color (eighth option in the *Standard Colors* section), apply bold formatting, and then click OK.
   g. Click OK at the New Formatting Rule dialog box.

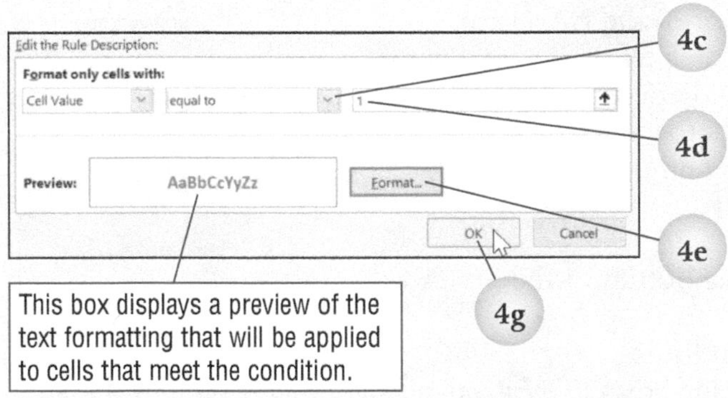

Rating	Claims
1	0
1	0
2	1
2	1
5	3
4	2
2	1
5	2
5	2
8	4
5	3
6	3
1	0
3	2
5	3
2	1
1	0

Bold dark red formatting has been applied to cells containing *0*, and bold blue formatting has been applied to cells containing *1*.

5

5. Click in any cell to deselect the range and review the conditionally formatted cells in the *Claims* column.
6. Save **1-ACInsce**.

Check Your Work

Tutorial

Editing and Deleting a Conditional Formatting Rule

Editing and Deleting a Conditional Formatting Rule

To edit or delete a formatting rule, select the range, click the Conditional Formatting button in the Styles group on the Home tab, and then click the *Manage Rule* option to open the Conditional Formatting Rules Manager dialog box. By default, *Show formatting rules for* is set to *Current Selection* when the

Quick Steps

Edit Formatting Rule

1. Select range.
2. Click Conditional Formatting button.
3. Click *Manage Rules*.
4. Click rule.
5. Click Edit Rule button.
6. Make changes.
7. Click OK two times.

Quick Steps

Remove Conditional Formatting

1. Select range.
2. Click Quick Analysis button.
3. Click Clear Format button.

Conditional Formatting Rules Manager dialog box is opened. If a range was not selected and no rules display, click the option box arrow and then select *This Worksheet* to show all the formatting rules in the current sheet. To edit the comparison rule criteria and/or formatting options, click to select the rule to change and then click the Edit Rule button. At the Edit Formatting Rule dialog box, make the required changes and then click OK two times. To remove a rule, click to select the rule to delete, click the Delete Rule button, and then click OK.

Another way to remove conditional formatting is to select the range, click the Conditional Formatting button, point to *Clear Rules* at the drop-down list, and then click either *Clear Rules from Selected Cells* or *Clear Rules from Entire Sheet*. Conditional formatting can also be removed using the Quick Analysis button. Once the range has been selected, click the Quick Analysis button, which appears at the bottom right corner of the selected data, and then click the Clear Format button in the drop-down gallery. The Quick Analysis gallery can also be accessed using the keyboard shortcut Ctrl + Q. Formatting applied to the cells by the deleted rule(s) will be removed.

Activity 2b Creating, Editing, and Deleting a Conditional Formatting Rule — Part 2 of 6

1. With **1-ACInsce** open, create a new formatting rule to add a fill color to the cells in the *No. of Autos* column for those auto insurance policy holders who have more than two cars by completing the following steps:
   a. Select the range C4:C20.
   b. Click the Conditional Formatting button and then click *New Rule* at the drop-down list.
   c. Click *Format only cells that contain* in the *Select a Rule Type* list box.
   d. In the *Edit the Rule Description* section, change the parameters for the rule to format only cells with values greater than 2. (If necessary, refer to Activity 2a, Steps 3e–3f, for assistance.)
   e. Click the Format button and then click the Fill tab at the Format Cells dialog box.
   f. Click the *Orange* color (third column, bottom row in the *Background Color* palette) and then click OK.
   g. Click OK to close the New Formatting Rule dialog box.

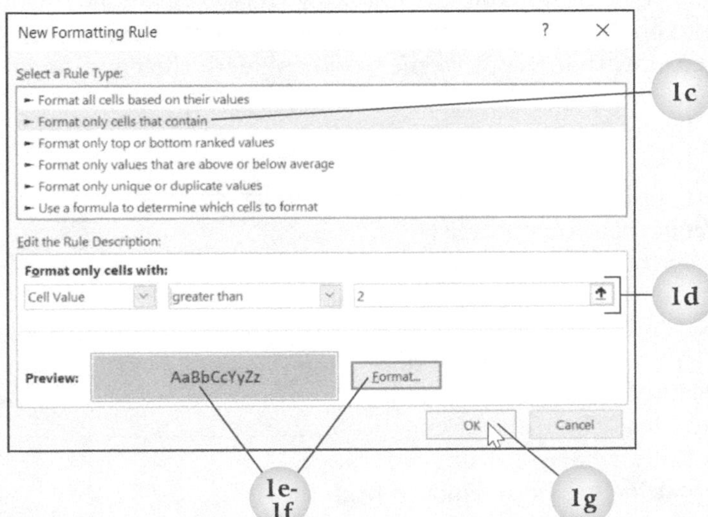

   h. Click in any cell to deselect the range.

2. After the formatted cells have been reviewed, it is decided that cells should be formatted for all policy holders with two or more cars. Edit the formatting rule to include the value *2* by completing the following steps:
   a. Select the range C4:C20.
   b. Click the Conditional Formatting button and then click *Manage Rules* at the drop-down list.
   c. Click *Cell Value > 2* in the Conditional Formatting Rules Manager dialog box to select the rule and then click the Edit Rule button.

Customer ID	Policy ID	No. of Autos
C-025	6512485	2
C-055	6123584	1
C-072	6583157	2
C-085	6124893	3
C-094	3481274	1
C-114	4956875	2
C-124	3354867	1
C-131	6598642	3
C-148	4668457	3
C-155	8512475	4
C-168	6984563	2
C-171	4856972	1
C-184	5124876	1
C-190	6845962	1
C-199	8457326	1
C-201	4968532	2
C-212	2698715	2

Formatting has been applied to cell values greater than 2.

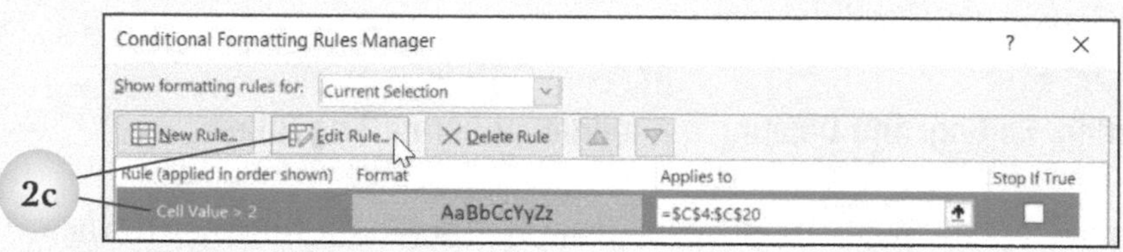

   d. Click the second option box arrow (which displays *greater than*) and then click *greater than or equal to* at the drop-down list.
   e. Click OK.
   f. Click OK to close the Conditional Formatting Rules Manager dialog box.
   g. Click in any cell to deselect the range.

Edit the Rule Description:
Format only cells with:
Cell Value
greater than or equal to
=2
Preview:
AaBbCcYyZz
Format...
OK
Cancel
2d
2e

3. Save and print the worksheet.
4. To prepare for experimenting with another method of formatting the data, save the revised worksheet with a new name and then delete the formatting rule in the original worksheet by completing the following steps:
   a. Save the workbook with the name **1-ACInsce-Autos2+**. Saving the workbook with a new name ensures that a copy of the workbook with the conditional formatting applied in this activity is kept.
   b. Close **1-ACInsce-Autos2+**.
   c. Open **1-ACInsce**.
   d. Click the Conditional Formatting button and then click *Manage Rules* at the drop-down list.
   e. Click the *Show formatting rules for* option box arrow and then click *This Worksheet*.
   f. Click *Cell Value >= 2* to select the rule and then click the Delete Rule button.
   g. Click OK to close the Conditional Formatting Rules Manager dialog box. Notice that the formatting has been removed from the cells in the *No. of Autos* column.

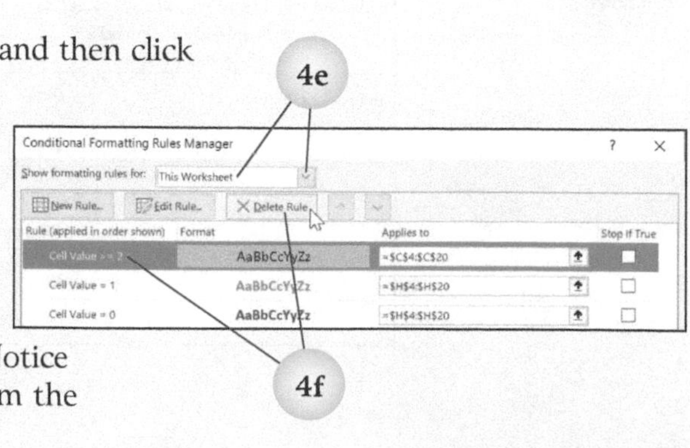

5. Save **1-ACInsce**.

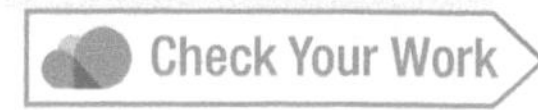

Applying Conditional Formatting Using an Icon Set

Applying Conditional Formatting Using an Icon Set

Format a range of values using an icon set to organize data into three to five categories. When this type of conditional formatting is applied, Excel places an icon in a cell to visually portray the value of the cell relative to the values of the other cells within the selected range. Using an icon set, similar data are categorized to easily identify high points, low points, and other trends. Icons are assigned to cells based on default threshold values for the selected range. For example, if the *3 Arrows (Colored)* icon set option is selected, icons are assigned as follows:

Green Up Arrow

Red Down Arrow

Yellow Sideways Arrow

- Green up arrows for values greater than or equal to 67%
- Red down arrows for values less than 33%
- Yellow sideways arrows for values between 33% and 67%

The available icon sets, shown in Figure 1.3, are organized into four sections: *Directional*, *Shapes*, *Indicators*, and *Ratings*. Choose the icon set that best represents the number of categories within the range and symbol type, such as directional colored arrows, traffic light shapes, flag indicators, star ratings, and so on. Modify the default threshold values or create unique icon sets by opening the Manage Rules dialog box and editing an existing rule or creating a new rule.

Quick Steps

Apply Conditional Formatting Using Icon Set

1. Select range.
2. Click Conditional Formatting button.
3. Point to *Icon Sets*.
4. Click icon set.
5. Deselect range.

Figure 1.3 Conditional Formatting Icon Sets Gallery

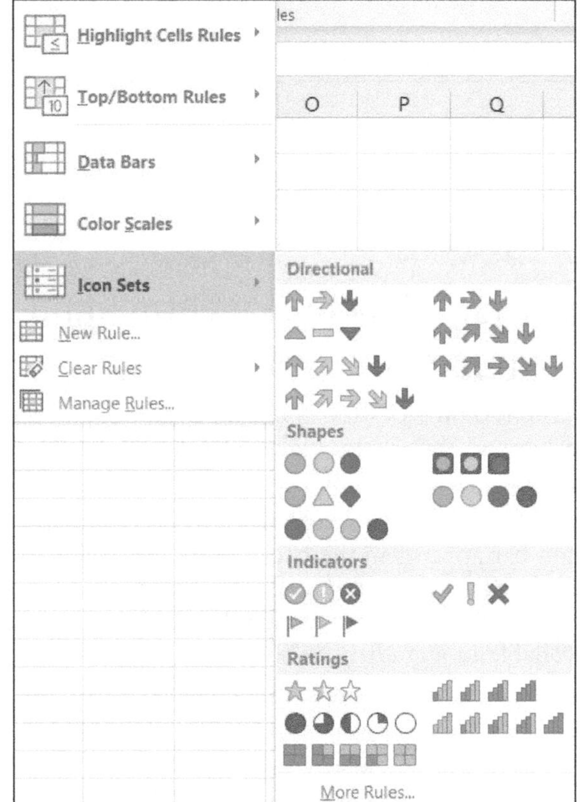

Activity 2c Applying Conditional Formatting Using an Icon Set

Part 3 of 6

1. With **1-ACInsce** open, select the range C4:C20.
2. Use an icon set to organize the number of automobiles into categories by completing the following steps:
   a. Click the Conditional Formatting button.
   b. Point to *Icon Sets* and then click *Red To Black* (first column, third row in the *Shapes* section) at the drop-down gallery.
   c. Click in any cell to deselect the range. Notice that Excel assigns an icon to each cell and that these icons correlate with the values of the cells. For example, all cells containing the value *1* have the same icon, all cells containing the value *2* have the same icon, and so on.

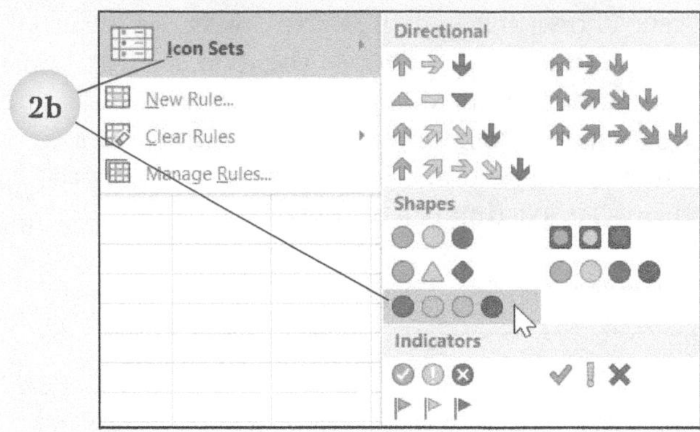

2c

No. of Autos
2
1
2
3
1
2
1
3
3
4
2
1
1
1
1
2
2

3. Save **1-ACInsce.**

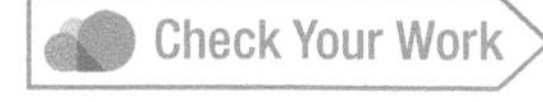

Applying Conditional Formatting Using Data Bars and Color Scales

Applying Conditional Formatting Using Data Bars and Color Scales

Excel also provides the ability to conditionally format cells using data bars, two-color scales, and three-color scales, to provide visual guides for identifying distributions or variations within a range.

Use data bars to easily identify the highest and lowest values within a range. A data bar appears in the background of a cell and the length of the bar depends on the value within the cell. A cell with a higher value within the range displays a longer bar than a cell with a lower value. Excel offers six colors for data bars and each color is available in a gradient or solid fill.

Hint Be careful not to use too many icon sets, color scales, and/or data bars. Readers can quickly lose focus when too many items compete for their attention.

Color scales format a range using a two-color or three-color palette. Excel provides 12 color scale gradients, half of which are two-color combinations and half of which are three-color combinations. The gradation of color applied to a cell illustrates its value relative to the rest of the range. Color scales are useful for reviewing the distribution of data. In a two-color scale, the shade applied to a cell represents either a higher or lower value within the range. In a three-color scale, the shade applied to a cell represents a higher, middle, or lower value within the range.

Activity 2d Applying Conditional Formatting Using Data Bars

Part 4 of 6

1. With **1-ACInsce** open, select the range I4:I20.
2. Apply gradient blue data bar formatting to the premium values to easily identify the higher and lower premiums by completing the following steps:
   a. Click the Conditional Formatting button.
   b. Point to *Data Bars* and then click *Blue Data Bar* (first option in the *Gradient Fill* section) at the drop-down gallery.
   c. Click in any cell to deselect the range. Notice that the lengths of the colored bars in the cells reflect various premium amounts, with longer bars representing higher premiums.

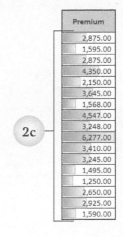

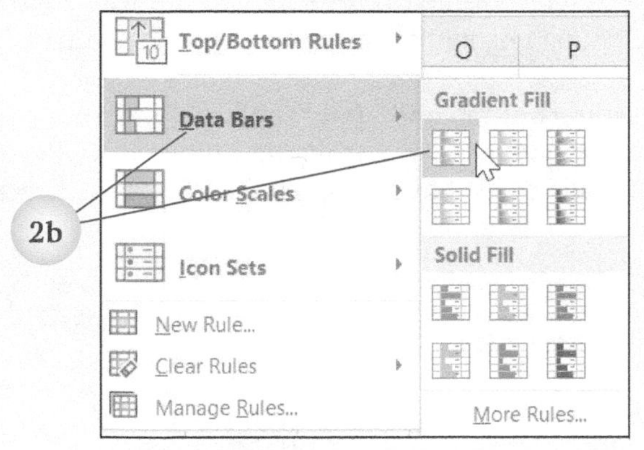

2c

Premium
2,875.00
1,595.00
2,875.00
4,350.00
2,150.00
3,645.00
1,568.00
4,547.00
3,248.00
6,277.00
3,410.00
3,245.00
1,495.00
1,250.00
2,650.00
2,925.00
1,590.00

3. Save **1-ACInsce**.

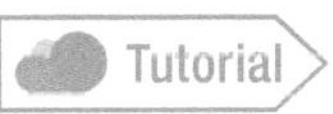

Applying Conditional Formatting Using a Formula

Applying Conditional Formatting Using a Formula

Use conditional formatting and a formula to format a cell based on the value in another cell or using some logical test. At the New Formatting Rule dialog box, choose *Use a formula to determine which cells to format* in the *Select a Rule Type* list box. Enter a formula, such as an IF statement, to determine whether a cell will be formatted.

For example, in Activity 2e, the premium values in column I of the insurance worksheet are formatted based on the rating values for the policies stored in column G. In this activity, the IF statement allows a premium to be conditionally formatted if the rating value for the policy is greater than 3. The IF function's logical test returns only a true or false result. The value in the rating cell is either greater than 3 (true) or not greater than 3 (false). Excel conditionally formats only those cells in the *Premium* column for which the conditional test returns a true result.

The formula that is entered into the New Formatting Rule dialog box in Activity 2e is *=IF(G4:G20>3,TRUE,FALSE)*. Excel treats any formula entered for conditional formatting as an array formula, which means one rule needs to be added for the range G4:G20. In the first cell in the selected range (cell I4), Excel will perform the following test: *Is the value in G4 greater than 3?* In the first row, this test returns a false result, so Excel will not conditionally format the value in cell I4. Excel will apply bold formatting and the standard red font color to those cells in column I for which the test returns a true result based on the corresponding cell in column G.

Activity 2e Applying Conditional Formatting Using a Formula

Part 5 of 6

1. With **1-ACInsce** open, select the range I4:I20.
2. The owner of AllClaims Insurance Brokers would like the premiums for those clients with ratings higher than 3 to stand out in the worksheet. Conditionally format the premiums in column I using a formula that checks the ratings in column G by completing the following steps:
   a. Click the Conditional Formatting button and then click *New Rule* at the drop-down list.
   b. At the New Formatting Rule dialog box, click *Use a formula to determine which cells to format* in the *Select a Rule Type* list box.
   c. Click in the *Format values where this formula is true* text box in the *Edit the Rule Description* section of the New Formatting Rule dialog box and then type =if(g4:g20>3,true,false).
   d. Click the Format button.
   e. At the Format Cells dialog box, click the Font tab and apply the Red font color (second option in the *Standard Colors* section), apply bold formatting, and then click OK.
   f. Click OK to close the New Formatting Rule dialog box and apply the rule to the selected cells.

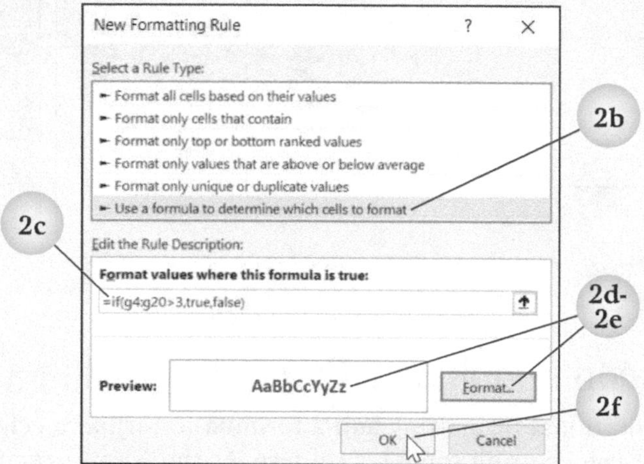

   g. Click in any cell to deselect the range. Notice that the cells in column I with bold formatting and the standard red font color are those for which the corresponding rating values in column G are greater than 3. For the most part, the higher ratings correspond to higher premiums, which are identified by the longer blue data bars.
3. Save **1-ACInsce**.

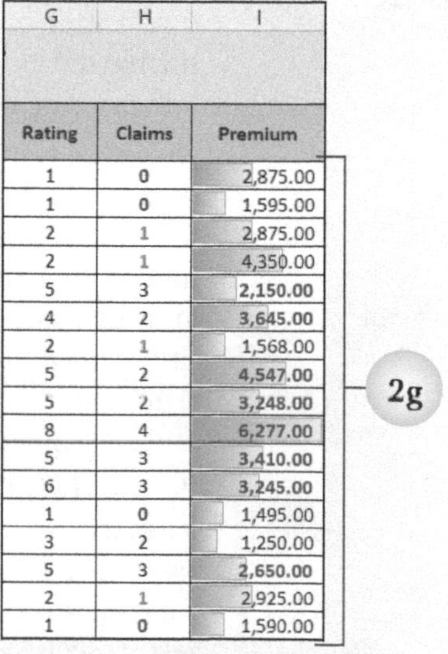

G	H	I
Rating	Claims	Premium
1	0	2,875.00
1	0	1,595.00
2	1	2,875.00
2	1	4,350.00
5	3	2,150.00
4	2	3,645.00
2	1	1,568.00
5	2	4,547.00
5	2	3,248.00
8	4	6,277.00
5	3	3,410.00
6	3	3,245.00
1	0	1,495.00
3	2	1,250.00
5	3	2,650.00
2	1	2,925.00
1	0	1,590.00

Check Your Work

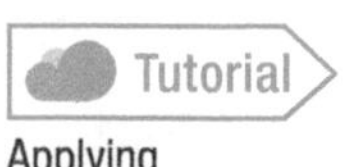

Applying Conditional Formatting Using Quick Analysis

Quick Analysis

Applying Conditional Formatting Using Quick Analysis

Use the Quick Analysis button to quickly apply preset conditional formatting. After the data is selected, the Quick Analysis button appears near the fill handle at the bottom right corner of the selection and the options shown in Figure 1.4 become available. Use these options to apply conditional formatting, create charts, add totals, create tables, and add Sparklines. With predefined conditional formatting rules, Excel can quickly analyze and format the data. If more options are required than those provided by the Quick Analysis button, access the rules from the Conditional Formatting button drop-down list.

Figure 1.4 Quick Analysis Button Options

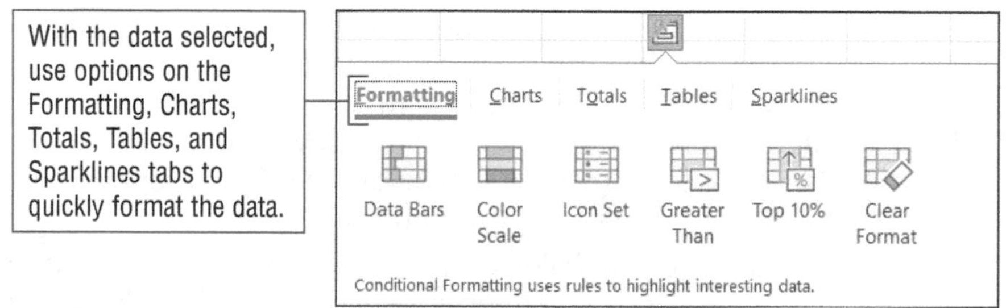

Activity 2f **Apply Conditional Formatting Using the Quick Analysis Button** Part 6 of 6

1. With **1-ACInsce** open, apply conditional formatting to apply a light red fill with dark red text for the number of drivers over three by completing the following steps:
   a. Select the range F4:F20.
   b. Click the Quick Analysis button at the bottom right of the selected range.
   c. Click the Greater Than button on the Formatting tab.

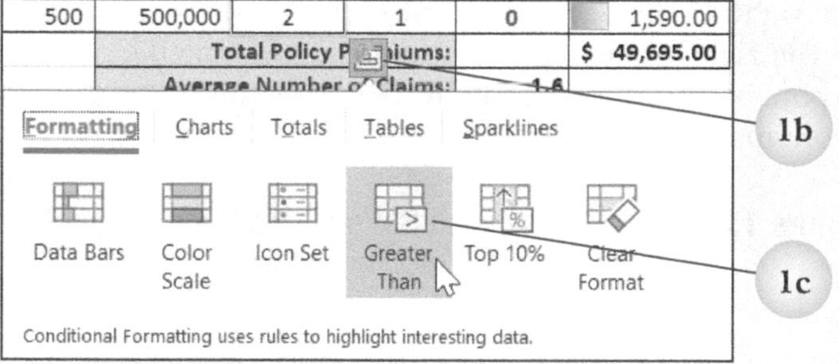

   d. At the Greater Than dialog box with the text already selected in the *Format cells that are GREATER THAN* text box, type 3.
   e. With *Light Red Fill with Dark Red Text* selected, click OK.
   f. Click in any cell to deselect the range. Review the cells that have been conditionally formatted. Notice that cells with values over 3 are formatted with a light red fill and dark red text.
2. Save, print, and then close **1-ACInsce**.

Activity 3 **Use Fraction and Scientific Formatting Options for a Lesson Plan Worksheet** — **1 Part**

Using two lesson plan worksheets, you will format cells in a solution column to display the answers for a math tutor.

Applying Fraction and Scientific Formatting

Review: Applying Number Formatting

Quick Steps

Apply Fraction Formatting

1. Select range.
2. Click Number group dialog box launcher.
3. Click *Fraction* in *Category* list box.
4. Click option in *Type* list box.
5. Click OK.
6. Deselect range.

Apply Scientific Formatting

1. Select range.
2. Click *Number Format* option box arrow.
3. Click *Scientific*.
4. Deselect range.

Applying Fraction Formatting and Scientific Formatting

Most worksheet values are formatted using the Accounting Number Format, Percent Style, or the Comma Style button in the Number group on the Home tab. However, some worksheets contain values that require other number formats. When clicked, the *Number Format* option box arrow in the Number group on the Home tab displays a drop-down list with additional format options, including date, time, fraction, scientific, and text options.

Click the Number group dialog box launcher at the bottom right of the Number group on the Home tab to open the Format Cells dialog box with the Number tab active, as shown in Figure 1.5. This dialog box may also be opened by clicking *More Number Formats* at the *Number Format* drop-down list or by using the keyboard shortcut Ctrl + 1. At this dialog box, specify additional parameters for the number format categories. For example, with the *Fraction* category selected, choose the type of fraction to be displayed.

Scientific formatting converts a number to exponential notation. Part of the number is replaced with *E+n*, where *E* means "exponent" and *n* represents the power. For example, the number *1,500,000.00* formatted in scientific number format displays as *1.50E+06*. In this example, *+06* means "Add six zeros to the right of the number left of *E* and then move the decimal point six places to the right." Scientists, mathematicians, engineers, and statisticians often use exponential notation to write very large numbers and very small numbers in a more manageable way.

Figure 1.5 Format Cells Dialog Box with the Number Tab Selected and the *Fraction* Category Active

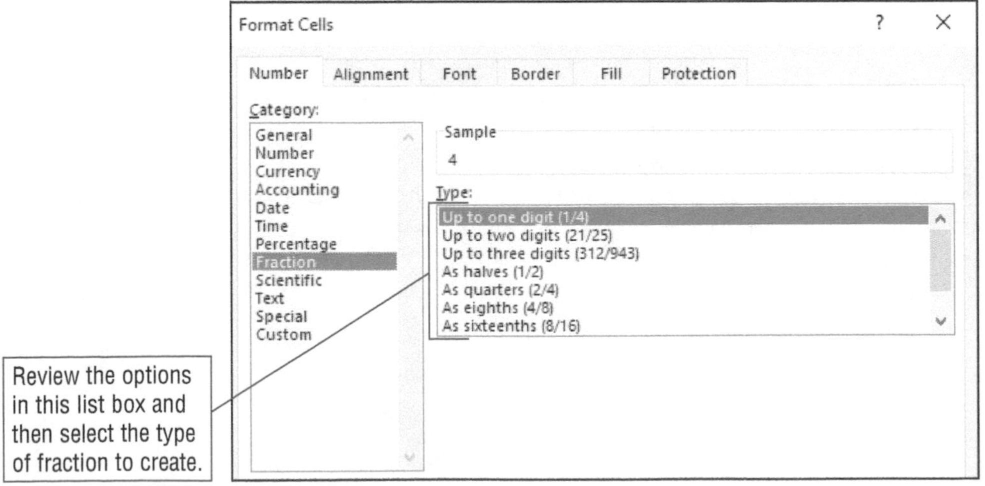

Activity 3 Applying Fraction Formatting and Scientific Formatting

1. Open **JTutor.**
2. Save the workbook with the name **1-JTutor**.
3. Make Fractions the active worksheet by clicking the Fractions sheet tab.
4. Apply fraction formatting to the values in column D to create the solution column for the math tutor by completing the following steps:
   a. Select the range D11:D19.
   b. Click the Number group dialog box launcher on the Home tab.
   c. At the Format Cells dialog box with the Number tab selected, click *Fraction* in the *Category* list box.
   d. Click *Up to two digits (21/25)* in the *Type* list box.

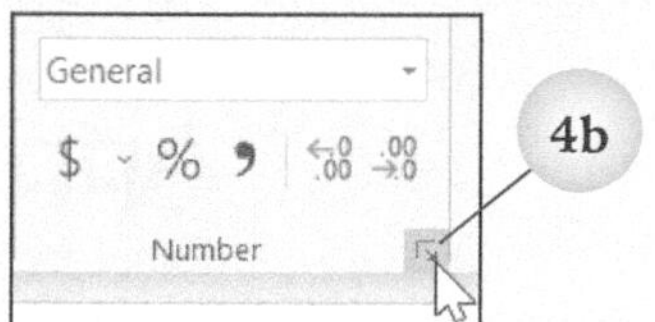

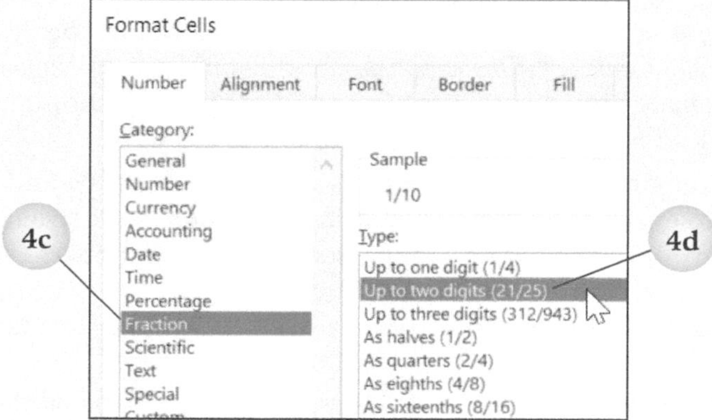

   e. Click OK.
   f. Click in any cell to deselect the range.
5. Click the Exponents sheet tab.
6. Apply scientific formatting to the values in column D to create the solution column for the math tutor by completing the following steps:
   a. Select the range D11:D25.
   b. Click the *Number Format* option box arrow (which displays *Custom*) in the Number group on the Home tab and then click *Scientific* at the drop-down list.
   c. Click in any cell to deselect the range.
7. Print the workbook.
8. Save and then close **1-JTutor**.

Examples	Converted to Scientific Notation
1,000,000,000	1.00E+09
100,000,000	1.00E+08
10,000,000	1.00E+07
1,000,000	1.00E+06
100,000	1.00E+05
10,000	1.00E+04
1,000	1.00E+03
100	1.00E+02
10	1.00E+01
1	1.00E+00
0.1	1.00E-01
0.01	1.00E-02
0.001	1.00E-03
0.0001	1.00E-04
0.00001	1.00E-05

6a-6c

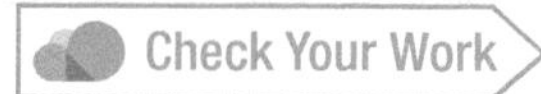

Activity 4 Apply Advanced Formatting Options to a Products Worksheet **2 Parts**

You will update a products worksheet by formatting telephone numbers and creating a custom number format to add descriptive characters before and after values.

Applying Special Number Formatting

Quick Steps

Apply Special Number Formatting

1. Select range.
2. Click Number group dialog box launcher.
3. Click *Special* in *Category* list box.
4. Click option in *Type* list box.
5. Click OK.
6. Deselect range.

Excel provides special number formats that are specific to countries and languages at the Format Cells dialog box with the Number tab active. As shown in Figure 1.6, when *Special* is selected in the *Category* list box and *English (United States)* is selected in the *Locale (location)* option box, the *Type* list box includes *Zip Code, Zip Code + 4, Phone Number,* and *Social Security Number*. When the *English (Canadian)* option is selected in the *Locale (location)* option box, the *Type* list box includes *Phone Number* and *Social Insurance Number*.

Applying special number formatting can save time and keystrokes, as well as help to ensure consistent formatting. For example, if special social security number formatting is applied to a range, social security numbers can be typed into the range without hyphens because Excel will add them. Typing *000223456* will enter *000-22-3456* in the cell with social security number formatting applied.

Figure 1.6 Format Cells Dialog Box with the Number Tab Selected and the *Special* Category Active

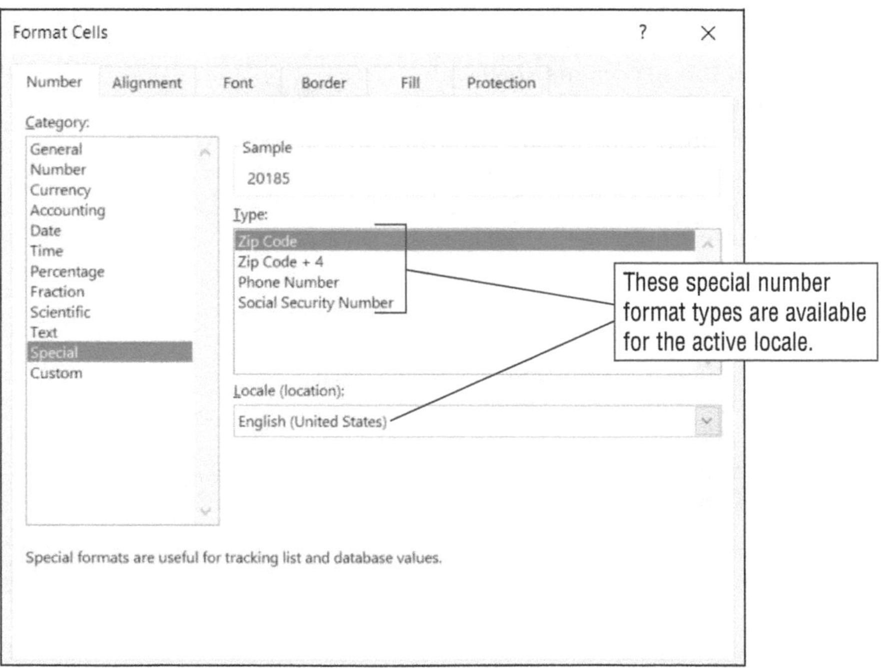

Activity 4a Applying Special Number Formatting

Part 1 of 2

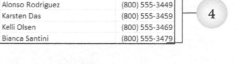

1. Open **Precision**.
2. Save the workbook with the name **1-Precision**.
3. Format the range that will contain telephone numbers to include brackets around each area code and a hyphen between the first three and last four digits of each number by completing the following steps:
   a. Select the range C15:C20.
   b. Click the Number group dialog box launcher.
   c. At the Format Cells dialog box with the Number tab selected, click *Special* in the *Category* list box.
   d. Click *Phone Number* in the *Type* list box and make sure the *Locale (location)* option box is set to *English (United States)*.
   e. Click OK.
   f. Click in cell C15 to deselect the range and make the first cell to contain a telephone number the active cell.
4. Type the telephone numbers for the sales representatives as follows:

   C15: 8005553429
   C16: 8005553439
   C17: 8005553449
   C18: 8005553459
   C19: 8005553469
   C20: 8005553479
5. Save **1-Precision**.

14	Regional Sales Representatives		
15	North	Jordan Lavoie	(800) 555-3429
16	South	Pat Gallagher	(800) 555-3439
17	East	Alonso Rodriguez	(800) 555-3449
18	West	Karsten Das	(800) 555-3459
19	Canada	Kelli Olsen	(800) 555-3469
20	International	Bianca Santini	(800) 555-3479

Creating a Custom Number Format

Creating a Custom Number Format

Quick Steps

Create Custom Number Format

1. Select range.
2. Click Number group dialog box launcher.
3. Click *Custom* in *Category* list box.
4. Select *General* in *Type* text box.
5. Press Delete.
6. Type custom format code.
7. Click OK.
8. Deselect range.

Hint Custom number formats are stored in the workbook in which they are created.

Use a custom number format for a worksheet to enter values that do not conform to predefined number formats or values to which punctuation, text, or formatting such as color is to be added. For example, in Activity 4b, a custom number format is created to automatically add two product category letters before each model number.

Formatting codes are used in custom formats to specify the types of formatting to apply. Type unique custom number format codes or select from a list of custom formats and modify the codes as necessary. Table 1.1 displays commonly used format codes along with examples of their uses.

Once a custom format has been created, it can be applied elsewhere within the workbook. To do this, select the text to be formatted, open the Format Cells dialog box with the Number tab selected, select the *Custom* category, scroll down to the bottom of the *Type* list box, click to select the custom format code, and then click OK.

Text, numbers, and punctuation added as part of a custom number format are not saved as part of the cell value. In Activity 4b, a custom number format that displays *PD-* in front of each model number is created. The value in cell A5 displays as *PD-1140* but *1140* is the actual value that is stored. This is important to remember when searching for or filtering data.

Table 1.1 Examples of Custom Number Format Codes

Format Code	Description	Custom Number Format Example	Display Result
#	Represents a digit; type one for each number. Excel rounds numbers if necessary to fit the number of digits after the decimal point.	###.###	Typing *145.0068* displays *145.007*.
0	Also represents a digit. Excel rounds numbers to fit the number of digits after the decimal point but also fills in leading zeros.	000.00	Typing *50.45* displays *050.45*.
?	Rounds numbers to fit the number of digits after the decimal point but also aligns numbers vertically on the decimal point by adding spaces.	???.???	Typing *123.5*, *.8*, and *55.356* one below the other in a column aligns the numbers vertically on the decimal points.
"text"	Adds the characters between the quotation marks to the entry.	"Model No." ##	Typing *58* displays *Model No. 58*.
[color]	Applies the font color specified in square brackets to the cell entry.	[Blue]##.##	Typing *55.346* displays *55.35*.
;	Separates the positive value format from the negative value format.	[Blue];[Red]	Typing *25* displays as *25* and typing *-25* displays as *25*.

Quick Steps

Delete Custom Number Format

1. Click Number group dialog box launcher.
2. Click *Custom* in *Category* list box.
3. Click custom format code.
4. Press Delete.
5. Click OK.

To delete a custom number format, open the workbook in which the custom format code was created, open the Format Cells dialog box with the Number tab selected, click *Custom* in the *Category* list box, scroll down the list of custom formats in the *Type* list box to the bottom of the list, click the custom format code that was added, and then click the Delete button. Deleting the formatting code also removes the custom formatting from any cells to which it was applied.

Activity 4b Creating a Custom Number Format

Part 2 of 2

1. With **1-Precision** open, select the range A5:A12.
2. Create a custom number format to insert *PD-* before each model number by completing the following steps:
   a. Click the Number group dialog box launcher.
   b. Click *Custom* in the *Category* list box in the Format Cells dialog box with the Number tab selected.

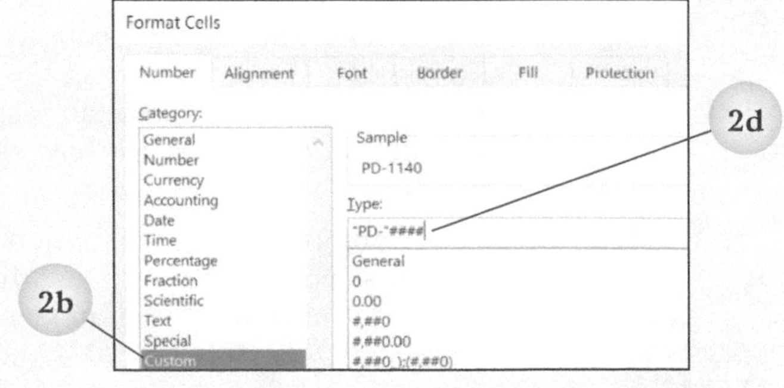

c. Scroll down the list of custom formats in the *Type* list box and notice the various combinations of format codes for numbers, dates, and times.
d. Select *General* in the *Type* text box and then type "PD-"####.
e. Click OK.
f. With the range A5:A12 still selected, click the Center button in the Alignment group on the Home tab.
g. Click in any cell to deselect the range.

	Model Number
4	
5	PD-1140
6	PD-2185
7	PD-3695
8	PD-4415
9	PD-5367
10	PD-6418
11	PD-7459
12	PD-8854

2f-2g

3. Create a custom number format to insert *lbs* after the weights in columns D and E by completing the following steps:
a. Select the range D5:E12.
b. Click the Number group dialog box launcher.
c. Click *Custom* in the *Category* list box.
d. Select *General* in the *Type* text box and then type ### "lbs". Make sure to include one space after ###.
e. Click OK.
f. Click in any cell to deselect the range.

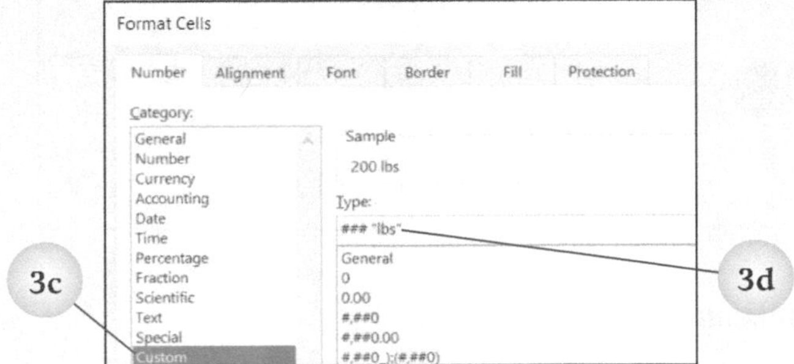

Test Weight in pounds	Recommended Weight in pounds
200 lbs	100 lbs
200 lbs	125 lbs
200 lbs	70 lbs
350 lbs	150 lbs
275 lbs	250 lbs
275 lbs	500 lbs
200 lbs	65 lbs
200 lbs	100 lbs

3f

4. Save, print, and then close **1-Precision**.

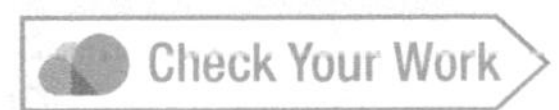

Activity 5 Filter and Sort Insurance and Payroll Data on Values, Icon Sets, and Colors — 4 Parts

You will filter an insurance policy worksheet to show policies based on a range of liability limits and by number of claims, filter policies based on the number of automobiles, and filter and sort a payroll worksheet by font and cell colors. You will also remove a filter.

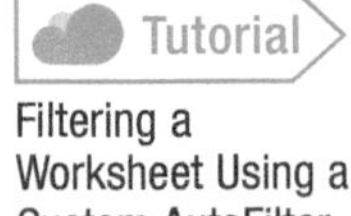

Filtering a Worksheet Using a Custom AutoFilter

Filtering a Worksheet Using a Custom AutoFilter

The Custom AutoFilter feature is used to display only the rows that meet specific criteria defined using the filter arrow at the top of each column. Rows that do not meet the criteria are temporarily hidden from view. At the top of each column in

Quick Steps

Filter Using Custom AutoFilter

1. Select range.
2. Click Sort & Filter button.
3. Click *Filter*.
4. Deselect range.
5. Click filter arrow at top of column to be filtered.
6. Point to *Number Filters*.
7. Click filter category.
8. Enter criteria at Custom AutoFilter dialog box.
9. Click OK.

Sort & Filter

the selected range or table, click a filter arrow to display a drop-down list of all the unique field values that exist within the column. To filter the values by more than one criterion using a comparison operator, open the Custom AutoFilter dialog box, shown in Figure 1.7. Use the ? and * wildcard characters in a custom filter. For example, filter a list of products by a product number beginning with *P* by using *P** as the criteria.

To display the Custom AutoFilter dialog box, select the range to filter, click the Sort & Filter button in the Editing group on the Home tab, and then click *Filter* at the drop-down list to add filter arrows. Filter arrows can also be added using the keyboard shortcut Ctrl + Shift + L. Click the filter arrow in the column that contains the criteria. Point to *Number Filters* or *Text Filters* and then choose one of the options at the drop-down list. The type of filter and options available depend on the type of data in the column—for example, text or numbers.

Figure 1.7 Custom AutoFilter Dialog Box

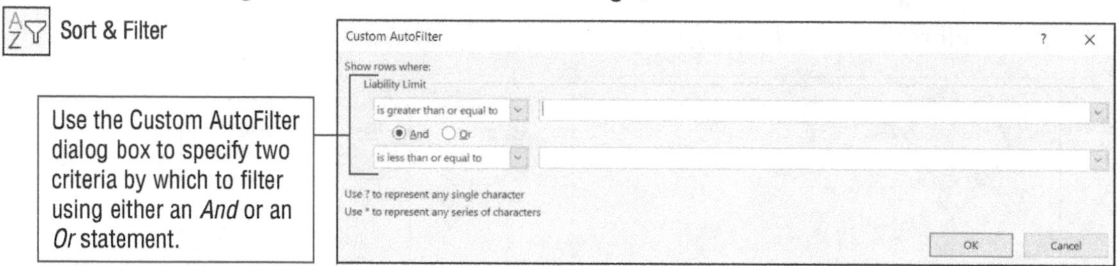

Activity 5a Filtering Policy Information Using a Custom AutoFilter

Part 1 of 4

1. Open **1-ACInsce**.
2. Save the workbook with the name **1-ACInsce-LL**.
3. The owner of AllClaims Insurance Brokers wants to review policies with liability limits from $500,000 to $1,000,000 that have had more than one claim to determine if customers should increase their coverage. Filter the policy information to produce the list of policies that meet the owner's request by completing the following steps:
   a. Select the range A3:I20.
   b. Click the Sort & Filter button in the Editing group on the Home tab.
   c. Click *Filter* at the drop-down list. A filter arrow displays at the top of each column.
   d. Deselect the range.
   e. Click the filter arrow next to *Liability Limit* in cell E3.
   f. Point to *Number Filters* and then click *Between* at the drop-down list.

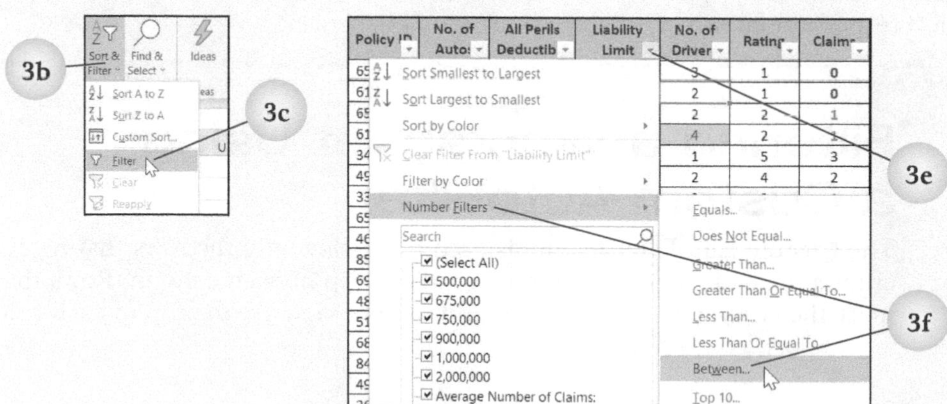

g. At the Custom AutoFilter dialog box with the insertion point positioned in the blank text box next to *is greater than or equal to*, type 500000.
h. Notice that *And* is the option selected between the criteria. This is correct, since the owner wants a list of policies with liability limits greater than or equal to $500,000 *and* less than or equal to $1,000,000.
i. Click in the blank text box next to *is less than or equal to* and type 1000000.

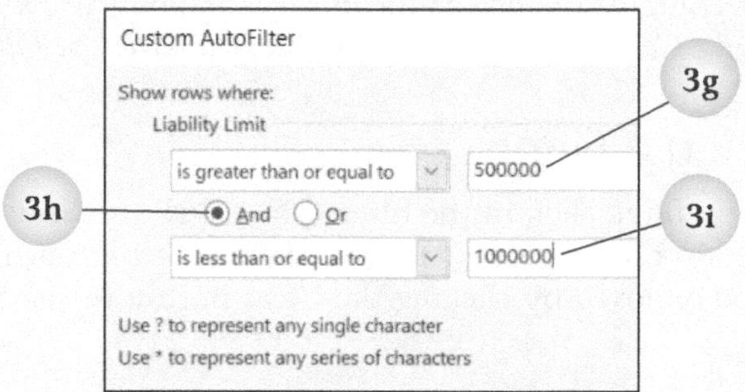

j. Click OK to close the Custom AutoFilter dialog box. The range is filtered to display the rows for customers with liability limits from $500,000 to $1,000,000.
k. Click the filter arrow next to *Claims* in cell H3.
l. Point to *Number Filters* and then click *Greater Than* at the drop-down list.
m. At the Custom AutoFilter dialog box with the insertion point positioned in the blank text box next to *is greater than*, type 1 and then click OK.

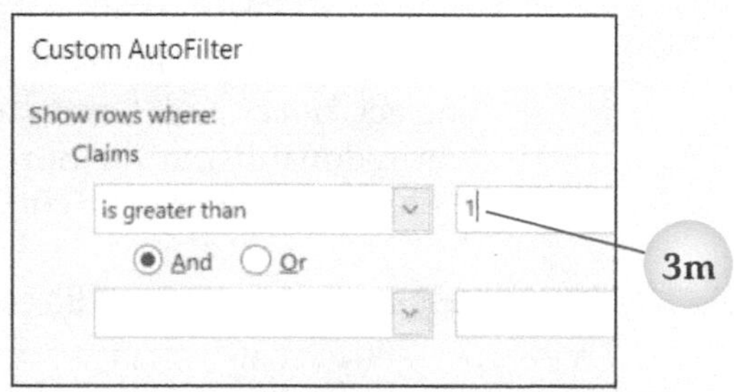

4. Print the filtered worksheet.
5. Save **1-ACInsce-LL.**

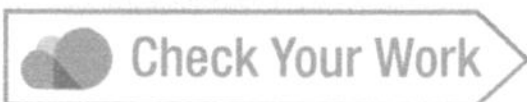

Filtering Data Using Conditional Formatting or Cell Attributes

Filtering and Sorting Data and Removing a Filter

A worksheet with cells that have been formatted manually or by conditional formatting to change the cell or font color can be filtered by color. In addition, a worksheet conditionally formatted using an icon set can be filtered using an icon. When the data needs to be redisplayed, remove the filter.

Hint If an error message about merged cells needing to be the same size appears when sorting, select the range to be sorted and do a custom sort.

Filtering and Sorting Data Using Conditional Formatting or Cell Attributes

To filter by color or icon, select the range, click the Sort & Filter button, click *Filter*, and then deselect the range. Click the filter arrow in the column to filter and then point to *Filter by Color* at the drop-down list. Depending on the formatting that has been applied, the list contains cell colors, font colors, or icon sets. Click the specific color or icon option to filter the column.

Quick Steps
Filter or Sort by Color or Icon Set
1. Select range.
2. Click Sort & Filter button.
3. Click *Filter.*
4. Deselect range.
5. Click filter arrow at top of column to be filtered.
6. Point to *Filter by Color* or *Sort by Color.*
7. Click color or icon.

The filter drop-down list also contains a *Sort by Color* option to sort rows within a range or table by a specified cell color, font color, or cell icon. To sort by color, follow steps similar to those used to filter by color. For example, to sort a column by font color, point to *Sort by Color* from the column filter drop-down list and then click the specific font color. Excel sorts the column by placing cells with the specified font color at the top. The list does not sort itself within the different color groupings.

The shortcut menu can also be used to sort or filter data. To do this, right-click a cell that contains the color or icon to filter, point to *Filter*, and then click *Filter by Selected Cell's Color*, *Filter by Selected Cell's Font Color*, or *Filter by Selected Cell's Icon*.

Removing a Filter

Quick Steps
Remove Filter
1. Click in filtered list.
2. Click Sort & Filter button.
3. Click *Clear* at drop-down list.

Clear

To remove a filter, click in the filtered list, click the Sort & Filter button in the Editing group on the Home tab, and then click *Clear* at the drop-down list. A filter can also be removed by clicking the Clear button in the Sort & Filter group on the Data tab.

Defining a Custom Sort

Define a custom sort in a worksheet when more than one cell or font color is applied to a column. Select the range, click the Sort & Filter button in the Editing group on the Home tab, and then click *Custom Sort* at the drop-down list. At the Sort dialog box, shown in Figure 1.8, define the color by which to sort first and then add a level for each other color in the order in which the sorting is to occur. Select *Values*, *Cell Color*, *Font Color*, or *Conditional Formatting Icon* from the *Sort On* drop-down list at the Sort dialog box. Figure 1.8 illustrates a sort definition for a column in which four conditional formatting icons have been used.

Figure 1.8 Sort Dialog Box with a Four-Color Sort Defined

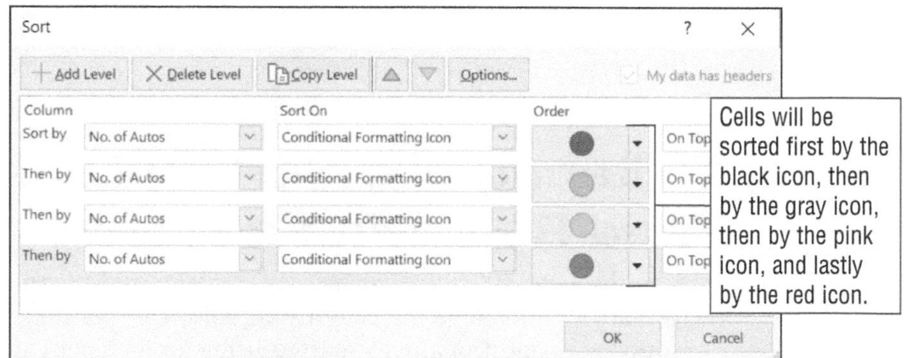

Activity 5b **Clearing a Filter and Filtering by an Icon Set** Part 2 of 4

1. With **1-ACInsce-LL** open, save the workbook as **1-ACInsce-1Auto**.
2. Remove the filter by completing the following steps:
   a. Click in the filtered list.
   b. Click the Sort & Filter button.
   c. Click *Clear* at the drop-down list.

3. Filter the worksheet to display the customers with coverage for only one automobile by completing the following steps:
   a. In Activity 2c, the Red to Black icon set was applied to the data in column C. Note that the black circle icon represents the *1* data set. Click the filter arrow next to *No. of Autos* in cell C3.
   b. Point to *Filter by Color* at the drop-down list.
   c. Click the black circle icon in the *Filter by Cell Icon* list.

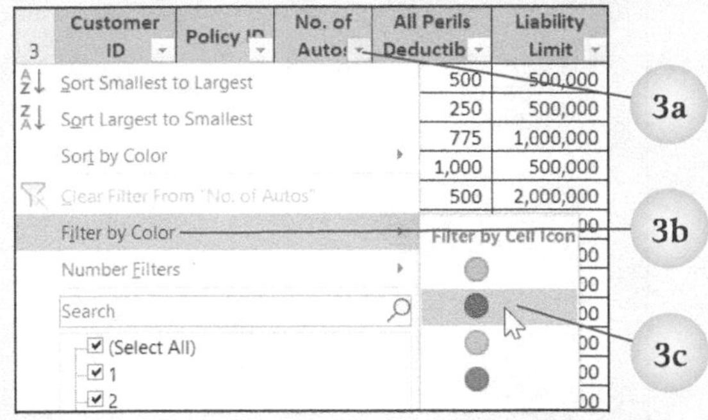

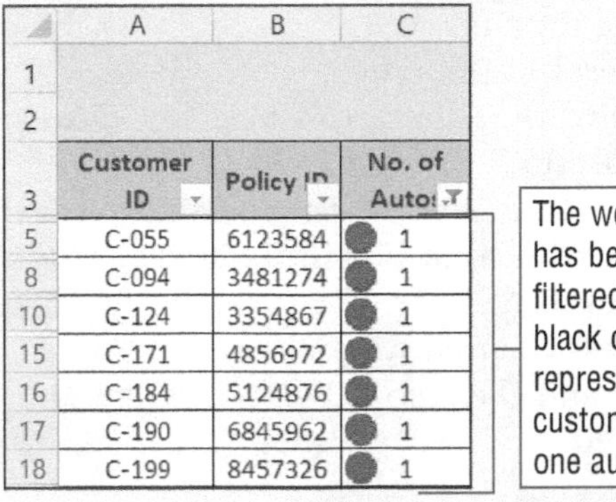

4. Print the filtered worksheet.
5. Save **1-ACInsce-1Auto**.

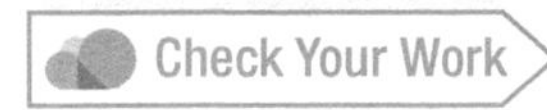

Activity 5c Filtering by Font Color

Part 3 of 4

1. With **1-ACInsce-1Auto** open, further filter the list to display the customers that have had zero claims. Recall that zero claims were conditionally formatted by applying a red font color and bold formatting to cells with values equal to 0. Filter the worksheet by the conditional formatting by completing the following steps:
   a. Right-click in cell H5 (or in any other cell in column H with a red font color).
   b. Point to *Filter* and then click *Filter by Selected Cell's Font Color* at the shortcut menu.

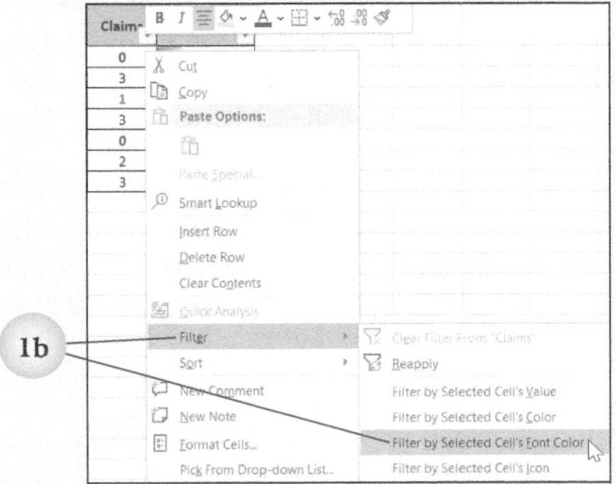

2. Print the filtered worksheet.
3. Save and then close **1-ACInsce-1Auto**.

Activity 5d Sorting by Cell Color

Part 4 of 4

1. Open **1-VRPay-Oct23**.
2. Save the workbook with the name **1-VRPay-Oct23-Sorted**.
3. Sort the payroll worksheet by cell color by completing the following steps:
   a. Select the range A5:M23, click the Sort & Filter button, and then click *Filter* at the drop-down list.
   b. Deselect the range.
   c. Click the filter arrow next to *Gross Pay* in cell M5.
   d. Point to *Sort by Color* and then click the pink fill color box in the *Sort by Cell Color* section.
4. Print the sorted worksheet.
5. Save and then close **1-VRPay-Oct23-Sorted**.

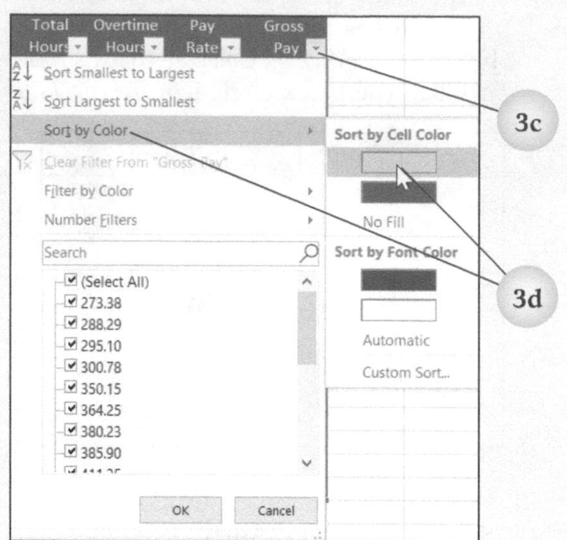

Activity 6 Apply an Advanced Filter to Create a Client List

2 Parts

You will use an advanced filter to create a list of clients of an insurance company who have a good rating with no claims and filter the same list using And and Or logical operators.

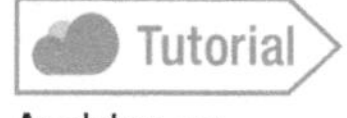

Applying an Advanced Filter

Applying an Advanced Filter

Use an advanced filter when a range needs to be filtered on complex criteria. An advanced filter allows the data to be filtered using the And or Or logical operator on more than one field. The list can either be filtered in place or copied to a new location.

To filter a range using an advanced filter, insert five or six rows at the top of the worksheet and then copy the column header row to the new row 1. If your worksheet has a title, insert the rows and the column header row under the title. Enough rows are needed at the top of the worksheet to enter all the required criteria and allow at least one blank row between the criteria range and the data to be filtered. Enter the filter criteria under the appropriate column headers. Click the Data tab and then click the Advanced button in the Sort & Filter group to display the Advanced Filter dialog box. Use options at the dialog box to indicate the filter criteria, as shown in Figure 1.9, and then click OK.

When using the And operator, enter criteria on the same row, and when using the Or operator, enter the criteria in separate rows.

Quick Steps

Apply Advanced Filter in Place

1. Select rows 1 through 5.
2. Right-click and then click *Insert.*
3. Select column header row.
4. Press Ctrl + C.
5. Click in cell A1.
6. Press Ctrl + V.
7. Enter filter criteria under appropriate column headers.
8. Click Data tab.
9. Click Advanced button.
10. Type range to be filtered.
11. Press Tab key.
12. Type range that contains criteria.
13. Click OK.

If you need to filter a range using a criterion that falls between two values in the same field, copy the field name and place it in the first empty cell in the row of the copied column header row. The worksheet in Figure 1.10 has been filtered to show the policies that have at least one claim and a premium between $3,000 and $4,000.

Figure 1.9 Advanced Filter Dialog Box

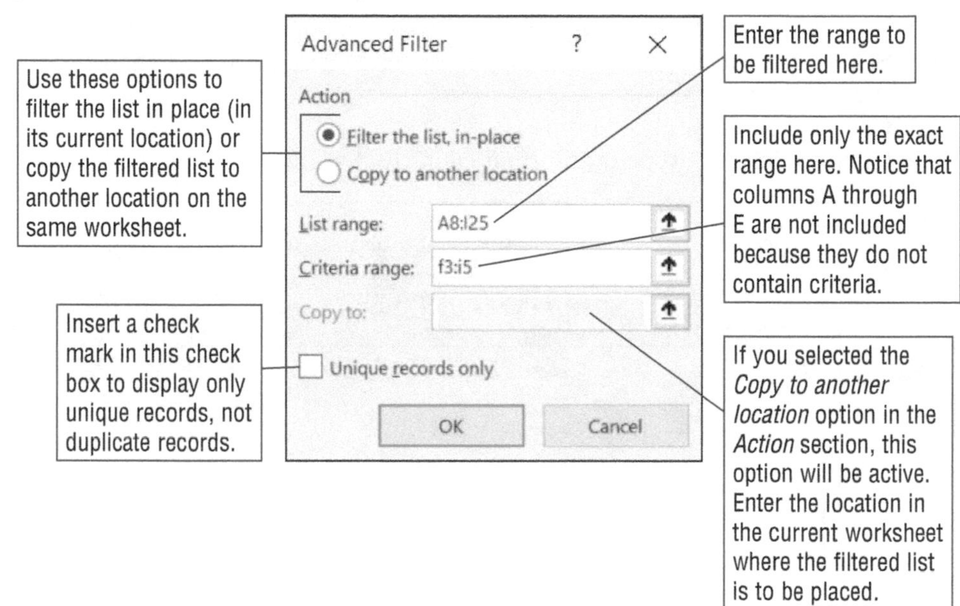
Advanced Filter
?
Action
Filter the list, in-place
Copy to another location
List range:
A8:I25
Criteria range:
f3:i5
Copy to:
Unique records only
OK
Cancel
Use these options to filter the list in place (in its current location) or copy the filtered list to another location on the same worksheet.
Insert a check mark in this check box to display only unique records, not duplicate records.
Enter the range to be filtered here.
Include only the exact range here. Notice that columns A through E are not included because they do not contain criteria.
If you selected the *Copy to another location* option in the *Action* section, this option will be active. Enter the location in the current worksheet where the filtered list is to be placed.

Figure 1.10 Between Filter Applied Using the Advanced Filter Feature

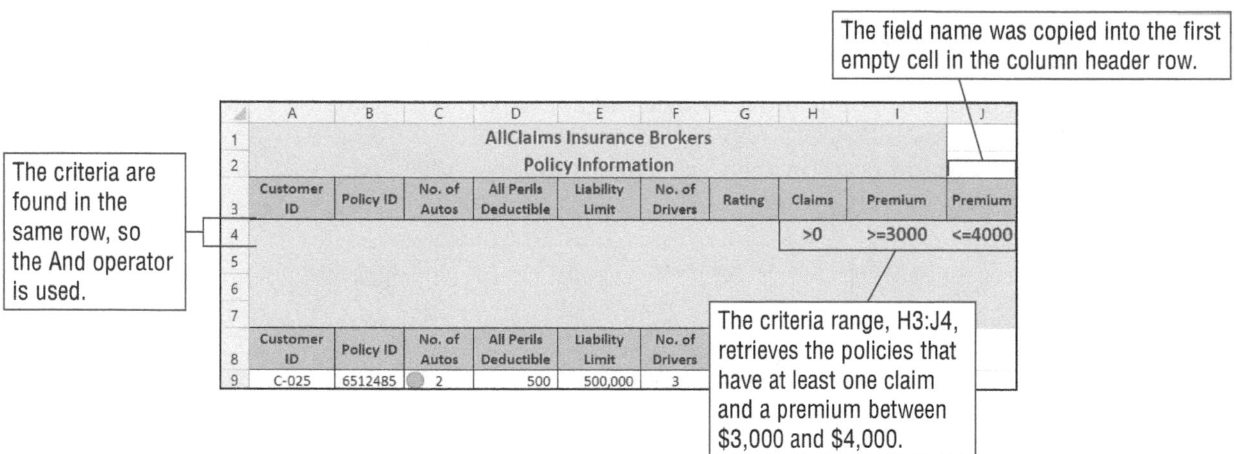
The field name was copied into the first empty cell in the column header row.
AllClaims Insurance Brokers
Policy Information
Customer ID
Policy ID
No. of Autos
All Perils Deductible
Liability Limit
No. of Drivers
Rating
Claims
Premium
Premium
>0
>=3000
<=4000
C-025
6512485
2
500
500,000
3
The criteria are found in the same row, so the And operator is used.
The criteria range, H3:J4, retrieves the policies that have at least one claim and a premium between $3,000 and $4,000.

Activity 6a Applying an Advanced Filter in Another Location

Part 1 of 2

1. Open **1-ACInsce**.
2. Save the workbook with the name **1-ACInsce-AF**.
3. Filter the range and copy the results to a new location for those clients with a rating of 1 who have zero claims by completing the following steps:
   a. Select rows 3 through 7.
   b. Right-click in the selected range and then click the *Insert* option.
   c. Select the range A8:I8, press Ctrl + C, click in cell A3, and then press Ctrl + V. Press the Esc key.
   d. Click in cell G4 and then type 1.
   e. Click in cell H4, type 0 and then click the Enter button on the Formula bar.

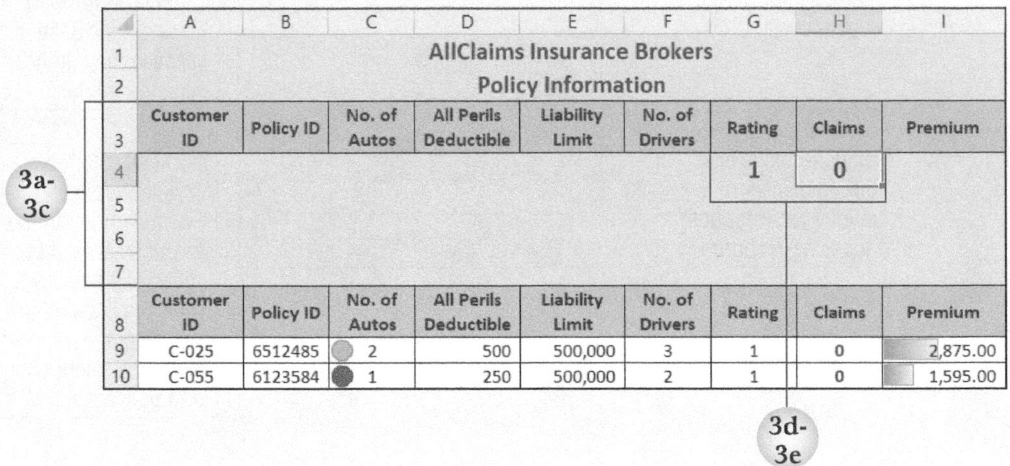

   f. Click the Data tab and then click the Advanced button in the Sort & Filter group.
   g. If a Microsoft Excel message box displays, click OK.
   h. Click the *Copy to another location* radio button.
   i. Select the text in the *List range* text box, type a8:i25 and then press the Tab key.
   j. With the insertion point in the *Criteria range* text box, type g3:h4 and then press the Tab key.
   k. With the insertion point in the *Copy to* text box, type a30.
   l. Click OK.

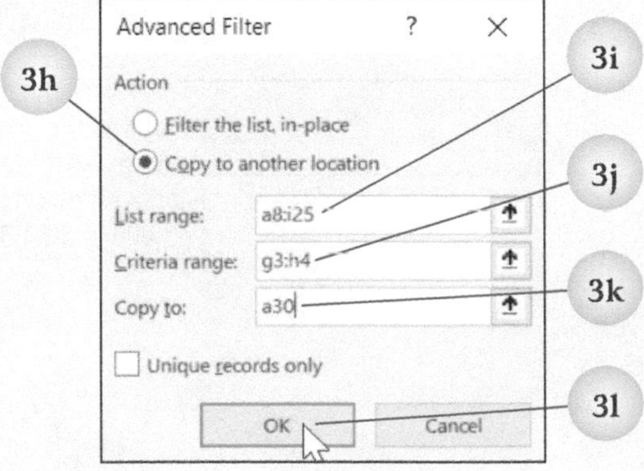

4. Save **1-ACInsce-AF**.

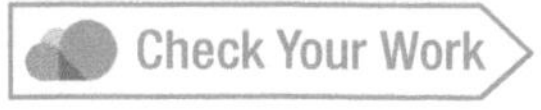

Activity 6b Apply an Advanced Filter in Place

1. With **1-ACInsce-AF** open, filter the range in its current location to show the records for policies that have a rating higher than two and more than one claim or that have a premium greater than 3,500 by completing the following steps:
   a. Delete the contents of cell G4 and H4.
   b. Click in cell G4 and then type >2.
   c. Click in cell H4 and then type >1.
   d. Click in cell I5 and type >3500, and then press the Enter key.

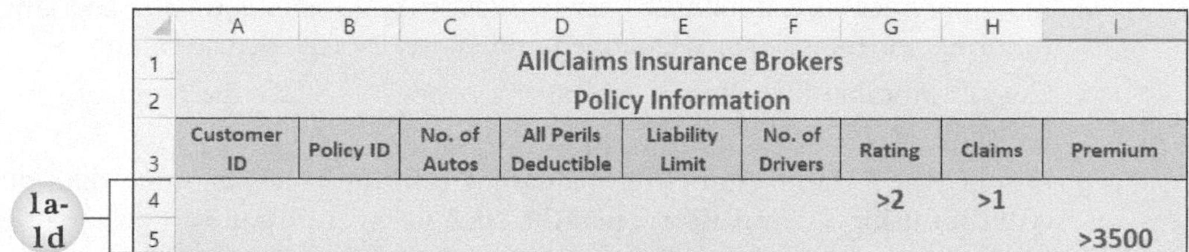

	A	B	C	D	E	F	G	H	I
1	AllClaims Insurance Brokers								
2	Policy Information								
3	Customer ID	Policy ID	No. of Autos	All Perils Deductible	Liability Limit	No. of Drivers	Rating	Claims	Premium
4							>2	>1	
5									>3500

   e. Click the Advanced button in the Sort & Filter group.
   f. Verify that the *Filter the list, in-place* radio button contains a bullet.
   g. Verify that the text in the *List range* text box is *$A$8:$I$25* and then press the Tab key.
   h. With the text selected in the *Criteria range* text box, type f3:i5.
   i. Click OK.
2. Save, print, and then close **1-ACInsce-AF**.

Chapter Summary

- Conditional formatting applies special formatting to cells based on a condition; cells that meet the condition have the formatting applied, and cells that do not meet the condition remain unformatted.
- Conditional formats can be based on values, dates, text entries, or duplicated values.
- Use the *Top/Bottom Rules* option at the Conditional Formatting button drop-down list to conditionally format based on the top 10 or bottom 10 value or percent or by above average or below average values.
- Use the *Highlight Cells Rules* option at the Conditional Formatting button drop-down list to conditionally format based on a value comparison.
- Conditional formats are based on rules that define criteria by which cells are selected for formatting and include the formatting attributes that are applied to cells that meet the criteria.
- Create a new conditional formatting rule by selecting *New Rule* at the Conditional Formatting button drop-down list.
- Edit or delete a rule at the Conditional Formatting Rules Manager dialog box.
- Apply conditional formatting using data bars, color scales, or icon sets to add small bar charts, gradations of color, or icons, respectively, to cells to make it easier to identify certain data.
- Apply conditional formatting using a formula to apply formatting to a cell based on the value in another cell or using some logical test. Excel treats any formula entered for conditional formatting as an array formula, which means one rule needs to be added for a selected range.

- An IF statement can be used to conditionally format those cells for which the conditional test returns a true result.
- Use the Quick Analysis button to quickly apply preset conditional formatting.
- Fraction formatting converts decimal values to fractions. To choose the type of fraction to create, open the Format Cells dialog box with the Number tab selected and the *Fraction* category active.
- Scientific formatting displays numbers in exponential notation, in which part of the number is replaced with $E+n$, where E stands for "exponent" and n represents the power.
- Excel provides special number formats that are specific to countries and languages to format entries such as telephone numbers and social security numbers.
- Custom number formats use formatting codes to specify the types of formatting to apply.
- Display the Custom AutoFilter dialog box to filter values by more than one criterion using a comparison operator, such as greater than (>) or equal to (=).
- A worksheet with cells that have been formatted manually or by conditional formatting can be filtered by color or icon.
- To remove a filter, click anywhere in the filtered list, click the Sort & Filter button in the Editing group on the Home tab, and then click *Clear* at the drop-down list.
- To specify the order of the sorted colors, define a custom sort if the worksheet contains more than one cell color, font color, or cell icon.
- Apply an advanced filter when a range needs to be filter on complex criteria. An advanced filter allows filtering the data using the And or Or logical operator on more than one field. The criteria in an advanced filter are entered directly in the worksheet and establish the criteria range.

Commands Review

FEATURE	RIBBON TAB, GROUP	BUTTON	KEYBOARD SHORTCUT
apply advanced filter	Data, Sort & Filter		
clear all filters	Home, Editing OR Data, Sort & Filter		
conditional formatting	Home, Styles OR Quick Analysis		Ctrl + Q
custom AutoFilter	Home, Editing		Ctrl + Shift + L
custom number format	Home, Number		Ctrl + 1
fraction formatting	Home, Number		Ctrl + 1
scientific formatting	Home, Number		Ctrl + 1
special number formatting	Home, Number		Ctrl + 1

Microsoft®

Excel®

Advanced Functions and Formulas

CHAPTER 2

Performance Objectives

Upon successful completion of Chapter 2, you will be able to:

1. Create and manage names for ranges of cells
2. Write formulas with the COUNTBLANK, COUNTIF, and COUNTIFS statistical functions
3. Write formulas with the AVERAGEIF and AVERAGEIFS statistical functions
4. Write formulas with the SUMIF and SUMIFS math and trigonometry functions
5. Write formulas with the VLOOKUP and HLOOKUP lookup functions
6. Write formulas with the PPMT financial function
7. Write formulas with the nested IF, AND, and OR logical functions and the IFS logical function
8. Write formulas with the ROUND math and trigonometry function
9. Expand the Formula bar to view longer formulas

To help make complex calculations easier to perform, Excel provides numerous preset formulas called *functions*. These are grouped into thirteen different categories to facilitate calculations in worksheets containing financial, logical, mathematical, statistical, or other types of data. The Insert function dialog box provides options for locating and building formulas with various functions. The structure of a function formula includes an equals sign (=) followed by the name of the function and then the function argument. *Argument* is the term given to the values to be included in the calculation. The structure of the argument is dependent on the type of function being used and can include references to values in a single cell, a range, multiple ranges, or any combination of these.

Before beginning chapter work, copy the EL2C2 folder to your storage medium and then make EL2C2 the active folder.

The online course includes additional training and assessment resources.

Activity 1 Calculate Statistics and Sums Using Conditional Formulas for an Insurance Claims Worksheet — 6 Parts

You will manage range names in an insurance claims worksheet and use the range names in statistical formulas that count, average, and sum based on single and multiple criteria.

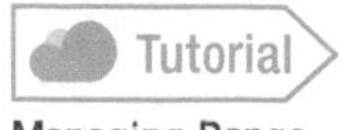

Managing Range Names

Review: Naming and Using a Range

Name Manager

Quick Steps

Modify Range Name and Reference

1. Click Formulas tab.
2. Click Name Manager button.
3. Click range name.
4. Click Edit button.
5. Type new range name in *Name* text box.
6. Type new range address at *Refers to* text box.
7. Click OK.
8. Click Close.

Hint The Formulas tab contains a Create from Selection button in the Defined Names group that can be used to automatically create range names for a list or table. Select the list or table and click the button. Excel uses the names in the top row or left-most column as the range names.

Managing Range Names

Recall that a range name is a name assigned to a cell or range of cells. Range names provide the option of referencing a source using a descriptive label, rather than the cell address or range address, when creating a formula, printing a worksheet, or navigating in a worksheet. Creating range names makes the task of managing complex formulas easier and helps others who may work in or edit a worksheet to understand the purpose of a formula more quickly.

By default, a range name is an absolute reference to a cell or range of cells. This means that if the formula is copied or moved to a different location, the references will not change. Later in this chapter, when creating a lookup formula, take advantage of the absolute referencing of a range name when including a group of cells in the formula that stay fixed when the formula is copied. A range name also includes the worksheet reference by default; therefore, typing the range name in the formula automatically references the correct worksheet. For example, assume that cell A3 in Sheet 2 has been named *ProductA* and cell A3 in Sheet 3 has been named *ProductB*. To add the two values, type the formula =*ProductA*+*ProductB* in the formula cell. Notice that the worksheet references do not need to be included.

The Name Manager dialog box, shown in Figure 2.1, is opened by clicking the Name Manager button in the Defined Names group on the Formulas tab or by using the keyboard shortcut Ctrl + F3. The Name Manager dialog box can be used to create, edit, and delete range names. A range name can be edited by changing the name or modifying the range address associated with it. A range name can also be deleted, but extra caution should be used when doing so. Cells that include a deleted range name in the formula will display the error text *#NAME?* Also use the Name Manager dialog box to add new range names to a worksheet.

Figure 2.1 Name Manager Dialog Box

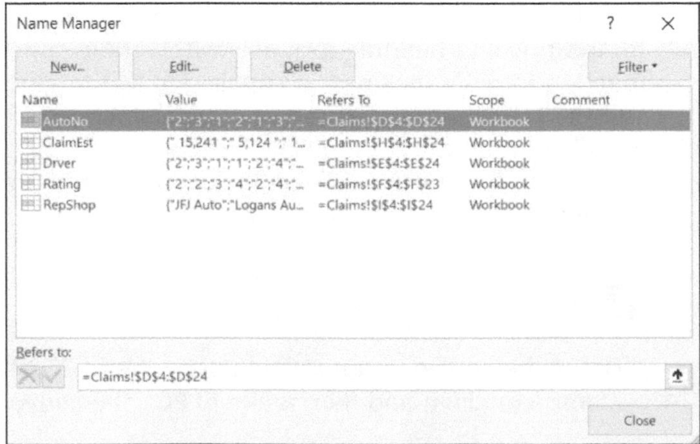

Activity 1a Modifying and Deleting Range Names

1. Open **ACOctVehRpt**.
2. Save the workbook with the name **2-ACOctVehRpt**.
3. Named ranges have been created for the auto number, driver number, rating, claim estimate, and repair shop data. Modify the range name *Drver* by completing the following steps:
   a. Click the Formulas tab.
   b. Click the Name Manager button in the Defined Names group.
   c. Click *Drver* in the *Name* column and then click the Edit button.
   d. At the Edit Name dialog box with *Drver* selected in the *Name* text box, type DriverNo and then click OK.

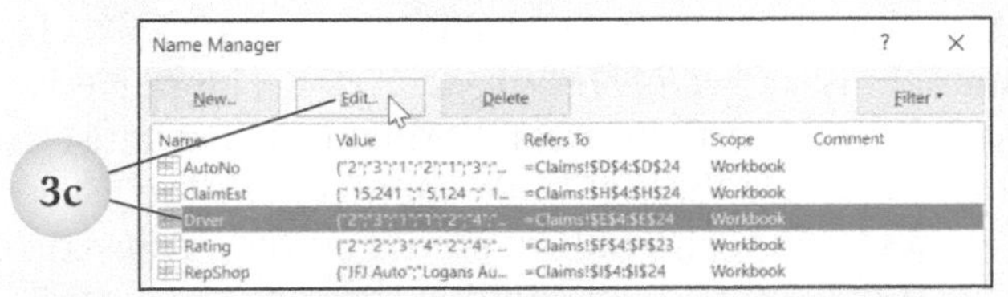

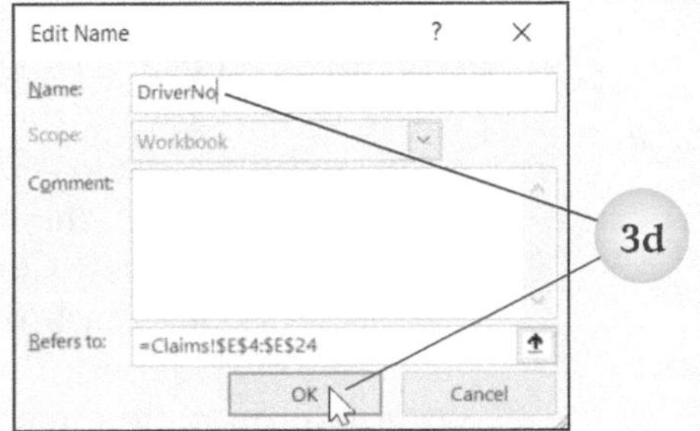

4. Modify the references in the range named *Rating* to include cell F24 by completing following steps:
   a. Click *Rating* at the Name Manager dialog box and then click the Edit button.
   b. At the Edit Name dialog box, click right of the text in the *Refers to* text box (which displays *Claims!$F$4:$F:$23*), press the Backspace key, type 4, and then click OK.

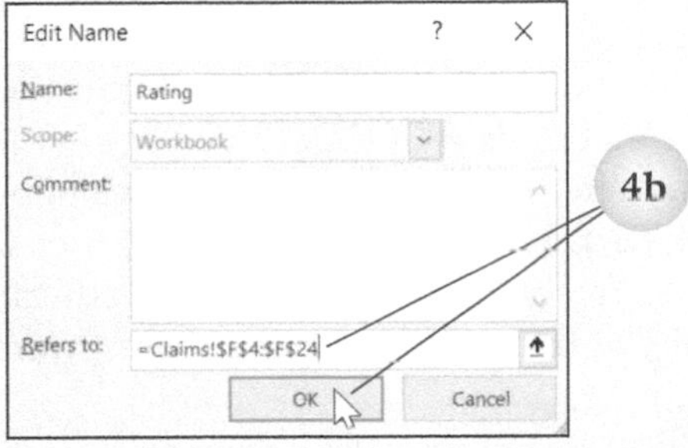

5. Delete the range name *AutoNo* by completing the following steps:
   a. Click *AutoNo* at the Name Manager dialog box and then click the Delete button.
   b. Click OK.
6. Click the Close button.
7. Save **2-ACOctVehRpt**.

Review: Using Statistical Functions

Using Statistical Functions

Commonly used statistical functions include AVERAGE, MAX, and MIN. AVERAGE returns the arithmetic mean, MAX returns the largest value, and MIN returns the smallest value in the range. Other common functions, COUNT and COUNTA, return the number of cells based on what is contained in the cells. COUNT is used when the cells contain numbers or dates and COUNTA is used when the cells contain text or a combination of text and numbers. Excel provides additional AVERAGE and COUNT functions, such as the COUNTBLANK function to find counts or averages for a range based on a criterion. The COUNTBLANK function counts the number of empty cells in range.

Open the Insert Function Dialog box by clicking the Insert Function button in the Formula bar or in the Insert Function group on the Formulas tab or by using the shortcut combination of Shift + F3. At the Insert Function dialog box, change the *Or select a category* option to *Statistical* and then scroll down the list of available functions or click the More Functions button in the Function Library group on the Formulas tab, click the *Statistical* option, and then scroll down the list of available functions.

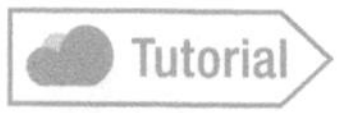

Using Statistical Functions: COUNTIF and COUNTIFS

Quick Steps

Create COUNTIF Formula

1. Make cell active.
2. Click Insert Function button.
3. Change category to *Statistical*.
4. Select *COUNTIF*.
5. Click OK.
6. Enter range or range name in *Range* text box.
7. Enter condition expression or text in *Criteria* text box.
8. Click OK.

Create COUNTIFS Formula

1. Make cell active.
2. Click Insert Function button.
3. Change category to *Statistical*.
4. Select *COUNTIFS*.
5. Click OK.
6. Enter range or range name in *Criteria_range1* text box.
7. Enter condition expression or text in *Criteria1* text box.
8. Enter range or range name in *Criteria_range2* text box.
9. Enter condition expression or text in *Criteria2* text box.
10. Continue adding criteria range expressions and criteria as needed.
11. Click OK.

Using Statistical Functions: COUNTIF and COUNTIFS

Use the COUNTIF function to count cells within a range that meet a single criterion or condition. For example, in a grades worksheet, use a COUNTIF function to count the number of students who achieved greater than 75%. The structure of a COUNTIF function is *=COUNTIF(range,criteria)*. The range is where to look for the data. The criteria defines a conditional test that must be passed (what to look for) in order for the cell to be counted. For the grades worksheet example, the formula to count the cells of students who achieved greater than 75% is *=COUNTIF(grades,">75")*, assuming the range name *grades* has been defined. Each time Excel finds a grade greater than 75, the count increases by 1. Notice that the syntax of the argument requires enclosing the criteria in quotation marks. If the Insert Function dialog box is used to create a formula, Excel adds the required syntax automatically. A cell reference may also be used as the criterion. A cell reference is not enclosed in quotation marks and should only contain the exact criterion.

The COUNTIFS function is used to count cells when more than one condition must be met. The formula uses the same structure as COUNTIF but includes additional ranges and criteria within the argument. The structure of a COUNTIFS function is *=COUNTIFS(range1,criteria1,range2,criteria2,. . .)*. For every range (where to look), there is a corresponding criteria or conditional test (what to look for). If all the conditions are met for each range, then the count increases by 1. Figure 2.2 shows a nursing education worksheet with a single-criterion COUNTIF to count the number of nurses (RNs) and a multiple-criteria

Figure 2.2 COUNTIF and COUNTIFS Formulas

	A	B	C	D	E	F	G	H	I	J	K
1	Department of Human Resources										
2	Full-Time Nursing Education Worksheet										
3	Employee Number	Employee Last Name	Employee First Name	Title	Unit	Extension	Years Experience	PD Current?		Nursing Educational Statistical Summary	
4	FT02001	Santos	Susan	RN	Med/Surg	36415	30	Yes		Number of RNs	16
5	FT02002	Daniels	Jasmine	RN	Med/Surg	36415	27	No		Number of LPNs	12
6	FT02003	Walden	Virgina	RN	ICU	34211	22	No			
7	FT02004	Jaffe	Paul	LPN	CSRU	36418	24	Yes		RNs who are current with PD	9
8	FT02005	Salvatore	Terry	LPN	ICU	34211	22	Yes		LPNs who are current with PD	7
9	FT02006	Mander	Kaitlynn	RN	ICU	34211	24	Yes			
10	FT02007	Friesen	Jessica	LPN	ICU	34211	20				
11	FT02008	Lavigne	Gisele	RN	CSRU	36418	20				
12	FT02009	Gauthier	Jacqueline	RN	PreOp	32881	19				
13	FT02010	Williamson	Forman	RN	CSRU	36418	19	Yes			
14	FT02011	Orlowski	William	RN	Ortho	31198	22	No			
15	FT02012	Kadri	Ahmed	LPN	Ortho	31198	21	No			
16	FT02013	El-Hamid	Lianna	LPN	Med/Surg	36415	20	No			
17	FT02014	Vezina	Ursula	LPN	Ortho	31198	20	No			
18	FT02015	Adams	Sheila	LPN	Med/Surg	36415					
19	FT02016	Jorgensen	Macy	RN	Med/Surg	36415					
20	FT02017	Pieterson	Eric	RN	ICU	34211					
21	FT02018	Keller	Douglas	RN	ICU	34211	10	No			
22	FT02019	Costa	Michael	RN	Ortho	31198	10	No			
23	FT02020	Li-Kee	Su-Lynn	LPN	PreOp	32881	8	No			
24	FT02021	Besterd	Mary	RN	PreOp	32881	7	Yes			

formula
=COUNTIF(Title,"RN")

formula
=COUNTIFS(Title,"RN",PDCurrent,"Yes")

COUNTIFS to count the number of RNs who are current with their professional development (PD) activities. The formulas shown in Figure 2.2 (on page 34) include range names for which *Title* references the entries in column D and *PDCurrent* references the entries in column H. The ranges do not have to be adjacent but they must have the same number of rows and columns.

Activity 1b Creating COUNTBLANK and COUNTIF Formulas

Part 2 of 6

1. With **2-ACOctVehRpt** open, make cell I25 active.
2. Create a COUNTBLANK function to count any cells in which repair shop information has not been entered by completing the following steps:
   a. Click the Insert Function button in the Formula bar.
   b. At the Insert Function dialog box, click the *Or select a category* option box arrow and then click *Statistical* at the drop-down list. ***Note: Skip this step if Statistical is already selected as the category.***
   c. Scroll down the Select a function list box and then click *COUNTBLANK*.
   d. Read the formula description below the function list box and then click OK.
   e. At the Function Arguments dialog box with the insertion point positioned in the *Range* text box type repshop. Recall from Activity 1a that a range name exists for the entries in column I. ***Note: If the dialog box is obscuring the view of the worksheet, drag the Function Arguments dialog box title bar left or right.***
   f. Click OK. Excel returns the value 0 in cell I25 as all the repair shop information has been entered.
3. Click in cell L4.
4. Create a COUNTIF function to count the number of auto insurance claims for which Dunbar Auto is the repair shop by completing the following steps:
   a. Click the Insert Function button in the Formula bar.
   b. With *Statistical* selected in the *Or select a category* option box, scroll down the *Select a function* list box and then click *COUNTIF*.
   c. Read the formula description below the function list box and then click OK.

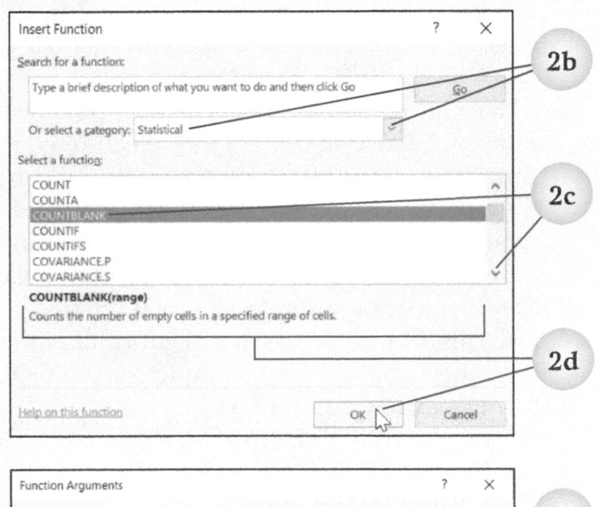

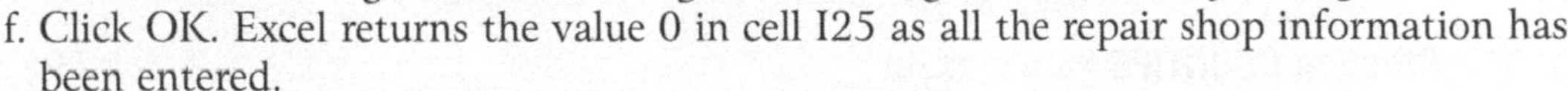

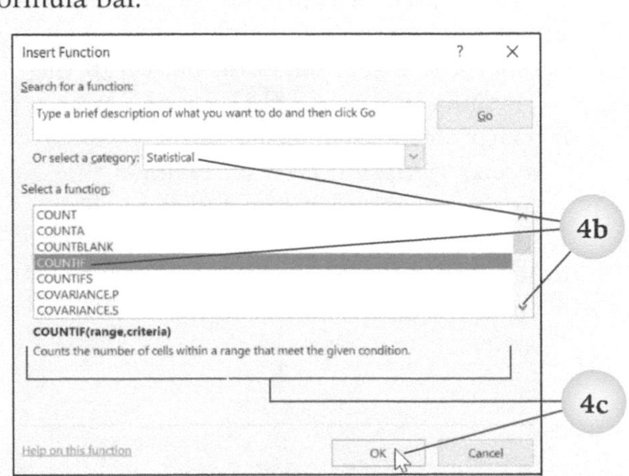

d. At the Function Arguments dialog box with the insertion point positioned in the *Range* text box, type repshop and then press the Tab key.

e. With the insertion point positioned in the *Criteria* text box, type Dunbar Auto and then press the Tab key. When the Tab key is pressed, Excel adds quotation marks around the criteria text.

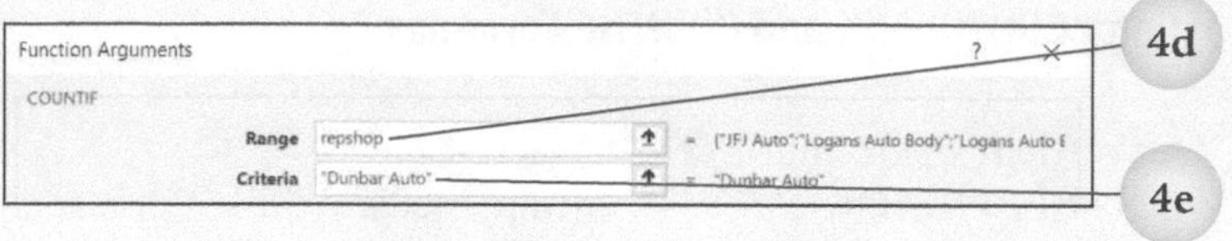

f. Click OK. Excel returns the value *3* in cell L4.

g. Look at the formula in the Formula bar created by the Function Arguments dialog box: *=COUNTIF(RepShop,"Dunbar Auto")*.

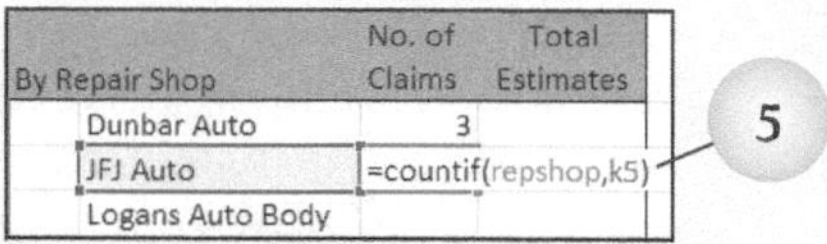

5. Make cell L5 active. The repair shop names are in the range K4:K7. Use cell K5 as the cell reference for JFJ Auto by typing the formula =countif(repshop,k5) and then press the Enter key. (When entering a formula, type the cell references and range names in lowercase letters. Excel will automatically display uppercase letters once the formula has been entered.)

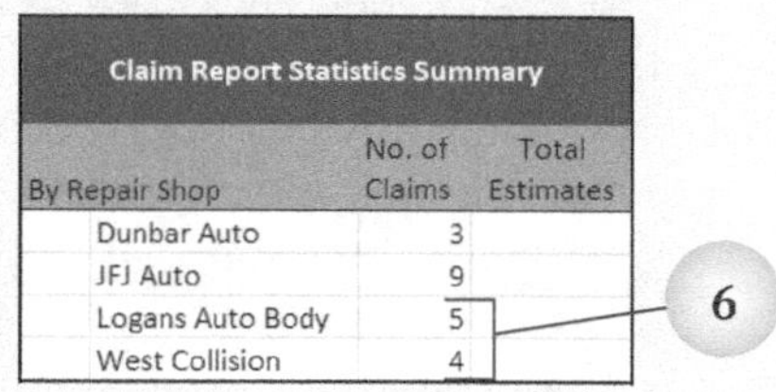

Claim Report Statistics Summary		
By Repair Shop	No. of Claims	Total Estimates
Dunbar Auto	3	
JFJ Auto	9	
Logans Auto Body	5	
West Collision	4	

6. Use the fill handle to copy the formula in cell L5 to the range L6:L7. When completed, the COUNTIF formulas will be as follows:
   L6: *=COUNTIF(RepShop,K6)*
   L7: *=COUNTIF(RepShop,K7)*
7. Save **2-ACOctVehRpt**.

Activity 1c Creating COUNTIFS Formulas

Part 3 of 6

1. With **2-ACOctVehRpt** open, make cell L10 active.
2. Create a COUNTIFS function to count the number of auto insurance claims for which the repair shop is JFJ Auto and the claims estimate is greater than $5,000 by completing the following steps:
   a. Click the Insert Function button in the Formula bar.
   b. With *Statistical* selected in the *Or select a category* option box, scroll down the *Select a function* list box and then click *COUNTIFS*.
   c. Read the formula description below the function list box and then click OK.

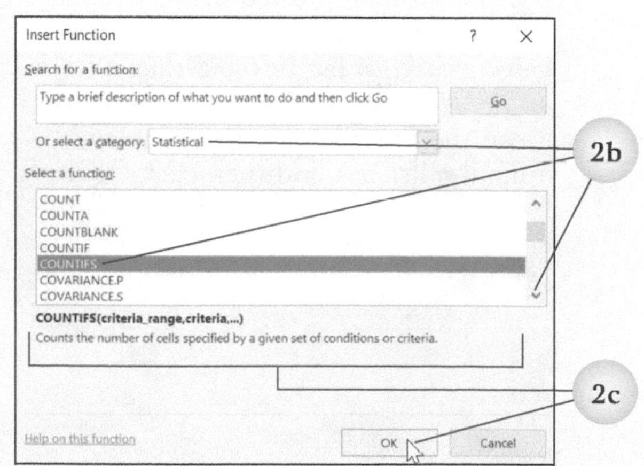

d. At the Function Arguments dialog box with the insertion point positioned in the *Criteria_range1* text box, type repshop and then press the Tab key. After the Tab key is pressed, a *Criteria_range2* text box is added to the dialog box.
e. With the insertion point positioned in the *Criteria1* text box, type k10 as the cell reference for JFJ Auto and then press the Tab key. After the Tab key is pressed, a *Criteria2* text box is added to the dialog box.
f. With the insertion point positioned in the *Criteria_range2* text box, type claimest and then press the Tab key. After the Tab key is pressed, a *Criteria_range3* text box is added to the dialog box.
g. With the insertion point positioned in the *Criteria2* text box, type >5000 and then press the Tab key. When the Tab key is pressed, Excel adds quotation marks around the criteria text.
h. Click OK. Excel returns the value *5* in cell L10.

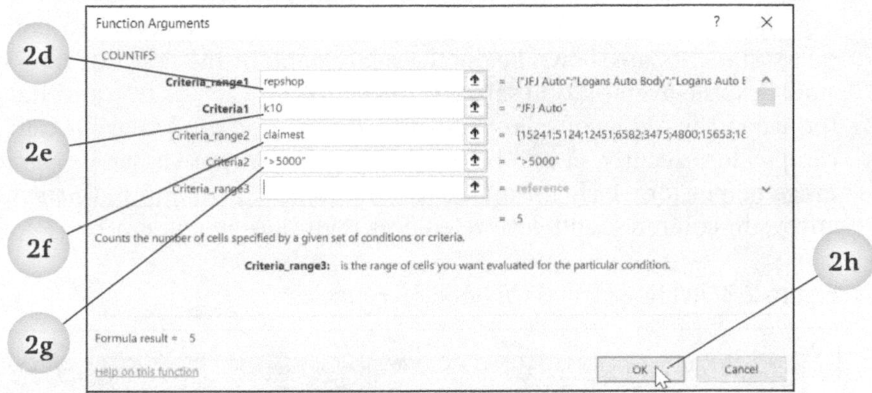

3. Look at the formula in the Formula bar created by the Function Arguments dialog box: *=COUNTIFS(RepShop,K10,ClaimEst,">5000")*.
4. In cell L13, enter a COUNTIFS formula to count the number of claims for which the repair shop is JFJ Auto and the rating is greater than 3 by using the Insert Function dialog box or by typing the following formula into the cell: =countifs(repshop,k13,rating,">3").

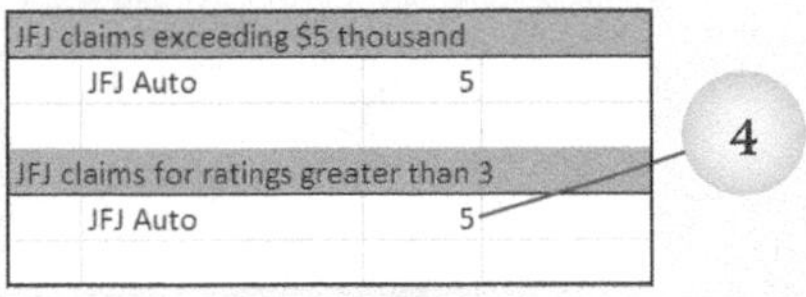

JFJ claims exceeding $5 thousand
JFJ Auto 5
JFJ claims for ratings greater than 3
JFJ Auto 5
4

5. Save **2-ACOctVehRpt**.

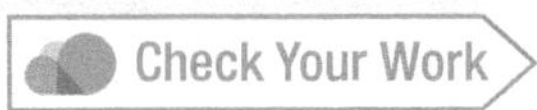

Using Statistical Functions: AVERAGEIF and AVERAGEIFS

Using Statistical Functions: AVERAGEIF and AVERAGEIFS

The AVERAGEIF function is used to find the arithmetic mean of the cells within a specified range that meet a single criterion or condition. The structure of an AVERAGEIF function is *=AVERAGEIF(range,criteria,average_range)*. *Range* is the cells to be tested for the criterion or where to look for the data. *Criteria* is the conditional test that must be passed (what to look for). *Average_range* is the range containing the values to average. If *average_range* is omitted, the cells in the *range* are used to calculate the average. The AVERAGEIFS function is used to average cells that meet multiple criteria using the formula *=AVERAGEIFS(average_range,criteria_range1,criteria1,criteria_range2,criteria2,. . .)*. Notice that the *average_range* (what to actually average) is at the beginning of the formula. It is followed by pairs of ranges (where to look for the specific condition) and criteria (the conditions that must be met).

Figure 2.3 shows an executive management salary report for a hospital. Average salary statistics are shown below the salary data. In the first two rows of salary statistics, the average total salary is calculated for each of two hospital campuses. In the second two rows of salary statistics, the average total salary is calculated for each campus for executives hired before 2018. The formulas shown in Figure 2.3 include range names for which *Year* references the values in column E, *Campus* references the entries in column F, and *Total* references the values in column I.

Quick Steps

Create AVERAGEIF Formula

1. Make cell active.
2. Click Insert Function button.
3. Change category to *Statistical*.
4. Select *AVERAGEIF*.
5. Click OK.
6. Enter range or range name in *Range* text box.
7. Enter condition expression or text in *Criteria* text box.
8. Enter range or range name to average in *Average_range* text box.
9. Click OK.

Create AVERAGEIFS Formula

1. Make cell active.
2. Click Insert Function button.
3. Change category to *Statistical*.
4. Select *AVERAGEIFS*.
5. Click OK.
6. Enter range or range name to average in *Average_range* text box.
7. Enter range or range name in *Criteria_range1* text box.
8. Enter condition expression or text in *Criteria1* text box.
9. Enter range or range name in *Criteria_range2* text box.
10. Enter condition expression or text in *Criteria2* text box.
11. Continue adding criteria range expressions and criteria as needed.
12. Click OK.

Figure 2.3 AVERAGEIF and AVERAGEIFS Formulas

	A	B	C	D	E	F	G	H	I
1				Columbia River General Hospital					
2				Executive Management Salary Report					
3				For the fiscal year 2021-2022					
4				Job Title	Year Hired	Campus	Salary	Benefits	Total
5	Ms.	Michelle	Tan	Chief Executive Officer	2001	Sunnyside	$ 231,750	$ 25,894	$ 257,644
6	Mr.	Douglas	Brown	Legal Counsel	2013	Sunnyside	137,975	23,595	161,570
7	Mrs.	Lauren	Quandt	Chief Financial Officer	2016	Portland	164,898	23,474	188,372
8	Dr.	Dana	Pembroke	Medical Director	2018	Portland	167,015	18,937	185,952
9	Mrs.	Gina	Wright	Director of Nursing	2010	Portland	137,945	18,937	156,881
10	Mr.	Fernando	Ortiega	Director of Patient Care Services	2011	Sunnyside	133,598	16,547	150,144
11	Mr.	Joshua	Vitello	Director of Facilities	2020	Sunnyside	130,270	12,828	143,098
12	Miss	Carin	Ledicke	Director of Human Resources	2006	Portland	130,270	12,828	143,098
13	Mr.	William	Formet	Director of Planning	2019	Portland	130,270	12,828	143,098
14	Mr.	Paul	Unraue	Director, Community Relations	1999	Sunnyside	120,270	11,070	131,340
15									
16							$ 1,484,260	$ 176,936	$ 1,661,196
17									
18				Salary Statistics					
19				Average executive total salary at Portland campus			$ 163,480		
20				Average executive total salary at Sunnyside campus			$ 168,759		
21									
22				Average executive total salary at Portland campus hired before 2018			$ 162,784		
23				Average executive total salary at Sunnyside campus hired before 2018			$ 175,175		

formula
=AVERAGEIFS(Total,Campus,"Sunnyside",Year,"<2018")

formula
=AVERAGEIF(Campus,"Portland",Total)

Activity 1d Creating AVERAGEIF Formulas

1. With **2-ACOctVehRpt** open, make cell M16 active.
2. Create an AVERAGEIF function to calculate the average auto insurance claim estimate for those claims with a rating of 1 by completing the following steps:
   a. Click the Insert Function button in the Formula bar.
   b. With *Statistical* selected in the *Or select a category* option box, click *AVERAGEIF* in the *Select a function* list box.
   c. Read the formula description below the function list box and then click OK.
   d. At the Function Arguments dialog box with the insertion point positioned in the *Range* text box, type rating and then press the Tab key.
   e. With the insertion point positioned in the *Criteria* text box, type 1 and then press the Tab key.
   f. With the insertion point positioned in the *Average_range* text box, type claimest.
   g. Click OK. Excel returns the value *2691* in cell M16.

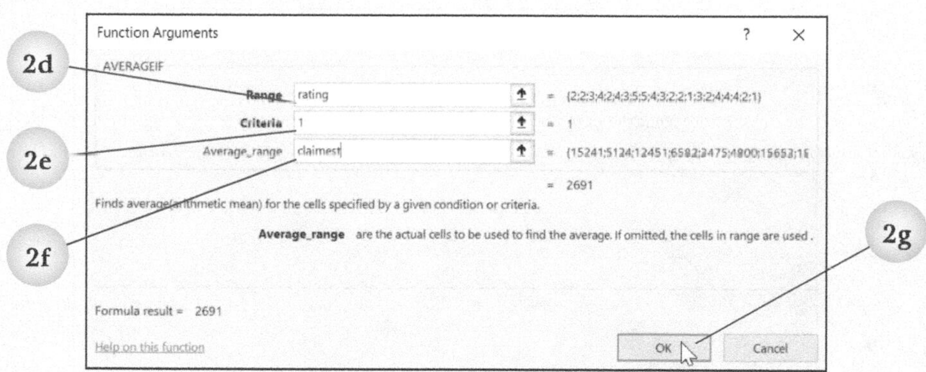

   h. Look at the formula in the Formula bar created by the Function Arguments dialog box: *=AVERAGEIF(Rating,1,ClaimEst)*.
3. Apply the Comma format with no digits after the decimal point to cell M16.
4. Make cell M17 active, type the formula =averageif(rating,k17,claimest), and then press the Enter key.
5. Apply the Comma format with no digits after the decimal point to cell M17.
6. With cell M17 active, drag the fill handle into cell M20. When completed, the AVERAGEIF formulas will be as follows:
   M18: *=AVERAGEIF(Rating,K18,ClaimEst)*
   M19: *=AVERAGEIF(Rating,K19,ClaimEst)*
   M20: *=AVERAGEIF(Rating,K20,ClaimEst)*
7. Save **2-ACOctVehRpt**.

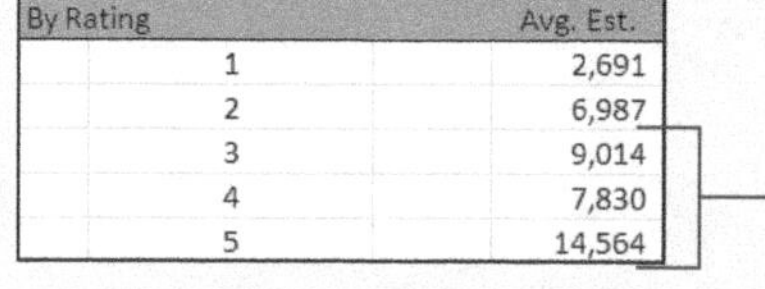

By Rating	Avg. Est.
1	2,691
2	6,987
3	9,014
4	7,830
5	14,564

Activity 1e Creating AVERAGEIFS Formulas

1. With **2-ACOctVehRpt** open, make cell M22 active.
2. Create an AVERAGEIFS function to calculate the average auto insurance claim estimate for those claims with a rating of 2 and a driver number of 1 by completing the following steps:
   a. Click the Insert Function button in the Formula bar.
   b. With *Statistical* selected in the *Or select a category* option box, click *AVERAGEIFS* in the *Select a function* list box.
   c. Read the formula description and then click OK.
   d. At the Function Arguments dialog box with the insertion point positioned in the *Average_range* text box, type claimest and then press the Tab key.
   e. Type rating in the *Criteria_range1* text box and then press the Tab key.
   f. Type 2 in the *Criteria1* text box and then press the Tab key.
   g. Type driverno in the *Criteria_range2* text box and then press the Tab key.
   h. Type 1 in the *Criteria2* text box.
   i. Click OK. Excel returns the value *6272.6667* in cell M22.

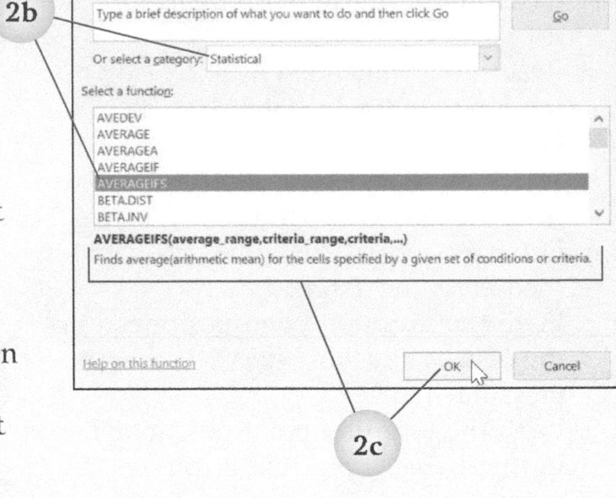

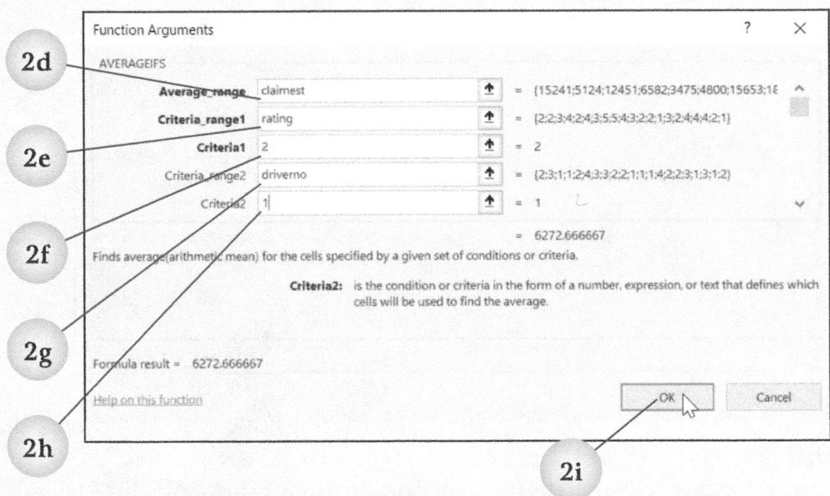

   j. Apply the Comma format with no digits after the decimal point to cell M22.
3. Copy the AVERAGEIFS formula in cell M22 and paste it into cell M23.
4. Edit the formula in cell M23 to change the rating criterion from *2* to *3*. When completed, the AVERAGEIFS formula will be *=AVERAGEIFS(ClaimEst,Rating,3,DriverNo,1)*.
5. Save **2-ACOctVehRpt.**

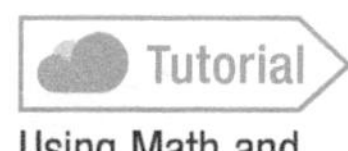

Using Math and Trigonometry Functions: SUMIF and SUMIFS

 Math & Trig

Using Math and Trigonometry Functions: SUMIF and SUMIFS

Excel provides several math and trigonometry functions, such as ABS to return the absolute value of a number, SQRT to find the square root of a number, and RAND to return a random number between 0 and 1, to name a few. At the Insert Function dialog box, change the *Or select a category* option to *Math & Trig* or click the Math & Trig button in the Function Library group and then scroll down the list of available functions.

Quick Steps

Create SUMIF Formula

1. Make cell active.
2. Click Formulas tab.
3. Click Math & Trig button.
4. Scroll down and click *SUMIF*.
5. Enter range or range name in *Range* text box.
6. Enter condition expression or text in *Criteria* text box.
7. Enter range or range name to add in *Sum_range* text box.
8. Click OK.

Within the category of math and trigonometry functions, Excel includes SUMIF to add the cells within a range that meet a single criterion or condition and SUMIFS to add the cells within a range that meet multiple criteria or conditions. The structure of the SUMIF function is *=SUMIF(range,criteria,sum_range)*, where *range* is where to look for the data, *criteria* is the conditional statement (the conditions that must be met or what to look for), and *sum_range* is the range containing the values to add. The SUMIFS function is used to add cells that meet multiple criteria using the formula *=SUMIFS(sum_range,criteria_range1,criteria1,criteria_range2,criteria2,. . .)*. Similar to the AVERAGEIFS function, the *sum_range* (what to actually sum) appears at the beginning of the formula. It is followed by pairs of ranges (where to look for the specific conditions) and criteria (the conditions that must be met).

Figure 2.4 shows how the SUMIF and SUMIFS formulas are used in the standard cost worksheet for examination room supplies at a medical clinic. Right of the clinic supplies inventory data, a SUMIF formula adds up the costs of items by supplier number. A SUMIFS formula adds up the costs by supplier number for items that require a minimum stock quantity of more than four. The formulas shown in Figure 2.4 include the range names *Supplier*, which references the entries in column C; *MinQty*, which references the values in column E; and *StdCost*, which references the values in column F.

Figure 2.4 SUMIF and SUMIFS Formulas

	A	B	C	D	E	F	G	H	I
1	North Shore Medical Clinic								
2	Clinic Supplies Inventory Units and Price								
3	Item	Unit	Supplier Number	Price	Minimum Stock Qty	Standard Cost		Exam Room Cost Analysis	
4	Sterile powder-free synthetic gloves, size Small	per 100	101	45.95	4	183.80	Cost by Supplier		
5	Sterile powder-free synthetic gloves, size Medium	per 100	101	45.95	8	367.60		Supplier Number 101	2,061.40
6	Sterile powder-free synthetic gloves, size Large	per 100	101	45.95	10	459.50		Supplier Number 155	874.33
7	Sterile powder-free latex gloves, size Small	per 100	101	26.25	4	105.00		Supplier Number 201	2,058.00
8	Sterile powder-free latex gloves, size Medium	per 100	101	26.25	8	210.00		Supplier Number 350	1,030.80
9	Sterile powder-free latex gloves, size Large	per 100	101	26.25	10	262.50			
10	Sterile powder-free vinyl gloves, size Small	per 100	101	21.50	4	86.00			
11	Sterile powder-free vinyl gloves, size Medium	per 100	101	21.50	8	172.00	Cost by Supplier with		
12	Sterile powder-free vinyl gloves, size Large	per 100	101	21.50	10	215.00	Minimum Qty over 4		
13	Disposable earloop mask	per 50	155	15.61	8	124.88		Supplier Number 101	1,686.60
14	Disposable patient gown	per dozen	155	17.90	16	286.40		Supplier Number 155	790.80
15	Disposable patient slippers	per dozen	155	14.27	16	228.32		Supplier Number 201	1,430.00
16	Cotton patient gown	per dozen	201	143.00	10	1,430.00		Supplier Number 350	859.00
17	Cotton patient robe	per dozen	201	157.00	4	628.00			
18	Disposable examination table paper	per roll	155	18.90	8	151.20			
19	Lab coat, size Small	each	350	42.95	4	171.80			
20	Lab coat, size Medium	each	350	42.95	8	343.60			
21	Lab coat, size Large	each	350	42.95	12	515.40			
22	Disposable shoe cover	per 300	155	47.75	1	47.75			
23	Disposable bouffant cap	per 100	155	17.89	2	35.78			
24	TOTAL STANDARD EXAM ROOM SUPPLIES COST:					6,024.53			

formula
=SUMIF(Supplier,"101",StdCost)

formula
=SUMIFS(StdCost,Supplier,"350",MinQty,">4")

Activity 1f **Creating SUMIF Formulas** Part 6 of 6

Note: In Step 4, check with your instructor before printing to see if two copies of the worksheets for the activities in this chapter need to be printed: one as displayed and another displaying the cell formulas. Save the worksheet before displaying formulas (Ctrl + `) so that column widths can be adjusted as necessary and then close without saving the changes.

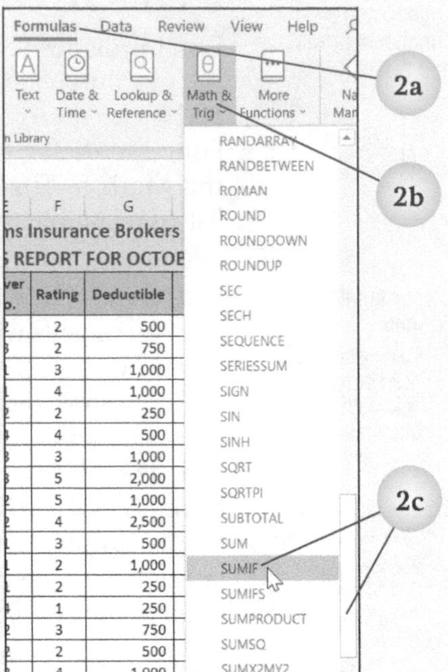

1. With **2-ACOctVehRpt** open, make cell M4 active.
2. Create a SUMIF function to add up the auto insurance claim estimates for those claims being repaired at Dunbar Auto by completing the following steps:
   a. Click the Formulas tab.
   b. Click the Math & Trig button in the Function Library group.
   c. Scroll down the drop-down list and then click *SUMIF*.
   d. At the Function Arguments dialog box with the insertion point positioned in the *Range* text box, type repshop and then press the Tab key.
   e. Designate cell K4 as the cell reference for Dunbar Auto by typing k4 in the *Criteria* text box and then press the Tab key.
   f. Type claimest in the *Sum_range* text box.
   g. Click OK. Excel returns the value *16656* in cell M4.

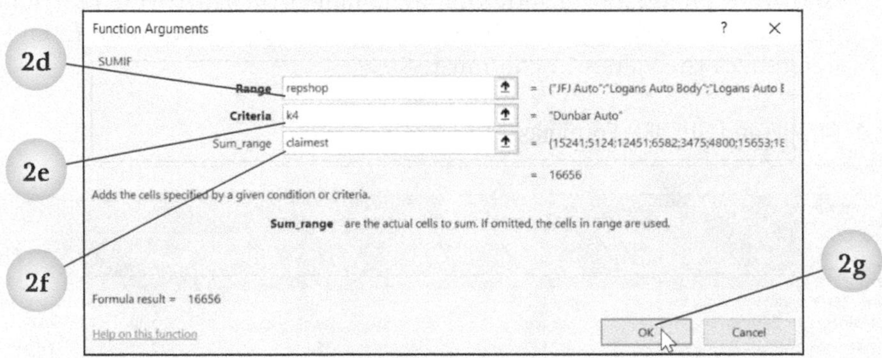

   h. Apply the Comma format with no digits after the decimal point to cell M4.
3. Use the fill handle to copy the formula in cell M4 to the range M5:M7. When completed, the SUMIF formulas will be as follows:
   M5: *=SUMIF(RepShop,K5,ClaimEst)*
   M6: *=SUMIF(RepShop,K6,ClaimEst)*
   M7: *=SUMIF(RepShop,K7,ClaimEst)*
4. Save, print, and then close **2-ACOctVehRpt**.

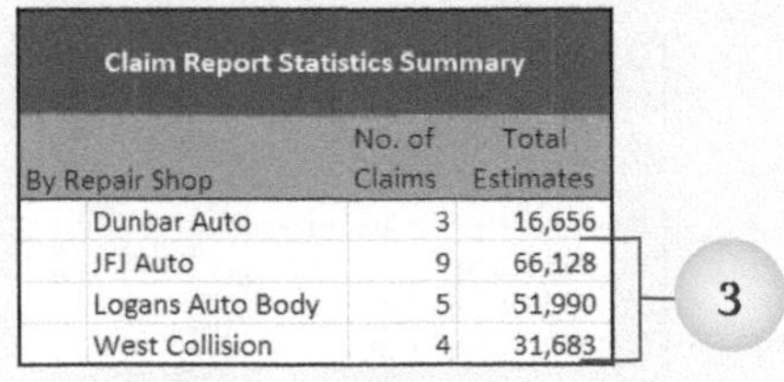

Claim Report Statistics Summary		
By Repair Shop	No. of Claims	Total Estimates
Dunbar Auto	3	16,656
JFJ Auto	9	66,128
Logans Auto Body	5	51,990
West Collision	4	31,683

Activity 2 Populate Cells by Looking Up Data in a Discount Table 1 Part

You will use a lookup formula to automatically enter discounts for containers and then calculate net prices.

Using Lookup Functions

Lookup & Reference

Using Lookup Functions

The Lookup & Reference functions provide formulas for looking up values in a range and can be found by clicking the Lookup & Reference button in the Function Library group. For example, in a grades worksheet, a letter grade can be generated by looking up the final numerical score in a range of cells that contain the letter grades with corresponding numerical scores. Being able to look up a value automates data entry in large worksheets and, when used properly, can prevent inaccuracies caused by data entry errors.

Excel provides the VLOOKUP and HLOOKUP functions, which refer to vertical and horizontal lookups, respectively. The layout of the lookup range (referred to as a *lookup table*) determines whether to use VLOOKUP or HLOOKUP. VLOOKUP is used more commonly, since most lookup tables are arranged with comparison data in columns (which means Excel searches for the lookup value in a vertical order). HLOOKUP is used when the lookup range contains comparison data in rows (which means Excel searches for the lookup value in a horizontal order).

Using the VLOOKUP Function

The structure of a VLOOKUP function is *=VLOOKUP(lookup_value,table_array,col_index_num,range_lookup)*. Table 2.1 explains all the parameters of a VLOOKUP argument.

The VLOOKUP function is easier to understand when explained using an example. In the worksheet shown in Figure 2.5, VLOOKUP is used to return the starting salary for new hires at a medical center. Each new hire is assigned a salary grid number depending on his or her education and years of work experience. This

Table 2.1 VLOOKUP Argument Parameters

Argument Parameter	Description
lookup_value	The value that Excel should search for in the lookup table. Enter a value or cell reference to a value.
table_array	The range address or range name for the lookup table that Excel should search for. Do not include column headers in the range. Use range names or absolute cell referencing.
col_index_num	The column number from the lookup table that contains the data to be placed in the formula cell.
range_lookup	Enter TRUE to instruct Excel to find an exact or approximate match for the lookup value. If this parameter is left out of the formula, Excel assumes TRUE, which means if an exact match is not found, Excel returns the value for the last category into which the known value fits. For the formula to work properly, the first column of the lookup table must be sorted in ascending order. Enter FALSE to instruct Excel to return only exact matches to the lookup value.

salary grid number determines the new hire's starting salary. The lookup table contains the grid numbers with the corresponding starting salaries. In column E, VLOOKUP formulas automatically insert the starting salary for each new employee based on his or her salary grid rating in column D. In the formula shown in Figure 2.5, a range named *Grid* represents the lookup table in the range G4:H8.

Quick Steps

Create VLOOKUP Formula

1. Make cell active.
2. Click Formulas tab.
3. Click Lookup & Reference button.
4. Click *VLOOKUP*.
5. Enter cell address, range name, or value in *Lookup_value* text box.
6. Enter range or range name in *Table_array* text box.
7. Type column number to return values from in *Col_index_num* text box.
8. Type false or leave blank for TRUE in *Range_lookup* text box.
9. Click OK.

Figure 2.5 VLOOKUP Example

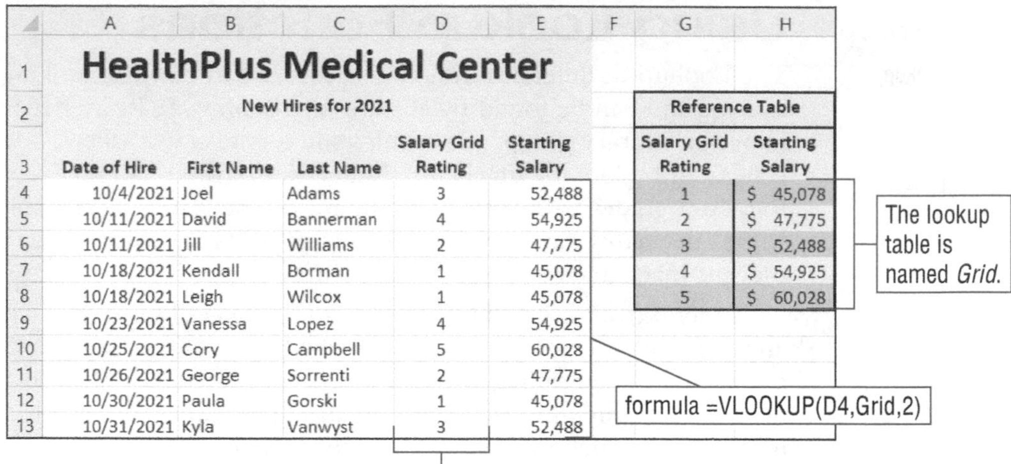

	A	B	C	D	E
1	HealthPlus Medical Center				
2	New Hires for 2021				
3	Date of Hire	First Name	Last Name	Salary Grid Rating	Starting Salary
4	10/4/2021	Joel	Adams	3	52,488
5	10/11/2021	David	Bannerman	4	54,925
6	10/11/2021	Jill	Williams	2	47,775
7	10/18/2021	Kendall	Borman	1	45,078
8	10/18/2021	Leigh	Wilcox	1	45,078
9	10/23/2021	Vanessa	Lopez	4	54,925
10	10/25/2021	Cory	Campbell	5	60,028
11	10/26/2021	George	Sorrenti	2	47,775
12	10/30/2021	Paula	Gorski	1	45,078
13	10/31/2021	Kyla	Vanwyst	3	52,488

Reference Table	
Salary Grid Rating	Starting Salary
1	$ 45,078
2	$ 47,775
3	$ 52,488
4	$ 54,925
5	$ 60,028

Activity 2 Creating a VLOOKUP Formula

Part 1 of 1

1. Open **PrecisionPrices**.
2. Save the workbook with the name **2-PrecisionPrices**.
3. Create a VLOOKUP formula to find the correct discount value for each product by completing the following steps:
   a. Select the range H4:I8 and name it *DiscTable*. DiscTable is the range name used for the lookup table.
   b. Make cell E4 active and then click the Formulas tab.
   c. Click the Lookup & Reference button in the Function Library group.
   d. Click *VLOOKUP* at the drop-down list.
   e. If necessary, drag the Function Arguments dialog box out of the way so that the first few rows of the product price list and discount table data can be seen.

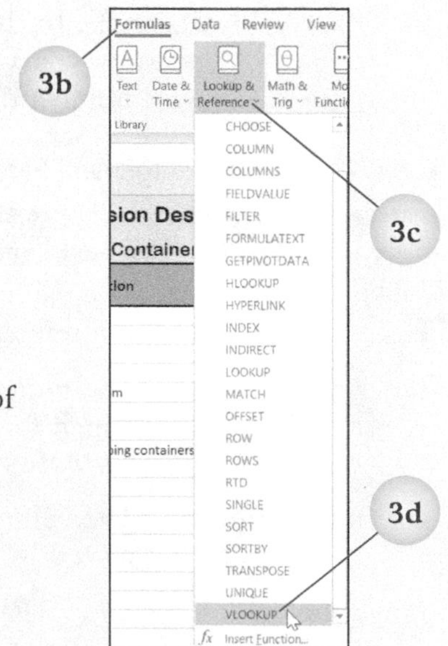

f. With the insertion point positioned in the *Lookup_value* text box, type c4 and then press the Tab key. Product discounts are categorized by letter codes. To find the correct discount, Excel needs to look for the matching category letter code found in cell C4 within the first column of the discount table. Notice that the letter codes in the discount table are listed in ascending order.

g. Type disctable in the *Table_array* text box and then press the Tab key. Using a range name for a reference table is a good idea, since the formula will be copied and absolute references are needed for the cells in the lookup table.

h. Type 2 in the *Col_index_num* text box and then press the Tab key. The discount percentage in column 2 of DiscTable will be placed in cell E4.

i. Type false in the *Range_lookup* text box (Entering *false* instructs Excel to return values for exact matches only. Should a discount category be typed into a cell in column C for which no entry exists in the discount table, Excel will return *#N/A* in the formula cell; this is an alert that an error has occurred in the data entry.)

j. Click OK.

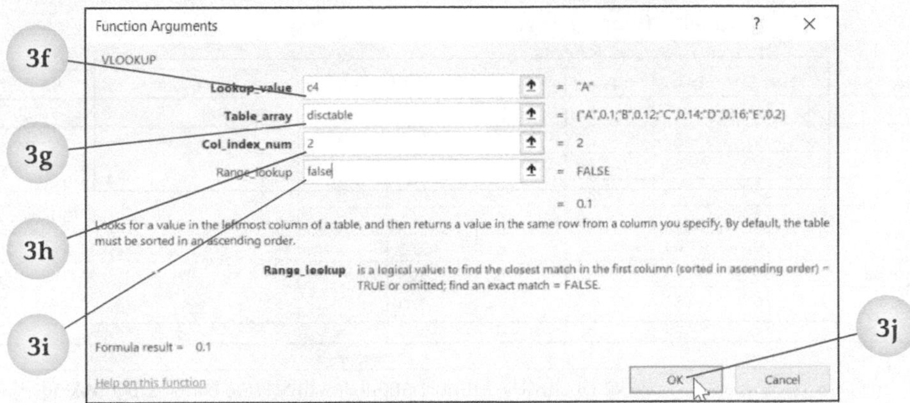

4. Look at the formula in the Formula bar: *=VLOOKUP(C4,DiscTable,2,FALSE)*.
5. Apply the Percent format to cell E4.
6. Make cell F4 active, type the formula =d4-(d4*e4) to calculate the net price, and then press the Enter key.

and Packaging

ducts Price List

Discount Category	List Price	Discount	Net Price
A	18.67	10%	=d4-(d4*e4)
C	22.50		
B	14.53		
D	5.25		
A	18.54		

Discount Table	
Discount Category	Discount Percent
A	10%
B	12%
C	14%
D	16%
E	20%

6

7. Select the range E4:F4 and then drag the fill handle into row 21.
8. Deselect the range.
9. Print the worksheet.
10. Save and then close **2-PrecisionPrices**.

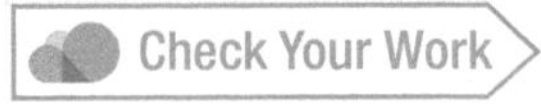

Using the HLOOKUP Function

The HLOOKUP function uses the same argument parameters as the VLOOKUP function. Use HLOOKUP when the table being searched for a comparison value is arranged horizontally, like the one shown in the range J3:O4 in Figure 2.6. Excel searches across the table in the first row for a matching value and then returns to the formula cell the value from the same column.

The structure of an HLOOKUP function is *=HLOOKUP(lookup_value,table_array,row_index_num,range_lookup)*. The argument parameters are similar to the VLOOKUP parameters described in Table 2.1 on page 43. Excel searches the first row of the table for the lookup value. When a match is found, Excel returns the value from the same column in the row number specified in the *row_index_num* argument.

Figure 2.6 HLOOKUP Example

formula
=HLOOKUP(F4,GradeTable,2)

	A	B	C	D	E	F	G
1	Math by Janelle Tutoring Service						
2	Student Progress Report						
3	Student Name	Test 1	Test 2	Test 3	Test 4	Total	Grade
4	Dana Rosenthal	51	48	55	50	51.0	D
5	Kelsey Williams	75	82	66	72	73.8	B
6	Hilary Orbet	81	88	79	83	82.8	A
7	Jose Alvarez	67	72	65	78	70.5	B
8	Linden Porter	42	51	40	55	47.0	F
9	Carl Quenneville	65	44	72	61	60.5	C
10	Andrewa Desmond	55	48	60	50	53.3	D
11	Kylie Winters	78	82	67	71	74.5	B
12	Lindsay Cortez	82	78	85	88	83.3	A

I	J	K	L	M	N	O
Score	0	50	60	70	80	90
Grade	F	D	C	B	A	A+

The lookup table is named *GradeTable*.

The HLOOKUP formula populates the range G4:G12 by looking up the total value in column F in the first row in the lookup table (GradeTable). The formula stops at the largest value in the table that is less than or equal to the lookup value. For example, looking for *62.3* would make Excel stop at *60*.

Activity 3 Analyze an Expansion Project Loan — 1 Part

You will use a financial function to calculate the principal portion of an expansion loan payment for two lenders. You will then calculate the total loan payments and analyze the results.

Using the PPMT Financial Function

Review: Using Financial Functions

Financial

Using the PPMT Financial Function

Financial functions can be used to perform a variety of financial analyses, including loan amortizations, annuity payments, investment planning, depreciation, and so on and can be found by clicking the Financial button in the Function Library group. The PMT function is used to calculate a payment for a loan based on a constant interest rate and constant payments for a set period. Excel provides two related financial functions: PPMT, to calculate the principal portion of the loan payment, and IPMT, to calculate the interest portion.

Quick Steps

Create PPMT Formula

1. Make cell active.
2. Click Formulas tab.
3. Click Financial button.
4. Click *PPMT*.
5. Enter value, cell address, or range name for interest rate in *Rate* text box.
6. Enter number representing payment to find principal for *Per* text box.
7. Enter value, cell address, or range name for total number of payments in *Nper* text box.
8. Enter value, cell address, or range name for amount borrowed in *Pv* text box.
9. Click OK.

Knowing the principal portion of a loan payment is useful in determining the amount of the payment being used to reduce the principal balance owed. The difference between the loan payment and the PPMT value represents the interest cost. The function returns the principal portion of a specific payment for a loan. For example, calculate the principal on the first payment, last payment, or any payment in between. The structure of a PPMT function is *=PPMT(rate,per,nper,pv,fv,type)*, where

- *rate* is the interest rate per period,
- *per* is the period for which to find the principal portion of the payment,
- *nper* is the number of payment periods,
- *pv* is the amount of money borrowed,
- *fv* is the balance at the end of the loan (if left blank, 0 is assumed), and
- *type* is either 0 (payment at end of period) or 1 (payment at beginning of period).

Make sure to be consistent with the units for the interest rate and payment periods. If the interest rate is divided by 12 for a monthly rate, the payment period should also be expressed monthly. For example, multiply the term by 12 if the amortization is entered in the worksheet in years.

Activity 3 Calculating Principal Portions of Loan Payments Using the PPMT Function Part 1 of 1

1. Open **DExpansion**.
2. Save the workbook with the name **2-DExpansion**.
3. Calculate the principal portion of the first loan payment for two loan proposals to fund a building expansion activity by completing the following steps:
   a. Make cell C10 active.
   b. If necessary, click the Formulas tab.
   c. Click the Financial button in the Function Library group.
   d. Scroll down the drop-down list and then click *PPMT*.
   e. If necessary, move the Function Arguments dialog box to the right side of the screen so that all the values in column C can be seen.

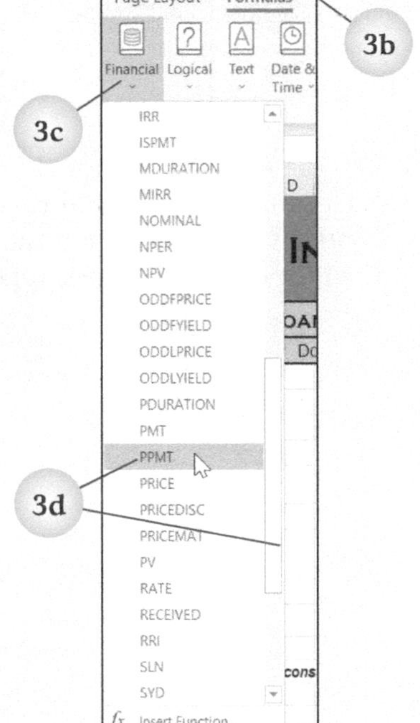

f. With the insertion point positioned in the *Rate* text box, type c4/12 and then press the Tab key. Since the interest rate is stated per annum (per year), dividing the rate by 12 calculates the monthly rate.
g. Type 1 in the *Per* text box to calculate the principal for the first loan payment and then press the Tab key.
h. Type c5*12 in the *Nper* text box and then press the Tab key. Since a loan payment is made each month, the number of payments is 12 times the amortization period.
i. Type c6 in the *Pv* text box. *Pv* refers to present value; in this example, it means the loan amount for which the payments are being calculated. It is positive because it represents cash received by the company.
j. Click OK. Excel returns the value *-1853.05* in cell C10. Payments are shown as negative numbers because they represent cash that is paid out. In this worksheet, negative numbers have been formatted to display in red and enclosed in parentheses.

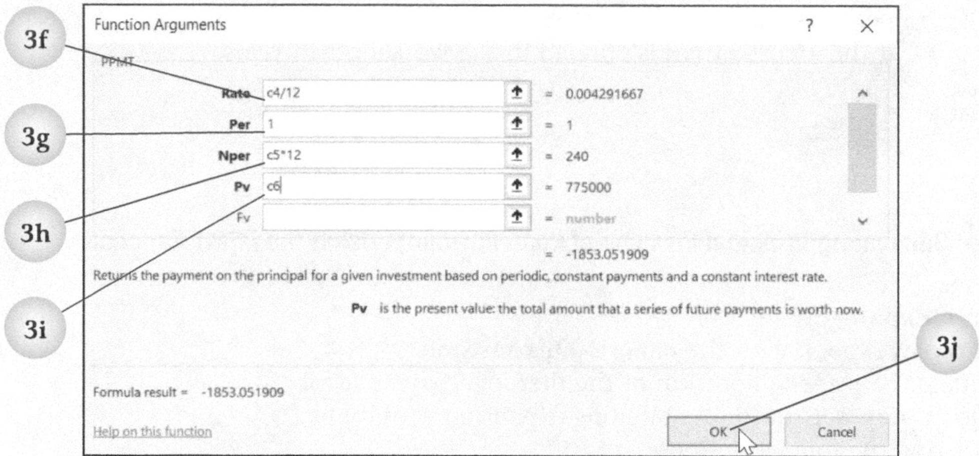

4. Copy and paste the formula from cell C10 into cell E10 and then press the Esc key to remove the scrolling marquee from cell C10.
5. Make cell C12 active, type =c8*12*c5, and then press the Enter key.

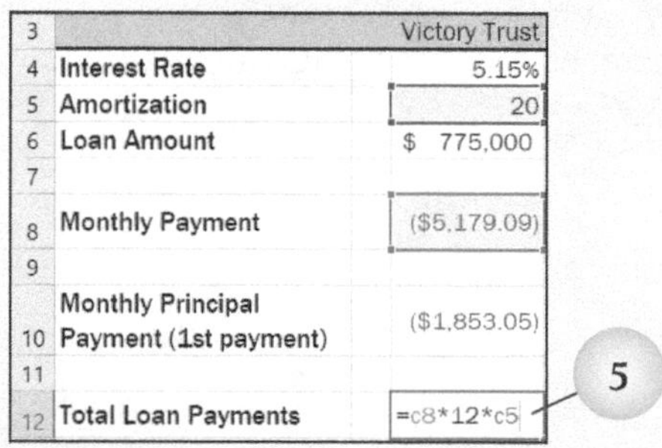

3		Victory Trust
4	Interest Rate	5.15%
5	Amortization	20
6	Loan Amount	$ 775,000
7		
8	Monthly Payment	($5,179.09)
9		
10	Monthly Principal Payment (1st payment)	($1,853.05)
11		
12	Total Loan Payments	=c8*12*c5

6. Copy and paste the formula from cell C12 into cell E12. Press the Esc key to remove the scrolling marquee from cell C12 and then AutoFit the width of column E. Notice that the loan from Dominion Trust is a better choice for Deering Industries, assuming the company can afford the higher monthly payments. Although the interest rate is higher than that for the Victory Trust loan, the shorter term means the loan will be repaid sooner and at a lesser total cost.
7. Print the worksheet.
8. Save and then close **2-DExpansion**.

Activity 4 Calculate Benefit Costs Using Conditional Logic **3 Parts**

You will create formulas to calculate the employee benefit costs and bonuses for ViewRite using logical functions to test multiple conditions.

Using the Nested IF Logical Function

Review: Using Logical IF Functions

Logical

Using and Nesting Logical Functions

Using conditional logic in a formula requires Excel to perform a calculation based on the outcome of a logical or conditional test. One calculation is performed if the test proves true and another calculation is performed if the test proves false. For example, the following is an IF formula using named ranges that could be used to calculate a salesperson's bonus if his or her sales exceed a target: *=IF(Sales>Target,Bonus,0)*. Excel first tests the value in the cell named *Sales* to see if it is greater than the value in the cell named *Target*. If the condition proves true, then Excel returns the value of the cell named *Bonus*. If the sales value is not greater than the target value, then the condition proves false and Excel places a *0* in the cell. The structure of the IF function is *=IF(logical_test,value_if_true,value_if_false)*. Logical functions can be found by clicking the Logical button in the Function Library group.

Using the Nested IF Logical Function

Quick Steps

Create IF Formula

1. Make cell active.
2. Click Formulas tab.
3. Click Logical button.
4. Click *IF*.
5. Type conditional test argument in *Logical_test* text box.
6. Type argument in *Value_if_true* text box.
7. Type argument in *Value_if_false* text box.
8. Click OK.

Hint If you type a nested IF function directly into a cell, Excel color-codes the parentheses for the different IF functions so you can keep track of them separately.

Hint The number of right parentheses needed to end a nested IF statement equals the number of times IF appears in the formula.

When more than two outcomes are possible or a decision is based on more than one field, a nested IF statement is used. A nested IF function is one IF function inside another. The structure of a nested IF statement is *=IF(logical_test,value_if_true,IF(logical_test,value_if_true,value_if_false))*. Excel evaluates the first *logical_test*. If the answer is true, then depending on what is entered for the *value_if_true*, a calculation is performed and text or numbers are entered; if the *value_if_true* is omitted, a 0 is entered. If the first *logical_test* is not true, then the next *logical_test* is evaluated and if the answer is true, the *value_if_true* is placed in the cell. Excel stops evaluating the formula once the *logical_test* has been answered as true. If the answer is never true, then depending on what is entered as the *value_if_false*, a calculation is performed and text or numbers are entered; if the *value_if_false* is omitted, then a 0 is entered.

For example, assume that a company has three sales commission rates based on the level of sales achieved by the salesperson. If sales are less than $40,000, the salesperson earns a 5% commission; if sales are greater than or equal to $40,000 but less than $80,000, the salesperson earns a 7% commission; and if sales are greater than or equal to $80,000, the salesperson earns a 9% commission. Since there are three possible sales commission rates, a single IF function will not work. To correctly calculate the sales commission rate, two conditional tests must be created. The last level (or in this case, the third commission rate of 9%) is used for the *value_if_false*.

Consider the following formula: *=IF(Sales<40000,Sales*5%,IF(Sales<80000, Sales*7%,Sales*9%))*. This formula includes two IF functions. In the first IF function, the conditional test is to determine if the sales value is less than $40,000 (*Sales<40000*). If the test proves true (for example, sales are $25,000), then Excel calculates the sales times 5% and returns the result in the active cell. If the test is

Quick Steps
Create AND Formula
1. Make cell active OR nest formula in IF statement *Logical_test* text box.
2. Type =and(or and(if nesting in IF statement.
3. Type first conditional test argument.
4. Type ,.
5. Type second conditional test argument.
6. Repeat Steps 4–5 for remaining conditions.
7. Type).

not true, then Excel reads the next section of the argument, which is the next IF function that includes the conditional test to determine if sales are less than $80,000 (*Sales<80000*). If this second conditional test proves true, then Excel calculates the sales times 7%. If the test proves false, then Excel calculates the sales times 9%. Since these are the only three possible actions, the formula ends. While up to 64 IF functions can be nested, doing this would create a very complex formula. Consider using a VLOOKUP or HLOOKUP to test different conditions.

Any function can be nested inside another function. For example, in the PPMT formula discussed in the previous section, Excel returns a negative value for the principal portion of the payment. The PPMT formula can be nested inside the ABS formula to have the principal payment displayed without a negative symbol. ABS is the function used to return the absolute value of a number (that is, the number without its sign). For example, *=ABS(PPMT(C4/12,1,C5*12,C6))* displays the payment calculated in Activity 3 as *$1,853.05* instead of *-$1,853.05*.

Using Logical Functions: Nested IF, AND, and OR

Hint Nest an AND or OR function with an IF function to test multiple conditions.

Quick Steps
Create OR Formula
1. Make cell active OR nest formula in IF statement *Logical_test* text box.
2. Type =or(or or(if nesting in IF statement.
3. Type first conditional test argument.
4. Type ,.
5. Type second conditional test argument.
6. Repeat Steps 4–5 for remaining conditions.
7. Type).

Using Logical Functions: Nested IF, AND, and OR

Other logical functions offered in Excel include AND and OR. These functions use Boolean logic to construct a conditional test in a formula to be either true or false. Table 2.2 describes how each function works to test a statement and provides an example of each function.

Table 2.2 AND and OR Logical Functions

Logical Function	Description	Example
AND	All conditions must be true for a result of *TRUE*. If any are false, the function returns *FALSE*.	*=AND(Sales>Target,NewClients>5)* Returns *TRUE* if both test true Returns *FALSE* if *Sales* is greater than *Target* but *NewClients* is less than 5. Returns *FALSE* if *Sales* is less than *Target* but *NewClients* is greater than 5.
OR	Returns *TRUE* if any of the conditions tests true; returns *FALSE* only when all conditions are false.	*=OR(Sales>Target,NewClients>5)* Returns *TRUE* if *Sales* is greater than *Target* or *NewClients* is greater than 5. Returns *FALSE* only if *Sales* is not greater than *Target* and *NewClients* is not greater than 5.

Using the ROUND Function

ROUND is another example of a function that can easily be nested with other functions. Excel uses the entire number stored in the cell and not just the visible number in any calculations. The function ROUND is used to modify the actual number of characters by rounding the value. The structure of this function is *=ROUND(number,num_digits). Number* can be a number or a formula. The *num_digits* number can be positive or negative. A positive number rounds the decimal value (the numbers right of the decimal point) to the designated number of places. A negative number rounds the numbers left of the decimal point to the nearest ones, tens, hundreds, and so on. Table 2.3 demonstrates how positive and negative *num_digits* are handled.

When nesting the ROUND function, make sure that the original function is working before rounding the final result. In Activity 4a, the nested IF AND formula used to calculate the pension contributions returns some values with three digits after the decimal point. The ROUND function will be added after the IF AND statement.

Table 2.3 Examples of Applying the ROUND Function

Example	Description	Result
=ROUND(1625.09,1)	Rounds *1625.09* to one digit past the decimal point.	*1625.1*
=ROUND(1625.1,0)	Rounds *1625.1* to zero digits past the decimal point.	*1625*
=ROUND(1625,-1)	Rounds *1625* to the nearest tens value.	*1630*

Activity 4a **Calculating Pension Costs Using Nested IF, AND, and ROUND Functions** Part 1 of 3

1. Open **VRSalCost**.
2. Save the workbook with the name **2-VRSalCost**.
3. ViewRite contributes 5.575% of an employee's salary into a privately managed company retirement account if the employee works full time and earns more than $50,000 a year. Calculate the pension benefit costs for eligible employees by completing the following steps:
   a. Make cell H6 the active cell.
   b. Click the Formulas tab.
   c. Click the Logical button in the Function Library group and then click *IF* at the drop-down list.
   d. If necessary, drag the Function Arguments dialog box down until all of row 6 can be seen in the worksheet.

e. With the insertion point positioned in the *Logical_test* text box, type and(c6="FT",g6>50000) and then press the Tab key. An AND function is required, since both conditions must be true for the company to contribute to the pension plan. The two conditions—being a full-time (FT) employee and having a salary over $50,000—are separated by a comma. ***Note: Excel requires having quotation marks around text when it is used in a conditional test formula.***

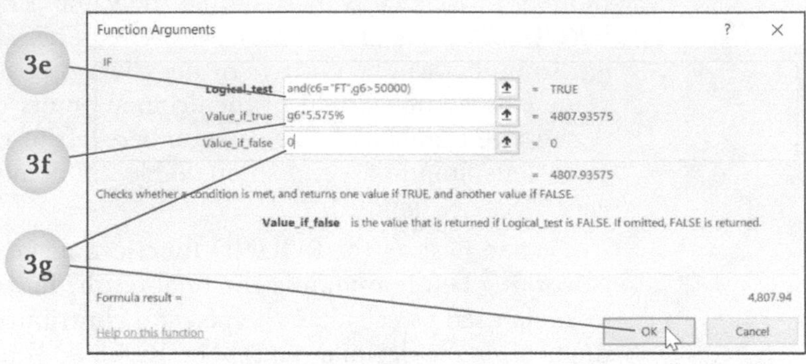

f. Type g6*5.575% in the *Value_if_true* text box and then press the Tab key.

g. Type 0 in the *Value_if_false* text box and then click OK.

h. Look at the formula *=IF(AND(C6="FT",G6>50000),G6*5.575%,0)* in the Formula bar. Notice that the AND function is nested within the IF function. Since both conditions for the first employee tested true, the pension cost is calculated.

4. With cell H6 selected, increase the number of digits after the display point to three. Use the ROUND function to round the pension amount to the nearest penny by completing the following steps:

=ROUND(IF(AND(C6="FT",G6>50000),G6*5.575%,0),2) — 4c

a. Click to the right of the equals sign in the Formula bar.

b. Type round(and then press the End key to move to the end of the formula.

c. Type ,2) and then press the Enter key.

d. Select cell H6, decrease the number of digits after the decimal point to two, and then copy the formula in cell H6 to the range H7:H14. Deselect the range. Notice that only the first four employees have pension benefit values. This is because they are the only employees who both work full time and earn over $50,000 a year in salary.

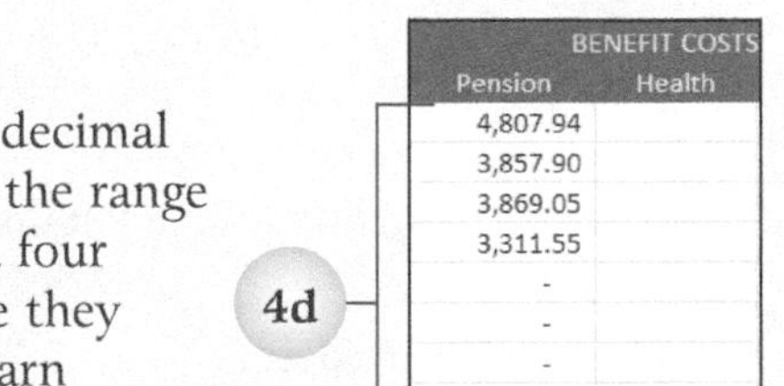

BENEFIT COSTS
Pension
Health
4,807.94
3,857.90
3,869.05
3,311.55
-
-
-
-
-
15,846.44
-
4d

5. Save **2-VRSalCost.**

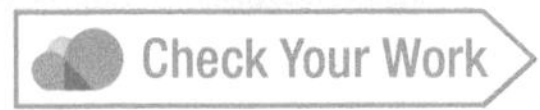

Activity 4b Calculating Health and Dental Costs Using Nested IF and OR Functions   Part 2 of 3

1. With **2-VRSalCost** open, make cell I6 the active cell.

2. ViewRite offers to pay the annual health premiums for employees not covered by other medical plans. The company pays $3,600 per year per employee for family coverage, $2,580 per year per employee for single coverage, and $0 per year if the employee declines coverage. Calculate the cost for each employee who chose to join the health plan by completing the following steps:

BENEFIT COSTS			Total	Salary +
Pension	Health	Dental	Benefits	Benefits
4,807.94	=if(d6="Family",3600,if(d6="Single",2580,0))			
3,857.90			3,857.90	73,057.90

2a

a. This formula requires a nested IF statement, since the result will be *$3,600, $2,580,* or *0* depending on the contents of cell D6. (An OR statement will not work for this formula, since two different health premiums are used.) In cell I6, type =if(d6="Family",3600,if(d6="Single",2580,0)) and then press the Enter key. ***Note: Recall that Excel requires the use of quotation marks around text entries within an IF function.***

   b. Copy the formula in cell I6 to the range I7:I14. Notice the cells in column I for which no values are entered. In column D in the corresponding row, the text *Declined* displays. Excel returned a value of *0* in column I because the conditions *D6="Family"* and *D6="Single"* both proved false.

3. ViewRite has negotiated a flat fee with its dental benefit service provider. The company pays $2,750 per year for each employee, regardless of the type of coverage. However, the service provider requires ViewRite to report each person's coverage as *Family* or *Single* for audit purposes. The dental plan is optional and some employees have declined coverage. Calculate the cost of the dental plan by completing the following steps:
   a. Make cell J6 the active cell.
   b. If necessary, click the Formulas tab.
   c. Click the Logical button and then click *IF* at the drop-down list.
   d. If necessary, drag the Function Arguments dialog box down until all of row 6 can be seen in the worksheet.
   e. With the insertion point positioned in the *Logical_test* text box, type or(e6="Family",e6="Single") and then press the Tab key. An OR function is appropriate for calculating this benefit, since either condition can be true for the company to contribute to the dental plan. The two conditions—being a family or being single—are separated by a comma.
   f. Type 2750 in the *Value_if_true* text box and then press the Tab key.
   g. Type 0 in the *Value_if_false* text box and then click OK.
   h. Look at the formula *=IF(OR(E6="Family", E6="Single"),2750,0)* in the Formula bar. Notice that the OR function is nested within the IF function. Since cell E6 contains neither *Family* nor *Single*, the OR statement tests false and *0* is returned in cell J6.

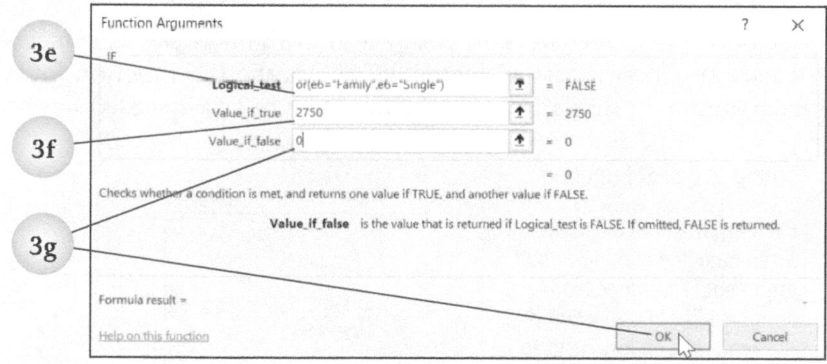

   i. Copy the formula in cell J6 to the range J7:J14 and then deselect the range.

3i

BENEFIT COSTS			Total	Salary +
Pension	Health	Dental	Benefits	Benefits
4,807.94	3,600.00	-	8,407.94	94,648.94
3,857.90	2,580.00	2,750.00	9,187.90	78,387.90
3,869.05	-	-	3,869.05	73,269.05
3,311.55	2,580.00	2,750.00	8,641.55	68,041.55
-	3,600.00	2,750.00	6,350.00	44,750.00
-	3,600.00	-	3,600.00	43,000.00
-	2,580.00	-	2,580.00	49,180.00
-	-	-	-	49,900.00
-	-	2,750.00	2,750.00	49,754.00
15,846.44	18,540.00	11,000.00	45,386.44	550,931.44

4. Save **2-VRSalCost**.

Using the IFS Logical Function

An alternative to using a nested IF function is to use an IFS function. The result of the IFS function must test true; in contrast, the last argument of the IF function tests false. If you can change the last argument to test true, then the IFS function can be used instead of a nested IF function. If no condition tests true, then the IFS function returns the error code *#NA*. The IFS function can test up to 127 conditions. Unlike a nested IF function, an IFS function does not require each argument to be enclosed in parentheses. This difference makes the IFS function easier to read.

Quick Steps

Create IFS Formula

1. Make cell active.
2. Click Formulas tab.
3. Click Logical button.
4. Click *IFS*.
5. Type conditional test argument in *Logical_test1* text box.
6. Type argument in *Value_if_true1* text box.
7. Add necessary pairs of *Logical_tests* and *Value_if true*.
8. Click OK.

The structure of the IFS function is *=IFS(logical_test1,value_if_true1,logical_test2,value_if_true2,...)*. Just as with a nested IF statement, Excel evaluates the first *logical_test*. If the answer is true, then depending on what is entered for the *value_if_true*, a calculation is performed and text or numbers are entered. If the first *logical_test* is not true, then the next *logical_test* is evaluated and if the answer is true, the *value_if_true* is placed in the cell. Excel stops evaluating the formula once the *logical_test* has been answered as true. If the answer is never true, then *#NA* is placed in the cell.

Viewing Long Formulas in the Formula Bar

Formulas containing nested or lengthy functions can get quite long and be difficult to read when viewed in the Formula bar. To make a formula easier to read, place each logical test on a separate line and expand the Formula bar.

To place an argument or logical test on a new line in the Formula bar, place the insertion point immediately before the logical test and then press Alt + Enter. To expand the Formula bar, hover the mouse pointer over the bottom of the bar until the pointer turns into a two-headed arrow, click and hold down the left mouse button, drag the border down until the new size is achieved, and then release the mouse button. Figure 2.7 shows the IFS function for Activity 4c with each argument displayed on a separate line in an expanded Formula bar.

Figure 2.7 IFS Function

Each argument is displayed on a separate line and individual arguments are separated by commas. The IFS function does not require each argument to be enclosed in parentheses.

```
fx  =IFS(C5>749999,1.5%,
    C5>499999,1%,
    C5>349999,0.75%,
    C5>199999,0.5%,
    C5>0,0)
```

Activity 4c Calculating Bonuses Using an IFS Function

1. With **2-VRSalCost** open, click the Bonus worksheet tab and then click in cell D5.
2. ViewRite offers an employee bonus based on sales. Enter a formula that uses an IFS function using the following data:

Sales	Bonus Percentage
>$749,999	1.5%
>$499,999	1%
>$349,999	0.75%
>$199,999	0.5%
Between $0 and $199,000	0%

Follow these steps to create the formula:

a. If necessary, click the Formulas tab.
b. Click the Logical button and then click *IFS* at the drop-down list.
c. Type c5>749999 in the *Logical_test1* text box and then press the Tab key.
d. Type 1.5% in the *Value_if_true1* text box and then press the Tab key.
e. Type c5>499999 in the *Logical_test2* text box and then press the Tab key.
f. Type 1% in the *Value_if_true2* text box and then press the Tab key.
g. With the insertion point in the *Logical_test3* text box, type c5>349999 and then press the Tab key.

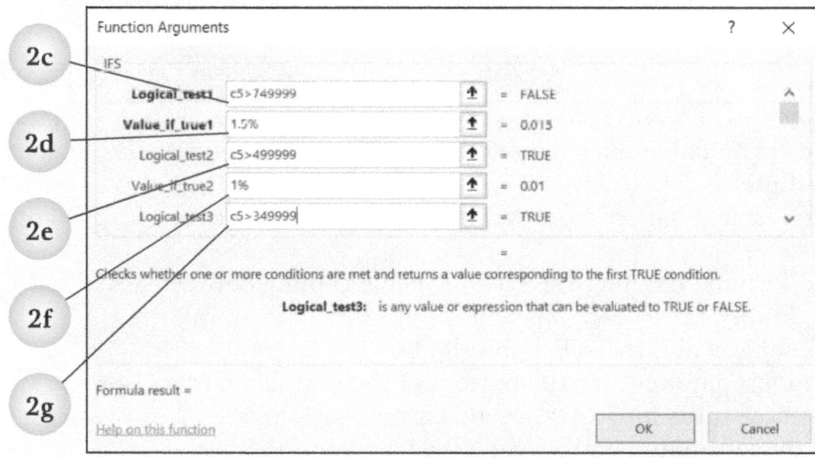

h. Type 0.75% in the *Value_if_true3* text box and then press the Tab key.
i. In the *Logical_test4* text box type c5>199999 and then press the Tab key.
j. Type 0.5% in the *Value_if_true4* text box and then press the Tab key.
k. In the *Logical_test5* text box type c5>0 and then press the Tab key.
l. Type 0% in the *Value_if_true5* text box and then click OK.

3. Look at the formula in the Formula bar created by the Function Arguments dialog box: *=IFS(C5>749999,1.5%,C5>499999,1%,C5>349999,0.75%,C5>199999,0.5%,C5>0,0%)*.

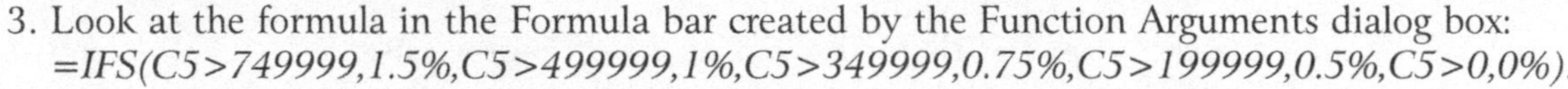

4. Apply the Percent format, increase the number of decimals to two digits after the decimal point, and then drag the fill handle into row 15.
5. View each argument on a separate line and then expand the Formula bar by completing the following steps:
   a. Click in the Formula bar after the second comma between *1.5%* and *C5* and then press Alt + Enter.

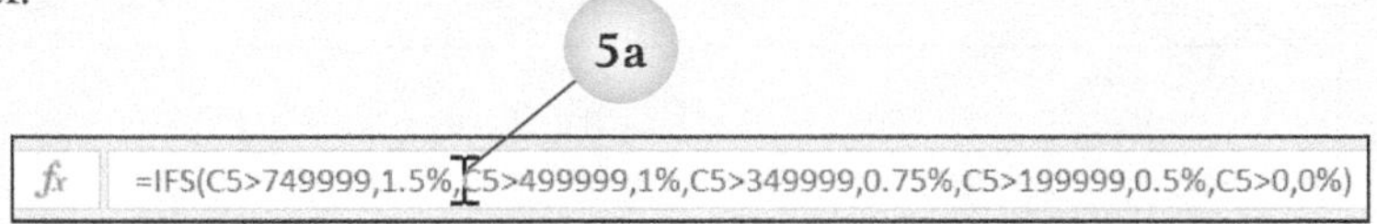

   b. Click in the Formula bar after the second visible comma between *1%* and *C5* and then press Alt + Enter.
   c. Click in the formula bar after the second visible comma between *0.75%* and *C5* and then press Alt + Enter.
   d. Click in the formula bar after the second visible comma between *0.5%* and *C5* and then press Alt + Enter.
   e. Press the Enter key and then click in cell D5.
   f. Hover the mouse pointer over the bottom of the Formula bar until the pointer turns into a two-headed arrow, click and hold down the left mouse button, drag the bottom of the bar down until all the rows of the formula can be seen, and then release the mouse button.
6. Collapse the Formula bar by completing the following steps:
   a. Hover the mouse pointer over the bottom of the Formula bar until the pointer turns into a two-headed arrow.
   b. Click and hold down the left mouse button, drag the bottom of the bar up until only one row is displayed, and then release the mouse button.
7. Save, print and then close **2-VRSalCost**.

Chapter Summary

- Using range names in formulas makes it easier to manage complex formulas and helps others who work in or edit a worksheet to understand the purpose of a formula more quickly.
- Click the Name Manager button in the Defined Names group on the Formulas tab to open the Name Manager dialog box. Use options at the Name Manager dialog box to create, edit, or delete a range name or edit the cells that a range name references.
- To insert a formula click the Insert Function button in the Formula bar, click the name of the function at the drop-down list, and then enter arguments at the Insert Function dialog box. Alternatively, you can click a button in the Function Library group on the Formulas tab, click the name of the function at the drop-down list, and then enter arguments at the Insert Function dialog box.
- The COUNTBLANK function counts the number of empty cells in a range. The COUNTIF statistical function counts cells within a range that meet a single criterion or condition; the COUNTIFS statistical function counts cells within a range that meet multiple criteria or conditions.
- Find the arithmetic mean of a range of cells that meet a single criterion or condition using the AVERAGEIF statistical function. Use the AVERAGEIFS statistical function to find the arithmetic mean for a range that meet multiple criteria or conditions.
- The math function SUMIF adds cells within a range that meet a single criterion or condition. To add cells within a range based on multiple criteria or conditions, use the SUMIFS math function.
- The Lookup & Reference functions VLOOKUP and HLOOKUP look up data in a reference table and return in the formula cell a value from a column or row, respectively, in the lookup table.
- The PPMT financial function returns the principal portion of a specified loan payment within the term based on an interest rate, total number of payments, and loan amount.
- Using conditional logic in a formula requires Excel to perform a calculation based on the outcome of a logical or conditional test, in which one calculation is performed if the test proves true and another calculation is performed if the test proves false.
- A nested function is one function inside another function. Nest an IF function to test an additional condition.
- Use the ROUND function to modify the number of characters by rounding the value.
- Use the AND logical function to test multiple conditions. Excel returns *TRUE* if all the conditions test true and *FALSE* if any of the conditions tests false.
- The OR logical function also tests multiple conditions. The function returns *TRUE* if any of the conditions tests true and *FALSE* if all the conditions test false.
- The IFS logical function is similar to the IF function, but the IFS function does not require each argument to be enclosed in parentheses and the results of the IFS function must test true.
- To make a formula containing a long function easier to read, place each logical test on a separate line and expand the Formula bar.

Commands Review

FEATURE	RIBBON TAB, GROUP	BUTTON	KEYBOARD SHORTCUT
financial functions	Formulas, Function Library		
Insert Function dialog box	Formulas, Function Library	*fx*	Shift + F3
logical functions	Formulas, Function Library	?	
lookup and reference functions	Formulas, Function Library		
math and trigonometry functions	Formulas, Function Library	θ	
Name Manager dialog box	Formulas, Defined Names		Ctrl + F3

Microsoft®

Excel®

CHAPTER 3

Working with Tables and Data Features

Performance Objectives

Upon successful completion of Chapter 3, you will be able to:

1. Create a table in a worksheet
2. Expand a table to include new rows and columns
3. Add a calculated column in a table
4. Format a table by applying table styles and table style options
5. Name a table
6. Add a *Total* row to a table and formulas to sum cells
7. Sort and filter a table
8. Use Data Tools to split the contents of a cell into separate columns
9. Remove duplicate records
10. Restrict data entry by creating validation criteria
11. Convert a table to a normal range
12. Create and modify subtotals of data and select data from different outline levels
13. Group and ungroup data

A *table* is a range that can be managed separately from other rows and columns in a worksheet. Data in a table can be sorted, filtered, and totaled as a separate unit. A worksheet can contain more than one table, which allows managing multiple groups of data separately within the same workbook. In this chapter, you will learn how to use the table feature to manage a range. You will use tools to validate data, search for and remove duplicate records, and convert text to a table. You will also convert a table back to a normal range and use data tools such as grouping related records and calculating subtotals.

Data Files

Before beginning chapter work, copy the EL2C3 folder to your storage medium and then make EL2C3 the active folder.

The online course includes additional training and assessment resources.

Activity 1 Create and Modify a Table in a Billing Summary Worksheet — 4 Parts

You will convert data in a billing summary worksheet to a table and then modify the table by adding a row and calculated columns, applying table styles and sorting and filtering the data.

Creating, Formatting, and Naming a Table

Quick Steps

Create Table

1. Select range.
2. Click Quick Analysis button.
3. Click Tables tab.
4. Click Table button.
5. Deselect range.

Formatting Data as a Table

A table in Excel is similar in structure to a database. Columns are called *fields*. Each field is used to store a single unit of information about a person, place, or object. The first row of a table contains the column headings and is called the *field names row* or *header row*. Each column heading in the table should be unique. Below the field names, data is entered in rows called *records*. A record contains all the field values related to the single person, place, or object that is the topic of the table. No blank rows exist within the table, as shown in Figure 3.1.

To create a table in Excel, enter the data in the worksheet and then define the desired range as a table using the Table button in the Tables group on the Insert tab, the Format as Table button in the Styles group on the Home tab, Ctrl + T, or the Table button on the Tables tab in the Quick Analysis button at the bottom right of the selected range. Before converting a range to a table, delete any blank rows between the column headings and the data or within the data range.

Figure 3.1 Worksheet with the Range Formatted as a Table

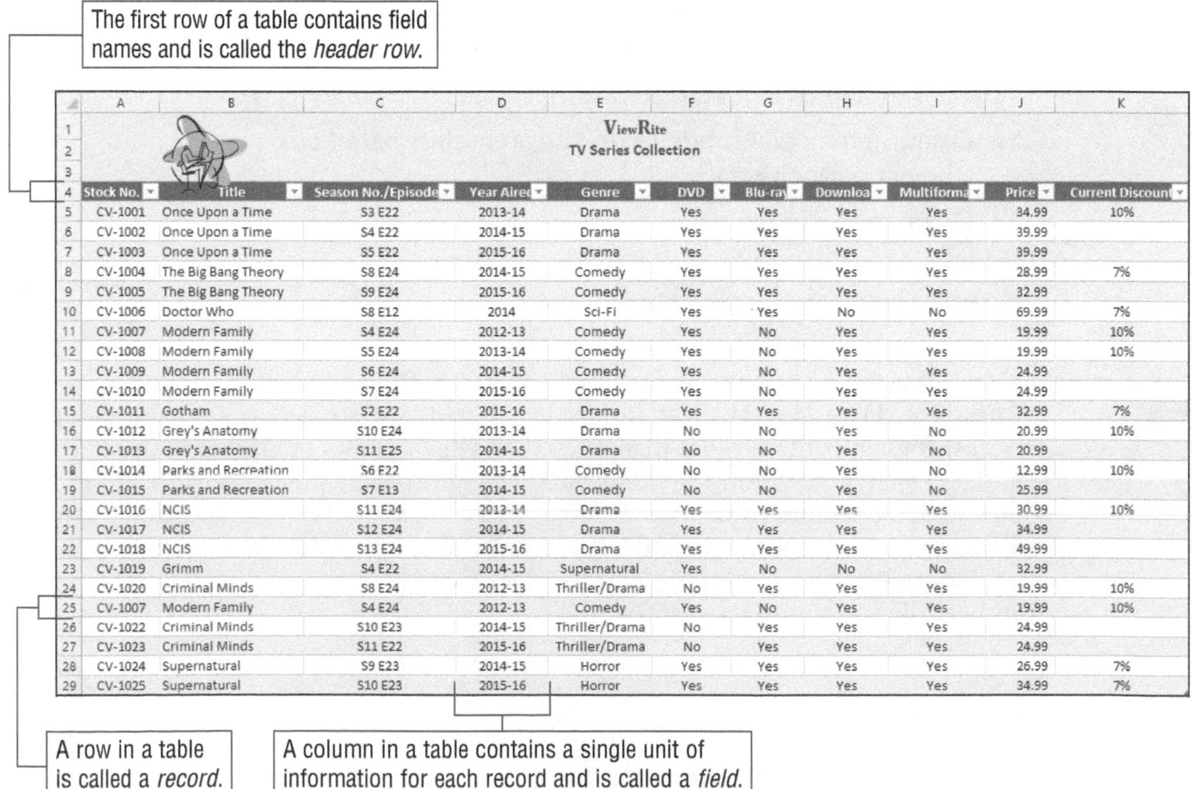

ViewRite
TV Series Collection

	A	B	C	D	E	F	G	H	I	J	K
4	Stock No.	Title	Season No./Episode	Year Aired	Genre	DVD	Blu-ray	Downloa	Multiforma	Price	Current Discount
5	CV-1001	Once Upon a Time	S3 E22	2013-14	Drama	Yes	Yes	Yes	Yes	34.99	10%
6	CV-1002	Once Upon a Time	S4 E22	2014-15	Drama	Yes	Yes	Yes	Yes	39.99	
7	CV-1003	Once Upon a Time	S5 E22	2015-16	Drama	Yes	Yes	Yes	Yes	39.99	
8	CV-1004	The Big Bang Theory	S8 E24	2014-15	Comedy	Yes	Yes	Yes	Yes	28.99	7%
9	CV-1005	The Big Bang Theory	S9 E24	2015-16	Comedy	Yes	Yes	Yes	Yes	32.99	
10	CV-1006	Doctor Who	S8 E12	2014	Sci-Fi	Yes	Yes	No	No	69.99	7%
11	CV-1007	Modern Family	S4 E24	2012-13	Comedy	Yes	No	Yes	Yes	19.99	10%
12	CV-1008	Modern Family	S5 E24	2013-14	Comedy	Yes	No	Yes	Yes	19.99	10%
13	CV-1009	Modern Family	S6 E24	2014-15	Comedy	Yes	No	Yes	Yes	24.99	
14	CV-1010	Modern Family	S7 E24	2015-16	Comedy	Yes	No	Yes	Yes	24.99	
15	CV-1011	Gotham	S2 E22	2015-16	Drama	Yes	Yes	Yes	Yes	32.99	7%
16	CV-1012	Grey's Anatomy	S10 E24	2013-14	Drama	No	No	Yes	No	20.99	10%
17	CV-1013	Grey's Anatomy	S11 E25	2014-15	Drama	No	No	Yes	No	20.99	
18	CV-1014	Parks and Recreation	S6 E22	2013-14	Comedy	No	No	Yes	No	12.99	10%
19	CV-1015	Parks and Recreation	S7 E13	2014-15	Comedy	No	No	Yes	No	25.99	
20	CV-1016	NCIS	S11 E24	2013-14	Drama	Yes	Yes	Yes	Yes	30.99	10%
21	CV-1017	NCIS	S12 E24	2014-15	Drama	Yes	Yes	Yes	Yes	34.99	
22	CV-1018	NCIS	S13 E24	2015-16	Drama	Yes	Yes	Yes	Yes	49.99	
23	CV-1019	Grimm	S4 E22	2014-15	Supernatural	Yes	No	No	No	32.99	
24	CV-1020	Criminal Minds	S8 E24	2012-13	Thriller/Drama	No	Yes	Yes	Yes	19.99	10%
25	CV-1007	Modern Family	S4 E24	2012-13	Comedy	Yes	No	Yes	Yes	19.99	10%
26	CV-1022	Criminal Minds	S10 E23	2014-15	Thriller/Drama	No	Yes	Yes	Yes	24.99	
27	CV-1023	Criminal Minds	S11 E22	2015-16	Thriller/Drama	No	Yes	Yes	Yes	24.99	
28	CV-1024	Supernatural	S9 E23	2014-15	Horror	Yes	Yes	Yes	Yes	26.99	7%
29	CV-1025	Supernatural	S10 E23	2015-16	Horror	Yes	Yes	Yes	Yes	34.99	7%

Activity 1a Converting a Range to a Table

Part 1 of 4

1. Open **BillSumOctWk1**.
2. Save the workbook with the name **3-BillSumOctWk1**.
3. Convert the billing summary data to a table by completing the following steps:
   a. Select the range A4:I24.
   b. Click the Insert tab.
   c. Click the Table button in the Tables group.
   d. At the Create Table dialog box with *=$A$4:$I$24* selected in the *Where is the data for your table?* text box and the *My table has headers* check box selected, click OK.
   e. Deselect the range.
4. Select columns A through I and AutoFit the column widths.
5. Deselect the columns.
6. Save **3-BillSumOctWk1**.

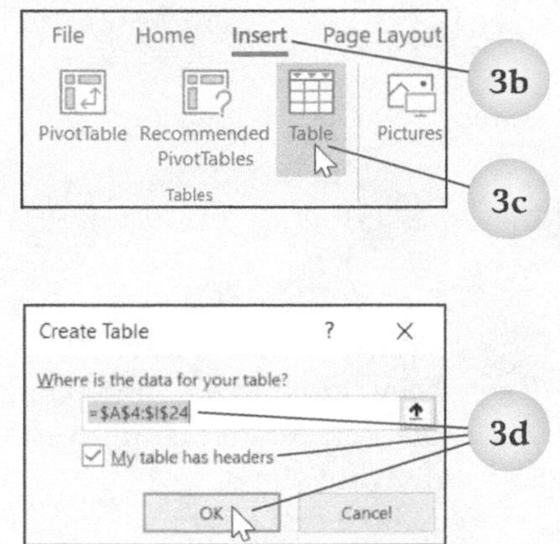

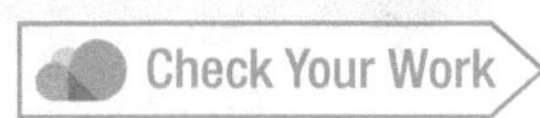

Adding a Row to a Table

Applying Table Style Options and Adding a Calculated Column

Quick Steps

Add Calculated Column

1. Type formula in first record in column.
2. Press Enter key.

Modifying a Table

Once a table has been defined, typing new data in the row immediately below the last row of the table or in the column immediately right of the last column causes the table to automatically expand to include the new entries. Excel displays the AutoCorrect Options button when the table is expanded. Click the button to display a drop-down list with the options *Undo Table AutoExpansion* and *Stop Automatically Expanding Tables*. To add data near a table without having the table expand, leave a blank column or row between the table and the new data.

Typing a formula in the first record of a new table column automatically creates a calculated column. In a calculated column, Excel copies the formula from the first cell to the remaining cells in the column immediately after the formula is entered. The AutoCorrect Options button appears when Excel converts a column to a calculated column. Click the button to display the options *Undo Calculated Column*, *Stop Automatically Creating Calculated Columns*, and *Control AutoCorrect Options*. If the formula is entered by typing the cell references, as in Activity 1b, a normal formula is entered. If the formula is entered by selecting the cells or ranges involved, Excel inserts a structured reference using the column name instead of the cell or range reference. For example, if the formula entered in Activity 1b Step 2b were entered by selecting the cells instead of typing the references, the formula in cell J5 would be *=[@[Billable Hours]]*[@Rate]* instead of *H5*I5*.

Activity 1b Adding a Row and Calculated Columns to a Table

Part 2 of 4

1. With **3-BillSumOctWk1** open, add a new record to the table by completing the following steps:
   a. Make cell A25 active, type RE-522, and then press the Tab key. Excel automatically expands the table to include the new row and displays the AutoCorrect Options button.

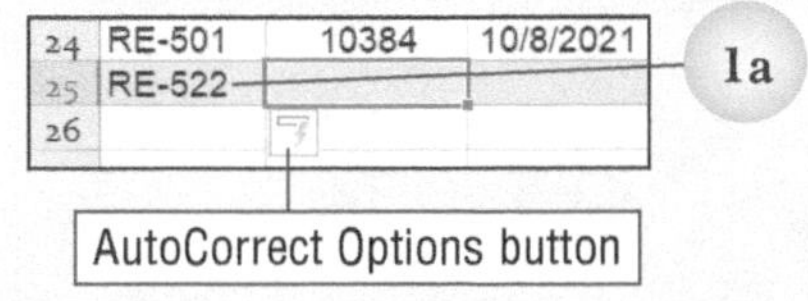

b. With cell B25 active, type the remainder of the record as follows. Press the Tab key to move from column to column in the table.

Client	10512
Date	10/8/2021
Client Name	Connie Melanson
Attorney FName	Kyle
Attorney LName	Williams
Area	Real Estate
Billable Hours	2.5

c. With cell I25 active, type 250 and then press the Enter key. (If you press the Tab key, a new table row will be created.)

2. Add a calculated column to multiply the billable hours times the rate by completing the following steps:
   a. Make cell J4 active, type Fees Due, and then press the Enter key. Excel automatically expands the table to include the new column.
   b. With cell J5 active, type =h5*i5 and then press the Enter key. Excel creates a calculated column and copies the formula to the rest of the rows in the table.
   c. Double-click the column J boundary to AutoFit the column.
3. Calculate the 6.5% tax owing using a structured reference and a ROUND function that rounds the result to two digits after the decimal point by completing the following steps:
   a. Make cell K4 active, type Taxes Due, and then press the Enter key.
   b. With cell K5 active, type =round(, click in cell J5, type *.065,2), and then press the Enter key. Excel creates a calculated column using a structured reference and copies the formula to the rest of the rows in the table.
   c. Double-click the column K boundary to AutoFit the column.

2a

2b

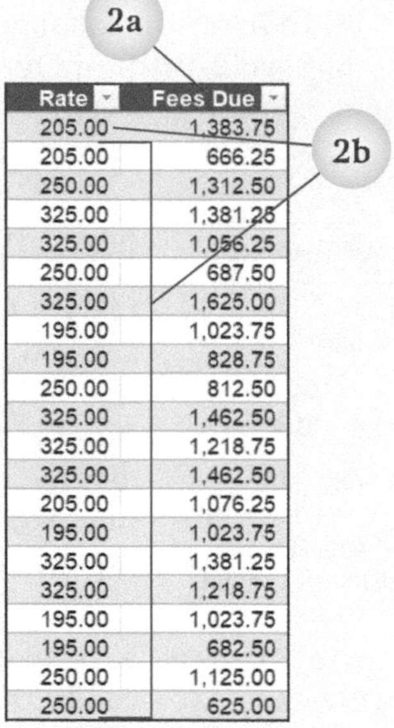

Rate	Fees Due
205.00	1,383.75
205.00	666.25
250.00	1,312.50
325.00	1,381.25
325.00	1,056.25
250.00	687.50
325.00	1,625.00
195.00	1,023.75
195.00	828.75
250.00	812.50
325.00	1,462.50
325.00	1,218.75
325.00	1,462.50
205.00	1,076.25
195.00	1,023.75
325.00	1,381.25
325.00	1,218.75
195.00	1,023.75
195.00	682.50
250.00	1,125.00
250.00	625.00

4. Adjust the centering and fill color of the titles across the top of the table by completing the following steps:
   a. Select the range A1:K1 and then click the Merge & Center button in the Alignment group on the Home tab two times.
   b. Select the range A2:K2 and then press the F4 function key to repeat the command to merge and center row 2 across columns A through K.
   c. Select the range A3:K3 and then press the F4 function key to repeat the command to merge and center row 3 across columns A through K.
5. Save **3-BillSumOctWk1**.

Check Your Work

Applying Table Styles, Table Style Options, and Table Properties

The contextual Table Tools Design tab, shown in Figure 3.2, contains options for formatting the table. Apply a different visual style to a table using the Table Styles gallery. Excel provides several table styles, which are categorized by *Light*, *Medium*, and *Dark* color themes. By default, Excel bands the rows within the table, which means that even-numbered rows are formatted differently from odd-numbered rows. Banding rows or columns makes it easier to read data across a row or down a column in a large table. The banding can be removed from the rows and/or added to the columns. Insert a check mark in the *First Column* or *Last Column* check box in the Table Style Options group to add emphasis to the first or last column in the table by formatting them differently from the rest of the table. Use the *Header Row* check box to show or hide the column headings in the table. Use the *Filter Button* check box to remove the filter arrows from the header row.

Click the *Total Row* check box or click the keyboard shortcut Ctrl + Shift + T to add a total row. Adding a *Total* row causes Excel to add the word *Total* in the leftmost cell of a new row at the bottom of the table. A Sum function is added automatically to the last numeric column in the table. Click in a cell in the *Total* row to display an option box arrow that when clicked displays a pop-up list; a function formula can be selected from this list.

A table name is a unique name used to reference an entire table and helps users easily identify the table if the workbook contains more than one. The table name appears in the *Table Name* text box. To name a table, click in any cell in the table, type the name in the *Table Name* text box in the Properties group on the Table Tools Design tab, and then press the Enter key. To select a table, click its name in the Name box. If a cell within a table is referenced in a formula in another cell outside the table then the name of the table is included in the formula.

Quick Steps

Change Table Style
1. Make table cell active.
2. If necessary, click Table Tools Design tab.
3. Click style in Table Styles gallery.
   OR
3. Click More button in Table Styles gallery.
4. Click desired style at drop-down gallery.

Add *Total* Row
1. Make table cell active.
2. If necessary, click Table Tools Design tab.
3. Click *Total Row* check box.
4. Click in cell in *Total* row.
5. Click option box arrow.
6. Click function.

Name Table
1. Make table cell active.
2. If necessary, click Table Tools Design tab.
3. Type table name in *Table Name* text box.
4. Press Enter key.

Figure 3.2 Table Tools Design Tab

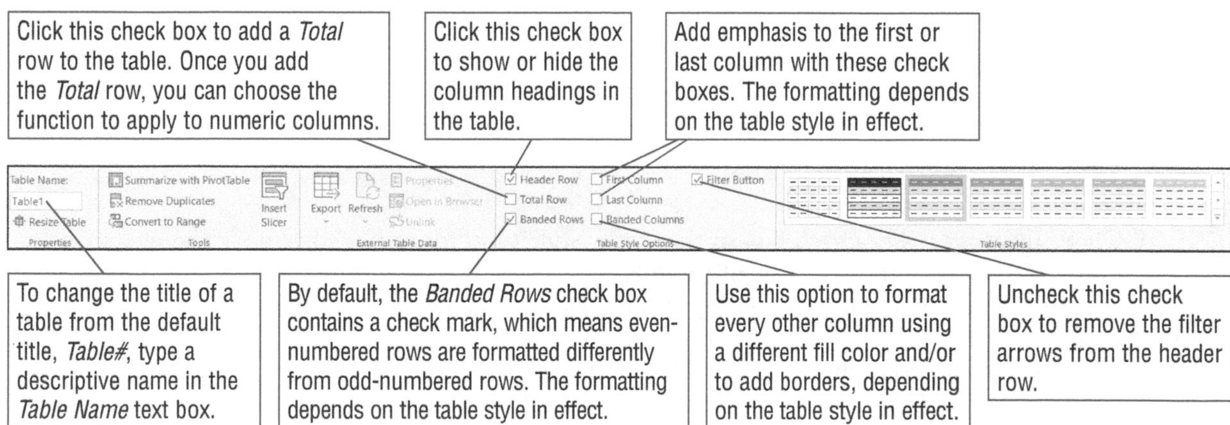

Click this check box to add a *Total* row to the table. Once you add the *Total* row, you can choose the function to apply to numeric columns.
Click this check box to show or hide the column headings in the table.
Add emphasis to the first or last column with these check boxes. The formatting depends on the table style in effect.
To change the title of a table from the default title, *Table#*, type a descriptive name in the *Table Name* text box.
By default, the *Banded Rows* check box contains a check mark, which means even-numbered rows are formatted differently from odd-numbered rows. The formatting depends on the table style in effect.
Use this option to format every other column using a different fill color and/or to add borders, depending on the table style in effect.
Uncheck this check box to remove the filter arrows from the header row.

Activity 1c Formatting a Table and Adding a *Total* Row and a Structured Reference Formula

Part 3 of 4

1. With **3-BillSumOctWk1** open, change the table style by completing the following steps:
   a. Click in any cell in the table to activate the table.
   b. Click the Table Tools Design tab.
   c. Click the More button in the Table Styles gallery.
   d. Click *White, Table Style Medium 15* at the drop-down gallery (first column, third row in the *Medium* section). Notice that the header row stays a dark blue and does not change to black.

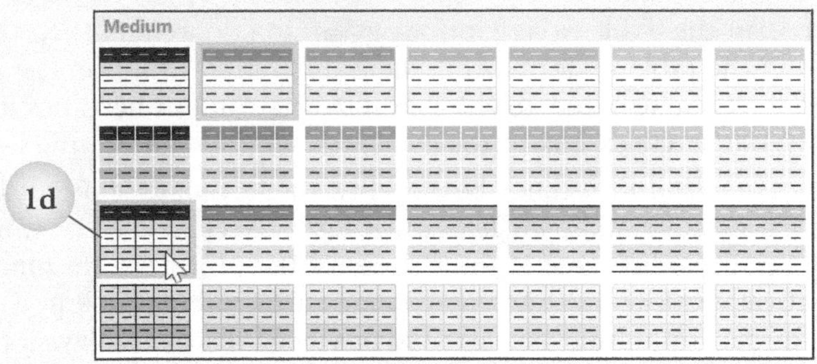

2. Change the table style options to remove the row banding, insert column banding, and emphasize the first column by completing the following steps:
   a. Click the *Banded Rows* check box in the Table Style Options group on the Table Tools Design tab to remove the check mark. All the rows in the table are now formatted the same.
   b. Click the *Banded Columns* check box in the Table Style Options group to insert a check mark. Every other column in the table is now formatted differently.
   c. Click the *First Column* check box in the Table Style Options group to insert a check mark. Notice that a darker fill color and reverse font color are applied to the first column.

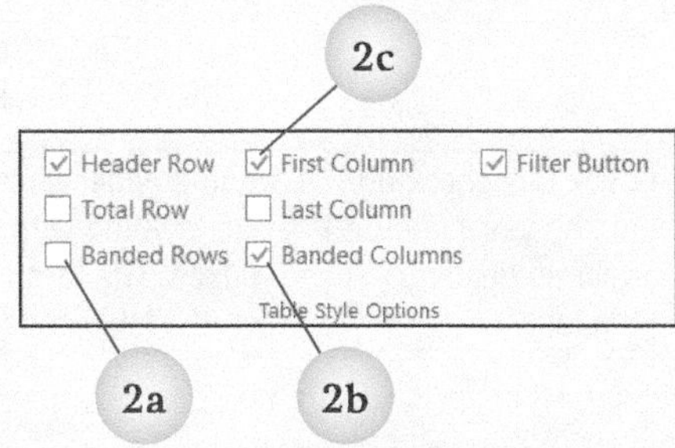

   d. Click the *Header Row* check box in the Table Style Options group to remove the check mark. Notice that the first row of the table (the row containing the column headings) disappears and is replaced with empty cells. The row is also removed from the table range definition.
   e. Click the *Header Row* check box to insert a check mark and redisplay the column headings.
   f. Click in the *Table Name* text box in the Properties group, type OctWk1, and then press the Enter key.

3. Add a *Total* row and add function formulas by completing the following steps:
   a. Click the *Total Row* check box in the Table Style Options group to add a *Total* row to the bottom of the table. Excel formats row 26 as a *Total* row, adds the label *Total* in cell A26, and automatically creates a Sum function in cell K26.
   b. Select the range K5:K26 and then apply comma formatting.
   c. In the *Fees Due* column, make cell J26 active, click the option box arrow that appears just right of the cell, and then click *Sum* at the pop-up list.
   d. Make cell B26 active, click the option box arrow that appears, and then click *Count* at the pop-up list.

None	69.96
Average	66.54
Count	89.78
Count Numbers	79.22
Max	66.54
Min	44.36
Sum	73.13
StdDev	40.63
Var	
More Functions...	1,500.04

3c

The *Taxes Due* column automatically sums when a *Total* row is added in Step 3a.

18	FL-385	None	0/7/2021	Lana Moore	Marty	O'Donovan	Separation	5.25	205.00	1,076.25	69.96
19	CL-412	Average	0/8/2021	Hilary Schmidt	Toni	Sullivan	Corporate	5.25	195.00	1,023.75	66.54
20	IN-801	Count	0/8/2021	Paul Sebastian	Rosa	Martinez	Insurance	4.25	325.00	1,381.25	89.78
21	EP-685	Count Numbers	0/8/2021	Frank Kinsela	Rosa	Martinez	Estate	3.75	325.00	1,218.75	79.22
22	CL-412	Max	0/8/2021	Hilary Schmidt	Toni	Sullivan	Corporate	5.25	195.00	1,023.75	66.54
23	CL-450	Min	0/8/2021	Henri Poissant	Toni	Sullivan	Corporate	3.50	195.00	682.50	44.36
24	RE-501	Sum StdDev	0/8/2021	Jade Eckler	Kyle	Williams	Real Estate	4.50	250.00	1,125.00	73.13
25	RE-522	Var More Functions...	0/8/2021	Connie Melanson	Kyle	Williams	Real Estate	2.50	250.00	625.00	40.63
26	Total									23,077.50	1,500.04

3d

4. Click in cell M4 and type Proposed Tax Rate and then press the Enter key.
5. With the insertion point in cell M5 create a structured reference formula that calculates a proposed tax decrease of 15% on the current taxes due by completing the following steps:
   a. Type =round(, click in cell K5, type *0.85,2), and then press the Enter key. Excel creates a structured reference formula using the table name and the column name.
   b. Click in cell M5 and look at the formula *=ROUND(OctWk1[@[Taxes Due]]*0.85,2)* in the Formula bar.
   c. Copy the formula down into cell M25.
   d. Apply Comma formatting and then deselect the range.
6. Click the Page Layout tab and change the *Width* option to *1 page* in the Scale to Fit group.
7. Preview and then print the worksheet.
8. Delete the data in column M.
9. Save **3-BillSumOctWk1**.

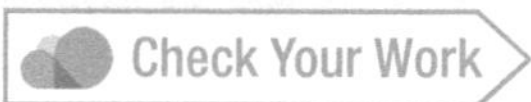
Check Your Work

Sorting and Filtering a Table

Sorting a Table

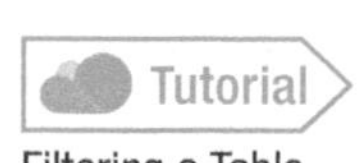
Filtering a Table

Tutorial

Filtering a Table with a Slicer

Slicer

By default, Excel displays a filter arrow next to each label in the table header row. Click the filter arrow to display a drop-down list with the same sort and filter options used in Chapter 1.

A table can also be filtered using the Slicer feature. When a Slicer is added, a Slicer pane containing all the unique values for the specified field is opened. Click an option in the Slicer pane to immediately filter the table. Add several Slicer panes to filter by more than one field, as needed.

To insert a Slicer pane, make any cell within the table active, click the Table Tools Design tab if necessary, and then click the Insert Slicer button in the Tools group. Excel opens the Insert Slicers dialog box, which contains a list of the fields

Quick Steps

Sort or Filter Table
1. Click filter arrow.
2. Click sort or filter options.
3. Click OK.

Custom Sort Table
1. Click Sort & Filter button.
2. Click *Custom Sort*.
3. Define sort levels.
4. Click OK.

in the table with a check box next to each field. Click to insert a check mark in the check box for each field to be filtered and then click OK. Click the option that the list is to be filtered on. Use the Shift and Ctrl keys to select several adjacent and nonadjacent options respectively or click the Multi-Select button at the top of the Slicer pane.

Activity 1d Sorting and Filtering a Table

Part 4 of 4

1. With **3-BillSumOctWk1** open, filter the table by attorney last name to print a list of billable hours for O'Donovan by completing the following steps:
   a. Click the filter arrow next to *Attorney LName* in cell F4.
   b. Click the *(Select All)* check box to remove the check mark.
   c. Click the *O'Donovan* check box to insert a check mark and then click OK. The table is filtered to display only those records with *O'Donovan* in the *Attorney LName* field. The Sum functions in columns J and K reflect the totals for the filtered records only.
   d. Print the filtered worksheet.
2. Redisplay all the records by clicking the *Attorney LName* filter arrow and then clicking *Clear Filter From "Attorney LName"* at the drop-down list.
3. Click the *Filter Button* check box in the Table Style Options group on the Table Tools Design tab to remove the check mark. Notice that the filter arrows disappear from the header row.
4. Filter the table with Slicers using the area of law by completing the following steps:
   a. With any cell active in the table, click the Insert Slicer button in the Tools group.
   b. At the Insert Slicers dialog box, click the *Area* check box to insert a check mark and then click OK. Excel inserts a Slicer pane in the worksheet with all the areas of law listed.
   c. If necessary, position the mouse pointer at the top of the Area Slicer pane until the pointer changes to a four-headed arrow and then drag the pane to an empty location at the right of the table.

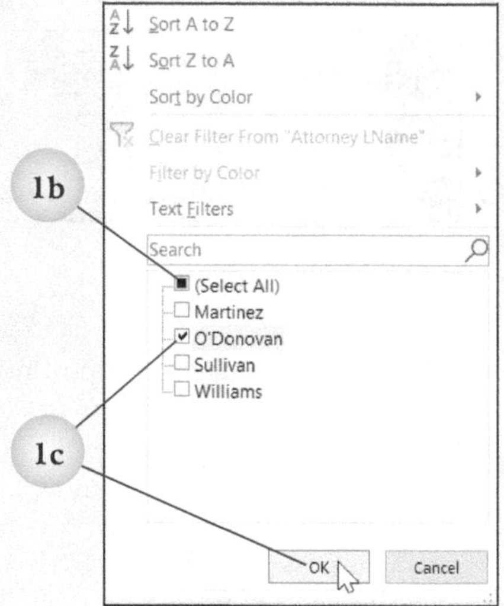

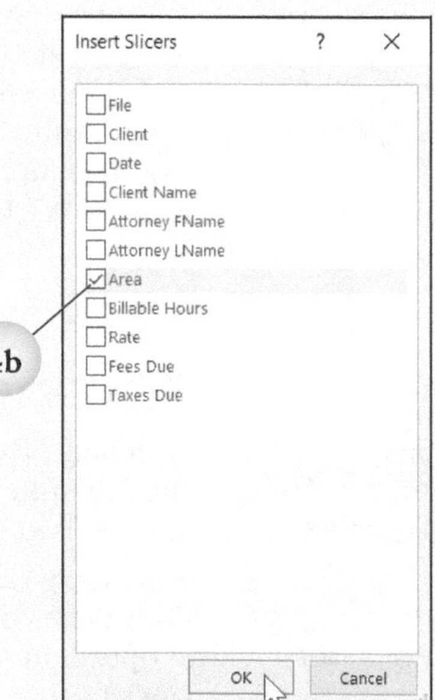

d. Click *Corporate* in the Area Slicer pane to filter the table. Excel filters the table by the *Corporate* area.
e. Click the Multi-Select button in the Slicer pane and then click *Employment*. Excel adds the *Employment* area to the filter.

5. Print the filtered worksheet.
6. Click the Clear Filter button at the top right of the Area Slicer pane to redisplay all the data.

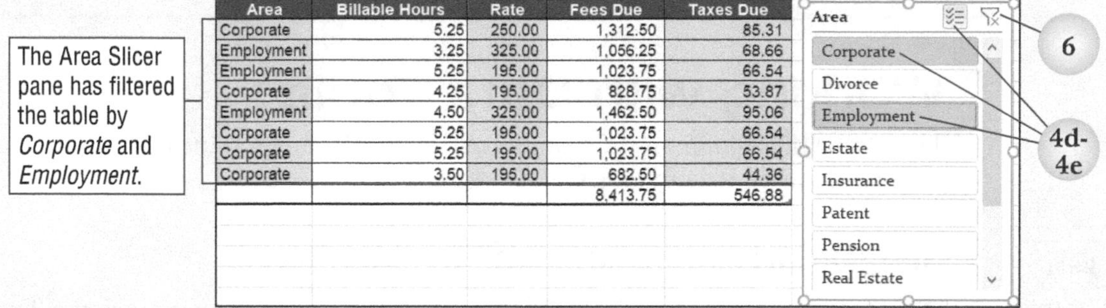

7. Click in the Area Slicer pane and then press the Delete key to remove the Slicer pane.
8. Use the Sort dialog box to sort the table first by attorney last name, then by area of law, and then by client name by completing the following steps:
   a. With any cell within the table active, click the Home tab.
   b. Click the Sort & Filter button in the Editing group and then click *Custom Sort* at the drop-down list.
   c. At the Sort dialog box, click the *Sort by* option box arrow in the *Column* section and then click *Attorney LName* at the drop-down list. The default options for *Sort On* and *Order* are correct since the cell values are to be sorted in ascending order.
   d. Click the Add Level button.
   e. Click the *Then by* option box arrow and then click *Area* at the drop-down list.
   f. Click the Add Level button.
   g. Click the second *Then by* option box arrow and then click *Client Name* at the drop-down list.
   h. Click OK.

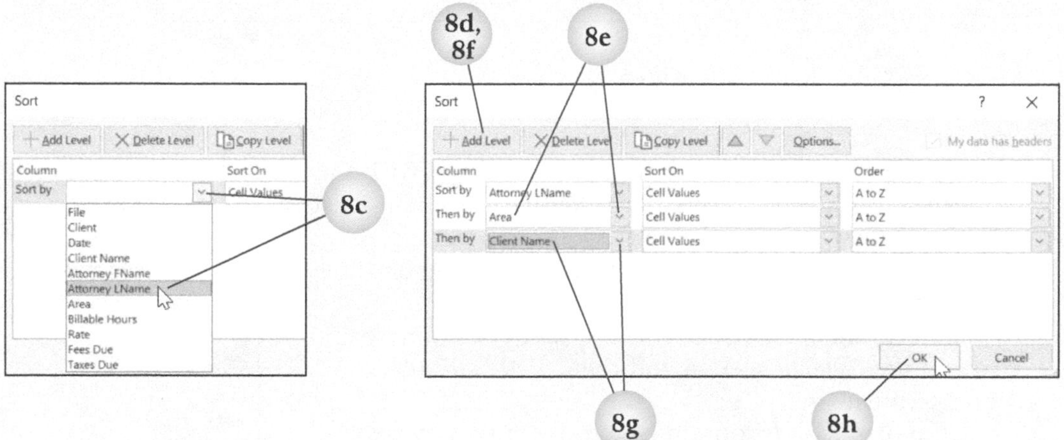

9. Print the sorted table.
10. Save **3-BillSumOctWk1**.

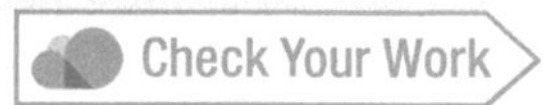

Activity 2 Use Data Tools to Split Data and Ensure Data Integrity in a Billing Summary Workbook for a Law Office — 5 Parts

You will use Excel's data tools in a billing summary workbook to split clients' first and last names into two columns, remove duplicate records, and restrict the type of data that can be entered into a field.

Working with Data Tools

The Data Tools group on the Data tab, shown in Figure 3.3, includes useful features for working with data in tables.

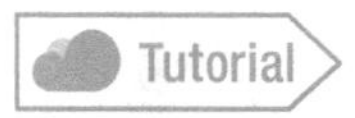

Separating Data Using Text to Columns

Text to Columns

Quick Steps

Split Text into Multiple Columns

1. Insert column(s).
2. Select data to be split.
3. Click Data tab.
4. Click Text to Columns button.
5. Click Next at first dialog box.
6. Select delimiter check box.
7. Click Next.
8. Click Finish.

Separating Data Using Text to Columns

When data in one field needs to be separated in multiple columns, use the Text to Columns feature. For example, a column that has first and last names in the same cell can be split so the first name appears in one column and the last name appears in a separate column. Breaking up the data into separate columns better facilitates sorting and other data management tasks.

Before using the Text to Columns feature, insert the required number of blank columns to separate the data immediately right of the column to be split. Select the column to be split and then click the Text to Columns button to start the Convert Text to Columns Wizard. Work through the three dialog boxes of the wizard to separate the data.

Figure 3.3 Data Tools Group on the Data Tab

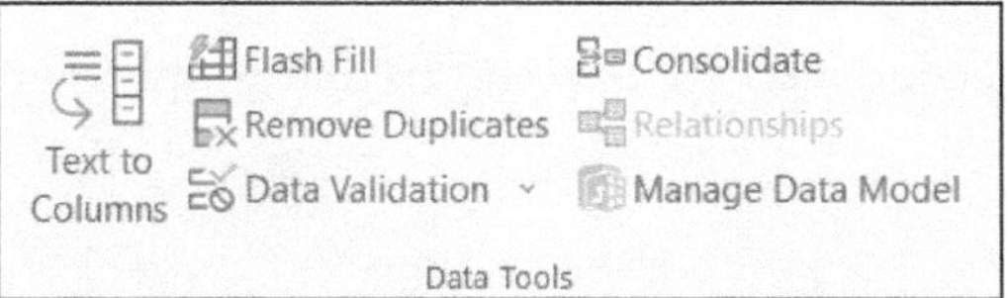

Activity 2a Separating Client Names into Two Columns — Part 1 of 5

1. With **3-BillSumOctWk1** open, save the workbook with the name **3-BillSumOctWk1-2**.
2. Modify the custom sort to sort the table first by date (oldest to newest) and then by client (smallest to largest) by completing the following steps:
   a. Click the Sort & Filter button in the Editing group on the Home tab and then click *Custom Sort* at the drop-down list.
   b. At the Sort dialog box, click the first *Sort by* option box arrow in the *Column* section and then click *Date* at the drop-down list.
   c. Click the first *Then by* option box arrow in the *Column* section and then click *Client* at the drop-down list.
   d. Click the second *Then by* on the third line and then click the Delete Level button.
   e. Click OK.

3. Split the client first and last names in column D into two columns by completing the following steps:
   a. Right-click column letter *E* at the top of the worksheet area and then click *Insert* at the shortcut menu to insert a blank column between the *Client Name* and *Attorney FName* columns in the table.
   b. Select the range D5:D25.
   c. Click the Data tab.
   d. Click the Text to Columns button in the Data Tools group.
   e. At the Convert Text to Columns Wizard - Step 1 of 3 dialog box, with *Delimited* selected in the *Choose the file type that best describes your data* section, click Next.

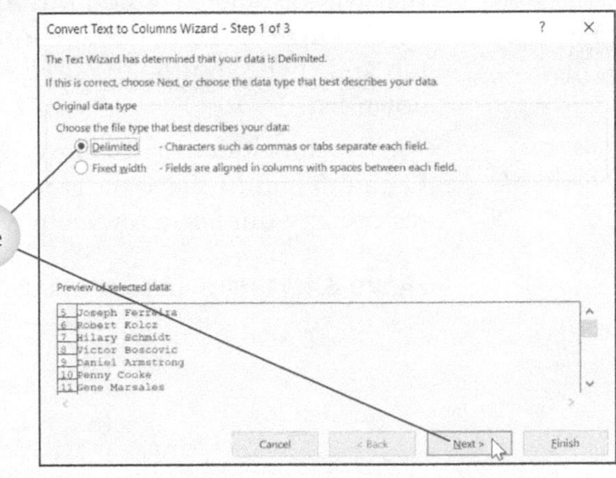

   f. In the *Delimiters* section of the Convert Text to Columns Wizard - Step 2 of 3 dialog box, click the *Space* check box to insert a check mark and then click Next. The *Data preview* section of the dialog box updates after the *Space* check box is clicked to show the names split into two columns.

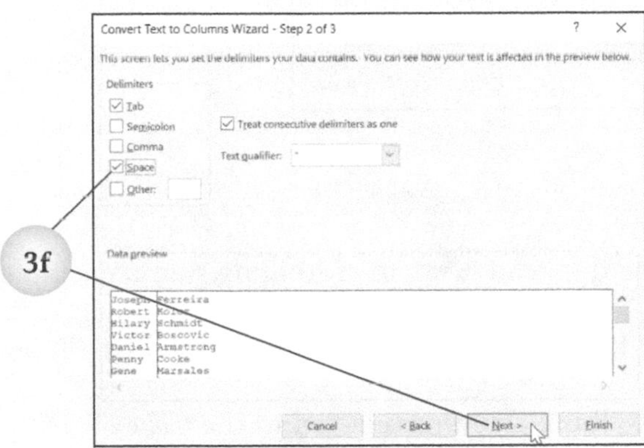

Client FName	Client LName
Joseph	Ferreira
Robert	Kolcz
Hilary	Schmidt
Victor	Boscovic
Daniel	Armstrong
Penny	Cooke
Gene	Marsales
Dana	Fletcher
Alexander	Torrez
Jean	Sauve
Victor	Boscovic
Daniel	Armstrong
Lana	Moore
Sam	Tonini
Hilary	Schmidt
Hilary	Schmidt
Paul	Sebastian
Henri	Poissant
Jade	Eckler
Frank	Kinsela
Connie	Melanson

4 5

Client first and last names are split into two columns in Steps 6a–6g.

   g. Click Finish at the last Convert Text to Columns Wizard dialog box to accept the default General data format for both columns.
   h. Deselect the range.
4. Make cell D4 active, change the label to *Client FName*, and then AutoFit the column width.
5. Make cell E4 active, change the label to *Client LName*, and then AutoFit the column width.
6. Save **3-BillSumOctWk1-2**.

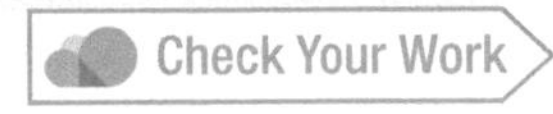

Identifying and Removing Duplicate Records

Identifying and Removing Duplicate Records

Excel can compare records within a worksheet and automatically delete duplicate rows based on the columns selected that might contain duplicate values. All the columns are selected by default when the Remove Duplicates dialog box, shown in

Quick Steps

Remove Duplicate Rows

1. Select range or make cell active in table.
2. Click Data tab.
3. Click Remove Duplicates button.
4. Select columns to compare.
5. Click OK two times.

Remove Duplicates

Figure 3.4, is opened. Click the Unselect All button to remove the check marks from all the columns, click the individual columns to compare, and then click OK. Excel automatically deletes the rows that contain duplicate values, and when the operation is completed, it displays a message with the number of rows that were removed from the worksheet or table and the number of unique values that remain.

Consider conditionally formatting duplicate values first to view the records that will be deleted. To do this, use the *Duplicate Values* option. Access this option by clicking the Conditional Formatting button in the Styles group on the Home tab and then pointing to *Highlight Cells Rules* at the Conditional Formatting drop-down list.

Excel includes the Remove Duplicates button in the Data Tools group on the Data tab and in the Tools group on the Table Tools Design tab. Click Undo to restore any duplicate rows removed by mistake.

Figure 3.4 Remove Duplicates Dialog Box

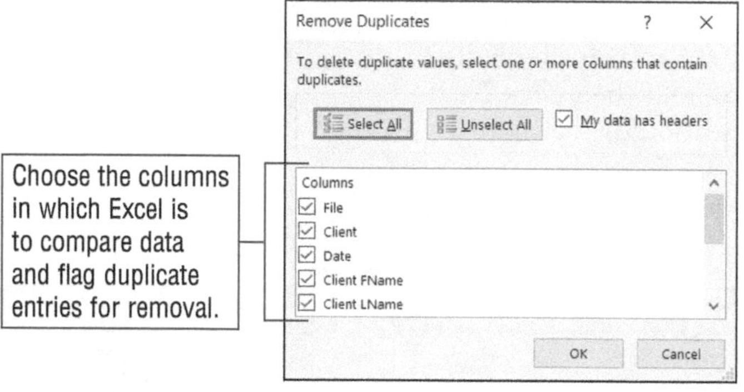

Activity 2b **Removing Duplicate Rows**

Part 2 of 5

1. With **3-BillSumOctWk1-2** open, remove the duplicate rows in the billing summary table by completing the following steps:
   a. With any cell in the table active, click the Remove Duplicates button in the Data Tools group on the Data tab.
   b. At the Remove Duplicates dialog box with all the columns selected in the *Columns* list box, click the Unselect All button.
   c. In the billing summary table, only one record should be assigned per file per date, since the attorneys record once per day the total hours spent on each file. (Records are duplicates if the same values exist in the two columns that store the file number and date). Click the *File* check box to insert a check mark.
   d. Click the *Date* check box to insert a check mark and then click OK.
   e. Click OK at the Microsoft Excel message box stating that a duplicate value was found and removed and that 20 unique values remain.

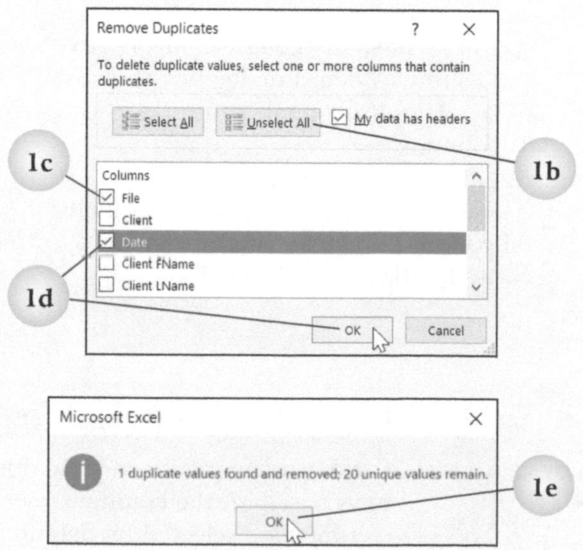

2. Scroll down the worksheet to view the total in cell L25. Compare the total with the printout from Activity 1d, Step 5. Notice that the total of the taxes due is now *1,433.50* compared with *1,500.04* in the printout.
3. Save **3-BillSumOctWk1-2**.

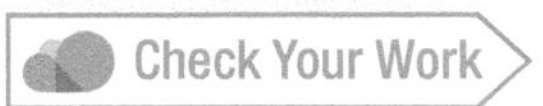

Validating Data Entry

Data Validation

Create Data Validation Rule

1. Select range.
2. Click Data tab.
3. Click Data Validation button.
4. Specify validation criteria in Settings tab.
5. Click Input Message tab.
6. Type input message title and text.
7. Click Error Alert tab.
8. Select error style.
9. Type error alert title and message text.
10. Click OK.

Validating Data Entry

Excel's data validation feature allows controlling the type of data that is accepted for entry in a cell. The type of data can be specified, along with parameters that validate whether the entry is within a certain range of acceptable values, dates, times, or text lengths. A list of values can also be set up that displays as a drop-down list when the cell is made active.

To do this, click the Data Validation button in the Data Tools group on the Data tab. At the Data Validation dialog box, shown in Figure 3.5, choose the type of data to be validated in the *Allow* option box on the Settings tab. Additional list or text boxes appear in the dialog box depending on the option chosen in the *Allow* drop-down list.

If a custom number format adds punctuation or text that appears in a cell, ignore the added characters when validating or restricting data entry. For example, a cell that contains the number *1234*, has a custom number format "*PD-*"*####*, and displays as *PD-1234* has a text length equal to four characters.

In addition to defining acceptable data entry parameters, there is the option of adding an input message and an error alert message to the range. Customized text can be added to define these messages.

When a cell to which data validation rules apply is made active, an input message displays. This kind of message is informational in nature. An error alert message appears when incorrect data is entered in a cell. There are three styles of error alerts, and a description and example of each type is provided in Table 3.1. If an error alert message has not been defined, Excel displays the Stop error alert with this default error message: *The value you entered is not valid. A user has restricted values that can be entered into this cell.*

Figure 3.5 Data Validation Dialog Box with the Settings Tab Selected

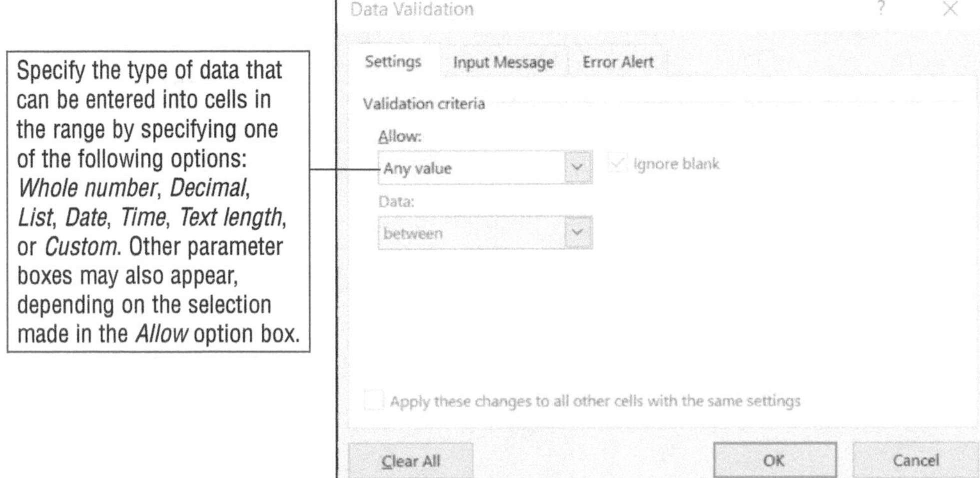

Table 3.1 Data Validation Error Alert Message Styles

Error Alert Icon	Error Alert Style	Description	Message Box Example
⊗	Stop	Prevents the data from being entered into the cell. The error alert message box provides three buttons to ensure that new data is entered.	Date is outside accepted range. × Please enter a date from October 4 to October 8, 2021. Retry Cancel Help
⚠	Warning	Does not prevent the data from being entered into the cell. The error alert message box provides four buttons below the prompt *Continue?*	Check number of hours × The hours you have entered are greater than 8. Continue? Yes No Cancel Help
ⓘ	Information	Does not prevent the data from being entered into the cell. The error alert message box provides three buttons below the error message.	Verify hours entered × The hours you have entered are outside the normal range. OK Cancel Help

Activity 2c **Restricting Data Entry to Dates within a Range** Part 3 of 5

1. With **3-BillSumOctWk1-2** open, create a validation rule, input message, and error alert for dates in the billing summary worksheet by completing the following steps:
   a. Select the range C5:C24.
   b. Click the Data Validation button in the Data Tools group on the Data tab.
   c. With Settings the active tab in the Data Validation dialog box, click the *Allow* option box arrow (displays *Any value*) and then click *Date* at the drop-down list. Validation options are dependent on the *Allow* setting. When *Date* is chosen, Excel adds *Start date* and *End date* text boxes to the *Validation criteria* section.
   d. With *between* selected in the *Data* option box, click in the *Start date* text box and then type 10/4/2021.
   e. Click in the *End date* text box and then type 10/8/2021. (Since the billing summary worksheet is for the work week of October 4 to 8, 2021, entering this validation criteria will ensure that only dates between the start date and end date are accepted.)
   f. Click the Input Message tab.
   g. Click in the *Title* text box and then type Billing Date.
   h. Click in the *Input message* text box and then type This worksheet is for the week of October 4 to October 8 only.
   i. Click the Error Alert tab.

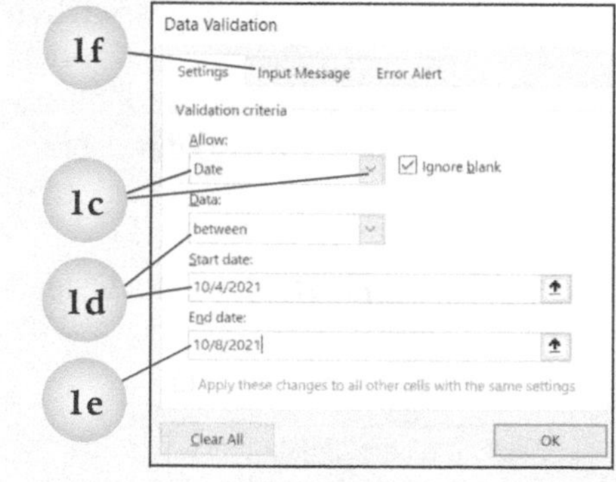

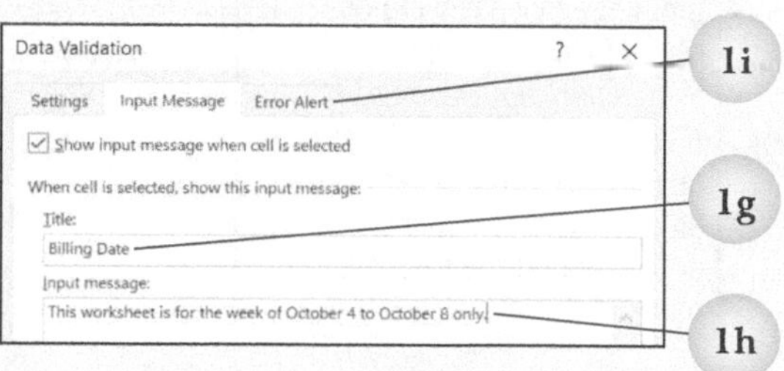

j. With *Stop* selected in the *Style* option box, click in the *Title* text box and then type Date is outside accepted range.

k. Click in the *Error message* text box and then type Please enter a date from October 4 to October 8, 2021.

l. Click OK. Since the range is active for which the data validation rules apply, the input message box appears.

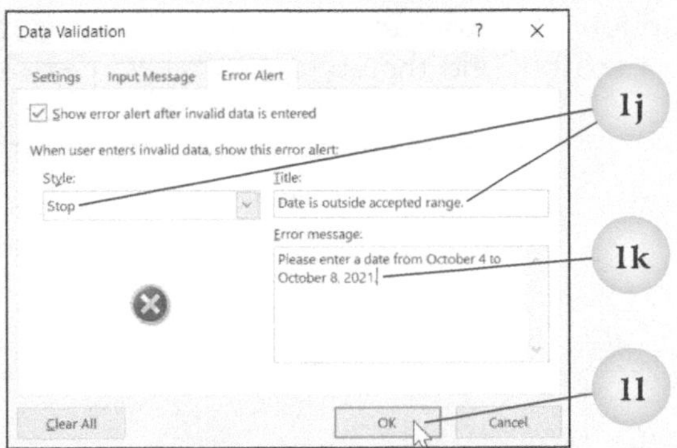

m. Deselect the range.

2. Add a new record to the table to test the date validation rule by completing the following steps:
   a. Right-click row number *25* and then click *Insert* at the shortcut menu to insert a new row into the table.
   b. Make cell A25 active, type PL-348, and then press the Tab key.
   c. Type 10420 in the *Client* column and then press the Tab key. The input message title and text appear when the *Date* column is made active.
   d. Type 10/15/2021 and then press the Tab key. Since the date entered is invalid, the error alert message box appears.
   e. Click the Retry button.
   f. Type 10/8/2021 and then press the Tab key.
   g. Enter the data in the remaining fields as follows (pressing the Tab key to move from column to column and pressing the Enter key after the fees due calculation is done):

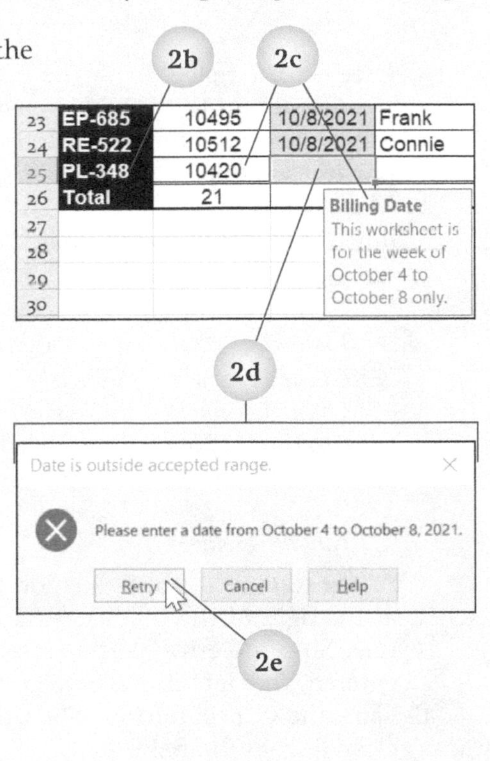

Client FName	Alexander
Client LName	Torrez
Attorney FName	Rosa
Attorney LName	Martinez
Area	Patent
Billable Hours	2.25
Rate	325.00

3. Save **3-BillSumOctWk1-2**.

Check Your Work

Activity 2d Restricting Data Entry to Values within a List

1. With **3-BillSumOctWk1-2** open, create a list of values allowed in a cell by completing the following steps:
   a. Select the range J5:J25.
   b. Click the Data Validation button in the Data Tools group on the Data tab.
   c. If necessary, click the Settings tab.
   d. Click the *Allow* option box arrow and then click *List* at the drop-down list.
   e. Click in the *Source* text box and then type 195.00,205.00,250.00,325.00.
   f. Click OK.

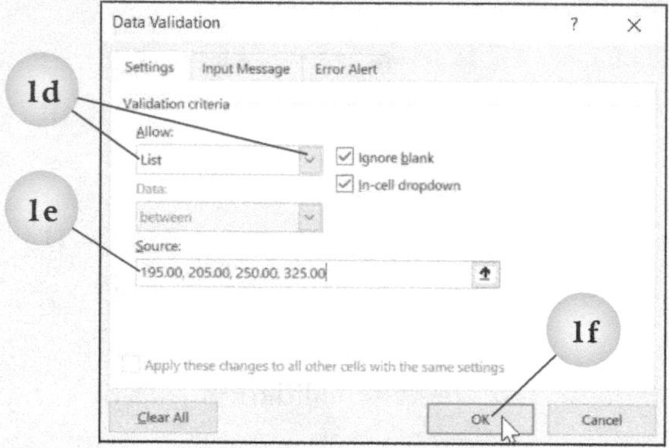

   g. Deselect the range.
2. Add a new record to the table to test the rate validation list by completing the following steps:
   a. Right-click row number *26* and then click *Insert* at the shortcut menu to insert a new row in the table.
   b. Make cell A26 active and then type data in the fields as follows (pressing the Tab key to move from column to column):

File	IN-745
Client	10210
Date	10/8/2021
Client FName	Victor
Client LName	Boscovic
Attorney FName	Rosa
Attorney LName	Martinez
Area	Insurance
Billable Hours	1.75

   c. At the *Rate* field, the validation list becomes active and an option box arrow appears at the right of the cell. Type 225.00 and then press the Tab key to test the validation rule. Since no error alert message was entered, the default message appears.
   d. Click the Cancel button. The value is cleared from the field.
   e. Make cell J26 the active cell, click the option box arrow at the right of the cell, click *325.00* at the drop-down list.
3. Save **3-BillSumOctWk1-2**.

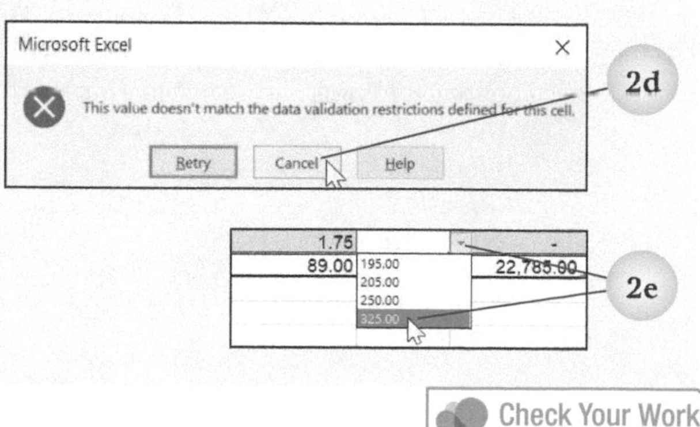

Check Your Work

Activity 2e Ensuring Data Entered Is a Specified Text Length

Part 5 of 5

1. With **3-BillSumOctWk1-2** open, create a validation rule to ensure that all client identification numbers are five characters (to be compatible with the firm's accounting system) by completing the following steps:
   a. Select the range B5:B26 and then click the Data Validation button in the Data Tools group on the Data tab.
   b. With the Settings tab active, click the *Allow* option box arrow and then click *Text length* at the drop-down list.
   c. Click the *Data* option box arrow and then click *equal to* at the drop-down list.
   d. Click in the *Length* text box and then type 5.
   e. Click OK.

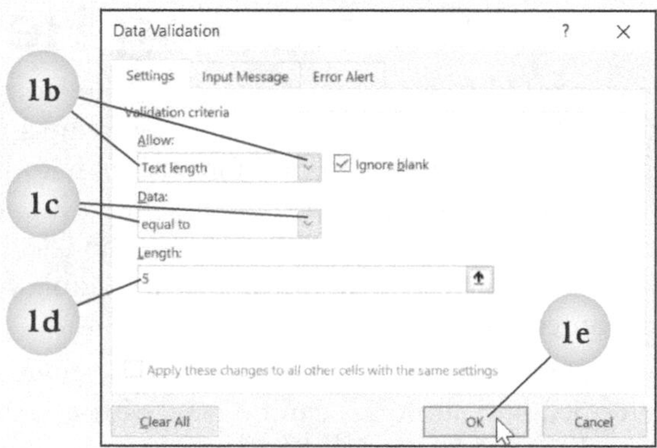

   f. Deselect the range.
2. Add a new record to the table to test the client identification validation rule by completing the following steps:
   a. Right-click row number *27* and then click *Insert* at the shortcut menu.
   b. Make cell A27 active, type FL-325, and then press the Tab key.
   c. Type 1010411 in cell B27 and then press the Tab key. Since this value is greater than the number of characters allowed in the cell, the default error message appears.
   d. Click the Retry button.
   e. Delete the selected text, type 1010, and then press the Tab key. Since this value is less than the specified text length, the default error message appears again. (Using a Text Length validation rule ensures that all entries in the range have the same number of characters. This rule is useful for validating customer numbers, employee numbers, inventory numbers, or any other data that requires a consistent number of characters.)
   f. Click the Cancel button, type 10104, and then press the Tab key. Since this entry is five characters in length, Excel moves to the next field.
   g. Enter the remaining fields as follows:

Date	10/8/2021
Client FName	Joseph
Client LName	Ferreira
Attorney FName	Marty
Attorney LName	O'Donovan
Area	Divorce
Billable Hours	5.75
Rate	205.00

3. Save and then print **3-BillSumOctWk1-2**.

Activity 3 Group and Subtotal Related Records in a Billing Summary Workbook for a Law Office

4 Parts

You will open a billing summary workbook and convert the billing summary table to a normal range, sort the rows by the attorney names, and then add subtotals to display total fees due, a count of fees, and the average billable hours and fees due for each attorney.

Converting a Table to a Normal Range and Subtotaling Related Data

Quick Steps

Convert Table to Range
1. Make table cell active.
2. Click Table Tools Design tab.
3. Click Convert to Range button.
4. Click Yes.

Create Subtotal
1. Select range.
2. Click Data tab.
3. Click Subtotal button.
4. Select field to group by in *At each change in* option box.
5. Select function in *Use function* option box.
6. Select field(s) to subtotal in *Add subtotal to* list box.
7. Click OK.

Converting a Table to a Normal Range and Subtotaling Related Data

A table can be converted to a normal range using the Convert to Range button in the Tools group on the Table Tools Design tab. Convert a table to a range to use the Subtotal feature or when the data no longer needs to be treated as a table, independent of the data in the rest of the worksheet. Remove some or all the table styles before converting the table to a range. Use the Clear button in the Table Styles gallery or click the individual options in the Table Style Options group to remove any unwanted formatting.

A range of data with a column that has multiple rows with the same field value can be grouped and subtotals can be created for each group automatically by using the Subtotal button in the Outline group on the Data tab. For example, a worksheet with multiple records with the same department name in a field can be grouped by department name and a subtotal of a numeric field can be calculated for each department. Choose from a list of functions for the subtotal, such as Average and Sum. Before creating subtotals, sort the data by the fields in which the records are to be grouped. Remove any blank rows within the range that is to be grouped and subtotaled.

Excel displays a new row with a summary total when the field value for the specified subtotal column changes. A grand total is also automatically included at the bottom of the range. Excel displays the subtotals with buttons along the left of the worksheet area. These buttons are used to show or hide the details for each group using the Outline feature. Excel can create an outline with up to eight levels.

Figure 3.6 illustrates the data that will be grouped and subtotaled in Activity 3a; the data is displayed with the worksheet at level 2 of the outline. Figure 3.7 shows the same worksheet with two attorney groups expanded to show the detail records.

Figure 3.6 Worksheet with Subtotals by Attorney Last Name Displayed at Level 2 of Outline

outline level buttons

O'Donovan & Sullivan Law Associates
Associate Billing Summary
October 4 to 8, 2021

	File	Client	Date	Client FName	Client LName	Attorney FName	Attorney LName	Area	Billable Hours	Rate	Fees Due	Taxes Due
15							Martinez Total				12,106.25	684.61
20							O'Donovan Total				4,305.00	268.78
26							Sullivan Total				4,871.25	371.56
31							Williams Total				3,250.00	269.67
32							Grand Total				24,532.50	1,594.62

Hide Detail button

Show Detail button

Figure 3.7 Worksheet with Subtotals by Attorney Last Name with Martinez and Sullivan Groups Expanded

O'Donovan & Sullivan Law Associates
Associate Billing Summary
October 4 to 8, 2021

	A	B	C	D	E	F	G	H	I	J	K	L
4	File	Client	Date	Client FName	Client LName	Attorney FName	Attorney LName	Area	Billable Hours	Rate	Fees Due	Taxes Due
5	IN-745	10210	10/5/2021	Victor	Boscovic	Rosa	Martinez	Insurance	4.25	325.00	1,381.25	68.66
6	IN-745	10210	10/7/2021	Victor	Boscovic	Rosa	Martinez	Insurance	4.50	325.00	1,462.50	89.94
7	IN-745	10210	10/8/2021	Victor	Boscovic	Rosa	Martinez	Insurance	1.75	325.00	568.75	52.81
8	EL-632	10225	10/5/2021	Daniel	Armstrong	Rosa	Martinez	Employment	3.25	325.00	1,056.25	95.06
9	EL-632	10225	10/7/2021	Daniel	Armstrong	Rosa	Martinez	Employment	4.50	325.00	1,462.50	76.62
10	PL-512	10290	10/7/2021	Sam	Tonini	Rosa	Martinez	Pension	3.75	325.00	1,218.75	69.96
11	IN-801	10346	10/8/2021	Paul	Sebastian	Rosa	Martinez	Insurance	4.25	325.00	1,381.25	66.54
12	PL-348	10420	10/6/2021	Alexander	Torrez	Rosa	Martinez	Patent	5.00	325.00	1,625.00	47.53
13	PL-348	10420	10/8/2021	Alexander	Torrez	Rosa	Martinez	Patent	2.25	325.00	731.25	73.13
14	EP-685	10495	10/8/2021	Frank	Kinsela	Rosa	Martinez	Estate	3.75	325.00	1,218.75	44.36
15							**Martinez Total**				12,106.25	684.61
20							**O'Donovan Total**				4,305.00	268.78
21	CL-412	10125	10/4/2021	Hilary	Schmidt	Toni	Sullivan	Corporate	5.25	250.00	1,312.50	36.97
22	CL-412	10125	10/8/2021	Hilary	Schmidt	Toni	Sullivan	Corporate	5.25	195.00	1,023.75	85.31
23	CL-521	10334	10/6/2021	Gene	Marsales	Toni	Sullivan	Corporate	4.25	195.00	828.75	89.78
24	CL-501	10341	10/6/2021	Dana	Fletcher	Toni	Sullivan	Employment	5.25	195.00	1,023.75	105.63
25	CL-450	10358	10/8/2021	Henri	Poissant	Toni	Sullivan	Corporate	3.50	195.00	682.50	53.87
26							**Sullivan Total**				4,871.25	371.56
31							**Williams Total**				3,250.00	269.67
32							**Grand Total**				24,532.50	1,594.62

Activity 3a Converting a Table to a Normal Range and Subtotaling Related Data

Part 1 of 4

1. With **3-BillSumOctWk1-2** open, save the workbook with the name **3-BillSumOctWk1-3**.
2. Remove style options and convert the table to a normal range to group and subtotal the records by completing the following steps:
   a. Click in any cell in the table and then click the Table Tools Design tab.
   b. Click the *Total Row* check box in the Table Style Options group to remove the *Total* row from the table. The Subtotal feature includes a grand total automatically, so the *Total* row is no longer needed.
   c. Click the *Banded Columns* check box in the Table Style Options group to remove the banded formatting.
   d. Click the Convert to Range button in the Tools group.
   e. Click Yes at the Microsoft Excel message box asking if you want to convert the table to a normal range.

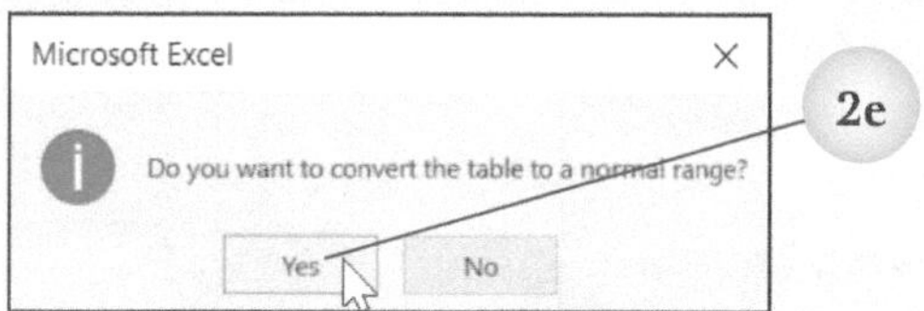

3. Sort the data by the fields to be subtotaled and grouped by completing the following steps:
   a. Select the range A4:L27.
   b. Click the Sort & Filter button in the Editing group on the Home tab and then click *Custom Sort* at the drop-down list.

c. At the Sort dialog box, define three levels to group and sort the records as follows:

Column	*Sort On*	*Order*
Attorney LName	Cell Values	A to Z
Client	Cell Values	Smallest to Largest
Date	Cell Values	Oldest to Newest

d. Click OK.

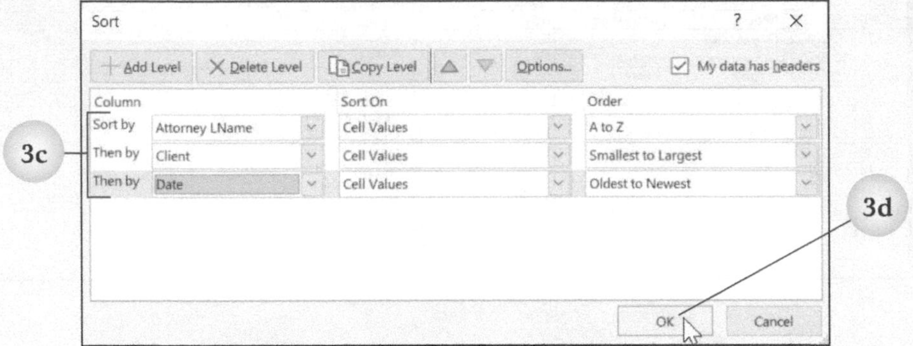

4. Create a subtotal for the fees and taxes due at each change in attorney last name by completing the following steps:
   a. With the range A4:L27 still selected, click the Data tab.
   b. Click the Subtotal button in the Outline group.
   c. At the Subtotal dialog box, click the *At each change in* option box arrow (which displays *File*), scroll down the list, and then click *Attorney LName*.
   d. Click the *Fees Due* check box in the *Add subtotal to* list box to add a checkmark. Excel adds subtotals to the *Fees Due* and *Taxes Due* columns.
   e. With *Use function* set to *Sum*, click OK.

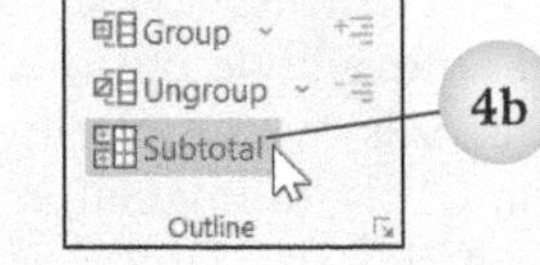

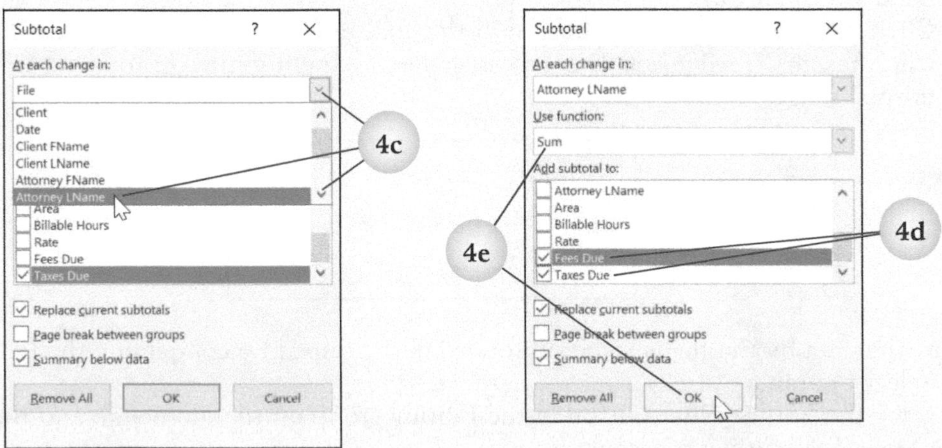

   f. Deselect the range.
5. Select columns A through L and AutoFit the column widths. Deselect the columns.
6. Print the worksheet.
7. Save **3-BillSumOctWk1-3**.

Activity 3b Working with Outline Levels

1. With **3-BillSumOctWk1-3** open, show and hide levels in the outlined worksheet by completing the following steps:
   a. Click the level 1 button at the top left of the worksheet area below the Name text box. Excel collapses the worksheet to display only the grand total of the *Fees Due* and *Taxes Due* columns.

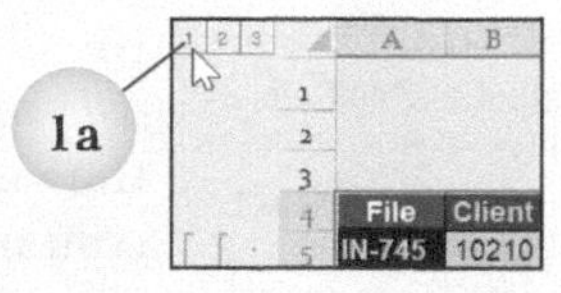

   b. Click the level 2 button to display the subtotals by attorney last names. Notice that a button with a plus symbol (+) displays next to each subtotal in the *Outline* section at the left of the worksheet area. The button with the plus symbol is the Show Detail button and the button with the minus symbol (–) is the Hide Detail button. Compare your worksheet with the one shown in Figure 3.6 (on page 76).
   c. Click the Show Detail button (which displays as a plus symbol) next to the row with the Martinez subtotal. The detail rows for the group of records for Martinez are displayed.

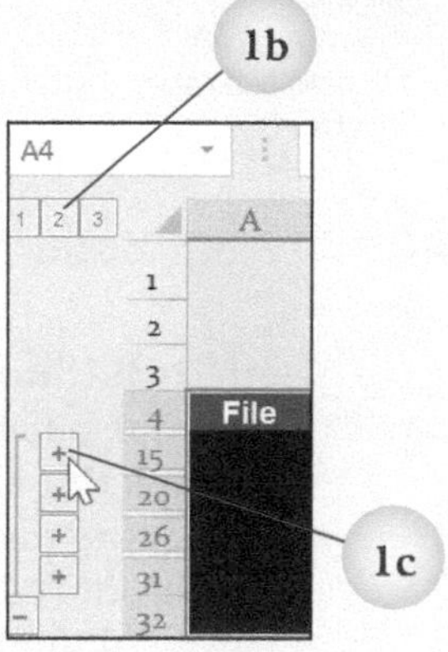

   d. Click the Show Detail button next to the row with the Sullivan subtotal.
   e. Compare your worksheet with the one shown in Figure 3.7 (on page 77).
   f. Click the level 3 button to display all the detail rows.
2. Save **3-BillSumOctWk1-3**.

Modifying Subtotals

Quick Steps

Add Additional Subtotal

1. Select range.
2. Click Data tab.
3. Click Subtotal button.
4. Select field to group by in *At each change in* option box.
5. Select function in *Use function* option box.
6. Select field(s) to subtotal in *Add subtotal to* list box.
7. Click *Replace current subtotals* check box to remove check mark.
8. Click OK.

Modify subtotals to include more than one type of calculation. For example, if subtotals are inserted that sum data, subtotals that count and average the same data can be added. When a new subtotal is added, it is placed above the existing subtotal or subtotals.

To add a subtotal to a data range that already has one or more subtotals, select a cell in the range that has been subtotaled and then click the Subtotal button in the Outline group on the Data tab. Select the field to insert the new subtotal at the *At each change in* drop-down list, select a function for the new subtotal at the *Use function* drop-down list, click the check box to insert a check mark for the field to which you are adding a subtotal, click the *Replace current subtotals* check box to remove the check mark, and then click OK.

To replace all the subtotals, click in a cell in the range; display the Subtotal dialog box; select the location, function, and field or fields for the replacement; verify that the *Replace current subtotals* check box contains a check mark; and then click OK.

To remove all the subtotals, select a cell in the range that has been subtotaled, click the Subtotal button, and then click the Remove All button.

Selecting Data from Different Outline Levels

Find & Select

Quick Steps

Select Visible Cells Only

1. Click Find & Select button.
2. Click *Go to Special* option.
3. Click *Visible cells only* radio button.
4. Click OK.

By default, when a subtotal or grand total is selected in a collapsed outline, the underlying data is also selected. To select only specific subtotals and/or grand totals, click the Find & Select button in the Editing group on the Home tab, click the *Go To Special* option to display the Go To Special dialog box, click the *Visible cells only* radio button to insert a bullet, and then click OK. After you have selected the visible subtotals, you can copy them to a new range or format the cells containing them.

Activity 3c **Modifying and Formatting Subtotals**

Part 3 of 4

1. With **3-BillSumOctWk1-3** open, add a subtotal to count the number of billable records for each attorney for the week by completing the following steps:
   a. Select the range A4:L32 and then click the Subtotal button in the Outline group on the Data tab. The Subtotal dialog box opens with the settings used for the subtotals created in Activity 3a.
   b. Click the *Replace current subtotals* check box to remove the check mark. With this check box cleared, Excel adds another subtotal row to each group.
   c. Click the *Use function* option box arrow and then click *Count* at the drop-down list.
   d. Click the *Fees Due* check box in the *Add subtotal to* list box to remove the check mark.
   e. With *Attorney LName* still selected in the *At each change in* list box and *Taxes Due* still selected in the *Add subtotal to* list box, click OK. Excel adds a new subtotal row to each group with the count of records displayed.
2. Add a subtotal to calculate the average billable hours and average fees due for each attorney by completing the following steps:
   a. With the data range still selected, click the Subtotal button.
   b. Click the *Use function* option box arrow and then click *Average* at the drop-down list.
   c. Click the *Billable Hours*, *Fees Due*, and *Taxes Due* check boxes in the *Add subtotal to* list box to insert check marks in the *Billable Hours* and *Fees Due* check boxes and to remove the check mark from the *Taxes Due* check box.
   d. Click OK. Excel adds a new subtotal row to each group with the average billable hours and average fees due for each attorney.

Attorney LName	Area	Billable Hours	Rate	Fees Due	Taxes Due
Martinez	Insurance	4.25	325.00	1,381.25	68.66
Martinez	Insurance	4.50	325.00	1,462.50	89.94
Martinez	Insurance	1.75	325.00	568.75	52.81
Martinez	Employment	3.25	325.00	1,056.25	95.06
Martinez	Employment	4.50	325.00	1,462.50	76.62
Martinez	Pension	3.75	325.00	1,218.75	69.96
Martinez	Insurance	4.25	325.00	1,381.25	66.54
Martinez	Patent	5.00	325.00	1,625.00	47.53
Martinez	Patent	2.25	325.00	731.25	73.13
Martinez	Estate	3.75	325.00	1,218.75	44.36
Martinez Average		3.73		1,210.63	
Martinez Count					10
Martinez Total				12,106.25	684.61

The averages of the *Billable Hours* and *Fees Due* columns are added to the subtotals for all the attorneys in Steps 2a–2c. The data for the Martinez group is shown.

3. Format the average, count, total, and grand total subtotals by completing the following steps:
   a. Click the level 4 outline button.
   b. Select the range G15:L42, click the Home tab, and then click the Find & Select button in the Editing group.
   c. Click the *Go To Special* option.
   d. Click the *Visible cells only* radio button and then click OK.
   e. Apply bold formatting and the *White, Background 1, Darker 15%* fill (first column, third row). ***Note that you will have to click the Bold button twice to apply Bold formatting.***
   f. Click the level 5 outline button.
   g. Deselect the range.

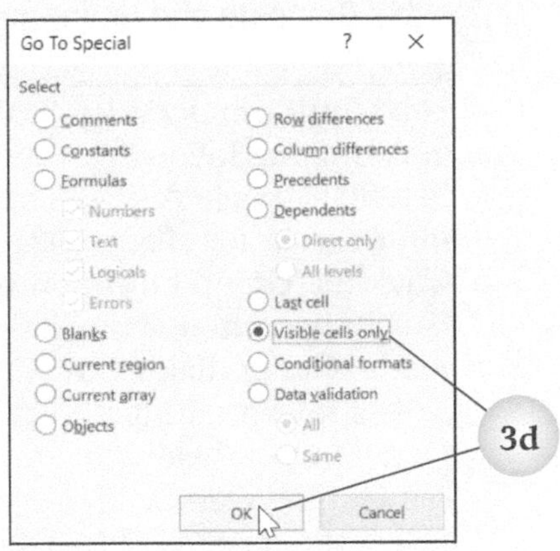

4. Click the Page Layout tab and scale the height of the worksheet to 1 page.
5. Save the revised workbook with the name **3-BillSumOctWk1-3c**.
6. Print and then close **3-BillSumOctWk1-3c**.

Grouping and Ungrouping Data

Group

Ungroup

Quick Steps

Group Data by Rows

1. Select range to be grouped within outlined worksheet.
2. Click Data tab.
3. Click Group button.
4. Click OK.

Ungroup Data by Rows

1. Select grouped range within outlined worksheet.
2. Click Data tab.
3. Click Ungroup button.
4. Click OK.

Grouping and Ungrouping Data

Use the Group and Ungroup buttons in the Outline group on the Data tab to further collapse and expand subgroups of records at various levels or use the keyboard shortcuts Shift + Alt + Right Arrow key to group data and Shift + Alt + Left Arrow key to ungroup data. For example, in an outlined worksheet with detailed rows displayed, a group of records can be further grouped by selecting a group of records and clicking the Group button to open the Group dialog box, shown in Figure 3.8. Clicking OK with *Rows* selected adds a further group feature to the selection. Selecting records that have been grouped and clicking the Ungroup button removes the group feature added to the selection and removes the Hide Detail button.

Columns can also be grouped and ungrouped. The outline section with the level numbers and the Show Detail and Hide Detail buttons displays across the top of the worksheet area. For example, in a worksheet in which two columns are used to arrive at a formula, the source columns can be grouped and the details hidden so that only the formula column with the calculated results is displayed in an outlined worksheet.

Figure 3.8 Group Dialog Box

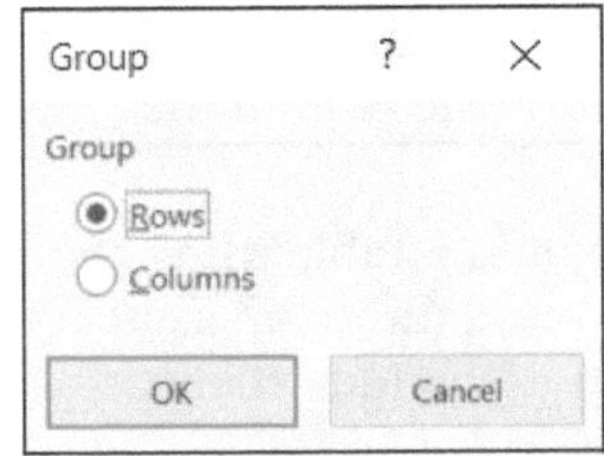

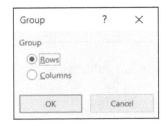

Activity 3d Grouping and Ungrouping Data

Part 4 of 4

1. Open **3-BillSumOctWk1-3.** Group client data within the Martinez attorney group by completing the following steps:
   a. Select the range A5:L7. These three rows contain billing information for client 10210.
   b. Click the Group button in the Outline group on the Data tab. (Click the button and not the button arrow.)
   c. At the Group dialog box with *Rows* selected, click OK. Excel adds a fourth outline level to the worksheet and a Hide Detail button below the last row of the grouped records in the Outline section.
   d. Select the range A12:L13, click the Group button, and then click OK at the Group dialog box.
   e. Deselect the range.
2. Experiment with the Hide Detail buttons in the Martinez group by hiding the detail for client 10210 and then hiding the detail for client 10420.
3. Redisplay the detail rows by clicking the Show Detail button for each client.
4. Select the range A5:L7, click the Ungroup button (click the button and not the button arrow), and then click OK at the Ungroup dialog box.

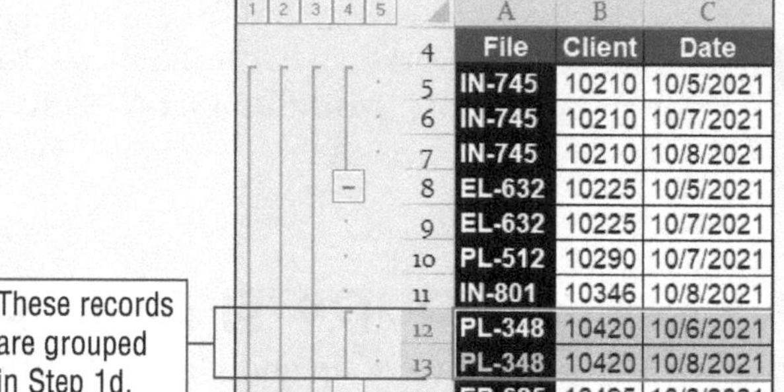

These records are grouped in Step 1d.
1 2 3 4 5
A B C
4 File Client Date
5 IN-745 10210 10/5/2021
6 IN-745 10210 10/7/2021
7 IN-745 10210 10/8/2021
8 EL-632 10225 10/5/2021
9 EL-632 10225 10/7/2021
10 PL-512 10290 10/7/2021
11 IN-801 10346 10/8/2021
12 PL-348 10420 10/6/2021
13 PL-348 10420 10/8/2021
14 EP-685 10495 10/8/2021

5. Select the range A12:L13, click the Ungroup button, and then click OK at the Ungroup dialog box.
6. Select the range A5:L14, click the Ungroup button, and then click OK at the Ungroup dialog box. Notice that the Hide Detail button is removed for the entire Martinez group.
7. Deselect the range and then click the level 4 button at the top of the outline section. Notice that the data for the Martinez records do not collapse like the others, since they are no longer grouped.
8. Save the revised workbook with the name **3-BillSumOctWk1-3d.**
9. Print and then close **3-BillSumOctWk1-3d.**

Chapter Summary

- A table in Excel is a range of cells similar in structure to a database in which there are no blank rows and the first row of the range contains column headings.
- Columns in a table are called *fields* and rows are called *records*. The first row of a table contains the column headings and is called the *field names row* or *header row*.
- Define a range as a table using the Table button in the Tables group on the Insert tab. Type data in adjacent rows and columns and the table will expand automatically to include them.
- Typing a formula in the first record of a new column causes Excel to define the column as a calculated column and to automatically copy the formula to the remaining cells in the column.

- The contextual Table Tools Design tab contains options for formatting tables.
- The Table Styles gallery contains several options for changing the visual appearance of a table.
- Banding rows or columns formats every other row or column differently to make reading a large table easier.
- Insert check marks in the *First Column* and *Last Column* check boxes in the Table Style Options group to add emphasis to the first column or last column in a table.
- The row containing column headings in a table can be shown or hidden using the *Header Row* option in the Table Style Options group.
- Adding a *Total* row to a table causes Excel to add the word *Total* in the leftmost column and to create a Sum function in the last numeric column in the table. Additional functions can be added by clicking in a column in the *Total* row and selecting a function from the pop-up list.
- By default, Excel displays a filter arrow next to each label in the table header row. Use these arrows to filter and sort the table.
- Slicers are used to filter data in a table using a Slicer pane, which contains all the items in the designated field.
- A column containing text that can be split can be separated into multiple columns using the Text to Columns feature. The Convert Text to Columns Wizard contains three dialog boxes that define how to split the data.
- Use options at the Remove Duplicates dialog box to compare records within a worksheet and automatically delete rows that contain duplicate values.
- Data can be validated as it is being entered into a worksheet, and invalid data can be prevented from being stored or a warning can be issued stating that data has been entered that does not conform to the parameters.
- Define the validation criteria for a cell entry at the Settings tab in the Data Validation dialog box. Data can be allowed based on values, dates, times, and text lengths or restricted to values within a drop-down list.
- Define a message that pops up when a cell for which data is restricted becomes active at the Input Message tab in the Data Validation dialog box.
- Define the type of error alert to display and the content of the error message at the Error Alert tab in the Data Validation dialog box.
- Convert a table to a normal range using the Convert to Range button in the Tools group on the Table Tools Design tab. Convert a table to a range to use the Subtotal feature or when a range of cells no longer needs to be treated independently from the rest of the worksheet.
- Sort a worksheet by column(s) to group data for subtotals before opening the Subtotals dialog box.
- A range of data with a column that has multiple rows with the same field value can be grouped and subtotals created for each group automatically by using the Subtotal button in the Outline group on the Data tab.
- Excel adds a subtotal automatically at each change in content for the column specified as the subtotal field. A grand total is also automatically added to the bottom of the range.
- Display more than one subtotal row for a group to calculate multiple functions, such as Sum and Average.

- A subtotaled range is outlined and record details can be collapsed or expanded using the level number, Hide Detail, and Show Detail buttons.
- To select only specific subtotals and/or grand totals, click the Find & Select button in the Editing group on the Home tab, click the *Go To Special* option to display the Go To Special dialog box, click the *Visible cells only* radio button to insert a bullet, and then click OK.
- When a worksheet is outlined, use the Group and Ungroup buttons in the Outline group on the Data tab to manage the display of individual groups.

Commands Review

FEATURE	RIBBON TAB, GROUP	BUTTON	KEYBOARD SHORTCUT
convert table to range	Table Tools Design, Tools		
create table	Insert, Tables		Ctrl + T
group data	Data, Outline		Shift + Alt + Right Arrow key
remove duplicates	Data, Data Tools OR Table Tools Design, Tools		
sort and filter table	Home, Editing		
subtotals	Data, Outline		
table styles	Table Tools Design, Table Styles		
text to columns	Data, Data Tools		
Total row	Table Tools Design, Table Style Options		Ctrl + Shift + T
ungroup	Data, Outline		Shift + Alt + Left Arrow key
validate data	Data, Data Tools		
visible cells only	Home, Editing		Ctrl + G

Microsoft®

Excel®

CHAPTER 4

Summarizing and Consolidating Data

Performance Objectives

Upon successful completion of Chapter 4, you will be able to:

1 Summarize data by creating formulas with range names that reference cells in other worksheets
2 Summarize data by creating 3-D references
3 Create formulas that link to cells in other worksheets or workbooks
4 Edit a link to a source workbook
5 Edit or break a link to an external source
6 Use the Consolidate feature to summarize data from multiple worksheets in a master worksheet
7 Create, edit, and format a PivotTable
8 Filter a PivotTable using Slicers and Timelines
9 Create and format a PivotChart
10 Create and format Sparklines

While working with Excel, you may find it useful to summarize and report data from various worksheets. Data can be summarized by creating formulas that reference cells in other areas of the same worksheet or workbook, or by linking to cells in other worksheets or workbooks. The Consolidate feature can also be used to summarize data and consolidate it into a master worksheet. Once the data has been summarized, consider presenting or analyzing the data by creating and formatting a PivotTable or PivotChart. Also consider creating Sparklines, which are miniature charts inserted into cells that reveal trends or other patterns in the data. Timelines allow the filtering of a PivotTable or PivotChart using a specified timeframe. In this chapter, you will learn how to summarize and filter data using a variety of methods and then present visually summarized data for analysis.

Before beginning chapter work, copy the EL2C4 folder to your storage medium and then make EL2C4 the active folder.

The online course includes additional training and assessment resources.

Activity 1 Calculate Park Attendance Totals **5 Parts**

You will calculate total park attendance at three national parks by using data stored in separate worksheets and linking to a cell in another workbook. You will also edit a linked workbook and update and remove the link in the destination file.

Summarizing Data in Multiple Worksheets Using Range Names

Quick Steps

Sum Multiple Worksheets Using Range Names

1. Make formula cell active.
2. Type =sum(.
3. Type first range name.
4. Type comma ,.
5. Type second range name.
6. Type comma ,.
7. Continue typing range names separated by commas until finished.
8. Type).
9. Press Enter key.

Summarizing Data in Multiple Worksheets Using Range Names and 3-D References

A workbook that has been organized with data in separate worksheets can be summarized by creating formulas that reference cells in other worksheets. When a formula is created that references a cell in the same worksheet, the sheet name does not need to be included in the reference. For example, the formula *=A3+A4* causes Excel to add the value in cell A3 in the active worksheet to the value in cell A4 in the active worksheet. However, when a formula is created that references a cell in a different worksheet, the sheet name must be included in the formula.

Assume that Excel is to add the value in cell A3 that resides in Sheet2 to the value in cell A3 that resides in Sheet3 in the workbook. To do this, include the worksheet name in the formula by typing *=Sheet2!A3+Sheet3!A3* into the formula cell. This formula contains both worksheet references and cell references. The worksheet reference precedes the cell reference and is separated from the cell reference with an exclamation point. Without a worksheet reference, Excel assumes the cells are in the active worksheet.

A formula that references the same cell in a range that extends over two or more worksheets is often called a *3-D reference*. For a formula that includes a 3-D reference, the 3-D reference can be typed directly in a cell or entered using a point-and-click approach. Formulas that include 3-D references are sometimes referred to as *3-D formulas*.

As an alternative, consider using range names to simplify formulas that summarize data in multiple worksheets. Recall from Chapter 2 that a range name includes the worksheet reference by default; therefore, typing the range name in the formula automatically references the correct worksheet. Another advantage to using a range name is that the name can describe the worksheet with the source data. When range names are used, the two worksheets do not have to be made identical in organizational structure.

Activity 1a Summarizing Data in Multiple Worksheets Using Range Names **Part 1 of 5**

1. Open **MayEntries**.
2. Save the workbook with the name **4-MayEntries**.
3. Click each sheet tab and review the data. Attendance data for each park is entered as a separate worksheet.

4. In the workbook, range names have already been created. Check each range name to find out what it references.

4 — Name box: E7 | Formula bar: 68
Name box list: Bryce, Grand, Mesa

	A	B	C	D	E	F
1				Bryce Canyon National Park		
2				Utah		
3				http://www.nps.gov/brca		
4				May 2021		
5				Private Vehicle and Individual Entrances Only		
6	Day	Entries		Day	Entries	
7	1	40		17	68	
8	2	55		18	30	
9	3	35		19	47	
10	4	30		20	40	
11	5	56		21	65	
12	6	32		22	79	
13	7	22		23	58	
14	8	25		24	65	
15	9	46		25	44	
16	10	19		26	55	
17	11	25		27	58	
18	12	65		28	68	
19	13	24		29	88	
20	14	30		30	72	
21	15	33		31	91	
22	16	42				

These ranges are automatically selected when *Bryce* is selected in the Name box.

5. Create a formula to add the total attendance for May at all three parks by completing the following steps:
   a. Click the AttendanceSummary tab to activate the worksheet.
   b. If necessary, make cell F7 active, type =sum(bryce,grand,mesa), and then press the Enter key. Notice that in a SUM formula, multiple range names are separated with commas. Excel returns the result *10460* in cell F7 of the AttendanceSummary worksheet.

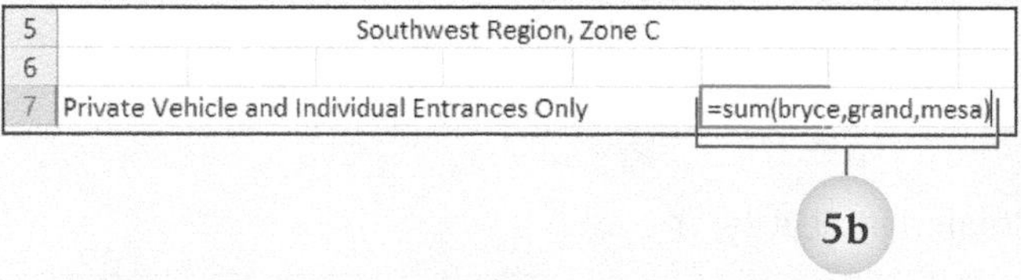

   c. Apply the Comma format with no digits after the decimal point to cell F7.
6. Save and then close **4-MayEntries.**

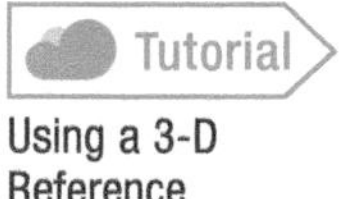

Using a 3-D Reference

A disadvantage to using range names emerges when several worksheets need to be summarized because the range name references must be created in each worksheet. If several worksheets need to be summarized, a more efficient method is to use a 3-D reference. Generally, when using a 3-D reference, it is a good idea to set up the data in each worksheet in identical cells. In Activity 1b, you will calculate the same attendance total for the three parks using a 3-D reference instead of range names.

Activity 1b Summarizing Data in Multiple Worksheets Using a 3-D Reference Formula

Part 2 of 5

1. Open **MayEntries**.
2. Save the workbook with the name **4-3D-MayEntries**.
3. Calculate the attendance total for the three parks using a point-and-click approach to create a 3-D reference by completing the following steps:
   a. In the AttendanceSummary worksheet, make cell F7 active and then type =sum(.
   b. Click the BryceCanyon sheet tab.
   c. Press and hold down the Shift key, click the MesaVerde sheet tab, and then release the Shift key. (Holding down the Shift key while clicking a sheet tab selects all the worksheets from the first sheet tab to the last sheet tab clicked.) Notice in the Formula bar that the formula reads *=sum('BryceCanyon:MesaVerde'!*
   d. With BryceCanyon the active worksheet, select the range B7:B22, press and hold down the Ctrl key, select the range E7:E21, and then release the Ctrl key.
   e. Type) and then press the Enter key. Excel returns the value *10460* in cell F7 in the AttendanceSummary worksheet.
   f. Apply the Comma format with no digits after the decimal point to cell F7.
4. With cell F7 the active cell, compare your formula with the one shown in Figure 4.1.
5. Save and then close **4-3D-MayEntries**.

	Day	Entries		Day	Entries	
7	1	40		17	68	
8	2	55		18	30	SUM(**number1**, [number2], ...)
9	3	35		19	47	
10	4	30		20	40	
11	5	56		21	65	
12	6	32		22	79	
13	7	22		23	58	
14	8	25		24	65	
15	9	46		25	44	
16	10	19		26	55	
17	11	25		27	58	
18	12	65		28	68	
19	13	24		29	88	
20	14	30		30	72	
21	15	33		31	91	
22	16	42				

3d

3b

AttendanceSummary | BryceCanyon | GrandCanyon | MesaVerde

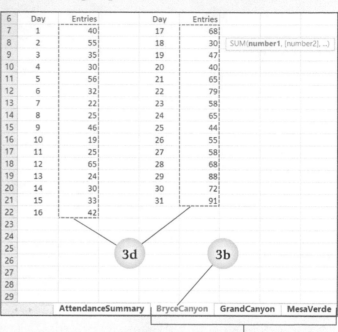

The three worksheets are grouped into the 3-D reference in Steps 3b and 3c.

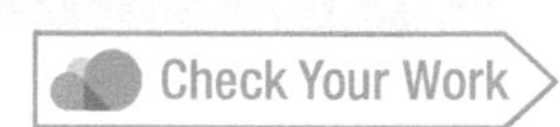

Figure 4.1 3-D Formula Created in Activity 1b

This 3-D formula is created in Activity 1b, Step 3, using a point-and-click approach.

F7 | =SUM(BryceCanyon:MesaVerde!B7:B22,BryceCanyon:MesaVerde!E7:E21)

	A	B	C	D	E	F	G	H	I	J
1	National Park Service									
2	U.S. Department of the Interior									
3	May 2021									
4	Attendance Summary									
5	Southwest Region, Zone C									
6										
7	Private Vehicle and Individual Entrances Only					10,460				

Linking Data

Summarizing Data by Linking to Ranges in Other Worksheets or Workbooks

Quick Steps

Create Link to External Source

1. Open source workbook.
2. Open destination workbook.
3. Arrange windows as desired.
4. Make formula cell active in destination workbook.
5. Type =.
6. Click to activate source workbook.
7. Click source cell.
8. Press Enter key.

Using a method similar to that used in Activity 1a or Activity 1b, data can be summarized in one workbook by linking to a cell, range, or range name in another worksheet or workbook. When data is linked, a change made in the source cell (the cell in which the original data is stored) is updated in any other cell to which the source cell has been linked. A link is established by creating a formula that references the source data. For example, entering the formula *=Sheet1!B10* into a cell in Sheet2 creates a link. The cell in Sheet2 displays the value in the source cell. If the data in cell B10 in Sheet1 is changed, the value in the linked cell in Sheet2 also changes.

As an alternative to creating a formula, copy the source cell to the Clipboard task pane. Make the destination cell active, click the Paste button arrow in the Clipboard group, and then click the Paste Link button in the *Other Paste Options* section of the drop-down gallery. Excel creates the link formula using an absolute reference to the source cell.

Linking to a cell in another workbook incorporates external references and requires adding a workbook name reference to the formula. For example, linking to cell A3 in a sheet named *ProductA* in a workbook named *Sales* requires entering *=[Sales.xlsx]ProductA!A3* in the cell. Notice that the workbook reference is entered first in square brackets. The workbook in which the external reference is added is called the *destination workbook*. The workbook containing the data that is linked to the destination workbook is called the *source workbook*. In Activity 1c, you will create a link to an external cell containing the attendance total for tour group entrances for the three parks.

The point-and-click approach to creating a linked external reference creates an absolute reference to the source cell. Delete the dollar symbols ($) in the cell reference if the formula is to be copied and the source cell needs to be relative. Note that the workbook and worksheet references remain absolute regardless.

Activity 1c Summarizing Data by Linking to Another Workbook — Part 3 of 5

1. Open **4-MayEntries**.
2. Open **MayGroupSales**. This workbook contains tour group attendance data for the three national parks. Tour groups are charged a flat-rate entrance fee, so their attendance values represent bus capacities rather than the actual numbers of patrons on the buses.
3. Click the View tab, click the Arrange All button in the Window group, click *Vertical* in the *Arrange* section of the Arrange Windows dialog box, and then click OK.
4. In the worksheet used in Activity 1a, create a linked external reference to the total attendance in the worksheet with the commercial tour vehicle attendance data by completing the following steps:
   a. Click in **4-MayEntries** to make the workbook active. Make sure the active worksheet is AttendanceSummary.
   b. Make cell A9 active, type Commercial Tour Vehicles Only, and then press the Enter key.
   c. Make cell F9 active and then type =.

d. Click the **MayGroupSales** title bar to activate the workbook and then click in cell F7. Notice that the formula being entered into the formula cell contains a workbook reference and a worksheet reference in front of the cell reference.
e. Press the Enter key.
f. Apply the Comma format with no digits after the decimal point to cell F9.
g. With cell F9 active, compare your worksheet with the 4-MayEntries worksheet shown below.

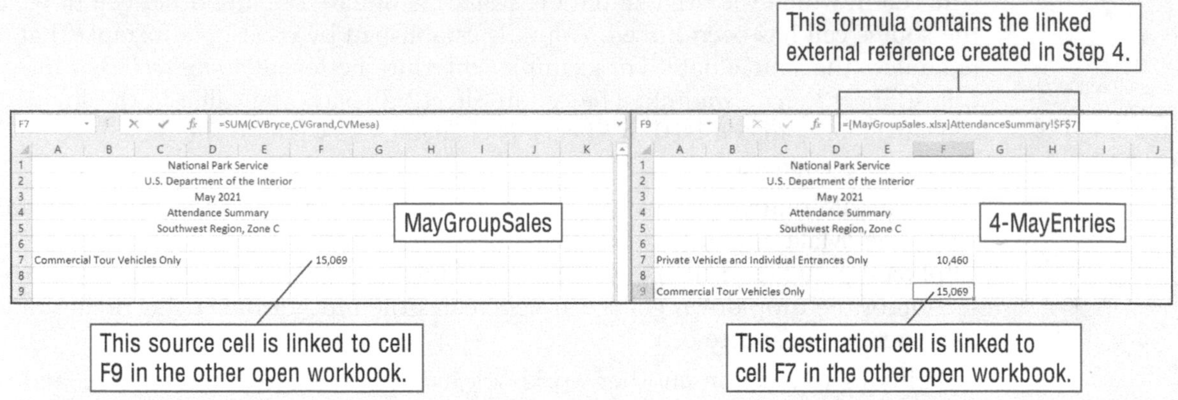
This formula contains the linked external reference created in Step 4.
MayGroupSales
4-MayEntries
This source cell is linked to cell F9 in the other open workbook.
This destination cell is linked to cell F7 in the other open workbook.

5. Click the Maximize button in the **4-MayEntries** title bar.
6. Make cell A11 active, type Total Attendance, and then press the Enter key.
7. Make cell F11 active and then create a formula to add the values in cells F7 and F9.
8. Print the AttendanceSummary worksheet in **4-MayEntries**. ***Note: If you submit your work as hard copy, check with your instructor to see if you need to print two copies of the worksheet, with one copy displaying the cell formulas.***
9. Save and then close **4-MayEntries**.
10. Close **MayGroupSales**. Click Don't Save if prompted to save changes.

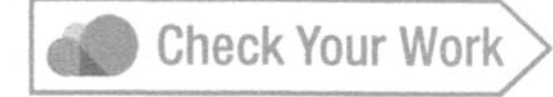
Check Your Work

Maintaining External References

Quick Steps

Edit Link to External Source

1. Open destination workbook.
2. Click Data tab.
3. Click Edit Links button.
4. Click link.
5. Click Change Source button.
6. Navigate to drive and/or folder.
7. Double-click source workbook file name.
8. Click Close button.
9. Save and close destination workbook.

Edit Links

In Excel, an *external reference* is a link to a cell or cells in another workbook. The reference includes a path to the specific drive or folder where the source workbook is located. If the source workbook is moved or the workbook name is changed, the link will no longer work. By default, when a linked workbook is opened, the automatic updates feature is disabled and Excel displays a security warning message in the Message bar area above the workbook. From the message bar, the content can be enabled so that links can be updated.

Links can be edited or broken at the Edit Links dialog box, shown in Figure 4.2. Open the dialog box by clicking the Edit Links button in the Queries & Connections group on the Data tab. If more than one link is present in the workbook, begin by clicking the link to be changed in the *Source* list. Click the Change Source button to open the Change Source dialog box and navigate to the drive and/or folder in which the source workbook was moved or renamed. Click the Break Link button to permanently remove the linked reference and convert the linked cells to their existing values. Links cannot be restored using the Undo feature. If a broken link needs to be restored, the linked formula will have to be recreated.

Quick Steps

Break Link to External Reference

1. Open destination workbook.
2. Click Data tab.
3. Click Edit Links button.
4. Click link.
5. Click Break Link button.
6. Click Break Links button.
7. Click Close button.
8. Save and close destination workbook.

Figure 4.2 Edit Links Dialog Box

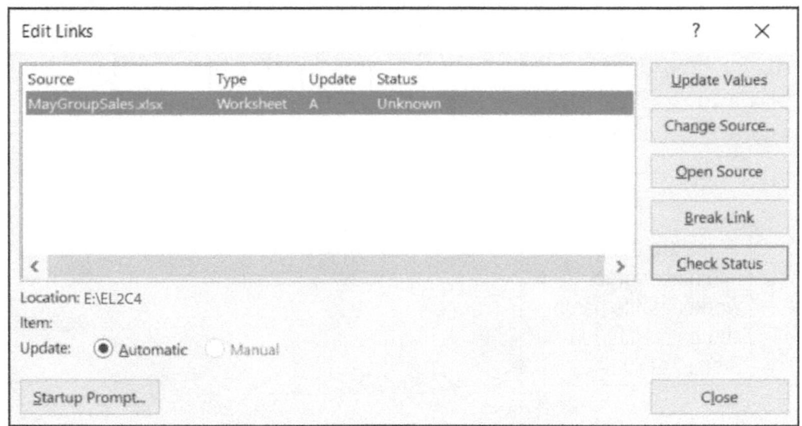

Activity 1d Editing Source Data and Updating an External Link

Part 4 of 5

1. Open **MayGroupSales** and maximize the screen.
2. Save the workbook with the name **4-Source**.
3. Edit the attendance data value at each park by completing the following steps:
   a. Click the BryceCanyon sheet tab.
   b. Make cell B8 active and then change the value from *55* to *361*.
   c. Click the GrandCanyon sheet tab.
   d. Make cell B20 active and then change the value from *275* to *240*.
   e. Click the MesaVerde sheet tab.
   f. Make cell E21 active and then change the value from *312* to *406*.
4. Click the AttendanceSummary tab. Note that the updated value in cell F7 is *15,434*.
5. Save and then close **4-Source**.
6. Open **4-MayEntries**. Notice the security warning in the Message bar above the worksheet area that states that the automatic update of links has been disabled. Instruct Excel to allow automatic updates for this workbook (since you are sure the content is from a trusted source) by clicking the Enable Content button next to the message. ***Note: If a Security Warning dialog box appears asking if you want to make the file a trusted document, click No.***

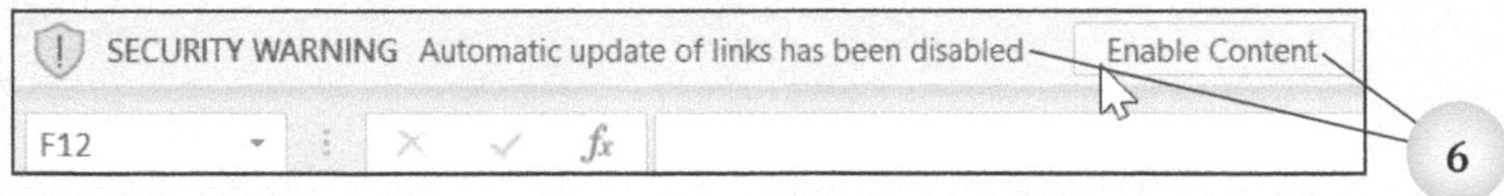

7. Edit the link to retrieve the data from the workbook you revised in Steps 2–5 by completing the following steps:
   a. Click the Data tab.
   b. Click the Edit Links button in the Queries & Connections group.

c. At the Edit Links dialog box, click the Change Source button.
d. If necessary, navigate to the EL2C4 folder. At the Change Source: MayGroupSales.xlsx dialog box, double-click ***4-Source*** in the file list box. Excel returns to the Edit Links dialog box and updates the source workbook file name and path.
e. Click the Close button.

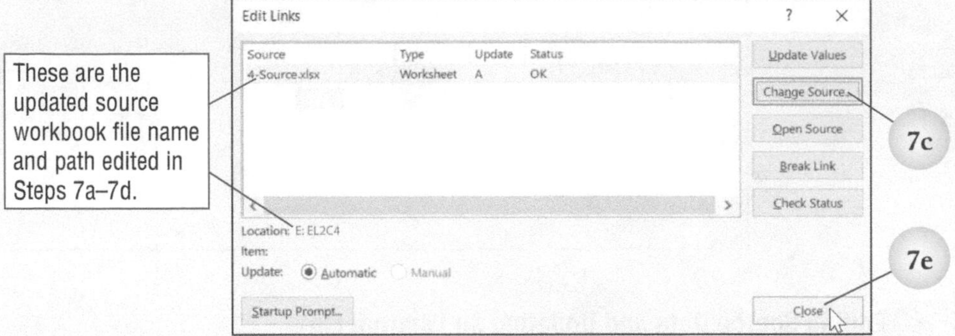

8. Click in cell F9 in the AttendanceSummary worksheet to view the updated linked formula. Notice that the workbook reference in the formula is *[4-Source.xlsx]* and the drive and path are included in the formula. (Your drive and/or path may vary from the one shown. If the entire formula is not shown, click the Expand Formula bar down arrow to show the entire formula and then click the Collapse Formula bar up arrow to return the formula bar to one line.)

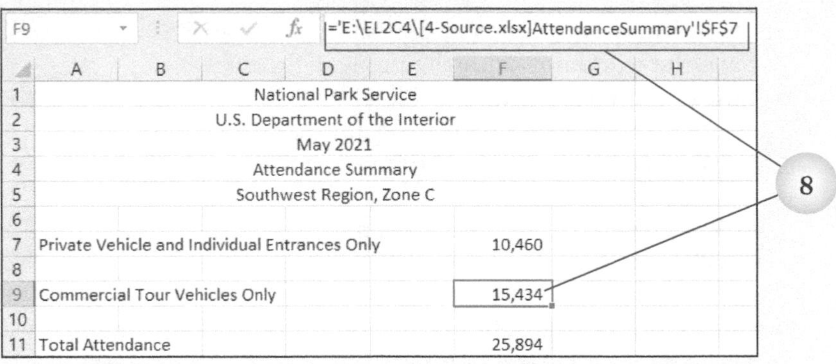

9. Print the AttendanceSummary worksheet.
10. Save and then close **4-MayEntries**.

Activity 1e Removing a Linked External Reference

Part 5 of 5

1. Open **4-MayEntries**.
2. At the Microsoft Excel message box that states that the workbook contains links to external sources, read the message text and then click the Update button to update the links. ***Note: Depending on the system settings on the computer you are using, this message may not appear. Proceed to Step 3.***

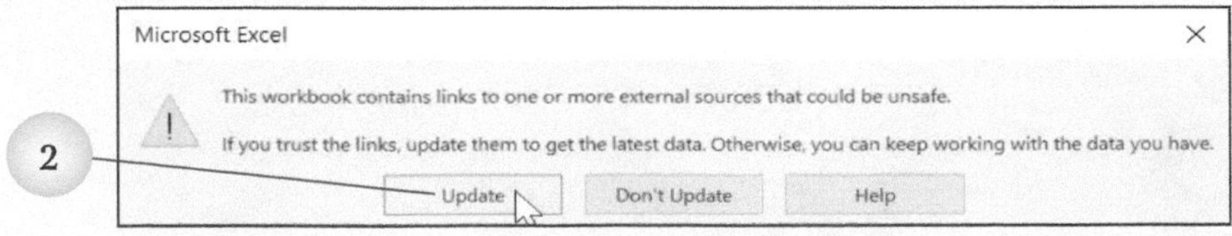

3. Remove the linked external reference to attendance values for commercial tour vehicles by completing the following steps:
   a. With the Data tab active, click the Edit Links button in the Queries & Connections group.
   b. Click the Break Link button at the Edit Links dialog box.
   c. Click the Break Links button at the Microsoft Excel message box warning that breaking links permanently converts formulas and external references to their existing values and asking if you are sure you want to break the links.

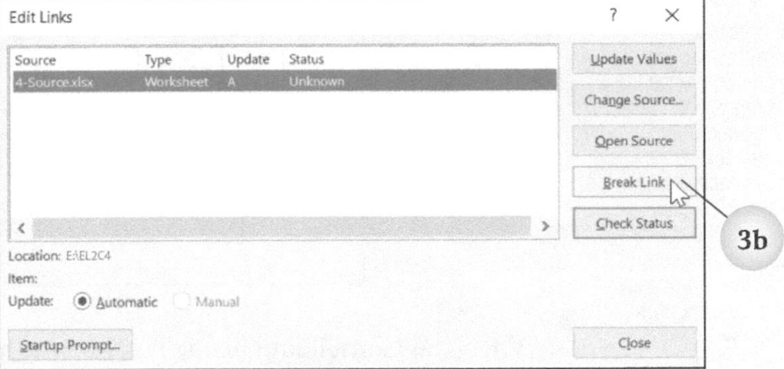

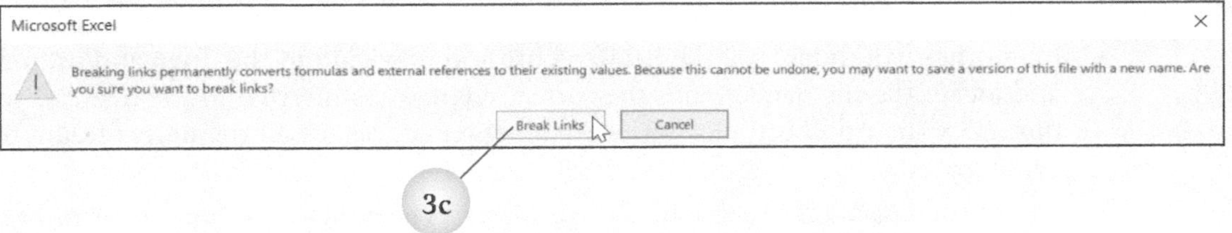

   d. Click the Close button at the Edit Links dialog box with no links displayed.
4. In the AttendanceSummary worksheet with cell F9 active, look in the Formula bar. Notice that the linked formula has been replaced with the latest cell value, *15434*.
5. Save and then close **4-MayEntries.**
6. Reopen **4-MayEntries**. Notice that since the workbook no longer contains a link to an external reference, the security warning no longer appears in the Message bar.
7. Close **4-MayEntries.** Click Don't Save if prompted to save changes.

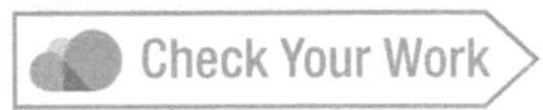

Activity 2 Calculate Total Fees Billed by Three Dentists — 1 Part

You will use the Consolidate feature to summarize the total dental fees billed by treatment category for three dentists.

Summarizing Data Using the Consolidate Feature

Consolidate

Summarizing Data Using the Consolidate Feature

The Consolidate feature is another tool that can be used to summarize data from multiple worksheets into a master worksheet. The worksheets can be located in the same workbook as the master worksheet or in a separate workbook. Open the Consolidate dialog box, shown in Figure 4.3, by clicking the Consolidate button in the Data Tools group on the Data tab.

Quick Steps

Consolidate Data

1. Make starting cell active.
2. Click Data tab.
3. Click Consolidate button.
4. If necessary, change function.
5. Enter first range in *Reference* text box.
6. Click Add button.
7. Enter next range in *Reference* text box.
8. Click Add button.
9. Repeat Steps 7–8 until all ranges have been added.
10. If necessary, click *Top row* and/or *Left column* check boxes.
11. If necessary, click *Create links to source data* check box.
12. Click OK.

Figure 4.3 Consolidate Dialog Box

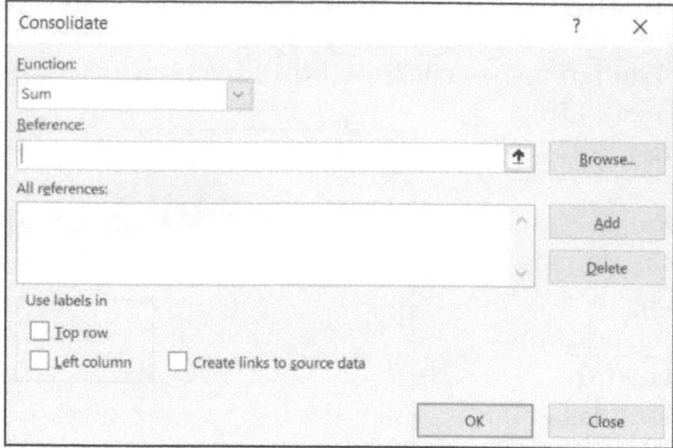

When the Consolidate dialog box opens, the Sum function is selected by default. Change to a different function, such as Count or Average, using the *Function* drop-down list. In the *Reference* text box, type the range name or use the Collapse Dialog button to navigate to the cells to be consolidated. If the cells are in another workbook, use the Browse button to navigate to the drive and/or folder and locate the file name. Once the correct reference is inserted in the *Reference* text box, click the Add button. Continue adding references for all the units of data to be summarized.

In the *Use labels in* section, click to insert a check mark in the *Top row* or *Left column* check boxes to indicate where the labels are located in the source ranges. Insert a check mark in the *Create links to source data* check box to instruct Excel to update the data automatically when the source ranges change. Make sure enough empty cells are available to the right of and below the active cell when the Consolidate dialog box is opened, since Excel populates the rows and columns based on the size of the source data.

Activity 2 Summarizing Data Using the Consolidate Feature

Part 1 of 1

1. Open **NADQ1Fees**.
2. Save the workbook with the name **4-NADQ1Fees**.
3. The workbook is organized with the first-quarter fees for each of three dentists entered in separate worksheets. Range names have been defined for each dentist's first-quarter earnings. Review the workbook structure by completing the following steps:
   a. Click the Name box arrow and then click *Popovich* at the drop-down list. Excel makes the Popovich worksheet active and selects the range A2:E12.
   b. Deselect the range.
   c. Display the defined range for the range name *Vanket* and then deselect the range.
   d. Display the defined range for the range name *Jones* and then deselect the range.
4. Use the Consolidate feature to total the fees billed by treatment category for each month by completing the following steps:
   a. Make FeeSummary the active worksheet.
   b. Make cell A4 active, if necessary, and then click the Data tab.
   c. Click the Consolidate button in the Data Tools group.

d. With *Sum* selected in the *Function* option box at the Consolidate dialog box and with the insertion point positioned in the *Reference* text box, type Popovich and then click the Add button.
e. With the text *Popovich* selected in the *Reference* text box, type Vanket and then click the Add button.
f. With the text *Vanket* selected in the *Reference* text box, type Jones and then click the Add button.
g. Click the *Top row* and *Left column* check boxes in the *Use labels in* section to insert check marks.
h. Click OK.

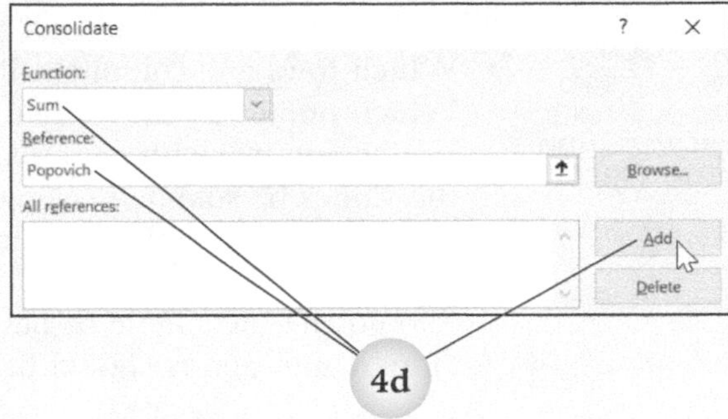

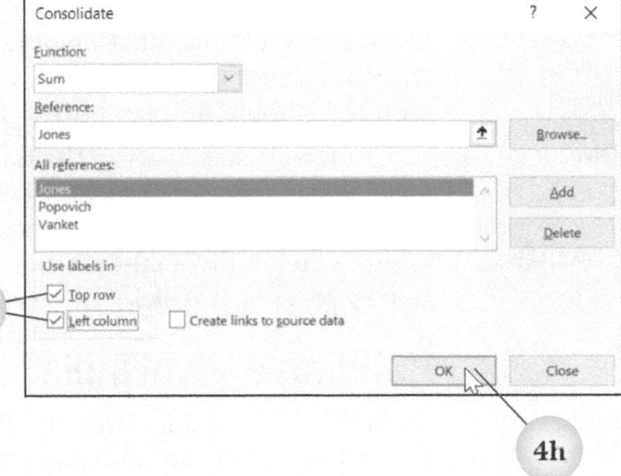

5. Deselect the consolidated range in the FeeSummary worksheet.
6. AutoFit the width of each column in the FeeSummary worksheet.
7. Use the Format Painter to apply the formatting options for the column headings and the *Total* row from any of the three dentist worksheets to the FeeSummary worksheet.
8. Print the FeeSummary worksheet.
9. Save and then close **4-NADQ1Fees**.

Activity 3 Analyze Fitness Equipment Sales Data in a PivotTable and PivotChart — 8 Parts

You will create and edit PivotTables and PivotCharts to analyze fitness equipment sales by region, product, manufacturer, and salesperson. You will change the PivotTable summary function and filter PivotTables using Slicers and a Timeline.

Creating PivotTables

Quick Steps

Create PivotTable

1. Select source range.
2. Click Insert tab.
3. Click PivotTable button.
4. Click OK.
5. Add fields as needed using PivotTable Fields task pane.
6. Modify and/or format as required.

PivotTable

A PivotTable is an interactive table that allows large worksheets to be manipulated in different ways. It organizes and summarizes data based on fields (column headings) and records (rows). A numeric column is selected and then grouped by the rows and columns category; the data is summarized using a function such as Sum, Average, or Count. PivotTables are useful management tools, since they allow data to be analyzed in a variety of scenarios by filtering a row or column category and instantly seeing the change in results. The interactivity of a PivotTable allows a variety of scenarios to be examined with just a few mouse clicks. Create a PivotTable using the PivotTable button in the Tables group on the Insert tab.

Hint Make sure that the source data contains no blank rows or columns and is structured in such a way that repeated data in columns or rows can be grouped.

Before creating a PivotTable, examine the source data and determine the following elements:

- Which rows and columns will define how to format and group the data?
- Which numeric field contains the values to be grouped?
- Which summary function will be applied to the values? For example, should the values be summed, averaged, or counted?
- Should it be possible to filter the report as a whole, as well as by columns or rows?
- Should the PivotTable be beside the source data or in a new sheet?
- How many reports should be extracted from the PivotTable by filtering fields?

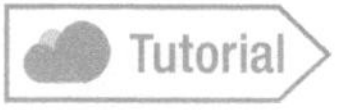

Creating, Modifying, and Filtering a Recommended PivotTable

Creating a Recommended PivotTable

Click the Recommended PivotTables button to show different PivotTable previews. After the PivotTable is created, it can then be edited and formatted further if required. (You will learn how to format a PivotTable in Activity 3c.)

Recommended PivotTables

To have Excel analyze the data and create a PivotTable using a recommended view, select the source range, click the Insert tab, change the source data if required, and then click the Recommended PivotTables button in the Tables group. Click a PivotTable in the left panel of the Recommended PivotTables dialog box to preview it. Click OK to insert the selected PivotTable.

Building a PivotTable

Building a PivotTable

To build a PivotTable using the PivotTable button in the Tables group on the Insert tab, select the source range or make sure the active cell is positioned within the list range, click the Insert tab, and then click the PivotTable button in the Tables group. At the Create PivotTable dialog box, confirm that the source range is correct and then select whether to place the PivotTable in the existing worksheet or a new worksheet. Figure 4.4 presents the initial PivotTable and PivotTable Fields task pane, in which the report layout is defined. Each column or row heading in the source range becomes a field in the PivotTable Fields task pane list. A PivotTable can also be created by using the Blank PivotTable button in the Tables tab on the Quick Analysis button.

Build a PivotTable by selecting fields in the PivotTable Fields task pane. Click the check box next to a field to insert a check mark and add it to the PivotTable. By default, non-numeric fields are added to the *Rows* box and numeric fields are added to the *Values* box in the layout section of the pane. Once a field has been added, it can be moved to a different box by dragging the field header or clicking the field to display a shortcut menu. As each field is added, the PivotTable updates to show the results. Check and uncheck the various field check boxes to view the data in different scenarios. Figure 4.5 displays the PivotTable built in Activity 3b.

Figure 4.4 PivotTable and PivotTable Fields Task Pane Used to Define the Report Layout

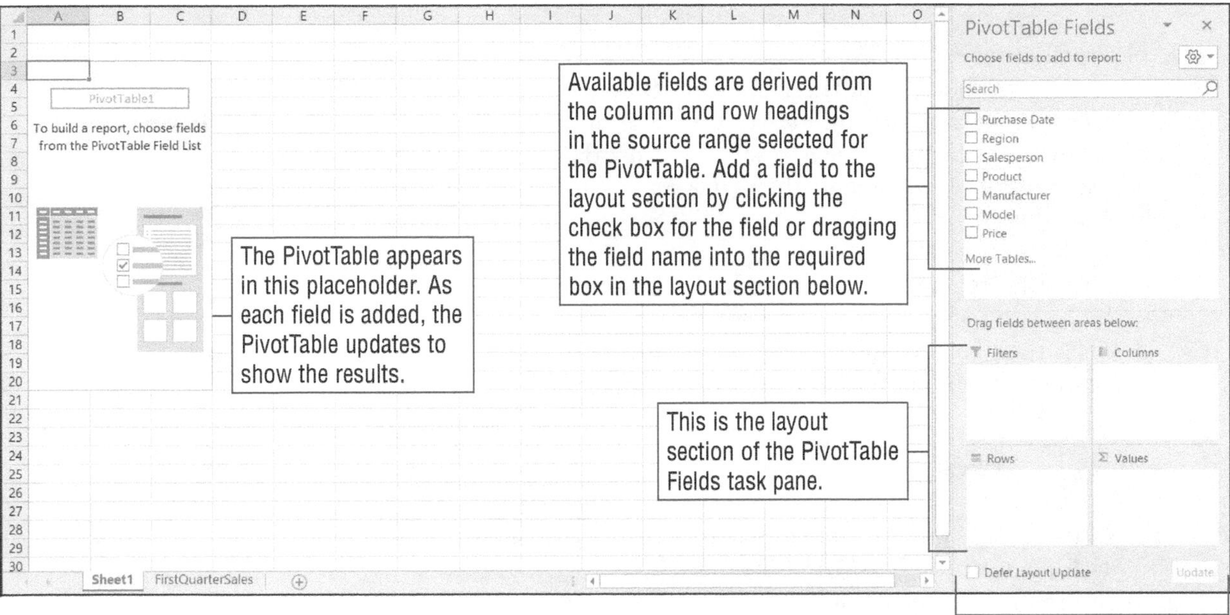

Figure 4.5 PivotTable for Activity 3b

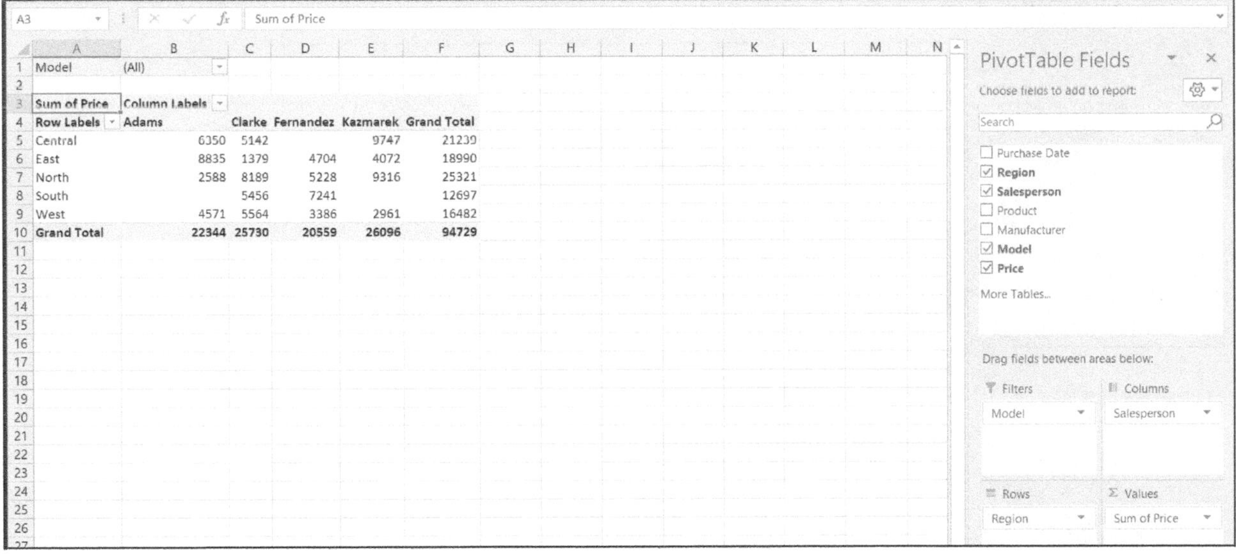

Model (All)

Sum of Price	Column Labels				
Row Labels	Adams	Clarke	Fernandez	Kazmarek	Grand Total
Central	6350	5142		9747	21239
East	8835	1379	4704	4072	18990
North	2588	8189	5228	9316	25321
South		5456	7241		12697
West	4571	5564	3386	2961	16482
Grand Total	**22344**	**25730**	**20559**	**26096**	**94729**

Activity 3a Creating a PivotTable Using Recommended PivotTables

Part 1 of 8

1. Open **PFSales**.
2. Save the workbook with the name **4-PFSales**.
3. Create a PivotTable to summarize the price by product by completing the following steps:
   a. A range has been defined to select the list data. Click the Name box arrow and then click *FirstQ* at the drop-down list.
   b. Click the Insert tab.
   c. Click the Recommended PivotTables button in the Tables group.
   d. Click the Change Source Data hyperlink at the bottom of the Recommended PivotTables dialog box to expand the range.

   e. At the Choose Data Source dialog box, with *FirstQuarterSales!$A$4:$G$47* entered in the *Table/Range* text box, click OK.
   f. Click the second PivotTable scenario in the left column to select the *Sum of Price by Product* PivotTable.
   g. Click OK to insert the PivotTable in a new worksheet.

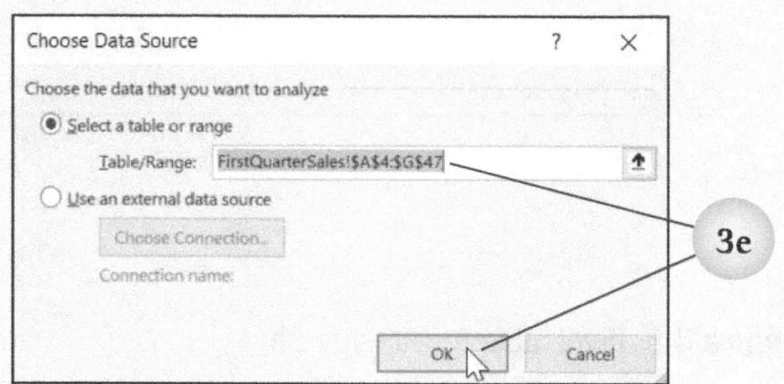

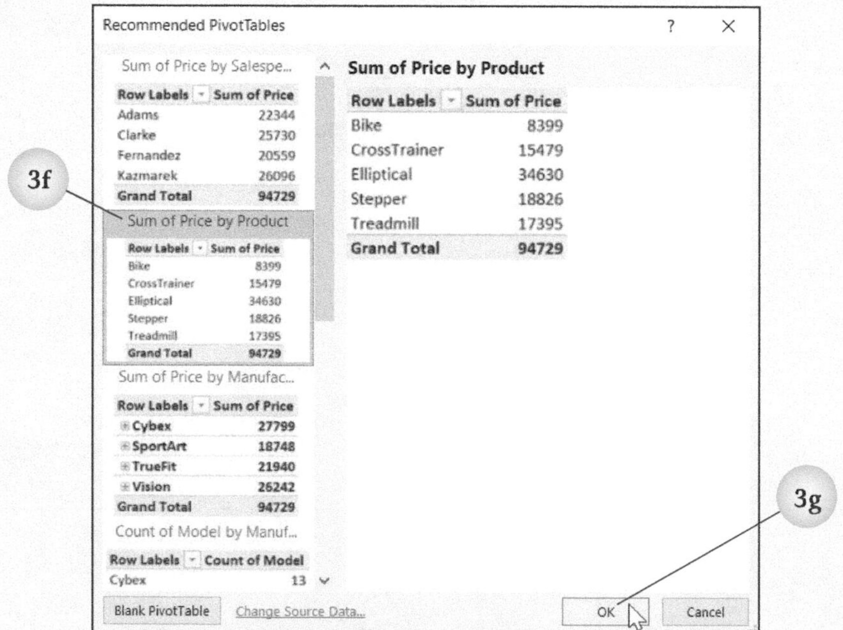

4. Apply the Comma format with no digits after the decimal point to the range B4:B9.
5. Rename the worksheet *PriceByProduct*.
6. Save **4-PFSales**.

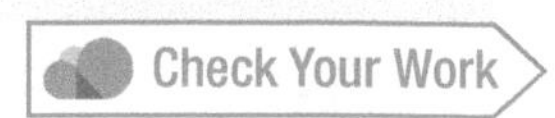

Activity 3b Building a PivotTable

1. With **4-PFSales** open, make the FirstQuarterSales worksheet active. The FirstQ range should still be selected.
2. Create a PivotTable to summarize fitness equipment sales by region and salesperson, as shown in Figure 4.5 (on page 97), by completing the following steps:
   a. Click the Insert tab.
   b. Click the PivotTable button in the Tables group.
   c. At the Create PivotTable dialog box, with *FirstQuarterSales!$A$4:$G$47* entered in the *Table/Range* text box and *New Worksheet* selected for *Choose where you want the PivotTable report to be placed*, click OK.
   d. Click the *Region* check box in the PivotTable Fields task pane. *Region* is added to the *Rows* list box in the layout section of the task pane and the report updates to show one row per region with a filter arrow at the top of the column and a *Grand Total* row automatically added to the bottom of the table. Since *Region* is a non-numeric field, Excel automatically places it in the *Rows* list box.
   e. Click the *Salesperson* check box in the PivotTable Fields task pane. Excel automatically adds *Salesperson* to the *Rows* list box in the layout section.
   f. Click the *Salesperson* field header in the *Rows* list box in the layout section and then click *Move to Column Labels* at the pop-up list. Notice that the layout of the report now displays one row per region and one column per salesperson.
   g. Hover the mouse pointer over *Model* in the PivotTable Fields task pane, click and hold down the left mouse button, drag the field into the *Filters* list box in the layout section, and then release the mouse button. Notice that *Model* is added as a filter at the top left of the PivotTable in the range A1:B1.
   h. Click the *Price* check box in the PivotTable Fields task pane. Since the field is numeric, Excel automatically adds it to the *Values* list box in the layout section and the report updates to show the Sum function applied to the grouped values in the PivotTable. Compare your results with the PivotTable shown in Figure 4.5.
3. Rename the worksheet *SalesByRegion*.
4. Save **4-PFSales**.

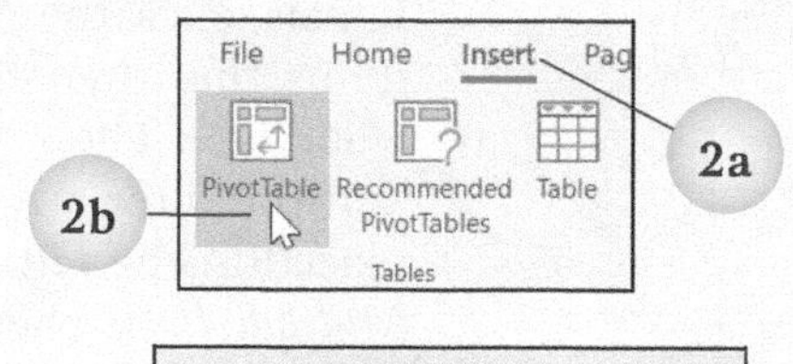

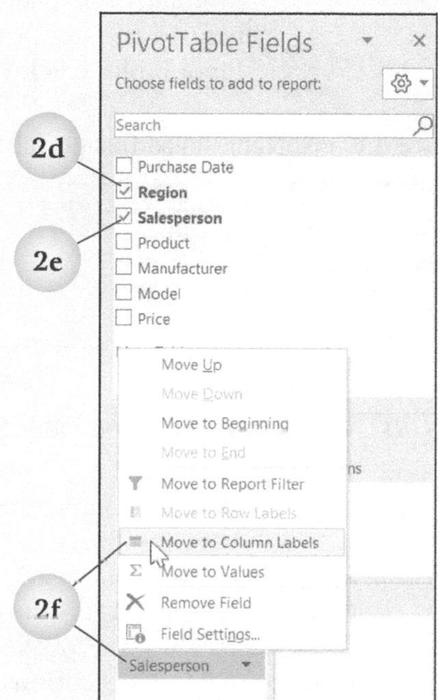

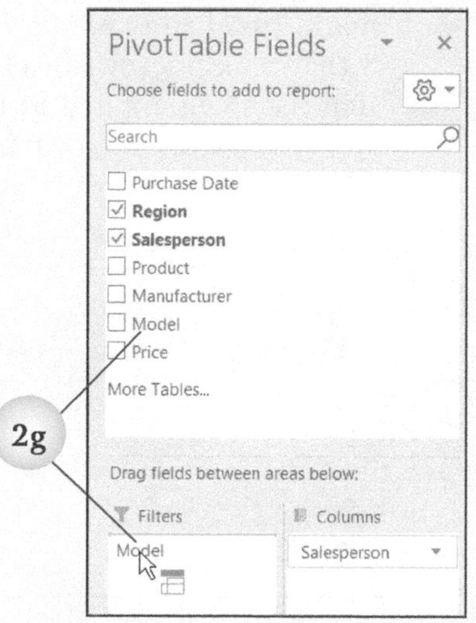

Formatting and Filtering a PivotTable

When the active cell is positioned inside a PivotTable, the contextual PivotTable Tools Analyze and PivotTable Tools Design tabs become available. The formatting features on the PivotTable Tools Design tab, shown in Figure 4.6, are similar to those on the Table Tools Design tab, which was discussed in Chapter 3.

To filter a PivotTable, click the filter arrow next to Row Labels or Column Labels, click the *(Select All)* check box to remove all the check marks next to the items, and then click the check boxes for the items to show in the PivotTable. Click OK. The PivotTable filters the data to show the items that were checked and the filter arrow changes to indicate that a filter is applied. If a field has been placed in the *Filters* list box, click the filter arrow next to *(All)*, click the *Select Multiple Items* check box, click the *(All)* check box to remove all the check marks next to the items, and then click the check boxes for the items to show in the PivotTable. Click OK.

Figure 4.6 PivotTable Tools Design Tab

File Home Insert Page Layout Formulas Data Review View Help Analyze Design Tell me what you want to do

Subtotals Grand Totals Report Layout Blank Rows — Layout

Row Headers Banded Rows Column Headers Banded Columns — PivotTable Style Options

PivotTable Styles

Activity 3c **Formatting and Filtering a PivotTable** — Part 3 of 8

1. With **4-PFSales** open and the SalesByRegion worksheet active, apply formatting options to the PivotTable to improve the appearance of the report by completing the following steps:
   a. With the active cell positioned in the PivotTable, click the PivotTable Tools Design tab.
   b. Click the More button in the PivotTable Styles gallery.
   c. Click *Light Orange, Pivot Style Medium 10* at the drop-down gallery (third column, second row of the *Medium* section).
   d. Click the *Banded Rows* check box in the PivotTable Style Options group to insert a check mark. Excel adds border lines between the rows in the PivotTable. Recall from Chapter 3 that banding rows or columns adds a fill color or border style, depending on the style that has been applied to the PivotTable.
   e. Apply the Comma format with no digits after the decimal point to the range B5:F10.
   f. Change the width of columns B through F to 12 characters.

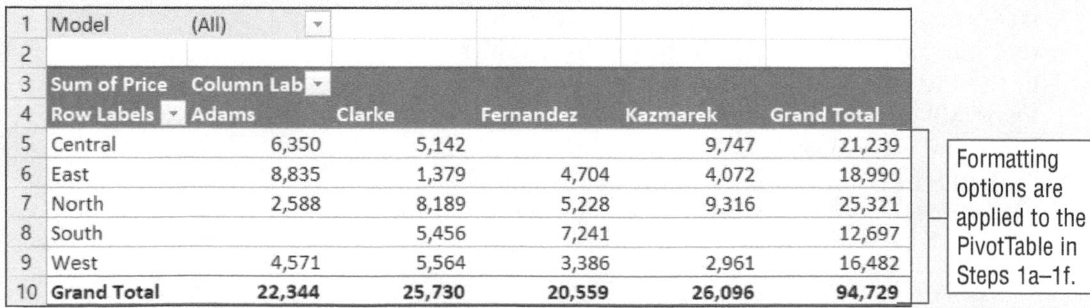

1	Model	(All)				
2						
3	Sum of Price	Column Lab				
4	Row Labels	Adams	Clarke	Fernandez	Kazmarek	Grand Total
5	Central	6,350	5,142		9,747	21,239
6	East	8,835	1,379	4,704	4,072	18,990
7	North	2,588	8,189	5,228	9,316	25,321
8	South		5,456	7,241		12,697
9	West	4,571	5,564	3,386	2,961	16,482
10	**Grand Total**	**22,344**	**25,730**	**20,559**	**26,096**	**94,729**

Formatting options are applied to the PivotTable in Steps 1a–1f.

   g. To stop Excel from using AutoFit to adjust the column widths after the cell content has been updated, right-click in the PivotTable and then click *PivotTable Options* at the shortcut menu. The PivotTable Options dialog box opens.

h. On the Layout & Format tab of the PivotTable Options dialog box, click the *Autofit column widths on update* check box to remove the check mark.
i. Click OK.

2. Filter the PivotTable to view sales for a group of product model numbers by completing the following steps:
    a. Click the filter arrow next to *(All)* in cell B1.
    b. Click the *Select Multiple Items* check box to insert a check mark and turn on the display of check boxes next to all the model numbers in the drop-down list.
    c. Click the *(All)* check box to remove the check marks next to all the model numbers.
    d. Click the check boxes for those model numbers that begin with *CX* to insert check marks. This selects all six models from Cybex.
    e. Click OK.
    f. Print the filtered PivotTable.
    g. Click the filter arrow next to *(Multiple Items)* in cell B1, click the *(All)* check box to select all the model numbers in the drop-down list, and then click OK.
    h. Experiment with the column labels and the row labels filter arrows to filter the PivotTable by region or salesperson.
    i. Make sure all the filters are cleared. ***Note: To remove all filters, click the* (All) *check box to insert a check mark.***
3. Save **4-PFSales**.

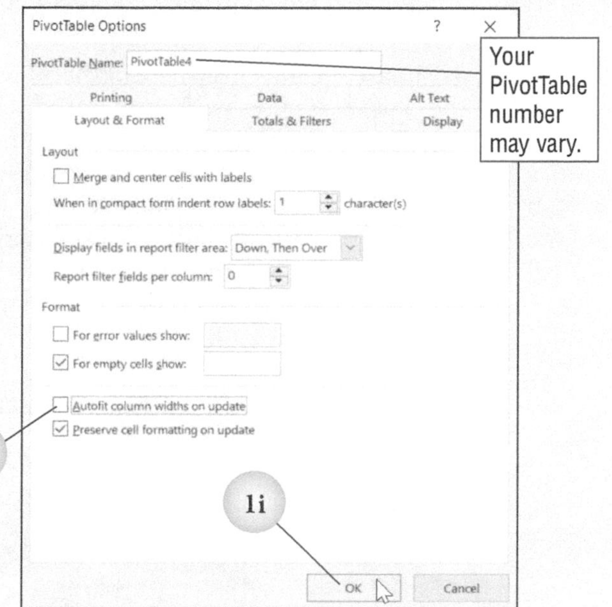

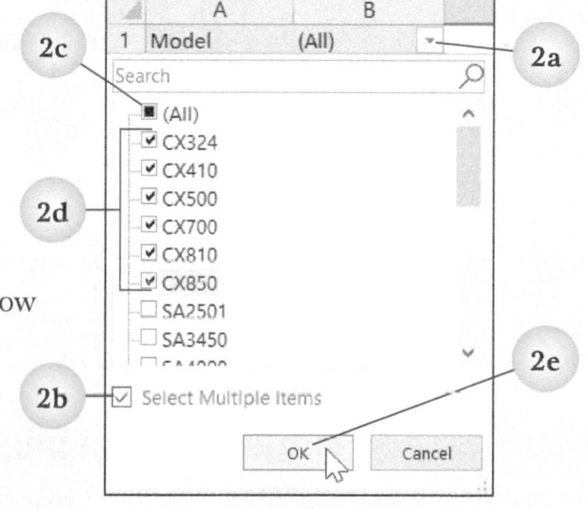

Changing the PivotTable Summary Function

Quick Steps

Change the PivotTable Summary Function

1. Make any PivotTable cell active.
2. Click PivotTable Tools Analyze tab.
3. Click Field Settings button.
4. Click function.
5. Click OK.

By default, Excel uses the Sum function to summarize the numeric value added to a PivotTable. To change Sum to another function, click any numeric value within the PivotTable or click the cell containing *Sum of [Fieldname]* at the top left of the PivotTable. Click the PivotTable Tools Analyze tab and then click the Field Settings button in the Active Field group. This opens the Value Field Settings dialog box, where a function other than Sum can be chosen. Alternatively, right-click any numeric value within the PivotTable, point to *Summarize Values By* at the shortcut menu, and then click a function name.

Activity 3d Changing the PivotTable Summary Function

Part 4 of 8

1. With **4-PFSales** open, save the workbook with the name **4-PFAvgSales.**
2. With the SalesByRegion worksheet active, change the function for the *Price* field from Sum to Average by completing the following steps:
   a. Make cell A3 the active cell in the PivotTable. This cell contains the label *Sum of Price*.
   b. Click the PivotTable Tools Analyze tab.
   c. Click the Field Settings button in the Active Field group.
   d. At the Value Field Settings dialog box with the Summarize Values By tab active, click *Average* in the *Summarize value field by* list box.
   e. Click OK.

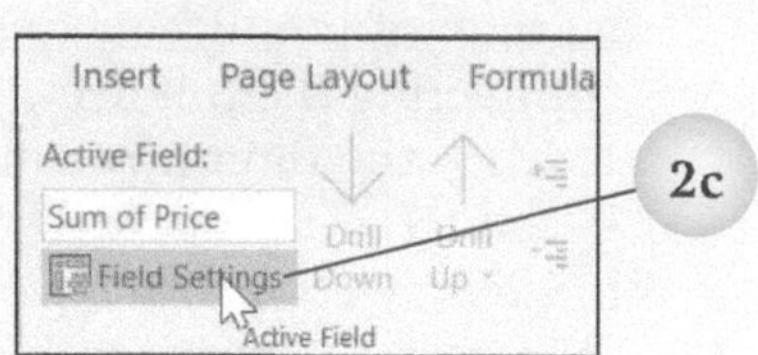

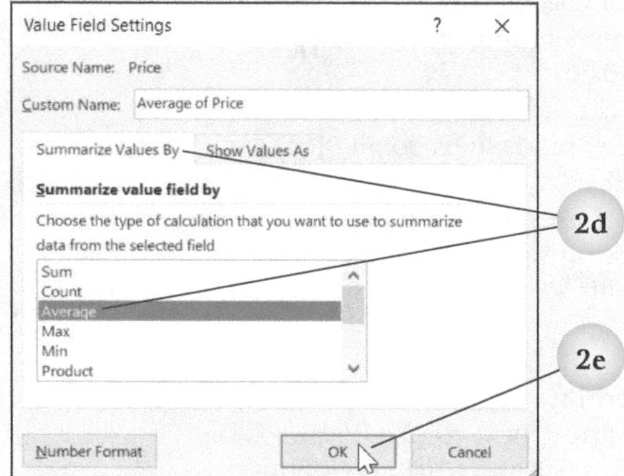

3. Change the page layout to Landscape orientation and then print the revised PivotTable.
4. Save and then close **4-PFAvgSales.**

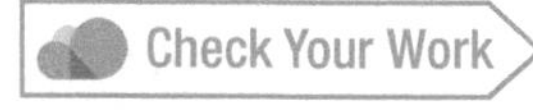

Filtering a PivotTable Using Slicers

Insert Slicer

Quick Steps

Add Slicer to PivotTable

1. Make any cell within PivotTable active.
2. Click PivotTable Tools Analyze tab.
3. Click Insert Slicer button.
4. Click check box for specific field.
5. Click OK.

Filtering a PivotTable Using Slicers

Recall from Chapter 3 that Slicers allow you to filter without using a filter arrow. When Slicers are added to a PivotTable or PivotChart, a Slicer pane containing all the unique values for the specified field is added to the window.

To insert a Slicer pane, make any cell within the PivotTable active, click the PivotTable Tools Analyze tab, and then click the Insert Slicer button in the Filter group. Excel opens the Insert Slicers dialog box, which contains a list of the fields in the PivotTable with a check box next to each field. Click to insert a check mark in the check box for each field to which a Slicer pane is to be added and then click OK.

Click to select one item that Excel should use to filter the list. To select more items, click the Multi-Select button at the top of the Slicer pane. Other ways to select items are to press and hold down the Ctrl key, click each additional item, and then release the Ctrl key or to press Ctrl + S and then select the items.

A Slicer pane can be customized with buttons on the Slicer Tools Options tab. Click a Slicer pane to activate this tab. Click the tab to display customization options, such as Slicer Styles. The height and width of the buttons in the Slicer pane and/or the height and width of the pane can also be changed with options on this tab.

Activity 3e Filtering a PivotTable Using Slicers

1. Open **4-PFSales**, make PriceByProduct the active worksheet, and then display a Slicer pane for the manufacturer by completing the following steps:
   a. Make any cell active within the PivotTable.
   b. Add *Manufacturer* to the *Filters* list box and *Region* to the *Columns* list box. (If necessary, refer to Activity 3b, Steps 2e–2g for assistance.)
   c. Click the PivotTable Tools Analyze tab.
   d. Click the Insert Slicer button in the Filter group.
   e. At the Insert Slicers dialog box, click the *Manufacturer* check box to insert a check mark.
   f. Click OK. Excel inserts a Slicer pane in the worksheet with all the manufacturer names.
2. If necessary, hover the mouse pointer at the top of the Manufacturer Slicer pane until the pointer changes to a four-headed arrow and then drag the pane into an empty area below the PivotTable.
3. Click *Vision* in the Manufacturer Slicer pane to filter the PivotTable. Excel filters the PivotTable by the *Vision* manufacturer. Notice that the *Manufacturer* filter arrow in cell B1 displays *Vision*.
4. Click the Multi-Select button in the Slicer pane and then click *Cybex* to add another manufacturer to the filter.
5. Click the Clear Filter button at the top right of the Manufacturer Slicer pane to redisplay all the data, and then click the Multi-Select button to deactivate it.

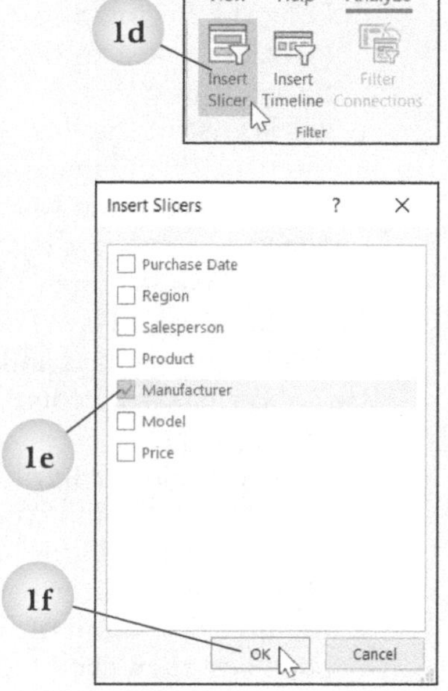

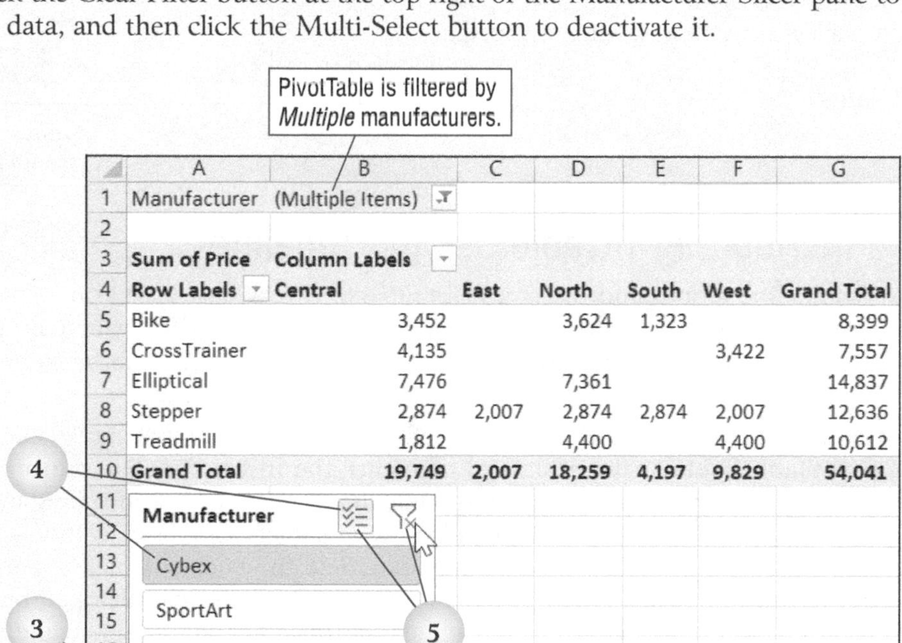

	A	B	C	D	E	F	G
1	Manufacturer	(Multiple Items)					
2							
3	**Sum of Price**	**Column Labels**					
4	**Row Labels**	**Central**	**East**	**North**	**South**	**West**	**Grand Total**
5	Bike	3,452		3,624	1,323		8,399
6	CrossTrainer	4,135				3,422	7,557
7	Elliptical	7,476		7,361			14,837
8	Stepper	2,874	2,007	2,874	2,874	2,007	12,636
9	Treadmill	1,812		4,400		4,400	10,612
10	**Grand Total**	**19,749**	**2,007**	**18,259**	**4,197**	**9,829**	**54,041**

6. Add a second Slicer pane and filter by two fields by completing the following steps:
   a. If necessary, make any cell active within the PivotTable.
   b. Click the PivotTable Tools Analyze tab and then click the Insert Slicer button.
   c. At the Insert Slicers dialog box, click the *Region* check box to insert a check mark and then click OK.
   d. Drag the Region Slicer pane below the PivotTable next to the Manufacturer Slicer pane.
   e. Click *West* in the Region Slicer pane to filter the PivotTable.
   f. Click *Vision* in the Manufacturer Slicer pane to filter West region sales by the Vision manufacturer.
7. Print the filtered PivotTable.
8. Redisplay all the data and remove the two Slicer panes by completing the following steps:
   a. Click the Clear Filter button at the top right of the Manufacturer Slicer pane.
   b. Click the Clear Filter button at the top right of the Region Slicer pane.
   c. Right-click the top of the Manufacturer Slicer pane and then click *Remove "Manufacturer"* at the shortcut menu.
   d. Right-click the top of the Region Slicer pane and then click *Remove "Region"* at the shortcut menu.
9. Save **4-PFSales**.

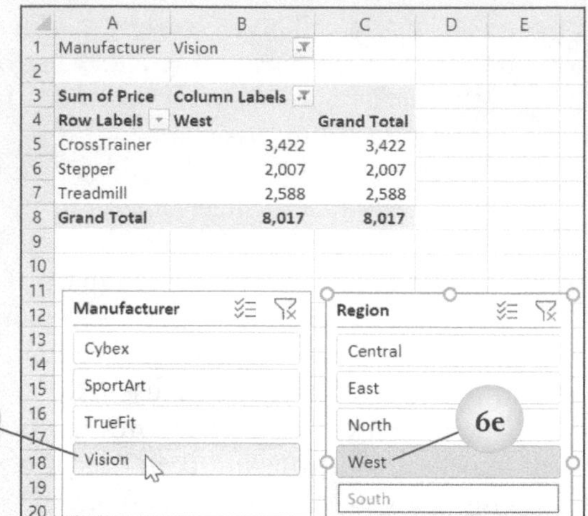

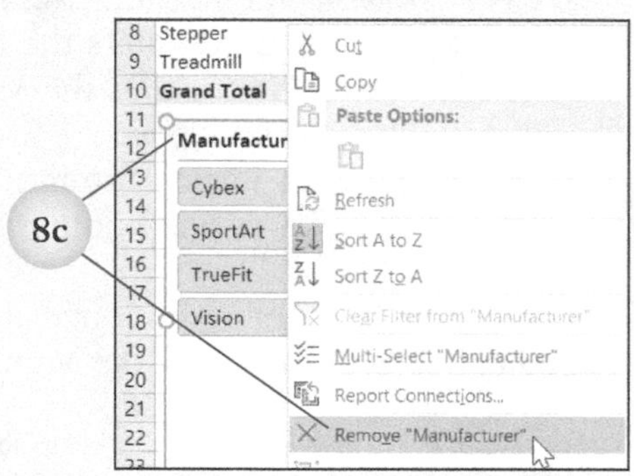

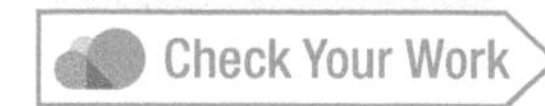

Filtering a PivotTable Using a Timeline

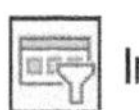

Insert Timeline

Add Timeline to PivotTable
1. Make any cell within PivotTable active.
2. Click PivotTable Tools Analyze tab.
3. Click Insert Timeline button.
4. Click check box for field.
5. Click OK.
6. Select timeframe.

Filtering a PivotTable Using a Timeline

A Timeline groups and filters a PivotTable or PivotChart based on a specific timeframe. Select a field formatted as a date and a Timeline pane containing a timeline slicer is added to the PivotTable. The timeframe can be extended or shortened to instantly filter the data by the selected date range.

To insert a Timeline, make any cell within the PivotTable active, click the PivotTable Tools Analyze tab, and then click the Insert Timeline button in the Filter group. Excel opens the Insert Timelines dialog box and displays any field that contains data formatted as a date along with a check box next to it. Click to insert a check mark in the check box of any date field to which a Timeline pane is to be added and then click OK. More than one Timeline pane can be open but the data can only be filtered using one Timeline at a time. The PivotTable will display the data for the time period that is selected. Use the Time Level indicator at the upper right of the pane to change the time period to years, quarters, months, or days.

Customize the Timeline pane with buttons on the Timeline Tools Options tab. Click a Timeline pane to activate the Timeline Tools Options tab. Click the tab to display customization options, such as Timeline styles. The height and width of the buttons in the Timeline pane and/or the height and width of the pane can also be changed.

Activity 3f Filtering a PivotTable Using a Timeline

Part 6 of 8

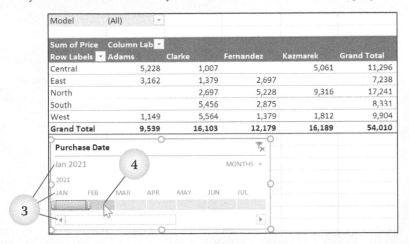

1. With **4-PFSales** open, make the SalesByRegion worksheet active. Display one Timeline for January and then another for February and March combined by completing the following steps:
   a. Make any cell active within the PivotTable.
   b. Click the PivotTable Tools Analyze tab.
   c. Click the Insert Timeline button in the Filter group. Excel displays an Insert Timelines dialog box with all the fields that have been formatted as dates.
   d. Click the check box next to *Purchase Date* in the Insert Timelines dialog box to insert a check mark.
   e. Click OK. Excel inserts a Timeline pane in the worksheet. The selection label displays *All Periods* to indicate that the PivotTable displays all periods.
2. If necessary, hover the mouse pointer at the top of the Timeline pane until the pointer changes to a four-headed arrow and then drag the pane into an empty area below the PivotTable.
3. Click the left scroll arrow at the bottom of the Timeline pane until JAN displays under 2021 and then click *JAN*. Excel filters the PivotTable by January. Notice that the selection label displays *Jan 2021*.
4. Click immediately right of the orange box on the Timeline to filter the PivotTable to include only the sales for February 2021. The selection label displays *Feb 2021*.

Model (All)

Sum of Price Row Labels	Column Labels Adams	Clarke	Fernandez	Kazmarek	Grand Total
Central	5,228	1,007		5,061	11,296
East	3,162	1,379	2,697		7,238
North		2,697	5,228	9,316	17,241
South		5,456	2,875		8,331
West	1,149	5,564	1,379	1,812	9,904
Grand Total	**9,539**	**16,103**	**12,179**	**16,189**	**54,010**

5. Hover the mouse pointer over the orange box representing February, click and hold down the left mouse button, drag the mouse pointer into the orange box representing March, and then release the mouse button. The February timeframe is extended to include March. The selection label displays *Feb - Mar 2021* to indicate that the PivotTable has been filtered to include data for February and March.

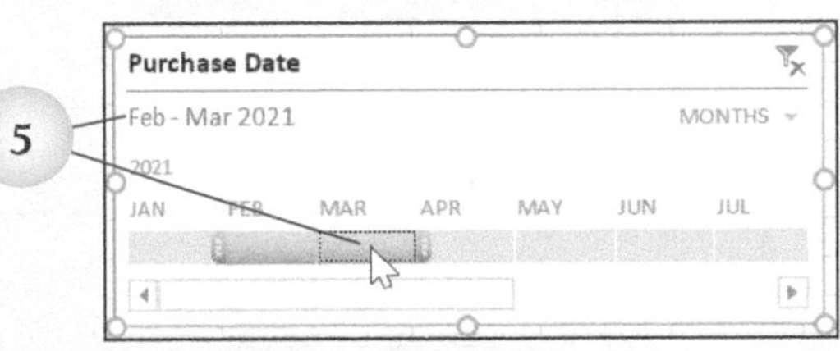

6. Change the page layout to Landscape orientation and then print the filtered PivotTable.
7. Redisplay all the data and remove the Timeline pane by completing the following steps:
   a. Click the Clear Filter button at the top right of the Timeline pane.
   b. Right-click the top of the Timeline pane and then click *Remove Timeline* at the shortcut menu.
8. Save **4-PFSales**.

Creating a PivotChart

PivotChart

Quick Steps

Create PivotChart from PivotTable

1. Make cell active within PivotTable.
2. Click PivotTable Tools Analyze tab.
3. Click PivotChart button.
4. Select chart type.
5. Click OK.

Creating a PivotChart

A *PivotChart* displays data in chart form. Like the data in a PivotTable, the data in a PivotChart can be filtered to examine various scenarios between categories. As changes are made to the PivotChart, the PivotTable associated with it also updates. Figure 4.7 displays the PivotChart you will create in Activity 3g.

In a worksheet that already contains a PivotTable, position the active cell anywhere in the PivotTable, click the PivotTable Tools Analyze tab, and then click the PivotChart button in the Tools group to create a chart from the existing summary data. The Insert Chart dialog box displays with a preview of the type of chart to create. Once the PivotChart has been generated, the PivotTable and PivotChart become connected. Making changes to the data by filtering in one causes the other to update with the same filter. For example, filtering the PivotChart by an individual salesperson name causes the PivotTable to filter by the same name.

If a PivotChart is created without a PivotTable, then Excel displays a blank chart, a PivotTable placeholder, and the PivotTable Fields task pane. Build the chart using the same techniques used to build a PivotTable. As the PivotChart is built, Excel also builds a PivotTable that is connected to the PivotChart.

Figure 4.7 PivotChart for Activity 3g

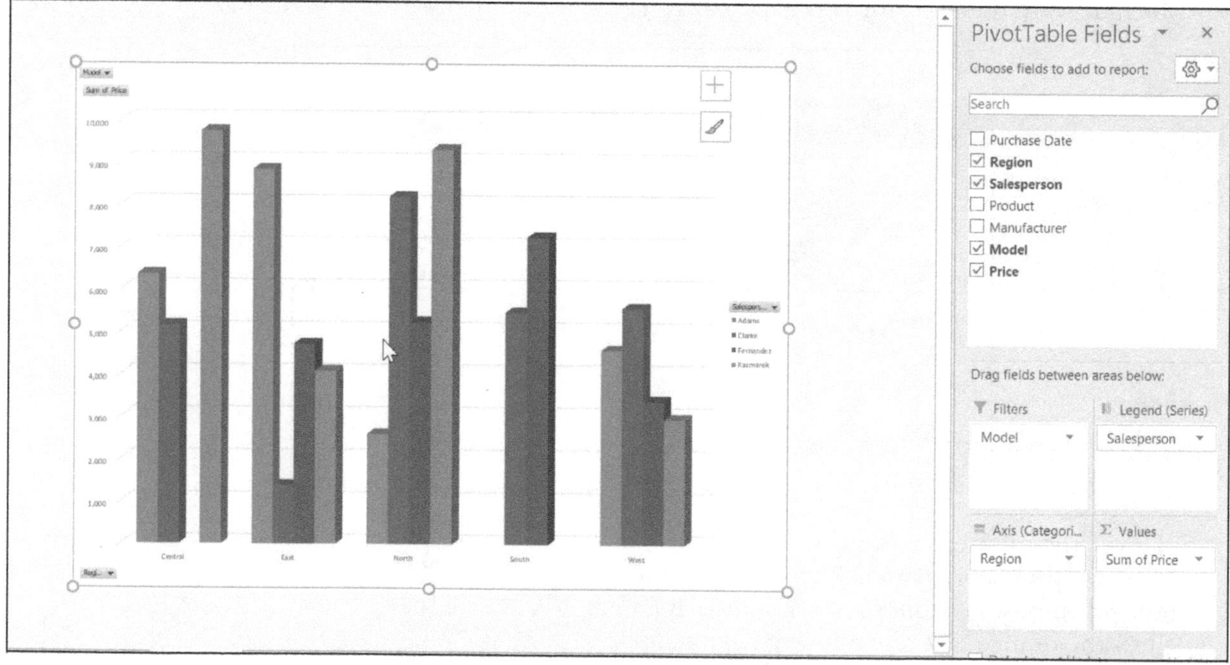

Quick Steps

Create PivotChart without Existing PivotTable

1. Select range containing data for chart.
2. Click Insert tab.
3. Click PivotChart button arrow.
4. Click *PivotChart*.
5. Click OK.
6. Add fields as needed in PivotTable Fields task pane to build chart.
7. Modify and/or format as required.

Move Chart

Before creating a PivotChart from scratch, examine the source data and determine the following:

- Which fields should display along the *x* (horizontal) axis? In other words, how should the data be compared when viewing the chart: by time period (such as months or years), by salesperson name, by department name, or by some other category?
- Which fields should display in the legend? In other words, how many data series (bars in a column chart) should be viewed in the chart: one for each region, product, salesperson, department, or other category?
- Which numeric field contains the values to graph in the chart?

Use the Chart Elements button and the Chart Styles button at the upper right corner of the PivotChart to add or remove titles, labels, or other chart elements and to apply a style or color scheme to the PivotChart. To move the chart to a new sheet, use the Move Chart button in the Actions group on the PivotChart Tools Analyze tab.

Activity 3g Creating a PivotChart Using a PivotTable

Part 7 of 8

1. With **4-PFSales** open, make the SalesByRegion sheet active, if necessary.
2. Create a PivotChart to visually present the data in the PivotTable by completing the following steps:
   a. If necessary, click in any cell within the PivotTable to activate the PivotTable Tools contextual tabs.
   b. Click the PivotTable Tools Analyze tab.
   c. Click the PivotChart button in the Tools group.
   d. At the Insert Chart dialog box with *Column* selected in the left pane, click *3-D Clustered Column* (fourth option above the preview) and then click OK.

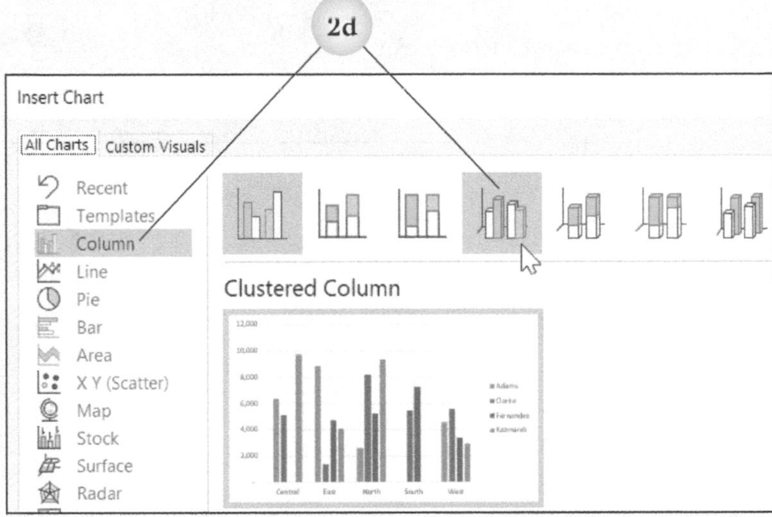

3. Filter the PivotChart to display sales for only one salesperson by completing the following steps:
   a. Click the Salesperson field button in the PivotChart. (This is the button above the salesperson names in the PivotChart legend.)
   b. Click the *(Select All)* check box to clear all the check boxes.
   c. Click the *Kazmarek* check box to insert a check mark.
   d. Click OK.
   e. Notice that the PivotTable behind the chart is also filtered to reflect the display of the chart. ***Note: If the chart is obscuring your view of the PivotTable, drag the PivotChart border to move it out of the way.***
   f. Click the Salesperson field button in the PivotChart and then click *Clear Filter From "Salesperson"*.

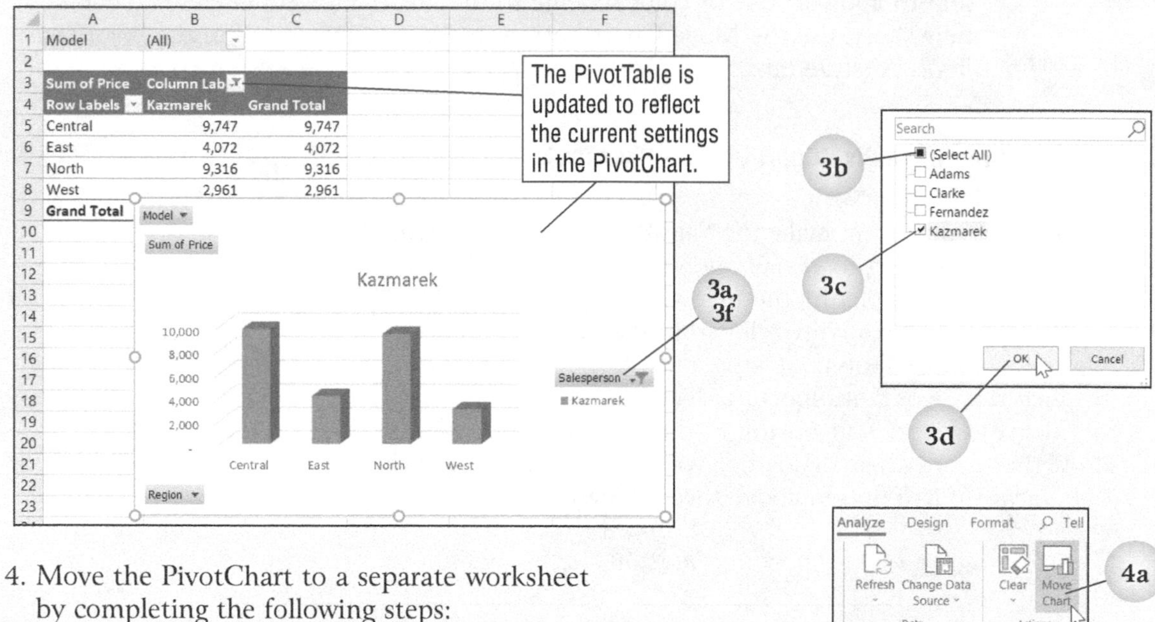

4. Move the PivotChart to a separate worksheet by completing the following steps:
   a. Click the Move Chart button in the Actions group on the PivotChart Tools Analyze tab.
   b. At the Move Chart dialog box, click the *New sheet* option and then type PivotChart in the *New sheet* text box.
   c. Click OK. Excel moves the PivotChart to a separate worksheet. Compare your PivotChart with the one shown in Figure 4.7 (on page 106).
5. Print the PivotChart.
6. Save **4-PFSales**.

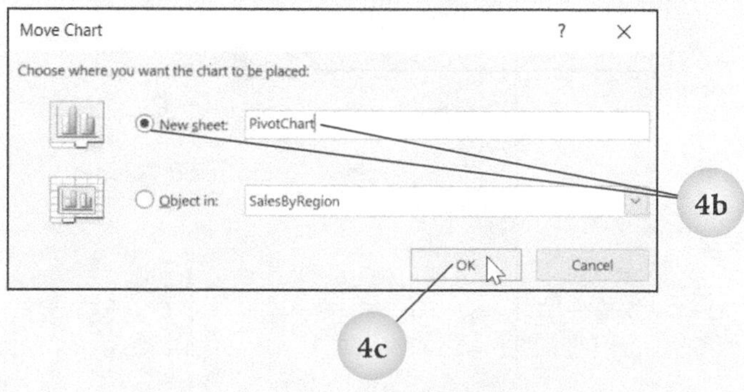

Activity 3h Creating a PivotChart from Scratch

1. With **4-PFSales** open, save the workbook with the name **4-PFChart**.
2. Create a PivotChart to display the sales by manufacturer by region by completing the following steps:
   a. Make the FirstQuarterSales worksheet active, select the named range *FirstQ*, and then click the Insert tab.
   b. Click the PivotChart button arrow in the Charts group and then click *PivotChart* at the drop-down list.
   c. At the Create PivotChart dialog box with *FirstQuarterSales!$A$4:$G$47* entered in the *Table/Range* text box and *New Worksheet* selected in the *Choose where you want the PivotChart to be placed* section, click OK.
   d. Excel displays a blank sheet with the PivotChart Fields task pane at the right side of the window. A PivotTable placeholder and chart placeholder appear in the worksheet area. As you build the PivotChart, notice that a PivotTable is created automatically.
   e. Click the *Manufacturer* check box in the PivotChart Fields task pane. Excel adds the field to the *Axis (Categories)* list box in the layout section.
   f. Click the *Region* check box in the PivotChart Fields task pane. Excel adds the field below *Manufacturer* in the *Axis (Categories)* list box in the layout section.
   g. Click the *Region* field header in the *Axis (Categories)* list box and then click *Move to Legend Fields (Series)* at the pop-up list. Excel moves the field and updates the chart and PivotTable.
   h. Click the *Price* check box in the PivotTable Fields task pane. Excel graphs the sum of the price values in the PivotChart and updates the PivotTable.
3. Point to the border of the PivotChart and then drag the PivotChart below the PivotTable.
4. Resize the chart to the approximate height and width of the chart shown below.
5. Experiment with the Chart Elements and Chart Styles buttons at the upper right corner of the chart. (See Level 1, Chapter 7 for more information on these buttons.)
6. Rename the sheet containing the PivotTable and PivotChart as *SummaryData*.
7. Deselect the PivotChart and then print the PivotTable and PivotChart worksheet.
8. Save and then close **4-PFChart**.

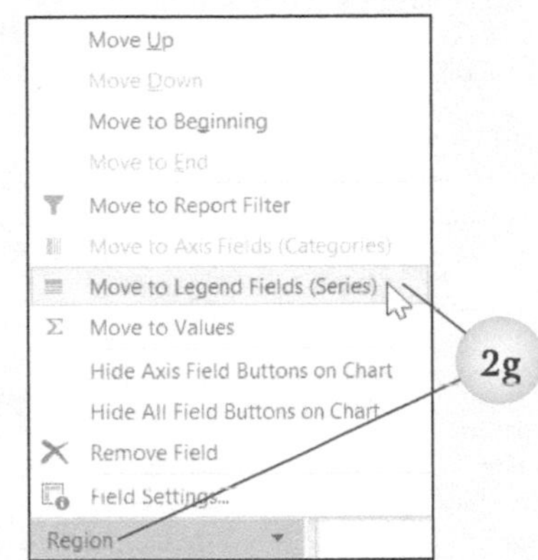

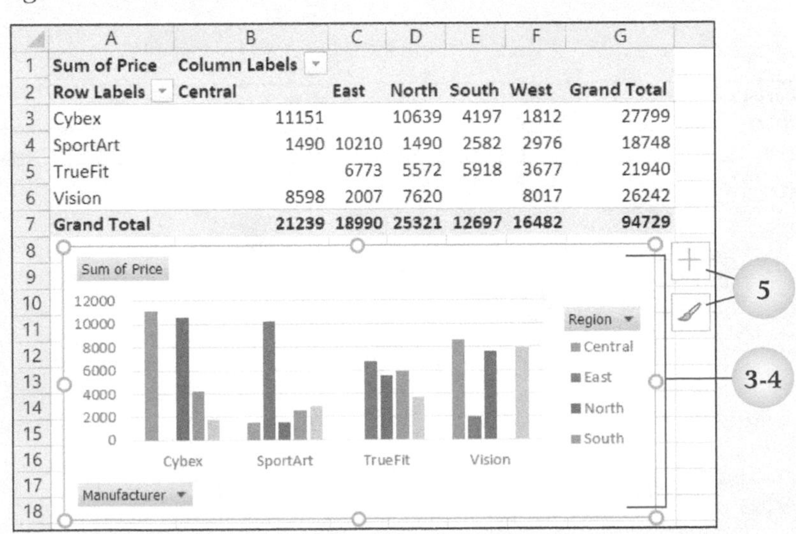

Sum of Price	Column Labels					
Row Labels	Central	East	North	South	West	Grand Total
Cybex	11151		10639	4197	1812	27799
SportArt	1490	10210	1490	2582	2976	18748
TrueFit		6773	5572	5918	3677	21940
Vision	8598	2007	7620		8017	26242
Grand Total	**21239**	**18990**	**25321**	**12697**	**16482**	**94729**

Check Your Work

Activity 4 Add Sparklines in a Worksheet to Show Trends **2 Parts**

You will add and format Sparklines to identify trends in fees for dental services over the first quarter.

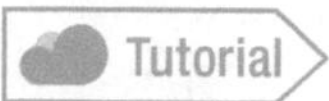

Summarizing Data with Sparklines

Quick Steps

Create Sparklines

1. Select empty range in which to insert Sparklines.
2. Click Insert tab.
3. Click Line, Column, or Win/Loss button in Sparklines group.
4. Type data range address or drag to select data range in *Data Range* text box.
5. Click OK.

Summarizing Data with Sparklines

Sparklines are miniature charts that can be embedded into the background of a cell. Entire charts exist in single cells. Since Sparklines can be placed directly next to the data set being represented, viewing them allows the quick determination of trends or patterns within the data. Consider using Sparklines to illustrate high and low values within a range, as well as trends and other patterns. Figure 4.8 illustrates the three buttons in the Sparklines group used to create Sparkline charts: Line, Column, and Win/Loss.

Creating Sparklines

To create Sparklines, select the empty cell range in which to insert the miniature charts, click the Insert tab, and then click either the Line, Column, or Win/Loss button in the Sparklines group. At the Create Sparklines dialog box, type or click the range of the cells that contain the data to graph in the *Data Range* text box and then click OK.

Figure 4.8 Line, Column, and Win/Loss Sparklines Added to a Worksheet

NewAge Dental Services

Fee Revenue Summary

	Q1 Fees	Q2 Fees	Q3 Fees	Q4 Fees	Fee Summary
Popovich	$ 72,148	$ 90,435	$ 95,123	$ 104,357	
Vanket	$ 35,070	$ 33,189	$ 31,876	$ 37,908	
Jones	$ 42,471	$ 47,845	$ 32,158	$ 38,452	
Total	$ 149,690	$ 171,469	$ 159,158	$ 180,717	Q4 set new record

Increase or Decease in Fees Compared to Last Year

Popovich	-3.0%	2.5%	4.5%	6.0%	
Vanket	5.5%	-8.0%	-10.0%	3.8%	
Jones	4.5%	6.4%	-12.0%	1.2%	

Use the Line or Column buttons to create Sparklines to show trends or patterns over a time period.

Since Sparklines are part of the background of a cell, text can be added to any cells that contain Sparklines.

Use the Win/Loss button to create Sparklines to show positive and negative values using bars. Notice that the bars are all the same height but that those quarters in which fees are lower than last year (negative percentages) show as red bars below the baseline.

Activity 4a Creating Sparklines

Part 1 of 2

1. Open **4-NADQ1Fees**.
2. Save the workbook with the name **4-NADQ1Fees-4**.
3. Create Sparklines to illustrate the trends in categories of dental service fees during the first quarter by completing the following steps:
   a. With the FeeSummary worksheet active, select the range F5:F13.
   b. Click the Insert tab.
   c. Click the Line button in the Sparklines group.
   d. At the Create Sparklines dialog box with the insertion point positioned in the *Data Range* text box, type b5:d13.
   e. Click OK. Excel inserts miniature line charts within the cells.
   f. Click in any cell to deselect the range.
4. Spend a few moments reviewing the Sparklines to determine what the charts indicate. Notice that the lines in cell F7 (*Teeth Whitening*) and cell F10 (*Crowns and Bridges*) slope up and then downward. This shows that these dental services peaked in February and then began to decline.
5. Save **4-NADQ1Fees-4**.

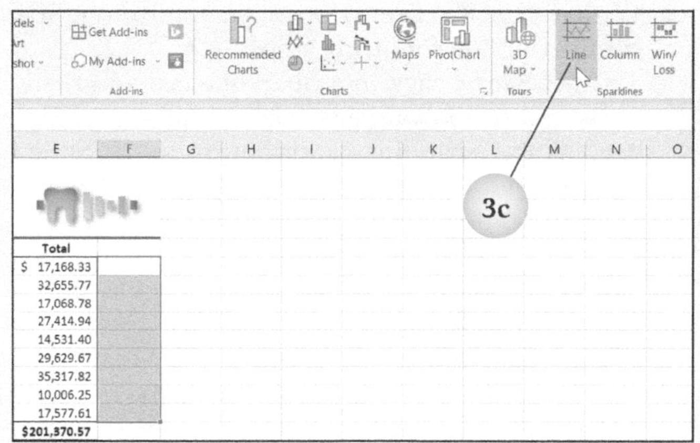

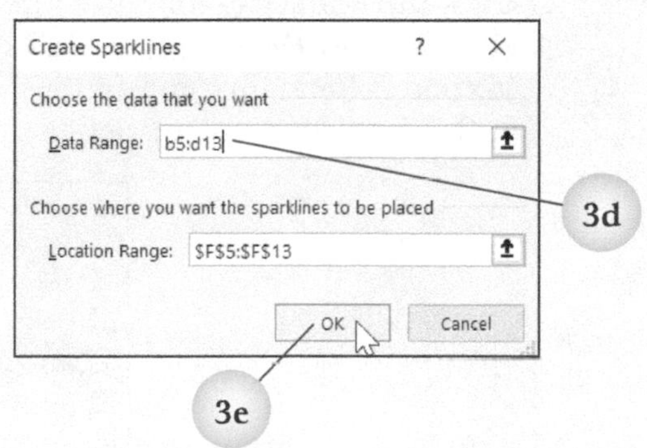

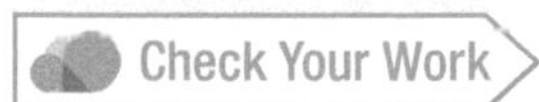

Customizing Sparklines

Quick Steps
Customize Sparklines
1. Click in any Sparkline cell.
2. Click Sparkline Tools Design tab.
3. Change chart type, show/hide points or markers, and change chart style, color, or marker color.

Activate any Sparkline cell and then click the Sparkline Tools Design tab to display the contextual tab shown in Figure 4.9. Click the Edit Data button to edit the range used to generate the Sparklines or instruct Excel how to graph hidden or empty cells in the data range. Use buttons in the Type group to change the chart type from Line to Column or Win/Loss. Click the check boxes in the Show group to show or hide data points in the chart or to show markers. Use options in the Style group to change the appearance of line and/or marker. Click the Axis button in the last group to customize the horizontal or vertical axis in the charts. Sparklines can be grouped, ungrouped, or cleared using the last three buttons on the tab.

Figure 4.9 Sparkline Tools Design Tab

Activity 4b Customizing Sparklines

Part 2 of 2

1. With **4-NADQ1Fees-4** open, customize the Sparklines by completing the following steps:
   a. If necessary, click in a Sparkline cell and then click the Sparkline Tools Design tab.
   b. Click the Sparkline Color button in the Style group and then click *Dark Red* (first option in the *Standard Colors* section) at the drop-down color palette.
   c. Click the *High Point* check box in the Show group to insert a check mark. Excel adds a marker at the highest point on each line graph.
   d. Click the *Markers* check box in the Show group to insert a check mark. Excel adds markers to all the other data points on each line.
   e. Click the Marker Color button in the Style group, point to *High Point*, and then click *Black, Text 1* (second column, first row in the *Theme Colors* section) at the drop-down color palette.

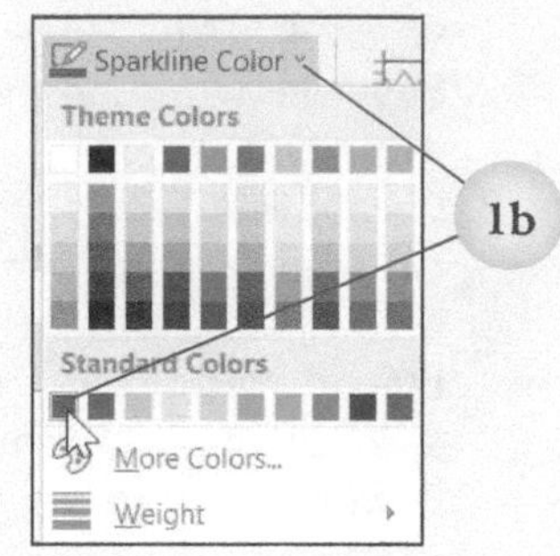

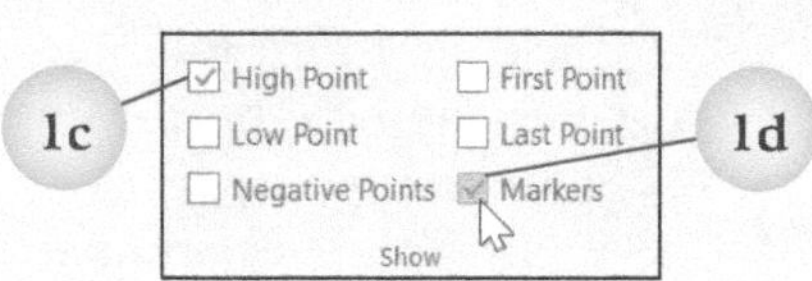

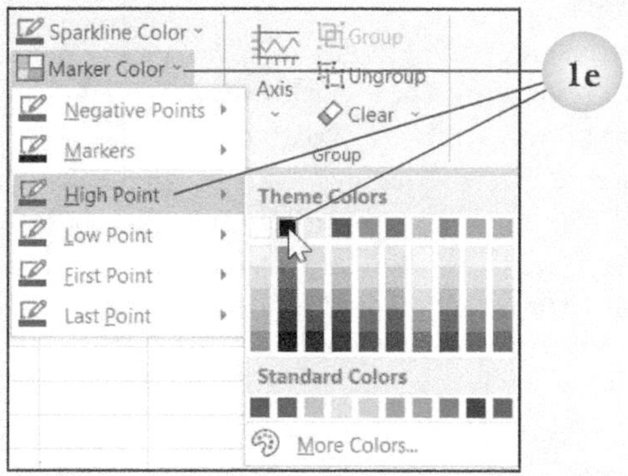

2. Widen the column and add a fill color to improve the appearance of the Sparklines by completing the following steps:
   a. Change the width of column F to 22 characters.
   b. Select the range F5:F13, click the Home tab, and then apply the Aqua, Accent 5, Lighter 80% fill color (ninth column, second row in the *Theme Colors* section) to the selected cells.
   c. Click in any cell to deselect the range.
3. Make cell F4 active, type January to March Trends, press the Enter key, and then, if necessary, format the title so it has the same formatting as the other titles in row 4.
4. Change the page layout to Landscape orientation and then print the FeeSummary worksheet.
5. Save and then close **4-NADQ1Fees-4**.

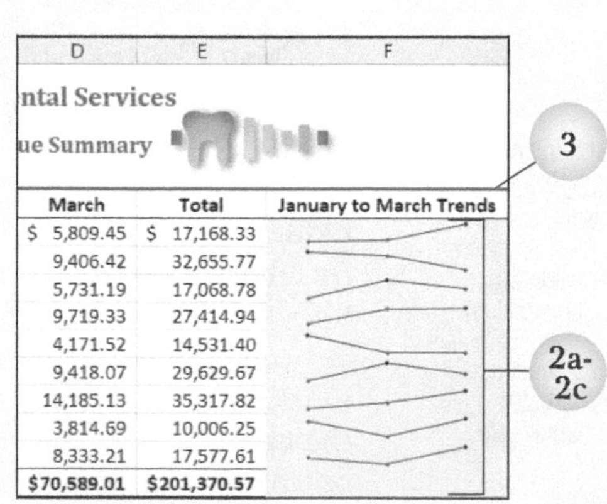

March	Total	January to March Trends
$ 5,809.45	$ 17,168.33	
9,406.42	32,655.77	
5,731.19	17,068.78	
9,719.33	27,414.94	
4,171.52	14,531.40	
9,418.07	29,629.67	
14,185.13	35,317.82	
3,814.69	10,006.25	
8,333.21	17,577.61	
$70,589.01	$201,370.57	

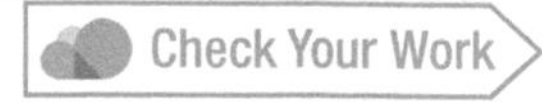

Chapter Summary

- A formula that references a cell in another worksheet within the same workbook contains a worksheet reference and a cell reference separated by an exclamation point.
- Range names can be used to simplify references to cells in other worksheets because the worksheet reference is automatically included in the definition of each range name.
- A disadvantage to using range names to reference other worksheets emerges if several worksheets are to be summarized because each name has to be defined before the formula can be created.
- A 3-D reference is used to summarize the same cell in a range that extends over two or more worksheets. A 3-D reference includes the starting worksheet name and ending worksheet name separated by a colon, similar to the method used to define a range of cells.
- A formula that references another worksheet is linked to that worksheet, so that a change made in the source cell is automatically made in the other worksheet. A formula that references a cell in another workbook must include a workbook reference before the worksheet and cell references. The workbook reference is enclosed in square brackets.
- The workbook in which the external reference is added is called the *destination workbook*. The workbook containing the data that is linked to the destination workbook is called the *source workbook*.
- When a formula that links to an external reference is created, Excel includes the drive and folder names in the path to the source workbook. If the source workbook is moved or the source workbook file name is changed, the link will no longer work.
- Open the Edit Links dialog box to edit or remove a linked external reference.
- The Consolidate feature is another tool that can be used to summarize the data from multiple worksheets into a master worksheet. Open the Consolidate dialog box by clicking the Consolidate button is in the Data Tools group on the Data tab.
- At the Consolidate dialog box, the Sum function is selected by default. Add the references containing the data to summarize, specify the location of the labels to duplicate, and indicate whether to create a link to the source data.
- A PivotTable is an interactive table that organizes and summarizes data based on categories in rows or columns. Create a PivotTable using the PivotTable button in the Tables group on the Insert tab.
- Preview different PivotTable scenarios by clicking the Recommended PivotTables button.
- Add fields to a PivotTable using the field name check boxes in the PivotTable Fields task pane.
- Use buttons on the contextual PivotTable Tools Analyze and PivotTable Tools Design tabs to format the PivotTable and/or edit the features used in it.
- Once created, a PivotTable can be used to view a variety of scenarios by filtering the row, column, or report headings.

- Slicers allow filtering data in a PivotTable or PivotChart without using a filter arrow. Because the Slicer pane contains all the items in the designated field, the report can be filtered with one mouse click. Click the Insert Slicer button in the Filter group on the PivotTable Tools Analyze tab to add a Slicer pane to a PivotTable.
- Timelines group and filter data in a PivotTable or PivotChart based on specific timeframes, such as years, quarters, months, and days. With any cell within the PivotTable active, click the PivotTable Analyze tab and then click the Insert Timeline button in the Filter group.
- A PivotChart displays data in chart form. As changes are made to the PivotChart, the PivotTable associated with it also updates. Filter a PivotChart using the legend or axis field buttons on the PivotChart.
- Sparklines are miniature charts inserted into the backgrounds of cells. Add Sparklines to a worksheet to show trends or high or low values in a range of source data.
- To create Sparklines, select the empty cell range in which to insert the miniature charts, click the Insert tab, and then click the chart type in the Sparklines group. At the Create Sparklines dialog box, type or click the range of cells that contain the values to graph and then click OK. Sparklines can be customized using options in the Sparkline Tools Design tab.

Commands Review

FEATURE	RIBBON TAB, GROUP	BUTTON	KEYBOARD SHORTCUT
Consolidate	Data, Data Tools		
edit links	Data, Queries & Connections		
PivotChart	Insert, Charts OR PivotTables Tools Analyze, Tools		
PivotTable	Insert, Tables		
Slicer	PivotTable Tools Analyze, Filter		
Sparklines	Insert, Sparklines		
Timelines	PivotTable Tools Analyze, Filter		

Microsoft®

Excel® Level 2

Unit 2

Managing and Integrating Data and the Excel Environment

Microsoft®

Excel®

CHAPTER 5

Using Data Analysis Features

Performance Objectives

Upon successful completion of Chapter 5, you will be able to:

1. Transpose data arranged in columns to rows and vice versa
2. Perform a mathematical operation during a paste routine
3. Populate cells using Goal Seek
4. Save and display various worksheet models using the Scenario Manager
5. Generate a scenario summary report
6. Create one-variable and two-variable data tables
7. Use auditing tools to view relationships between cells in formulas
8. Identify Excel error message codes and troubleshoot formulas using formula auditing tools
9. Use the Circle Invalid Data feature
10. Use the Watch Window to track cells affected by key formulas

Excel's Paste Special dialog box includes several options for pasting copied data. Choose to paste attributes of a copied cell or alter the paste routine to perform a more complex operation. Apply a variety of What-If Analysis tools to manage data and assist with decision-making and management tasks. Use formula-auditing tools to troubleshoot formulas or view dependencies between cells. By working through the activities in this chapter, you will learn about these tools and features available in Excel to assist with accurate data analysis.

Before beginning chapter work, copy the EL2C5 folder to your storage medium and then make EL2C5 the active folder.

The online course includes additional training and assessment resources.

Activity 1 Analyze Data from a Request for Proposal — 2 Parts

You will manipulate a worksheet containing vendor quotations for an enterprise resource-planning information system by copying and pasting using Paste Special options.

Pasting Data Using Paste Special Options

Paste

Pasting Data Using Paste Special Options

Clicking the Paste button arrow in the Clipboard group on the Home tab opens the Paste drop-down gallery. This gallery contains many options for pasting copied data and is divided into three sections: *Paste*, *Paste Values*, and *Other Paste Options*. The Paste drop-down gallery includes a live preview of how the data will be pasted to assist in choosing the correct paste option. Click *Paste Special* at the bottom of the Paste drop-down gallery to open the Paste Special dialog box, shown in Figure 5.1. Use options in this dialog box to paste specific attributes of the source data, perform a mathematical operation in the destination range based on values in the source range, or carry out a more complex paste sequence.

Several options in the Paste Special dialog box are also available by clicking a button at the Paste drop-down gallery. For example, to copy a range of cells that has border formatting applied and then paste the range without the borders, click the Paste button arrow and then click the No Borders button (first column, second row in the *Paste* section) at the drop-down gallery. This produces the same result as clicking the Paste button arrow, clicking *Paste Special* at the drop-down gallery, clicking *All except borders* in the *Paste* section of the Paste Special dialog box, and then clicking OK.

Figure 5.1 Paste Special Dialog Box

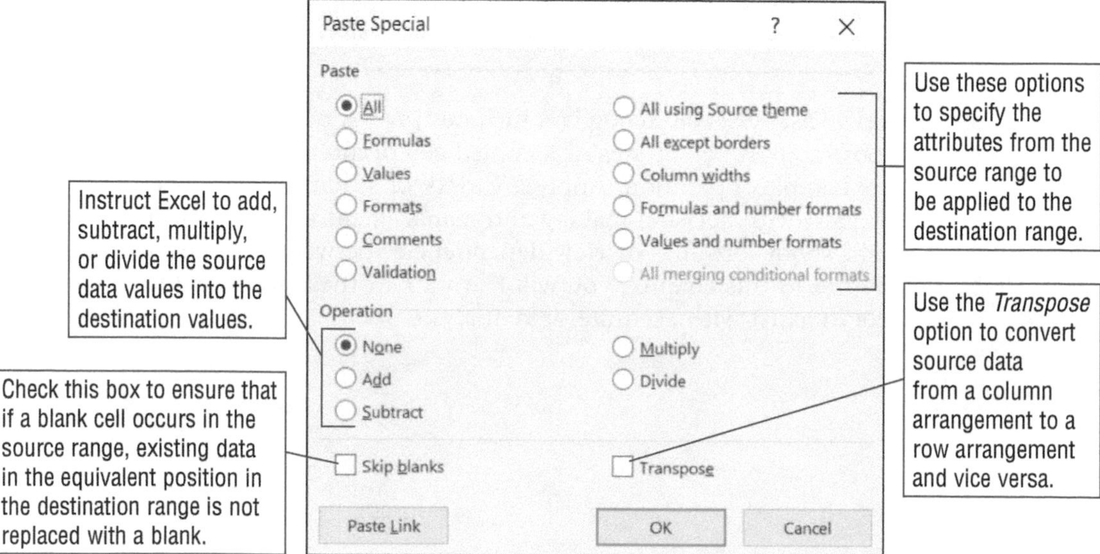

Selecting Other Paste Special Options

A variety of options can be selected at the Paste Special dialog box. Click *Formulas* or *Values* to paste only the source formulas or displayed values, click *Formats* to paste only the formatting options from the source, and click *Validation* to paste a validation rule. Click *All using Source theme* to apply the theme from the source, click *All except borders* to paste everything but the borders from the source, and click *Column widths* to adjust the destination cells to the same column widths as the source. To paste formulas or values including the number formats from the source, click the *Formulas and number formats* option or the *Values and number formats* option.

Transposing Data

Quick Steps

Transpose Range

1. Select source range.
2. Click Copy button.
3. Click starting cell in destination range.
4. Click Paste button arrow.
5. Click Transpose button.

Transpose

In some cases, the data in a worksheet is arranged in a way that is not suitable for performing the required analysis. For example, examine the worksheet shown in Figure 5.2. This is the worksheet used in Activity 1. Notice that each company that submitted a proposal appears in a separate column and the criteria for analysis (such as the cost of the hardware) are arranged in rows. At first glance, this layout may seem appropriate but consider that only those vendors that offer five-year contracts are to be examined. To use the filter feature on this data, the contract term needs to be displayed in a columnar format. Rearranging the data in this worksheet manually would be time consuming and risky due to the possibility of making errors. To avoid this, convert the columns to rows and the rows to columns using the Transpose button in the Paste button drop-down gallery or the Paste Special dialog box.

Figure 5.2 Activity 1 Worksheet

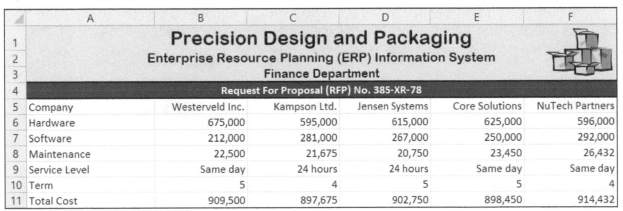

	A	B	C	D	E	F
1	Precision Design and Packaging					
2	Enterprise Resource Planning (ERP) Information System					
3	Finance Department					
4	Request For Proposal (RFP) No. 385-XR-78					
5	Company	Westerveld Inc.	Kampson Ltd.	Jensen Systems	Core Solutions	NuTech Partners
6	Hardware	675,000	595,000	615,000	625,000	596,000
7	Software	212,000	281,000	267,000	250,000	292,000
8	Maintenance	22,500	21,675	20,750	23,450	26,432
9	Service Level	Same day	24 hours	24 hours	Same day	Same day
10	Term	5	4	5	5	4
11	Total Cost	909,500	897,675	902,750	898,450	914,432

Activity 1a **Converting Data from Rows to Columns** Part 1 of 2

1. Open **PreERP**.
2. Save the workbook with the name **5-PreERP**.
3. Convert the worksheet to arrange the company names in rows and the criteria data in columns by completing the following steps:
   a. Select the range A5:F11.
   b. Click the Copy button.

c. Click in cell A13.

d. Click the Paste button arrow and then hover the mouse pointer over the Transpose button (third column, second row in the *Paste* section) at the drop-down gallery. A live preview shows how the copied data will be pasted. Click the Transpose button.

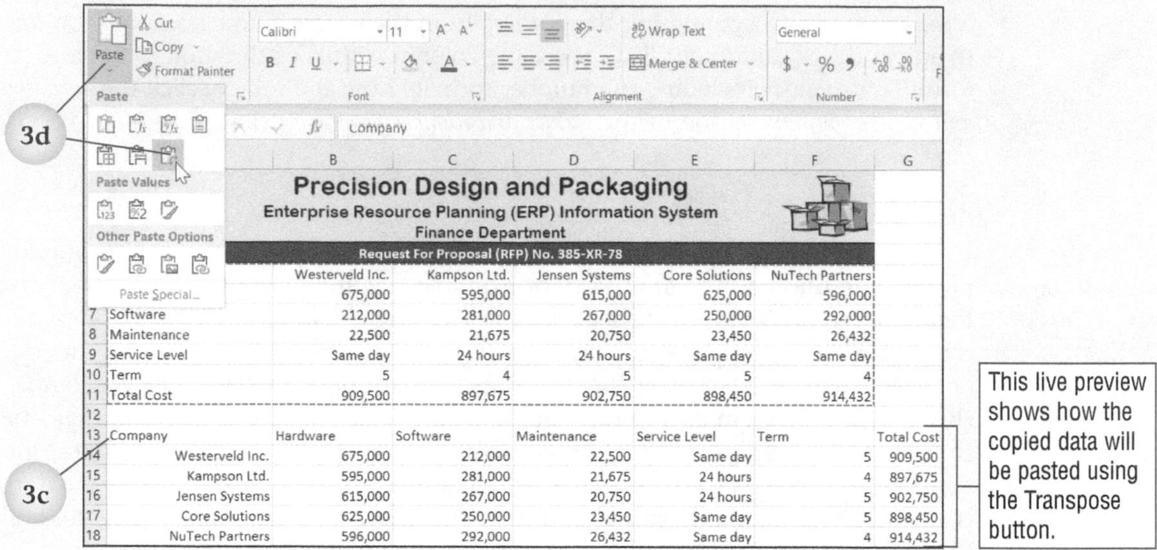

e. Press the Esc key to remove the scrolling marquee from the source range and then click in any cell to deselect the range.

4. Delete rows 5 through 12.
5. Correct the merge and centering in rows 1 through 4 to extend the titles across columns A through G. If necessary, move or otherwise adjust the position of the picture at the right side of the worksheet after merging and centering.
6. Add a thick bottom border to cells A3 and A4 separately.
7. Apply bold formatting to and center-align the labels in the range A5:G5.
8. Select the range A5:G10, turn on the Filter feature, and then click in any cell to deselect the range.
9. Filter the worksheet to display only those vendors offering five year contracts by completing the following steps:
   a. Click the filter arrow in cell F5.
   b. Click the *(Select All)* check box.
   c. Click the *5* check box and then click OK.

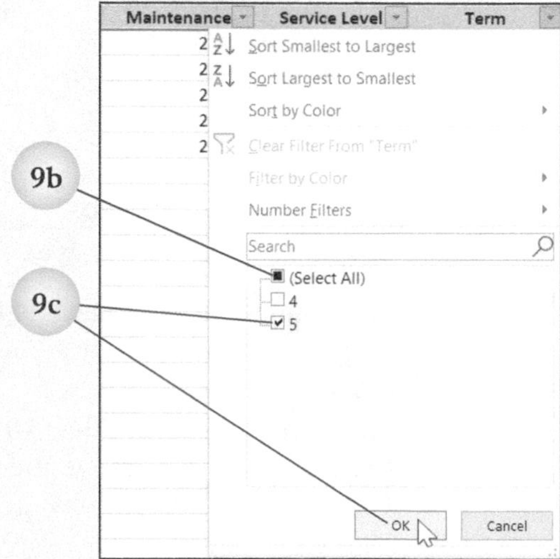

10. Click the filter arrow in cell E5 and then filter the remaining rows to display only those vendors offering same-day service using the same method utilized in Step 9.

Request For Proposal (RFP) No. 385-XR-78						
Company	Hardware	Software	Maintenance	Service Level	Term	Total C
Westerveld Inc.	675,000	212,000	22,500	Same day	5	909,500
Core Solutions	625,000	250,000	23,450	Same day	5	898,450

10

11. Print the filtered worksheet.
12. Turn off the Filter feature and then save **5-PreERP**.

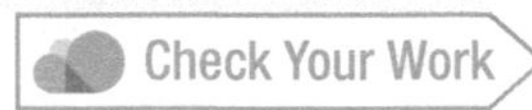

Performing a Mathematical Operation While Pasting

Quick Steps

Perform Mathematical Operation While Pasting

1. Select source range values.
2. Click Copy button.
3. Click starting cell in destination range.
4. Click Paste button arrow.
5. Click *Paste Special*.
6. Click mathematical operation.
7. Click OK.

A range of cells in a copied source range can be added to, subtracted from, multiplied by, or divided by the cells in the destination range. To do this, open the Paste Special dialog box and then select the mathematical operation to be performed. For example, in the worksheet for Activity 1a, the values in the *Maintenance* column are the annual maintenance fees charged by the various vendors. To compare the fees across all the vendors, the maintenance value for the life cycle of the contract must be known.

In Activity 1b, this calculation will be performed by copying and pasting using a multiply operation. Using this method makes it unnecessary to add a new column to the worksheet to show the maintenance fees for the entire term of the contract.

Activity 1b **Multiplying Source Cell Values by Destination Cell Values** Part 2 of 2

1. With **5-PreERP** open, select the range F6:F10. These cells contain the terms for each company's individual contract. The data in the *Maintenance* column contains the cost of yearly maintenance while the data in the *Hardware* and *Software* columns contain data for the entire duration of the term.
2. Click the Copy button.
3. Paste the source range and instruct Excel to multiply the values in the *Maintenance* column by the values in the *Term* column when pasting by completing the following steps:
   a. Click in cell D6.
   b. Click the Paste button arrow and then click *Paste Special* at the drop-down gallery.

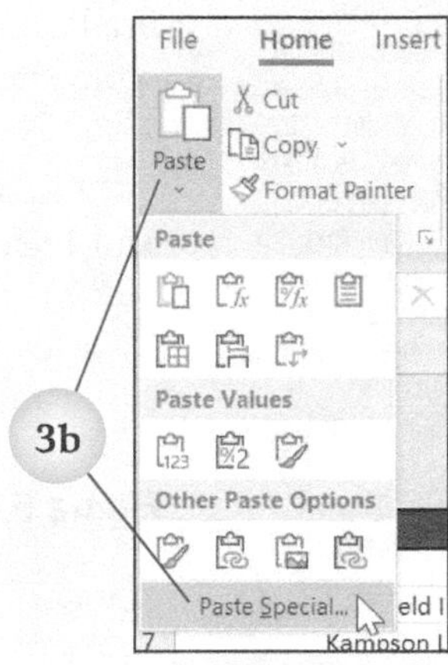

c. Click *Multiply* in the *Operation* section of the Paste Special dialog box and then click OK.
d. Press the Esc key to remove the scrolling marquee from the source range and then click in any cell to deselect the range.

4. Print the worksheet.
5. Save and then close **5-PreERP.**

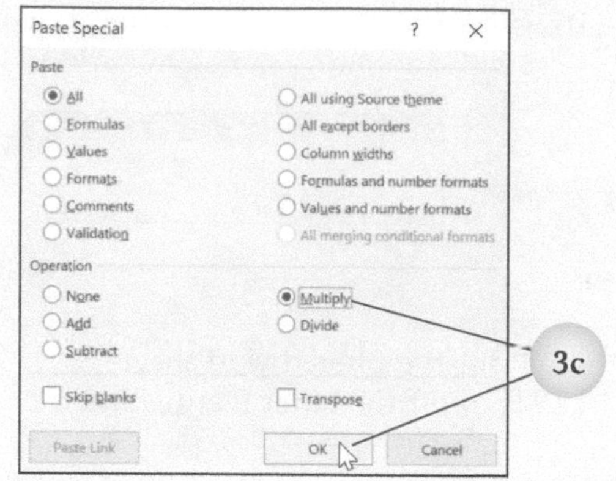

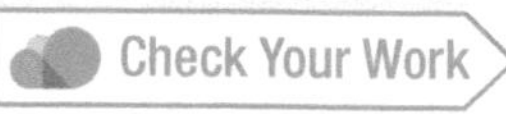

Activity 2 Calculate a Target Test Score — 1 Part

Using a grades worksheet, you will determine the score a student needs to earn on a final test to achieve a specified final average grade.

Using Goal Seek to Populate a Cell

Quick Steps

Use Goal Seek to Return Value

1. Make cell active.
2. Click Data tab.
3. Click What-If Analysis button.
4. Click *Goal Seek.*
5. Enter cell address in *Set cell* text box.
6. Enter target value in *To value* text box.
7. Enter dependent cell address in *By changing cell* text box.
8. Click OK.
9. Click OK or Cancel.

What-If Analysis

Using Goal Seek to Populate Cells

When the result of a formula is known, use the Goal Seek feature to determine what input value should be entered in one cell to achieve the result of the formula. For example, the worksheet shown in Figure 5.3 shows Whitney's grades on the first four tutoring assessments. The value in cell B11 (average grade) is the average of the five values in the range B5:B9. Note that the final test shows a grade of 0 even though the test has not yet occurred. Once the final test grade is entered, the value in cell B11 will update to reflect the average of all five scores. Suppose Whitney wants to achieve a final average grade of 76% in her tutoring assessments. Goal Seek will determine the score she needs to earn on the final test to achieve the 76% average. In Activity 2, Goal Seek will return a value in cell B9 based on the target value of cell B11.

Goal Seek causes Excel to calculate in reverse. The ending value is specified and Excel figures out the input numbers that will achieve the result that is wanted. Note that the cell in which Excel is to calculate the target value must be referenced by a formula in the *Set cell* text box. Goal Seek is useful for any situation in which the wanted result is known but the value needed to get it is not.

Figure 5.3 Activity 2 Worksheet

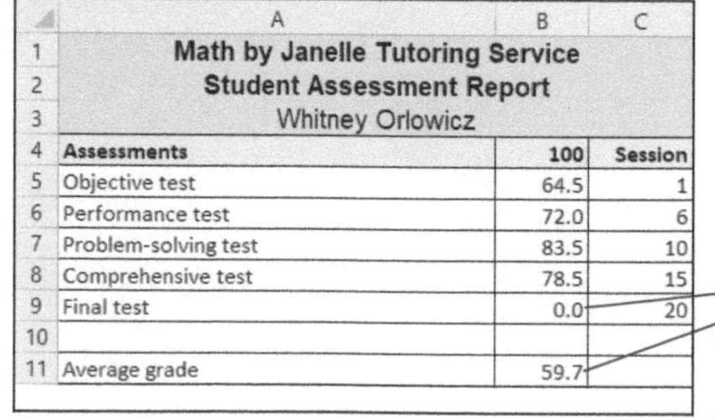

	A	B	C
1	**Math by Janelle Tutoring Service**		
2	**Student Assessment Report**		
3	Whitney Orlowicz		
4	**Assessments**	**100**	**Session**
5	Objective test	64.5	1
6	Performance test	72.0	6
7	Problem-solving test	83.5	10
8	Comprehensive test	78.5	15
9	Final test	0.0	20
10			
11	Average grade	59.7	

Use Goal Seek to determine the value needed in cell B9 for the final test to achieve the desired average grade in cell B11.

Activity 2 Using Goal Seek to Return a Target Value

Part 1 of 1

1. Open **JTutor.**
2. Save the workbook with the name **5-JTutor**.
3. Use Goal Seek to find the score Whitney needs to earn on the final test to achieve a 76% average grade by completing the following steps:
   a. Make cell B11 active.
   b. Click the Data tab.
   c. Click the What-If Analysis button in the Forecast group and then click *Goal Seek* at the drop-down list.
   d. If necessary, drag the Goal Seek dialog box so you can see all the values in column B.
   e. With *B11* already entered in the *Set cell* text box, click in the *To value* text box and then type 76.
   f. Press the Tab key and then type b9 in the *By changing cell* text box.
   g. Click OK.
   h. Click OK at the Goal Seek Status dialog box, which shows that Excel found a solution.

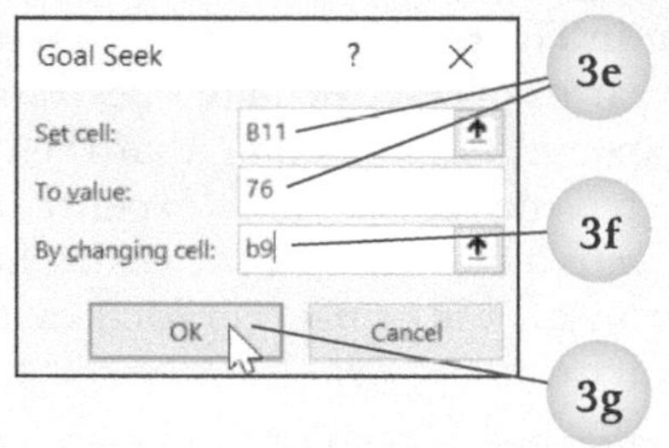

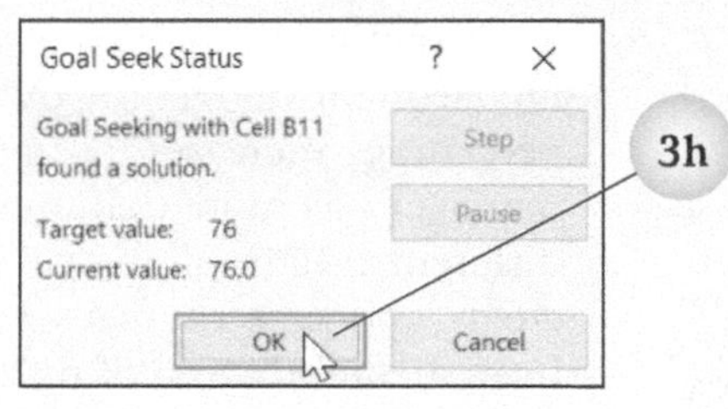

4. Notice that Excel entered the value *81.5* in cell B9. This is the score Whitney must earn to achieve a final average grade of 76%.
5. Assume that Whitney wants to achieve a final average grade of 80%. Use Goal Seek to find the score she will need to earn on the final test to accomplish the new target by completing the following steps:
   a. Click the What-If Analysis button and then click *Goal Seek* at the drop-down list.
   b. With *B11* already entered in the *Set cell* text box, click in the *To value* text box, type 80, and then press the Tab key.
   c. Type b9 in the *By changing cell* text box.
   d. Click OK.
   e. Notice that the value entered in cell B9 is *101.5*. This is the score Whitney needs on the final test to earn an 80% average grade.
   f. The final test is worth only 100, so Whitney will not be able to score 101.5. Restore the previous values in the report by clicking the Cancel button at the Goal Seek Status dialog box.

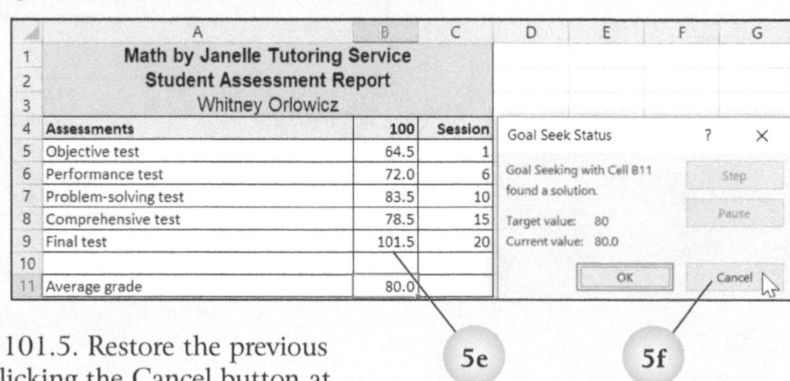

6. Save, print, and then close **5-JTutor.**

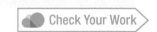

Check Your Work

Activity 3 Forecast a Budget Based on Various Inflation Rates **3 Parts**

You will determine how various rates of inflation impact a department's budget to determine the funding request to present to management to maintain service.

Adding Scenarios

Editing and Applying Scenarios

Quick Steps

Add Scenario

1. Click Data tab.
2. Click What-If Analysis button.
3. Click *Scenario Manager*.
4. Click Add button.
5. Type name in *Scenario name* text box.
6. Type or select variable cells in *Changing cells* text box.
7. Click OK.
8. Enter value for each changing cell.
9. Click OK.
10. Click Close button.

Hint Create a range name for each changing cell. This allows a descriptive reference next to the input text box, rather than a cell address, when adding a scenario.

Adding, Editing, and Applying Scenarios

The Scenario Manager allows storing multiple sets of assumptions about data and then viewing how each set of assumptions affects the worksheet. Switch between scenarios to test the various inputs on the worksheet model. Save each scenario using a descriptive name, such as *BestCase* or *WorstCase*, to indicate the type of data assumptions stored in it. Generally, the first scenario created should contain the original values in the worksheet, since Excel replaces the content of each changing cell when a scenario is shown.

Examine the worksheet shown in Figure 5.4. In it, the Computing Services Department budget for the next year has been calculated based on projected percentage increases for various expense items. Assume that the department manager has more than one projected increase for each expense item based on different inflation rates or vendor rate increases for next year. The manager can create and save various scenarios to view the impact on total costs that results from a combination of different forecasts.

Using the Scenario Manager dialog box, shown in Figure 5.5, create as many models as needed to test various what-if conditions. For example, two scenarios have been saved in the example shown in Figure 5.5: *LowInflation* and *HighInflation*. When a scenario is added, define which cells will change and then enter the data to be stored under the new scenario name.

Figure 5.4 Activity 3 Worksheet

	A	B	C	D
1	National Online Marketing Inc.			
2	Computing Services Department			
3		Current Budget	Projected Increase	New Budget
4	Wages and benefits	483,437	16,920	500,357
5	Computer supplies	195,455	2,931	198,386
6	Training and development	83,005	8,300	91,305
7	Other administrative costs	64,448	3,222	67,670
8	Total costs:	$ 826,345		$ 857,718

Figure 5.5 Scenario Manager Dialog Box and Scenario Values Dialog Box

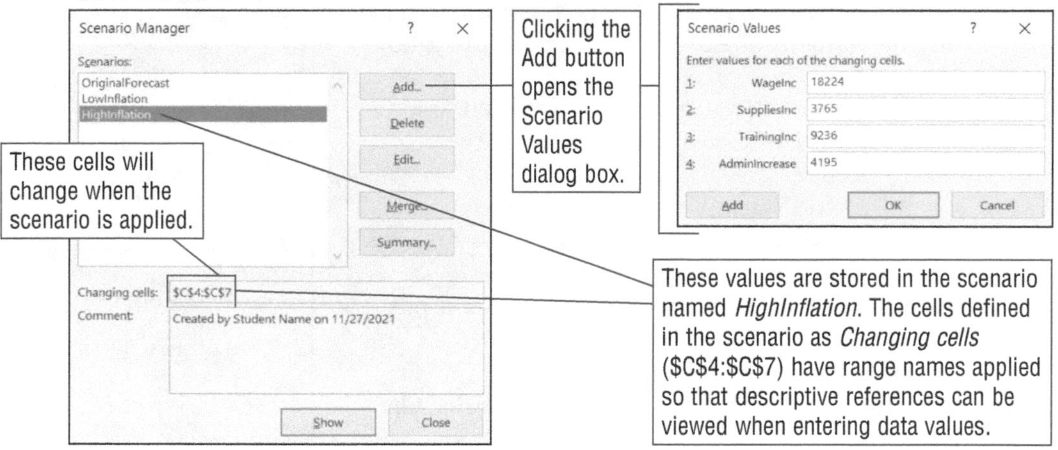

Activity 3a Adding Scenarios to a Worksheet Model

Part 1 of 3

1. Open **NationalBdgt.**
2. Save the workbook with the name **5-NationalBdgt.**
3. View the range names already created in the worksheet by clicking the Name box arrow and then clicking *WageInc* at the drop-down list. Cell C4 becomes active. A range name has been created for each data cell in column C, so a descriptive label displays when scenarios are added in Steps 4 and 5.
4. Add a scenario, named *OriginalForecast*, that contains the original worksheet values by completing the following steps:
   a. Click the Data tab.
   b. Click the What-If Analysis button and then click *Scenario Manager* at the drop-down list.
   c. Click the Add button at the Scenario Manager dialog box.
   d. At the Add Scenario dialog box with the insertion point positioned in the *Scenario name* text box, type OriginalForecast and then press the Tab key.
   e. Type c4:c7 in the *Changing cells* text box. (As an alternative, move the dialog box out of the way and select the cells that will change in the worksheet.)
   f. Click OK.

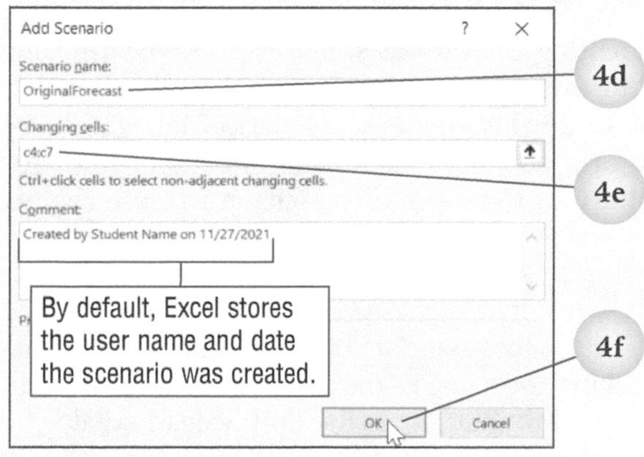

g. At the Scenario Values dialog box, notice that the original value is already entered in each text box. Click OK.

5. Add another scenario to the worksheet that assumes low inflation for next year by completing the following steps:
   a. Click the Add button at the Scenario Manager dialog box. Notice that the *Changing cells* text box already contains the range C4:C7.
   b. Type LowInflation in the *Scenario name* text box and then click OK.
   c. At the Scenario Values dialog box, with the insertion point positioned in the *1: WageInc* text box, type 14010 and then press the Tab key.
   d. Type 27500 and then press the Tab key.
   e. Type 5979 and then press the Tab key.
   f. Type 2005.
   g. Click OK.

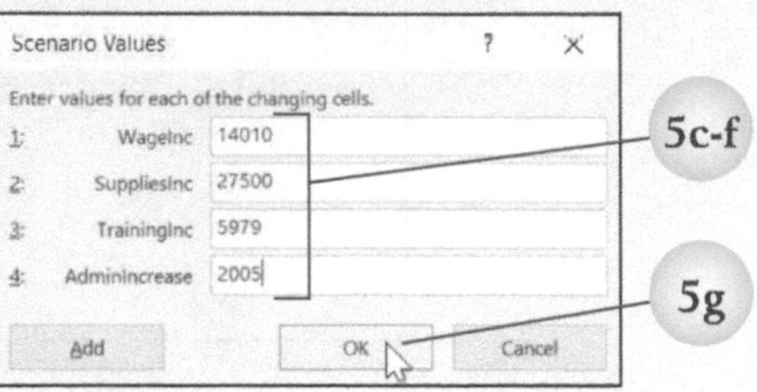

6. Add a third scenario named *HighInflation*, which assumes a high inflation rate, by completing the following steps:
   a. Click the Add button at the Scenario Manager dialog box.
   b. Type HighInflation in the *Scenario name* text box and then click OK.
   c. At the Scenario Values dialog box, type the following values into the text boxes indicated:

      1: WageInc 18224
      2: SuppliesInc 3765
      3: TrainingInc 9236
      4: AdminIncrease 4195

   d. Click OK.
7. Click the Close button to close the Scenario Manager dialog box.
8. Save **5-NationalBdgt.**

Applying a Scenario

Quick Steps

Apply Scenario
1. Click Data tab.
2. Click What-If Analysis button.
3. Click *Scenario Manager* at drop-down list.
4. Click scenario name.
5. Click Show button.
6. Click Close button.

After creating the various scenarios to save with the worksheet, apply the values stored in each scenario to the variable cells to view the effects on the worksheet model. To do this, open the Scenario Manager dialog box, click the name of the scenario that contains the values to be applied to the worksheet, and then click the Show button. Click the Close button to close the Scenario Manager dialog box.

Editing a Scenario

Change the values associated with a scenario by opening the Scenario Manager dialog box, clicking the name of the scenario that contains the values to be changed, and then clicking the Edit button. At the Edit Scenario dialog box, make any changes to the scenario name and/or changing cells and then click OK to open the Scenario Values dialog box to edit the individual value associated with each changing cell. When done, click OK and then click the Close button.

Deleting a Scenario

To delete a scenario, open the Scenario Manager dialog box, click the scenario to be removed, and then click the Delete button. Click the Close button to close the Scenario Manager dialog box.

Activity 3b Applying and Editing Scenario Values

Part 2 of 3

1. With **5-NationalBdgt** open, apply the scenario that assumes the low inflation rate by completing the following steps:
   a. With Data the active tab, click the What-If Analysis button and then click *Scenario Manager* at the drop-down list.
   b. If necessary, drag the Scenario Manager dialog box so you can see all the values in column D.
   c. Click *LowInflation* in the *Scenarios* list box and then click the Show button. Excel changes the values in the range C4:C7 to the values stored within the scenario. Notice that based on the assumption of a low inflation rate, the total cost of the new budget shown in cell D8 is $875,839.

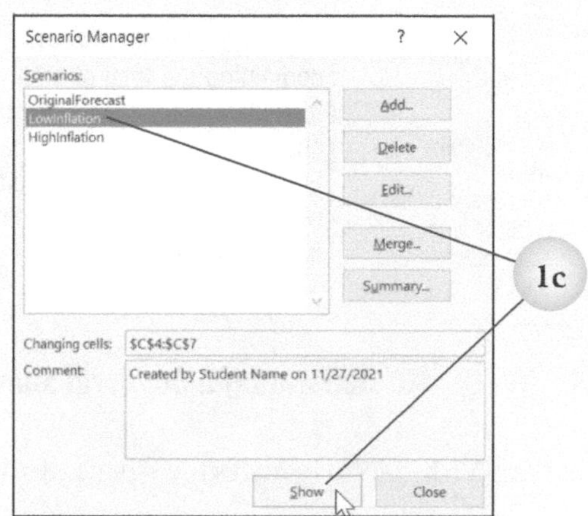

2. With the Scenario Manager dialog box still open, change the worksheet to display the scenario that assumes a high inflation rate by clicking *HighInflation* in the *Scenarios* list box and then clicking the Show button. Notice that in this high-inflation scenario, the total cost of the new budget is $861,765.
3. After the data are reviewed, it is decided that the projected increase for computer supplies should be $4,500. Edit the HighInflation scenario by completing the following steps:
   a. With *HighInflation* selected in the *Scenarios* list box, click the Edit button.
   b. Click OK at the Edit Scenario dialog box.
   c. Select *3765* in the *SuppliesInc* text box and then type 4500.
   d. Click OK and then click the Show button.

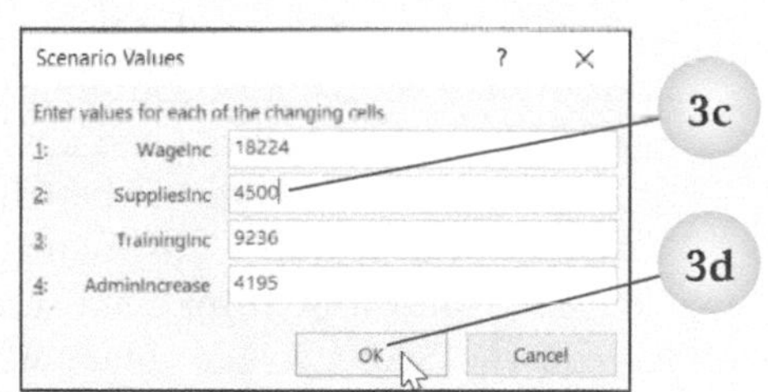

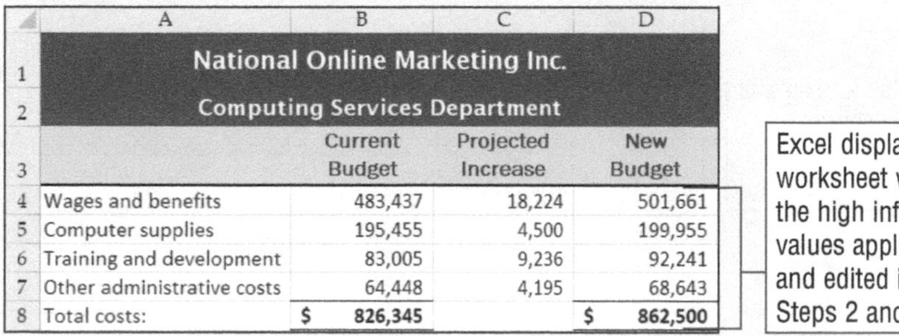

	A	B	C	D
1	National Online Marketing Inc.			
2	Computing Services Department			
3		Current Budget	Projected Increase	New Budget
4	Wages and benefits	483,437	18,224	501,661
5	Computer supplies	195,455	4,500	199,955
6	Training and development	83,005	9,236	92,241
7	Other administrative costs	64,448	4,195	68,643
8	Total costs:	$ 826,345		$ 862,500

Excel displays the worksheet with the high inflation values applied and edited in Steps 2 and 3.

4. Show the worksheet with the data values from the OriginalForecast scenario.
5. Click the Close button to close the Scenario Manager dialog box.
6. Save **5-NationalBdgt**.

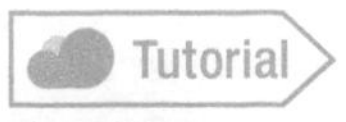

Generating a Scenario Summary Report

Generating a Scenario Summary Report

Create a scenario summary report to compare scenarios side by side in a worksheet or PivotTable. At the Scenario Summary dialog box, shown in Figure 5.6, enter in the *Result cells* text box the formula cell or cells that change when the data is applied in the various scenarios. Enter multiple cell addresses in this text box and use commas to separate them.

Quick Steps

Create Scenario Summary Report

1. Click Data tab.
2. Click What-If Analysis button.
3. Click *Scenario Manager*.
4. Click Summary button.
5. If necessary, change cell address in *Result cells* text box.
6. Click OK.

Figure 5.6 Scenario Summary Dialog Box

Enter the address of the cell containing the total or other formula results affected by the changing cells in each scenario. Enter cell addresses for multiple results separated by commas or use a range if applicable.

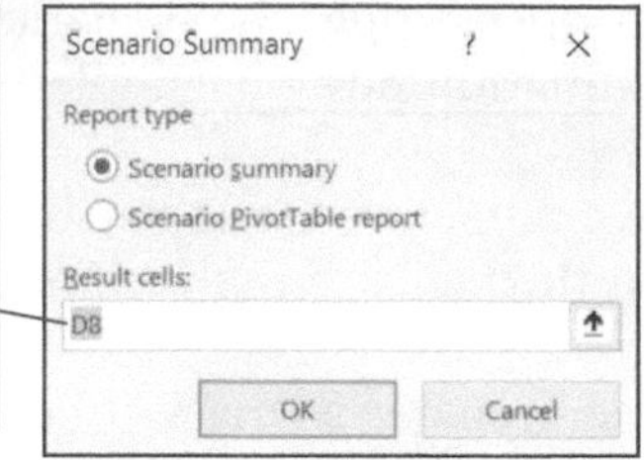

Activity 3c **Generating a Scenario Summary Report**

Part 3 of 3

1. With **5-NationalBdgt** open, display a scenario summary report by completing the following steps:
   a. With Data the active tab, click the What-If Analysis button and then click *Scenario Manager* at the drop-down list.
   b. Click the Summary button at the Scenario Manager dialog box.
   c. At the Scenario Summary dialog box, with the *Report type* set to *Scenario summary* and *Result cells* displaying the address *D8*, click OK.
2. Examine the Scenario Summary sheet added to the workbook. It displays each changing cell with the input for each scenario. Below the Changing Cells table, Excel displays the Result Cells, which provide the values that result from input from each scenario.
3. Print the Scenario Summary worksheet.
4. Save and then close **5-NationalBdgt.**

Scenario Summary

?

×

Report type

Scenario summary

Scenario PivotTable report

Result cells:

D8

OK

Cancel

1c

In Step 2, examine the Scenario Summary report created in Step 1.

Scenario Summary	Current Values:	OriginalForecast	LowInflation	HighInflation
Changing Cells:				
WageInc	16,920	16,920	14,010	18,224
SuppliesInc	2,931	2,931	27,500	4,500
TrainingInc	8,300	8,300	5,979	9,236
AdminIncrease	3,222	3,222	2,005	4,195
Result Cells:				
TotalNewCosts	$ 857,718	$ 857,718	$ 875,839	$ 862,500

Notes: Current Values column represents values of changing cells at time Scenario Summary Report was created. Changing cells for each scenario are highlighted in gray.

Activity 4 Compare the Effects of Various Inputs Related to Cost and Sales Pricing — 2 Parts

Using one-variable and two-variable data tables, you will analyze the effects on the cost per unit and the selling price per unit of a manufactured container.

Performing What-If Analysis Using Data Tables

The term *data table* refers to a range of cells that contains a series of input values. Excel calculates a formula substituting each input value in the data table range and places the result in the cell adjacent to the value. Either a one-variable or a two-variable data table can be created. A one-variable data table calculates a formula by modifying one input value in the formula. A two-variable data table calculates a formula substituting two input values. Using data tables provides a means of analyzing various outcomes in a calculation that occur as a result of changing a dependent value without creating multiple formulas.

Creating a One-Variable Data Table

Data Table

Quick Steps

Create One-Variable Data Table

1. Create variable data in column at right of worksheet.
2. Enter formula one row above and one cell right of variable data.
3. Select data range, including formula cell.
4. Click Data tab.
5. Click What-If Analysis button.
6. Click *Data Table.*
7. Type cell address for variable data in source formula in *Column input cell* text box.
8. Click OK.

Creating a One-Variable Data Table

Design a one-variable data table with the variable input data values in a series down a column or across a row. Examine the worksheet shown in Figure 5.7. Assume that management wants to calculate the effects on the cost per unit for a variety of production volumes given a standard set of costs per factory shift. The worksheet includes the total costs for direct materials, direct labor, and overhead.

The formula in cell B8 sums the three cost categories. Based on a standard production volume of 500,000 units, the cost per unit is $3.21, calculated by dividing the total cost by the production volume (cell B8 divided by cell B10). In the range E6:E12, the factory manager has input varying levels of production. The manager would like to see the change in the cost per unit for each level of production volume, assuming the costs remain the same. In Activity 4a, a data table is used to show the various costs. This data table will manipulate one input value—production volume—so it is a one-variable data table.

Figure 5.7 Activity 4a One-Variable Data Table

	A		B	C	D	E	F	G	H
1	Precision Design and Packaging								
2	Cost Price Analysis								
3	"E" Container Bulk Cargo Box								
4	Factory costs per shift					Variable unit production impact on cost			
5	Direct materials	$	580,000						
6	Direct labor		880,552			425,000			
7	Overhead		145,350			450,000			
8	Total cost	$	1,605,902			475,000			
9						500,000			
10	Standard production		500,000	units		525,000			
11						550,000			
12	Cost per unit	$	3.21			575,000			

In this area of the worksheet, calculate the change in cost per unit based on varying the production volume using a data table.

Activity 4a **Creating a One-Variable Data Table**

1. Open **PreEBoxCost.**
2. Save the workbook with the name **5-PreEBoxCost.**
3. Calculate the cost per unit for seven different production levels using a one-variable data table by completing the following steps:
   a. In a data table, the formula for calculating the various outcomes must be placed in the cell in the first row above and one column right of the table values. The data table values have been entered in the range E6:E12; therefore, make cell F5 active.
   b. The formula that calculates the cost per unit is *=B8/B10*. This formula has already been entered in cell B12. Link to the source formula by typing =b12 and then pressing the Enter key.
   c. Select the range E5:F12.
   d. Click the Data tab.
   e. Click the What-If Analysis button in the Forecast group and then click *Data Table* at the drop-down list.

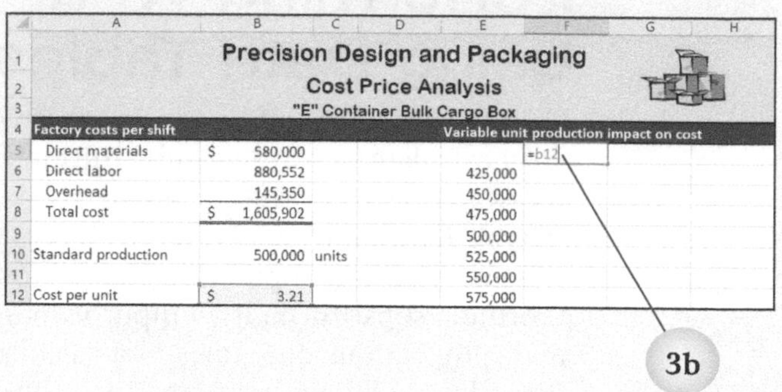

Precision Design and Packaging
Cost Price Analysis
"E" Container Bulk Cargo Box
Factory costs per shift
Variable unit production impact on cost
Direct materials $ 580,000
Direct labor 880,552
Overhead 145,350
Total cost $ 1,605,902
Standard production 500,000 units
Cost per unit $ 3.21
=b12
425,000
450,000
475,000
500,000
525,000
550,000
575,000
3b

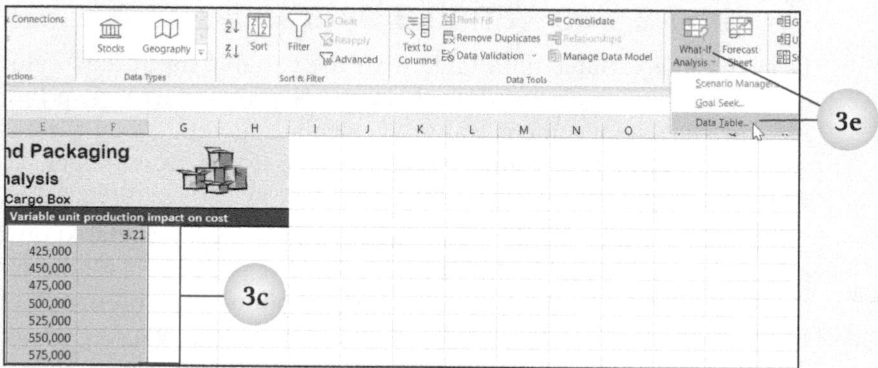

   f. At the Data Table dialog box, click in the *Column input cell* text box and then type b10. At the Data Table dialog box, Excel needs to know which reference in the source formula is the address where the variable data is to be inserted. (The production volume is cell B10 in the source formula.)
   g. Click OK.
   h. Click in any cell to deselect the range.
4. Print the worksheet.
5. Save and then close **5-PreEBoxCost.**

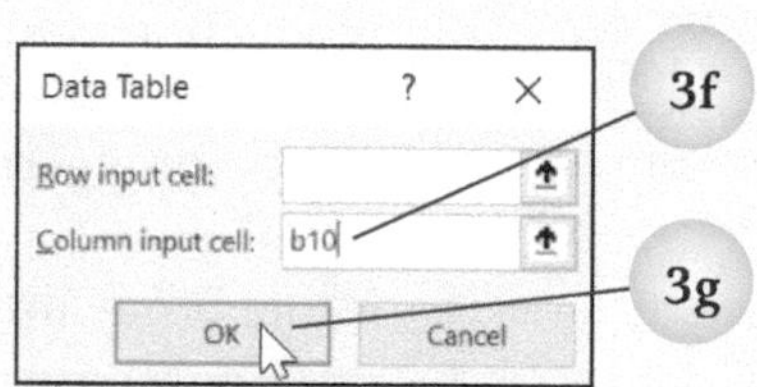

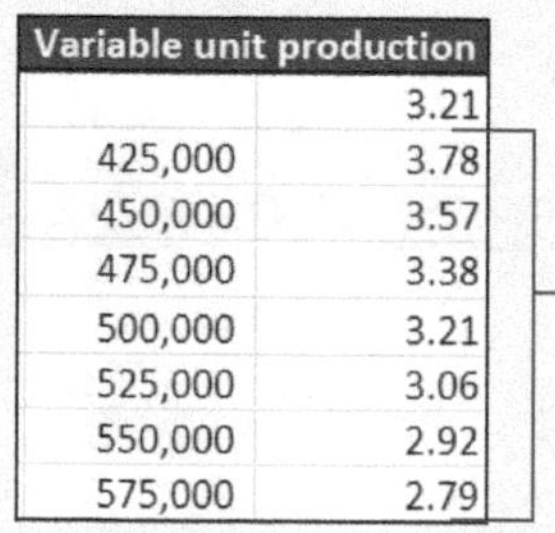

Variable unit production	
	3.21
425,000	3.78
450,000	3.57
475,000	3.38
500,000	3.21
525,000	3.06
550,000	2.92
575,000	2.79

The data table calculates costs at all the production volumes. Notice that the costs are higher at lower volumes and decrease as the production volume increases.

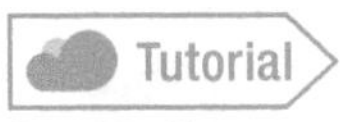

Creating Two-Variable Data Table

Quick Steps

Create Two-Variable Data Table

1. Create variable data at right of worksheet with one input series in column and another in row across top of table.
2. Enter formula in top left cell of table.
3. Select data table range.
4. Click Data tab.
5. Click What-If Analysis button.
6. Click *Data Table.*
7. Type cell address for variable data in source formula in *Row input cell* text box.
8. Press Tab key.
9. Type cell address for variable data in source formula in *Column input cell* text box.
10. Click OK.

Creating a Two-Variable Data Table

A data table can substitute two variables in a source formula. To modify two input cells, design the data table with a column along the left containing one set of variable input values and a row along the top containing a second set of variable input values. In a two-variable data table, the source formula is placed at the top left cell in the table. In the worksheet shown in Figure 5.8, the source formula will be inserted in cell E5, which is the top left cell in the data table.

Figure 5.8 Activity 4b Two-Variable Data Table

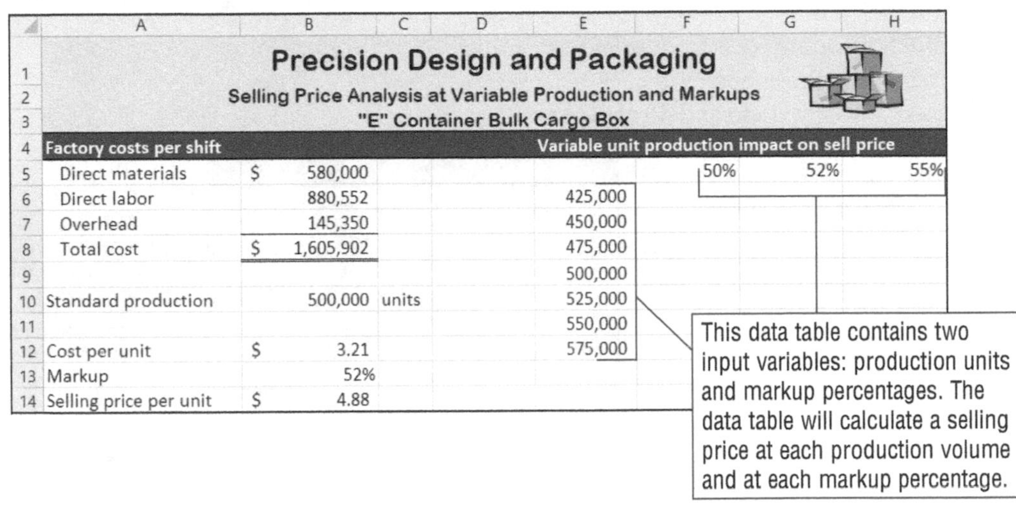

Precision Design and Packaging
Selling Price Analysis at Variable Production and Markups
"E" Container Bulk Cargo Box
Factory costs per shift
Variable unit production impact on sell price
Direct materials $ 580,000
Direct labor 880,552
Overhead 145,350
Total cost $ 1,605,902
Standard production 500,000 units
Cost per unit $ 3.21
Markup 52%
Selling price per unit $ 4.88
50% 52% 55%
425,000
450,000
475,000
500,000
525,000
550,000
575,000
This data table contains two input variables: production units and markup percentages. The data table will calculate a selling price at each production volume and at each markup percentage.

Activity 4b Creating a Two-Variable Data Table

Part 2 of 2

1. Open **PreEBoxSell.**
2. Save the workbook with the name **5-PreEBoxSell.**
3. Calculate the selling price per unit for seven different production levels and three different markups using a two-variable data table by completing the following steps:
   a. In a two-variable data table, the source formula must be placed in the top left cell in the data table; therefore, make cell E5 active.
   b. Type =b14 and then press the Enter key. The formula that Excel is to use to create the data table is in cell B14. The selling price per unit, found in cell B14, is calculated by adding the cost per unit (cell B12) to the result of multiplying the cost per unit (cell B12) by the markup (cell B13).
   c. Select the range E5:H12.
   d. Click the Data tab.
   e. Click the What-If Analysis button and then click *Data Table* at the drop-down list.

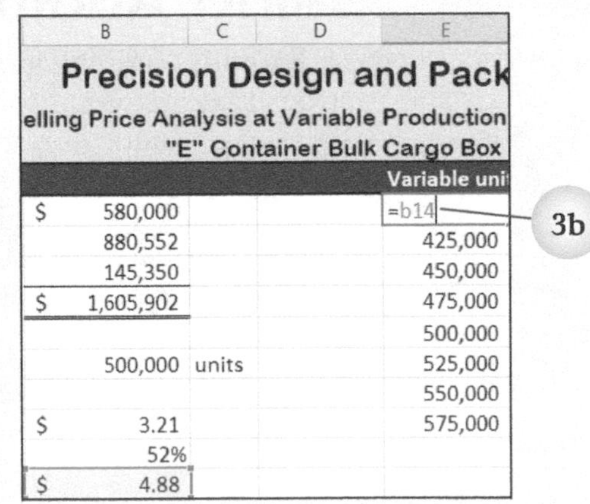

f. At the Data Table dialog box with the insertion point positioned in the *Row input cell* text box, type b13 and then press the Tab key. Excel needs to know which reference in the source formula is the address relating to the variable data in the first row of the data table. (The markup value is in cell B13 in the source formula.)

g. Type b10 in the *Column input cell* text box. As in Activity 4a, Excel needs to know which reference relates to the production volume in the source formula.

h. Click OK.

i. Click in any cell to deselect the range.

4. Print the worksheet.
5. Save and then close **5-PreEBoxSell.**

Data Table
Row input cell: b13 — 3f
Column input cell: b10 — 3g
OK — 3h
Cancel

Variable unit production impact on sell price			
$ 4.88	50%	52%	55%
425,000	5.67	5.74	5.86
450,000	5.35	5.42	5.53
475,000	5.07	5.14	5.24
500,000	4.82	4.88	4.98
525,000	4.59	4.65	4.74
550,000	4.38	4.44	4.53
575,000	4.19	4.25	4.33

The selling price is calculated by the data table at each production volume and each percentage markup.

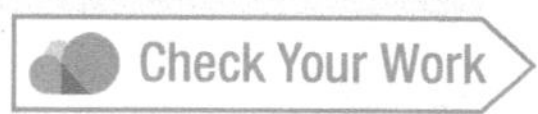

Activity 5 Audit a Worksheet to View and Troubleshoot Formulas — 3 Parts

You will use buttons in the Formula Auditing group to view relationships between cells that comprise a formula, identify error codes in a worksheet, and troubleshoot errors using error checking tools.

Using Auditing Tools

Using Auditing Tools

The Formula Auditing group on the Formulas tab, shown in Figure 5.9, contains options that are useful for viewing relationships between cells in formulas. Checking a formula for accuracy can be difficult when it is part of a complex sequence of operations. Opening a worksheet created by someone else can also present a challenge in understanding the relationships between sets of data. When Excel displays an error message in a cell, finding the source of the error can be made easier by viewing the relationships between the dependencies of cells.

Quick Steps

Trace Precedent Cells

1. Open worksheet.
2. Make cell active.
3. Click Formulas tab.
4. Click Trace Precedents button.
5. Continue clicking until all relationships are visible.

Trace Dependent Cells

1. Open worksheet.
2. Make cell active.
3. Click Formulas tab.
4. Click Trace Dependents button.
5. Continue clicking until all relationships are visible.

Figure 5.9 Formula Auditing Group on the Formulas Tab

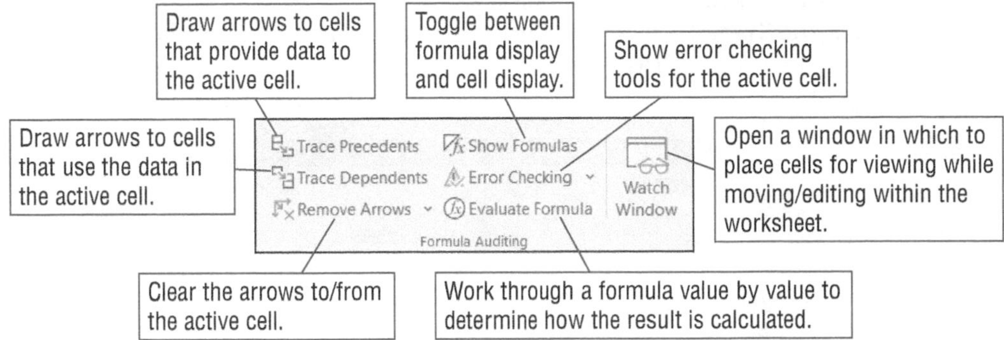
Draw arrows to cells that provide data to the active cell.
Toggle between formula display and cell display.
Show error checking tools for the active cell.
Draw arrows to cells that use the data in the active cell.
Trace Precedents
Show Formulas
Trace Dependents
Error Checking
Remove Arrows
Evaluate Formula
Watch Window
Formula Auditing
Open a window in which to place cells for viewing while moving/editing within the worksheet.
Clear the arrows to/from the active cell.
Work through a formula value by value to determine how the result is calculated.

Tracing Precedent and Dependent Cells

Precedent cells provide data to formula cells. For example, if cell B3 contains the formula =*B1*+*B2*, then cell B1 and cell B2 are precedent cells. Dependent cells contain formulas that refer to other cells. In the previous example, cell B3 is the dependent cell to cells B1 and B2, since cell B3 relies on the data from cells B1 and B2.

Trace Precedents

Click in a cell and then click the Trace Precedents button to draw tracer arrows that show direct relationships to a cell or cells that provide data to the active cell. Click the button a second time to show indirect relationships to a cell or cells that provide data to the active cell at the next level. Continue clicking the button until no further arrows are drawn. Excel will sound a beep if the button is clicked and no more relationships exist.

Trace Dependents

Remove Arrows

Show Formulas

Click in a cell and then click the Trace Dependents button to draw tracer arrows that show direct relationships to other cells in the worksheet that use the contents of the active cell. As with the Trace Precedents button, click a second time to show the next level of indirect relationships and continue clicking the button until no further tracer arrows are drawn.

Excel draws blue tracer arrows if no error is detected in the active cell and red tracer arrows if an error is detected within the active cell.

Activity 5a Viewing Relationships between Cells and Formulas

Part 1 of 3

1. Open **5-PreEBoxSell.**
2. Display tracer arrows between cells to view the relationships between cells and formulas by completing the following steps:
   a. Make cell B8 active.
   b. Click the Formulas tab.
   c. Click the Trace Precedents button in the Formula Auditing group. Excel draws a blue tracer arrow that shows the cells that provide data to cell B8.
   d. Click the Remove Arrows button in the Formula Auditing group. The blue tracer arrow leading to cell B8 is cleared.
   e. Make cell B14 active.

This blue precedent arrow is drawn to cell B8 in Step 2c.

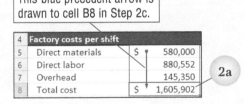

4	Factory costs per shift	
5	Direct materials	$ 580,000
6	Direct labor	880,552
7	Overhead	145,350
8	Total cost	$ 1,605,902

2a

f. Click the Trace Precedents button.
g. Click the Trace Precedents button a second time to show the next level of cells that provide data to cell B14.
h. Click the Trace Dependents button to view the cell dependent on cell B14.

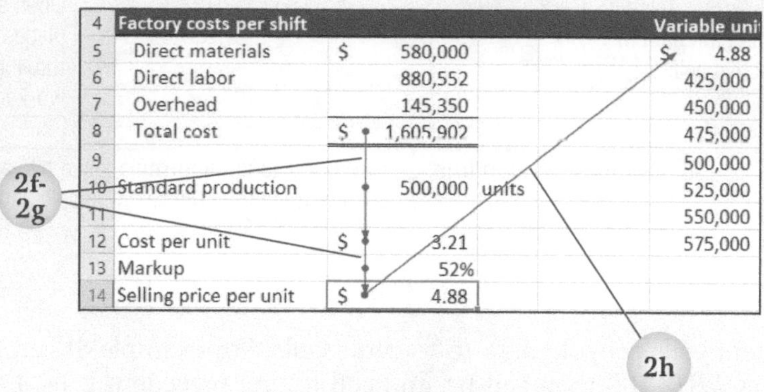

4	Factory costs per shift				Variable unit
5	Direct materials	$	580,000		$ 4.88
6	Direct labor		880,552		425,000
7	Overhead		145,350		450,000
8	Total cost	$	1,605,902		475,000
9					500,000
10	Standard production		500,000	units	525,000
11					550,000
12	Cost per unit	$	3.21		575,000
13	Markup		52%		
14	Selling price per unit	$	4.88		

3. Click the Remove Arrows button in the Formula Auditing group to clear all the arrows.
4. Click the Show Formulas button in the Formula Auditing group to display the cell formulas. Click the Show Formulas button again to turn off the display of formulas.
5. Close **5-PreEBoxSell.** Click the Don't Save button when prompted to save changes.

Troubleshooting Formulas

Quick Steps
Trace Errors
1. Click in cell containing error message.
2. Click Formulas tab.
3. Click arrow on Error Checking button.
4. Click *Trace Error.*

Hint Reference errors can also occur—for instance, when the formula uses correct syntax and logic but refers to the wrong data. These errors are difficult to find and only a thorough review and test of key figures will reveal them.

Formulas in Excel can contain various types of errors. Some errors are obvious because Excel displays an error message, such as *#VALUE!* Other errors occur without the display of an error message but are incorrect because the logic is flawed. For example, a formula could be entered in a cell that Excel does not flag as an error because the syntax is correct; however, the calculation could be incorrect for the data and the situation. Logic errors are difficult to find and require checking a worksheet by entering proof formulas or by manually checking the accuracy of each formula.

A proof formula is a formula entered outside the main worksheet area that checks key figures within the worksheet. For example, in a payroll worksheet, a proof formula to check the total net pay column could add the total net pay to the totals of all the deduction columns. The total displayed should be equal to the total gross pay amount in the worksheet.

Excel displays an error message code in a cell that is detected to have an error. Two types of error flags can occur. A green diagonal triangle in the upper left corner of a cell indicates an error condition. Activate the cell and an error checking button displays that can be used to access error checking tools. Errors can also be indicated with text entries, such as *#NAME?* Figure 5.10 displays a portion of the worksheet used in Activity 5b to troubleshoot errors. Table 5.1 describes the three types of error codes displayed in Figure 5.10.

Error Checking

Evaluate Formula

The Error Checking button in the Formula Auditing group can be used to help find the source of an error condition in a cell by displaying the Error Checking dialog box or drawing a red tracer arrow to locate the source cell that is contributing to the error. The Evaluate Formula button can be used to work through a formula value by value to determine where within the formula an error exists.

Figure 5.10 Activity 5b Partial Worksheet

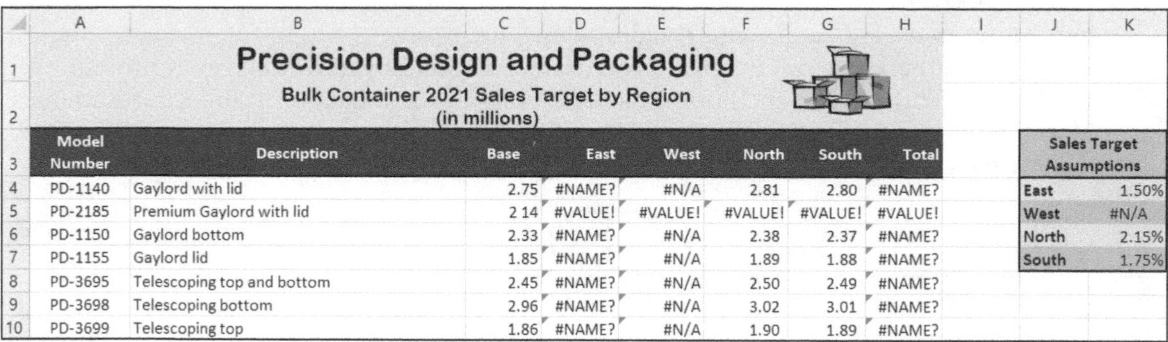

	A	B	C	D	E	F	G	H	I	J	K
1	Precision Design and Packaging										
2	Bulk Container 2021 Sales Target by Region (in millions)										
3	Model Number	Description	Base	East	West	North	South	Total		Sales Target Assumptions	
4	PD-1140	Gaylord with lid	2.75	#NAME?	#N/A	2.81	2.80	#NAME?		East	1.50%
5	PD-2185	Premium Gaylord with lid	2.14	#VALUE!	#VALUE!	#VALUE!	#VALUE!	#VALUE!		West	#N/A
6	PD-1150	Gaylord bottom	2.33	#NAME?	#N/A	2.38	2.37	#NAME?		North	2.15%
7	PD-1155	Gaylord lid	1.85	#NAME?	#N/A	1.89	1.88	#NAME?		South	1.75%
8	PD-3695	Telescoping top and bottom	2.45	#NAME?	#N/A	2.50	2.49	#NAME?			
9	PD-3698	Telescoping bottom	2.96	#NAME?	#N/A	3.02	3.01	#NAME?			
10	PD-3699	Telescoping top	1.86	#NAME?	#N/A	1.90	1.89	#NAME?			

Table 5.1 Types of Error Codes in Figure 5.10

Error Code	Description of Error Condition
#N/A	A required value for the formula is not available.
#NAME?	The formula contains an unrecognized entry.
#VALUE!	A value within the formula is of the wrong type or otherwise invalid.

Activity 5b Troubleshooting Formulas

Part 2 of 3

1. Open **PreSalesTrgt.**
2. Save the workbook with the name **5-PreSalesTrgt.**
3. Solve the #N/A error by completing the following steps:
   a. Make cell E4 active.
   b. Point to the Trace Error button next to the cell and read the ScreenTip below the button.
   c. Look in the Formula bar at the formula that has been entered into the cell. Notice that the formula includes a reference to a named cell. Tracer arrows will be used in the next step to locate the source of the named cell.

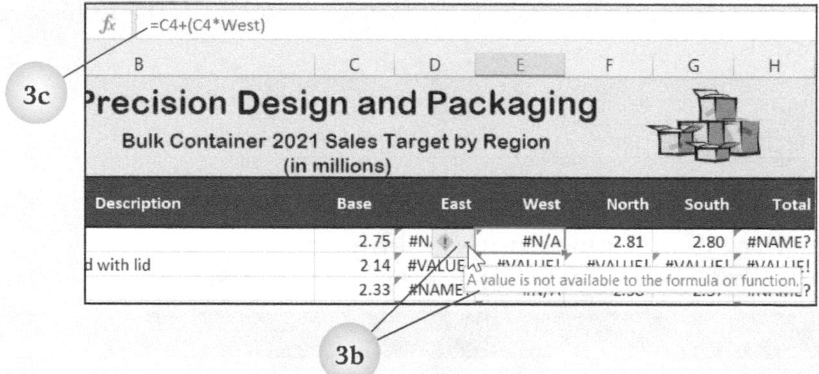

d. Click the Error Checking button arrow in the Formula Auditing group on the Formulas tab and then click *Trace Error* at the drop-down list.
e. Excel moves the active cell to cell K5 and draws a red tracer arrow from cell K5 to cell E4. Look in the Formula bar and notice that *#N/A* displays as the entry in cell K5. Also notice that the cell name *West* displays in the Name box. Since there is no value in the cell named *West*, which is cell K5, the dependent cell E4 is not able to calculate its formula.

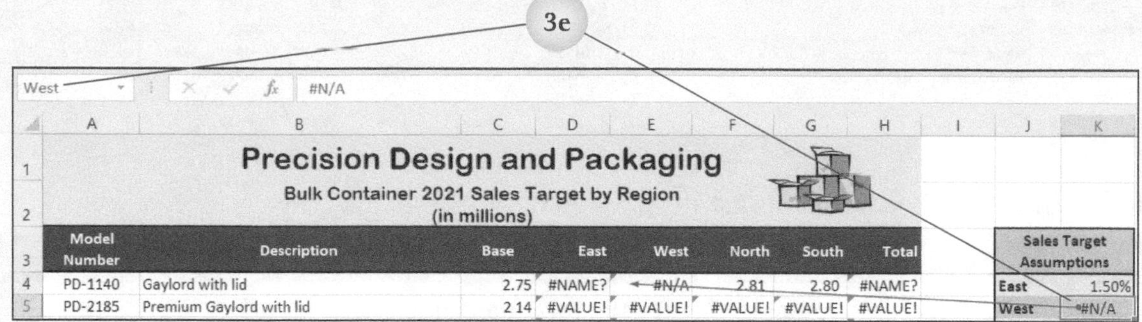

f. With cell K5 active, type 1.25% and then press the Enter key. The red tracer arrow changes to blue because the error is corrected and the #N/A error messages no longer display.
g. Click the Remove Arrows button to clear the blue tracer arrow and then right-align the entry in cell K5.

4. Solve the #NAME? error by completing the following steps:
   a. Make cell D4 active, point to the Trace Error button that appears, and then read the ScreenTip that appears. The message indicates that the formula contains unrecognized text.
   b. Look at the entry in the Formula bar: *=C4+(C4*East)*. Notice that the formula is the same as the one reviewed in Step 3c except that the named range is *East* instead of *West*. The formula appears to be valid.
   c. Click the Name box arrow and view the range names in the drop-down list. Notice that the range name *East* is not in the list.
   d. Click *North* at the Name box drop-down list. Cell K6 becomes the active cell. You know from this step and Step 3d that the named ranges should reference the percentage values within column K.
   e. Make cell K4 active, type East in the Name box, and then press the Enter key. The #NAME? error is resolved.

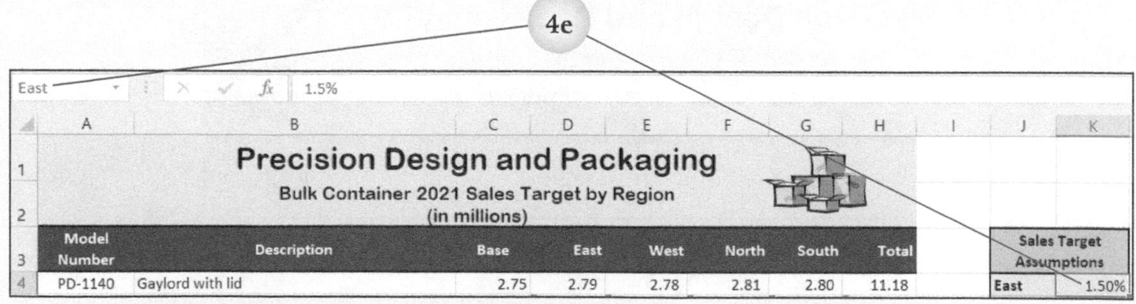

5. Solve the #VALUE! error by completing the following steps:
   a. Make cell D5 active, point to the Trace Error button that appears, and then read the ScreenTip that appears. The message indicates that a value within the formula is of the wrong data type.

b. Click the Trace Precedents button to display tracer arrows that show the source cells that provide data to cell D5. Two blue arrows appear, indicating that two cells provide the source values: cells K4 and C5.
c. Make cell K4 active and look at the entry in the Formula bar: *1.5%*. This value is valid.
d. Make cell C5 active and look at the entry in the Formula bar: *2 14*. Notice that there is a space instead of a decimal point between *2* and *1*.

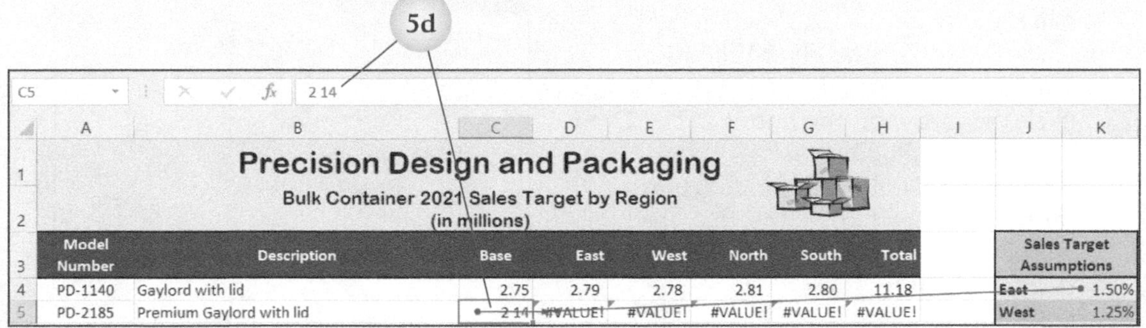

e. Click in the Formula bar and then edit the formula to delete the space between *2* and *1* and type a period (inserting a decimal point). Press the Enter key. The #VALUE! error is resolved.
f. Click the Remove Arrows button to clear the blue tracer arrows.
6. Save **5-PreSalesTrgt.**

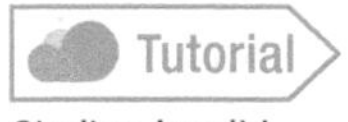

Circling Invalid Data and Watching a Formula Cell

Data Validation

Quick Steps
Circle Invalid Data
1. Open worksheet containing validation rules.
2. Click Data tab.
3. Click Data Validation button arrow.
4. Click *Circle Invalid Data.*

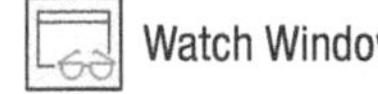
Watch Window

Quick Steps
Watch Formula Cell
1. Click Formulas tab.
2. Click Watch Window button.
3. Click Add Watch button.
4. Click in cell.
5. Click Add button.

Circling Invalid Data

Recall from Chapter 3 that the data validation feature is used to restrict cell entries. If data validation rules are set up after data has been entered, existing values will not be tested against the new rules. In this situation, use the Circle Invalid Data feature, which draws red circles around the cells that do not conform to the new rule. To circle invalid data, click the Data Validation button arrow in the Data Tools group on the Data tab, and then click the *Circle Invalid Data* option.

Watching a Formula Cell

In a large worksheet, a dependent cell may not always be visible while changes are being made to other cells that affect a formula. Open a Watch Window and add a dependent cell to it to view changes made to the cell as the worksheet is modified. Multiple cells can be added to the Watch Window to create a single window where cells affected by key formulas within a large worksheet can be tracked. To watch a cell, click the Watch Window button in the Formula Auditing group on the Formulas tab, click the Add Watch button, click to select the cell you want to watch, and then click the Add button.

Consider assigning a name to a cell to be tracked using the Watch Window. At the Watch Window, the cell name will appear in the *Name* column and provide a descriptive reference to the entry being watched. Expand the width of the *Name* column if a range name is not entirely visible.

The Watch Window can be docked at the top, left, bottom, or right edge of the worksheet area by clicking the top edge of the window and dragging it to the edge of the screen. When the Watch Window is docked, Excel changes it to a Watch Window task pane.

Activity 5c Circling Invalid Data and Watching a Formula Cell

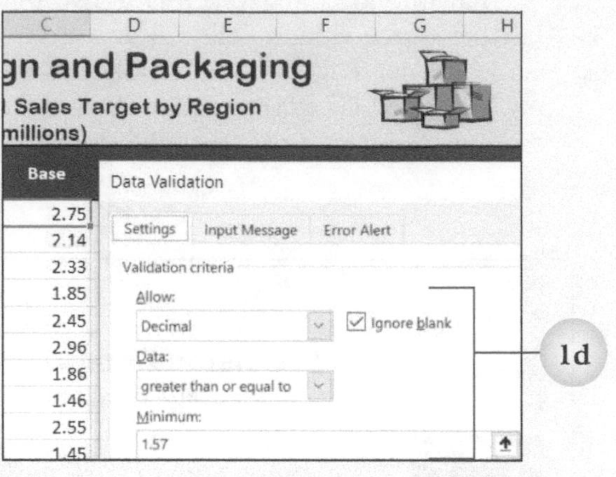

1. With **5-PreSalesTrgt** open, view the data validation rule in effect for column C by completing the following steps:
   a. If necessary, make active any cell containing a value in column C.
   b. Click the Data tab.
   c. Click the top of the Data Validation button in the Data Tools group. (Do not click the arrow on the button.) The Data Validation dialog box opens.
   d. Review the parameters for data entry on the Settings tab. Notice that the restriction is that values should be greater than or equal to 1.57.
   e. Click OK.

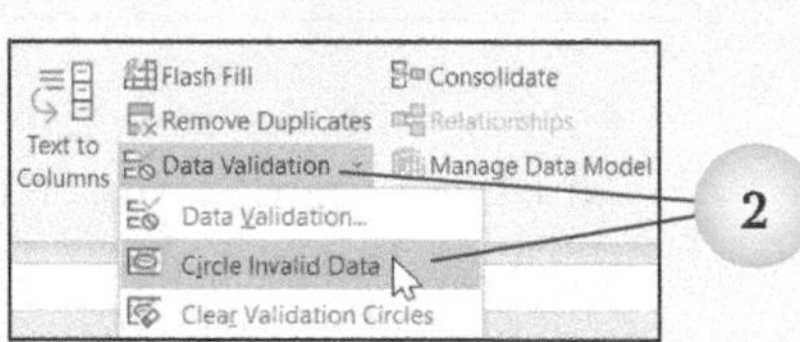

2. Click the Data Validation button arrow and then click *Circle Invalid Data* at the drop-down list. Three cells are circled in the worksheet: C11, C13, and C16.
3. Watch the total in cell H22 update as the invalid data is corrected by completing the following steps:
   a. Make cell H22 active and then click the Formulas tab.
   b. Click the Watch Window button in the Formula Auditing group. A Watch Window opens.
   c. Click the Add Watch button in the Watch Window.
   d. At the Add Watch dialog box, move the dialog box out of the way, if necessary, to view cell H22. Notice that cell H22 is entered by default as the watch cell. Click the Add button.

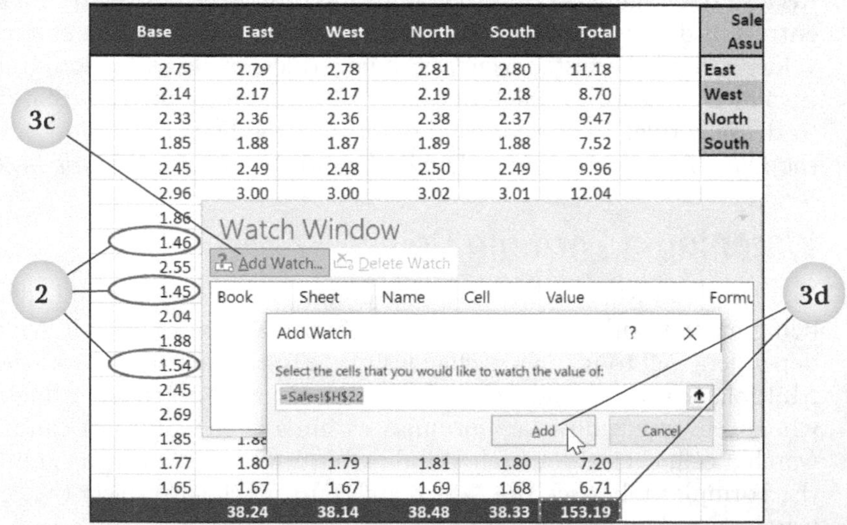

   e. Scroll up the worksheet, if necessary, until you can view cell C11. If necessary, drag the Watch Window out of the way so the cells being watched and the cells used in the formula are visible.
   f. Make cell C11 active, type 1.58, and then press the Enter key. Notice that the red circle disappears because a value has been entered that conforms to the validation rule. Look at the value for cell H22 in the Watch Window. The new value is *153.67*.

g. Make cell C13 the active cell, type 1.61, and then press the Enter key. Look at the updated value for cell H22 in the Watch Window.

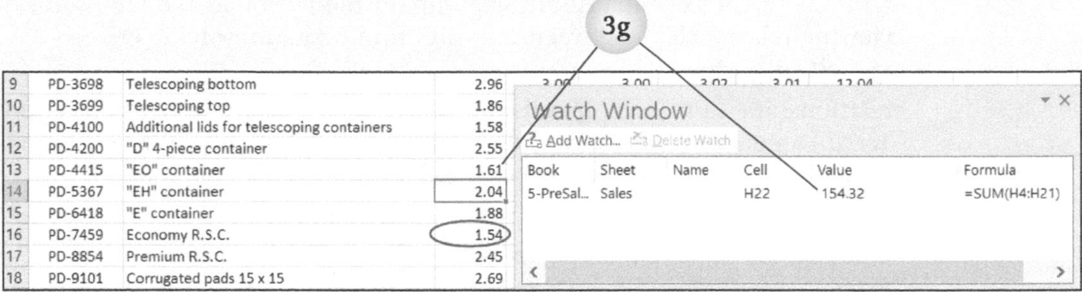

h. Make cell C16 active, type 1.57, and then press the Enter key.

i. Click the Watch Window button to close the Watch Window.

4. Print the worksheet.
5. Save and then close **5-PreSalesTrgt.**

Chapter Summary

- Click the Paste button arrow to open the Paste drop-down gallery, which contains many options for pasting copied data. Open the Paste Special dialog box to paste attributes of the source cell(s) or perform a mathematical operation during the paste.
- Transposing data during a paste routine means that data arranged in columns is converted to rows and data arranged in rows is converted to columns. Transpose data using the Transpose button in the Paste button drop-down gallery or the Paste Special dialog box.
- The Goal Seek feature returns a value in a cell based on a target value specified for another cell. The two cells must have a dependent relationship for Excel to calculate a value.
- Click the What-If Analysis button in the Forecast group on the Data tab to use the Goal Seek, Scenario Manager, or Data Table feature.
- The Scenario Manager allows storing multiple sets of assumptions about data and then viewing how each set affects the worksheet. Switch between scenarios to test the various inputs on the worksheet model.
- Create a scenario summary report to compare scenarios side by side in a worksheet or PivotTable. Enter the formula cell or cells that change when the data is applied in various scenarios at the Scenario Summary dialog box.
- A data table is a range of cells that contains a series of input values; a calculated formula result is placed adjacent to each input value. A one-variable data table calculates a formula by modifying one input value in the formula. A two-variable data table calculates a formula substituting two input values.
- Design a one-variable data table with the variable input data values in a series down a column or across a row. Enter the formula one row above and one column right of the variable data.

- Design a two-variable data table with a column along the left containing one set of variable input values and a row along the top containing a second set of variable input values. Enter the formula in the top left cell of the table.
- Options in the Formula Auditing group on the Formulas tab are useful for viewing relationships between cells and finding and resolving errors.
- Use the Trace Precedents button to draw tracer arrows that show direct relationships to the cell or cells that provide data to the active cell. Use the Trace Dependents button to draw tracer arrows that show direct relationships to another cell or other cells that use data from the active cell.
- Click the Trace Precedents or Trace Dependents button a second time to display an indirect set of relationship arrows at the next level.
- A logic error occurs when the formula is not correct for the data or situation. A reference error occurs when a formula refers to the wrong data.
- Use a proof formula to test the accuracy of key figures in a worksheet. A proof formula is entered outside the main worksheet area and double-checks key figures within the worksheet.
- Excel displays two types of error messages in a cell in which an error has been detected. A green diagonal triangle in the upper left corner of the cell indicates an error condition. Errors can also be indicated with text entries. For example, *#NAME?* means that the formula contains text that Excel cannot recognize.
- Other error codes include *#VALUE!*, which means a value within the formula is not valid, and *#N/A*, which means a value needed by the formula is not available.
- Use the Error Checking button in the Formula Auditing group to help find the source of an error in a cell. Display the Error Checking dialog box or draw a red tracer arrow to locate the source cell that is contributing to the error.
- If data validation rules are set up after data has been entered, existing values will not be tested against the new rules. Use the Circle Invalid Data feature from the Data Validation button to draw red circles around the cells that do not conform to the new rule.
- Open a Watch Window and add a dependent cell to it to view changes made to the cell as the worksheet is modified. Multiple cells can be added to create a single window where cells can be tracked.
- After completing a worksheet, take time to examine the data carefully for data entry errors, values that do not appear realistic, and other indications of potential errors that should be fixed.

Commands Review

FEATURE	RIBBON TAB, GROUP	BUTTON	KEYBOARD SHORTCUT
circle invalid data	Data, Data Tools		
data table	Data, Forecast		
display formulas	Formulas, Formula Auditing		Ctrl + `
Goal Seek dialog box	Data, Forecast		
Paste Special dialog box	Home, Clipboard		Ctrl + Alt + V
remove tracer arrow	Formulas, Formula Auditing		
Scenario Manager	Data, Forecast		
trace dependent cell	Formulas, Formula Auditing		Ctrl +]
trace error	Formulas, Formula Auditing		
trace precedent cell	Formulas, Formula Auditing		Ctrl + [
transpose data	Home, Clipboard		
Watch Window	Formulas, Formula Auditing		

Microsoft®

Excel®

CHAPTER 6

Exporting, Importing, and Transforming Data

Performance Objectives

Upon successful completion of Chapter 6, you will be able to:

1 Copy, embed, link, and unlink Excel data in a Word document
2 Copy, paste, and embed Excel data in a PowerPoint presentation
3 Copy and paste Excel data in an Access table
4 Export an Excel worksheet as a text file
5 Import data from an Access database
6 Modify imported data with the Query Editor
7 Import data from a text file
8 Refresh, modify, and delete queries
9 Use Flash Fill to transform data
10 Modify text using the text functions PROPER, UPPER, LOWER, SUBSTITUTE, RIGHT, LEFT, MID, TEXTJOIN, and CONCAT

Exchanging data between programs by exporting or importing eliminates duplication of effort and reduces the likelihood of data errors or missed entries, which could occur if the data was retyped. One of the advantages of working with a suite of programs such as Microsoft Word, Excel, Access, and PowerPoint is being able to easily integrate data from one program to another. In this chapter, you will learn how to export data in a worksheet to other programs and how to bring data into an Excel worksheet from external sources.

Before beginning chapter work, copy the EL2C6 folder to your storage medium and then make EL2C6 the active folder.

The online course includes additional training and assessment resources.

Activity 1 Export Data from Excel to Various Applications **6 Parts**

You will copy and paste data related to car inventory from an Excel worksheet to integrate with an Word report, a PowerPoint presentation, and an Access database. You will also save a worksheet as a comma-separated text file for use in a non-Microsoft program.

Exporting Data from Excel

Applications in Office 365 are designed for integration so that an object can easily be created in one application and copied to another application. For example, use Excel data in other Microsoft programs by copying cells to the Clipboard and then pasting them in the destination files. Integration is possible because the applications have a common interface that allows each application to understand another application's file format.

To use Excel data in Word, PowerPoint, or Access, use the copy and paste, copy and embed, or copy and link method. During an export or import, the file containing the original data is called the *source file*, and the file to which the original data is being copied, embedded, or linked is called the *destination file*.

To export Excel data for use in another program, open the Save As dialog box and then change the *Save as type* option to the desired file format. If the file format for the destination program does not appear in the *Save as type* list, try copying and pasting the data or go to the Microsoft Office Online website and search for a file format converter that can be downloaded and installed.

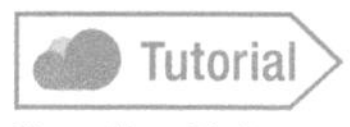

Exporting Data into Word

Quick Steps

Embed or Link Excel Data in Word Document

1. Select cells.
2. Click Copy button.
3. Open Word.
4. Position insertion point in document.
5. Click Paste button arrow.
6. Click Paste Special.
7. Click *Microsoft Excel Worksheet Object*.
8. Click OK to embed, or click *Paste link* and then OK to link.

Copying and Pasting Data into Word

Data from Excel can be copied and pasted directly into Word, or it can be copied and then pasted as an embedded or linked object. Use the simple copy and paste method if the data being brought into the Word document is not likely to be updated or edited later. Copy and embed the data to be able to edit it in Word using Excel. Copy and link the data to allow it to be updated whenever edits are made to the source file.

Embedding Excel Data in a Word Document To embed copied Excel data in a Word document, open the document, move the insertion point to where the copied Excel data should be inserted, and then open the Paste Special dialog box. At the Paste Special dialog box, click the option to paste as a *Microsoft Excel Worksheet Object* and then click OK.

To edit an embedded Excel object in Word, double-click the embedded object to open it for editing. The worksheet object opens in Excel. Click the Excel Close button to close Excel and make Word the active application. Any changes made to the Excel object in the Word document are not reflected in the Excel file containing the original data and vice versa.

Linking Excel Data to a Word Document When Excel data is linked to a Word document, the source data exists only in Excel. Word places a shortcut to the source data file name and range in the document. When a Word document is opened that contains one or more links, Word prompts the user to update the links. Since the data resides only in the Excel workbook, the original workbook that contains the original data should not be moved or renamed. If either happens, the link in the Word document will no longer work.

To paste copied Excel data as a link in a Word document, open the document, move the insertion point to where the cells should be linked, open the Paste Special dialog box, click *Microsoft Excel Worksheet Object*, click *Paste link*, and then click OK.

Activity 1a Embedding Excel Data in a Word Document

Part 1 of 6

1. Open **CRInventory.**
2. Copy and embed the data in the CarCosts worksheet in a Word document by completing the following steps:
   a. Make CarCosts the active worksheet, if necessary.
   b. Select the range A4:F9.
   c. Click the Copy button in the Clipboard group on the Home tab.
   d. Start Microsoft Word 365.
   e. Open **CRCarRptW** from the EL2C6 folder on your storage medium. If a security warning displays stating that the document is in Protected View, click the Enable Editing button.
   f. Save the document with the name **6-CRCarRptW**.
   g. Press Ctrl + End to move the insertion point to the end of the document.
   h. Click the Paste button arrow and then click *Paste Special* at the drop-down list.
   i. At the Paste Special dialog box, click *Microsoft Excel Worksheet Object* in the *As* list box and then click OK.

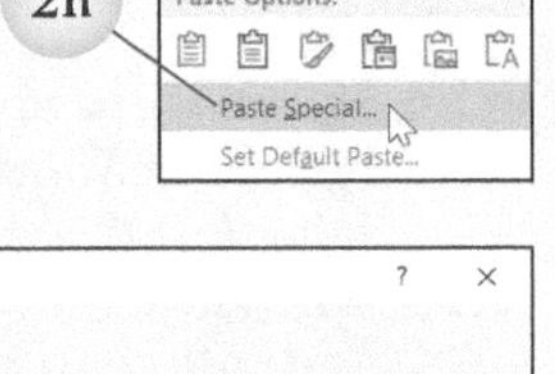

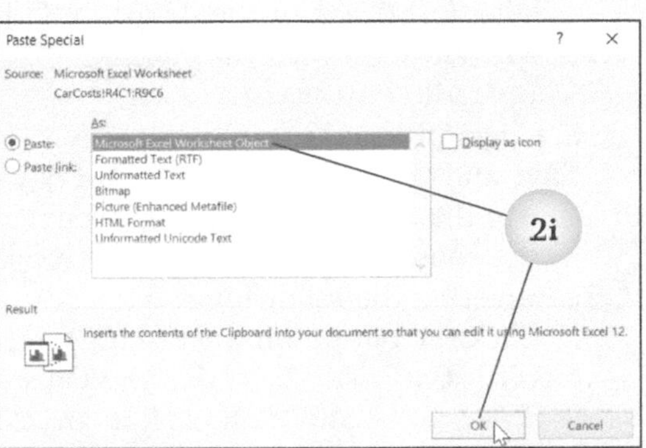

3. Save **6-CRCarRptW.**
4. When Paste Special is used, the copied cells are embedded as an object in the Word document. Edit the embedded object using Excel by completing the following steps:
   a. Double-click in a cell in the embedded worksheet object. The object opens in Excel. ***Note: Depending on your version of Office, an Excel ribbon may open within Word and your steps will vary slightly as you will need to click within the Word document to close the Excel ribbon.***
   b. Select the range B4:F4 and then click the Center button.
   c. Click the Excel Close button. If necessary, make Word the active application.

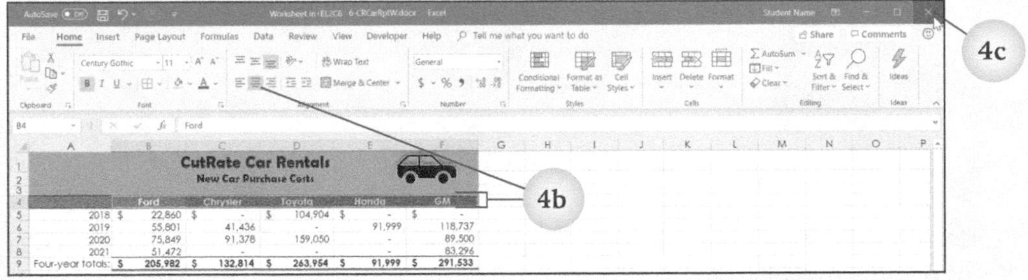

5. Save and then print **6-CRCarRptW**.
6. Close Word.
7. Click in any cell to deselect the range in the CarCosts worksheet and leave the **CRInventory** workbook open for the next activity.

Activity 1b Linking Excel Data to a Word Document

Part 2 of 6

1. With **CRInventory** open, copy and link the data in the CarCosts worksheet to a Word document by completing the following steps:
   a. With CarCosts the active worksheet, select the range A4:F9 and then click the Copy button.
   b. Start Microsoft Word 365.
   c. Open **CRCarRptW**.
   d. Save the document with the name **6-CRCarRptW-Linked**.
   e. Press Ctrl + End to move the insertion point to the end of the document.
   f. Click the Paste button arrow and then click *Paste Special* at the drop-down list.
   g. At the Paste Special dialog box, click *Microsoft Excel Worksheet Object* in the *As* list box and then click the *Paste link* radio button.
   h. Click OK.

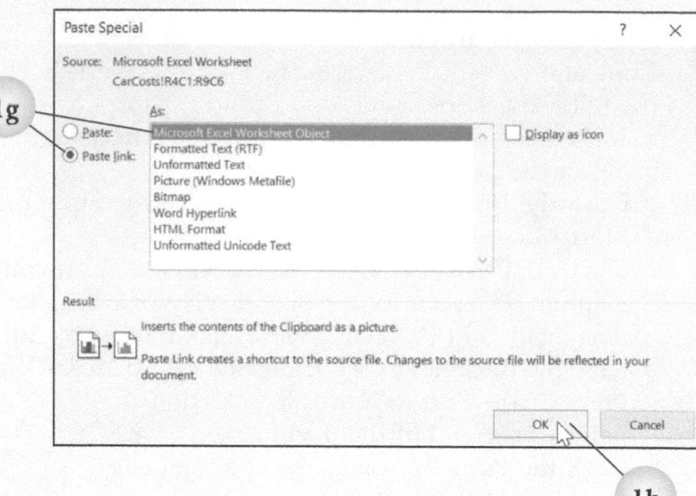

2. Save and then close **6-CRCarRptW-Linked**. When data is linked, it exists only in the source file. In the destination document, Word inserts a shortcut to the specified range in the source file. Edit the source range and view the update to the Word document by completing the following steps:
   a. Click the button on the taskbar representing the Excel workbook **CRInventory**.
   b. With CarCosts the active worksheet, press the Esc key to remove the scrolling marquee, if necessary, and then click in any cell to deselect the copied range.
   c. Make cell E5 active, type 85000, and then press the Enter key.
   d. Click the button on the taskbar representing Word.
   e. Open **6-CRCarRptW-Linked.**
   f. At the Microsoft Word message box asking whether to update the document with data from the linked files, click Yes.

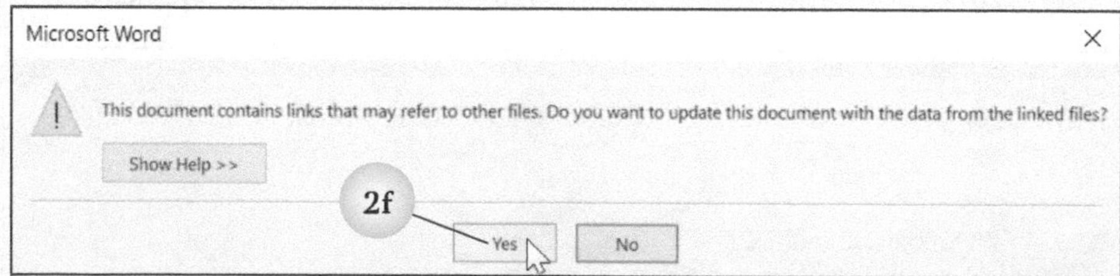

3. Notice that the data inserted in the Excel worksheet is also shown in the linked Word document.
4. Save and then print **6-CRCarRptW-Linked.**
5. Exit Word.
6. With CarCosts the active worksheet in **CRInventory**, delete the content of cell E5 and leave the workbook open for a later activity.

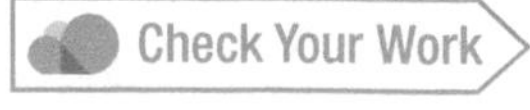

Breaking a Link to an Excel Object

Quick Steps

Break Link to Excel Object

1. Open Word document.
2. Right-click linked object.
3. Point to *Linked Worksheet Object.*
4. Click *Links.*
5. Click Break Link button.
6. Click Yes.
7. Save document.

If the Excel data in a Word document no longer needs to be linked, the connection between the source and destination files can be broken. Breaking the link means that the data in the Word document will no longer be connected to the data in the Excel workbook. If a change is made to the original data in Excel, the Word document will not reflect the update. Once the link to the document is broken, the prompt to update the object each time the Word document is opened will no longer appear.

To break a link, open the Word document, right-click the linked object, point to *Linked Worksheet Object,* and then click *Links* at the shortcut menu. This opens the Links dialog box. If more than one linked object exists in the document, click the source object for the link to be broken and then click the Break Link button. At the message box that appears, click Yes to confirm that the link is to be broken.

Activity 1c **Breaking a Link** Part 3 of 6

1. Start Word and open **6-CRCarRpt-Linked.**
2. At the message asking whether to update the links, click No.
3. Break the link between the Excel workbook and the linked object by completing the following steps:
   a. Right-click the linked Excel worksheet object.
   b. Point to *Linked Worksheet Object* and then click *Links* at the shortcut menu.
   c. At the Links dialog box with the linked object file name selected in the *Source file* list box, click the Break Link button.

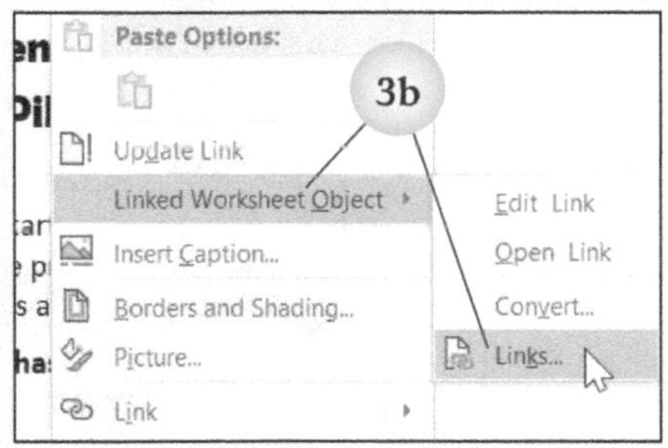

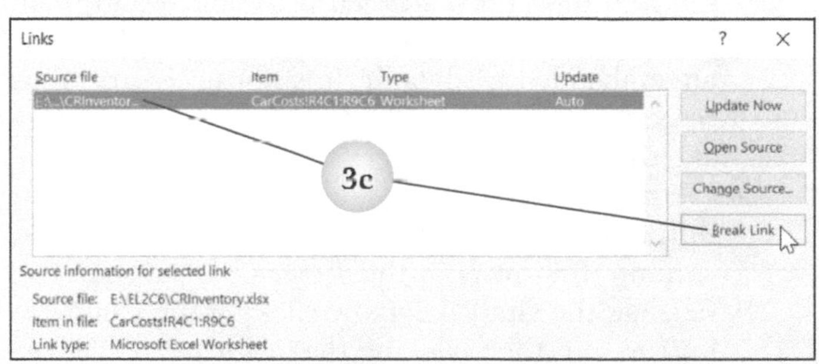

   d. At the Microsoft Word dialog box asking for confirmation to break the selected link, click Yes.
4. Save **6-CRCarRptW-Linked** and then exit Word.

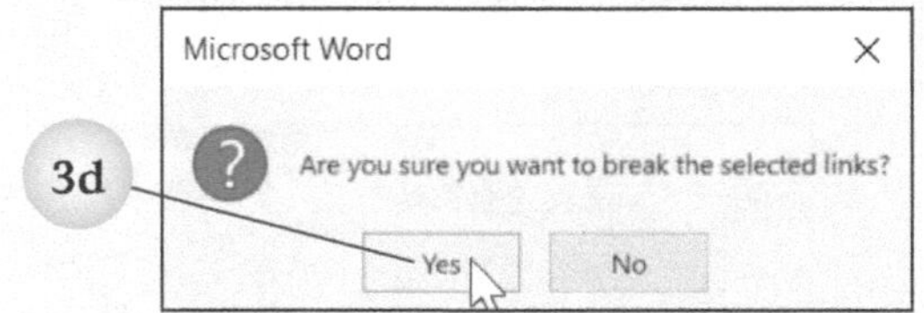

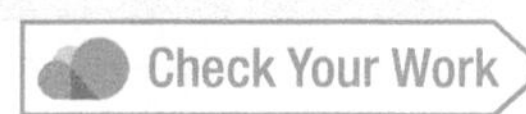

Copying and Pasting Data into PowerPoint

Copying and Pasting Data into PowerPoint

As they can with Word, users can copy and paste, copy and embed, or copy and link Excel data to slides in a PowerPoint presentation. Charts are often incorporated to presentations to visually depict numerical data in a graph format that is easy to understand. Although tables and charts can be created in PowerPoint slides, users may prefer to use Excel to create these items and then copy and paste them into PowerPoint. Depending on the version of Office 365 you are using, copy and paste is the best method to use if the chart will need to be formatted.

Quick Steps

Embed Excel Data in PowerPoint Presentation

1. Select cells.
2. Click Copy button.
3. Open PowerPoint presentation.
4. Make slide active.
5. Click Paste button arrow.
6. Click *Paste Special.*
7. Make sure *Microsoft Excel Worksheet Object* is selected in *As* list box.
8. Click OK.

Since the chart feature is fully integrated within Word, Excel, and PowerPoint, a chart that has been pasted in a PowerPoint presentation can be edited using the same techniques for editing a chart in Excel. Clicking a chart in a PowerPoint slide causes the contextual Chart Tools Design and Chart Tools Format tabs to become active with the same groups and buttons available as in Excel. Three buttons—Chart Elements, Chart Styles, and Chart Filter—are also available for editing.

Activity 1d Pasting and Embedding Excel Data into a PowerPoint Presentation

Part 4 of 6

1. With **CRInventory** open, copy and embed the chart from the CarCostsChart worksheet in a PowerPoint slide by completing the following steps:
   a. Make CarCostsChart the active worksheet.
   b. Click the Home tab and then click the Copy button.
   c. Start Microsoft PowerPoint 365.
   d. Open **CRCarPres.**
   e. Save the presentation with the name **6-CRCarPres**.
   f. Click Slide 3 in the slide thumbnails pane.
   g. Click in the *Click to add text* placeholder and then click the Paste button in the Clipboard group. Since all charts are embedded by default, it is not necessary to use Paste Special.

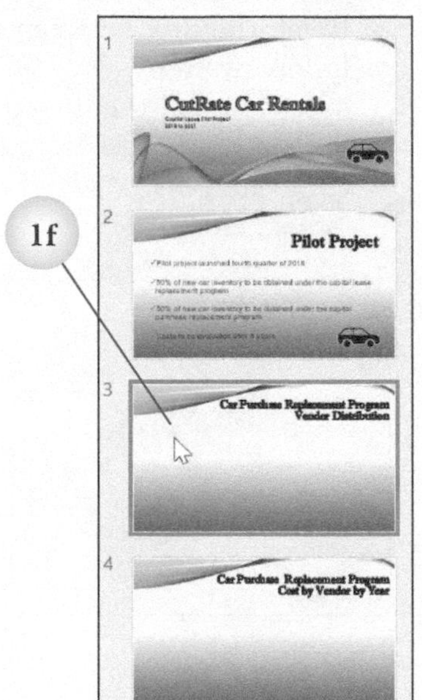

2. Make the following changes to the chart:
   a. With the object placeholder selected, click the font color option box arrow and then click *Black, Background 1* (first column, first row) in the *Theme Colors* section.
   b. Change the chart colors by clicking the Chart Styles button and then clicking the Color tab. Click the *Colorful Palette 2* option (second option in the *Colorful* section of the color palette).

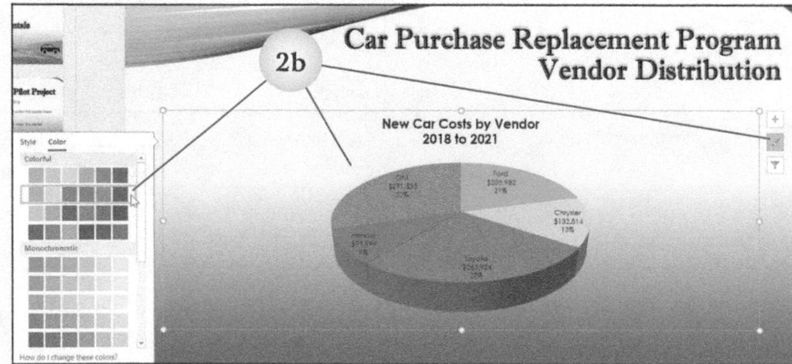

   c. Click outside the chart.

3. Copy the table used to generate the chart in the CarCosts worksheet and embed it in the next slide by completing the following steps:
   a. Click Slide 4 in the slide thumbnails pane.
   b. Click the button on the taskbar representing the Excel workbook **CRInventory**.
   c. Make CarCosts the active worksheet, select the range A1:F9, and then click the Copy button.
   d. Click the button on the taskbar representing the PowerPoint presentation **6-CRCarPres**.
   e. Click the Paste button arrow and then click *Paste Special* at the drop-down list.
   f. With *Microsoft Excel Worksheet Object* selected in the *As* list box, click OK.

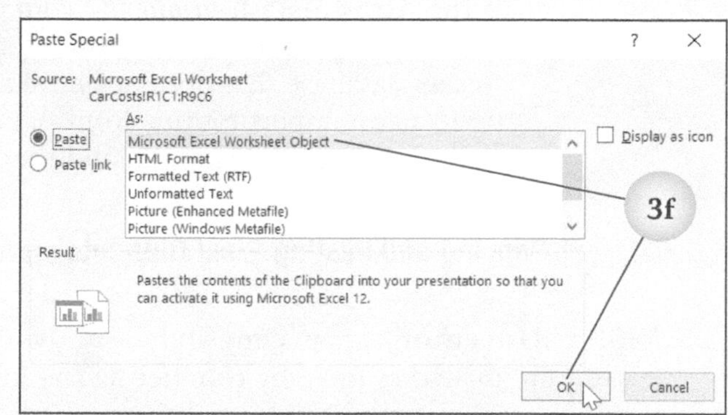

4. Resize and position the embedded table to the approximate height, width, and position shown at the right.

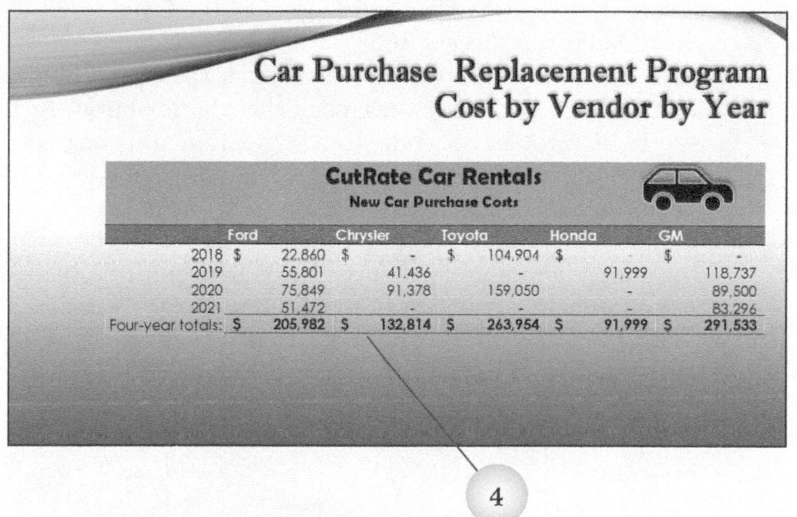

	Ford	Chrysler	Toyota	Honda	GM
2018	$ 22,860	$ -	$ 104,904	$ -	$ -
2019	55,801	41,436	-	91,999	118,737
2020	75,849	91,378	159,050	-	89,500
2021	51,472	-	-	-	83,296
Four-year totals:	$ 205,982	$ 132,814	$ 263,954	$ 91,999	$ 291,533

5. Click the File tab and then click the *Print* option. At the Print backstage area, click the button in the *Settings* category that reads *Full Page Slides* and then click *4 Slides Horizontal* at the drop-down list. Click the Print button.
6. Save **6-CRCarPres** and then exit PowerPoint.
7. Press the Esc key to remove the scrolling marquee and then click in any cell to deselect the range in the CarCosts worksheet. Leave the **CRInventory** workbook open for the next activity.

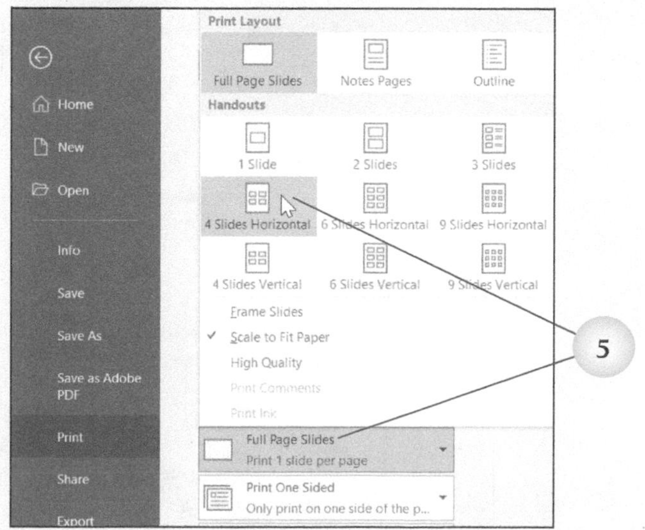

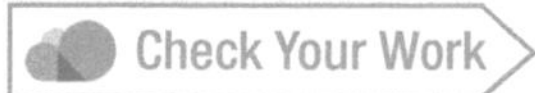

Copying and Pasting Data into Access

Copying and Pasting Data into Access

Data in an Excel worksheet can be copied and pasted into an Access table datasheet, query, or form using the Clipboard task pane. Before pasting data into a table datasheet, make sure that the column structures in the two programs match. If the Access datasheet already contains records, choose to replace the existing records or append the Excel data to the end of the table. To export Excel data to an Access database that does not have an existing table in which to receive the data, perform an import routine from Access. To do this, start Access, open the database, click the External Data tab, and then click the Import Excel spreadsheet button.

Activity 1e **Copying and Pasting Excel Data into an Access Datasheet** Part 5 of 6

1. With **CRInventory** open, copy and paste the rows in the Inventory worksheet to the bottom of an Access table by completing the following steps:
   a. Make Inventory the active worksheet.
   b. Select the range A5:G33 and then click the Copy button.
   c. Start Microsoft Access 365.
   d. At the Access 365 opening screen, click the *Open Other Files* option.
   e. At the Open backstage area, click the *Browse* option. At the Open dialog box, navigate to the EL2C6 folder on your storage medium and then double-click ***CRInventoryData***. If a security warning message displays below the ribbon stating that some active content has been disabled, click the Enable Content button.
   f. Double-click *CarInventory* in the Tables group in the Navigation pane at the left side of the Access window. This opens the CarInventory table in Datasheet view. Notice that the structure of the columns in the datasheet is the same as in the source worksheet in Excel.
   g. With the table open in Datasheet view, click the Paste button arrow in the Clipboard group and then click *Paste Append* at the drop-down list.

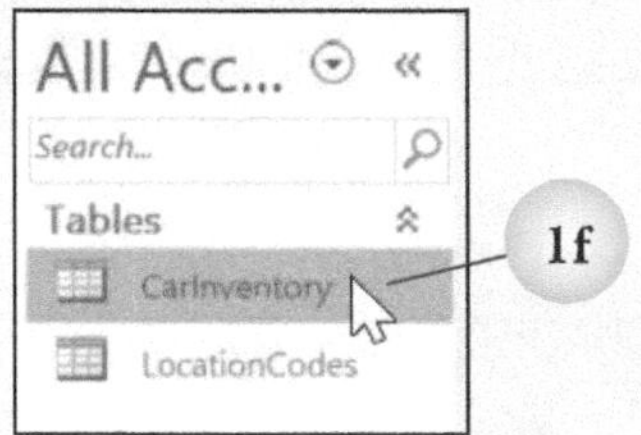

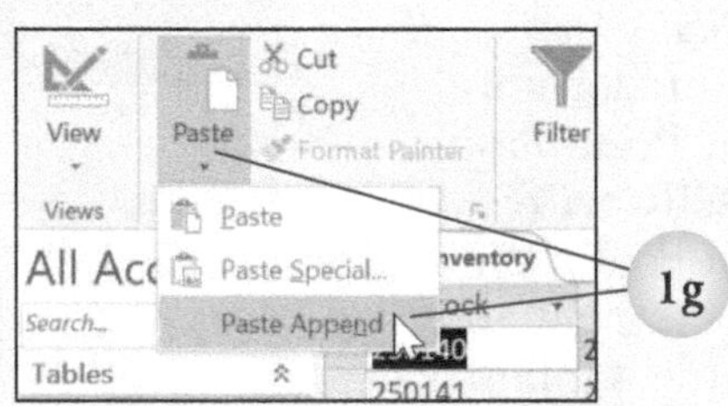

   h. At the Microsoft Access message box stating that you are about to paste 29 records and asking if you are sure, click Yes.

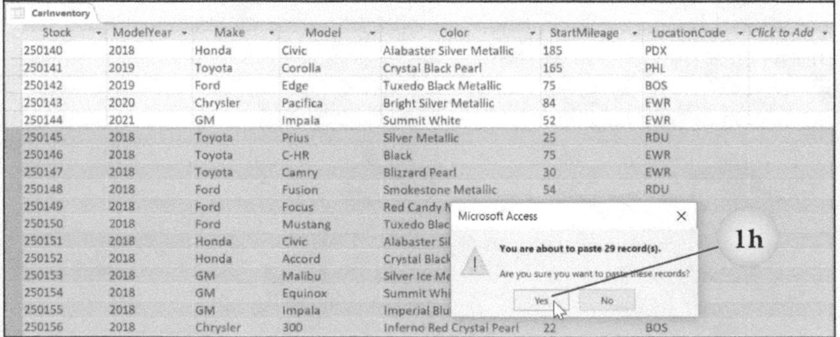

   i. Click in any cell within the datasheet to deselect the pasted records.

2. Print the Access datasheet in landscape orientation by completing the following steps:
   a. Click the File tab, click the *Print* option, and then click the *Print Preview* option.
   b. Click the Landscape button in the Page Layout group on the Print Preview tab.
   c. Click the Page Setup button in the Page Layout group.
   d. At the Page Setup dialog box with the Print Options tab selected, change the top and bottom margins to 0.5 inch. The left and right margins should already be set to 1 inch. Click OK.
   e. Click the Print button in the Print group and then click OK at the Print dialog box.
   f. Click the Close Print Preview button in the Close Preview group.
3. Click the Close button in the upper right corner to close Access.
4. Click in any cell to deselect the range in the Inventory worksheet and then press the Esc key to remove the scrolling marquee.
5. Leave the **CRInventory** workbook open for the next activity.

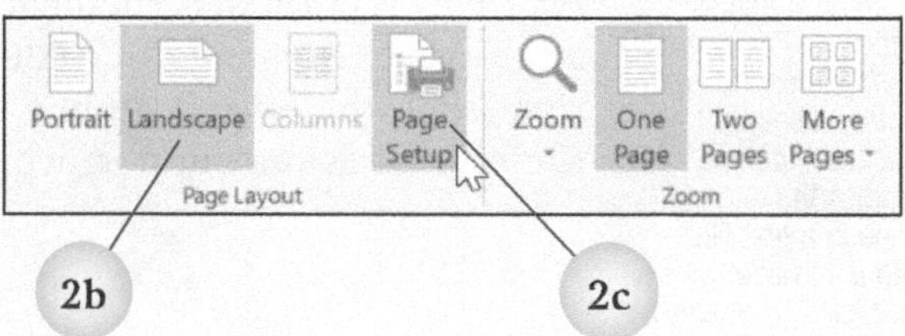

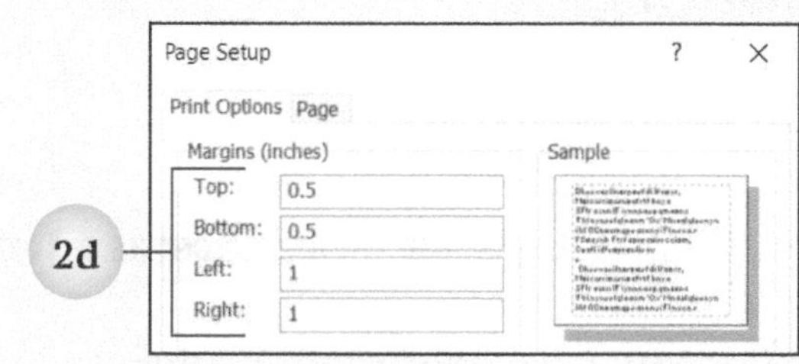

Exporting a Worksheet as a Text File

Quick Steps

Export Worksheet as Text File

1. Make sheet active.
2. Click File tab.
3. Click *Export* option.
4. Click *Change File Type*.
5. Click text file type in *Other File Types* section.
6. Click Save As button.
7. If necessary, navigate to drive and/or folder.
8. Type file name.
9. Click Save button.
10. Click OK.
11. Click Yes.

Exporting a Worksheet as a Text File

To exchange Excel data with someone who cannot import a Microsoft Excel worksheet or cannot copy and paste using the Clipboard task pane, save the data as a text file. Excel provides several text file options, including file formats suitable for computers that use the Apple operating system (Macintosh computers), as shown in Table 6.1. To save a worksheet as a text file, open the Save As dialog box and then change the file type to the correct option. Type a file name for the text file and then click the Save button. Click OK at the message box stating that only the active worksheet will be saved and then click Yes at the next message box to confirm saving the data as a text file.

Table 6.1 Supported Text File Formats for Exporting

Text File Format	File Extension
text (tab delimited)	.txt
unicode text	.txt
CSV (comma delimited)	.csv
formatted text (space delimited)	.prn
text (Apple)	.txt
text (MS-DOS)	.txt
CSV (Apple)	.csv
CSV (MS-DOS)	.csv

Hint Why are there so many text file formats? Although all systems support text files, there are differences across platforms. For example, the Apple operating system (used by Macintosh computers) denotes the end of a line in a text file with a carriage return character, Unix uses a linefeed character, and MS-DOS inserts both a linefeed and a carriage return character code at the end of each line.

Another way to save the current worksheet in a text file format is to click the File tab and then click the *Export* option. At the Export backstage area, click *Change File Type*. In the *Change File Type* section at the right, click *Text (Tab delimited)*, *CSV (Comma delimited)*, or *Formatted Text (Space delimited)* in the *Other File Types* section and then click the Save As button. If necessary, navigate to the appropriate drive and/or folder in the Save As dialog box. Type the file name and then click the Save button. Click OK at the message box stating that the selected file type does not support workbooks that contain multiple sheets.

Activity 1f **Exporting a Worksheet as a Text File** Part 6 of 6

1. With **CRInventory** open, export the Inventory worksheet data as a text file by completing the following steps:
   a. With Inventory the active worksheet, click the File tab and then click the *Export* option.
   b. Click the *Change File Type* option at the Export backstage area.
   c. Click the *CSV (Comma delimited)* option in the *Other File Types* section.
   d. Click the Save As button.

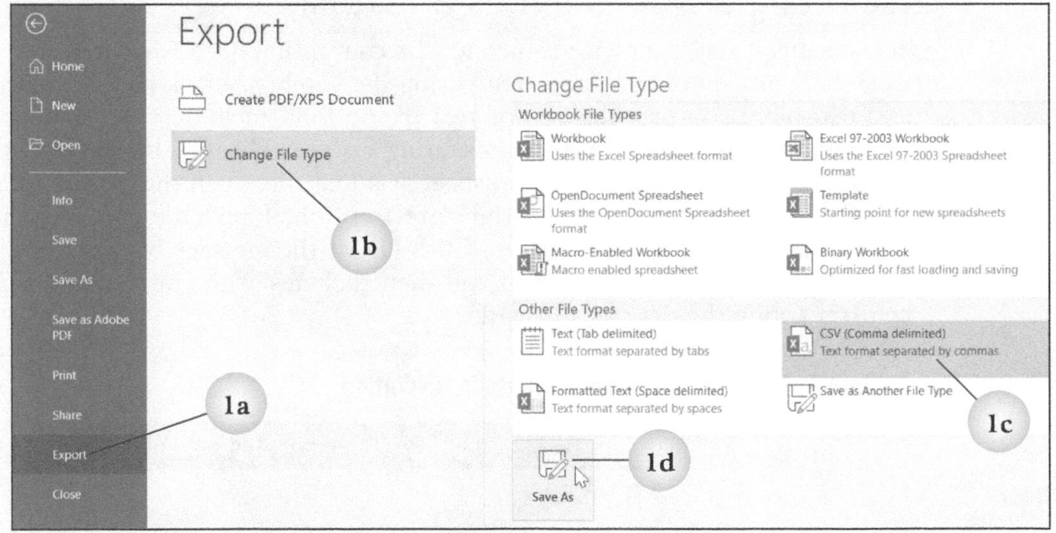

   e. Type 6-CRInventoryTxt in the *File name* text box.
   f. Click the Save button.

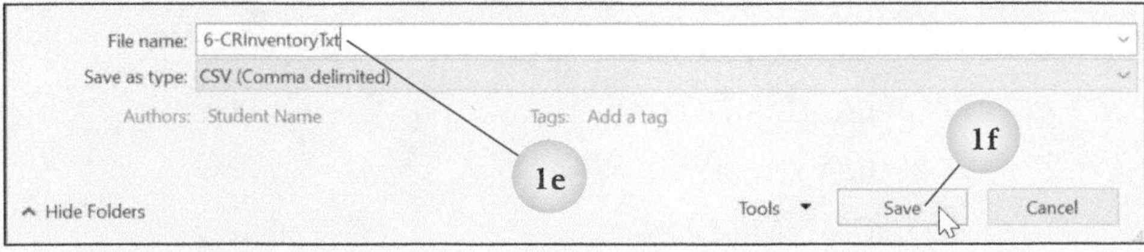

g. Click OK to save only the active sheet at the Microsoft Excel message box stating that the selected file type does not support workbooks that contain multiple sheets.

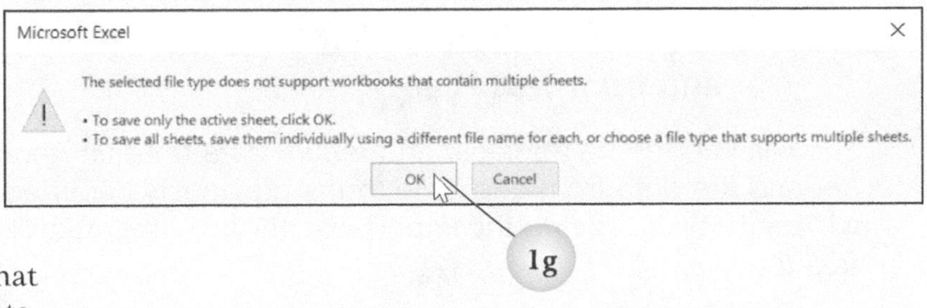

h. A message displays above the Formula bar stating that there is some possible data loss. Click the Message Close button.

1h

POSSIBLE DATA LOSS Some features might be lost if you save this workbook in the comma-delimited (.csv) format. To preserve these features, save it in an Excel file format. Don't show again Save As...

2. Close **6-CRInventoryTxt**. Click Don't Save when prompted to save changes. (The file does not need to be saved because no changes have been made since the file type was changed.)
3. Open Notepad and view the text file created in Step 1 by completing the following steps:
   a. Click the Start button. At the Start screen, start typing notepad. When *Notepad* appears in the *Best match* area, press the Enter key. (Depending on your operating system, these steps may vary. If Notepad is not available, use another text editor.)

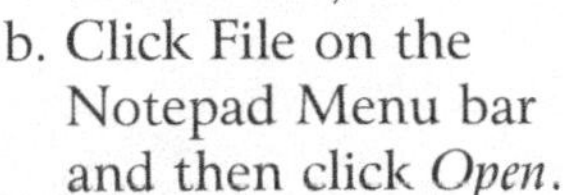

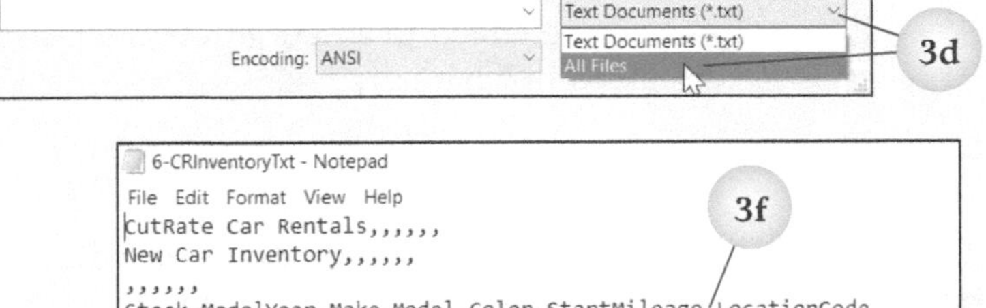

   b. Click File on the Notepad Menu bar and then click *Open*.
   c. Navigate to the EL2C6 folder on your storage medium.
   d. Click the *File type* option box arrow (which displays *Text Documents (*.txt)*) and then click *All Files* at the drop-down list.
   e. Double-click ***6-CRInventoryTxt***.
   f. If necessary, scroll down to view all the data in the text file. Notice that commas have been inserted between the items of data previously arranged in columns.

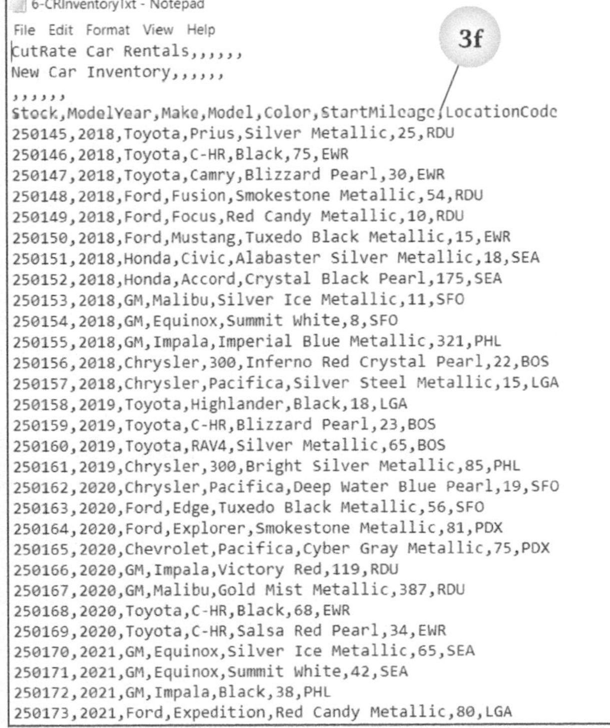


```
CutRate Car Rentals,,,,,,
New Car Inventory,,,,,,
,,,,,,
Stock,ModelYear,Make,Model,Color,StartMileage,LocationCode
250145,2018,Toyota,Prius,Silver Metallic,25,RDU
250146,2018,Toyota,C-HR,Black,75,EWR
250147,2018,Toyota,Camry,Blizzard Pearl,30,EWR
250148,2018,Ford,Fusion,Smokestone Metallic,54,RDU
250149,2018,Ford,Focus,Red Candy Metallic,10,RDU
250150,2018,Ford,Mustang,Tuxedo Black Metallic,15,EWR
250151,2018,Honda,Civic,Alabaster Silver Metallic,18,SEA
250152,2018,Honda,Accord,Crystal Black Pearl,175,SEA
250153,2018,GM,Malibu,Silver Ice Metallic,11,SFO
250154,2018,GM,Equinox,Summit White,8,SFO
250155,2018,GM,Impala,Imperial Blue Metallic,321,PHL
250156,2018,Chrysler,300,Inferno Red Crystal Pearl,22,BOS
250157,2018,Chrysler,Pacifica,Silver Steel Metallic,15,LGA
250158,2019,Toyota,Highlander,Black,18,LGA
250159,2019,Toyota,C-HR,Blizzard Pearl,23,BOS
250160,2019,Toyota,RAV4,Silver Metallic,65,BOS
250161,2019,Chrysler,300,Bright Silver Metallic,85,PHL
250162,2020,Chrysler,Pacifica,Deep Water Blue Pearl,19,SFO
250163,2020,Ford,Edge,Tuxedo Black Metallic,56,SFO
250164,2020,Ford,Explorer,Smokestone Metallic,81,PDX
250165,2020,Chevrolet,Pacifica,Cyber Gray Metallic,75,PDX
250166,2020,GM,Impala,Victory Red,119,RDU
250167,2020,GM,Malibu,Gold Mist Metallic,387,RDU
250168,2020,Toyota,C-HR,Black,68,EWR
250169,2020,Toyota,C-HR,Salsa Red Pearl,34,EWR
250170,2021,GM,Equinox,Silver Ice Metallic,65,SEA
250171,2021,GM,Equinox,Summit White,42,SEA
250172,2021,GM,Impala,Black,38,PHL
250173,2021,Ford,Expedition,Red Candy Metallic,80,LGA
```

4. Click File on the Notepad Menu bar and then click *Print*. Click the Print button at the Print dialog box.
5. Exit Notepad.
6. Close **CRInventory**.

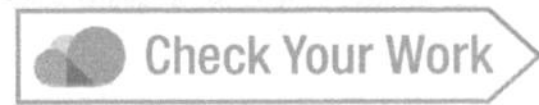

Activity 2 Import Data from an Access Database and from Text Files **5 Parts**

You will import site manager and tenant data from an Access database and then append the data from a text file to the previously imported tenant data. The data will be modified during the import. Rental listings data will also be imported from a text file.

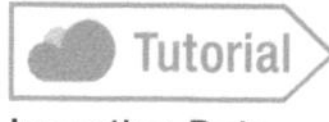

Importing Data into Excel

Importing Data into Excel

Importing data from other applications allows for the manipulation, organization, and analyzing of data in Excel in a variety of ways. Time and money are saved by not having to enter the information manually. Importing data also reduces errors that may be introduced during data entry.

The Get & Transform Data group on the Data tab contains buttons for importing data from external sources into an Excel worksheet using Power Query technology. To import data, make active the cell in which the imported data is to start and then click the button representing the source application or point to the Get Data button and then select the source from a drop-down list. Previously, Excel used wizards to import data. Those wizards are now called *legacy wizards* and can be added to a new group in an existing or new tab. Adding buttons is discussed in Chapter 7.

Importing Data from Access

Quick Steps

Import Access Table

1. Click Data tab.
2. Click Get Data button.
3. Point to *From Database.*
4. Click *From Microsoft Access Database.*
5. Navigate to drive and/or folder.
6. Double-click source database file name.
7. If necessary, click table name and then *Load.*

Exchanging data between Access and Excel is a seamless process, since the data in an Access datasheet is structured in the same row and column format as the data in an Excel worksheet. The imported data can be appended to an existing worksheet or placed in a new worksheet.

To import an Access table, click the Data tab, click the Get Data button, point to the *From Database* option at the drop-down list, and then click the *From Microsoft Access Database* option at the second drop-down list. Navigate to the drive and/or folder in which the source database resides and then double-click the Access database file name in the file list. At the Navigator dialog box, click the table containing the data to be imported. A preview of the data appears in the

Figure 6.1 Import Data Dialog Box

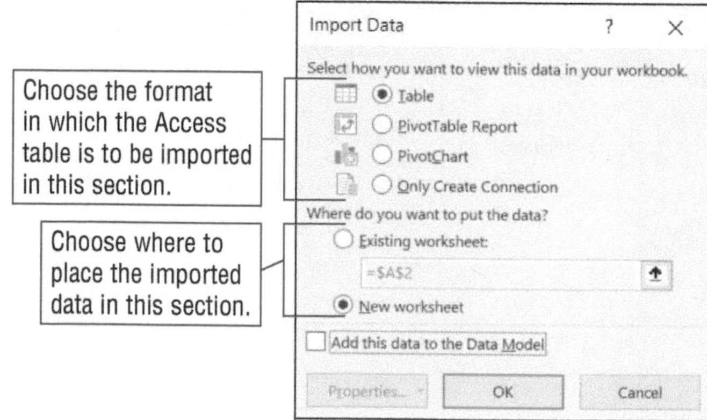

right panel. Click the Load button to import the data in a new worksheet, click the Load button arrow, and then click the *Load To* option at the drop-down list to open the Import Data dialog box, shown in Figure 6.1 (on page 154), to import the data in a different location, or click the Edit button to modify and then import the data.

Hint Only one table can be imported at a time. To import all the tables in the source database, repeat the import process for each table.

When data is imported into Excel, the data is imported in a table format and a query is created. The query specifies the import steps and any modifications made to the data. The Queries & Connections task pane displays with the Queries tab active and the new query selected.

Activity 2a Importing Data from an Access Database

Part 1 of 5

1. Open **PropMgt**.
2. Save the workbook with the name **6-PropMgt**.
3. Import the SiteManagers table stored in an Access database and place the information in the Site Managers worksheet by completing the following steps:
   a. If necessary, make cell A2 active.
   b. Click the Data tab.
   c. Click the Get Data button in the Get & Transform Data group. Point to the *From Database* option and then click the *From Microsoft Access Database* option at the second drop-down list.

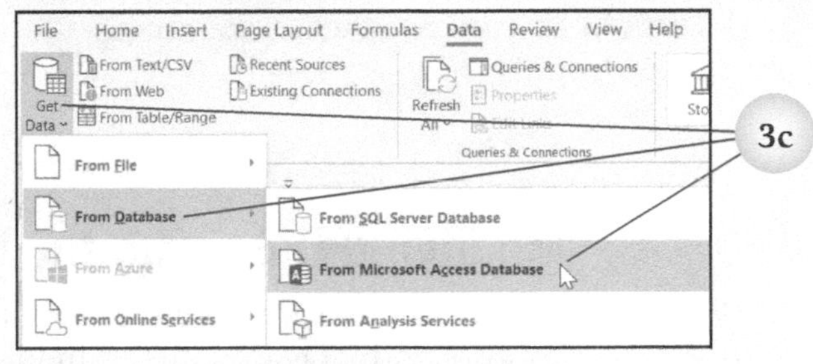

   d. If necessary, navigate to the EL2C6 folder on your storage medium and then double-click ***PropMgtData***.
   e. Click *SiteManagers* in the left panel. A preview of the table displays in the right panel.
   f. Click the Load button arrow and then click the *Load To* option.

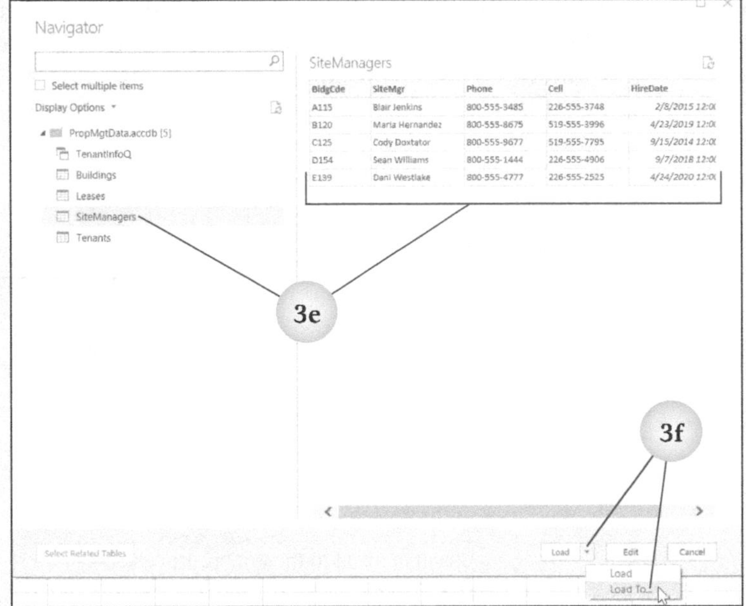

g. At the Import Data dialog box, click the Existing worksheet radio button.
h. With *=$A$2* in the *Existing worksheet* text box, click OK.

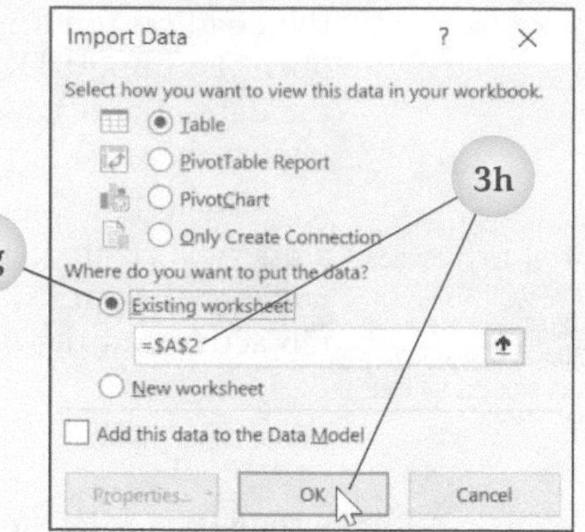

4. Look at the imported table data. Notice that the data is formatted as a table with filter arrows. The Queries & Connections panel displays the query with details of the new import.
5. With the Table Tools Design tab active, make the following changes to the worksheet:
   a. Remove the filter arrows.
   b. Change the table style to Blue, Table Style Light 9 (third column, second row in the *Light* section).
   c. Make the Home tab active and apply the Short Date format to the range E3:E7.

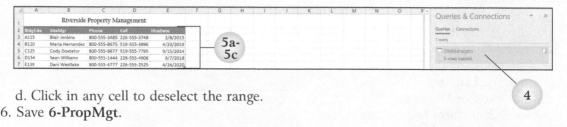

Riverside Property Management

BldgCde	SiteMgr	Phone	Cell	HireDate
A115	Blair Jenkins	800-555-3485	226-555-3748	2/8/2015
B120	Maria Hernandez	800-555-8675	519-555-3996	4/23/2019
C125	Cody Doxtator	800-555-9677	519-555-7795	9/15/2014
D154	Sean Williams	800-555-1444	226-555-4906	9/7/2018
E139	Dani Westlake	800-555-4777	226-555-2525	4/24/2020

5a-5c

Queries & Connections
SiteManagers
5 rows loaded.

4

   d. Click in any cell to deselect the range.
6. Save **6-PropMgt**.

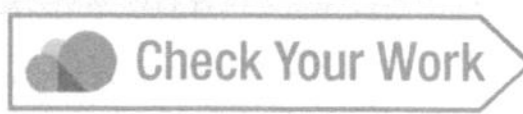

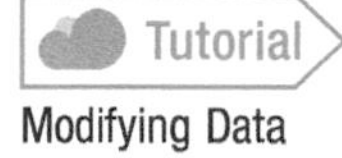

Modifying Data with the Power Query Editor

Modifying Data with the Power Query Editor

Use the Power Query Editor to transform data before it is imported into Excel. To display the Query Editor window before the data is imported, click the Edit button at the Navigator dialog box. Depending on the version of Excel, the Edit button may display as the Transform Data button. To transform data, use tools on the Home tab of the Power Query Editor window shown in Figure 6.2. For example, if a field contains both the first names and the last names of tenants, separate the field into two fields: one containing first names and the other containing last names. The steps used to transform the data are saved as part of the query in the APPLIED STEPS section at the Query Settings task pane in the Power Query Editor window. The steps in the APPLIED STEPS section will be reapplied to the data every time the data is refreshed.

Figure 6.2 Power Query Editor Window

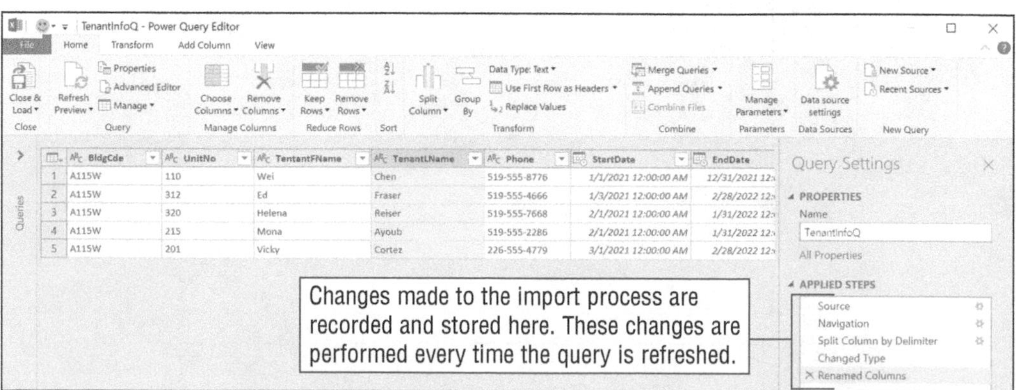

Activity 2b Importing and Modifying Data from an Access Database

1. With **6-PropMgt** open, import the *TenantInfoQ* query from the **PropMgtData** database into a new worksheet by completing the following steps:
   a. With any cell active, click the Data tab.
   b. Click the Get Data button.
   c. Point to the *From Database* option and then click the *From Microsoft Access Database* option at the second drop-down list.
   d. If necessary, navigate to the EL2C6 folder on your storage medium and then double-click to select the file **PropMgtData**.
   e. Click *TenantInfoQ* in the left panel. A preview of the query displays in the right panel.
   f. Click the Edit button in the right panel. ***Note: Depending on the version of Excel, the Edit button may display as the Transform Data button.***
   g. Click in any cell in the *TenantName* column, click the Split Column button in the Transform group on the Home tab, and then click the *By Delimiter* option at the drop-down list.

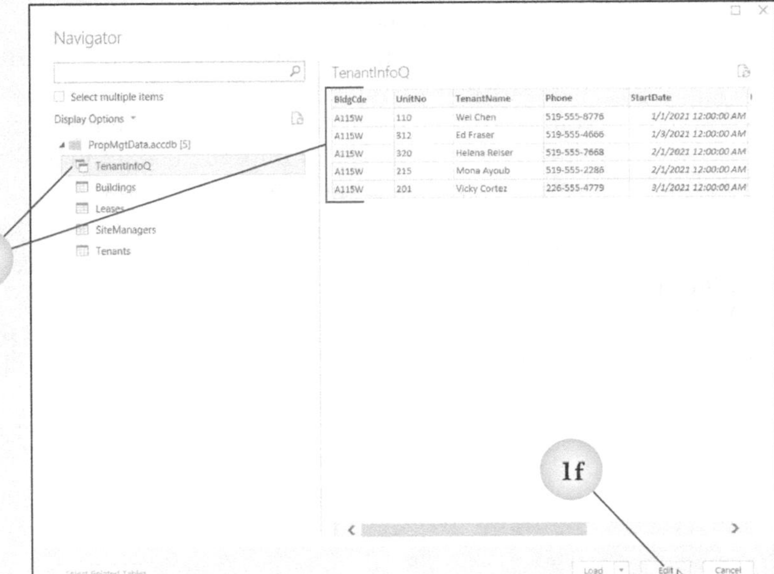

   h. With the *Space* option appearing in the *Select or enter delimiter* option box and a bullet appearing in the *Each occurrence of the delimiter* radio button, click OK.

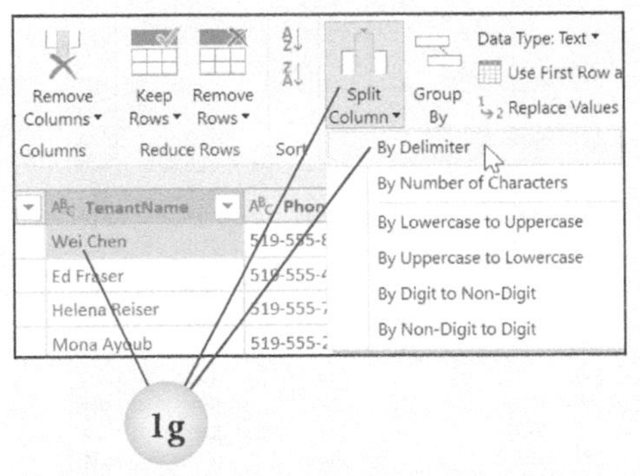

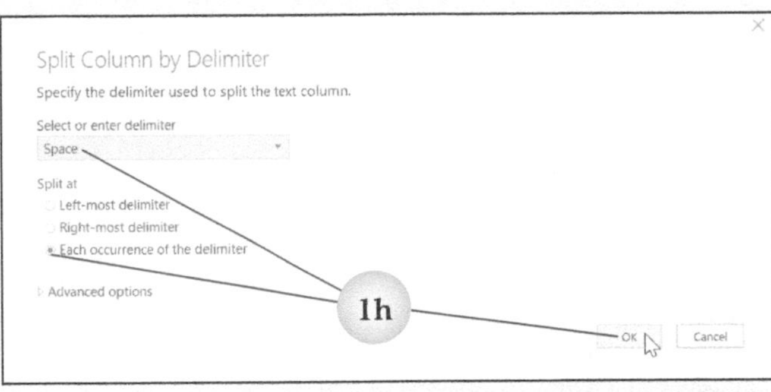

   i. Right-click the *TenantName.1* column header, click the *Rename* option, type TenantFName, and then press the Enter key.
   j. Right-click the *TenantName.2* column header, click the *Rename* option, type TenantLName, and then press the Enter key.
   k. Click the Close & Load button in the Close group.
2. Rename the worksheet **Tenants**.
3. Save **6-PropMgt**.

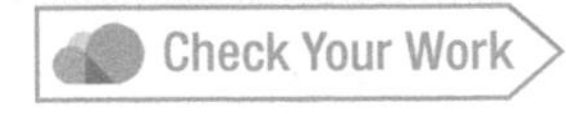

Importing Data from a Text File

Hint Most programs can export data in a text file. To use data from a program that is not compatible with Excel, check the program's export options for a text file format.

As noted when exporting, a text file is often used to exchange data between different programs because the file format is recognized by nearly all applications. Text files contain no formatting and consist only of letters, numbers, punctuation symbols, and a few control characters. Two commonly used text file formats separate fields with tabs (delimited file format) or commas (comma-separated file format). One of the text files used in Activity 2c is shown in a Notepad window in Figure 6.3. If necessary, view and edit a text file in Notepad before importing it.

From Text/CSV

To import a text file into Excel, use the From Text/CSV button in the Get & Transform Data group on the Data tab and then select the source file at the Import Data dialog box. Excel displays in the file list any file in the active folder that ends with the file extension *.prn, .txt,* or *.csv*. Once the source file is selected, Excel displays a preview of the file. Click the Load button to import the data in a new worksheet, click the Load button arrow, and then click the *Load To* option at the drop-down list to import the data in a different location, or click the Edit button to edit and then import the data.

Quick Steps

Import Data from Delimited Text File

1. Click Data tab.
2. Click From Text/CSV button.
3. Double-click text file name.
4. Click Load.

Non-native files—including but not limited to web pages, extensible markup language (XML) files, text files, and data sources—can also be opened directly in Excel. To open a non-native file directly in Excel, click the File tab and then click the *Open* option. Click the file location and then click the *Browse* option to display the Open dialog box. Navigate to the specific folder and then click the *File Type* option box to display a drop-down list of all the different file types that can be opened in Excel. Click the specific file type and then double-click the file name. If the exact file type is not known, select *All Files* to display all the available files. Save the file as an Excel workbook, or if changes were made, resave it as a text file (but note that some features might be lost).

Figure 6.3 Activity 2c Text File Content

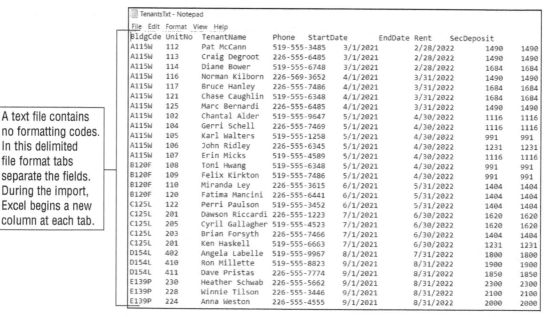

A text file contains no formatting codes. In this delimited file format tabs separate the fields. During the import, Excel begins a new column at each tab.

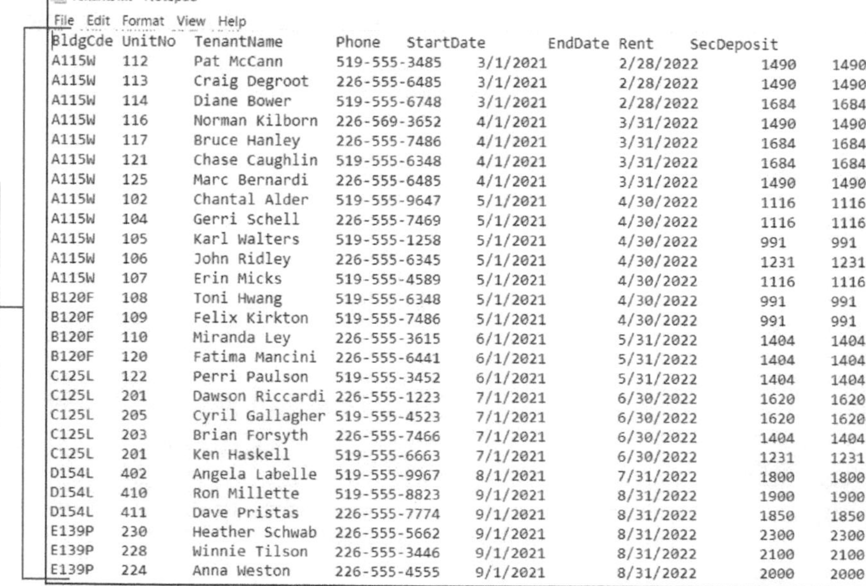

TenantsTxt - Notepad

File Edit Format View Help

BldgCde	UnitNo	TenantName	Phone	StartDate	EndDate	Rent	SecDeposit
A115W	112	Pat McCann	519-555-3485	3/1/2021	2/28/2022	1490	1490
A115W	113	Craig Degroot	226-555-6485	3/1/2021	2/28/2022	1490	1490
A115W	114	Diane Bower	519-555-6748	3/1/2021	2/28/2022	1684	1684
A115W	116	Norman Kilborn	226-569-3652	4/1/2021	3/31/2022	1490	1490
A115W	117	Bruce Hanley	226-555-7486	4/1/2021	3/31/2022	1684	1684
A115W	121	Chase Caughlin	519-555-6348	4/1/2021	3/31/2022	1684	1684
A115W	125	Marc Bernardi	226-555-6485	4/1/2021	3/31/2022	1490	1490
A115W	102	Chantal Alder	519-555-9647	5/1/2021	4/30/2022	1116	1116
A115W	104	Gerri Schell	226-555-7469	5/1/2021	4/30/2022	1116	1116
A115W	105	Karl Walters	519-555-1258	5/1/2021	4/30/2022	991	991
A115W	106	John Ridley	226-555-6345	5/1/2021	4/30/2022	1231	1231
A115W	107	Erin Micks	519-555-4589	5/1/2021	4/30/2022	1116	1116
B120F	108	Toni Hwang	519-555-6348	5/1/2021	4/30/2022	991	991
B120F	109	Felix Kirkton	519-555-7486	5/1/2021	4/30/2022	991	991
B120F	110	Miranda Ley	226-555-3615	6/1/2021	5/31/2022	1404	1404
B120F	120	Fatima Mancini	226-555-6441	6/1/2021	5/31/2022	1404	1404
C125L	122	Perri Paulson	519-555-3452	6/1/2021	5/31/2022	1404	1404
C125L	201	Dawson Riccardi	226-555-1223	7/1/2021	6/30/2022	1620	1620
C125L	205	Cyril Gallagher	519-555-4523	7/1/2021	6/30/2022	1620	1620
C125L	203	Brian Forsyth	226-555-7466	7/1/2021	6/30/2022	1404	1404
C125L	201	Ken Haskell	519-555-6663	7/1/2021	6/30/2022	1231	1231
D154L	402	Angela Labelle	519-555-9967	8/1/2021	7/31/2022	1800	1800
D154L	410	Ron Millette	519-555-8823	9/1/2021	8/31/2022	1900	1900
D154L	411	Dave Pristas	226-555-7774	9/1/2021	8/31/2022	1850	1850
E139P	230	Heather Schwab	226-555-5662	9/1/2021	8/31/2022	2300	2300
E139P	228	Winnie Tilson	226-555-3446	9/1/2021	8/31/2022	2100	2100
E139P	224	Anna Weston	226-555-4555	9/1/2021	8/31/2022	2000	2000

Activity 2c Importing, Editing, and Appending Data from Delimited Text and CSV Files — Part 3 of 5

1. With **6-PropMgt** open, import, edit, and then append the data to the Tenants list previously imported. Choose the data source and edit the data by completing the following steps:
   a. With any cell active in the Tenants worksheet, click the Data tab, if necessary.
   b. Click the From Text/CSV button in the Get & Transform Data group.
   c. At the Import Data dialog box, navigate to the EL2C6 folder on your storage medium, if necessary, and then double-click ***TenantsTxt*** in the file list.
   d. At the **TenantsTxt.txt** preview, click the Edit button.
   e. Click in any cell in the *TenantName* column, click the Split Column button, and then click the *By Delimiter* option at the drop-down list.
   f. With the *Space* option appearing in the *Select or enter delimiter* option box and a bullet appearing in the *Each occurrence of the delimiter* radio button, click OK.
   g. Right-click the *TenantName.1* column header, click the *Rename* option, type TenantFName, and then press the Enter key.
   h. Right-click the *TenantName.2* column header, click the *Rename* option, type TenantLName, and then press the Enter key.

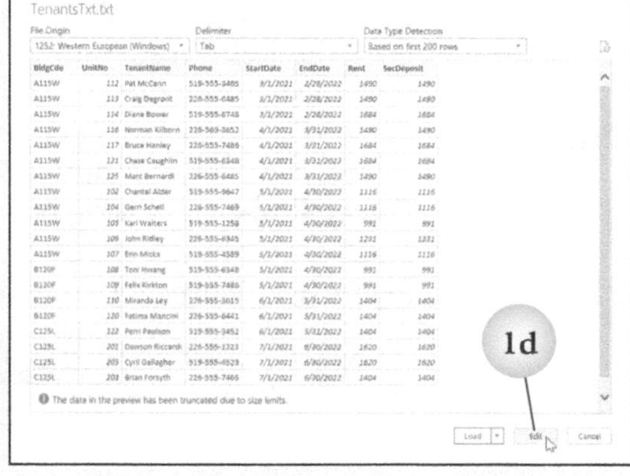

2. Append the data from the text file to the previously imported Access query by completing the following steps:
   a. Click the Append Queries button in the Combine group.
   b. Click the *Table to append* option box arrow, click the *TenantInfoQ* option, and then click OK.
   c. Click the Close & Load button.
3. Make the following changes to the data:
   a. Select the range B29:B33 and right-align the numbers.
   b. Select the range F2:G33 and apply the Short Date format.
   c. Select the range H2:I33 and apply Currency formatting with no digits past the decimal point.
   d. Sort the table in ascending order by the *BldgCde* field.
   e. Remove the filter arrows.
   f. Change the table style to Blue, Table Style Light 9 (third column, second row in the *Light* section).
   g. Rename the worksheet **All Tenants**.

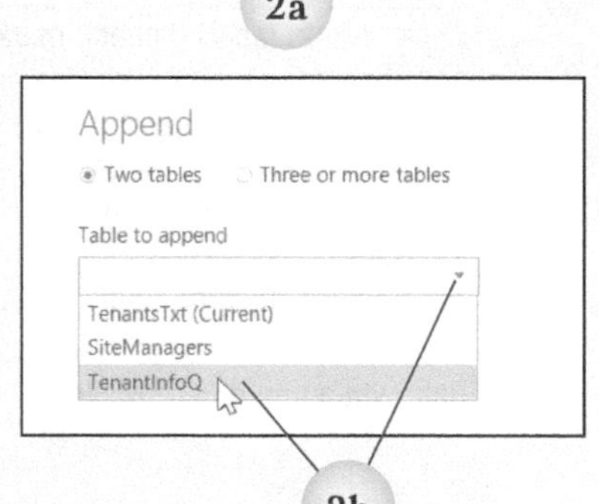

4. Import the RentalListingsCSV CSV file into a new worksheet by completing the following steps:
   a. Click the Data tab and then click the From Text/CSV button.
   b. At the Import Data dialog box, navigate to the EL2C6 folder on your storage medium, if necessary, and then double-click ***RentalListingsCSV*** in the file list.
   d. At the **RentalListingsCSV.csv** preview, click the Load button.
   e. Rename the worksheet **Rental Listings**.
5. Save **6-PropMgt**.

Refreshing and Deleting Queries

Refreshing, Modifying, and Deleting Queries

When data is imported into Excel, a connection is established between the source file and the destination file. If the file is imported using Power Query technology, the connection is created using a query. Refreshing, modifying, and removing queries helps maintain the data needed to make sound business decisions by ensuring the most current data is in the destination file. Editing a query allows further changes to be made to the data. Removing a connection allows for the data to be captured at a specific time.

Refresh All

To refresh a query, click the Refresh All button in the Queries & Connections group on the Data tab as shown in Figure 6.4. To refresh just the selected query, click the Refresh All button arrow and then click the *Refresh* option at the drop-down list. To modify the data to refresh at a specific time period or when the workbook is opened, click the Refresh All button arrow on the Data tab, click the *Connections Properties* option at the drop-down list, and then choose options at the Query Properties dialog box, shown in Figure 6.5.

Figure 6.4 Queries & Connections Group on the Data Tab

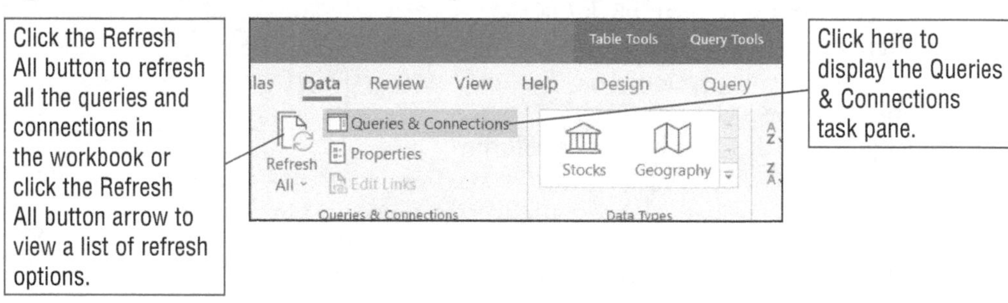

Figure 6.5 Query Properties Dialog Box

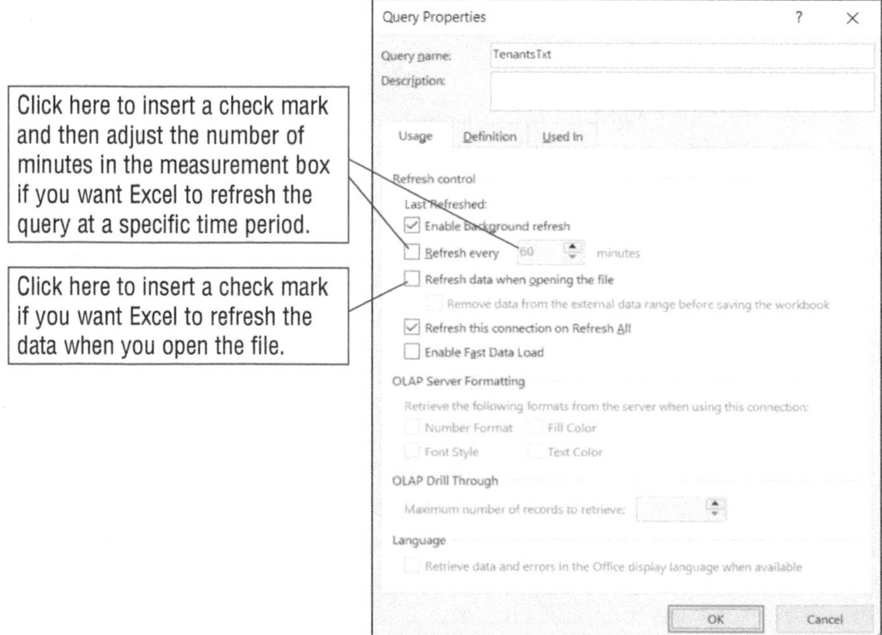

To redisplay the Query & Connections task pane, click the Queries & Connections button in the Queries & Connections group on the Data tab, as shown in Figure 6.4 (on page 160). Edit a query if further changes need to be made to the data on a query that will be refreshed. To edit a query, double-click the query item at the Queries & Connections task pane, make the necessary changes in the Query Editor window, and then click the Close & Load button in the Close group on the Home tab in the Power Query Editor window. The features on the Query Tools Query tab are also found at the pop-up menu when you right-click a query item at the Queries & Connections task pane.

To display the Query dialog box, as shown in Figure 6.6, point to the query at the task pane. The Query dialog box provides options for previewing, editing, and deleting a query.

To delete a query, right-click the query at the Queries & Connections task pane and then click the *Delete* option at the pop-up menu or click the Delete button in the Edit group on the Query Tools Query tab. If you convert the table to a range, a message box displays asking if you want to permanently remove the query definition.

Figure 6.6 Query Dialog Box

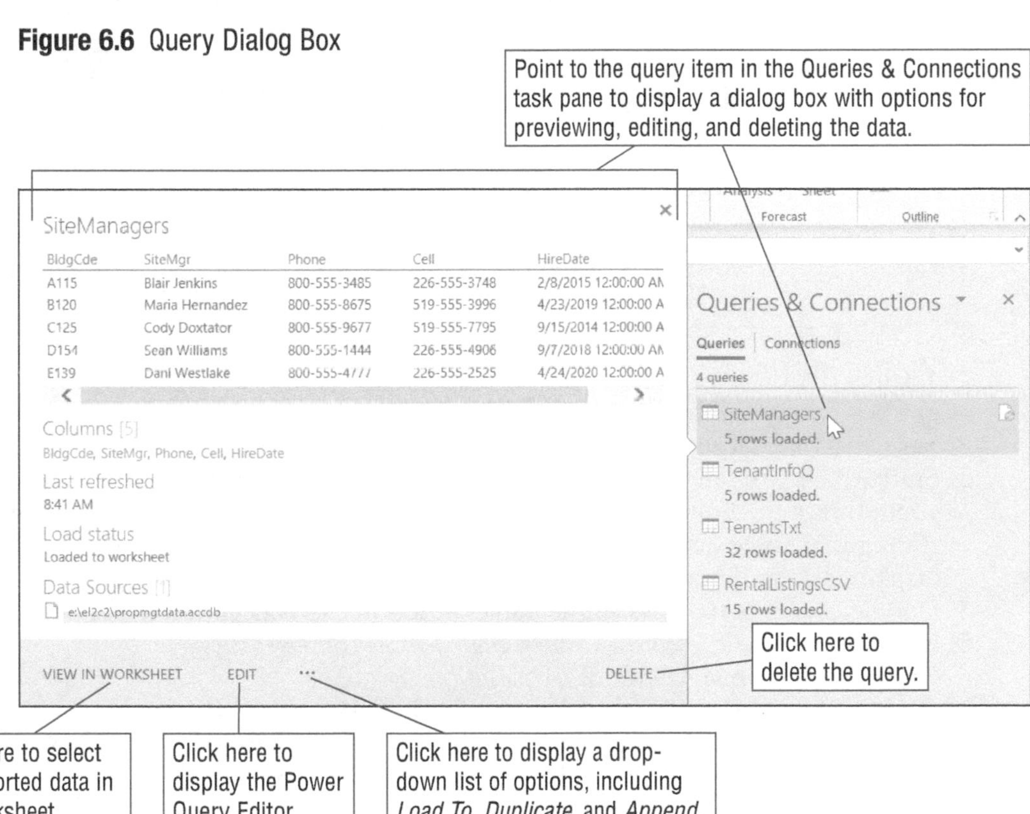

Activity 2d Editing a Query and Refreshing the Data

1. With **6-PropMgt** open, edit the SiteManagers query by completing the following steps:
   a. Make the Site Managers worksheet active.
   b. If the Queries & Connections panel is not open, click the Queries & Connections button in the Queries & Connections group on the Data tab.
   c. Double-click the *SiteManagers* query in the Queries & Connections task pane.
   d. Click in any cell in the *SiteMgr* column and then click the Sort Ascending button in the Sort group.
   e. Click in any cell in the *HireDate* column, click the *Data Type* option arrow in the Transform group, and then click the *Date* option.

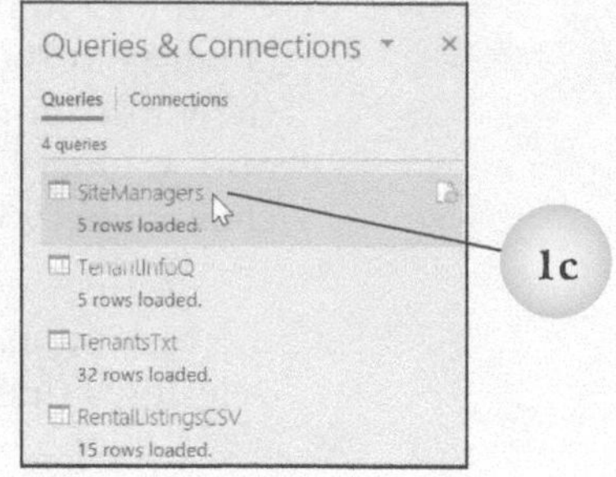

1c

1d 1e

   f. Click the Close & Load button.
   g. Click in any cell to deselect the range.
2. Save and then close **6-PropMgt**.
3. Start Access 365 and then open the data file **PropMgtData** from the EL2C6 folder on your storage medium. Click the Enable Content button if a security warning displays stating that some active content has been disabled. Click the Yes button if a message displays asking if you want to make this a trusted document.
4. Double-click *SiteManagers* in the Tables group in the Navigation pane.
5. In row 1, change the contact name *Blair Jenkins* to *Sherri Blythe*.
6. Close the **6-PropMgtData** database.
7. Open **6-PropMgt** and notice the name *Blair Jenkins* in cell B3.
8. Click the Data tab and then click the Refresh All button in the Queries & Connections group. *Blair Jenkins* has been replaced by *Sherri Blythe* in cell B7.
9. Save **6-PropMgt**.

	A	B	C	D	E
1	Riverside Property Management				
2	BldgCde	SiteMgr	Phone	Cell	HireDate
3	C125	Cody Doxtator	800-555-9677	519-555-7795	9/15/2014
4	E139	Dani Westlake	800-555-4777	226-555-2525	4/24/2020
5	B120	Maria Hernandez	800-555-8675	519-555-3996	4/23/2019
6	D154	Sean Williams	800-555-1444	226-555-4906	9/7/2018
7	A115	Sherri Blythe	800-555-3485	226-555-3748	2/8/2015

8

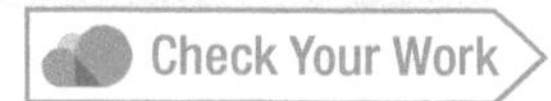

Activity 2e Deleting a Query

Part 5 of 5

1. With **6-PropMgt** open, delete the *TenantsTxt*, *TenantInfoQ*, and *RentalListingsCSV* queries by completing the following steps:
   a. If the Queries & Connections task pane is not open, click the Data tab and then click the Queries & Connections button.
   b. Right-click the *TenantsTxt* query item at the task pane.
   c. Click the *Delete* option.
   d. Click the Delete button at the Delete Query message box that asks if you are sure you want to delete the TenantsTxt query.

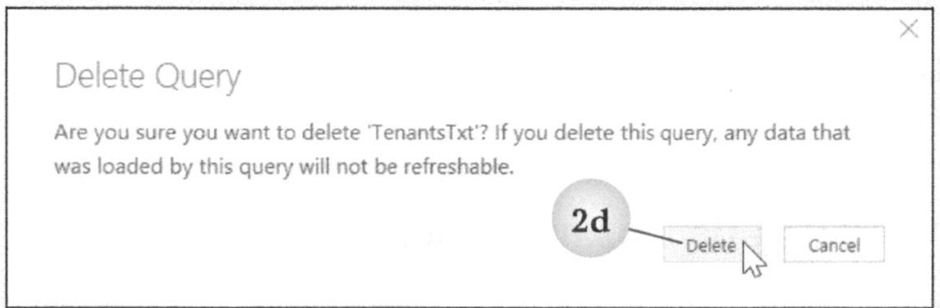

   e. Follow Steps 1b through 1d to delete the *TenantInfoQ* and the *RentalListingsCSV* queries.
2. Delete the Tenants worksheet.
3. Save **6-PropMgt**.

Editing or Removing the Source for a Query

If you move or rename a source, Excel will not know where to locate the file and a yellow triangle with an exclamation mark will appear beside the query item at the Queries & Connections task pane, as shown in Figure 6.7.

To edit the source, double-click the query item at the Queries & Connections task pane. Click the Data source settings button in the Data sources group on the Home tab in the Power Query Editor window. Click the Change Source button at the Data source settings dialog box, as shown in Figure 6.8. Click the File Path Browse button at the source information dialog box. Navigate to the folder containing the source file, click the source file in the file list box, and then click the OK button. Click the Close button at the Data source settings dialog box. Click the Close & Load button in the Close group on the Home tab at the Power Query Editor window to import the data from the new source file.

Figure 6.7 Source File Moved or Renamed

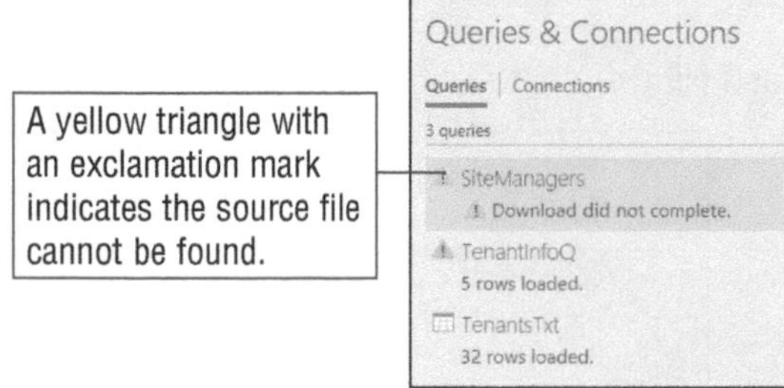

Figure 6.8 Data Source Settings Dialog Box

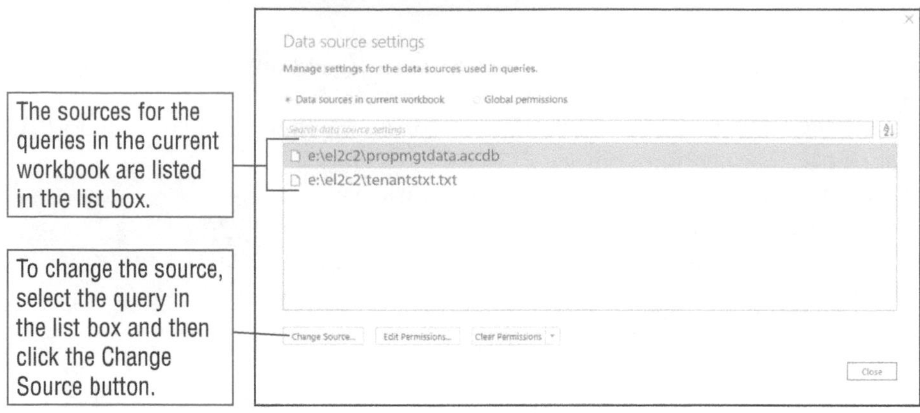

Activity 3 Transform Data Using Flash Fill and Text Functions — 4 Parts

You will continue working with a property management spreadsheet, using Flash Fill and text functions to split site managers' names into two fields and creating tenant IDs as well as new email addresses for site managers.

Populating Data Using Flash Fill

Quick Steps

Extract Data Using Flash Fill

1. Insert blank column(s) next to source data.
2. Type first record.
3. Press Enter key.
4. Start typing second record.
5. When grayed-out text appears, press Enter key.

Transforming Data Using Flash Fill

The Flash Fill feature extracts, joins, and inserts text, numbers, dates, and times. It is useful for organizing data that has been pasted or imported from another source. Join all or extract parts of the contents of cells. Flash Fill analyzes adjacent columns while entering data, detects any patterns, and suggests how the rest of the column should be completed.

Flash Fill can split columns, like the Text to Columns button in the Data Tools group on the Data tab or the Split Column feature in the Transform group on the Home tab of the Power Query Editor. To split a column using Flash Fill, insert two new columns. Type the first name *Cody* in column C, as shown in Figure 6.9. Press the Enter key and then type *D* to start the second name, *Dani*. Excel recognizes that the first word of the adjacent column B is to be extracted and suggests doing the same for the remaining cells in column C. Notice that the rest of the names are grayed out. Press the Enter key to accept the suggestion or continue typing to reject the suggestion. Repeat the process for the last name.

A few rows of data may need to be entered before Excel recognizes the pattern. Once the pattern is established, press the Enter key. Other methods for using Flash

Figure 6.9 Flash Fill

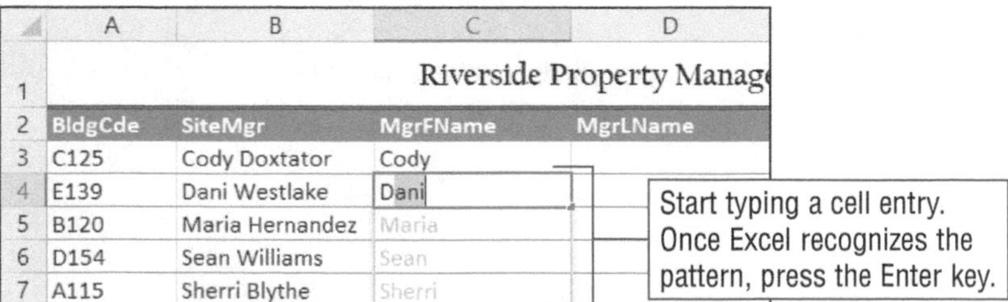

Flash Fill

Fill are to click the Fill button in the Editing group on the Home tab and then choose *Flash Fill* from the drop-down menu, to click the Flash Fill button in the Data Tools group on the Data tab, or to use the keyboard shortcut Ctrl + E.

Activity 3a **Separating Site Manager Names into Two Columns Using Flash Fill** Part 1 of 4

1. With **6-PropMgt** open, split the site managers' names in column B into two columns by completing the following steps:
   a. If necessary, make the Site Managers worksheet active.
   b. Insert two columns between the *SiteMgr* and *Phone* columns in the table. Type MgrFName in cell C2 and MgrLName in cell D2.
   c. In cell C3, type Cody and then press the Enter key.
   d. In cell C4, type D. Flash Fill recognizes the sequence and suggests how to fill the rest of the column.
   e. Press the Enter key to accept the suggestions. If Excel does not recognize the pattern right away, continue to type the first names or click the Flash Fill button in the Data Tools group on the Data tab.
   f. In cell D3, type Doxtator and then press the Enter key.
   g. In cell D4, type W. Flash Fill recognizes the sequence and suggests how to fill the rest of the column.
   h. Press the Enter key to accept the suggestions. If Excel does not recognize the pattern right away, continue to type the last names or click the Flash Fill button in the Data Tools group on the Data tab.
2. Delete column B.
3. Save **6-PropMgt.**

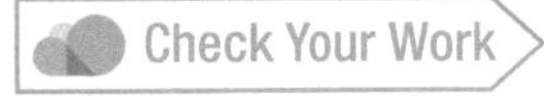
Check Your Work

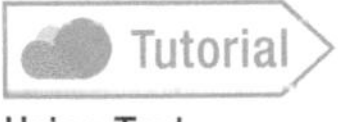
Using Text Functions

Text

Using Text Functions

Text can be formatted or modified using text functions. Insert a text function by typing it or by clicking the Text button in the Function Library group on the Formulas tab and then selecting a function from the drop-down list. For example, use the LOWER and UPPER functions to convert text from uppercase to lowercase and vice versa. Text that has incorrect capitalization can be changed to title case using the PROPER function. New text can be substituted for existing text using the SUBSTITUTE function.

Use text functions to extract the data when only some of the characters in a cell need to be copied. Text can be extracted from the rightmost, leftmost, or middle of a string of characters using the RIGHT, LEFT, or MID function, respectively. These three functions—along with the TRIM function, which removes extra spaces between characters—also can be used on data that has been imported or copied from another source. Table 6.2 provides more information about each text function.

Using the CONCAT Function

The CONCAT function was introduction in Excel 2016 and replaces the CONCATENATE function. The CONCATENATE function is still available for compatibility with earlier version of Excel. Use the CONCAT function to join the content of two or more cells, including text, numbers, or cell references. Additional information, including spaces and characters, can also be added to the combined data. After extracting data, you can use these functions to combine the data in different ways to make unique customer numbers, employee IDs, email addresses, and other useful strings of text. Spaces or characters (text, numbers, or symbols) added directly to the function are enclosed in quotation marks. Numbers do not need quotation marks. The TEXTJOIN function is similar to the CONCAT function in that it joins the contents of two or more cells. With the TEXTJOIN function a constant delimiter, such as a hyphen, is specified and is placed between the contents of each cell.

The formula used in Activity 3b, =TEXTJOIN("-",TRUE,K2,L2,M2), joins the middle three characters of *BldgCde*, a hyphen, the first three letters of the tenant's last name, a hyphen, and the last four digits of the tenant's phone number to create a new TenantID. TRUE instructs Excel to ignore any empty cells. If this parameter is left out of the formula, Excel assumes TRUE. In a TEXTJOIN or a CONCAT formula, cell references are separated by commas and any spaces or characters (text or symbols) added directly to the formula are enclosed in quotation marks.

Table 6.2 Examples of Text Functions

Text Function	Description	Example
=PROPER(text)	Capitalizes first letter of each word	=PROPER("annual budget") returns *Annual Budget* in formula cell OR A3 holds text *annual budget*; =PROPER(a3) entered in C3 causes C3 to display *Annual Budget*
=UPPER(text)	Converts text to uppercase	=UPPER("annual budget") returns *ANNUAL BUDGET* in formula cell OR A3 holds text *annual budget*; =UPPER(a3) entered in C3 causes C3 to display *ANNUAL BUDGET*
=LOWER(text)	Converts text to lowercase	=LOWER("ANNUAL BUDGET") returns *annual budget* in formula cell OR A3 holds text *ANNUAL BUDGET*; =LOWER(a3) entered in C3 causes C3 to display *annual budget*
=SUBSTITUTE(text)	Inserts new text in place of old text	A3 holds text *Annual Budget*; =SUBSTITUTE(a3,"Annual","2021") entered in C3 causes C3 to display *2021 Budget*
=RIGHT(text,num_chars)	Extracts requested number of characters, starting at rightmost character	=RIGHT("2021 Annual Budget",13) returns *Annual Budget* in formula cell OR A3 holds text *2021 Annual Budget*; =RIGHT(a3,13) entered in C3 causes C3 to display *Annual Budget*
=LEFT(text,num_chars)	Extracts requested number of characters, starting at leftmost character	=LEFT("2021 Annual Budget",4) returns *2021* in formula cell OR A3 holds text *2021 Annual Budget*; =LEFT(a3,4) entered in C3 causes C3 to display *2021*

Table 6.2 Examples of Text Functions—*Continued*

Text Function	Description	Example
=MID(text,start-num, num-chars)	Extracts requested number of characters, starting at given position	=MID("2021 Annual Budget",6,13) returns *Annual Budget* in formula cell OR A3 holds text *2021 Annual Budget*; =MID(a3,6,13) entered in C3 causes C3 to display *Annual Budget*
=CONCAT(text1, text2,text3...)	Joins contents of two of more cells plus additional information	=CONCAT("Sara","Jones","@ppi-edu.net") returns *SaraJones@ppi-edu.net* in formula cell OR A3 holds text *Sara*; A4 holds *Jones* =CONCAT(a3,a4,"@ppi-edu.net") entered in C5 causes C5 to display *SaraJones@ppi-edu.net*
=TEXTJOIN(delimeter, ignore_empty,text1,text2, text3...)	Joins contents of two or more cells and places a constant delimiter between each cell content	A3 holds text *115*, B3 holds text *112* and C3 holds text *McC* =TEXTJOIN("-",true,a3,b3,c3) returns *115-112-McC*
=LEN(text)	Returns the number of characters	A3 holds text *Annual Budget* =LEN(a3) entered in C3 causes C3 to display *13*

Activity 3b Extracting and Combining Text Using the RIGHT, LEFT, MID, and TEXTJOIN Functions

Part 2 of 4

1. With **6-PropMgt** open, make the All Tenants worksheet active.
2. Extract data and then combine it to create a TenantID number using the middle three letters or digits of *BldgCde*, followed by a hyphen, the first three letters of the tenant's last name, a hyphen, and the last four digits of the tenant's phone number (for example: *115-McC-3485*). To extract the middle three characters of *BldgCde*, complete the following steps:
   a. Click in cell K1, type BldgCde, and then press the Enter key.
   b. Click the Formulas tab and then click the Text button in the Function Library group.
   c. Click *MID* at the drop-down list.
   d. If necessary, drag the Function Arguments dialog box out of the way so that the first few rows of the worksheet can be seen.
   e. With the insertion point positioned in the *Text* text box, type a2 and then press the Tab key.
   f. Type 2 in the *Start-num* text box and then press the Tab key.
   g. Type 3 in the *Num_chars* text box and then click OK.

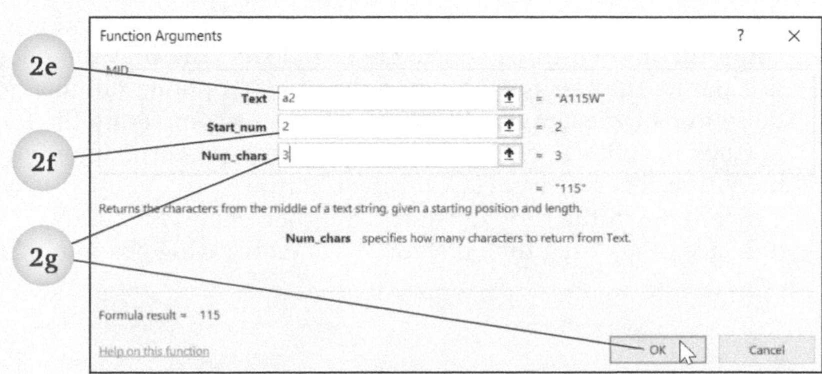

3. To extract the first three letters of the tenant's last name, complete the following steps:
   a. Click in cell L1, type TenantLName, and then press the Enter key.
   b. AutoFit the width of column L.
   c. With cell L2 active, click the Text button.
   d. Click *LEFT* at the drop-down list.
   e. If necessary, drag the Function Arguments dialog box out of the way so that the first few rows of the worksheet can be seen.
   f. With the insertion point positioned in the *Text* text box, type d2 and then press the Tab key.
   g. Type 3 in the *Num_chars* text box and then click OK.

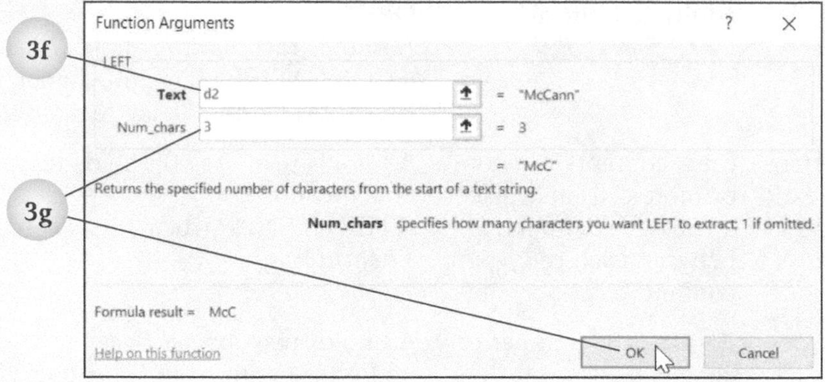

4. To extract the last four numbers of the tenant's phone number, complete the following steps:
   a. Click in cell M1, type Phone, and then press the Enter key.
   b. With cell M2 active, click the Text button.
   c. Click *RIGHT* at the drop-down list.
   d. If necessary, drag the Function Arguments dialog box out of the way so that the first few rows of the worksheet can be seen.
   e. With the insertion point positioned in the *Text* text box, type e2 and then press the Tab key.
   f. Type 4 in the *Num_chars* text box and then click OK.

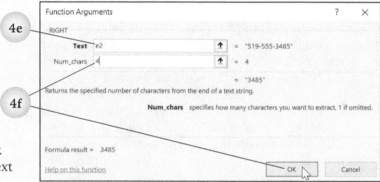

5. Use the TEXTJOIN function to combine the extracted data to create the new TenantID using the middle three characters of *BldgCde*, the first three letters of the tenant's last name, the last four digits of the tenant's phone number, and a hyphen as the delimiter—for example, *115-McC-3485*—by completing the following steps:
   a. Click in cell N1, type TenantID, and then press the Enter key.
   b. With cell N2 active, click the Text button.
   c. Scroll down the drop down-list and then click *TEXTJOIN*.
   d. If necessary, drag the Function Arguments dialog box out of the way.

e. With the insertion point positioned in the *Delimiter* text box, type - (a hyphen character) and then press the Tab key.
f. Type true in the *Ignore_empty* text box and then press the tab key.
g. Type k2 in the *Text1* text box and then press the Tab key.
h. Type l2 in the *Text2* text box and then press the Tab key.
i. Type m2 in the *Text3* text box and then click OK.

6. AutoFit the width of column N.
7. Copy the range K2:N2 to row 33 and then deselect the range.
8. Save **6-PropMgt.**

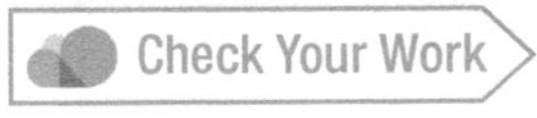

Activity 3c Converting Text Using the UPPER Function

Part 3 of 4

1. With **6-PropMgt** open, place the new TenantID within the table and convert all the letters in the *TenantID* column in a new column to uppercase by completing the following steps:
   a. Click in cell A1, right click, point to the *Insert* option, and then click *Table Columns to the Left* option.

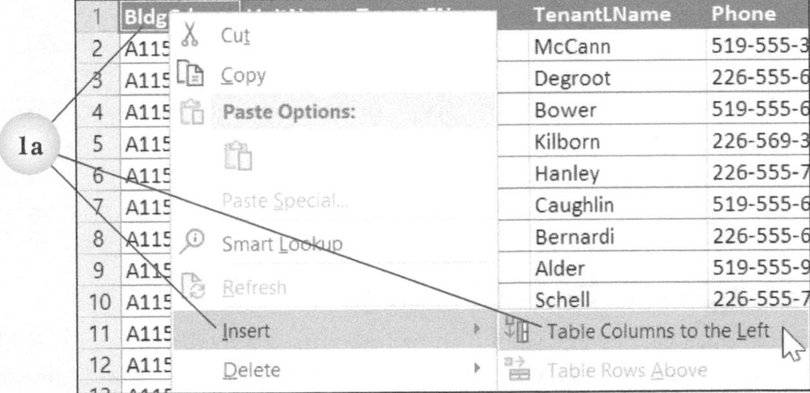

   b. With cell A1 active, type TenantID and then press the Enter key.
   c. With cell A2 active, type =upper(o2) and then press the Enter key. Excel fills the column with the formula.
2. AutoFit the width of columns A through O.
3. Save **6-PropMgt.**

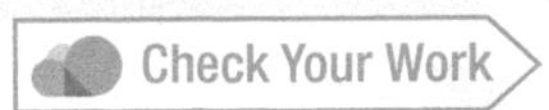

Activity 3d Create Email Addresses and Count the Characters Using the CONCAT, LOWER and LEN Functions

Part 4 of 4

1. With **6-PropMgt** open, create new email addresses for the site managers by completing the following steps:
   a. Make the Site Managers worksheet active.
   b. Click in cell G2, type Email, and then press the Enter key.
   c. Click the Formulas tab and then click the Text button.
   d. Click *CONCAT* at the drop-down list.
   e. If necessary, drag the Function Arguments dialog box out of the way so that the first few rows of the worksheet can be seen.
   f. With the insertion point positioned in the *Text1* text box, type b3 and then press the Tab key.
   g. Type . (a period) in the *Text2* text box and then press the Tab key. Excel will enter quotes around the period.
   h. Type c3 in the *Text3* text box and then press the Tab key.
   i. Type @ppi-edu.net in the *Text4* text box and then click OK.
   j. AutoFit the width of column G.
2. With cell G3 active, click in the Formula bar, click between the equal sign and the function CONCAT, and then type lower(. Press the End key, type), and then press the Enter key. The formula in the range G3:G7 is *=LOWER(CONCAT(B3,".",C3,"@ppi-edu.net"))*.

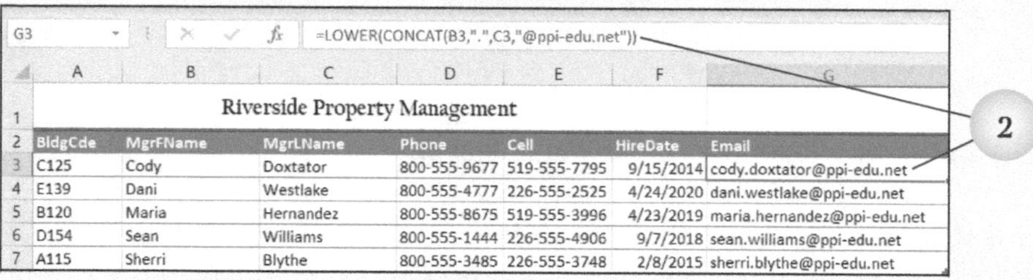

	A	B	C	D	E	F	G
1	Riverside Property Management						
2	BldgCde	MgrFName	MgrLName	Phone	Cell	HireDate	Email
3	C125	Cody	Doxtator	800-555-9677	519-555-7795	9/15/2014	cody.doxtator@ppi-edu.net
4	E139	Dani	Westlake	800-555-4777	226-555-2525	4/24/2020	dani.westlake@ppi-edu.net
5	B120	Maria	Hernandez	800-555-8675	519-555-3996	4/23/2019	maria.hernandez@ppi-edu.net
6	D154	Sean	Williams	800-555-1444	226-555-4906	9/7/2018	sean.williams@ppi-edu.net
7	A115	Sherri	Blythe	800-555-3485	226-555-3748	2/8/2015	sherri.blythe@ppi-edu.net

3. Count the number of characters in the email address by completing the following steps:
   a. Click in cell H2 and type Length and then press the Enter key.
   b. Click the Text button.
   c. Click *LEN* at the drop-down list.
   d. With the insertion point in the *Text* text box, type g3 and then click OK. The formula in the range H3:H4 is *=LEN(G3)*.
4. Change the All Tenants worksheet to Landscape orientation and then print the workbook.
5. Save and then close **6-PropMgt**.

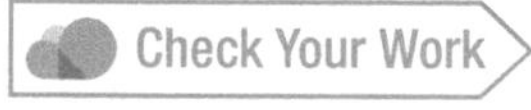

Chapter Summary

- Excel data can be embedded in or linked to a Word document. Embedding inserts a copy of the source data in the Word document and allows the object to be edited using Excel's tools within the Word environment. Linking the object inserts a shortcut in Word to the Excel workbook from which the source data is retrieved.
- To embed copied Excel data in a Word document, open the document, move the insertion point where the copied Excel data should be inserted, and then open the Paste Special dialog box. At the Paste Special dialog box, click *Microsoft Excel Worksheet Object* in the *As* list box and then click OK. To link data, follow the same steps for embedding, but click the *Paste link* radio button.

- Breaking a link involves removing the connection between the source file and destination file. This means that the data will no longer be updated in the destination file when the original data changes.
- To break a link in a Word document, right-click the linked object, point to *Linked Worksheet Object*, and then click *Links* at the shortcut menu. Click the source object for the link to be broken and then click the Break Link button. At the message box that appears, click Yes to confirm that the link is to be broken.
- Copy and paste, copy and embed, or copy and link Excel data into slides in a PowerPoint presentation using the same techniques used to embed cells in or link cells to a Word document.
- In Office 365, the charting tools are fully integrated. A chart copied and pasted from Excel to a PowerPoint presentation or Word document is embedded by default.
- Data in an Excel worksheet can be copied and pasted into an Access table datasheet, query, or form using the Clipboard task pane. Before pasting data into a table datasheet, make sure that the column structures in the two programs match.
- To exchange Excel data with someone who cannot import an Excel worksheet or cannot copy and paste using the Clipboard task pane, save the data as a text file.
- To save a worksheet as a text file, open the Save As dialog box and then change the file type to the correct option. Type a file name for the text file and then click the Save button. Click OK at the message box stating that only the active worksheet will be saved and then click Yes at the next message box to confirm saving the data as a text file.
- Excel provides several text file formats to accommodate differences across operating systems, which configure text files using various end-of-line character codes.
- The Get & Transform Data group on the Data tab contains buttons for importing data from external sources into an Excel worksheet using Power Query technology. To import data, make active the cell in which the imported data is to start and then click the button representing the source application or point to the Get Data button and select the source from a drop-down list.
- Exchanging data between Access and Excel is a seamless process, since the data in an Access datasheet is structured in the same row and column format as the data in an Excel worksheet. The imported data can be appended to an existing worksheet or placed in a new worksheet.
- When data is imported into Excel, the data is imported in a table format a query is created. The Queries & Connections task pane displays with the Queries tab active and the new query selected.
- Text files are often used to exchange data between different programs because the file format is recognized by nearly all applications. In a text file, the data between fields is generally separated with a tab character or a comma.
- If you move or rename a source, Excel will not know where to locate the file and a yellow triangle with an exclamation mark will appear beside the query item at the Queries & Connections task pane.
- Refreshing, modifying, and removing queries helps ensure that the most current data is in a destination file. Removing a connection allows the user to capture data at a specific time.

- Convert text from lowercase to uppercase or from uppercase to lowercase using the UPPER and LOWER text functions.
- Text that has incorrect capitalization can be changed to title case using the PROPER function. New text can be substituted for existing text using the SUBSTITUTE function.
- Extract data from a cell based on its position in a cell using the RIGHT, LEFT, or MID text functions.
- Combine the content of two or more cells using the TEXTJOIN or CONCAT function.
- Count the number of characters in a cell using the LEN function.
- Use the Flash Fill feature to extract, join, and insert text, numbers, dates, and times.

Commands Review

FEATURE	RIBBON TAB, GROUP/OPTION	BUTTON, OPTION	KEYBOARD SHORTCUT
copy	Home, Clipboard		Ctrl + C
embed Excel data in PowerPoint presentation or Word document	Home, Clipboard	, *Paste Special*	
export as a text file	File, *Export*		
Flash Fill	Home, Editing OR Data, Data Tools		Ctrl + E
import Access table	Data, Get & Transform Data		
import from text file	Data, Get & Transform Data		
insert text function (CONCAT, LEFT, LEN, LOWER, MID, PROPER, RIGHT, SUBSTITUTE, TEXTJOIN, UPPER)	Formulas, Function Library		
link Excel data to PowerPoint presentation or Word document	Home, Clipboard	, *Paste Special*	

Microsoft®

Excel®

CHAPTER 7

Automating Repetitive Tasks and Customizing Excel

Performance Objectives

Upon successful completion of Chapter 7, you will be able to:

1. Customize the display options for Excel
2. Minimize the ribbon
3. Customize the ribbon by creating a custom tab and adding buttons
4. Customize the Quick Access Toolbar by adding and removing buttons for frequently used commands
5. Create and apply custom views
6. Record, run, and edit a macro
7. Save a workbook containing macros as a macro-enabled workbook
8. Assign a macro to a shortcut key
9. Insert and configure form controls
10. Create and use templates
11. Customize save options to AutoRecover files
12. View Trust Center settings

Automating and customizing the Excel environment to accommodate preferences can increase efficiency. For example, create a macro if the same task is being frequently repeated to save time and ensure consistency. Add a button for a frequently used command to the Quick Access Toolbar to provide single-click access to it. Other ways to customize Excel include creating a custom template, ribbon tab, or view and modifying display and save options. By completing the activities in this chapter, you will learn how to effectively automate and customize the Excel environment.

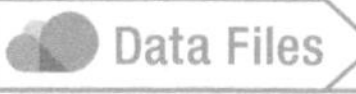

Before beginning chapter work, copy the EL2C7 folder to your storage medium and then make EL2C7 the active folder.

The online course includes additional training and assessment resources.

Activity 1 Customize the Excel Work Environment 7 Parts

You will customize the Excel environment by minimizing the ribbon, changing display options, importing and exporting custom settings for the Quick Access Toolbar and ribbon, creating a custom ribbon tab, adding buttons to the Quick Access Toolbar to make features more accessible, and then creating custom views.

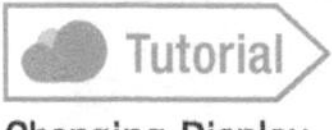

Changing Display Options

Quick Steps

Change Display Options

1. Click File tab.
2. Click *Options*.
3. Click *Advanced* in left pane.
4. Change display options as required.
5. Click OK.

Minimize Ribbon

Press Ctrl + F1.

OR

1. Click Ribbon Display Options button.
2. Click *Show Tabs*.

OR

Click Collapse the Ribbon button.

Changing Display Options

The Excel Options dialog box contains many options for customizing the environment to suit the user's needs. As shown in Figure 7.1, Excel groups options that affect the display by those that are global settings, those that affect the entire workbook, and those that affect only the active worksheet. Changes to workbook and/or worksheet display options are saved with the workbook.

Figure 7.1 Excel Options Dialog Box with the Display Options Shown

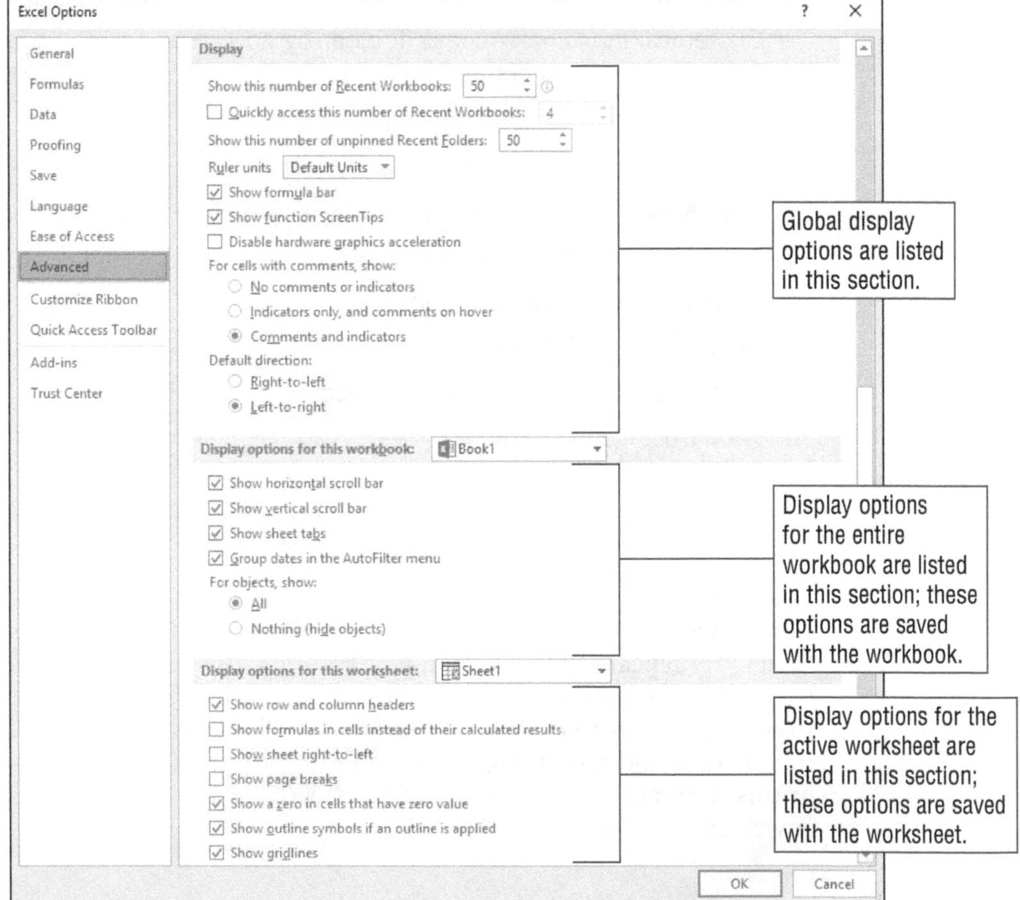

Minimizing the Ribbon

When working with a large worksheet, it may be easier to work with the ribbon minimized, which creates more space within the work area. Figure 7.2 shows the worksheet for Activity 1a with the customized display options and minimized ribbon.

Collapse the Ribbon

One way to minimize the ribbon is to click the Collapse the Ribbon button located at the right edge of the ribbon. With the ribbon minimized, clicking a tab temporarily redisplays it to allow selecting a feature. After the feature has been selected, the ribbon returns to the minimized state. Press Ctrl + F1 or double-click the ribbon to toggle it on or off.

Ribbon Display Options

Another way to minimize the ribbon is to click the Ribbon Display Options button, which remains in the upper right corner of the screen. Options under this button allow for quickly auto-hiding the ribbon (including tabs and commands), showing only the ribbon tabs (commands are hidden), or redisplaying the ribbon tabs and commands.

Activity 1a Changing Display Options and Minimizing the Ribbon

Part 1 of 7

1. Open **NWinterSch.**
2. Save the workbook with the name **7-NWinterSch.**
3. Turn off the display of the Formula bar (since there are no formulas in the workbook), turn off the display of sheet tabs (since there is only one sheet in the workbook), and turn off the display of row and column headers and gridlines by completing the following steps:
   a. Click the File tab.
   b. Click *Options*.
   c. Click *Advanced* in the left pane.
   d. Scroll down the Excel Options dialog box to the *Display* section and then click the *Show formula bar* check box to remove the check mark.
   e. Scroll down to the *Display options for this workbook* section and then click the *Show sheet tabs* check box to remove the check mark.
   f. Scroll down to the *Display options for this worksheet* section and then click the *Show row and column headers* check box to remove the check mark.
   g. Click the *Show gridlines* check box to remove the check mark.
   h. Click OK.
4. Press Ctrl + F1 to hide the ribbon.
5. Compare your screen with the one shown in Figure 7.2.
6. Save and then close **7-NWinterSch.**

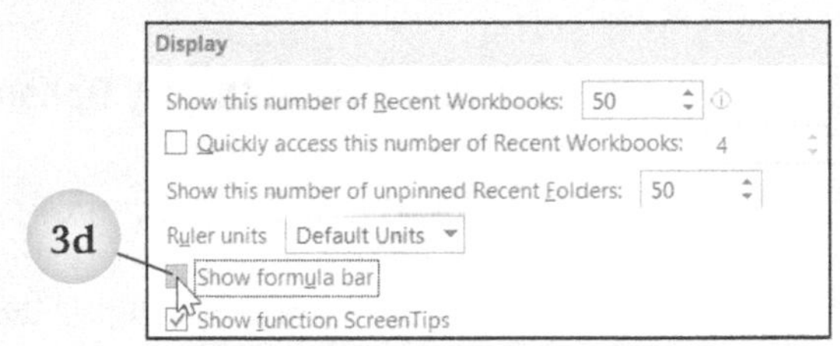

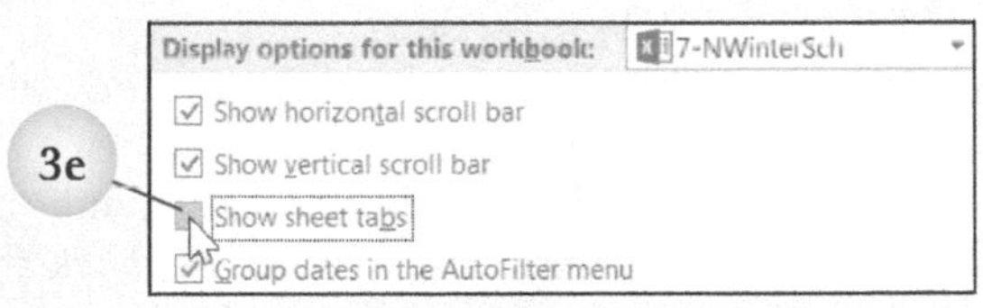

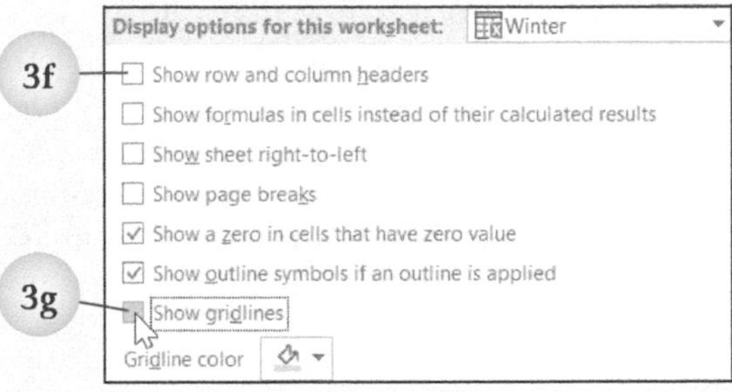

Figure 7.2 Activity 1a Worksheet with Customized Display Options and Minimized Ribbon

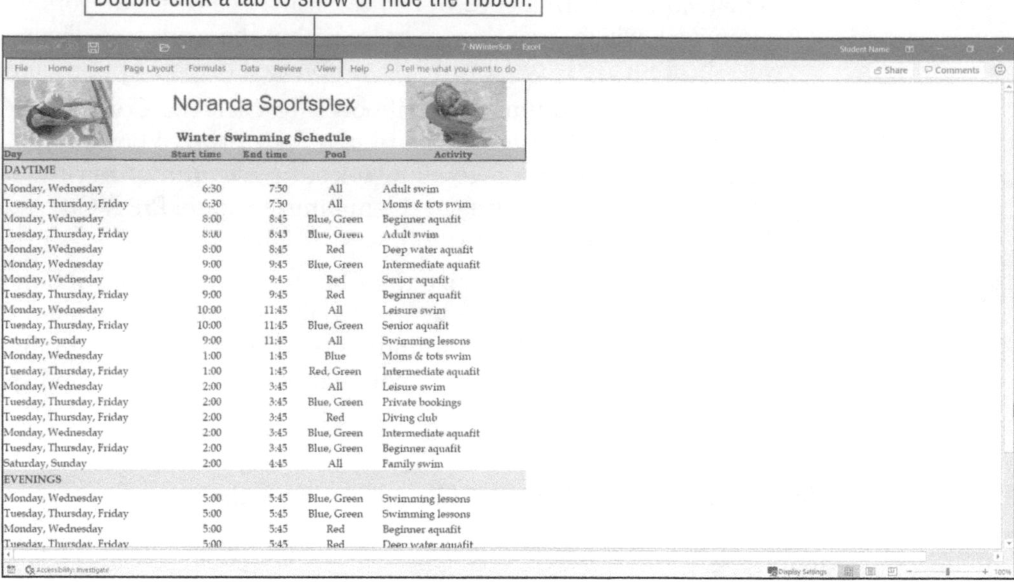

Day	Start time	End time	Pool	Activity
DAYTIME				
Monday, Wednesday	6:30	7:50	All	Adult swim
Tuesday, Thursday, Friday	6:30	7:50	All	Moms & tots swim
Monday, Wednesday	8:00	8:45	Blue, Green	Beginner aquafit
Tuesday, Thursday, Friday	8:00	8:45	Blue, Green	Adult swim
Monday, Wednesday	8:00	8:45	Red	Deep water aquafit
Monday, Wednesday	9:00	9:45	Blue, Green	Intermediate aquafit
Monday, Wednesday	9:00	9:45	Red	Senior aquafit
Tuesday, Thursday, Friday	9:00	9:45	Red	Beginner aquafit
Monday, Wednesday	10:00	11:45	All	Leisure swim
Tuesday, Thursday, Friday	10:00	11:45	Blue, Green	Senior aquafit
Saturday, Sunday	9:00	11:45	All	Swimming lessons
Monday, Wednesday	1:00	1:45	Blue	Moms & tots swim
Tuesday, Thursday, Friday	1:00	1:45	Red, Green	Intermediate aquafit
Monday, Wednesday	2:00	3:45	All	Leisure swim
Tuesday, Thursday, Friday	2:00	3:45	Blue, Green	Private bookings
Tuesday, Thursday, Friday	2:00	3:45	Red	Diving club
Monday, Wednesday	2:00	3:45	Blue, Green	Intermediate aquafit
Tuesday, Thursday, Friday	2:00	3:45	Blue, Green	Beginner aquafit
Saturday, Sunday	2:00	4:45	All	Family swim
EVENINGS				
Monday, Wednesday	5:00	5:45	Blue, Green	Swimming lessons
Tuesday, Thursday, Friday	5:00	5:45	Blue, Green	Swimming lessons
Monday, Wednesday	5:00	5:45	Red	Beginner aquafit
Tuesday, Thursday, Friday	5:00	5:45	Red	Deep water aquafit

Activity 1b **Restoring Default Display Options**

Part 2 of 7

1. Press Ctrl + N to open a new blank workbook.
2. Notice that the workbook and worksheet display options that were changed in Activity 1a are restored to the default options. The Formula bar remains hidden (since this is a global display option) and the ribbon remains minimized (since the display of the ribbon is a toggle on/off option).
3. Open **7-NWinterSch**.
4. Notice that the sheet tabs, row and column headers, and gridlines are hidden (since these display option settings are saved with the workbook).
5. Close **7-NWinterSch** without saving it.
6. With the blank workbook active, click the Ribbon Display Options button next to the Minimize button in the upper right corner of the screen and then click *Show Tabs and Commands* at the drop-down list.
7. Redisplay the Formula bar by completing the following steps:
   a. Click the File tab and then click *Options*.
   b. Click *Advanced* in the left pane.
   c. Scroll down the Excel Options dialog box to the *Display* section, click the *Show formula bar* check box to insert a check mark, and then click OK.
8. Close the workbook without saving it.

Customizing Ribbons and the Quick Access Toolbar

When working with Excel, a user may prefer to access frequently used features from the Quick Access Toolbar or in a new group within an existing or new ribbon. Activities 1d and 1e demonstrate how to customize both the ribbon and the Quick Access Toolbar.

Exporting and Importing Customizations

Exporting and Importing Customizations

The ribbon or the Quick Access Toolbar may already have been customized on the computers in your institution's computer lab. To be able to restore these customizations after making changes in the upcoming activities, Activity 1c will demonstrate how to save (export) them and Activity 1f will demonstrate how to reinstall (import) them.

To save the current ribbon and Quick Access Toolbar settings, click the File tab and then click *Options*. At the Excel Options dialog box, click *Customize Ribbon* in the left pane. The dialog box will display as shown in Figure 7.3. Click the Import/Export button in the lower right corner of the Excel Options dialog box. Click *Export all customizations* to save the file with the custom settings. Use this file to reinstall the saved settings in Activity 2f or to install customized settings on a different computer. Click the Import/Export button and then click *Import customization file*. Locate the file and reinstall the customized settings.

Activity 1c Exporting Customizations — Part 3 of 7

1. Press Ctrl + N to open a new blank workbook.
2. Save the current ribbon and Quick Access Toolbar settings to the desktop by completing the following steps:
   a. Click the File tab and then click *Options*.
   b. Click *Customize Ribbon* in the left pane of the Excel Options dialog box.
   c. Click the Import/Export button at the bottom right of the Excel Options dialog box.
   d. Click *Export all customizations* at the drop-down list.
   e. Click *Desktop* in the *This PC* list in the left panel of the File Save dialog box.
   f. Change the file name to **7-ExcelCustomizations** and then click the Save button. The file is saved as an Exported Office UI file with the name **7-ExcelCustomizations**.
   g. Click OK.
   h. Close the workbook. Click Don't Save if prompted to save changes.

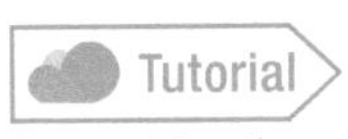

Customizing the Ribbon

Hint To save the mouse clicks used when switching tabs and choosing options from drop-down lists, create a custom tab with buttons used on a regular basis.

Customizing the Ribbon

To customize the ribbon by adding a new tab, group, or button, click the File tab and then click *Options*. At the Excel Options dialog box, click *Customize Ribbon* in the left pane. The dialog box will display as shown in Figure 7.3. The dialog box can also be accessed by right-clicking anywhere in the ribbon or Quick Access Toolbar and then choosing the *Customizing the Ribbon* option.

The commands shown in the left list box are dependent on the current option in the *Choose commands from* option box. Click the *Choose commands from* option box arrow (displays *Popular Commands*) to select from a variety of options, such as *Commands Not in the Ribbon* and *All Commands*. The tabs shown in the right list box are dependent on the current option in the *Customize the Ribbon* option box. Click the *Customize the Ribbon* option box arrow (displays *Main Tabs*) to select *All Tabs*, *Main Tabs*, or *Tool Tabs*.

Figure 7.3 Excel Options Dialog Box with *Customize Ribbon* Selected

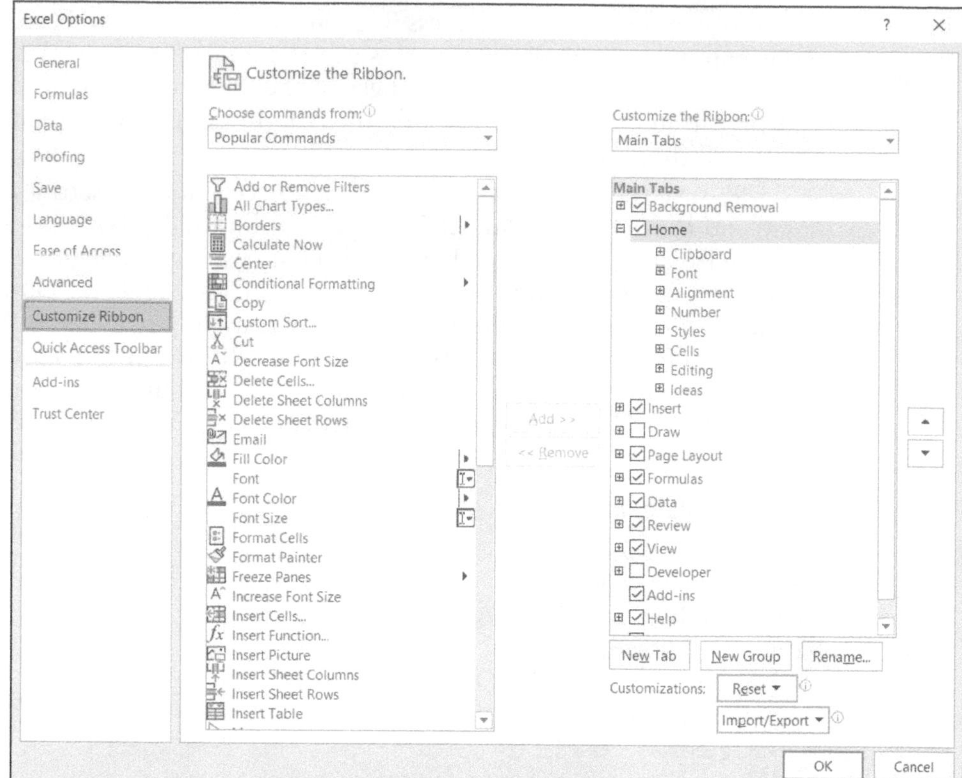

Create a new group in an existing tab and add buttons within the new group or create a new tab, create a new group within the tab, and then add buttons to the new group.

Creating a New Tab To create a new tab, click any tab in the list box and then click the New Tab button. The newly created tab will appear with the name *New Tab (Custom)* as shown in Figure 7.4. It will also include a new group, called *New Group (Custom)*. Rename the tab and group by clicking the Rename button and entering a new name (see below). Move the tab up or down in order by clicking on it and then clicking the Move Up or Move Down arrow buttons at the right side of the dialog box.

Adding Buttons to a Group Click the group name within the tab, click the desired command in the list box at the left, and then click the Add button that displays between the two list boxes. Remove commands in a similar manner: Click the command to be removed from the tab group and then click the Remove button between the two list boxes.

Renaming a Tab, Group, or Command Click the tab name in the *Main Tabs* list box and then click the Rename button below the *Main Tabs* list box. At the Rename dialog box, type the name for the tab and then press the Enter key or click OK. Display the Rename dialog box by right-clicking the tab name and then clicking *Rename* at the shortcut menu.

Complete similar steps to rename a group or command. The Rename dialog box for a group or command name contains the *Symbol* list box and the *Display name* text box. Type the new name for the group in the *Display name* text box and then press the Enter key or click OK. Using symbols helps to identify new buttons.

Quick Steps

Create New Tab and Group
1. Click File tab.
2. Click *Options*.
3. Click *Customize Ribbon* in left pane.
4. Click tab name to precede new tab.
5. Click New Tab button.

Add New Group to Existing Tab
1. Click File tab.
2. Click *Options*.
3. Click *Customize Ribbon* in left pane.
4. Click tab name on which to add new group.
5. Click New Group button.

Add Button to Group
1. Click File tab.
2. Click *Options*.
3. Click *Customize Ribbon* in left pane.
4. Click group name in which to insert new button.
5. Select *All Commands* in the drop-down list.
6. Click command.
7. Click Add button.

Rename Tab or Group
1. Click File tab.
2. Click *Options*.
3. Click *Customize Ribbon* in left pane.
4. Click tab or group to be renamed.
5. Click Rename button.
6. Type new name.
7. Click OK.

Figure 7.4 New Tab and Group Created in the Customize the Ribbon Pane at the Excel Options Dialog Box

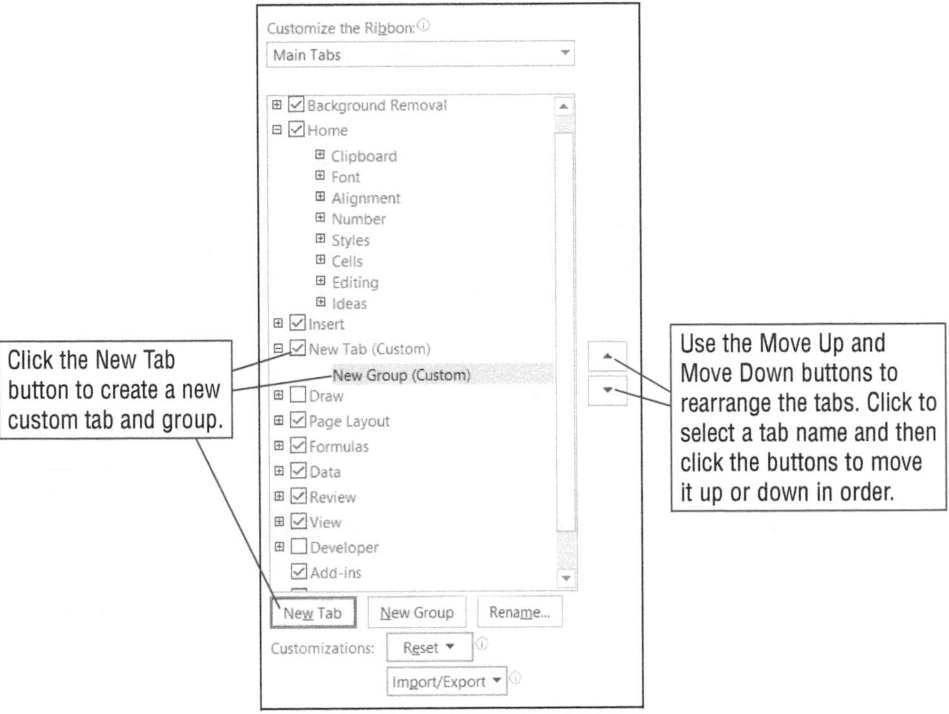

Activity 1d Customizing the Ribbon

Part 4 of 7

1. Open **NationalJE**.
2. Save the workbook with the name **7-NationalJE.**
3. Customize the ribbon by adding a new tab and a new group within the tab by completing the following steps. ***Note: The ribbon will be reset to its original settings in Activity 1f.***
   a. Click the File tab and then click *Options*.
   b. Click *Customize Ribbon* in the left pane of the Excel Options dialog box.
   c. Click *Insert* in the *Main Tabs* list box at the right of the dialog box.
   d. Click the New Tab button below the list box. (This inserts a new tab below the Insert tab and a new group below the new tab.)

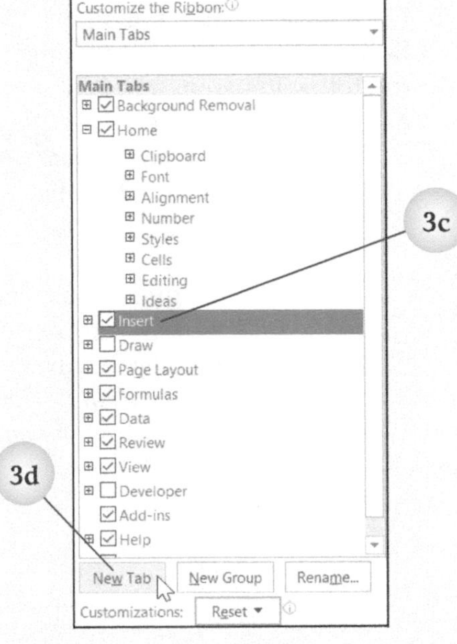

4. Rename the tab and the group by completing the following steps:
   a. Click to select *New Tab (Custom)* in the *Main Tabs* list box.
   b. Click the Rename button below the list box.
   c. At the Rename dialog box, type your first and last names and then click OK.
   d. Click to select the *New Group (Custom)* group name below the new tab.
   e. Click the Rename button.
   f. At the Rename dialog box, type Borders in the *Display name* text box and then click OK. (The Rename dialog box for a group or button displays symbols in addition to the *Display name* text box. You will apply a symbol to a button in a later step.)

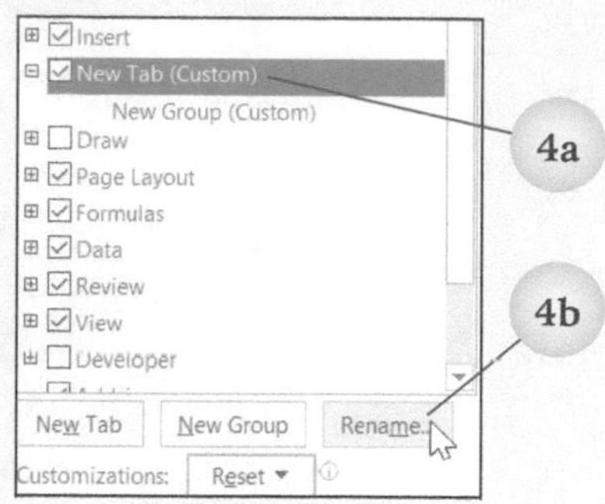

5. Add buttons to the *Borders (Custom)* group by completing the following steps:
   a. With *Borders (Custom)* selected, click the *Choose commands from* option box arrow (displays *Popular Commands*) and then click *All Commands* at the drop-down list.
   b. Scroll down the *All Commands* list box (the commands display alphabetically), click *Thick Bottom Border*, and then click the Add button between the two list boxes. (This inserts the command below the *Borders (Custom)* group name.)
   c. With the *Thick Outside Borders* option selected, click the Add button.
   d. Scroll down the *All Commands* list box, click *Top and Double Bottom Border*, and then click the Add button.

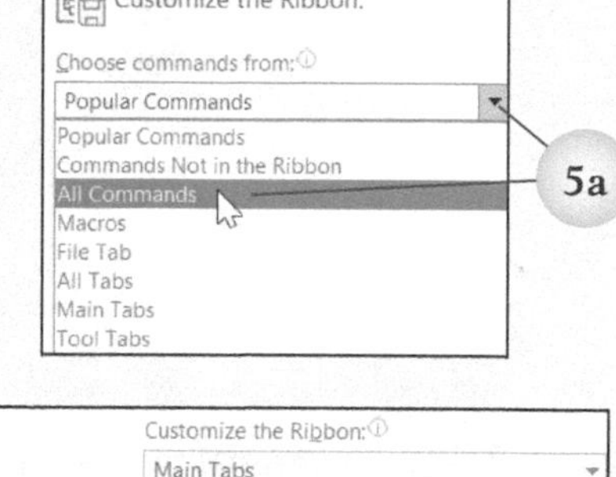

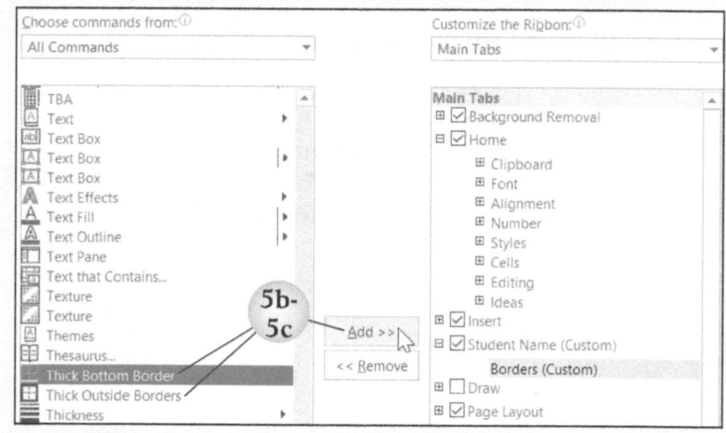

6. Rename the Thick Outside Borders button by completing the following steps:
   a. Right-click *Thick Outside Borders* below *Thick Bottom Border* in the *Main Tabs* list box and then click *Rename* at the shortcut menu.
   b. At the Rename dialog box, click the white square with a black outline symbol in the *Symbol* list box (seventh row, second column) and then click OK. ***Note: The position of the symbol may vary on your computer.***

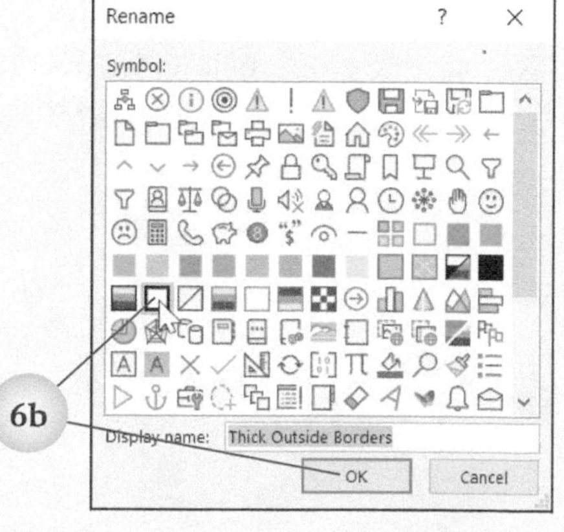

7. Click OK to close the Excel Options dialog box.
8. Use buttons on the custom tab to format the worksheet by completing the following steps:
   a. Select the range A1:A3, click the custom tab labeled with your name, and then click the Thick Outside Borders button in the Borders group.

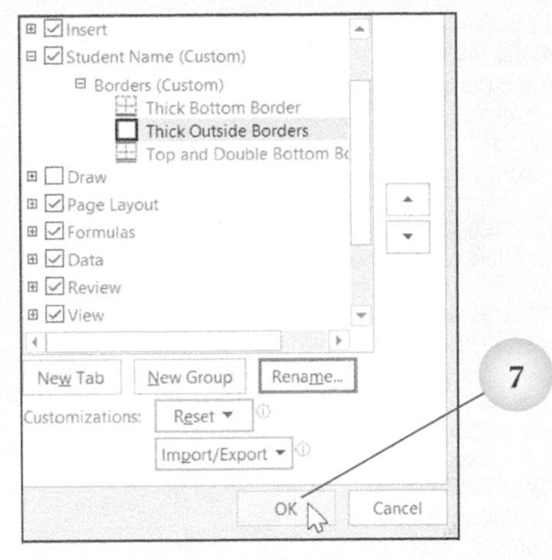

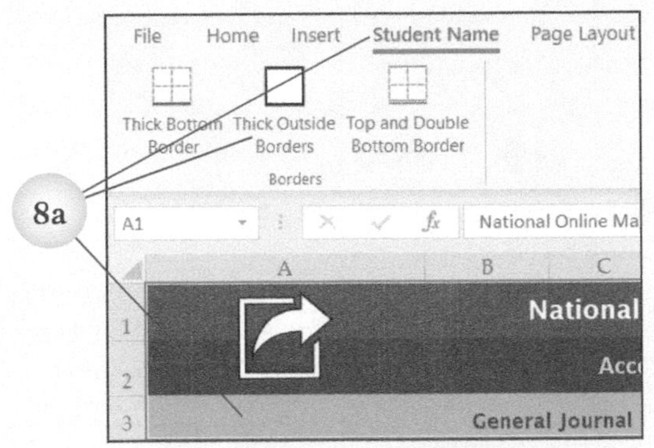

   b. Select the range B6:H6 and then click the Thick Bottom Border button in the Borders group.
   c. Make cell D18 the active cell and then click the Top and Double Bottom Border button in the Borders group.
9. Save **7-NationalJE.**
10. In a new Excel workbook, insert a screenshot of the worksheet showing the custom tab by using either the Screenshot feature (Insert tab, Screenshot button in Illustrations group) or the Windows key + Shift + S with Paste. Type your name below the screenshot.
11. Save the workbook with the name **7-NationalScreenshot.**
12. Print the first page of **7-NationalScreenshot** and then close the workbook.
13. Print and then close **7-NationalJE.**

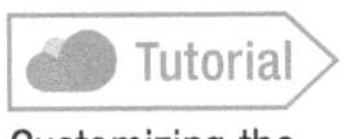

Customizing the Quick Access Toolbar

Customize Quick Access Toolbar

Customizing the Quick Access Toolbar

Click the Customize Quick Access Toolbar button at the right side of the Quick Access Toolbar to open the Customize Quick Access Toolbar drop-down list, as shown in Figure 7.5. Click *More Commands* at the drop-down list to open the Excel Options dialog box with *Quick Access Toolbar* selected in the left pane, as shown in Figure 7.6. Change the list of commands shown in the left list box by clicking the *Choose commands from* option box arrow and then clicking the appropriate category. Scroll down the list box to locate the command and then double-click the command name to add it to the Quick Access Toolbar.

A few of Excel's less popular features are available only by adding buttons to the Quick Access Toolbar. If a feature is not available in any tab on the ribbon, search for it in the *All Commands* list box.

Delete a button from the Quick Access Toolbar by clicking the Customize Quick Access Toolbar button and then clicking the command at the drop-down list. If the command is not in the drop-down list, click the *More Commands* option. At the Excel Options dialog box, double-click the command in the right list box.

Quick Steps

Add Button to Quick Access Toolbar

1. Click Customize Quick Access Toolbar button.
2. Click button.

OR

1. Click Customize Quick Access Toolbar button.
2. Click *More Commands.*
3. Click *Choose commands from* option box arrow.
4. Click category.
5. Double-click command in commands list box.
6. Click OK.

Remove Button from Quick Access Toolbar

1. Click Customize Quick Access Toolbar button.
2. Click command.

OR

1. Click Customize Quick Access Toolbar button.
2. Click *More Commands.*
3. Click command in right list box.
4. Click Remove button.
5. Click OK.

Figure 7.5 Customize Quick Access Toolbar Drop-Down List

Figure 7.6 Excel Options Dialog Box with *Quick Access Toolbar* Selected

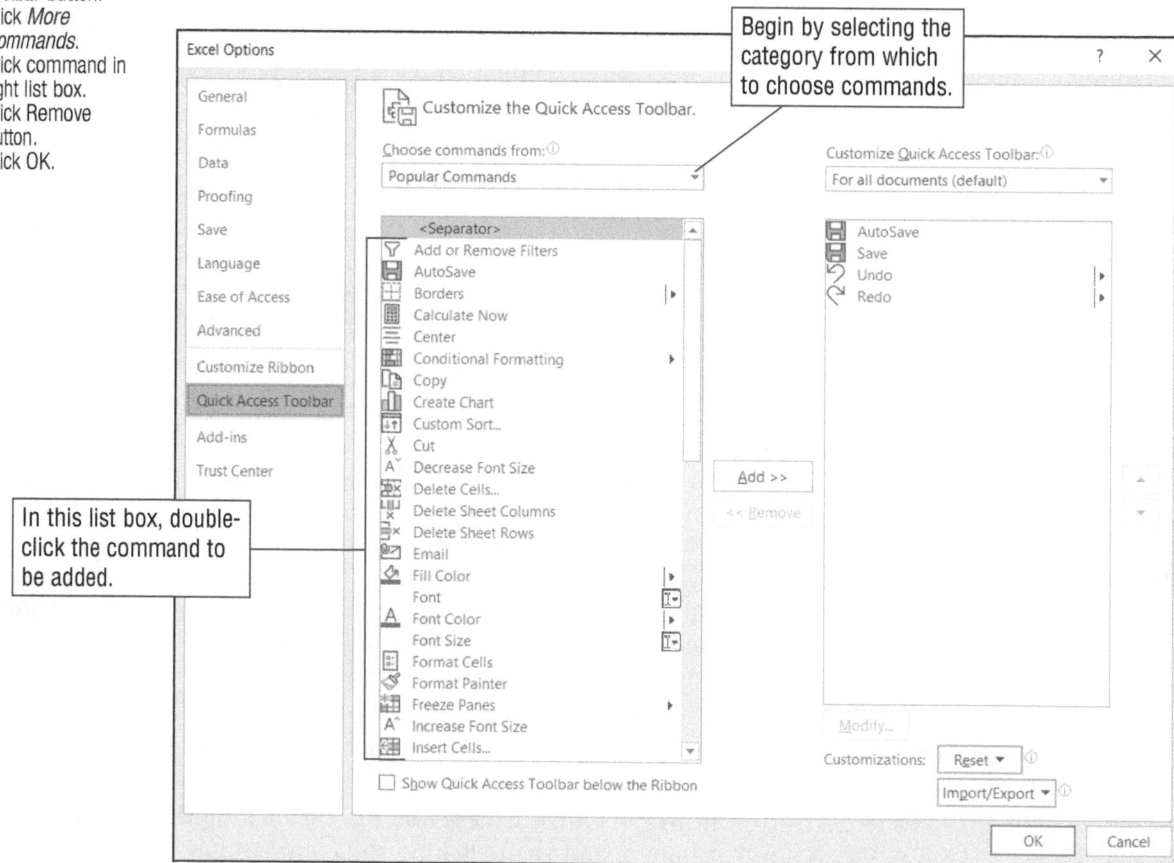

Activity 1e Adding Commands to the Quick Access Toolbar

Part 5 of 7

1. Press Ctrl + N to open a new blank workbook and then add the Print Preview and Print and Sort commands to the Quick Access Toolbar by completing the following steps. ***Note: You will reset the Quick Access Toolbar to the original settings in Activity 1f.***
   a. Click the Customize Quick Access Toolbar button at the right side of the Quick Access Toolbar.
   b. Click *Print Preview and Print* at the drop-down list. The Print Preview and Print button is added to the end of the Quick Access Toolbar. ***Note: Skip to Step 1d if the Print Preview and Print button already appears on your Quick Access Toolbar.***
   c. Click the Customize Quick Access Toolbar button.
   d. Click *More Commands* at the drop-down list.
   e. At the Excel Options dialog box with *Quick Access Toolbar* selected in the left pane, click the *Choose commands from* option box arrow and then click *All Commands*.

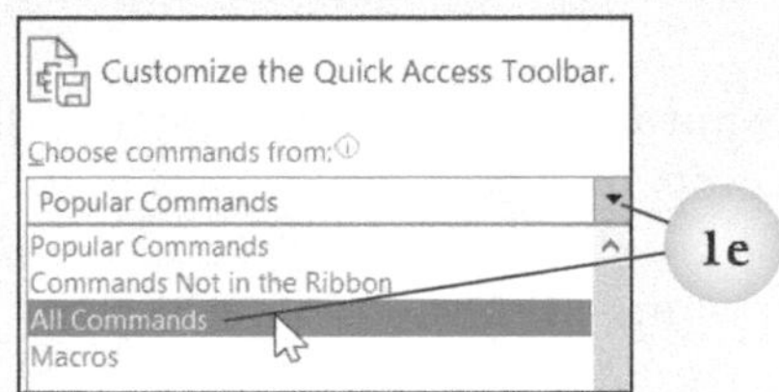

   f. Scroll down the *All Commands* list box and then double-click the second *Sort* option, which displays the ScreenTip *Data Tab | Sort & Filter | Sort...(SortDialog)*. ***Note: The commands are organized in alphabetical order; you will need to scroll far down the list to find this option.***

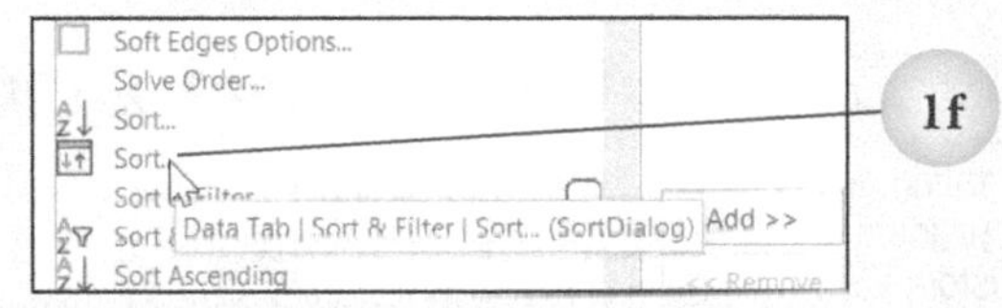

   g. Click OK. The Sort button is added to the end of the Quick Access Toolbar.
2. Type your name in cell A1, press the Enter key, and then click the Print Preview and Print button on the Quick Access Toolbar to display the Print backstage area.
3. Press Esc to close the Print backstage area.
4. Click the Sort button on the Quick Access Toolbar to open the Sort dialog box.
5. Click the Cancel button at the Sort dialog box.
6. Close the workbook. Click the Don't Save button when prompted to save changes.

Resetting the Ribbons and the Quick Access Toolbar

Restore the ribbons and Quick Access Toolbar to the original settings that came with Excel 365 by clicking the Reset button below the *Main Tabs* list box in the Excel Options dialog box with *Customize Ribbon* selected. Clicking the Reset button displays two options: *Reset only selected Ribbon tab* and *Reset all customizations*. Click *Reset all customizations* to restore the ribbons and Quick Access Toolbar to their original settings and then click Yes at the message box that displays the question *Delete all Ribbon and Quick Access Toolbar customizations for this program?* To remove a tab that was created previously, right-click the tab and then click *Customize the Ribbon*. Right-click the tab in the *Main Tabs* list box and then click *Remove*.

To restore the ribbons and Quick Access Toolbar to your institution's original settings, import the settings exported in Activity 1c. Click the Import/Export button in the lower right corner of the Excel Options dialog box and then click *Import customization file*. Locate the file and reinstall the customized settings.

Activity 1f Importing Ribbon and Quick Access Toolbar Customizations — Part 6 of 7

1. Import the ribbon and Quick Access Toolbar customizations you saved in Activity 1c to reset your institution's original settings by completing the following steps:
   a. Press Ctrl + N to open a new blank workbook.
   b. Click the File tab and then click *Options*.
   c. Click *Customize Ribbon* in the left pane of the Excel Options dialog box.
   d. Click the Import/Export button at the bottom right of the Excel Options dialog box.
   e. Click *Import customization file* at the drop-down list.
   f. Click *Desktop* in the *This PC* list in the left panel of the File Open dialog box.
   g. Click **7-ExcelCustomizations.**
   h. Click Open.
   i. Click Yes at the message asking if you want to replace all the existing ribbon and Quick Access Toolbar customizations for this program.
   j. Click OK.
2. Close the workbook. Click Don't Save if prompted to save changes.

Creating and Applying a Custom View

Quick Steps

Create Custom View

1. Change display and print settings as desired.
2. Click View tab.
3. Click Custom Views.
4. Click Add button.
5. Type name for view.
6. Choose *Include in view* options.
7. Click OK.

Custom Views

Quick Steps

Apply Custom View

1. Click View tab.
2. Click Custom Views button.
3. Click view name.
4. Click Show button.

Hint A custom view cannot be used in a worksheet with a table.

Creating and Applying a Custom View

A custom view saves display and print settings for the active worksheet. These settings can involve column widths, row heights, hidden rows and/or columns, filter settings, cell selections, windows settings, page layout options, and print areas. Create multiple custom views for the same worksheet and access stored views using the Custom Views dialog box. In Activity 1g, three custom views are created that store display settings, hidden rows, and a row height for a swimming schedule. Switch between views to show different portions of the worksheet, such as only the daytime swimming activities.

Begin creating a custom view by applying the required settings to the active worksheet, clicking the cell to be active, and displaying the rows and columns to be shown on the screen. When finished, click the View tab, click the Custom Views button in the Workbook Views group, click the Add button, type a name for the custom view, and then click OK.

Change a worksheet to display the settings for a custom view by opening the Custom Views dialog box, selecting the view name in the *Views* list box, and then clicking the Show button. Another method for displaying the settings is to double-click the view name. If a different worksheet is active, Excel will switch to the worksheet to which the view applies. A custom view can be applied only to the worksheet in which it was created.

If a custom view is no longer required, delete it by opening the Custom Views dialog box, selecting the custom view name in the *Views* list box, and then clicking the Delete button.

Activity 1g Creating and Applying Custom Views

Part 7 of 7

1. Open **7-NWinterSch**.
2. Save the workbook with the name **7-NWinterSch-CV** and then redisplay the row and column headers in the worksheet. Refer to Activity 1b for assistance with this step.
3. Create a custom view with display settings for all the swimming sessions by completing the following steps:
   a. Select rows 4 through 37, click the Format button in the Cells group on the Home tab, click *Row Height* at the drop-down list, type 20 in the *Row height* text box at the Row Height dialog box, and then click OK.
   b. Press Ctrl + Home.
   c. Click the View tab.
   d. Click the Custom Views button in the Workbook Views group.
   e. Click the Add button at the Custom Views dialog box.
   f. With the insertion point positioned in the *Name* text box at the Add View dialog box, type AllSessions.
   g. Make sure that the *Print settings* and *Hidden rows, columns and filter settings* check boxes contain check marks and then click OK.

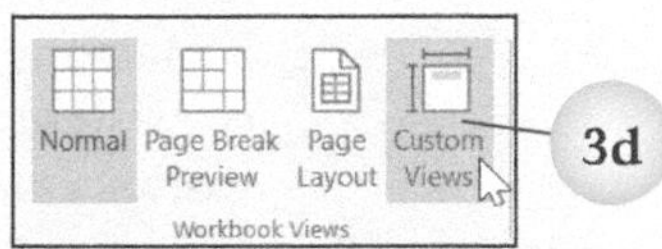

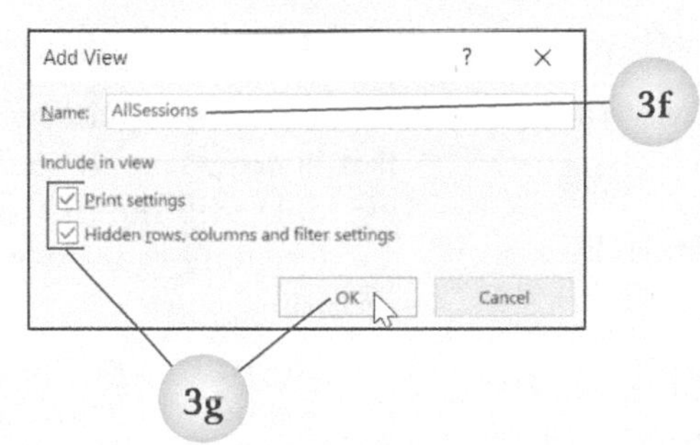

4. Create a second custom view to display the daytime swimming activities and hide the evening activities by completing the following steps:
   a. Select rows 24 through 37 and then press Ctrl + 9 to hide the rows.
   b. Press Ctrl + Home.
   c. Click the Custom Views button.
   d. At the Custom Views dialog box, click the Add button.
   e. At the Add View dialog box, type DaytimeSessions in the *Name* text box.
   f. Make sure that the *Print settings* and *Hidden rows, columns and filter settings* check boxes contain check marks and then click OK.

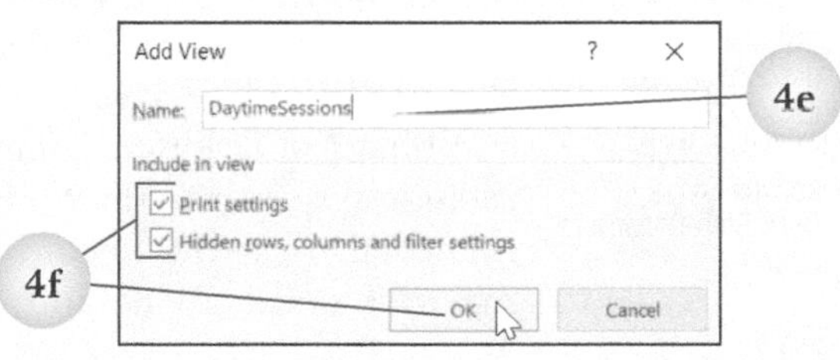

5. Click the Custom Views button in the Workbook Views group.
6. With *AllSessions* selected in the *Views* list box, click the Show button to apply the custom view.

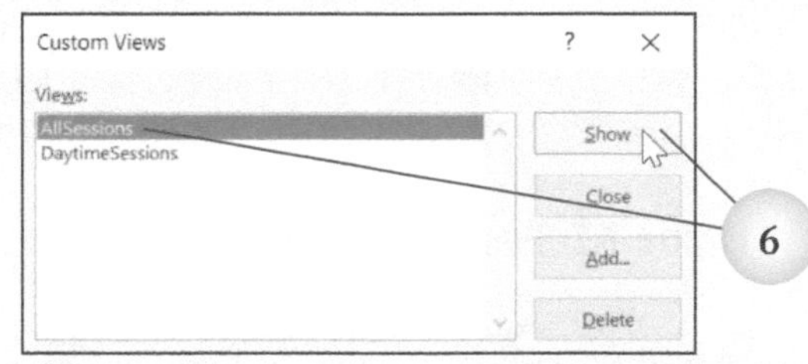

7. Create a third custom view to show only the evening swimming sessions by completing the following steps:
   a. Select rows 4 through 23 and hide the rows by completing a step similar to Step 4a.
   b. Create a custom view named *EveningSessions* by completing steps similar to Steps 4b–4f.
8. Click the Custom Views button and then double-click *DaytimeSessions* in the *Views* list box at the Custom Views dialog box.
9. Show the *EveningSessions* custom view.
10. Show the *AllSessions* custom view.
11. Save and then close **7-NWinterSch-CV**.

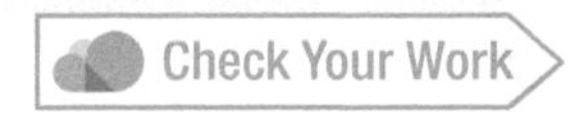

Activity 2 Create Macros in a New Workbook — 4 Parts

You will create, run, edit, and delete macros to automate tasks; assign a macro to a shortcut key; and then store frequently used macros in a macro workbook.

Automating Tasks Using Macros

A macro is a series of instructions stored in sequence that can be recalled and carried out whenever the need arises. Consider creating a macro to perform the same task repeatedly without variation. Saving the instructions for a task in a macro not only saves time, but it also ensures that the steps are performed consistently every time. This can prevent errors in data entry, formatting, or other worksheet tasks.

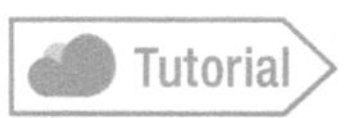

Creating a Macro

Quick Steps

Create Macro
1. Click View tab.
2. Click Macros button arrow.
3. Click *Record Macro.*
4. Type macro name.
5. Click in *Description* text box and type description text.
6. Click OK.
7. Perform required actions.
8. Click Stop Recording button.

Macros

Creating a Macro

Before recording a new macro, take a few moments to plan the steps. Also consider if it is necessary to specify which cell must be active when the macro is run. For example, will the first step in the macro involve making a specific cell active? If so, designate the active cell using a shortcut key or Go To command during the recording.

To create a macro, begin by turning on the macro recorder by clicking the Macros button arrow in the macros group on the View tab and then clicking *Record Macro* at the drop-down list. This opens the Record Macro dialog box, as shown in Figure 7.7. Identify the macro by assigning a unique name to the steps that will be saved. A macro name must begin with a letter and can be a combination of letters, numbers, and underscore characters. A macro name cannot include spaces; use the underscore character to separate the words in a macro name. Also use the Record Macro dialog box to choose the location in which the macro is saved. By default, Excel saves the macro within the current workbook.

A macro can be assigned to a shortcut key combination. Doing so allows the user to run the macro more quickly by pressing the Ctrl key plus the chosen lowercase or uppercase letter. Enter a description of the purpose of a macro to provide information to other users who might use or edit it. In a macro workbook

Figure 7.7 Record Macro Dialog Box

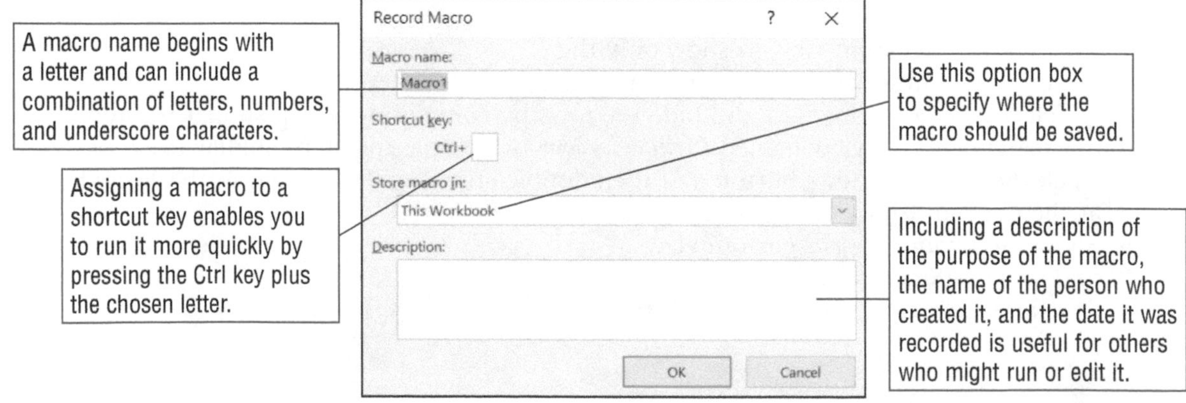

Hint When a macro is being recorded, the mouse clicks for select tabs within the ribbon are not saved.

Stop Recording

that will be shared, also consider entering the creator's name and the creation date into the description box for reference purposes. Click OK when finished identifying the macro and the recorder will begin saving the text and/or steps that are performed. Do not be concerned with making typing mistakes or canceling a dialog box while recording a macro. Correct mistakes as they happen, since only the result is saved. After completing the tasks to be saved, click the Stop Recording button on the Status bar to end the recording.

Saving Workbooks Containing Macros

Quick Steps

Save Macro-Enabled Workbook

1. Click File tab.
2. Click *Save As*.
3. Click *Browse*.
4. Navigate to appropriate folder.
5. Type file name in *File name* text box.
6. Click *Save as type* list arrow.
7. Click *Excel Macro-Enabled Workbook*.
8. Click Save.

When a macro is created in Excel, the commands are written and saved in a language called Microsoft Visual Basic for Applications (VBA). A workbook that contains a macro should be saved using the macro-enabled file format (.xlsm). The default XML-based file format (.xlsx) cannot store the macro code. The macro recorder used when creating a macro converts the actions to VBA statements behind the scenes. View and edit the VBA code or create macros from scratch by using the VBA Editor in Microsoft Visual Basic for Applications, which can be opened through the Macros dialog box. Activity 2d looks at the VBA statements created for the PrintInv macro and edits an instruction.

To save a new or existing workbook as a macro-enabled workbook, perform one of the following actions:

- *New workbook*. Click the Save button on the Quick Access Toolbar or click the File tab and then click the *Save As* option. At the Save As backstage area, click the *Browse* option to display the Save As dialog box and then navigate to the appropriate folder. Type the file name and then change the *Save as type* option to *Excel Macro-Enabled Workbook*. Click the Save button.
- *Existing workbook*. Click the File tab and then click the *Save As* option. At the Save As backstage area, click the *Browse* option to display the Save As dialog box and then navigate to the appropriate folder. Type the file name and then change the *Save as type* option to *Excel Macro-Enabled Workbook*. Click the Save button.

Activity 2a **Creating a Macro and Saving a Workbook as a Macro-Enabled Workbook** Part 1 of 4

1. You work in the Accounting Department at a large company. The company has a documentation standard for all Excel workbooks that requires each worksheet to show the department name, author's name, creation date, and revision history. To standardize the documentation, you decide to create a macro that will insert row labels for this data. Begin by opening a new blank workbook.
2. Create the documentation macro by completing the following steps:
   a. Make cell C4 the active cell and then click the View tab. (Make a cell other than A1 active so you can move the active cell to the top left cell in the worksheet during the macro.)
   b. Click the Macros button arrow in the Macros group.
   c. Click *Record Macro* at the drop-down list.

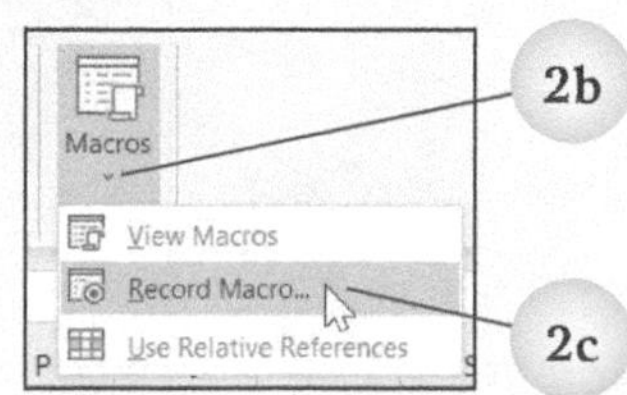

d. At the Record Macro dialog box with the insertion point positioned in the *Macro name* text box, type AcctgDocumentation.

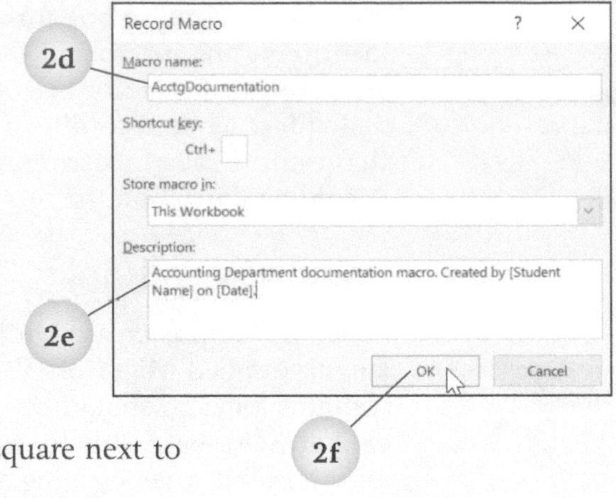

e. Click in the *Description* text box and then type Accounting Department documentation macro. Created by [Student Name] on [Date]. Substitute your name for *[Student Name]* and the current date for *[Date]*.

f. Click OK. The macro recorder is now turned on, as indicated by the appearance of the Stop Recording button in the Status bar (which displays as a gray square next to *Ready*).

g. Press Ctrl + Home to move the active cell to cell A1. Including this command in the macro ensures that the documentation will begin at cell A1 in every workbook.

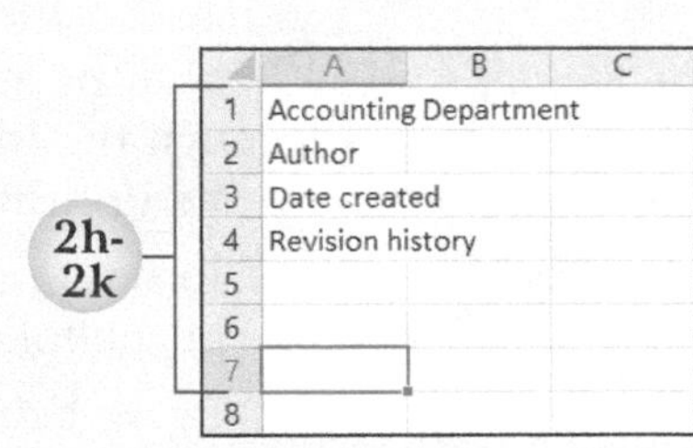

h. Type Accounting Department and then press the Enter key.

i. With cell A2 active, type Author and then press the Enter key.

j. With cell A3 active, type Date created and then press the Enter key.

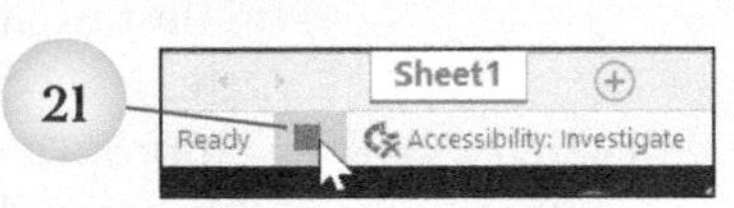

k. With cell A4 active, type Revision history and then press the Enter key three times to leave two blank rows before the start of the worksheet.

l. Click the Stop Recording button at the left side of the Status bar, next to *Ready.*

3. Save the workbook as a macro-enabled workbook by completing the following steps:
   a. Click the Save button on the Quick Access Toolbar.
   b. At the Save As backstage area, click the *Browse* option.
   c. At the Save As dialog box, navigate to the EL2C7 folder in the Navigation pane and then double-click the *EL2C7* folder in the Content pane.
   d. Click in the *File name* text box and then type 7-Macros.
   e. Click the *Save as type* option box, scroll up or down the pop-up list, and then click *Excel Macro-Enabled Workbook.*
   f. Click the Save button.

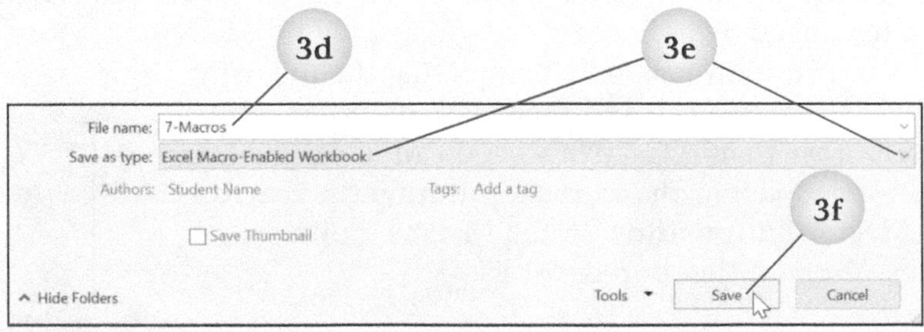

Running a Macro

Quick Steps

Run Macro

1. Click View tab.
2. Click Macros button.
3. Double-click macro name.

Running a Macro

Running a macro is sometimes referred to as *playing a macro*. Since a macro is a series of recorded tasks, running a macro involves instructing Excel to *play back* the recorded tasks. Think of a macro as a video. When the video is played, the same thing happens every time.

To run (play) a macro, view the list of macros by clicking the Macros button in the Macros group on the View tab. This opens the Macro dialog box, shown in Figure 7.8. Click the name of the macro to run and then click the Run button or double-click the name of the macro in the *Macro name* list box.

Figure 7.8 Macro Dialog Box

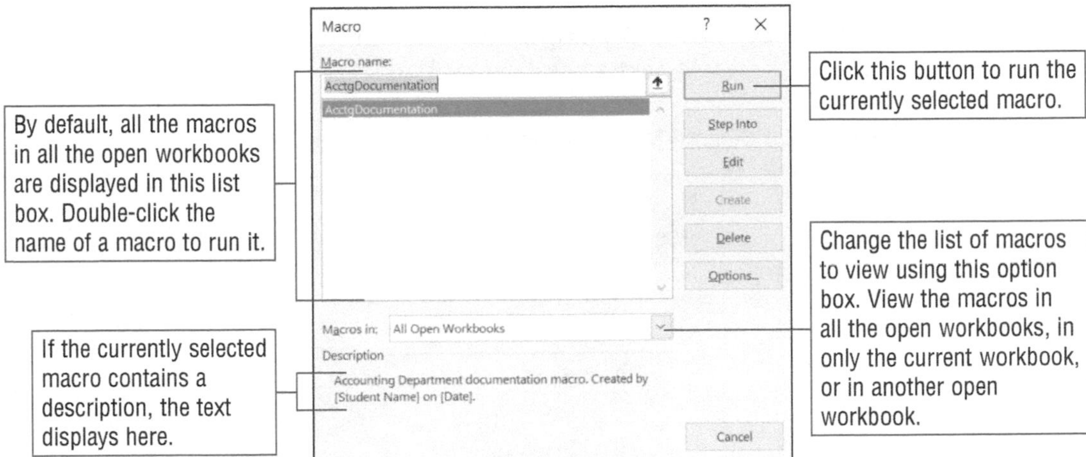

Activity 2b Running a Macro

Part 2 of 4

1. With **7-Macros** open, run the AcctgDocumentation macro to test that it works correctly by completing the following steps:
   a. Select the range A1:A4 and then press the Delete key to erase the cell contents.
   b. To test the Ctrl + Home command in the macro, make sure cell that A1 is not active when the macro begins playing. Click in any cell other than cell A1 to deselect the range.
   c. Click the Macros button in the Macros group on the View tab. Make sure to click the button and not the button arrow.
   d. At the Macro dialog box with *AcctgDocumentation* already selected in the *Macro name* list box, click the Run button.
2. Save and then close **7-Macros**.

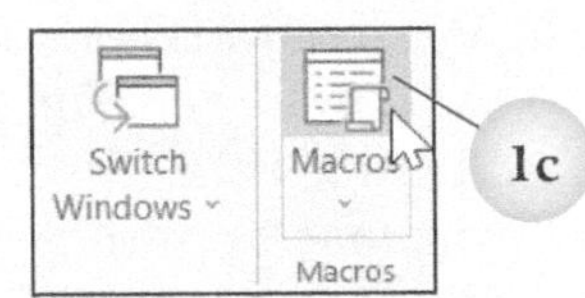

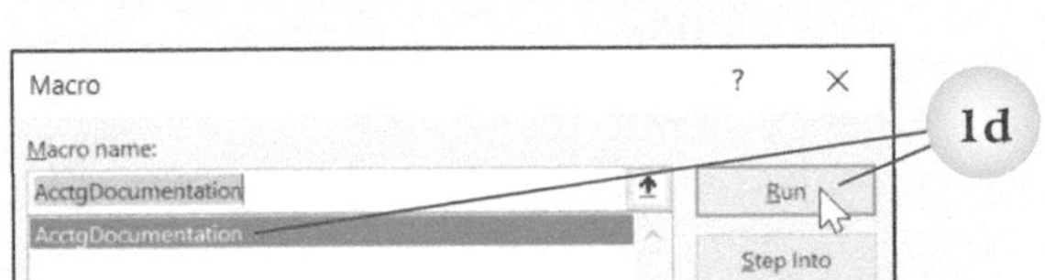

Assigning a Macro to a Shortcut Key

Quick Steps

Assign Macro to Shortcut Key

1. Click View tab.
2. Click Macros button arrow.
3. Click *Record Macro*.
4. Type macro name.
5. Click in *Shortcut key* text box.
6. Type a letter.
7. Click in *Description* text box.
8. Type description text.
9. Click OK.
10. Perform actions.
11. Click Stop Recording button.

When a macro is being recorded, it can be assigned to a Ctrl key combination. A macro assigned to a keyboard shortcut can be run without displaying the Macro dialog box. To create a keyboard shortcut, choose any lowercase or uppercase letter. Excel distinguishes the case of the letter when typing it in the *Shortcut key* text box at the Record Macro dialog box. For example, if an uppercase O is typed, Excel defines the shortcut key as *Ctrl* + *Shift* + *O*, as shown in Figure 7.9.

If an Excel feature is already assigned to the chosen key combination, the macro will override the feature. For example, pressing Ctrl + p in Excel causes the Print backstage area to display. If a macro is assigned to Ctrl + p, using this keyboard shortcut will run the new macro instead of displaying the Print backstage area. View a list of Excel-assigned keyboard shortcuts in Help by typing *keyboard shortcuts* in the *Search* text box. Point to *Get Help on "keyboard shortcuts"*. Choose *Keyboard shortcuts in Excel for Windows* in the results list.

Figure 7.9 Record Macro Dialog Box with a Shortcut Key Assigned

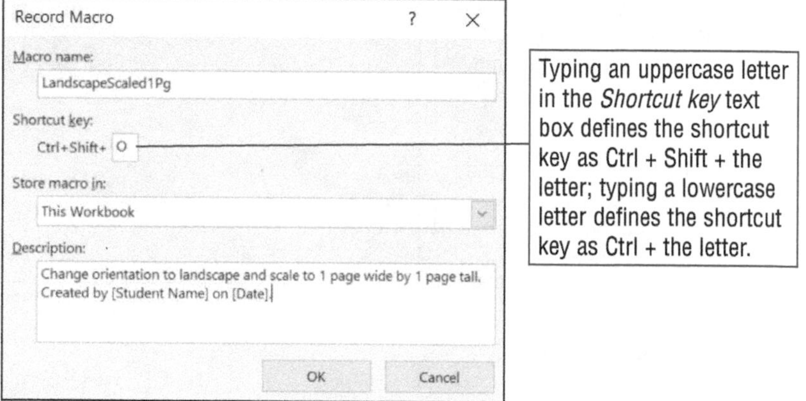

Activity 2c Creating and Running a Macro Using a Shortcut Key

Part 3 of 4

1. Open **7-Macros**.
2. When a workbook that contains a macro is opened, the default security setting is *Disable all macros with notification*. This causes a security warning to appear in the message bar (between the ribbon and the formula bar) stating that macros have been disabled. Enable the macros in the workbook by clicking the Enable Content button.

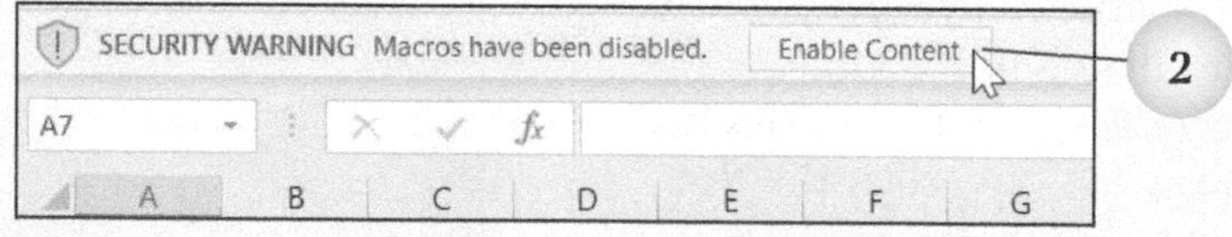

3. Create a macro that changes the print options for a worksheet and assign it to a shortcut key by completing the following steps:
   a. Once the recording of a macro has stopped in an Excel session, the Stop Recording button in the Status bar changes to the Record New Macro button. Click the Record New Macro button at the left side of the Status bar next to *Ready*. (If you exited Excel before starting this activity, start a new macro by clicking the View tab, clicking the Macros button arrow, and then clicking *Record Macro*.)

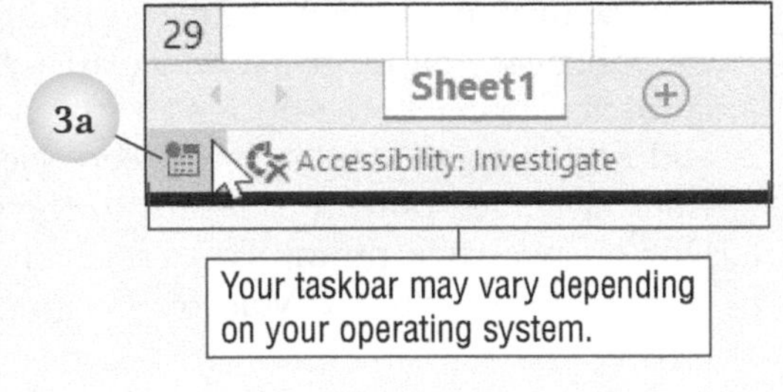

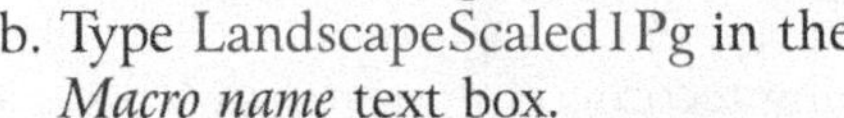

   b. Type LandscapeScaled1Pg in the *Macro name* text box.
   c. Click in the *Shortcut key* text box, press and hold down the Shift key, type the letter O, and then release the Shift key.
   d. Click in the *Description* text box and then type Change orientation to landscape and scale to 1 page wide by 1 page tall. Created by [Student Name] on [Date]. Substitute your name for *[Student Name]* and the current date for *[Date]*.

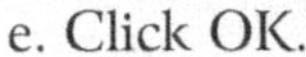

   e. Click OK.
   f. Click the Page Layout tab.
   g. Click the Page Setup dialog box launcher at the bottom right of the Page Setup group.
   h. At the Page Setup dialog box with the Page tab selected, click *Landscape* in the *Orientation* section.
   i. Click *Fit to* in the *Scaling* section to scale the printout to 1 page wide by 1 page tall.
   j. Click OK.

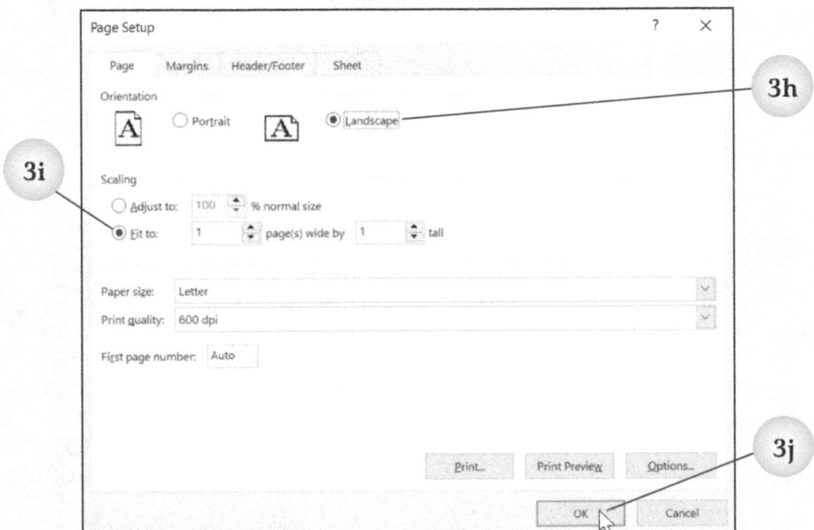

   k. Click the Stop Recording button.

4. Press Ctrl + N to open a new blank workbook.
5. Press Ctrl + Shift + O to run the LandscapeScaled1Pg macro.
6. Type your name in cell A1, press the Enter key, and then press Ctrl + F2 to display the worksheet in the Print backstage area. Notice in Print Preview that the page orientation is landscape. Review the options in the Settings category. Notice that *Landscape Orientation* and *Fit Sheet on One Page* have been selected by the macro.
7. Click the Back button to return to the worksheet and then close the workbook. Click Don't Save when prompted to save changes.
8. Save and then close **7-Macros**.

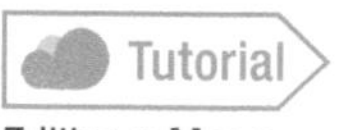

Editing a Macro

Quick Steps

Edit Macro

1. Open workbook containing macro.
2. Click View tab.
3. Click Macros button.
4. Click macro name.
5. Click Edit button.
6. Make changes in VBA code window.
7. Click Save button.
8. Click File.
9. Click *Close and Return to Microsoft Excel.*

Editing a Macro

The actions performed while a macro is being recorded are stored in VBA code. Each macro is saved as a separate module within a VBAProject for the workbook. A module can be described as a receptacle for the macro instructions. Figure 7.10 displays the window containing the VBA code module for the macro created in Activity 2a.

Use the module to edit a macro if the change needed is easy to decipher within the VBA statements. If several changes to a macro are required or if you do not feel comfortable with the VBA code, re-record the macro. When a new macro has been recorded and is being saved with the same name as an existing macro, Excel prompts the user to replace the existing macro. Save the re-recorded macro by overwriting the original macro.

Figure 7.10 Microsoft Visual Basic for Applications Window for Activity 2a AcctgDocumentation Macro

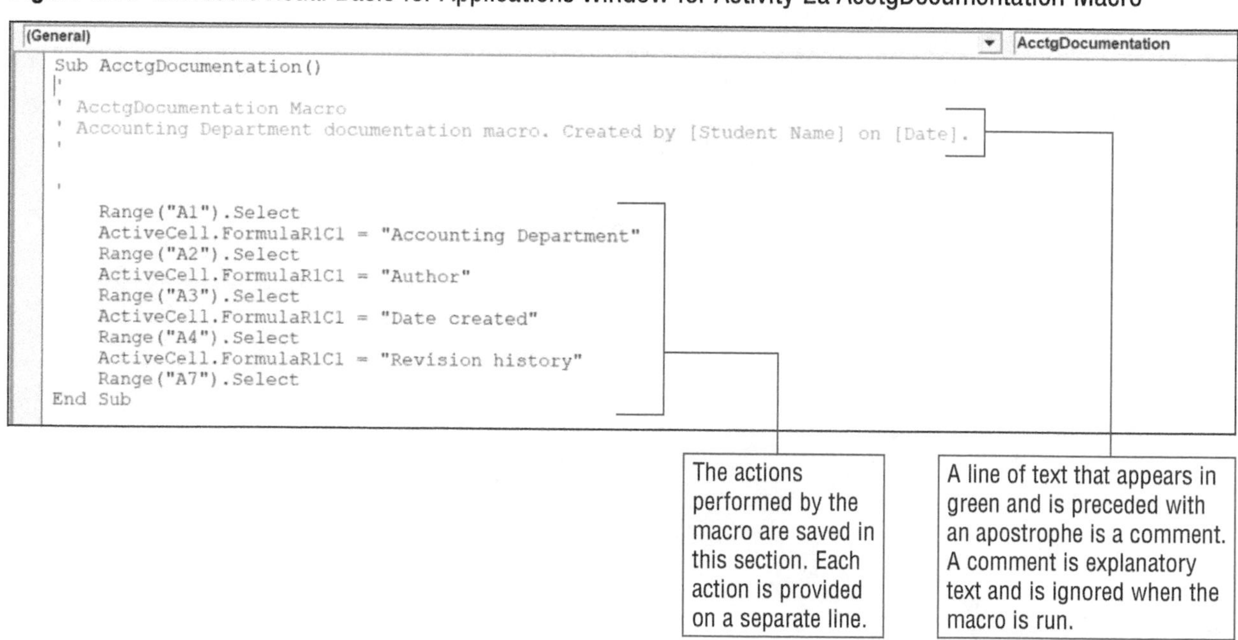

Activity 2d Editing a Macro

Part 4 of 4

1. Open **NationalInv** and enable the content, if necessary.
2. Save the workbook with the name **7-NationalInv**.
3. The workbook contains a macro called *PrintInv* that automatically prints the invoice. Modify the macro to have the invoice display in print preview when the macro is run by completing the following steps:
   a. If necessary, click the View tab.
   b. Click the Macros button.
   c. At the Macro dialog box with *PrintInv* already selected in the *Macro name* list box, click the Edit button. A Microsoft Visual Basic for Applications window opens with the program code displayed for 7-NationalInv.xlsm - [Module1 (Code)].
   d. Read the statements between the *Sub* and *End Sub* statements. *Sub* indicates the beginning of the procedure and *End Sub* indicates the end of the procedure. A procedure is a set of VBA statements that perform actions. The name of the procedure appears after the opening *Sub* statement and is the macro name. Each line beginning with a single apostrophe (') is a comment. A comment is used in programming to insert explanatory text that describes the logic or purpose of a statement. A statement that begins with an apostrophe is ignored when the macro is run. The commands that are executed when the macro is run display as indented lines of text below the comments.
   e. Remove the command that has Excel print one copy of the selected worksheet by selecting the text after the second period in the commands, starting with the word *Printout* and ending with the world *False*, and then press the Delete key.
   f. Type PrintPreview. The new command now reads *ActiveWindow.SelectedSheets.PrintPreview*. ***Note: Do not include the period after* PrintPreview.**

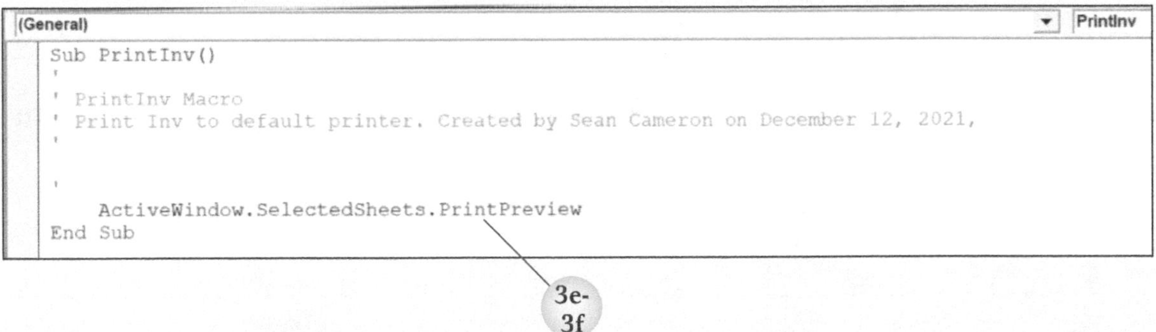
(General)
PrintInv
Sub PrintInv()
'
' PrintInv Macro
' Print Inv to default printer. Created by Sean Cameron on December 12, 2021,
'
'
ActiveWindow.SelectedSheets.PrintPreview
End Sub
3e-3f

   g. Click the Save button on the toolbar.

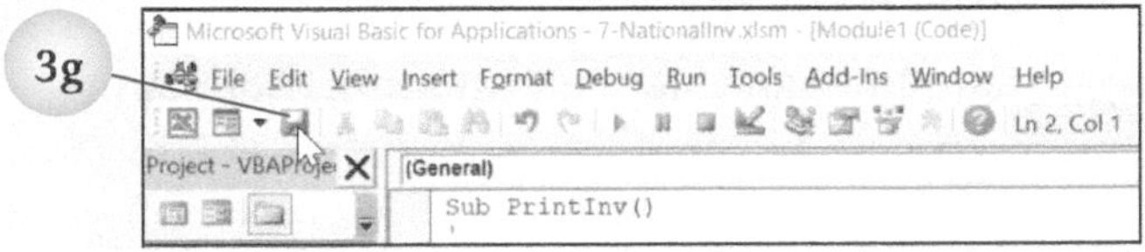
3g
Microsoft Visual Basic for Applications - 7-NationalInv.xlsm - [Module1 (Code)]
File Edit View Insert Format Debug Run Tools Add-Ins Window Help
Ln 2, Col 1
Project - VBAProje
(General)
Sub PrintInv()

4. Click File and then click *Close and Return to Microsoft Excel*.
5. Test the edited macro to make sure that the invoice displays in print preview by completing the following steps:
   a. Click the Macros button.
   b. At the Macro dialog box, double-click *PrintInv* in the *Macro name* list box.
   c. Click the Close Print Preview button.
6. Save **7-NationalInv.**

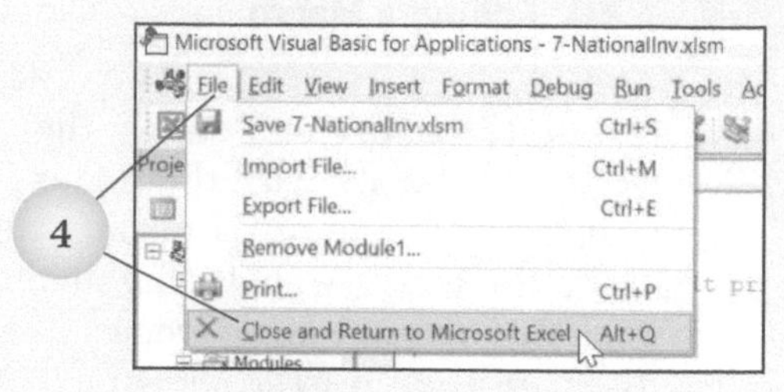

Managing and Deleting Macros

Quick Steps

Delete Macro
1. Open Macro dialog box.
2. Click macro name.
3. Click Delete button.
4. Click Yes.

By default, a macro is stored within the workbook that is active when it is recorded. When the workbook is closed, the macros within it are no longer available. For example, if the file 7-Macros is closed, the AcctgDocumentation macro will not be available in a new workbook. To continue using the macros, leave the workbook that contains them open, since by default, the Macro dialog box displays the macros for all the open workbooks in the *Macro name* list box.

Consider creating a macros workbook with a set of standard macros, similar to the macros workbook created or modified in Activities 2a through 2d. Open this workbook when working in Excel and the macros stored within it will be available for all the files that are created or edited during the Excel session. Create one macros workbook and copy it to other computers so a set of standard macros can be distributed to others for use.

If a macro is no longer needed, delete it in the Macro dialog box. Open the Macro dialog box, select the macro name in the *Macro name* list box, and then click the Delete button.

Activity 3 Insert and Configure Form Controls in an Invoice Workbook — 3 Parts

You will insert a combo box form control, a check box form control, and a macro button form control into an invoice workbook.

Inserting and Configuring Form Controls

Insert a form control to allow users to enter information in a worksheet. For example, insert a combo box form control or a list box form control to allow users to select an option from a list, or insert a check box form control to allow users to select an option by inserting a check mark in a check box. After inserting a form control in a worksheet, configure the control to define how it will be used; also size the control and align multiple controls.

Inserting Form Controls

Insert

Quick Steps

Insert Form Control

1. Click Developer tab.
2. Click Insert button.
3. Click control.
4. Draw control.

To insert a form control in an active worksheet, click the Insert button in the Controls group on the Developer tab, click an option in the *Form Controls* section at the drop-down list, and then draw a box in the worksheet. The size of the form control box depends on the control options. For example, a form control that allows users to select from a drop-down list of two-letter state abbreviations (AL, AK, etc.) will be narrower than a form control that offers a drop-down list of city names (eg., Abbeville, Aberdeen, etc.). Table 7.1 describes selected types of form controls.

Configuring Form Controls

To configure and add options to a form control, right-click the control, click the *Format Control* option at the pop-up menu, and then enter information on the Control tab at the Format Control dialog box. The information entered at the Format Control dialog box depends on the type of form control. Figure 7.11 shows the Format Control dialog box for a combo box form control.

Table 7.1 Selected Types of Form Controls

Type of Form Control	Display	How to Use	Example
combo box form control	an option box with an arrow	Click the option box arrow to see a drop-down list of available options and then click an option.	Method of Payment e-Transfer Check Visa MC
list box form control	a box containing all the available options—with scroll bars, if necessary	Click an option in the list box to select it. The control can be configured to allow the user to select more than one option.	Method of Payment e-Transfer Check Visa MC
check box form control	a check box with a text label	Click the check box to insert or remove a check mark.	Ship to: Same as billing address
button form control	a button with a label and with a macro assigned to it	Click the button to run the macro.	Print Preview
option button form control	a radio button with a label	Click the radio button to insert or remove a bullet.	Option Button 3

Figure 7.11 Control Tab at the Format Control Dialog Box for a Combo Box Form Control

Format Control
Size | Protection | Properties | Alt Text | Control
Input range: MOP
Cell link: C11
Drop down lines: 4
3-D shading
OK | Cancel

Enter the defined name, or range reference for the worksheet cells that contain the options to be displayed.

Enter the cell reference that will store the value chosen.

Enter the number of options to display. If the number entered is less than the number of items in the Input range, a scroll bar will appear at the drop-down list for the form control.

	A	B
1	Method of Payment	
2	e-Transfer	1
3	Check	2
4	Visa	3
5	MC	4

Activity 3a Inserting a Combo Box Form Control

Part 1 of 3

1. With **7-NationalInv** open, add the Developer tab to the toolbar by completing the following steps:
   a. Right-click on any part of the ribbon.
   b. Click the *Customize the Ribbon* option.
   c. Click the *Developer* check box in the *Main Tabs* list box to insert a check mark and then click OK.
2. Add a combo box form control to include the different methods of payment by completing the following steps:
   a. Click the Developer tab and then click the Insert button in the Controls group.
   b. Click the *Combo Box (Form Control)* option (second column, first row in the *Form Controls* section).
   c. Draw a box in cell A11 that is the same width and height as the cell.

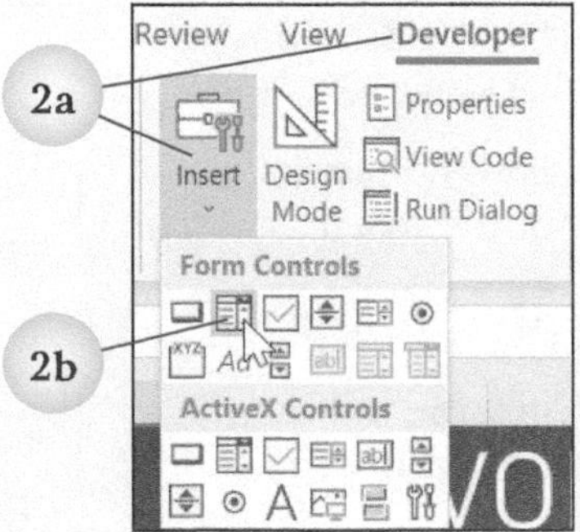

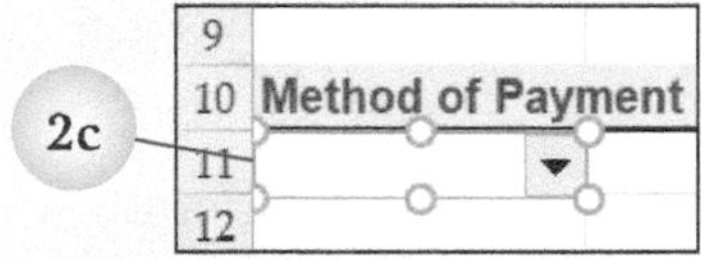

d. Right-click the border of the combo box and then click the *Format Control* option at the pop-up menu.
e. Click in the *Input range* text box, type MOP, and then press the Tab key.
f. Type a11 in the *Cell link* text box and then press the Tab key.
g. Type 4 in the *Drop down lines* text box and then click OK.
h. Click in any worksheet cell outside the form control.
3. Save **7-NationalInv**.

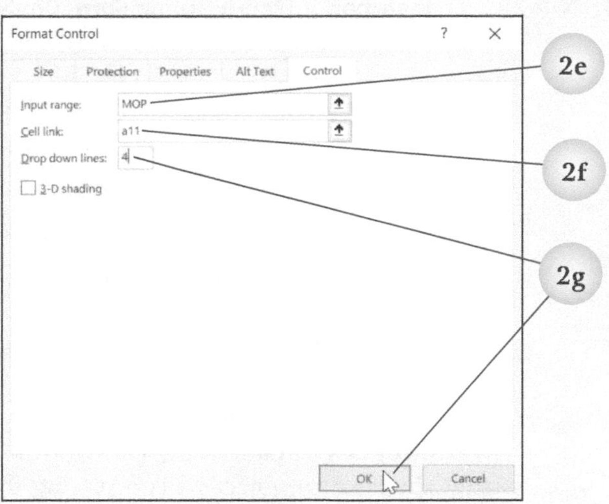

Activity 3b Inserting a Check Box Form Control

Part 2 of 3

1. With **7-NationalInv** open, insert a check box form control to have customers indicate that the shipping address is the same as the billing address by completing the following steps:
   a. Click the Insert button in the Controls group.
   b. Click the *Check Box (Form Control)* option (third column, first row in the *Form Controls* section).
   c. Draw a box in cell B8 that is the same width and height as the cell.

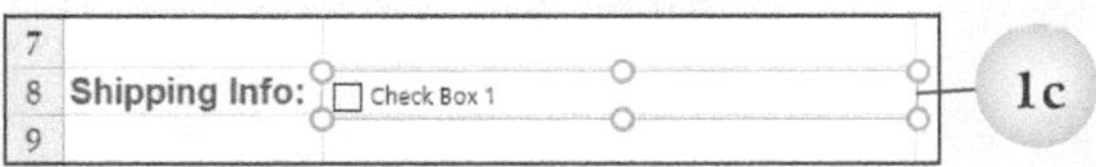

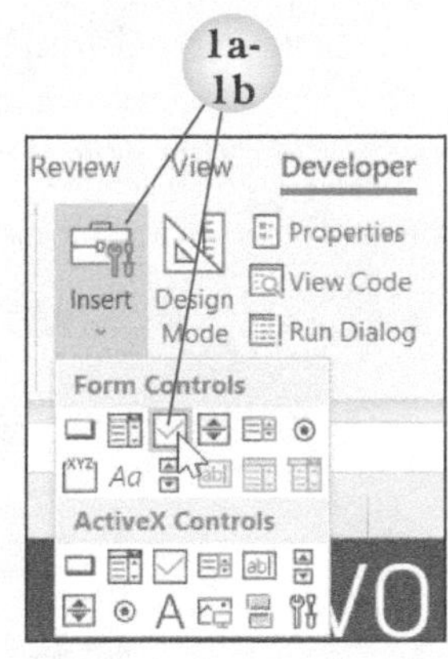

2. Change the text of the check box form control by clicking in the check box form control, selecting the text, and then typing Same as billing address.
3. Click in any worksheet cell outside the form control.
4. Save **7-NationalInv**.

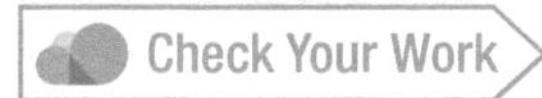

Creating a Macro Button Form Control

A macro can be assigned to a button form control that allows the user to quickly run the macro without having to remember the shortcut key combination or ribbon commands.

To create a button form control with a macro assigned to it, click the Insert button in the Controls group on the Developer tab, click the *Button (Form Control)* option, draw the button, click the macro name in the *Macro name* list box at the Assign Macro dialog box, and then click OK. Macro button form controls do not display in Print Preview and do not print.

Activity 3c Inserting a Macro Button Form Control Part 3 of 3

1. With **7-NationalInv** open, insert a macro form control to have customers indicate that the shipping address is the same as the billing address by completing the following steps:
   a. Click the Insert button in the Controls group on the Developer tab.
   b. Click the *Button (Form Control)* option (first column, first row in the *Form Controls* section).
   c. Draw a box in cell A30 that is the same width and height as the cell.
   d. Click the *PrintInv* option in the *Macro name* list box and then click OK.
   e. Type Print Preview and then click in any worksheet cell outside the form control.

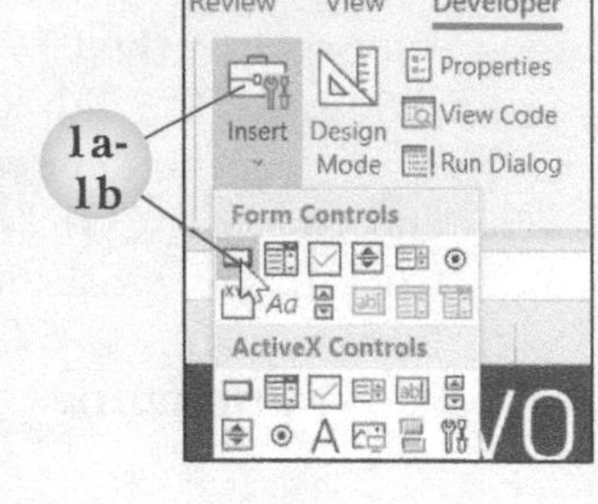

2. Format the control object by completing the following steps:
   a. Right-click the Print Preview button form control and then click the *Format Control* option at the pop-up menu.
   b. Click the Font tab, if necessary; click the *Color* option box arrow; click the *Dark Red* option (first column, second row) at the drop-down gallery; and then click OK.
   c. Click in any worksheet cell outside the Print Preview button form control.
3. Save **7-NationalInv.**

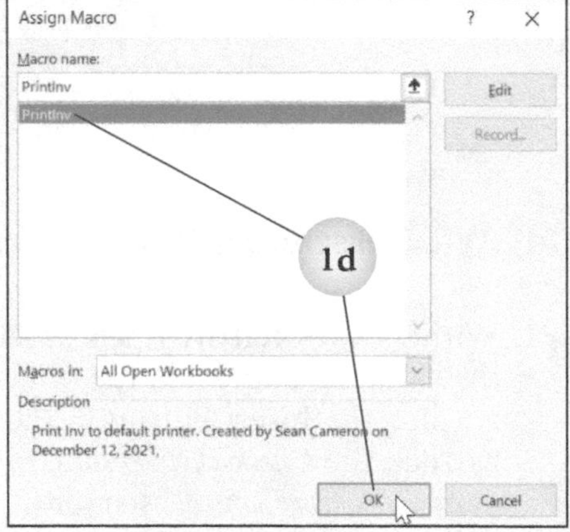

Activity 4 Save a Workbook as a Template 2 Parts

You will save a workbook as a template and then use the template to create a new invoice.

Saving a Workbook as a Template

Save Workbook as Template
1. Open workbook.
2. Make changes.
3. Click File tab.
4. Click *Save As.*
5. Click *Browse.*
6. Change *Save as type* to *Excel Template.*
7. Type file name.
8. Click Save button.

Saving a Workbook as a Template

A template is a workbook that contains standard text, formulas, and formatting. Cell entries are created and formatted for all the data that does not change. Cells that will contain variable information have formatting applied but are left empty, since they will be filled in when the template is used to generate a worksheet. Examples of worksheets that are well suited to templates include invoices, purchase orders, time cards, and expense forms. These types of worksheets are usually filled in with the same kinds of data but the data itself varies.

Several templates have already been created and are installed with Excel or can be installed after they are downloaded. To use a template to create a worksheet, first check the New backstage area to see if the template already exists. Another option is to search online for templates using categories such as *Budget*, *Invoice*, *Calendars*, and *Expenses*. Once a topic has been selected in the *Suggested Searches* section of the New backstage area, either download one of the templates shown or choose another topic from the Category task pane.

If none of the existing templates meets your needs, create a custom template. To do this, create a workbook that contains all the standard data, formulas, and formatting. Leave the cells empty for any information that is variable but format those cells as required. Save the workbook as a template at the Save As dialog box by changing the *Save as type* option to *Excel Template (*.xltx)* or *Excel Macro-Enabled Template (*.xltm)* if the workbook contains macros. Before saving the worksheet as a template, consider protecting it by locking all the cells except those that will hold variable data.

Activity 4a Saving a Workbook as a Template

Part 1 of 2

1. With **7-NationalInv** open, save the workbook as a template containing macros by completing the following steps:
   a. Click the File tab.
   b. Click *Save As*.
   c. Select the current text in the *File name* text box and then type NationalTemplate-StudentName, substituting your name for *StudentName*.
   d. Click the *Save as type* option box arrow and then click *Excel Macro-Enabled Template (*.xltm)* at the pop-up list.
   e. Click the Save button.
2. Close **NationalTemplate-StudentName**.

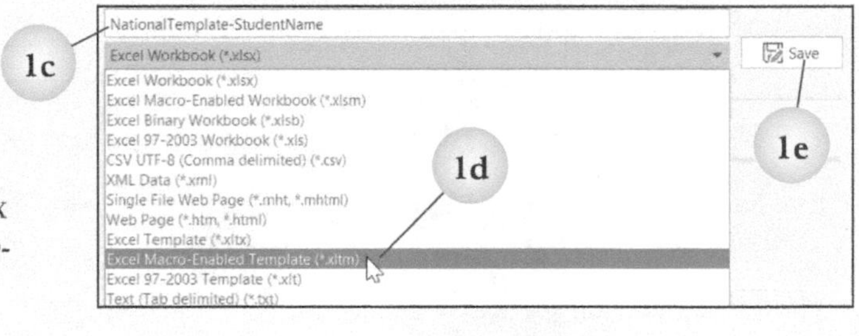

Using a Custom Template

Quick Steps

Use Custom Template
1. Click File tab.
2. Click *New*.
3. Click *Personal*.
4. Double-click template.

Delete Custom Template
1. Click File tab.
2. Click *Open*.
3. Click *Computer*.
4. Click Browse button.
5. Navigate to [c:]\Users*username*\Documents\Custom Office Templates.
6. Right-click template name.
7. Click *Delete*.
8. Click Cancel.

To use a template that you created, click the File tab and then click *New*. At the New backstage area, click *Personal*. This opens the Personal template section, as shown in Figure 7.12. Double-click the name of the template to open it. A workbook opens with the name of the template followed by a *1*. Save the document with a more descriptive name.

Figure 7.12 New Backstage Area with the *Personal* Template Section Selected

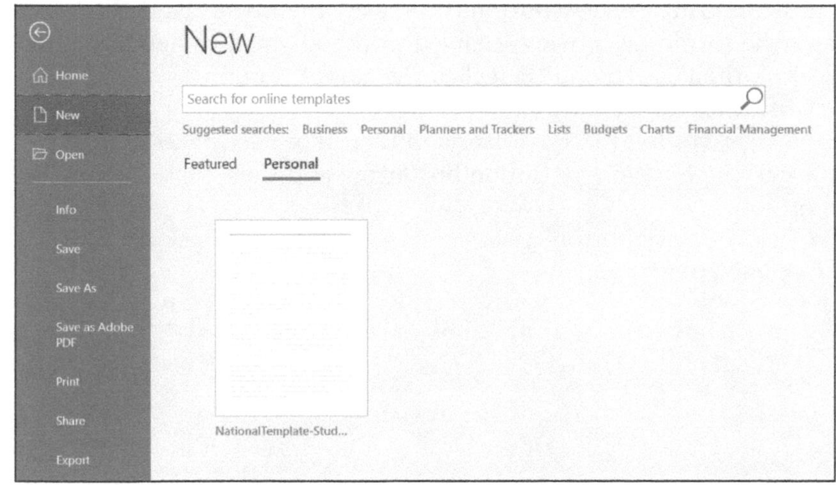

Deleting a Custom Template

To delete a custom template that is no longer needed, use the Open dialog box to navigate to [c:]\Users*username*\Documents\Custom Office Templates. Right-click the name of the template to be deleted and then click *Delete* at the shortcut menu. Click Cancel to close the Open dialog box.

Activity 4b **Using a Custom Template** — Part 2 of 2

1. At a blank Excel screen, open the template created in Activity 4a by completing the following steps:
   a. Click the File tab.
   b. Click *New*.
   c. At the New backstage area, click *Personal*.
   d. In the *Personal* template section, click *NationalTemplate-StudentName.* (Your template will have your name in place of *StudentName*.)

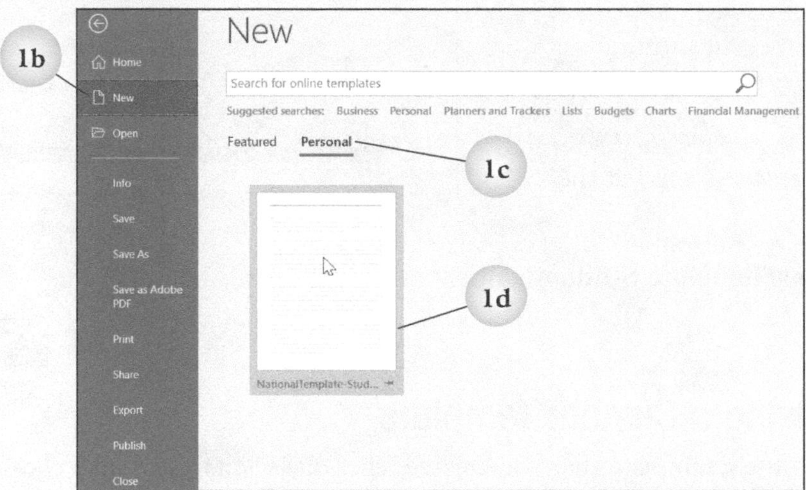

2. Look at the workbook name in the title bar. Notice that Excel has added *1* to the end of the name.
3. Enable the content.
4. Fill in the invoice as shown in Figure 7.13. ***Note: Add a formula in the Line Total column for each item.***
5. Click the Print Preview button to preview the invoice and then print the invoice.
6. Save the invoice as a macro-enabled workbook by completing the following steps:
   a. Click the File tab and then click the *Save As* option.
   b. Click the Browse button.
   c. Navigate to the EL2C7 folder and then type 7-NInv2035 in the *File name* text box.
   d. Click the *Save as type* option box arrow and then click the *Excel Macro-Enabled Workbook* option.
   e. Click the Save button.
7. Close **7-NInv2035**.

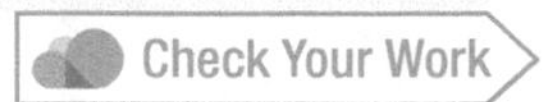

Figure 7.13 Invoice for Activity 4b

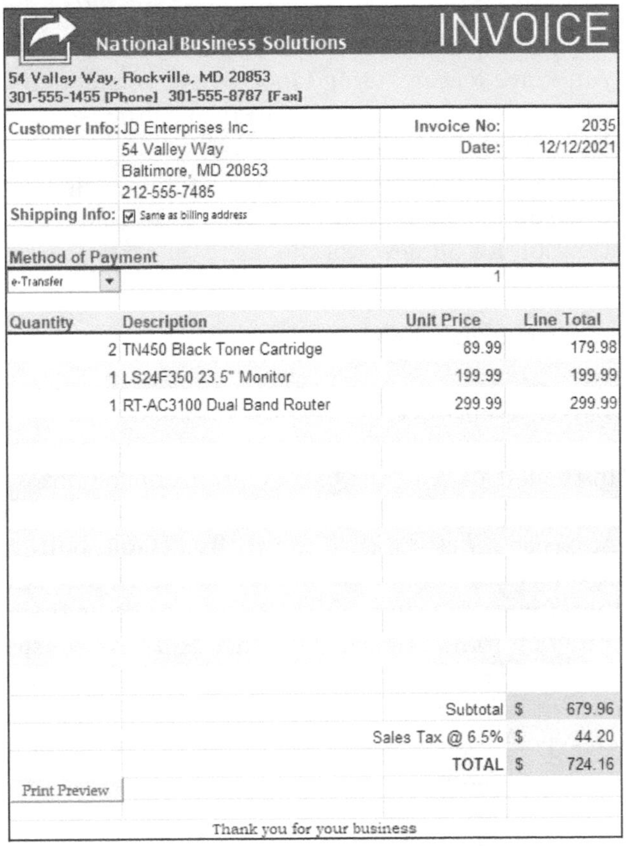

National Business Solutions		INVOICE	
54 Valley Way, Rockville, MD 20853 301-555-1455 [Phone] 301-555-8787 [Fax]			
Customer Info:	JD Enterprises Inc.	Invoice No:	2035
	54 Valley Way	Date:	12/12/2021
	Baltimore, MD 20853		
	212-555-7485		
Shipping Info:	☑ Same as billing address		
Method of Payment			
e-Transfer		1	
Quantity	Description	Unit Price	Line Total
2	TN450 Black Toner Cartridge	89.99	179.98
1	LS24F350 23.5" Monitor	199.99	199.99
1	RT-AC3100 Dual Band Router	299.99	299.99
		Subtotal	$ 679.96
		Sales Tax @ 6.5%	$ 44.20
		TOTAL	$ 724.16
Print Preview			
	Thank you for your business		

Activity 5 Manage Excel's Save Options and Trust Center Settings **3 Parts**

You will review Excel's current save options, modify the AutoRecover options, and then recover an unsaved workbook. You will also explore the default settings in the Trust Center.

Customizing Save Options

Quick Steps

Customize Save Options

1. Click File tab.
2. Click *Options*.
3. Click *Save* in left pane.
4. Change save options.
5. Click OK.

The AutoRecover feature saves versions of your work at a specified time interval. This will be beneficial in case changes are not saved or Excel closes unexpectedly (such as during a power outage). When Excel restarts, the opening screen displays a *Recovered* section below the Recent list. Click the Recovered unsaved workbooks hyperlink and the Document Recovery task pane opens with a list of workbooks for which AutoRecover files exist.

By default, Excel's AutoRecover feature is turned on and will automatically save AutoRecover information every 10 minutes. The time interval can be adjusted to suit the user's needs. Keep in mind that data loss can still occur with AutoRecover turned on. For example, suppose the time interval is set at 20 minutes and a power outage occurs 15 minutes after an AutoRecover save. When Excel restarts, the recovered file will not contain the last 15 minutes of

Hint Do not rely on AutoRecover as you work. Saving regularly to minimize data loss and protect against unforeseen events is the best practice.

work if the workbook was not saved manually. Open the Excel Options dialog box and select *Save* in the left pane to view and/or change the AutoRecover options.

In conjunction with AutoRecover, Excel provides to Office 365 users the AutoSave feature, using OneDrive or SharePoint Online to store their files. The files are saved in real-time. To turn AutoSave on, click the AutoSave Off button located on the Quick Access Toolbar.

The save options at the Excel Options dialog box also allow changing the drive and/or folder in which to store AutoRecovered files, as well as the default file location for all new workbooks.

Activity 5a Customizing Save Options

Part 1 of 3

1. At a blank Excel screen, click the File tab and then click *Options* to open the Excel Options dialog box.
2. Click *Save* in the left pane of the Excel Options dialog box.
3. Note the current settings for *Save AutoRecover information every [ ] minutes* and *Keep the last AutoRecovered version if I close without saving*. By default, both check boxes should be checked and the time interval should be 10 minutes; however, the settings may have been changed on the computer you are using. If that is the case, write down the options so you can restore the program to its original state once you have finished this activity.
4. If necessary, insert check marks in the two check boxes to turn on the AutoRecover features.
5. Select the current value in the *Save AutoRecover information every [ ] minutes* measurement box and then type 2 to change the time interval to two minutes.

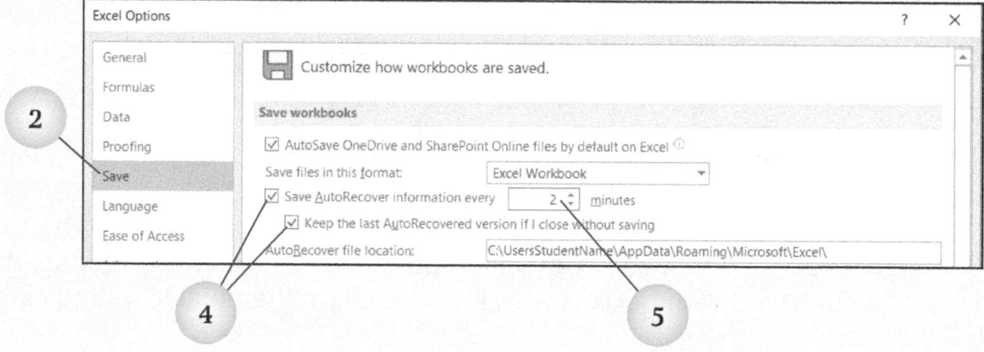

6. Click OK.

Activity 5b Recovering a Workbook

Part 2 of 3

1. Open **7-NationalJE**.
2. Save the workbook with the name **7-NationalJE-5**.
3. Note the system time in the bottom right corner of the screen. You will use this time to make sure that more than two minutes elapse before you interrupt the Excel session.

4. Make the following changes to the worksheet:
    a. Select the range A7:A17 and apply the standard dark red font color (first color in the *Standard Colors* section of the drop-down color palette).
    b. Select the range E7:E17 and apply the standard dark red font color.

	A	B	C	D	E	F	G	H
4	Internal Chargeback for Computing Services Department							
5	Batch Technical Service Requests (TSRs)						GL Account	Journal Entry
6		Parts	Labor	Total	TSR	Dept Code	Number	Number
7	Accounting	$ -	$1,525.00	$ 1,525.00	CS-4042	225	011475	160101
8	Executive Administration	1,564.27	985.50	2,549.77	CS-4043	216	011482	160102
9	Finance	964.32	635.50	1,599.82	CS-4044	166	011435	160103
10	Human Resources	397.45	225.50	622.95	CS-4045	187	011485	160104
11	Graphics Design	417.45	175.50	592.95	CS-4046	210	011415	160105
12	Electronic Production	215.48	475.50	690.98	CS-4047	350	011443	160106
13	Marketing	1,048.57	725.50	1,774.07	CS-4048	452	011409	160107
14	Web Programming	975.85	854.50	1,830.35	CS-4049	284	011462	160108
15	Planning and Development	161.45	132.50	293.95	CS-4050	310	011473	160109
16	President's Office	-	425.00	425.00	CS-4051	105	011455	160110
17	Purchasing	415.87	175.50	591.37	CS-4052	243	011428	160111
18				$12,496.21				

4a

4b

5. Make sure more than two minutes has elapsed since you checked the system time in Step 3. If necessary, wait until you are sure an AutoRecover file has been saved.
6. Press Alt + Ctrl + Delete.
7. At the Windows screen, select *Task Manager*.
8. At the Task Manager dialog box, click *Microsoft Excel (32 bit)* in the task list box and then click the End task button.
9. Close the Task Manager dialog box.
10. Restart Microsoft Excel. At the opening screen, click the Recover unsaved workbooks hyperlink in the *Recent* section. Two files are available: the original version of the file used in this activity and the AutoRecovered version.

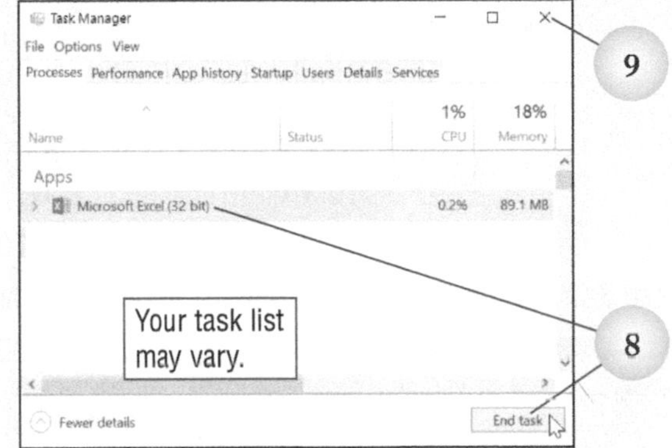

11. Point to the first file in the Document Recovery task pane. A ScreenTip displays stating that the first file is the AutoRecover version.
12. Point to the second file in the Document Recovery task pane. A ScreenTip displays stating that the second file is the original document.

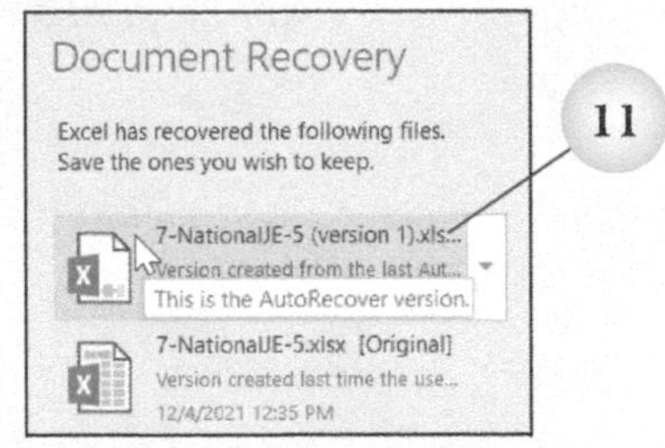

13. Click the first file in the Document Recovery task pane. Notice that the edited version of the file appears. Look at the additional information next to the file name in the Title bar. Excel includes *(version 1)* and *[AutoRecovered]* in the file name.

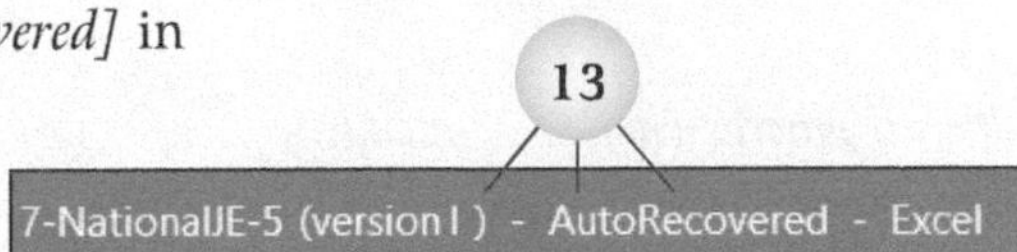

14. Click the option box arrow next to the AutoRecovered document, click the *Save As* option, and then click *Save* at the Save As dialog box to accept the default name *7-NationalJE-5 (AutoRecovered)*.
15. Open the Excel Options dialog box. If necessary, restore the save options to the settings you wrote down in Activity 5a. Close the Excel Options dialog box.
16. Close **7-NationalJE-5**.

Check Your Work

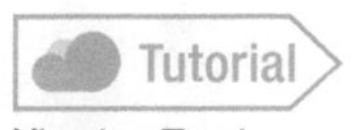

Viewing Trust Center Settings

Quick Steps

View Trust Center Settings

1. Click File tab.
2. Click *Options*.
3. Click *Trust Center* in left pane.
4. Click Trust Center Settings button.
5. Click desired trust center category in left pane.
6. View and/or modify options.
7. Click OK two times.

Hint Changing the macro security setting in Excel does not affect the macro security setting in other Microsoft programs, such as Word and Access.

Viewing Trust Center Settings

In Excel, the Trust Center is responsible for blocking unsafe content when a workbook is opened. Recall the security warning that sometimes appears in the message bar when a workbook is opened. That warning is generated by the Trust Center and it can be closed by clicking the Enable Content button. The Trust Center also allows the user to view and/or modify the security options that protect the computer from malicious content.

The Trust Center maintains a Trusted Locations list of locations from which content can be considered trusted. When a location is added to the Trusted Locations list, Excel treats any files opened from that location as safe. A workbook opened from a trusted location does not cause a security warning to display in the message bar and none of its content is blocked.

If a workbook contains macros, the Trust Center checks for a valid and current digital signature from an entity in the Trusted Publishers list before enabling macros. The Trusted Publishers list is maintained by the user on the computer being used. To add a publisher to the list, enable content from that publisher and then click the option *Trust all content from this publisher*.

Depending on the active macro security setting, if the Trust Center cannot match the digital signature information with an entity in the Trusted Publishers list or the macro does not contain a digital signature, a security warning displays in the message bar. The default macro security setting is *Disable all macros with notification*. Table 7.2 describes the four macro security settings. In some cases, the user may decide to change the default macro security setting. This can be done at the Trust Center dialog box.

Table 7.2 Macro Security Settings for Workbooks Not Opened from Trusted Locations

Macro Setting	Description
Disable all macros without notification	All macros are disabled; security alerts do not appear.
Disable all macros with notification	All macros are disabled; security alerts appear with the option to enable content if the source of the file is trusted. This is the default setting.
Disable all macros except digitally signed macros	A macro that does not contain a digital signature is disabled; security alerts do not appear. If the macro is digitally signed by a publisher in the Trusted Publishers list, the macro is allowed to run. If the macro is digitally signed by a publisher not in the Trusted Publishers list, a security alert appears.
Enable all macros (not recommended, potentially dangerous code can run)	All macros are allowed; security alerts do not appear.

Activity 5c Viewing Trust Center Settings

Part 3 of 3

1. To explore the settings in the Trust Center, complete the following steps:
   a. Click the File tab and then click *Options*.
   b. Click *Trust Center* in the left pane of the Excel Options dialog box.
   c. Click the Trust Center Settings button in the *Microsoft Excel Trust Center* section.

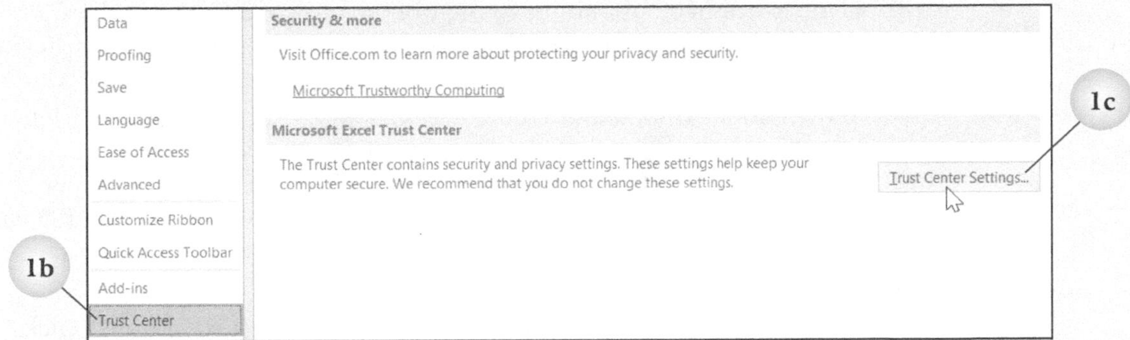

   d. At the Trust Center dialog box, click *Macro Settings* in the left pane.
   e. Review the options in the *Macro Settings* section. Note which option is active on the computer you are using. The default option is *Disable all macros with notification*. ***Note: The security setting on the computer you are using may be different from the default setting. Do not change the security setting without your instructor's permission.***
   f. Click *Trusted Publishers* in the left pane. If any publishers have been added to the list on the computer you are using, their names will appear in the list box. If the list box is empty, no trusted publishers have been added.

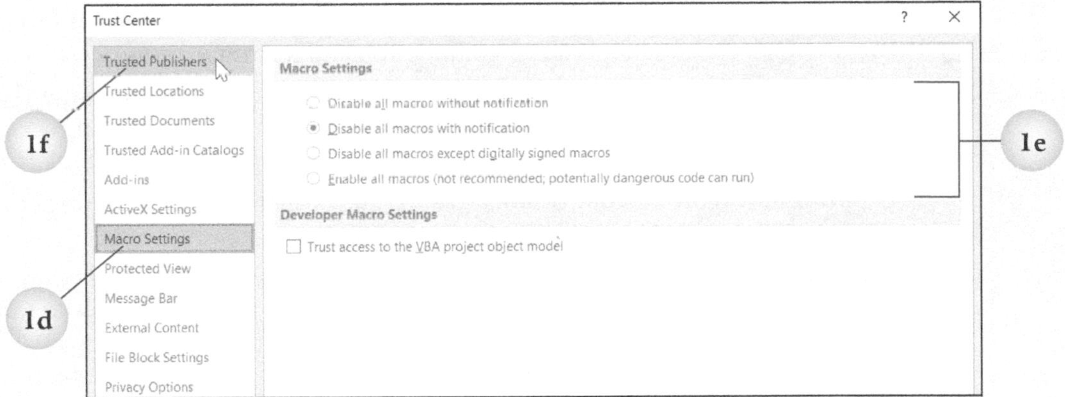

   g. Click *Trusted Locations* in the left pane. Review the paths and descriptions of the folders in the *Trusted Locations* list box. By default, Excel adds the folder created upon installation that contains the templates provided by Microsoft. Additional folders that have been added by a system administrator or network administrator may also appear.
   h. Click OK to close the Trust Center dialog box.
2. Click OK to close the Excel Options dialog box.

Chapter Summary

- Display options, found in the Excel Options dialog box in Excel are grouped as global display options, options that affect the current workbook, and options that affect only the active worksheet. Customized workbook and worksheet display options are saved with the file.
- Minimize the ribbon to provide more space in the work area when working with a large worksheet. To minimize the ribbon, click the Collapse the Ribbon button, click the Ribbon Display Options button, or Press Ctrl + F1. Clicking a tab temporarily redisplays the ribbon to allow a feature to be selected.
- To save the current ribbon and Quick Access Toolbar settings, click the File tab and then click *Options*. At the Excel Options dialog box, click *Customize Ribbon* in the left pane. Click the Import/Export button in the lower right corner of the Excel Options dialog box. Click *Export all customizations* to save the file with the custom settings. Click *Import all customizations* to import previously saved customizations.
- To customize the ribbon, open the Excel Options dialog box and then click *Customize Ribbon* in the left pane. Customize the ribbon by creating a new tab, adding buttons to a group, and/or renaming a tab, group, or command.
- Create a new tab by clicking the tab name in the *Main Tabs* list box that will precede the new tab and then clicking the New Tab button. A new group is automatically added with the new tab.
- Add buttons to a group by clicking the group name, selecting the desired command in the commands list box, and then clicking the Add button between the two list boxes.
- Rename a tab by selecting the tab name in the *Main Tabs* list box, clicking the Rename button, typing the new name, and then pressing the Enter key or clicking OK. Rename a group or command using a similar process.
- Add buttons to or delete buttons from the Quick Access Toolbar using the Customize Quick Access Toolbar button. Locate a command to add by opening the Excel Options dialog box with *Quick Access Toolbar* selected in the left pane.
- Export and import customizations to save and restore previous settings on the ribbons and Quick Access Toolbar.
- A custom view saves display and print settings so they can be applied to a worksheet when needed. Multiple custom views can be created for the same worksheet at the Custom Views dialog box. Open this dialog box by clicking the Custom Views button in the Workbook Views group on the View tab.
- Create a macro for a task that is repeated frequently and for which the steps do not vary.
- To begin recording a new macro, click the View tab, click the Macros button arrow in the Macros group, and then click *Record Macro*. At the Record Macro dialog box, assign the macro a name, an optional shortcut key, and a description. Click OK to turn on the macro recorder and close the Record Macro dialog box. All the commands and keystrokes will be recorded until the Stop Recording button is clicked.
- Workbooks that contain macros are saved in the Excel Macro-Enabled Workbook (*.xlsm) file format.

- Run a macro by opening the Macro dialog box and double-clicking the macro name. Run a macro assigned to a shortcut key by pressing Ctrl + the assigned letter. If a macro and an Excel feature are both assigned to the same shortcut key, the macro overrides the feature.
- The instructions for a macro are recorded in Visual Basic for Applications (VBA) program code. To edit a macro, open the Macro dialog box, click the macro name to be edited, and then click the Edit button. A Microsoft Visual Basic for Applications window opens, displaying a code module in which the program code for the macro can be edited. After editing the macro, save the changes, click File, and then click *Close and Return to Microsoft Excel*.
- An alternative to editing a macro in VBA is recording a new macro and then saving it with the same name to replace the existing macro.
- Delete a macro at the Macro dialog box.
- A macro is stored in the workbook in which it was created. When the Macro dialog box is open, all the macros from all the open workbooks are accessible. Therefore, to use a macro stored in another workbook, open that workbook first.
- Another option for making macros accessible to other workbooks is to create a macros workbook with a set of standard macros and then open the macros workbook when working in Excel.
- Inserting a form control allows users to enter information in a worksheet. For example, a combo box form control allows users to select an option from a list. A check box form control allows users to select an option by inserting a check mark in a check box.
- To configure and add options to a form control, right-click the control, click the *Format Control* option at the pop-up menu, and then enter information on the Control tab at the Format Control dialog box.
- Assigning a macro to a button form control allows users to quickly run the macro without having to remember the shortcut key combination or ribbon command.
- A template is a workbook that contains standard text, formatting, and formulas.
- Check the New backstage area to see if the template already exists or search online for templates using the different categories.
- Create a custom template from an existing workbook by selecting *Excel Template (*.xltx)* or *Excel Macro-Enabled Template (*.xltm)* in the *Save as type* option box at the Save As dialog box. To use a custom template, open the New backstage area, click *Personal* to display the templates, and then double-click the custom template name.
- By default, Excel's AutoRecover feature saves an open file every 10 minutes. If an Excel session is unexpectedly terminated or a file is closed without saving, the file can be recovered at the Document Recovery task pane.
- The AutoRecover feature saves the last version of a workbook in a temporary file. If a workbook is closed without saving or an earlier version is wanted, the autosaved version can be recovered using the Recover Unsaved Workbooks hyperlink.
- View and modify security options at Excel's Trust Center, which is responsible for blocking unsafe content when a workbook is opened.

Commands Review

FEATURE	RIBBON TAB, GROUP/OPTION	BUTTON	KEYBOARD SHORTCUT
customize display options	File, *Options*		
customize Quick Access Toolbar	File, *Options*		
customize ribbons	File, *Options*		
customize save options	File, *Options*		
customize view	View, Workbook Views		
delete macro	View, Macros		Alt + F8
edit macro	View, Macros		Alt + F8
insert control	Developer, Controls		
minimize ribbon			Ctrl + F1
record macro	View, Macros	OR	
ribbon display options			Ctrl + F1
save as macro-enabled workbook	File, *Save As*		F12
use custom template	File, *New*		

Microsoft®

Excel®

CHAPTER 8

Protecting and Distributing a Workbook

Performance Objectives

Upon successful completion of Chapter 8, you will be able to:

1. Add information to a workbook's properties
2. Protect cells within a worksheet to prevent changes from being made
3. Protect and unprotect the structure of a workbook
4. Require a password to open a workbook
5. Check a workbook for accessibility issues
6. Scan and remove private or confidential information from a workbook
7. Mark a workbook as final
8. Use the Compatibility Checker to check a workbook for loss of functionality or fidelity with earlier versions of Excel
9. Publish an Excel workbook as a PDF or XPS file
10. Publish an Excel worksheet as a web page
11. Create an XML schema and export and import XML data

In this chapter, you will learn several ways to prepare a workbook to be shared with others, including adding to a workbook's properties, locking worksheets and ranges, and checking for accessibility and compatibility. In a collaborative work environment, adding information to a workbook's properties can help provide other users with information about the structure and purpose of the workbook. Locking worksheets and ranges can help to protect data from accidental changes when a workbook is accessed by multiple users, and checking for accessibility and compatibility is an important step that can help ensure the data can be read by everyone. Finally, you will learn how to publish worksheets in different formats for electronic distribution, including importing and exporting worksheet data in XML code.

Before beginning chapter work, copy the EL2C8 folder to your storage medium and then make EL2C8 the active folder.

The online course includes additional training and assessment resources.

Activity 1 Add Workbook Properties and Insert Comments in a Car Rental Rates Workbook

1 Part

You will add the author's name and other descriptive information in a workbook's properties.

Adding Workbook Properties

Add Information to Properties

1. Click File tab.
2. Click *Info* option.
3. Click *Add a [property]* next to property name.
4. Type text.
5. Click outside property box.

Adding Workbook Properties

Workbook properties include information about the workbook, such as the author's name, the title, the subject, the category to which the workbook is related (such as finance), and general comments about the workbook. This information is added to the file at the Info backstage area, shown in Figure 8.1. The document information panel found in previous versions of Excel does not exist in Excel 365.

Some information is automatically added to a workbook's properties by Excel. For example, Excel maintains statistics such as the date the workbook was created, the date the workbook was last modified, and the name of the last person to save the workbook. Workbook properties are sometimes referred to as *metadata*—a term used to identify descriptive information about data.

To add an author's name or other descriptive information about a workbook, click the File tab and then click the *Info* option. Excel displays the Info backstage area with the workbook's properties displayed at the right side of the screen. By default, when a new workbook is created, Excel inserts in the *Author* property box the name of the computer user (as defined when Microsoft Office is installed). To add another author or make a change to a workbook property (such as the title), click to open the text box next to the property's name. For example, click *Add a title* next to the Title property name. Type the appropriate title in the text box. Click outside the text box to end the entry. Properties that do not display with the message *Add a [property]* cannot be edited. Click the Show All Properties hyperlink at the bottom of the right section in the Info backstage area to add more properties.

Figure 8.1 Properties in the Info Backstage Area

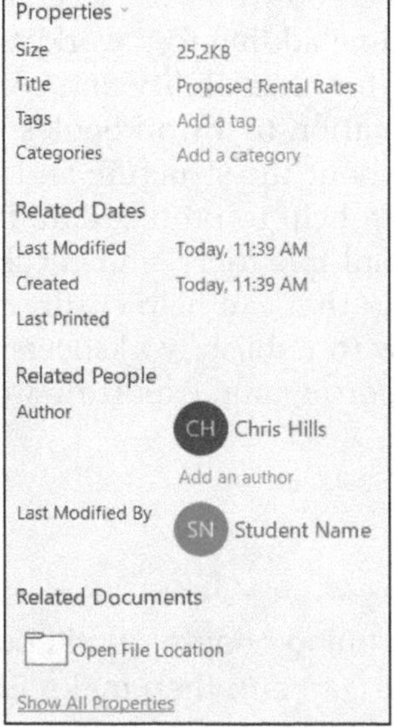

Quick Steps

Add Advanced Properties

1. Click File tab.
2. Click *Info* option.
3. Click Properties button.
4. Click *Advanced Properties.*
5. Add or edit properties as required.
6. Click OK.

To display the advanced properties shown in Figure 8.2, click the Properties button at the top of the right section in the Info backstage area and then click *Advanced Properties* at the drop-down list. Add other properties, including but not limited to information regarding the date completed, the editor, and the person who checked the document.

Having personal information available can be useful when browsing a list of files. The words *Authors, Size,* and *Date Modified* appear in a ScreenTip when the mouse pointer hovers over a workbook name in the Open dialog box. This information helps users to select the correct file.

Figure 8.2 Advanced Properties

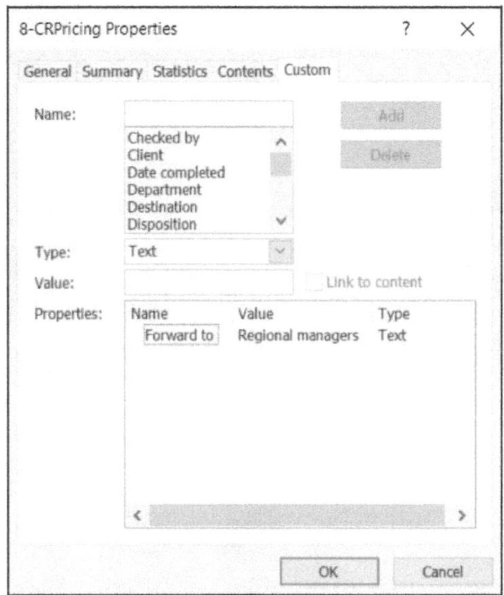

Activity 1 Adding Workbook Properties

Part 1 of 1

1. Open **CRPricing**.
2. Save the workbook with the name **8-CRPricing**.
3. Add an additional author's name, as well as a title, subject, and comments associated with the workbook, by completing the following steps:
   a. Click the File tab and then click the *Info* option.
   b. At the Info backstage area, open an *Author* text box by clicking the *Add an author* text box below the current author's name in the *Related People* section.
   c. Type Chris Hills. If the message *We couldn't find the person you were looking for* displays, ignore it.
   d. Click outside the *Author* text box to close it.
   e. Click *Add a title* in the *Title* text box, type Proposed Rental Rates, and then click outside the text box.

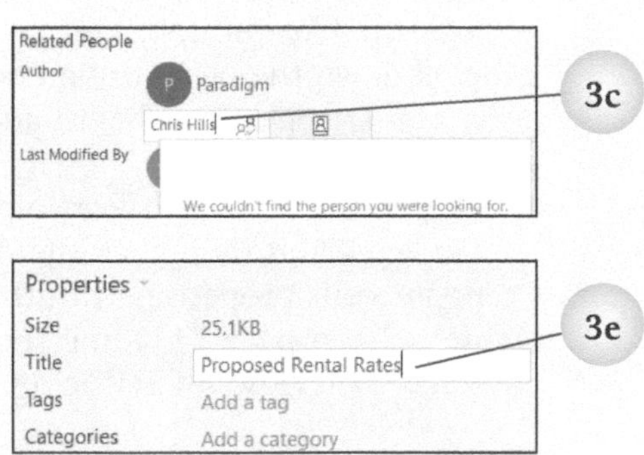

f. Click the Show All Properties hyperlink below the *Related Documents* section to display additional properties.

g. Click *Specify the subject* in the *Subject* text box, type Rental Rates for May 2021, and then click outside the text box.

h. Click *Add comments* in the *Comments* text box, type Proposed rental rates sent for review to regional managers., and then click outside the text box.

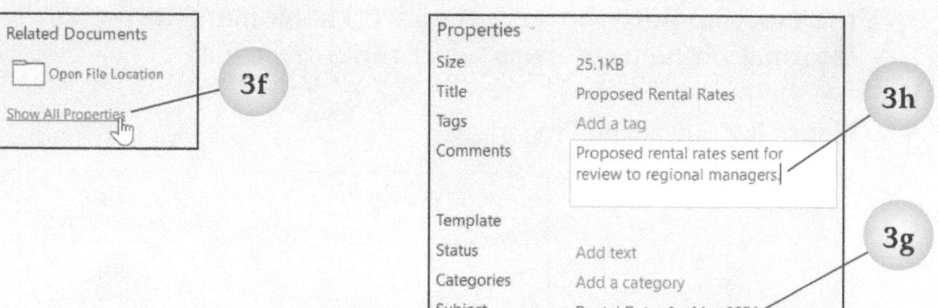

4. Right-click *Paradigm* next to the *Author* text box and then click *Remove Person* at the shortcut menu.
5. Click the Show Fewer Properties hyperlink at the bottom of the properties.

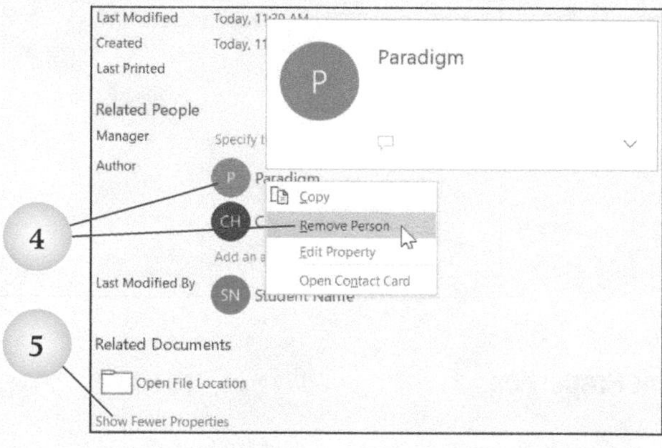

6. Compare your properties with those shown in Figure 8.1 (on page 210). The dates may vary.
7. Add advanced properties by completing the following steps:
   a. Click the Properties button above the workbook properties and then click *Advanced Properties* at the drop-down list.
   b. Click the Custom tab.
   c. Scroll down the *Name* option box until *Forward to* appears in the list and then click this option.
   d. Click in the *Value* text box, type Regional managers, and then click the Add button.

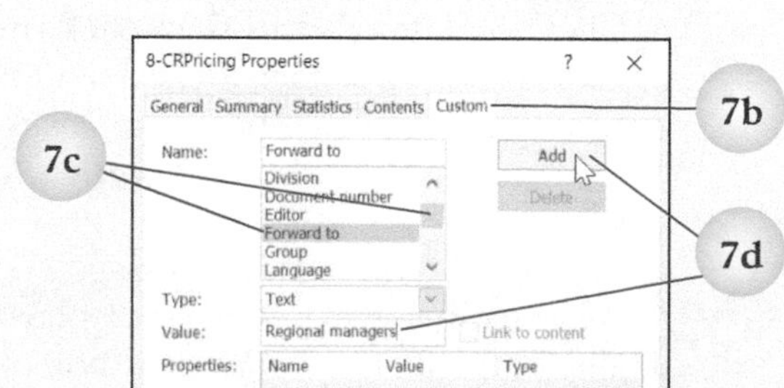

8. Compare your properties with those shown in Figure 8.2 (on page 211) and then click OK.
9. Save and then close **8-CRPricing**.

Activity 2 Lock and Unlock a Workbook, Worksheet, and Ranges in a Car Rental Rates Workbook — 4 Parts

You will protect a worksheet, unlock ranges, prevent changes to the structure of a workbook, and then add a password to open a workbook.

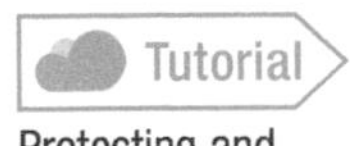

Protecting and Unprotecting Worksheets

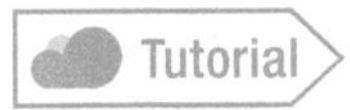

Unlocking Cells and Protecting a Worksheet

Format

Protect Sheet

Quick Steps

Protect Worksheet

1. Open workbook.
2. Activate sheet.
3. Click Review tab.
4. Click Protect Sheet button.
5. Type password.
6. Choose allowable actions.
7. Click OK.
8. Retype password if entered in Step 5.
9. Click OK.

Unlock Cell

1. Select cell(s) to be unlocked.
2. Click Home tab.
3. Click Format button.
4. Click *Lock Cell*.
5. Deselect cell(s).

Protecting and Unprotecting Worksheets

Protecting a worksheet prevents other users from accidentally deleting or modifying cells that should not be changed. By default, when a worksheet is protected, each cell in it is locked. This means that no one can insert, delete, or modify the content. In most cases, some of the cells within a worksheet contain data that other users can change. Therefore, in a collaborative environment, protecting a worksheet generally involves two steps:

1. Clear the lock attribute on those cells that are allowed to be edited.
2. Protect the worksheet.

To clear the lock attribute from the cells that are allowed to be edited, select the cells to be unlocked, click the Home tab, and then click the Format button in the Cells group. Click *Lock Cell* in the *Protection* section of the drop-down list to turn off the lock attribute. To turn on worksheet protection, click the Review tab and then click the Protect Sheet button in the Protect group. At the Protect Sheet dialog box, shown in Figure 8.3, select the actions to be allowed and then click OK. A password can be assigned to unprotect the sheet. Be cautious about adding a password, since the worksheet cannot be unprotected if the password is forgotten. If necessary, write down the password and store it in a secure location.

Figure 8.3 Protect Sheet Dialog Box

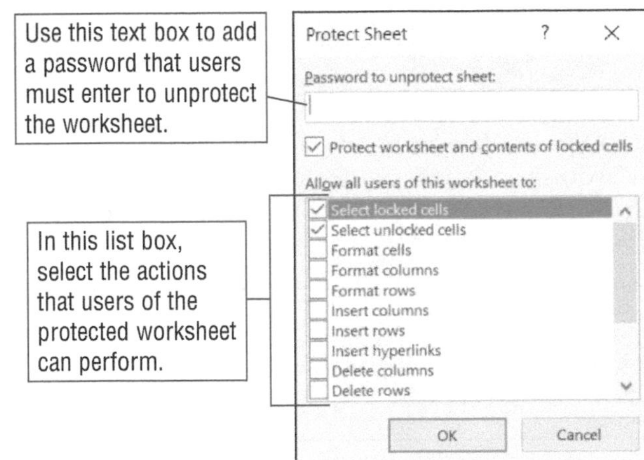

When a worksheet has protection turned on, the Protect Sheet button in the Protect group on the Review tab turns into the Unprotect Sheet button. To remove worksheet protection, click the Unprotect Sheet button or click the Unprotect hyperlink in the Info backstage area. If a password was entered when the worksheet was protected, the Unprotect Sheet dialog box appears, as shown in Figure 8.4. Type the password and then press the Enter key or click OK.

Figure 8.4 Unprotect Sheet Dialog Box

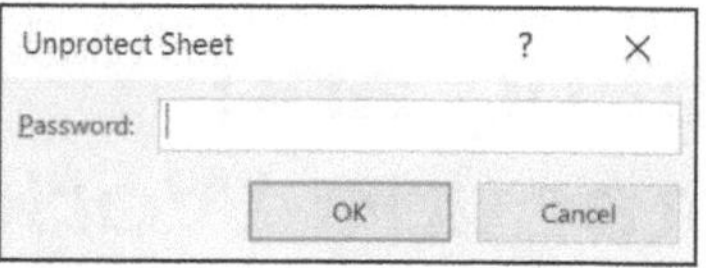

Activity 2a **Protecting an Entire Worksheet** Part 1 of 4

1. Open **CRFinalPrices** and save it with the name **8-CRFinalPrices.**
2. Protect the entire FinalPrices worksheet by completing the following steps:
   a. Make sure FinalPrices is the active sheet.
   b. Click the Review tab.
   c. Click the Protect Sheet button in the Protect group.
   d. At the Protect Sheet dialog box with the insertion point positioned in the *Password to unprotect sheet* text box, type eL2-C8 and then click OK.
   e. At the Confirm Password dialog box with the insertion point positioned in the *Reenter password to proceed* text box, type eL2-C8 and then click OK.

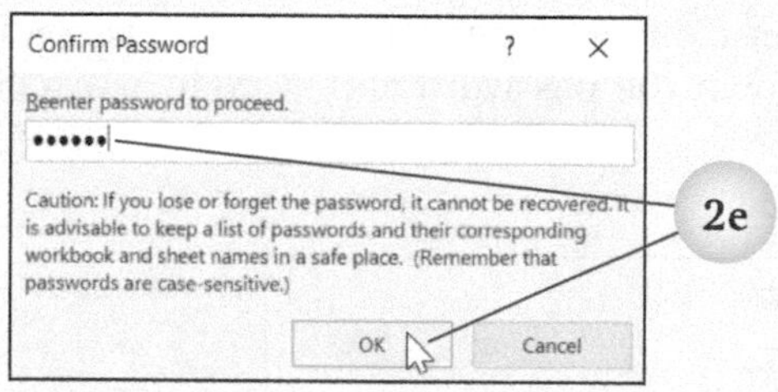

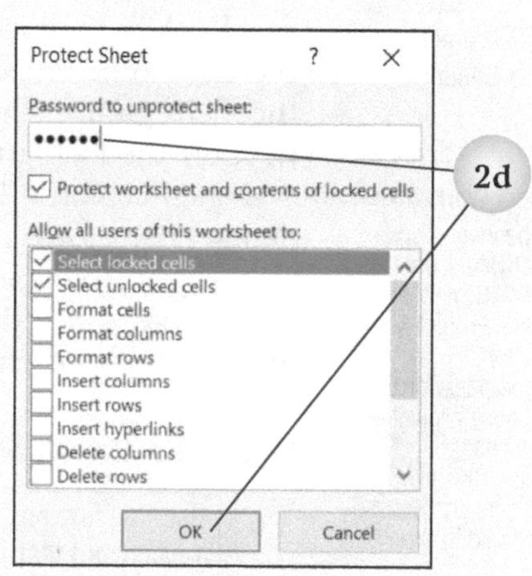

   f. Make any cell active in the FinalPrices sheet and attempt to delete the data or type new data. Since the entire worksheet is now protected, all the cells are locked. A Microsoft Excel message appears stating that the cell or chart trying to be changed is on a protected worksheet. Click OK.

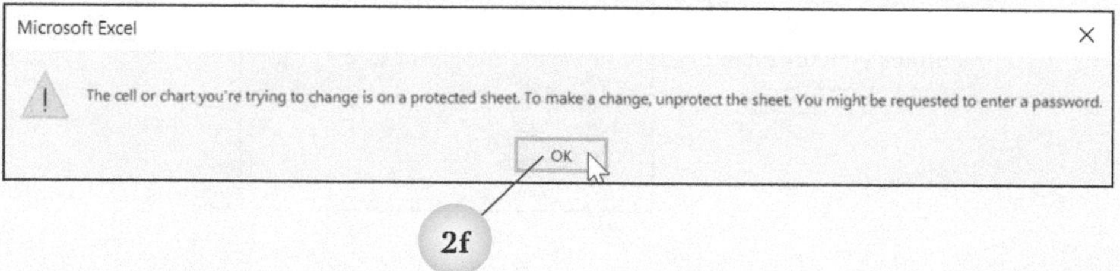

3. Notice that the Protect Sheet button changes to the Unprotect Sheet button when a worksheet has been protected.
4. Save **8-CRFinalPrices.**

Activity 2b **Unlocking Cells and Protecting a Worksheet** Part 2 of 4

1. With **8-CRFinalPrices** open, make TargetRevenue the active sheet.
2. Unlock the weekday target rental data cells for editing by completing the following steps:
   a. Select the range C5:C10.
   b. Click the Home tab.
   c. Click the Format button in the Cells group.
   d. At the Format button drop-down list, look at the icon next to *Lock Cell* in the *Protection* section. The highlighted icon indicates that the lock attribute is turned on.
   e. Click *Lock Cell* at the Format button drop-down list to turn the lock attribute off for the selected range.
   f. Click in any cell within the range C5:C10 and then click the Format button in the Cells group. Look at the icon next to *Lock Cell* in the drop-down list. The icon is no longer highlighted, which indicates that the cell is unlocked.
   g. Click within the worksheet area to close the drop-down list.

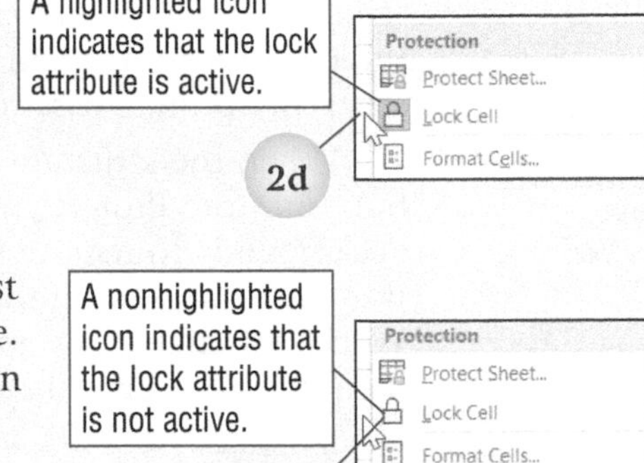

3. Unlock the remaining target rental ranges for editing by completing the following steps:
   a. Select the range F5:F10, press and hold down the Ctrl key, select the ranges I5:I10 and L5:L10, and then release the Ctrl key.
   b. Press the F4 function key to repeat the command to unlock the cells or click the Format button in the Cells group and then click *Lock Cell* at the drop-down list.
   c. Click in any cell to deselect the ranges.
4. Protect the TargetRevenue worksheet by completing the following steps:
   a. Click the Review tab.
   b. Click the Protect Sheet button in the Protect group.
   c. Type eL2-C8 in the *Password to unprotect sheet* text box.
   d. Click OK.
   e. Type eL2-C8 in the *Reenter password to proceed* text box.
   f. Click OK.
5. Save **8-CRFinalPrices**.
6. Test the worksheet protection applied to the TargetRevenue sheet by completing the following steps:
   a. Make cell B8 active and then press the Delete key.
   b. Click OK at the Microsoft Excel message box stating that the protected cell cannot be changed.
   c. Make cell C8 active and then press the Delete key. Since cell C8 is unlocked, its contents are deleted and its dependent cells are updated.
   d. Click the Undo button on the Quick Access Toolbar to restore the contents of cell C8.
7. Save **8-CRFinalPrices**.

6c

4	Category	Weekday (Mo to Th)	Target Rentals	Target Revenue
5	Compact	$ 45.99	675	$ 31,043
6	Mid-size	48.99	880	43,111
7	Full-size	50.99	425	21,671
8	Minivan	85.99		-
9	SUV	99.99	198	19,798
10	Luxury	109.99	86	9,459
11	TOTAL		Weekday:	$ 125,082

Protecting and Unprotecting the Structure of a Workbook

Protect Workbook

Quick Steps

Protect Workbook Structure

1. Open workbook.
2. Click Review tab.
3. Click Protect Workbook button.
4. Type password.
5. Click OK.
6. Retype password if entered at Step 4.
7. Click OK.

Protecting and Unprotecting the Structure of a Workbook

Use the Protect Workbook button in the Protect group on the Review tab to prevent changes to the structure of a workbook, such as inserting a new sheet, deleting a sheet, or unhiding a hidden worksheet. At the Protect Structure and Windows dialog box, shown in Figure 8.5, turn on protection for the workbook's structure. Click the *Windows* check box to prevent a user from resizing or changing the positions of the windows in the workbook. As with protecting a worksheet, enter an optional password that will protect the workbook.

When the structure of a workbook has been protected, the Protect Workbook button in the Protect group on the Review tab displays with a gray shaded background. To remove workbook protection, click the Protect Workbook button. If a password was entered when the workbook was protected, the Unprotect Workbook dialog box appears, as shown in Figure 8.6. Type the password and then press the Enter key.

Figure 8.5 Protect Structure and Windows Dialog Box

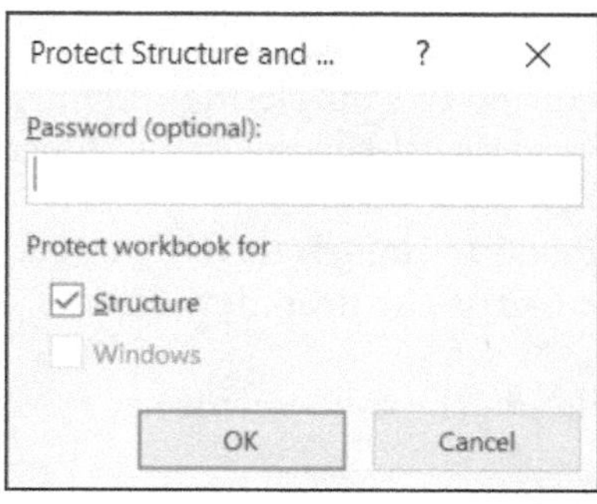

Figure 8.6 Unprotect Workbook Dialog Box

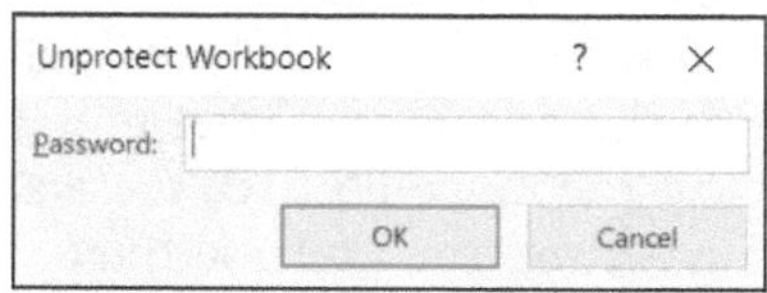

Activity 2c Protecting the Structure of a Workbook

Part 3 of 4

1. With **8-CRFinalPrices** open, protect the workbook structure by completing the following steps:
   a. If necessary, click the Review tab.
   b. Click the Protect Workbook button in the Protect group.
   c. At the Protect Structure and Windows dialog box with the insertion point positioned in the *Password (optional)* text box, type eL2-C8.
   d. Click OK.
   e. At the Confirm Password dialog box with the insertion point positioned in the *Reenter password to proceed* text box, type eL2-C8.
   f. Click OK.

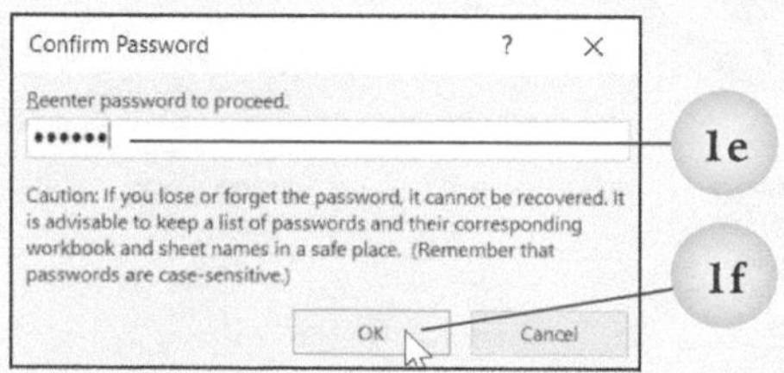

2. To test the workbook protection, attempt to insert a new worksheet by completing the following steps:
   a. Right-click the TargetRevenue sheet tab.
   b. Look at the shortcut menu. Notice that all the options related to managing worksheets are dimmed, which means they are unavailable.
   c. Click within the worksheet area to close the shortcut menu.
3. Save **8-CRFinalPrices.**

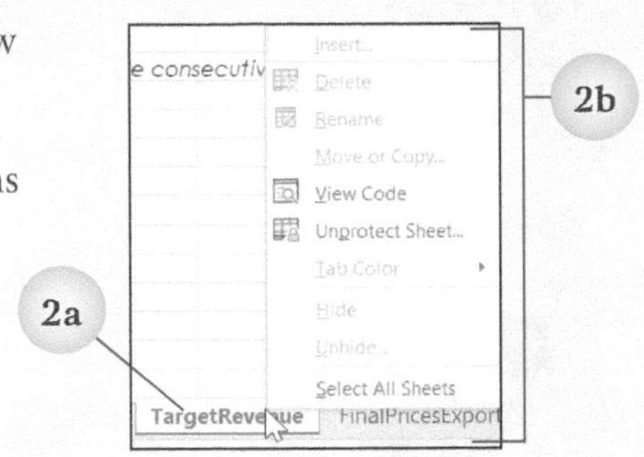

Adding a Password to Open a Workbook

Protect Workbook

Adding and Removing a Password to Open a Workbook

Prevent unauthorized access to Excel data by requiring a password to open a workbook. The password to open a workbook is encrypted. In an encrypted password, the plain text that is typed is converted into a scrambled format called *ciphertext*, which prevents unauthorized users from retrieving the password. To add an encrypted password to an open workbook, click the File tab and then click the *Info* option. At the Info backstage area, shown in Figure 8.7, click the Protect Workbook button in the *Protect Workbook* section. Click *Encrypt with Password* at the drop-down list to open the Encrypt Document dialog box, shown in Figure 8.8. Save the workbook after typing and confirming the password.

Figure 8.7 Info Backstage Area with the Protect Workbook Drop-Down List

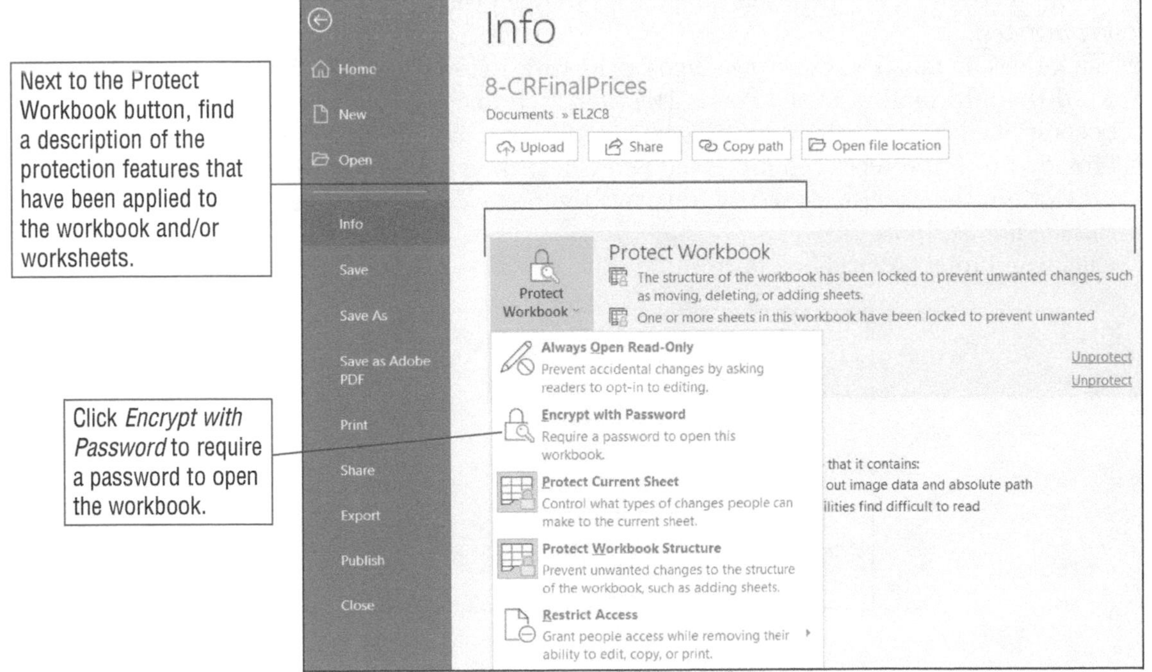

Figure 8.8 Encrypt Document Dialog Box

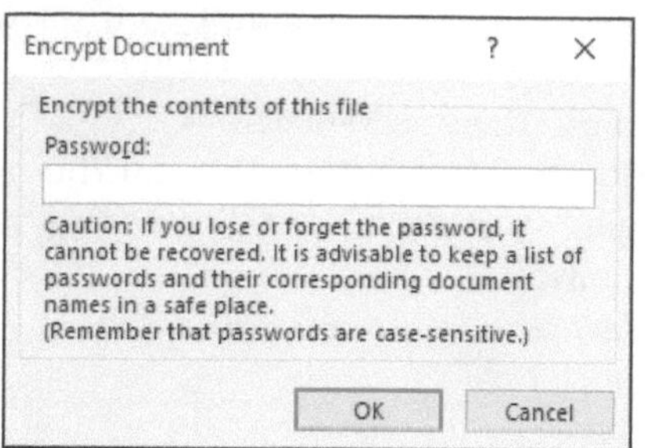

Quick Steps

Add Workbook Password

1. Open workbook.
2. Click File tab.
3. Click *Info* option.
4. Click Protect Workbook button.
5. Click *Encrypt with Password.*
6. Type password.
7. Click OK.
8. Retype password if entered in Step 6.
9. Click OK.
10. Save workbook.

When creating a password, it is good practice to use a combination of four types of characters: uppercase letters, lowercase letters, symbols, and numbers. A password constructed using these elements is considered secure and more difficult to crack. Note that if the password is forgotten, the workbook cannot be opened. If necessary, write down the password and store it in a secure location.

To remove a password from a workbook, open the workbook using the password. At the Info backstage area, click the Protect Workbook button. Click *Encrypt with Password* at the drop-down list to open the Encrypt Document dialog box. Delete the password, click OK, and then save the workbook.

Activity 2d Adding a Password to Open a Workbook

Part 4 of 4

1. With **8-CRFinalPrices** open, add a password to open the workbook by completing the following steps:
   a. Click the File tab. The backstage area opens with the *Info* option selected.
   b. Read the information in the *Protect Workbook* section. Since protection has already been applied to this workbook, the existing features are described and a hyperlink is provided to unprotect each protected worksheet. In a workbook with no pre-existing protection, the *Permissions* section displays the text *Control what types of changes people can make to this workbook.*
   c. Click the Protect Workbook button.

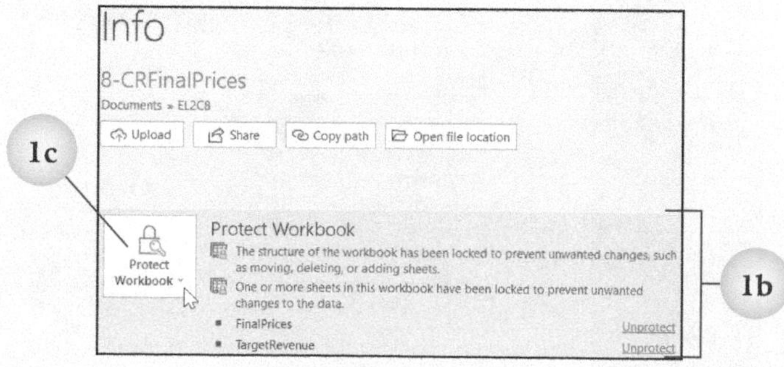

d. Click *Encrypt with Password* at the drop-down list.
e. At the Encrypt Document dialog box with the insertion point positioned in the *Password* text box, type eL2-C8.
f. Click OK.

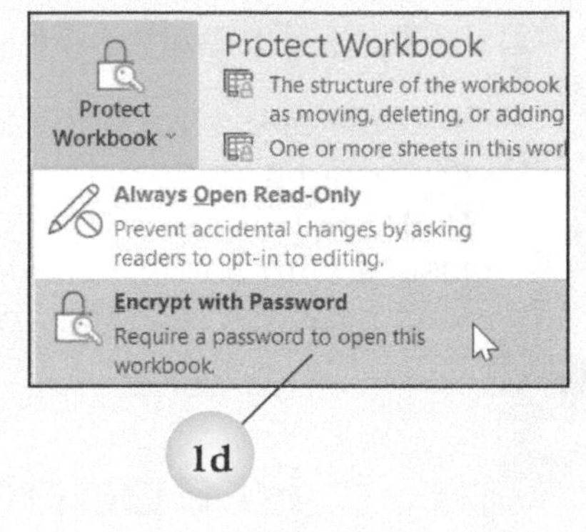

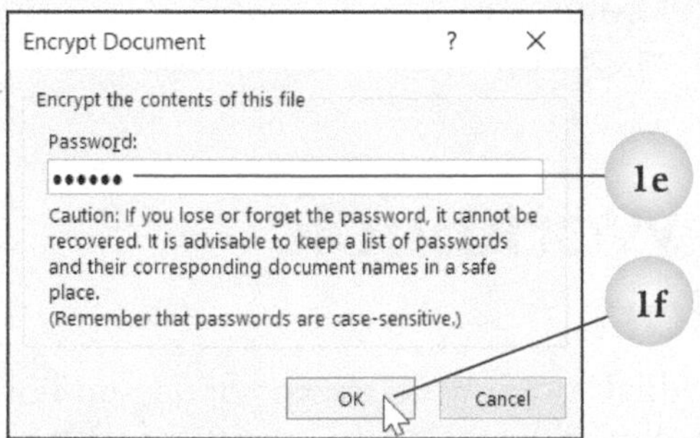

g. At the Confirm Password dialog box with the insertion point positioned in the *Reenter password* text box, type eL2-C8.
h. Click OK.
i. Notice that the description next to the Protect Workbook button now includes the text *A password is required to open this workbook.*
j. Click the Back button to return to the worksheet.

2. Save and then close **8-CRFinalPrices.**
3. Test the password security on the workbook by completing the following steps:
   a. Open **8-CRFinalPrices.**
   b. At the Password dialog box with the insertion point positioned in the *Password* text box, type a password that is incorrect for the file.
   c. Click OK.
   d. At the Microsoft Excel message box stating that the password is not correct, click OK.
   e. Open **8-CRFinalPrices.**
   f. Type eL2-C8 in the *Password* text box.
   g. Click OK.
4. Close **8-CRFinalPrices.**

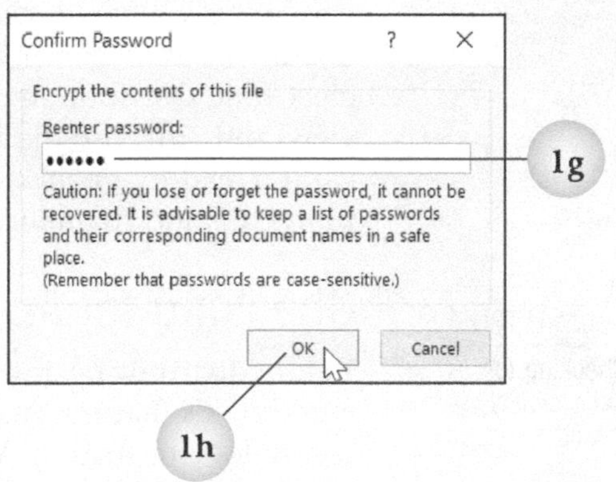

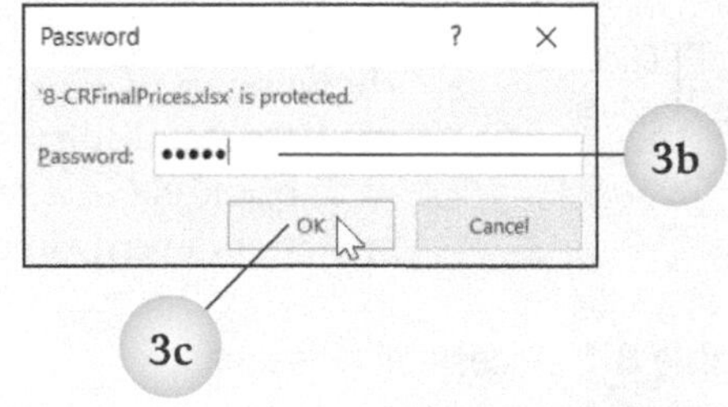

Activity 3 Prepare a First-Quarter Sales Workbook for Distribution **4 Parts**

You will check for and fix any accessibility issues in a workbook, remove confidential information from a workbook, and mark the workbook as final to prepare it for distribution. In another workbook, you will check for compatibility issues with earlier versions of Excel before sending the workbook to someone who uses Excel 2003. You will also explore the default settings in the Trust Center.

Preparing a Workbook for Distribution

In today's workplace, individuals often work as part of a team both within and outside an organization. Excel workbooks are frequently exchanged between coworkers via email message attachments; saving to a shared network folder, document management server, or company website; or using other means of electronic distribution. Before making a workbook available for others to open, view, and edit, use the features provided by Excel to ensure that the workbook can be read by people with accessibility issues and that confidentiality will be protected and maintained.

Checking for Accessibility Issues

Check Accessibility

Check for Issues

Checking for Accessibility Issues

Before distributing a workbook, be sure to determine whether any of the workbook's features may make it difficult for someone who requires assistive technology to read it. After opening the file, run the Accessibility Checker by clicking the Check Accessibility button in the Accessibility group on the Review tab or click the File tab and then click the *Info* option. Click the Check for Issues button and then click *Check Accessibility* in the drop-down list. Depending on the version of Excel, a message will appear in the Status bar notifying the user of the accessibility status of the workbook. It will either notify the user that the workbook is *Good to go* or prompt the user to *Investigate*. There are three levels of errors; a description and example of each is provided in Table 8.1.

Table 8.1 Accessibility Issues

Accessibility Issue	Description	Example
Error	Workbook will be very difficult if not impossible for people with accessibility issues to understand.	Each object must have alternative text. Examples of objects are pictures, charts, tables, and shapes without text.
Warning	Workbook will be difficult in some cases for people with accessibility issues to understand.	Sheet tabs are named. Remove split or merged cells.
Tip	Workbook can be understood by people with accessibility issues but making changes might make it better organized and easier to understand.	Closed captions are included for inserted audio and video.

Inspection Results

Quick Steps

Check Accessibility

1. Click Review tab.
2. Click *Check Accessibility*.
3. Click issue.
4. Follow steps to fix issue.

After running the Accessibility Checker, refer to the Accessibility Checker task pane on the right side of the screen for a list of inspection results, as shown in Figure 8.9. The flagged object or cell, including the name of the sheet in which it is located, is listed under the relevant issue (*Errors*) and problem (*Missing alternative text*). Click a problem and Excel selects the portion of the worksheet affected by the issue, if possible. For example, objects like the table in Figure 8.9 are selected but sheet tabs are not. Once a problem is selected, an option box arrow appears. Click the arrow and choose an option to correct the problem or review the instructions in the *Why Fix?* and *Steps To Fix* sections, which appear in the *Additional Information* section at the bottom of the Accessibility Checker task pane. Once an issue has been corrected, it will no longer appear in the inspection results. Microsoft continues to update the Accessibility Checker to ensure compatibility with assistive technology, so steps may vary in the following activities.

Figure 8.9 Accessibility Checker Task Pane with Inspection Results Shown

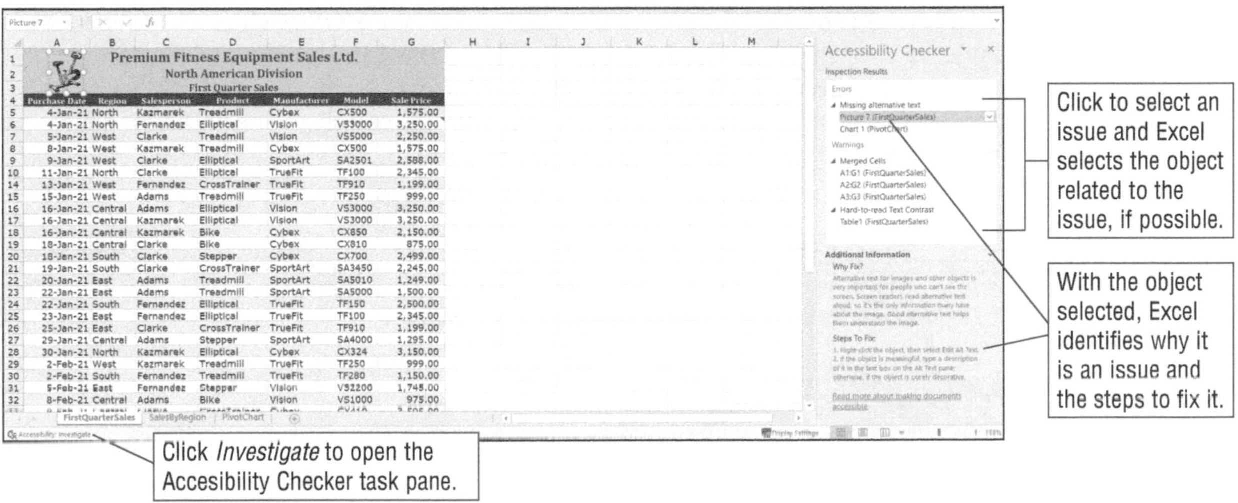

Activity 3a **Inspecting a Workbook for Accessibility Issues** Part 1 of 4

1. Open **PFSales**.
2. Save the workbook with the name **8-PFSales**.
3. Examine the workbook for accessibility issues by completing the following steps:
   a. Click the Review tab and then click the Check Accessibility button in the Accessibility group.
   b. Expand the Errors and Warnings, if necessary, by clicking the expand button at the left of the error.
   c. Read the inspection results in the Accessibility Checker task pane.
4. Correct the errors listed in the inspection results by completing the following steps:
   a. Click *Picture 7 (FirstQuarterSales)* under *Missing alternative text*. The picture left of the title in row 1 in the FirstQuarterSales worksheet is selected.
   b. Click the option box arrow and then click the *Mark as decorative* option. The issue is removed from the *Errors* list in the *Inspection Results* section.

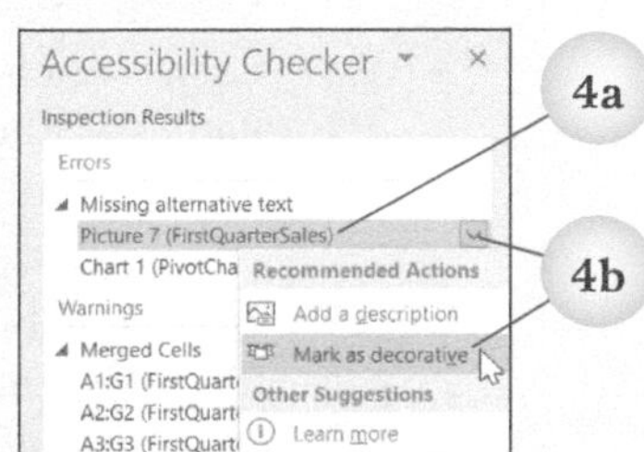

c. Click *Chart 1 (PivotChart)* under *Missing alternative text.* The Pivot Chart is selected.
d. Click the option box arrow and then click the *Add a description* option.
e. At the Alt Text task pane, click in the text box and type the following description: PivotChart depicting the first-quarter sales by region and by salesperson. The issue is removed from the *Errors* list.
f. Click the Alt Text task pane Close button.

5. Click *Table1 (FirstQuarterSales)* under *Hard-to-read Text Contrast.* Read the *Steps To Fix* and note that a style that has higher contrast between the text and the background is suggested.
6. Correct the issue by completing the following steps:
   a. Click *Table1 (FirstQuarter Sales)* under *Hard-to-read Text Contrast.*
   b. Click the option box arrow, hover the mouse pointer over *Quick Styles,* and then choose a style that has a higher contrast between the text and the background. Experiment with different styles until the issue disappears from the inspection results. Click the Light Orange, Table Style Light 16 table style (third column, third row in the *Light* section) since it meets the requirements to pass the accessibility check.
7. Close the Accessibility Checker task pane by clicking the Accessibility Checker task pane Close button.

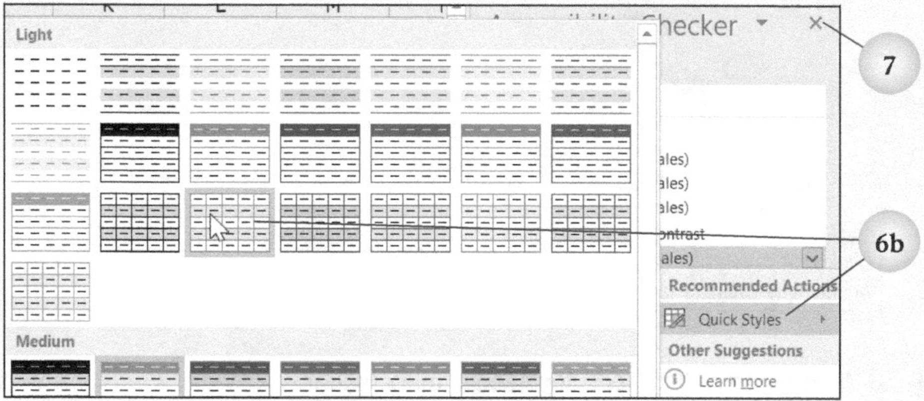

8. Save **8-PFSales**.

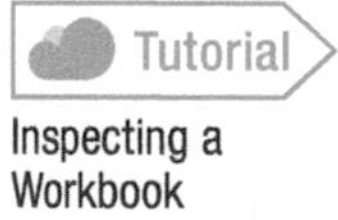

Inspecting a Workbook

Inspecting a Workbook and Removing Information before Distributing It

Before distributing a workbook electronically, consider using the Document Inspector to scan the workbook for personal data and hidden information that others should not view, including information that is tracked automatically by Excel, such as the names of the individuals who have accessed and edited a workbook, or headers, footers, hidden items, and other invisible data that may not need to be viewed.

If any of this sensitive or hidden information should remain confidential, remove it before distributing the file. Before doing so, save a copy of the original file retaining all the content. To inspect the document, click the File tab and then click the *Info* option. At the Info backstage area, click the Check for Issues button in the *Inspect Workbook* section and then click *Inspect Document* at the drop-down

Quick Steps

Use Document Inspector to Remove Private Information

1. Open workbook.
2. Click File tab.
3. Click the *Info* option.
4. Click Check for Issues button.
5. Click *Inspect Document*.
6. Clear check boxes for items not to be scanned.
7. Click Inspect button.
8. Click Remove All button in sections to be removed.
9. Click Close button.

list. This opens the Document Inspector dialog box, shown in Figure 8.10. By default, all the check boxes are selected. Clear the check boxes for those items that are not to be scanned or removed and then click the Inspect button.

The Document Inspector scans the workbook to look for all the checked items. When the scan is completed, a dialog box like the one in Figure 8.11 appears. Excel displays check marks in the sections for which no items were found and red exclamation marks in the sections for which items were found. Click the Remove All button in the section that contains content to be removed. Click OK when finished and then distribute the workbook as needed. If you require information such as authors and other metadata to be saved in the future, click the Allow this information to be saved in our file hyperlink in the *Inspect Workbook* section of the Info backstage area.

Figure 8.10 Document Inspector Dialog Box

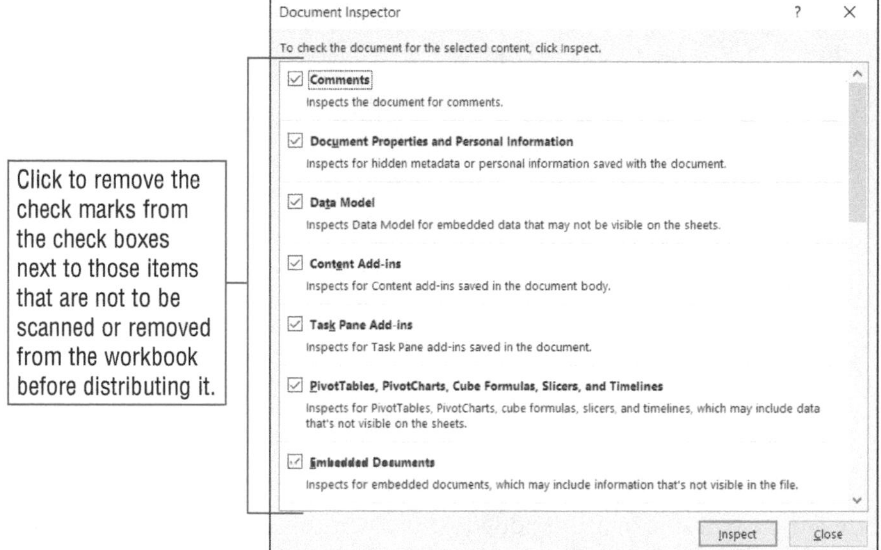

Figure 8.11 Document Inspector Dialog Box with Inspection Results Shown

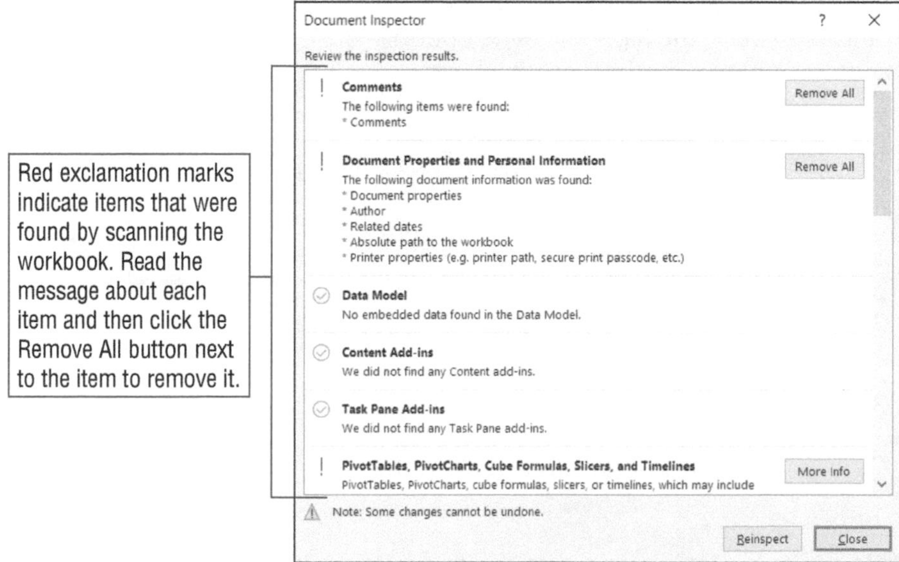

Activity 3b Removing Private and Confidential Data from a Workbook

Part 2 of 4

1. With **8-PFSales** open, examine the workbook for private and other confidential information by completing the following steps:
   a. Click the File tab and then click the *Info* option.
   b. Read the property information in the fields in the *Properties* section at the right side of the screen.
   c. Click the Properties button and then click *Advanced Properties* at the drop-down list.
   d. Click the Custom tab in the 8-PFSales Properties dialog box.
   e. Hover the mouse pointer over the right column boundary for the *Value* column in the *Properties* list box until the pointer changes to a left-and-right-pointing arrow with a vertical line in the middle. Drag the column width to the right until all the text in the column can be read.

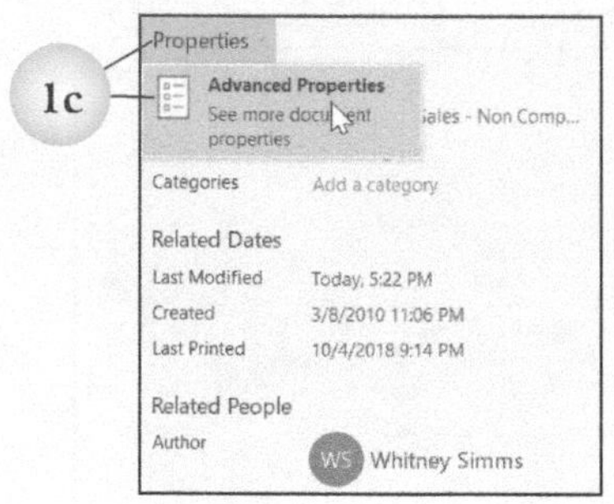

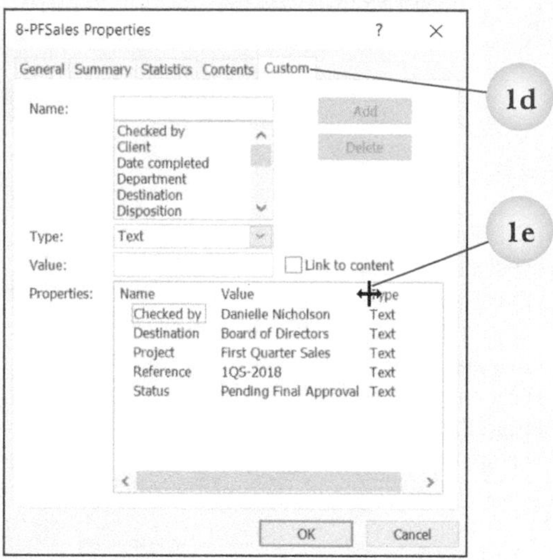

   f. Notice that the extra information added to the workbook properties contains names and other data that should perhaps remain confidential.
   g. Click OK.
   h. Press the Esc key or click the Back button.
   i. With the FirstQuarterSales worksheet active, click the Review tab, click the Notes button, and then click the *Show All Notes* option.
   j. Read the note displayed in the worksheet area.

Manufacturer	Model	Sale Price
Cybex	CX500	1,575.00
Vision	VS3000	3,250.00
Vision	VS5000	2,250.00
Cybex	CX500	1,575.00
SportArt	SA2501	2,588.00

Whitney Simms:
Price increase expected next year.

1j

2. Use the Document Inspector to scan the workbook for other confidential information by completing the following steps:
   a. Click the File tab, click the Check for Issues button in the *Inspect Workbook* section at the Info backstage area, and then click *Inspect Document* at the drop-down list.
   b. At the message box stating that the file contains changes that have not been saved, click Yes to save the file.
   c. At the Document Inspector dialog box with all the check boxes selected, click the Inspect button to look for all the items.
   d. Read the messages in the first two sections of the Document Inspector dialog box, which display with red exclamation marks.
   e. Click the Remove All button in the *Document Properties and Personal Information* section. Excel deletes the metadata and the section displays with a check mark, indicating the information has been removed.

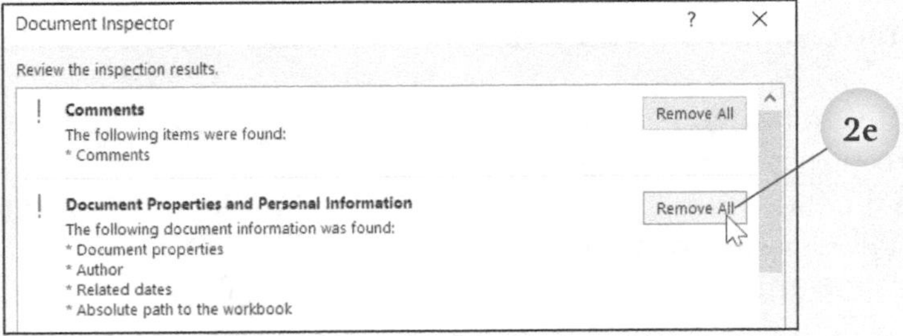

   f. Scroll down and read the message for the *PivotTables, PivotCharts, Cube Formulas, Slicers, and Timelines* section. The PivotTable and PivotChart will not be altered.
   g. Scroll down further and notice that the inspection results indicate that a header and three hidden rows were found. Review these items but do not click the Remove All buttons. Click the Close button to close the Document Inspector dialog box.
3. Display the worksheet in Page Layout view and view the header. Switch back to Normal view.
4. Look at the row numbers in the worksheet area. Notice that after row 10, the next row number is 14. Select row numbers 10 and 14, right-click the selected rows, and then click *Unhide* at the shortcut menu to display rows 11 through 13.

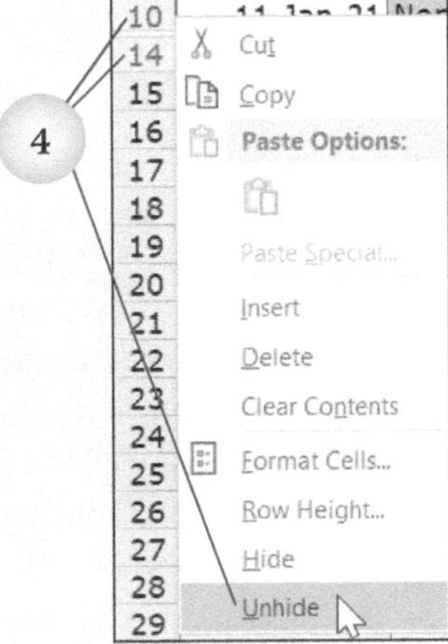

5. Click in any cell to deselect the range. Review the information in the rows that were hidden.
6. You decide that the rows that were initially hidden should remain displayed but you want to prevent reviewers of the workbook from seeing the header and comments. Use the Document Inspector to remove these items by completing the following steps:
   a. Click the File tab, click the *Info* option, click the Check for Issues button, click *Inspect Document* at the drop-down list, and then click the Yes button to save the changes to the workbook.
   b. Remove the check marks from all the check boxes except those next to the sections *Comments* and *Headers and Footers*.
   c. Click the Inspect button.
   d. Click the Remove All button in the *Comments* section.
   e. Click the Remove All button in the *Headers and Footers* section.
   f. Click the Close button.
7. Notice that the comments and/or notes and the header have been deleted from the worksheet.
8. Click the Notes button and then the *Show All Notes* option in the Notes group on the Review tab to turn off the feature.
9. Allow personal information to be saved with the workbook by completing the following steps.
   a. Click the File tab and then click the *Info* option.
   b. Click the Allow this information to be saved in your file hyperlink.

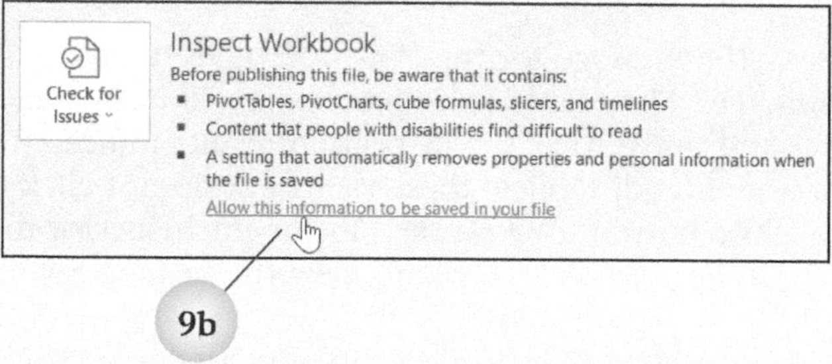

10. Save **8-PFSales**.

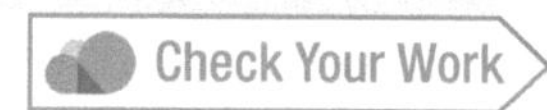

Marking a Workbook as Final

Quick Steps
Mark Workbook as Final
1. Open workbook.
2. Click File tab.
3. Click Protect Workbook button.
4. Click *Mark as Final*.
5. Click OK two times.

A workbook that will be distributed to others can be marked as final, which means it is protected from additions, deletions, and modifications. When a workbook is marked as final, it is changed to a read-only file and the status property is set to *Final*. In addition to protecting the workbook, marking it as final also indicates to the recipients that the content is considered complete.

To mark a workbook as final, click the File tab and then click the *Info* option. At the Info backstage area, click the Protect Workbook button and then click *Mark as Final* at the drop-down list. (Note that marking a workbook as final is not as secure as using password-protected, locked ranges.)

A workbook marked as final displays with the ribbon minimized and a message above the Formula bar that informs the user that the author has marked the workbook as final to discourage editing. Click the Edit Anyway button in the message bar to remove the Mark as Final feature, redisplay the ribbon, and allow changes to be made to the workbook.

Activity 3c Marking a Workbook as Final

1. With **8-PFSales** open, save the workbook with the name **8-PFSalesFinal**.
2. Mark the workbook as final to prevent changes from being made and set the Status property to *Final* by completing the following steps:
   a. Click the File tab, click the *Info* option, click the Protect Workbook button in the Info backstage area, and then click *Mark as Final* at the drop-down list.

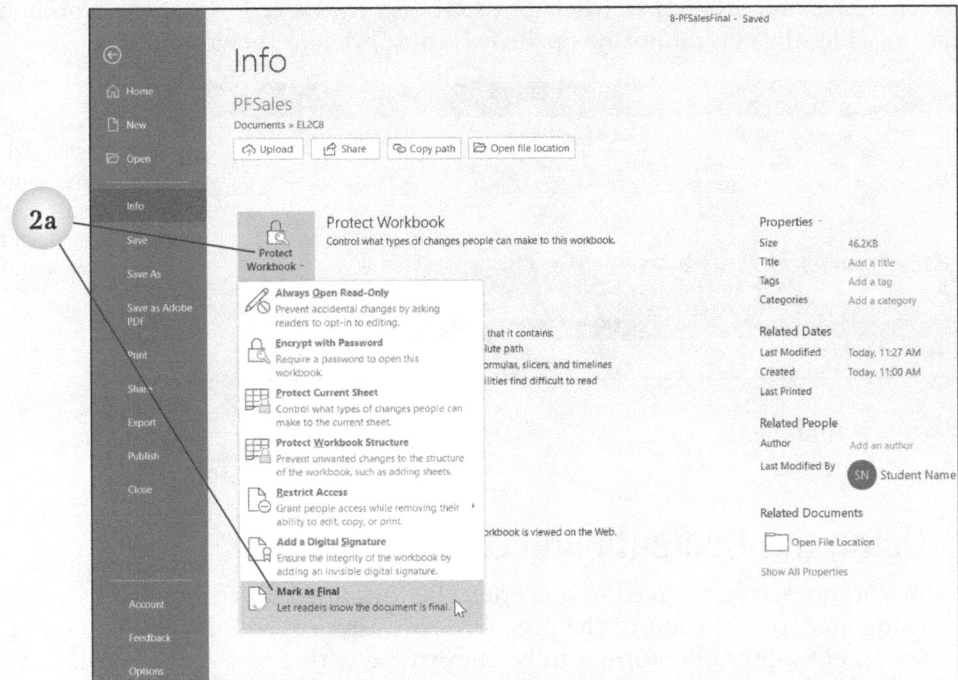

   b. Click OK at the message box stating that the workbook will be marked as final and then saved.

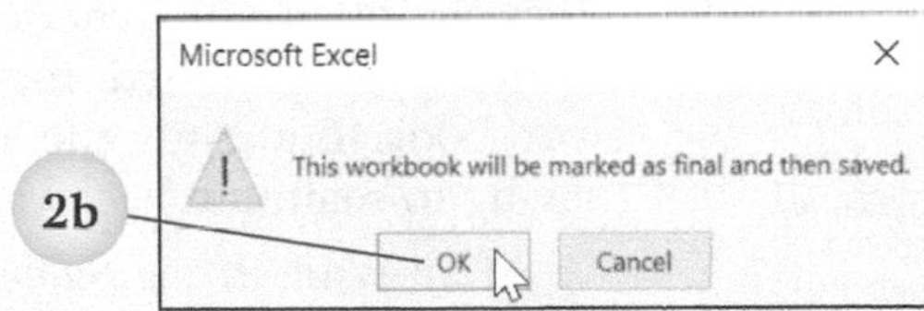

   c. Click OK at the second message box stating that the workbook has been marked as final to indicate that editing is complete and this is the final version of the file. ***Note:** If this message box does not appear, it has been turned off by a previous user who clicked the* **Don't show this message again** ***check box.***

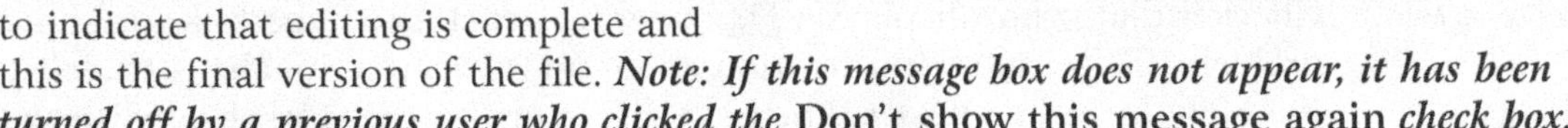

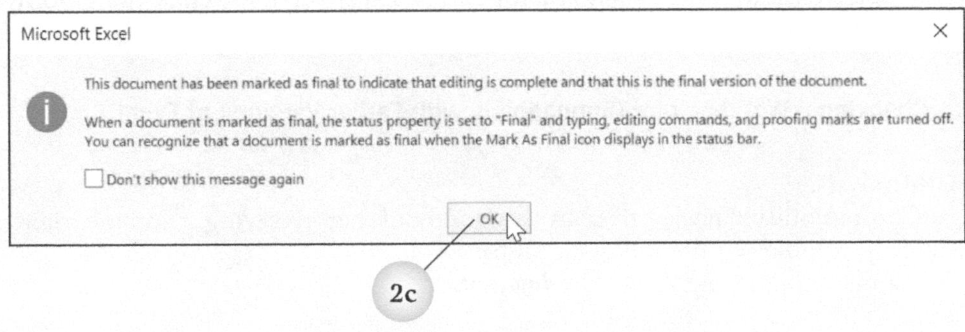

3. Click the File tab. Notice that the *Protect Workbook* section of the Info backstage area displays in yellow with a message stating that the workbook has been marked as final. Click the Back button and notice the addition of *Read-Only* next to the file name in the Title bar.
4. The ribbon is minimized and a message displays above the Formula bar indicating that the workbook has been marked as final to discourage editing. An additional message or icon may display in the Status bar.
5. Make any cell active and attempt to insert or delete text in the cell. Since the workbook is now a read-only file, the cell cannot be opened to edit or delete the contents.

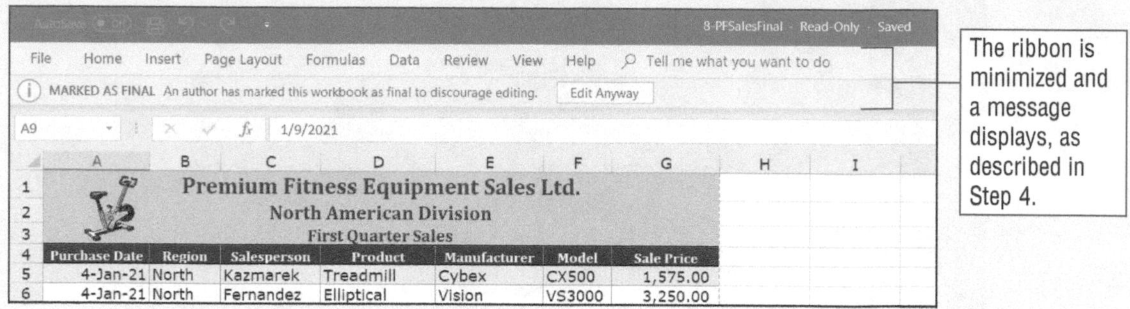

6. Close **8-PFSalesFinal**.

Using the Compatibility Checker

Quick Steps

Check Workbook for Compatibility
1. Open workbook.
2. Click File tab.
3. Click *Info* option.
4. Click Check for Issues button.
5. Click *Check Compatibility*.
6. Read information in *Summary* list box.
7. Click *Copy to New Sheet* button.
   OR
   Click Close.

A workbook can be saved in an earlier file format so it can be read by people using an earlier version of the program. For instance, a workbook can be saved as an Excel 97-2003 file format to be compatible with Excel versions prior to 2007. When a file is saved in the file format of an earlier version, Excel automatically does a compatibility check and provides prompts about any loss of functionality or fidelity. If preferred, use the Compatibility Checker feature before saving the workbook to identify the areas of the worksheet that may need changes before saving to maintain backward compatibility.

If an issue in the *Summary* list box at the Microsoft Excel - Compatibility Checker dialog box displays a Fix hyperlink, click the hyperlink to resolve the problem. To get more information about a loss of functionality or fidelity, click the Help hyperlink next to the issue. To return to the worksheet with the cells selected that are problematic for earlier Excel versions, click the Find hyperlink next to the issue.

Activity 3d Checking a Workbook for Compatibility with Earlier Versions of Excel — Part 4 of 4

1. Open **CRAnalysis**.
2. Run the Compatibility Checker to scan the workbook before saving it in an earlier Excel file format by completing the following steps:
   a. Click the File tab and then click the *Info* option.

b. Click the Check for Issues button in the Info backstage area.
c. Click *Check Compatibility* at the drop-down list.
d. At the Microsoft Excel - Compatibility Checker dialog box, read the information in the *Summary* list box in the *Significant loss of functionality* section.
e. Scroll down and read the information in the *Minor loss of fidelity* section.
f. Scroll back up to the top of the *Summary* list box.
g. Click the Copy to New Sheet button.

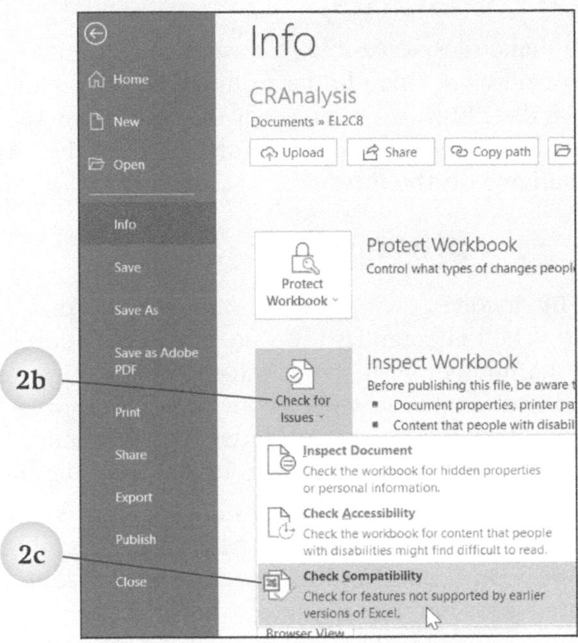

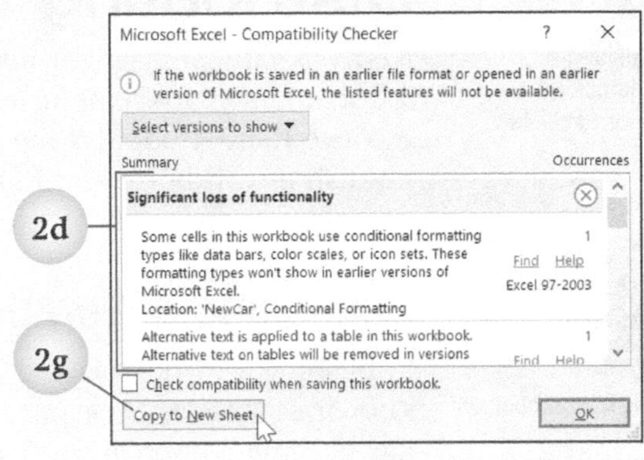

3. At the Compatibility Report sheet, read the information in the box with the hyperlink NewCar'!D13:D16 and then click the hyperlink. The NewCar worksheet becomes active with those cells selected that have conditional formatting applied that is not supported in the earlier version of Excel (the range D13:D16).

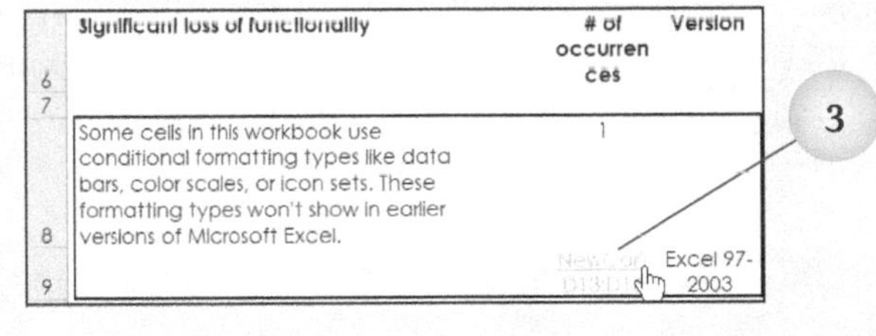

4. Make the Compatibility Report sheet active and then print the worksheet with the worksheet scaled to *Fit Sheet on One Page*.
5. Save the revised workbook with the name **8-CRAnalysisCompChk**.
6. Make NewCar the active worksheet and then deselect the range.
7. To save the workbook in an earlier version of Excel, click the File tab, click the *Export* option, click *Change File Type*, click *Excel 97-2003 Workbook* in the *Workbook File Types* section, and then click the Save As button. Click the Save button at the Save As dialog box to accept the default file name. Click the Continue button at the Compatibility Checker dialog box.
8. Close **8-CRAnalysisCompChk**.

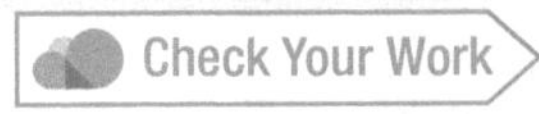

Activity 4 Distribute a First-Quarter Sales Workbook 3 Parts

You will publish a workbook as a PDF file and an XPS file. You will also publish a worksheet as a web page.

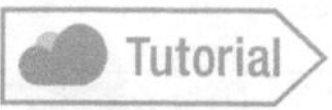

Publishing a Workbook as a PDF or XPS File

Distributing Workbooks

Many organizations that need to make files accessible to several users create a document management server or network share folder from which users can retrieve files. A popular method of distributing content over the internet is to publish a workbook as a PDF or XPS file. A workbook can also be published as a web page to make the content available on the internet.

Publishing a Workbook as a PDF File

Quick Steps

Publish Workbook as PDF File

1. Open workbook.
2. Click File tab.
3. Click *Export*.
4. Click Create PDF/XPS button.
5. Click Publish button.

Hint Publish a multisheet workbook as a multipage PDF file by clicking the Options button in the Publish as PDF or XPS dialog box and then clicking *Entire workbook* in the *Publish what* section of the Options dialog box.

Publishing a workbook as a PDF file involves saving it in a fixed-layout format known as *Portable Document Format*. The PDF standard was developed by Adobe and has become a popular format for sharing files with people outside an organization. Creating a PDF file of a workbook ensures that it will look the same on most computers, with all the fonts, formatting, and images preserved. The recipient of the file does not have to have Microsoft Excel on his or her computer to read the file.

To open and view a PDF file, the recipient must have Adobe Acrobat Reader DC on his or her computer or an Internet browser such as Microsoft Edge. The reader is a free application available from Adobe and can be downloaded and installed if the computer being used does not already have it installed. (Go to http://adobe.com and click *Adobe Acrobat Reader DC* to download and install the latest version of the software.)

A PDF file can also be opened with Word 365. It converts a PDF to an editable file, converting any formulas to values and any charts to objects. The file may not look exactly like the original PDF file, however.

Activity 4a Publishing a Workbook as a Multipage PDF File Part 1 of 3

1. Open **8-PFSales**.
2. Publish the workbook as a PDF file by completing the following steps:
   a. Click the File tab.
   b. Click the *Export* option.
   c. With *Create PDF/XPS Document* selected in the Export backstage area, click the Create PDF/XPS button.

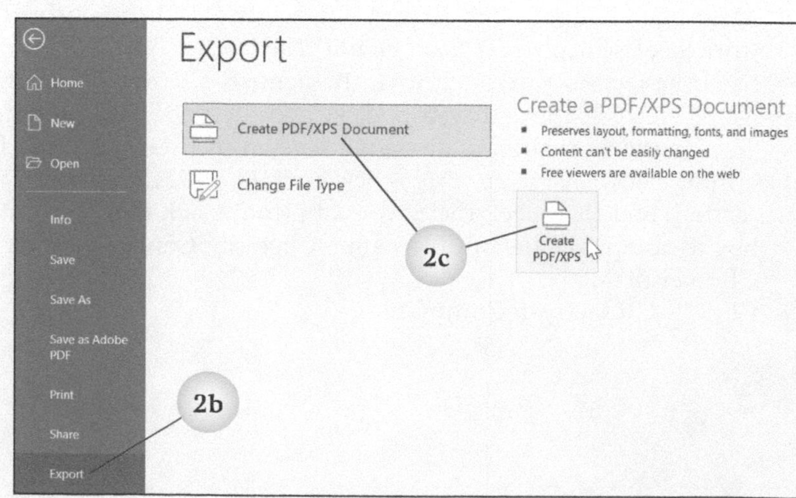

d. Click the *Open file after publishing* check box at the bottom of the Publish as PDF or XPS dialog box to insert a check mark, if necessary.

e. Click the Options button and then click the *Entire workbook* option in the *Publish what* section of the Options dialog box. This will create a PDF with three pages. Click OK.

f. With *PDF* in the *Save as type* option box and *8-PFSales* in the *File name* text box, click the Publish button.

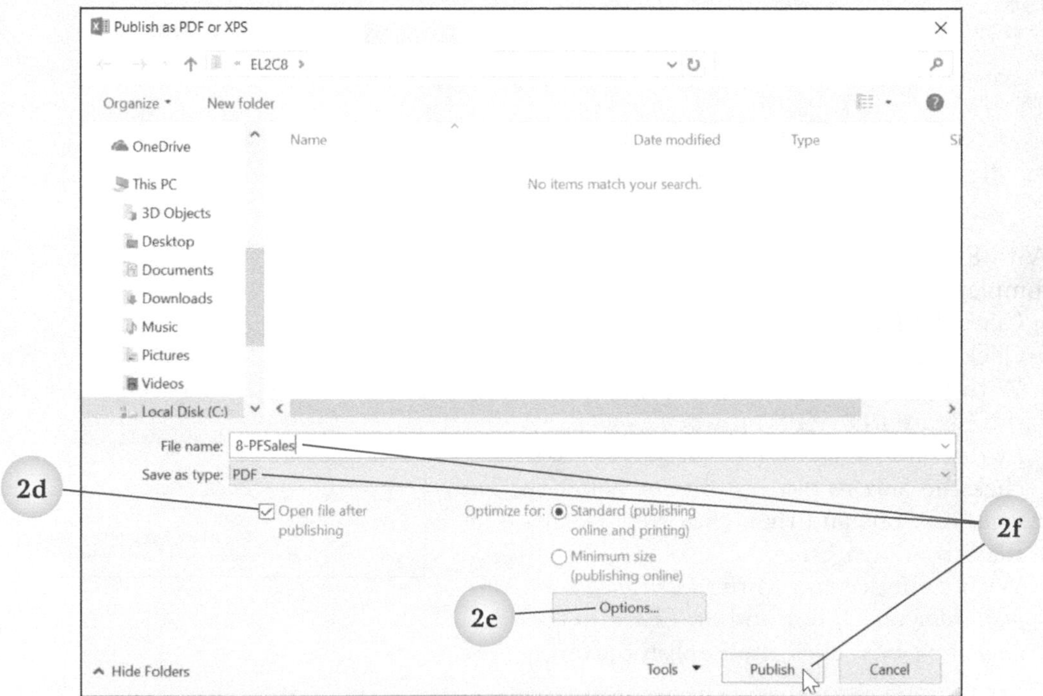

3. An internet browser such as Microsoft Edge or an Adobe Acrobat Reader DC application window opens with the published workbook displayed. Notice that the workbook has retained all the Excel formatting and other visual features and contains three pages.

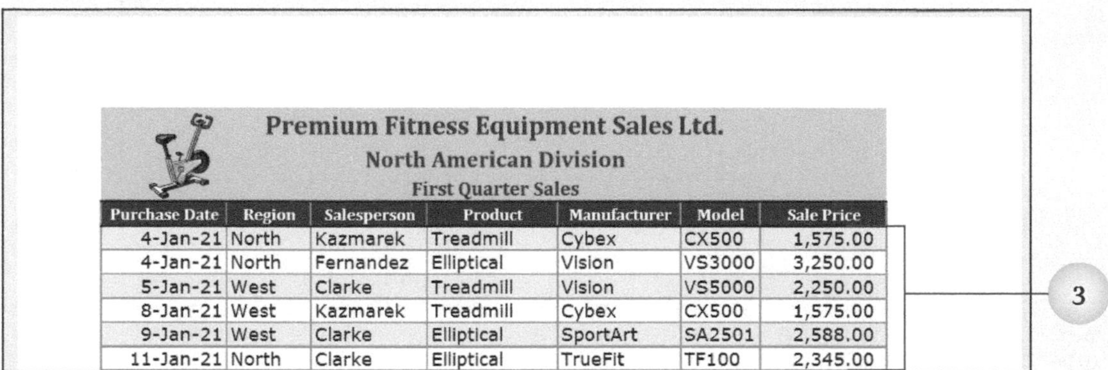

Premium Fitness Equipment Sales Ltd.
North American Division
First Quarter Sales

Purchase Date	Region	Salesperson	Product	Manufacturer	Model	Sale Price
4-Jan-21	North	Kazmarek	Treadmill	Cybex	CX500	1,575.00
4-Jan-21	North	Fernandez	Elliptical	Vision	VS3000	3,250.00
5-Jan-21	West	Clarke	Treadmill	Vision	VS5000	2,250.00
8-Jan-21	West	Kazmarek	Treadmill	Cybex	CX500	1,575.00
9-Jan-21	West	Clarke	Elliptical	SportArt	SA2501	2,588.00
11-Jan-21	North	Clarke	Elliptical	TrueFit	TF100	2,345.00

4. Close the application window.
5. Return to Excel and leave **8-PFSales** open for the next activity.

Publishing a Workbook as an XPS File

Quick Steps

Publish Workbook as XPS File

1. Open workbook.
2. Click File tab.
3. Click *Export*.
4. Click Create PDF/XPS button.
5. Click *Save as type* option box.
6. Click *XPS Document*.
7. Click Publish button.

XPS stands for *XML paper specification*, which is another fixed-layout format that has all the same advantages as PDF. XPS was developed by Microsoft with the Office 2007 suite. Similar to PDF files, which require Adobe Acrobat Reader DC for viewing, XPS files require the XPS viewer. The viewer is provided by Microsoft and is packaged with Windows 10, Windows 8, Windows 7, and Windows Vista.

Activity 4b Publishing a Worksheet as an XPS File

Part 2 of 3

1. With **8-PFSales** open, publish the FirstQuarterSales worksheet as an XPS file by completing the following steps:
   a. Click the File tab.
   b. Click the *Export* option.
   c. With the *Create PDF/XPS Document* option selected in the Export backstage area, click the Create PDF/XPS button.
   d. At the Publish as PDF or XPS dialog box, click the *Save as type* option box below the *File name* text box and then click *XPS Document* at the drop-down list.
   e. With a check mark in the *Open file after publishing* check box and *8-PFSales* in the *File name* text box, click the Publish button.

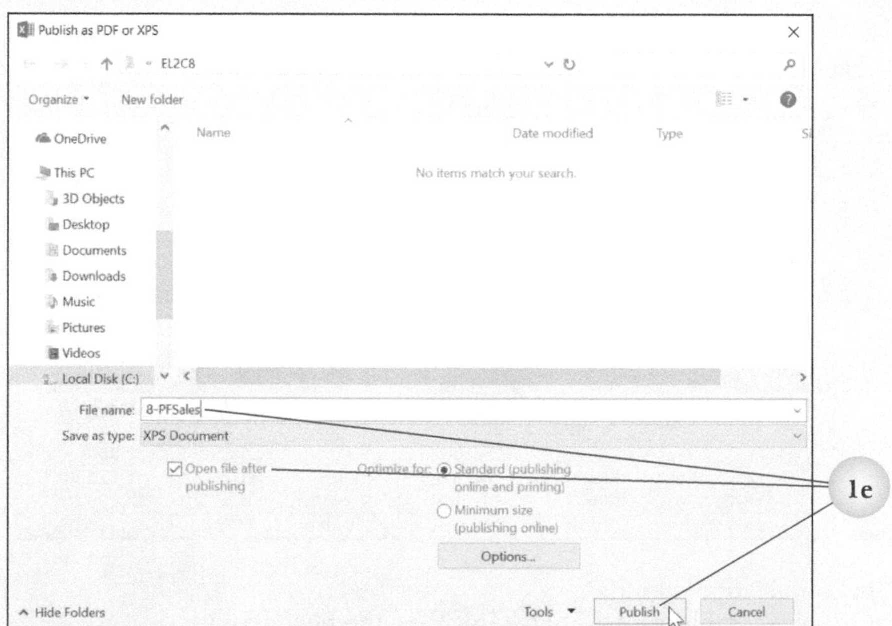

2. The XPS Viewer application window opens with the published worksheet displayed. ***Note: Choose the XPS Viewer application if a dialog box opens asking which application should be used to view the file.***
3. Close the XPS Viewer application window.

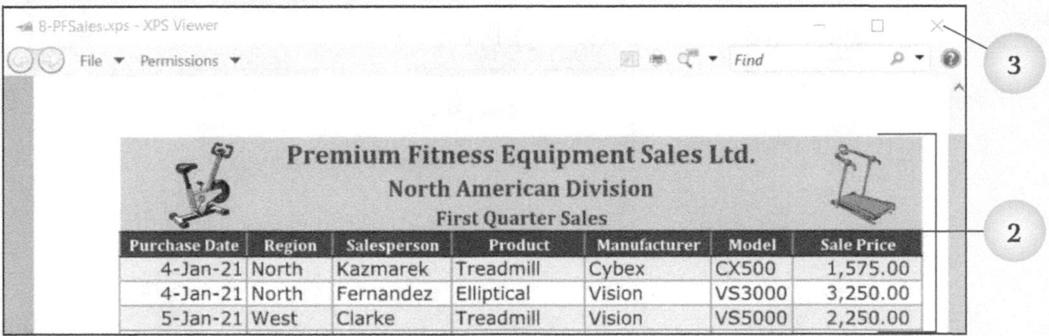

Purchase Date	Region	Salesperson	Product	Manufacturer	Model	Sale Price
4-Jan-21	North	Kazmarek	Treadmill	Cybex	CX500	1,575.00
4-Jan-21	North	Fernandez	Elliptical	Vision	VS3000	3,250.00
5-Jan-21	West	Clarke	Treadmill	Vision	VS5000	2,250.00

4. Leave **8-PFSales** open for the next activity.

Publishing a Worksheet as a Web Page

Quick Steps

Publish Worksheet as Web Page

1. Open workbook.
2. Click File tab.
3. Click *Export*.
4. Click *Change File Type*.
5. Click *Save as Another File Type* option.
6. Click Save As button.
7. Click *Save as type* option box.
8. Click *Web Page*.
9. If necessary, change drive, folder, and/or file name.
10. Click Change Title button, type title, and then click OK.
11. Click Publish button.
12. Set options.
13. Click Publish.

Publish the worksheet in the traditional Hypertext Markup Language (HTML) file format for web pages by changing the *Save as type* option to *Web Page*. In the *html* option, Excel creates additional files for supplemental data and saves them in a subfolder. Alternatively, publish a worksheet as a web page by changing the *Save as type* option to *Single File Web Page*. In this format, all the data in the worksheet, including graphics and other supplemental data, is saved in a single file that can be uploaded to a web server.

When a web page option is chosen at the *Save as type* list, the Save As dialog box changes, as shown in Figure 8.12. At this dialog box, specify whether to

Figure 8.12 Save As Dialog Box with File Type Changed to *Web Page*

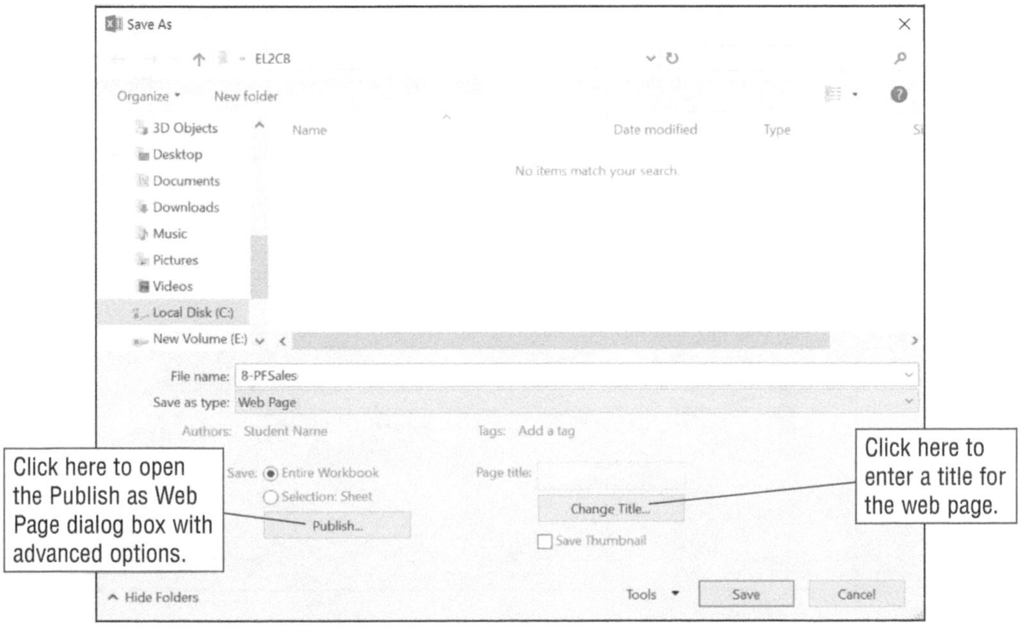

Hint Not all browsers support the single file (.mht) web page format. If the page will not be viewed in Microsoft Edge, consider using the traditional .htm or .html web page format.

publish the entire workbook or only the active sheet. Click the Change Title button to add a title to the web page. The page title displays in the Title bar of the browser window and on the Microsoft Edge tab when the page is viewed online. Click the Publish button and the Publish as Web Page dialog box appears, as shown in Figure 8.13, providing additional options.

Figure 8.13 Publish as Web Page Dialog Box

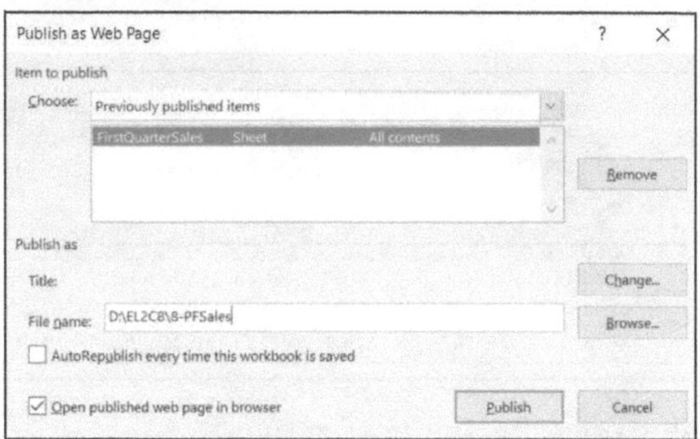

Activity 4c Publishing a Worksheet as a Web Page

Part 3 of 3

1. With **8-PFSales** open, prepare the worksheet to be published as a web page by completing the following steps:
   a. Select the range G5:G47; click the Home tab, if necessary; and then click the Alignment dialog box launcher.
   b. Click the Horizontal option box arrow and then click the *Right (Indent)* option.
   c. Click the *Indent* measurement up arrow once so that *1* displays in the *Indent* measurement box.
   d. Click OK and then click in any cell to deselect the range.
2. Publish the worksheet as a web page by completing the following steps:
   a. Click the File tab.
   b. Click the *Export* option.
   c. Click the *Change File Type* option and then click the *Save as Another File Type* option in the *Other File Types* section.
   d. Click the Save As button.
   e. Click the *Save as type* option box and then click *Web Page* at the drop-down list.
   f. Click the Change Title button.
   g. At the Enter Text dialog box, type Premium Fitness Equipment Sales Ltd. 1st Q Sales in the *Page title* text box and then click OK.
   h. Click the Publish button.

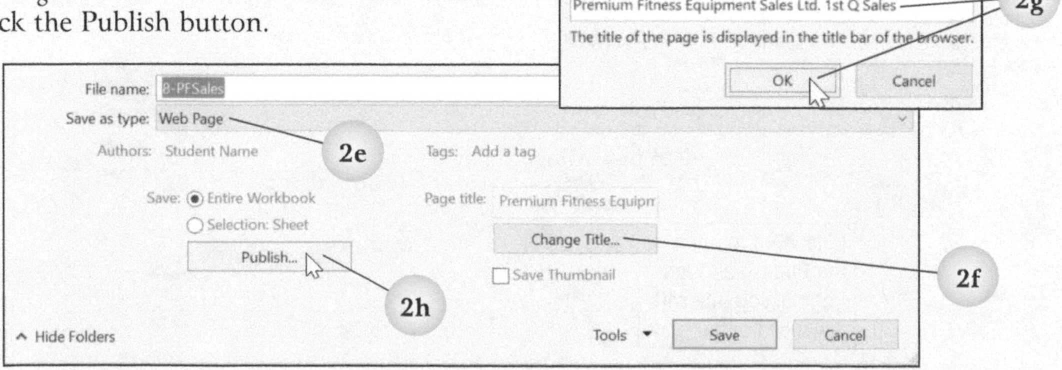

i. At the Publish as Web Page dialog box, click the *Open published web page in browser* check box to insert a check mark and then click the Publish button. Choose how you want to view the web page.
3. After viewing the web page, close the browser window.
4. Save and close **8-PFSales**.

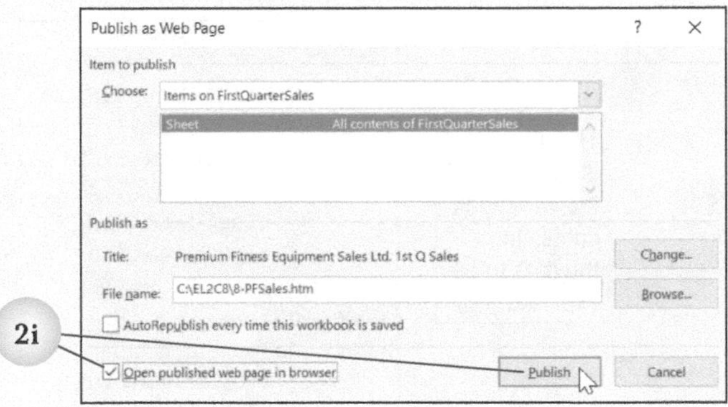

Activity 5 Export a Final Prices Worksheet in XML Format and Import an XML File Containing Customer Data — 2 Parts

You will create a schema and convert final prices data to an XML file and then import customer information from an XML file.

Exporting and Importing XML Data

Extensible Markup Language (XML) defines a set of rules that allows users to customize the markup language used to encode the data in a worksheet. XML code is easily understood and can be used to present workbook data in a browser. The standards of XML coding are developed and maintained by the World Wide Web Consortium (W3C), an international organization.

Creating an XML Schema

To export an Excel worksheet as an XML file, you first need to create an XML schema for the worksheet, as shown in Figure 8.14. It is created in a text editor, such as Notepad. The first two lines of code for an XML schema contain the XML declaration, which provides information on the XML version, the encoding being used to denote the characters, whether the document needs information from external sources, the file name, and where information about the standards can be found.

XML code is written using tags. Each tag is enclosed in angle brackets (< and >), and tags must be used in pairs, with an opening tag and a closing tag. The closing tag includes a forward slash (/). Use the basic code shown in Figure 8.14 as a template for writing an XML schema. Provide code for at least two records, with the opening tag <record> indicating the start of a record and the closing tag </record> indicating the end of a record. Excel will complete the schema based on the pattern established for those records.

Figure 8.14 Basic Schema Code

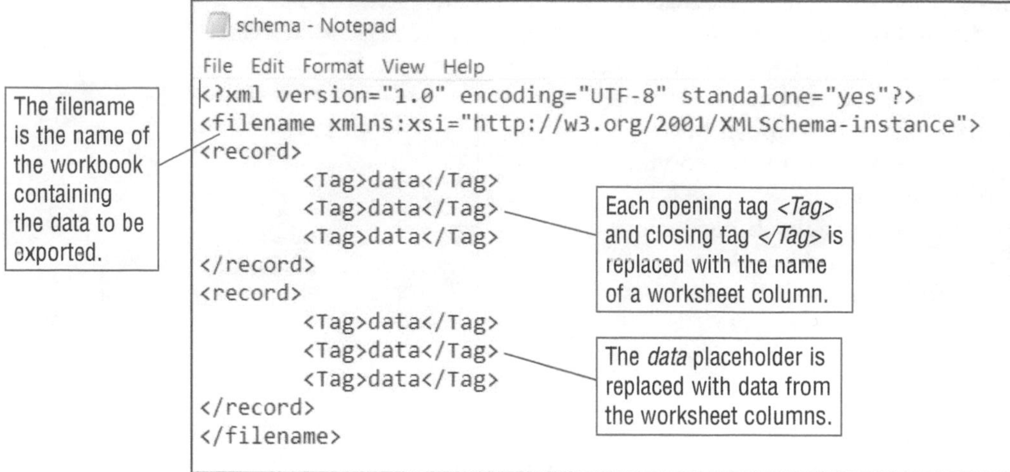

```
schema - Notepad
File Edit Format View Help
<?xml version="1.0" encoding="UTF-8" standalone="yes"?>
<filename xmlns:xsi="http://w3.org/2001/XMLSchema-instance">
<record>
        <Tag>data</Tag>
        <Tag>data</Tag>
        <Tag>data</Tag>
</record>
<record>
        <Tag>data</Tag>
        <Tag>data</Tag>
        <Tag>data</Tag>
</record>
</filename>
```

The filename is the name of the workbook containing the data to be exported.
Each opening tag <*Tag*> and closing tag </*Tag*> is replaced with the name of a worksheet column.
The *data* placeholder is replaced with data from the worksheet columns.

Figure 8.15 Schema Code for Activity 5a

```
crschema - Notepad
File Edit Format View Help
<?xml version="1.0" encoding="UTF-8" standalone="yes"?>
<crfp xmlns:xsi="http://www.w3.org/2001/XMLSchema-instance">
<record>
        <Category>Compact</Category>
        <Weekday>35.99</Weekday>
        <Weekend>55.99</Weekend>
        <Weekly>175.99</Weekly>
        <Monthly>675.99</Monthly>
        <Corporate>12%</Corporate>
</record>
<record>
        <Category>Mid-size</Category>
        <Weekday>38.99</Weekday>
        <Weekend>62.99</Weekend>
        <Weekly>185.99</Weekly>
        <Monthly>692.99</Monthly>
        <Corporate>15%</Corporate>
</record>
</crfp>
```

The columns must be listed in the same order in the schema as they are in the worksheet, but the column names do not have to be exactly the same.

Provide at least two examples of records in the schema. When the data is imported, Excel will fill in the rest.

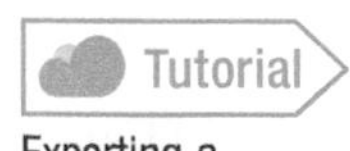

Tutorial

Exporting a Worksheet as an XML File

Source

Exporting a Worksheet as an XML File

To export data in an Excel worksheet as an XML file, complete the following steps:

1. Click the Source button in the XML group on the Developer tab.
2. Click the XML Maps button at the XML Source task pane, shown in Figure 8.16.
3. Click the Add button at the SML Maps dialog box, navigate to the XML schema file at the Select XML Source dialog box, click the XML schema file in the file list pane, and then click the Open button.
4. Click the OK button at the message box that displays, stating that the specific XML source does not refer to a schema and that Excel will create a schema based on the XML source data.

Export

5. Click the OK button at the XML Maps dialog box.
6. Drag each element in the *XML maps in this workbook* list box at the XML Source task pane to its corresponding column header in the worksheet.
7. Click the Developer tab and then click the Export button in the XML group.
8. Type the file name in the *File name* text box and then click the Export button.

When the schema file is added to the workbook, each <*Tag*> in the XML code appears as an XML element in the *XML maps in the workbook* list box at the XML Source task pane. An XML data map connects the schema file to the worksheet. Create an XML data map by dragging each element from the list box at the XML Source task pane to its respective column header in the worksheet. When a worksheet column has been mapped to an XML element, it becomes an XML element and changes to a table format.

If an Error in XML message box displays, stating that Excel cannot load the specified XML or schema source, click the Details button, read the information about the error at the XML Error dialog box, and then click the OK button to close the dialog box. Correct the error and then add the schema file again.

Figure 8.16 XML Source Task Pane

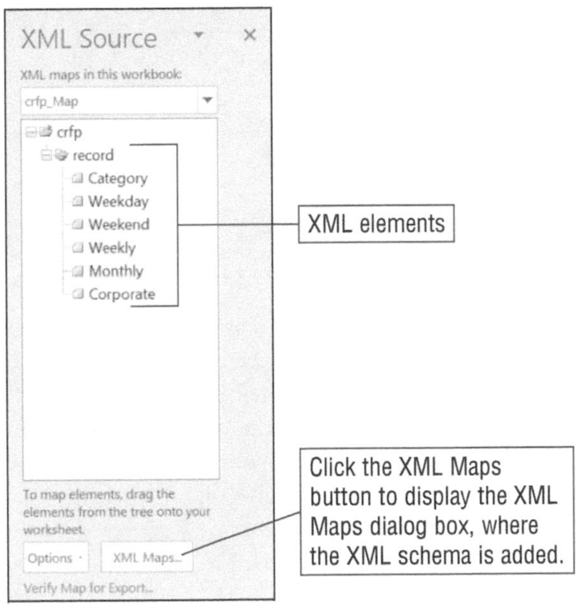

Activity 5a Exporting an XML File

Part 1 of 2

1. Open the data file **crschema** in Notepad.
2. Move the insertion point to the beginning of the first blank line and then type the following code, using the Tab key to indent the lines as shown:

```
<record>
	<Category>Compact</Category>
	<Weekday>35.99</Weekday>
	<Weekend>55.99</Weekend>
	<Weekly>175.99</Weekly>
```

```
        <Monthly>675.99</Monthly>
        <Corporate>12%</Corporate>
    </record>
    <record>
        <Category>Mid-size</Category>
        <Weekday>38.99</Weekday>
        <Weekend>62.99</Weekend>
        <Weekly>185.99</Weekly>
        <Monthly>692.99</Monthly>
        <Corporate>15%</Corporate>
    </record>
    </crfp>
```

3. Compare your schema with Figure 8.15 (on page 236). Save and then close **crschema** and Notepad.
4. Open **8-CRFinalPrices** using the password *eL2-C8* and then save the file with the name **CRFP**. Make the FinalPricesExport worksheet active.
5. Add the Developer tab to the ribbon, if necessary, by completing the following steps:
   a. Right-click on any part of the ribbon and then click the *Customize the Ribbon* option.
   b. Click the *Developer* check box in the *Main Tabs* list box and then click OK.
6. Click the Developer tab and then click the Source button in the XML group.

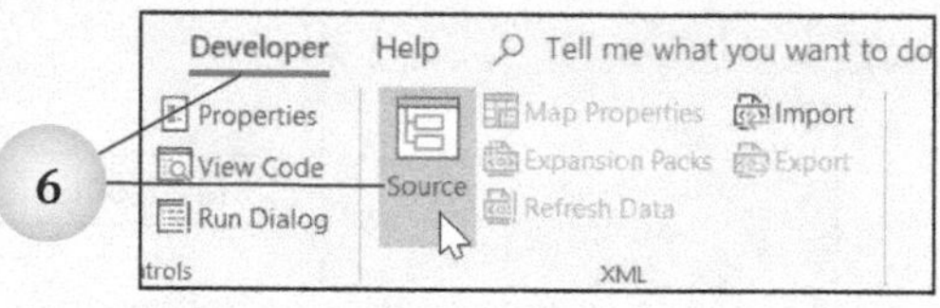

7. Click the XML Maps button in the XML Source task pane.
8. At the XML Maps dialog box, click the Add button.
9. Navigate to your EL2C8 folder at the Select XML Source dialog box, click the *All XML Data Sources* option box arrow, click the *All Files* option at the drop-down list, click **crschema** in the file list pane, and then click the Open button.
10. Click the OK button at the message box stating that the XML source does not refer to a schema and that Excel will create a schema based on the XML source data.
11. Click the OK button at the XML Maps dialog box.

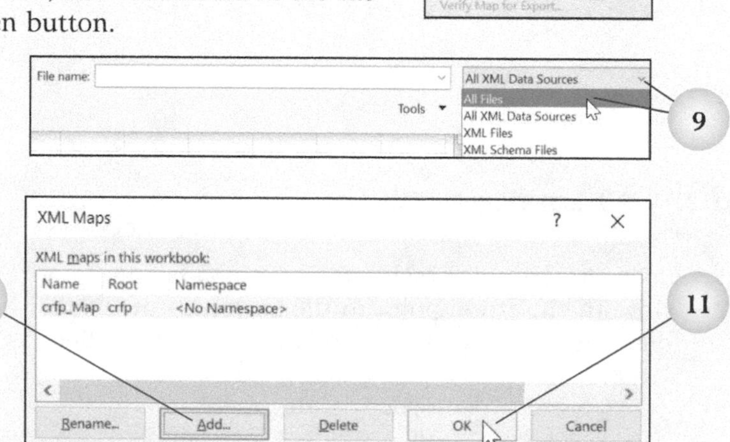

12. Drag the *Category* element in the list box at the XML Source task pane to cell A4.

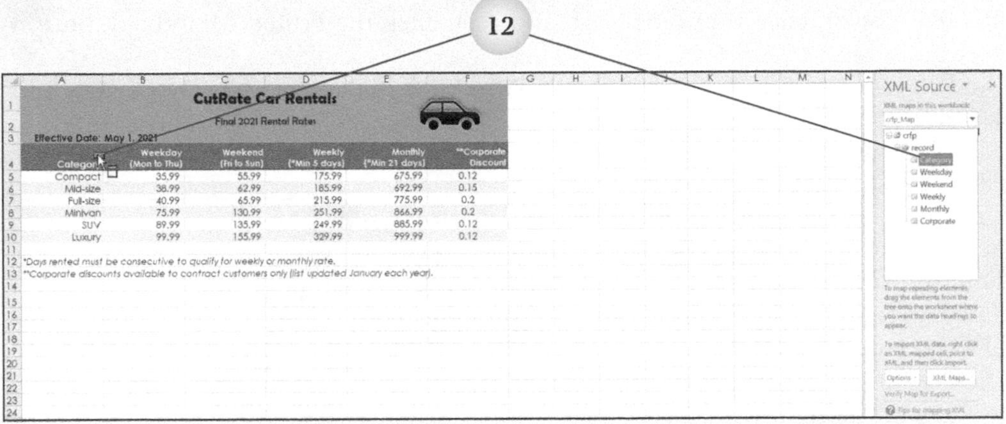

13. Drag the *Weekday* element in the list box to cell B4.
14. Repeat Step 11 to map the *Weekend, Weekly, Monthly*, and *Corporate* elements in the list box at the XML Source task pane to the corresponding column headers in the worksheet.
15. Click the Developer tab, click the Export button in the XML group, navigate to your EL2C8 folder, click in the *File name* text box, type FinalPrices, and then click the Export button.
16. Open File Explorer, navigate to your EL2C8 folder, and then double-click the data file **FinalPrices** in the file list pane. Choose an application to open the file, if necessary.
17. Scroll through the file and notice that Excel added the rest of the categories and prices.
18. Click the Close button on the **FinalPrices** file and then click the Close button on the File Explorer window.
19. Save **CRFP**.

Check Your Work

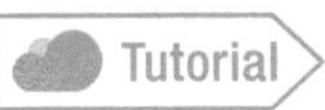
Tutorial
Importing an XML File

GetData

Importing an XML File

To import an XML file, click the Data tab, click the Get Data button, point to the *From File* option at the drop-down list, and then click the *From XML* option at the second drop-down list. At the Import Data dialog box, navigate to the drive and/or folder in which the source file resides and then double-click the XML file name in the file list. At the Navigator dialog box, click the record that contains the data to be imported (it is named *record*). Click the Load button to import the data into a new worksheet, or click the Load button arrow and then click the *Load To* option to open the Import Data dialog box, which contains more options for viewing and placing the data. Another option is to click the Edit button to edit and then import the data. This process is similar to importing an Access table into Excel, where a query is created.

Activity 5b Importing Data from an XML File

Part 2 of 2

1. With **CRFP** open, click the Review tab and then click the Protect Workbook button in the Protect group.
2. At the *Password* text box in the Unprotect Workbook dialog box, type eL2-C8 and then click OK.
3. Import the Customers XML file into a new worksheet by completing the following steps:
   a. Click the Data tab.
   b. Click the Get Data button in the Get & Transform group. Point to the *From File* option and then click the *From XML* option at the second drop-down list.
   c. Navigate to your EL2C8 folder and then double-click **CRCustomers**.
   d. Click *record* in the left panel. A preview of the data displays in the right panel.
   e. Click the Load button.
   f. Rename the worksheet **Customers**.
   g. Print the worksheet.
   h. Save and then close **CRFP**.

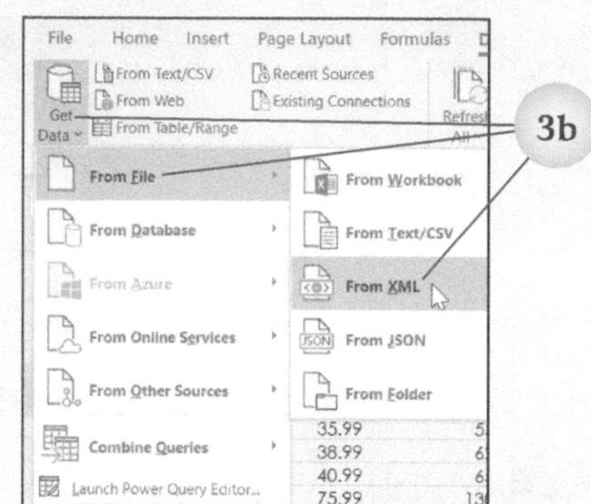

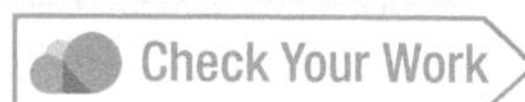

Chapter Summary

- Workbook properties include descriptive information about the workbook, such as the author's name and the workbook title, subject, category, and comments. Display the Info backstage area to add information to a workbook's properties. Workbook properties are sometimes referred to as *metadata*.
- When Microsoft Office is installed, a user name is defined for the computer. Excel automatically inserts this name in the *Author* property box when a new workbook is created.
- Protect an entire worksheet to prevent other users from accidentally inserting or deleting data. Protect a worksheet using the Protect Sheet button in the Protect group on the Review tab.
- By default, each cell in a worksheet has a lock attribute that activates when the worksheet is protected. To allow editing of individual cells in a protected worksheet, select the cells and turn off the lock attribute before protecting the worksheet. Add a password to unprotect a worksheet.
- Use the Protect Workbook button in the Protect group on the Review tab to prevent changes to the structure of a workbook, such as inserting, deleting, renaming, or otherwise managing worksheets within it. To remove workbook protection, click the Protect Workbook button. If a password was entered when the workbook was protected, the Unprotect Workbook dialog box appears. Type the password and then press the Enter key.
- Prevent unauthorized access to an Excel workbook by requiring a password to open it. The plain text of the password is encrypted, which prevents unauthorized users from retrieving it.
- Add a password at the Info backstage area by clicking the Protect Workbook button and then clicking *Encrypt with Password*. Save the workbook after typing and confirming the password.

- Before distributing a workbook for others to open, view, and edit, use Excel features to ensure that the file can be read by individuals who require assistive technology to read the workbook. Run the Accessibility Checker by clicking the Check Accessibility button in the Accessibility group on the Review tab or click the File tab and then click the *Info* option.
- Before distributing a workbook, also check it to ensure that confidentiality will be protected and maintained. The Document Inspector scans a workbook for personal or hidden information. Identify and then remove any information that should remain confidential at the Document Inspector dialog box.
- After a workbook has been inspected, Excel displays a red exclamation mark in each section in which Excel detected a requested item. Click the Remove All button to delete all such items from the workbook.
- Marking a workbook as final changes it to a read-only file and sets the status property as *Final*. To mark a workbook as final, click the File tab and the click the *Info* option. At the Info backstage area, click the Protect Workbook button and then click *Mark as Final* at the drop-down list.
- Run the Compatibility Checker before saving a workbook in an earlier version of Excel to identify areas of the worksheet that may need changes to maintain backward compatibility. The results of the compatibility check can be copied to a new worksheet for easy referencing and documentation purposes.
- Saving a workbook in a fixed-layout format such as PDF or XPS preserves all the Excel formatting and layout features. Adobe Acrobat Reader or Word 365 is required to open and view a workbook saved as a PDF file. The XPS Viewer is provided with Windows. Adobe Acrobat Reader can be downloaded for free from the Adobe website.
- To publish the current worksheet as a web page, open the Save As dialog box and change the *Save as type* option to *Web Page* or *Web Page*.
- Extensible Markup Language (XML) defines a set of rules that allows users to customize the markup language used to encode the data in a worksheet. To export an Excel worksheet as an XML file, the user first needs to create an XML schema for the worksheet. An XML schema is a document created in Notepad that defines the XML file structure. XML code is written using tags. Each tag is enclosed in angle brackets (< and >), and tags must be used in pairs, with an opening and a closing tag. An XML data map connects the schema file to the worksheet.
- To import an XML file, click the Data tab, click the Get Data button, point to the *From File* option at the drop-down list, and then click the *From XML* option at the second drop-down list. At the Import Data dialog box, navigate to the drive and/or folder in which the source file resides and then double-click the XML file name in the file list. At the Navigator dialog box, click the record containing the data to be imported. Click the Load button to import the data in a new worksheet, click the *Load to* button arrow and then click the *Load To* option at the drop-down list to open the Import Data dialog box, or click the Edit button to Edit and then import the data.

Commands Review

FEATURE	RIBBON TAB, GROUP/OPTION	BUTTON, OPTION	KEYBOARD SHORTCUT
Accessibility Checker	Review, Accessibility OR File, *Info*	, *Check for Issues* , *Check for Issues*	
Compatibility Checker	File, *Info*		
Document Inspector	File, *Info*	, *Check for Issues*	
export data as XML file	Developer, XML		
import XML file into Excel	Data, Get & Transform Data		
mark workbook as final	File, *Info*	, *Protect Workbook*	
protect workbook	Review, Protect		
protect worksheet	Review, Protect		
save as	File, *Save As*		F12
save as PDF/XPS	File, *Export* OR File, *Save As*		F12
save as web page	File, *Export* OR File, *Save As*		F12
unlock cells	Home, Cells		

Index

D

G

H

I

K

L

M

N

O

P

Q

R

S

T

Interior Photo Credits

Page GS-1 (banner image) © lowball-jack/GettyImages; *page GS-1, (in Figure G.1)* all images courtesy of Paradigm Education Solutions; *page GS-2*, © irbis picture/Shutterstock.com; *page GS-3*, © th3fisa/Shutterstock.com; *page GS-4*, © goldyg/Shutterstock.com; *page GS-5*, © Pressmaster/Shutterstock.com.